Psychological Testing and Assessment

Psychological Testing and Assessment

EIGHTH EDITION

LEWIS R. AIKEN
Pepperdine University

ALLYN AND BACON

Boston   London   Toronto   Sydney   Tokyo   Singapore

Vice President and Publisher: Susan Badger
Executive Editor: Laura Pearson
Editorial Assistant: Marnie Greenhut
Cover Administrator: Linda Dickinson
Manufacturing Buyer: Megan Cochran
Editorial-Production Service: Raeia Maes
Cover Designer: Design Ad Cetera

Copyright © 1994, 1991, 1988, 1985, 1982, 1979, 1976 by Allyn and Bacon
A Division of Simon & Schuster, Inc.
160 Gould Street
Needham Heights, Massachusetts 02194

The first edition was published under the title, *Psychological and Educational Testing,*
© 1971 by Allyn and Bacon, Inc.

Library of Congress Cataloging-in-Publication Data

Aiken, Lewis R.
    Psychological testing and assessment / Lewis R. Aiken.—8th ed.
        p.   cm.
    Includes bibliographical references and indexes.
    ISBN 0-205-13782-2
    1. Psychological tests.   I. Title.
BF176.A48 1994
150'.28'7—dc20   93-21509
                                                              CIP

Printed in the United States of America

10 9 8 7 6 5 4 3 2   98 97 96 95 94

Whatever exists at all exists in some amount.   *Thorndike, 1918*

Anything that exists in amount can be measured.   *McCall, 1939*

Contents

Preface

During the past three decades, there has been much criticism of psychological testing and assessment. The use of standardized tests in educational and employment contexts, in particular, has been repeatedly attacked. There have been numerous legal suits and court cases concerned with testing, and in certain states legislation pertaining to test standards and usage has been passed. The effects of these events, however, have been mainly salutary, and psychological testing has continued to flourish. Increased public and professional attention to the usefulness and limitations of testing has stimulated a desire for greater care in designing and distributing psychological tests and other assessment instruments. The need for the users of tests to be better trained and to have greater awareness of the personal and social consequences of testing has also become increasingly obvious. Psychometricians and other knowledgeable persons are concerned that tests be constructed and used not only with attention to their technical features but also with a sensitivity to the needs and rights of examinees and society as a whole. This outlook is reflected in *The Standards for Educational and Psychological Testing* (American Educational Research Association et al., 1985), the *Code of Fair Testing Practices in Education* (Fremer, Diamond, & Camara, 1989), and the *Principles for the Validation and Use of Personnel Selection Procedures* (Society for Industrial & Organizational Psychology, 1987).

Consistent with these concerns and aspirations, the major objective of this book is to improve the knowledge, understanding, and practices of those who construct tests, those who take tests, and those who ponder over the meaning and value of test scores. Like previous editions, the current volume is designed primarily as a textbook for college students, but it may also serve as a source of information and procedures for professional psychologists, educators, and others who use tests and test results. The material is appropriate for a one-semester course at the undergraduate or beginning graduate level.

In writing this textbook I have tried to be comprehensive without being exhaustive, so instructors who adopt the book will find that they have not been replaced by the written word. Ample opportunity remains for the instructor to serve as a selector and interpreter, as well as an elaborator on the text material. The *Exercises* and *Suggested Readings* at the end of each chapter may also extend and supplement the material discussed in the chapter.

The basic structure of the eighth edition of *Psychological Testing and Assessment* remains as it was in previous editions. Consequently, instructors who adopted earlier editions of the text will find themselves in familiar territory that has changed here and there, but not shifted radically. Since publication of the seventh edition several notable, if not revolutionary, changes in psychological and educational testing have occurred. It is hoped that this revision adequately reflects those changes. In addition to updating the descriptions of the most widely used standardized tests and other assessment instruments, some new contenders have been introduced. Increased attention has also been given to adaptive testing, fair testing practices, item response theory, the use of microcomputers in psychological assessment, neuropsychological testing, and applications of testing in various contexts. Issues such as the use of SAT scores to determine eligibility for participation in college sports and achievement testing to assess the attainment of national educational standards are discussed. Also considered are proposals for new psychometric approaches to teacher certification, newer approaches to the assessment of lying and cheating, and the latest edition (the eleventh) of *The Mental Measurements Yearbook.*

As with previous editions, my goal in preparing this eighth edition was to introduce psychological testing and assessment as an interesting, important field of study, not only to students who plan to become professional psychologists but also to those who plan to enter a wide range of educational, health-related, law-related, and other organizational contexts in the world of work. To assist in accomplishing this task, greater emphasis has been placed on applications of psychological testing in educational–school, clinical–counseling, and industrial–organizational settings. Although the uses of tests and other assessment instruments are discussed throughout the book, Chapter 11 is devoted exclusively to applications.

End-of-chapter exercises, some of which make use of computer programs written expressly for this text, have been included. Not only do these computer programs permit the computation of a variety of statistics and graphical displays of results, but they may also serve as aids in the construction, administration, and scoring of tests, inventories, and other psychometric devices. The programs and the accompanying guide to their use, *Computer Programs for Psychological Assessment,* are available free of charge to instructors who adopt the text. To obtain a diskette of computer programs, which are written in BASICA for IBM-PCs and compatible microcomputers, instructors should write directly to the author (Lewis R. Aiken, 12449 Mountain Trail Court, Moorpark, CA 93021). An *Instructor's Manual to Accompany Psychological Testing and Assessment (8th ed.),* containing several hundred multiple-choice and true–false items as well as other course-related materials and teaching suggestions, is available from the publisher. The manual is also available on computer diskette as an ASCII file for instructors who wish to construct course tests on a word processor. Write to the author for a copy of the diskette.

I am grateful to the many students and colleagues who worked their way through the seven previous editions of this book and provided constructive criticisms and suggestions. I also wish to thank the reviewers of this edition, Roberta Dihoff, Rowan College of New Jersey, George Domino, University of Arizona, Wendy Dunn, Coe College, Linda Hynan, Baylor University, Laura L. Koppes, University of Wisconsin-Oshkosh, Terry G. Newell, California State University-Fresno, Peter Rowe, College of Charleston, my production editor, Raeia Maes, and the copyeditor, William Thomas, for their untiring efforts and expertise. I sincerely hope that the results of their labors and mine are evident in the finished product.

L. R. A.

Psychological Testing and Assessment

PART ONE

METHODOLOGY OF ASSESSMENT

PART ONE

METHODOLOGY OF
ASSESSMENT

Chapter One

Foundations of Psychological Measurement

Anyone who has attended grade school or college, served in the armed forces, or applied for a job in the United States during the last 50 years or so has undoubtedly taken one or more psychological tests. Testing has come to have an important influence on the lives and careers of Americans and citizens of countries throughout the world. Whenever information is needed to help make decisions about people or to assist them in selecting courses of action pertaining to their future educational or occupational status, some form of test may be administered. Tests are used extensively in schools, psychological clinics, industry, and the civil and military services for diagnostic evaluation, selection, placement, and promotion purposes. In addition to their applications in practical decision making, tests are used extensively in research.

Considering its many functions, it is not surprising that testing itself has become a big business. The total sales figure for standardized tests administered in grades K–12 alone was an estimated $134 million in 1991 (data provided by Association of American Publishers). Professional organizations such as those listed in Appendix D specialize in publishing and distributing psychological tests and other instruments for assessing the abilities, personality, interests, and other characteristics of individuals of all ages and in various circumstances.

HISTORICAL PERSPECTIVE

The fact that people differ in their abilities, personalities, and behaviors and that these differences can be assessed in some way has probably been recognized since the beginning of human history. Plato and Aristotle wrote about individual differences nearly 2500 years ago, and even they were preempted by the ancient Chinese (Bowman, 1989; Doyle, 1974). As early as 2200 B.C. , a civil-service system was instituted by the Chinese emperor to determine if his officials were fit to perform their governmental duties. This system, according to which officials were examined every 3 years, was continued by later Chinese

3

emperors. During the nineteenth century, British and French officials patterned their civil-service examinations after the ancient Chinese system.

Interest in individual differences, at least from a scientific viewpoint, was almost nonexistent in Europe during the Middle Ages. In the social structure of medieval European society, a person's activities were dictated by the class into which he or she was born. Little freedom was provided for personal expression or development. By the sixteenth century, however, European society had become more capitalistic and less doctrinaire; the idea was growing that people are unique and entitled to assert their natural gifts and improve their lot in life. Thus, the Renaissance can be viewed not only as a period during which interest in learning was reawakened, but also as a rebirth of individualism. The spirit of freedom and individual worth, which flourished with the political and economic stimulation provided by capitalism and democracy, found expression in art, science, and government. Not until the late nineteenth century, however, did the scientific study of individual differences in mental abilities and personality actually begin.

Mental Measurement in the Nineteenth Century

Early in the nineteenth century, scientists generally viewed individual differences in sensorimotor and mental abilities as more of a nuisance than anything else. Before the invention of precise, automatic equipment for measuring and recording physical events, the accuracy of scientific measurements of time, distance, and other physical variables depended to a great extent on the perceptual abilities of human observers. These observers were usually highly trained and very careful in making such measurements, but the measurements made by different people and by the same person on different occasions could still vary appreciably. Because the search for general laws of nature is difficult when measurements of natural phenomena are unreliable, physical scientists directed their attention to the construction of instruments that would be more consistent and precise than unaided human observations.

Stimulated by the writings of Charles Darwin on the origin of species and by the emergence of scientific psychology, interest in the study of individual differences grew during the latter half of the nineteenth century. Darwin was an Englishman, but psychology was actually christened as a science in Germany during the last quarter of the century. During that time, Gustav Fechner, Wilhelm Wundt, Hermann Ebbinghaus, and other German experimental psychologists demonstrated that psychological phenomena could be expressed in quantitative, rational terms. Events occurring in France and the United States were also important to psychological testing. The research of French psychiatrists and psychologists on mental disorders influenced the development of clinical assessment techniques and tests, and the increased attention given to written examinations in U.S. schools resulted in the development of standardized measures of scholastic achievement.

As is true of the history of any field, many people in a number of countries played significant roles in the pioneering phase of mental measurement. Especially important during the late 1800s were Francis Galton, James Cattell, and Alfred Binet. Galton, a highly gifted cousin of Charles Darwin, was an English gentleman who became interested in the hereditary basis of intelligence and in techniques for measuring abilities. A particular concern of Galton was the inheritance of genius, but he also constructed a number of sensorimotor tests and devised several methods for investigating individual differences in abilities and temperament. Using these simple tests, he collected measurements on over 9000 people, ranging in age from 5 to 80 years. Among the many methodological contributions made by Galton was the technique of "co-relations," which has continued to be a popular method for analyzing test scores.

James M. Cattell was an American who, on returning from Germany after receiving his Ph.D. under Wilhelm Wundt, stopped over in England and became acquainted with Galton's methods and tests while serving as his assistant. Later, at Columbia University, Cattell tried relating scores on these *mental tests* of reaction time and sensory discrimination to school marks. The relationships, or correlations, between performance on these tests and scholastic achievement were, however, very low. It remained for a Frenchman, Alfred Binet, to construct the first mental test that proved to be an effective predictor of scholastic achievement.

Testing in the Early Twentieth Century

The psychologist Alfred Binet (Figure 1–1) and his physician-associate Theodore Simon were commissioned in 1904 by the Parisian minister of public instruction to develop a procedure for identifying children who presumably could not benefit sufficiently from instruction in regular school classes. For this purpose, Binet and Simon constructed an individually administered test consisting of 30 problems arranged in order of ascending difficulty. The problems on this first workable *intelligence test,* which was published in 1905, emphasized the ability to judge, understand, and reason. A revision of the test,

FIGURE 1–1 Alfred Binet.
(Reprinted by permission of Culver Pictures Inc.)

containing a large number of subtests grouped by age levels from 3 to 13 years, was published in 1908. In scoring the 1908 revision of the Binet–Simon Intelligence Scale, the concept of *mental age* was introduced as a way of quantifying an examinee's overall performance on the test. A further revision of the Binet–Simon scale, published after Binet's untimely death, extended the test to the adult level.

Among other pioneers in psychological testing and assessment were Charles Spearman in test theory, Edward L. Thorndike in achievement testing, Lewis Terman in intelligence testing, Robert Woodworth and Hermann Rorschach in personality testing, and Edward Strong in interest measurement. The work of Arthur Otis on group-administered tests of intelligence led directly to the construction of the Army Examinations Alpha and Beta by a committee of psychologists during World War I. These two tests, the Army Alpha for literates and the Army Beta for illiterates, were administered on a group basis to measure the mental abilities of thousands of U.S. soldiers during and after the war.

Since World War I, many individuals have contributed to the theory and practice of psychological and educational testing, a number of whom are referred to in Table 1–1. The names of these pioneers are still to be found in the titles of tests and in references to techniques, procedures, and other developments to which they contributed. Among these developments were improvements in statistical methodology and technological advances in the preparation and scoring of tests and the analysis of test results.

TABLE 1–1   Selected Events in the History of Psychological and Educational Assessment

2200 B.C.	Mandarins set up civil-service testing program in China.
A.D. 1219	First formal oral examinations in law held at University of Bologna.
1575	J. Huarte publishes book, *Examinen de Ingenios,* concerned with individual differences in mental abilities.
1636	Oral examinations for degree certification used at Oxford University.
1795	Astronomer Maskelyne of Greenwich Observatory fires assistant Kinnebrook when their observations of the transit time of Venus disagree.
1845	Printed examinations first used by Boston School Committee under guidance of the educator Horace Mann.
1864	George Fisher, an English schoolmaster, constructs a series of scales consisting of sample questions and answers as guides for evaluating students' answers to essay test questions.
1865	Establishment of the New York State Regents' Examination.
1869	Scientific study of individual differences begins with publication of Francis Galton's *Classification of Men According to Their Natural Gifts.*
1879	Founding of first psychological laboratory in the world by Wilhelm Wundt at University of Leipzig in Germany.
1884	Francis Galton opens Anthropometric Laboratory for International Health Exhibition in London.
1887	Gustav Fechner formulates first psychological law.

TABLE 1–1 *(continued)*

1888	J. M. Cattell opens testing laboratory at the University of Pennsylvania.
1893	Joseph Jastrow displays sensorimotor tests at Columbian Exhibition in Chicago.
1896	Emil Kraeplin proposes new classification of mental disorders. Hermann Ebbinghaus develops first completion test.
1897	J. M. Rice publishes research findings on spelling abilities of U.S. schoolchildren.
1900	College Entrance Examination Board founded.
1904	Charles Spearman describes two-factor theory of mental abilities. First major textbook on educational measurement, E. L. Thorndike's *Introduction to the Theory of Mental and Social Measurement,* published.
1905	First Binet–Simon Intelligence Scale published. Carl G. Jung uses word-association test for analysis of mental complexes.
1908	Revision of Binet–Simon Intelligence Scale published.
1908–1909	Objective arithmetic tests published by J. C. Stone and S. A. Courtis.
1908–1914	E. L. Thorndike develops standardized tests of arithmetic, handwriting, language, and spelling, including *Scale for Handwriting of Children* (1910).
1914	Arthur Otis develops first group test of intelligence, based on Terman's Stanford Revision of the Binet–Simon Scales.
1916	Stanford–Binet Intelligence Scale published by Lewis Terman.
1917	Army Alpha and Army Beta, first group intelligence tests, constructed and administered to U.S. Army recruits. Robert Woodworth's Personal Data Sheet, the first standardized personality inventory, used in military selection.
1919	Louis Thurstone's Psychological Examination for College Freshmen published.
1920	National Intelligence Scale published. Hermann Rorschach's Inkblot Test first published.
1923	Stanford Achievement Test first published. Pintner–Cunningham Primary Mental Test first published.
1924	Truman Kelly's *Statistical Method* published.
1925	Arthur Otis's *Statistical Method in Educational Measurement* published.
1926	Scholastic Aptitude Test first administered.
1927	First edition of Strong Vocational Interest Blank for Men published. Kuhlmann–Anderson Intelligence Tests first published.
1935	Development of the first IBM test-scoring machine.
1936	First volume of *Psychometrika* published.
1937	Revision of Stanford–Binet Intelligence Scale published.
1938	Henry Murray publishes *Explorations in Personality.* O. K. Buros publishes first *Mental Measurements Yearbook.*

TABLE 1–1   *(continued)*

1939	Wechsler–Bellevue Intelligence Scale published.
1942	Minnesota Multiphasic Personality Inventory published.
1947	Educational Testing Service founded.
1949	Wechsler Intelligence Scale for Children published.
1960	Form L–M of Stanford–Binet Intelligence Scale published.
1969	Arthur Jensen's paper on racial inheritance of IQ published in *Harvard Educational Review.*
1970–	Increasing use of computers in designing, administering, scoring, analyzing, and interpreting tests.
1971	Federal court decision requiring tests used for personnel selection purposes to be job relevant (*Griggs* v. *Duke Power*).
1974	Wechsler Intelligence Scale for Children–Revised published.
1975–	Growth of behavioral assessment techniques.
1980–	Development of item response theory.
1981	Wechsler Adult Intelligence Scale–Revised published.
1985	*Standards for Educational and Psychological Testing* published.
1987	California Psychological Inventory–Revised published. DSM–III–R published.
1989	MMPI–II published. Wechsler Preschool and Primary Test of Intelligence–Revised published.
1990	Wechsler Intelligence Scale for Children–III published.
1992	Eleventh edition of *The Mental Measurements Yearbook* published.

TESTING AS A PROFESSION

The field of psychological testing has grown rapidly since the 1920s, and hundreds of tests are now commercially produced and distributed. After World War II, standardized testing, especially the testing of academic achievement or performance, spread throughout the world. Many U.S.-made tests of ability and personality were translated into other languages. In addition to published standardized tests, hundreds of unpublished test materials are available. These tests, which are cited in professional journals and books, are in use in the United States, Europe, and many other countries.

Sources of Information

Information concerning psychological tests and other assessment devices can be found in the catalogs of companies that distribute tests (see Appendix D) or, in more detail, in manuals accompanying the tests themselves. A number of reference books dealing with tests are also available. *Tests in Print III* (Mitchell, 1983), for example, contains descriptive information on 2674 commercially published tests. Also important are the eleven editions of *The Mental Measurements Yearbook* (Buros, 1978 and earlier; Mitchell, 1985; Conoley & Kramer, 1989; Kramer & Conoley, 1992), a series of volumes containing descriptions and reviews of tests. Information on a wide variety of published tests may also be found in the volume *Tests* (Sweetland & Keyser, 1983, 1986), and reviews of tests are given in *Test Critiques* (Keyser & Sweetland, 1984–1988). Useful information on tests in specific areas (personality, reading, intelligence, English, foreign languages, mathematics, science, social studies, vocations) is provided in a series of monographs prepared by O. K. Buros (1970, 1975a, 1975b, and others) and in the ETS Test Collection Catalog (Educational Testing Service, Princeton, NJ). Also available in the ETS Test Collection are 200 annotated Test Collection Bibliographies and a quarterly newsletter, "News on Tests."

Among the many other books of annotated lists and reviews of published tests are *Test and Measurements in Child Development* (Johnson & Bommarito, 1971; Johnson, 1976), *Tests in Education: A Book of Critical Reviews* (Levy & Goldstein, 1984), *Testing Children* (Weaver, 1984), *Testing Adolescents* (Harrington, 1986), and *Testing Adults* (Swiercinsky, 1985). Information on available computer software and test-scoring services may be found in *Psychware Sourcebook* (Krug, 1988–1989) and *Computer Use in Psychology: A Directory of Software* (Stoloff & Couch, 1988). Computer databases containing information on published tests include the *Mental Measurements Online Database* (Buros Institute of Mental Measurements, Lincoln, NE) and the ETS Test Collection Database (The Test Collection, Educational Testing Service, Princeton, NJ).

Details on many unpublished tests and scales may be found in sources such as the *Directory of Unpublished Experimental Mental Measures* (Goldman & Busch, 1978, 1982; Goldman & Mitchell, 1990; Goldman & Osborne, 1985; Goldman & Saunders, 1974), *Measures for Psychological Assessment* (Chun, Cobb, & French, 1976), *Measuring Human Behavior* (Lake, Miles, & Earle, 1973), and *Tests in Microfiche* (Educational Testing Service).

Information on published and unpublished measures for clinical situations is given in *A Source Book for Mental Health Measures* (Comrey, Bacher, & Glaser, 1973) and the *Handbook of Psychiatric Rating Scales*, 2nd ed. (Lyerly, 1978). For information on unpublished measures of attitudes, the series of volumes produced at the University of Michigan's Institute for Social Research (Robinson, Athanasiou, & Head, 1974; Robinson, Rush, & Head, 1973; Robinson, Shaver & Wrightsman, 1991), in addition to the volume by Shaw and Wright (1967), should be consulted. The HAPI (*Health and Psychosocial Instruments*) and PsycINFO databases are other useful sources for information on unpublished instruments.

Reviews of selected tests are also published in a number of professional journals, for example, the *American Educational Research Journal, Journal of Educational Measurement, Measurement and Evaluation in Counseling and Development, Personnel Psychology*, and *Psychoeducational Assessment*. Articles on the development and evaluation of psychological tests and measures are included in such professional journals as *Applied Psychological Measurement, Educational and Psychological Measurement*, the *Journal of Clinical Psychology, Psychological Assessment: A Journal of Consulting and Clinical Psychology*, the *Journal of Counseling Psychology*, and the *Journal of Vocational Behavior*. Citations of sources of information on specific tests may also be found in *Psychological Abstracts, Education Index*, and *Current Index to Journals in Education*. In addition, entire books and series of books have been written on single tests, such as the Minnesota Multiphasic Personality Inventory (MMPI) and the Rorschach Inkblot Test.

Classification of Tests

As is true of any other profession, psychological testing has its own special vocabulary. The glossary in Appendix E provides definitions of the most frequently used terms, many of which refer to types of tests or methods of classifying tests. One such method of classification is the dichotomy *standardized versus nonstandardized*. A *standardized test* has fixed directions for administration and scoring, having been constructed by professional test makers and administered to a representative sample of examinees from the population for whom the test is intended. Various types of converted scores, or *norms*, may be computed from the raw test scores of this sample group (the *standardization group*) of examinees; these norms serve as a basis for interpreting the scores of subsequent examinees. Even more common than published standardized tests are nonstandardized classroom tests, which are usually constructed in an informal manner by school teachers.

Tests are also classified as *individual* or *group*. An *individual test*, such as the Binet–Simon Intelligence Scale, is administered to one examinee at a time. A *group test*, such as the Army Examination Alpha, can be administered simultaneously to many examinees.

Whereas the dichotomy *individual versus group* is related to the efficiency of administration, *speed versus power* pertains to the time limits of a test. A pure *speed test* consists of many easy items, but the time limits are very strict and almost no one finishes in the allotted time. The time limits on a *power test* are ample for most examinees, but the test contains more difficult items than a speed test.

A third classification dichotomy, *objective versus nonobjective*, is concerned with the method of scoring a test. An *objective test* has fixed, precise scoring standards and can be scored by a clerk. Scoring essay tests and certain types of personality tests is, on the other hand, quite subjective, and different scorers may obtain different results.

Tests may also be classified according to the content or task presented to examinees. Some tests contain only *verbal* materials (for example, vocabulary and sentences), whereas other tests consist of *nonverbal* materials (for example, diagrams and puzzles). A test may also require the examinees to manipulate objects, such as putting pegs into holes. This kind of instrument is called a *performance test*.

Another broad classification of tests according to content or process is *cognitive versus affective*. *Cognitive tests*, which attempt to quantify the processes and products of mental activity, may be classified as measures of achievement and aptitude. An *achievement test,* which assesses knowledge of some academic subject or occupation, focuses on the examinee's past behavior (what he or she has already learned or accomplished). An *aptitude test* focuses on future behavior, that is, what a person is capable of learning with appropriate training. Thus, tests of mechanical aptitude and clerical aptitude are designed to assess the ability to profit from further training in mechanical and clerical tasks, respectively. Achievement and aptitude, however, are not separate entities; what a person has accomplished in the past is usually a fairly good indicator of what can be expected of that person in the future. In fact, some psychologists prefer not to use the terms *achievement* and *aptitude* at all as ways of classifying tests; they refer to both kinds of tests as measures of *ability*.

Affective tests are designed to assess interests, attitudes, values, motives, temperament traits, and other noncognitive characteristics of personality. Various techniques, such as behavioral observation, paper-and-pencil inventories, and projective pictures, have been designed for this purpose.

Certain institutions and organizations that maintain collections of psychological and educational tests have formal systems for classifying these instruments. One of the most comprehensive classification systems is that of *The Mental Measurements Yearbook*. In this system, the major headings of which are listed in Table 1–2, tests are classified into 19 broad content categories.

Purposes and Uses of Testing

Psychological tests and other assessment devices are administered in a wide range of organizational contexts in contemporary society: schools and colleges, businesses and industries, psychological clinics and counseling centers, government and military organizations, and research contexts of various kinds. Thus, personnel psychologists, clinical psychologists, counseling psychologists, school psychologists, guidance and marriage counselors, and many other applied and research-oriented specialists in human behavior spend a substantial portion of their professional time administering, scoring, and interpreting psychological tests.

The primary purpose of psychological testing and assessment today is the same as it has been throughout this century: to evaluate behavior, mental abilities, and other personal characteristics in order to assist in making judgments, predictions, and decisions about people. More specifically, tests are used to (1) screen applicants for jobs and educational and training programs; (2) classify and place people in educational and employing contexts; (3) counsel and guide individuals for educational, vocational, and per-

TABLE 1–2   The Nineteen Major Categories of Tests Listed in *The Eleventh Mental Measurements Yearbook*

Achievement	Neuropsychological
Developmental	Personality
Education	Reading
English	Science
Fine Arts	Sensory–Motor
Foreign Languages	Social Studies
Intelligence and Scholastic Aptitude	Speech and Hearing
Mathematics	Vocations
Miscellaneous	Behavior Assessment
Multiaptitude	

Source: Reproduced from *The Eleventh Mental Measurements Yearbook* by permission of The Buros Institute of Mental Measurements of the University of Nebraska–Lincoln. Copyright 1992.

TABLE 1–3   Psychological Tests Used Most Frequently by Clinical Psychologists

Test	Usage rank
Wechsler Adult Intelligence Scale	1
Minnesota Multiphasic Personality Inventory	2
Bender Visual Motor Gestalt Test	3
Rorschach Inkblot Test	4
Thematic Apperception Test	5
Wechsler Intelligence Scale for Children–Revised	6
Peabody Picture Vocabulary Test	7.5
Sentence Completion Test (all kinds)	7.5
House–Tree–Person Test	9
Draw-a-Person Test	10
Wechsler Memory Scale	11
Rotter Sentence Completion Test	12
Memory for Designs	13
Vineland Social Maturity Scale	14
Stanford–Binet Intelligence Scale	15
Strong Vocational Interest Blank–Men	16
Bender Visual Retention Test	17.5
Edwards Personal Preference Schedule	17.5
Strong Vocational Interest Blank–Women	19
Children's Apperception Test	20.5
Progressive Matrices	20.5
Kuder Preference Record	22
Porteus Mazes	23
Full Range Picture Vocabulary Test	24
Differential Aptitude Tests	25
Gray Oral Reading Test	26
Wechsler–Bellevue Intelligence Scale	27
Cattell Infant Intelligence Test	28
Goldstein–Scheerer Tests of Abstract and Concrete Thinking	29
Blacky Pictures	30

Source: From B. Lubin, R.M. Larsen, & J.D. Matarazzo, 1984. Patterns of psychological test usage in the United States: 1935–1982. *American Psychologist, 39,* 451–454. Copyright 1984 by the American Psychological Association. Adapted by permission of the authors.

sonal counseling purposes; (4) retain or dismiss, promote, and rotate students or employees in educational and training programs and in job situations; (5) diagnose and prescribe psychological and physical treatments in clinics and hospitals; (6) evaluate cognitive, intra- and interpersonal changes due to educational, psychotherapeutic, and other behavior intervention programs; and (7) conduct research on changes in behavior over time and on the effectiveness of new programs or techniques. In addition to their applications in describing and analyzing individual characteristics, tests are used to assess psychological environments, social movements, and other psychosocial events.

No one knows exactly how many of each kind of commercially and noncommercially available tests are administered, and in what situations, for what purposes, and by whom these tests are administered during a given year. An indication of the nature of intent of test usage can be obtained, however, from the results of various surveys (for example, Brown & McGuire, 1976; Wade & Baker, 1977; Harrison et al., 1988; Piotrowski & Keller, 1989; Archer et al., 1991). Understandably, the findings of these surveys depend on the kinds of practitioners and/or researchers included in the survey sample. For example, the results given in Table 1–3 were obtained from a study of 221 psychologists employed in psychiatric hospitals, community mental health centers and clinics, schools for the mentally retarded, counseling centers, and Veterans Administration hospitals. The 30 most frequently mentioned tests are listed in order of frequency in Table 1–3. These data, which were collected in 1982, are similar to those reported some years earlier by Brown and McGuire (1976).

The results of a survey of randomly selected members of the Division of Counseling Psychology of the American Psychological Association (Watkins, Campbell, & McGregor, 1988) are summarized in Table 1–4. The 630 persons from whom these data were obtained were employed in private practice, college and university counseling centers, hospital settings, or community mental health centers. The findings reported in Tables 1–3 and 1–4 do not completely overlap, but we would not expect identical results. This is true not only because of differences in the times when the surveys were conducted, but also because different types of psychological practitioners were sampled in the two surveys. The results of another survey, this one of psychological tests administered to adolescents, are given in Table 1–5.

TABLE 1–4 Assessment Instrument Used Most Frequently by Counseling Psychologists

Test	Usage rank
Minnesota Multiphasic Personality Inventory	1
Wechsler Adult Intelligence Scale–Revised	2
Strong–Campbell Interest Inventory	3
Sentence Completion Blanks	4
Bender–Gestalt Test	5
Wechsler Intelligence Scale for Children–Revised	6
House–Tree–Person Test	7
Draw-a-Person Test	8
Thematic Apperception Test	9
Rorschach Inkblot Test	10.5
Sixteen Personality Factor Questionnaire	10.5
Wide Range Achievement Test	12
Edwards Personal Preference Schedule	13.5
Kuder Occupational Interest Survey	13.5
California Psychological Inventory	15
Wechsler Memory Scale	16
Wechsler Preschool and Primary Scale of Intelligence	17
Differential Aptitude Test	18

Source: Adapted from Watkins, Campbell, and McGregor, 1988.

TABLE 1–5   Psychological Assessment Instruments Used with Adolescents in Order of Usage Frequency

Wechsler Intelligence Scales
Rorschach Inkblot Test
Bender–Gestalt Test
Thematic Apperception Test
Sentence Completion Tests
Minnesota Multiphasic Personality Inventory
Human Figure Drawings
House–Tree–Person Test
Wide Range Achievement Test
Kinetic Family Drawing
Beck Depression Inventory
Millon Adolescent Personality Inventory
MacAndrew Alcoholism Scale
Child Behavior Checklist
Woodcock Johnson Psychoeducational Battery
Peabody Picture Vocabulary Test
Conners Behavior Rating Scale
Developmental Test of Visual–Motor Integration
Reynolds Adolescent Depression Scale
Children's Depression Inventory
Vineland Adaptive Behavior Scale
Vineland Social Maturity Scale
Roberts Apperception Test
Benton Visual Retention Test
Piers–Harris Children's Self-Concept Scale
Stanford–Binet Intelligence Scale
Personality Inventory for Children
Peabody Individual Achievement Test
Halstead–Reitan
High School Personality Inventory

Source: Archer et al., 1991.

TEST STANDARDS AND ETHICS

The increasing use of standardized tests of all kinds has brought with it a recognition of the need for greater public awareness of the advantages and limitations of tests and the motivations and practices of those who sell and use psychological and educational tests. It is a continuing concern of professional organizations of psychologists and educators that commercially available tests should be useful and measure what the test authors, publishers, and distributors claim. Contributing to this goal is a booklet of technical standards, the *Standards for Educational and Psychological Testing,* which was prepared by representatives of three professional organizations: The American Educational Research Association, the American Psychological Association, and the National Council on Measurement in Education (1985). Test authors, publishers, and consumers are well advised to become familiar with these *Standards,* which are referred to throughout this book. Also concerned with the matter of test standards are the *Guidelines for Computerbased Tests and Interpretations* (American Psychological Association, 1986) and the *Principles for the Validation and Use of Personnel Selection Procedures* (Society for Industrial and Organizational Psychology, Inc., 1987).

Qualifications of Test Users

Qualifications for administering, scoring, and interpreting tests are not uniform. They vary with the particular type of test, being more stringent for individually administered tests of intelligence and personality than for group-administered tests of achievement and special abilities. Whatever the qualifications or whoever the users may be, the ethical responsibility for ensuring that tests are sold only to qualified persons rests squarely on the shoulders of test publishers and distributors. The qualifications required to administer and interpret specific tests must be spelled out and adhered to by these organizations.

Reputable commercial test publishers require that their customers satisfy certain requirements, depending on the nature of the test and/or the degree of training needed to administer it. An example is the three-level (A, B, and C) qualification system of The Psychological Corporation. Level C tests may be purchased by schools and other organizations and by individuals certified or licensed to administer those tests. Qualification at level B requires a master's degree in psychology or education, equivalent training relevant to assessment, or membership in a professional association that requires appropriate training in assessment of its members. Qualification at level A, the highest level, requires a Ph.D. in psychology or education, the equivalent in training in assessment, or verification of licensure or certification requiring appropriate training and experience in psychological assessment.

Ethical Codes

The ethical use of tests can be controlled to some extent by a code of ethics to which professional testers and publishers subscribe. Both the American Psychological Association (APA) and the American Personnel and Guidance Association (APGA) have ethical codes pertaining to test administration and other psychological services. The APA and APGA ethical codes cover many of the same matters of test administration, standardization, reliability, and validity as the *Standards for Educational and Psychological Testing* (American Educational Research Association et al., 1985). Both codes stress the importance of considering the welfare of the examinee or client and guarding against the misuses of assessment instruments.

With respect to evaluation and assessment, the "Ethical Principles of Psychologists and Code of Conduct" (American Psychological Association, 1992) emphasize providing evaluation and diagnosis only in a professional context by trained, competent test users and the administration of appropriate tests. Emphasis is also placed on the applications of scientific procedures in designing and selecting tests and techniques that are appropriate for specified populations, the judicious interpretation of test results, the careful use of test scoring and interpretation services, the clear but careful explanation of assessment findings, and the need for maintaining test security.

The mere existence of high-quality tests and a set of standards or principles for test publishers, test distributors, and test consumers does not guarantee that tests will be administered and interpreted properly. Responsibility for using tests correctly rests with the test administrators and interpreters themselves, a responsibility that is being increasingly recognized by professional psychologists. Unfortunately, the skills and knowledge possessed by many counselors, clinicians, and other professionals are inadequate for administering certain tests. Therefore, mental testers must be made aware of the limitations of their professional qualifications, the need for further training, and the necessity of relying on other professionals and up-to-date sources of information for assistance. Furthermore, testers must be able to make sound ethical judgments by being sensitive to the needs of examinees and the institution as well as society as a whole.

In 1984, the three professional organizations (AERA, APA, and APGA) that were responsible for developing the *Standards for Educational and Psychological Testing* formed a Joint Committee on Test Practices (JCTP). The purpose of this committee was to work with test publishers in an attempt to improve the quality of testing practices in the public interest (Fremer, Diamond, & Camara, 1989). One result of the committee's efforts was a Code of Fair Testing Practices in Education. As shown in Figure 1–2, the 21 points of this code are listed in four sections: A. Developing/Selecting Appropriate Tests, B. Interpreting Scores, C. Striving for Fairness, and D. Informing Test Takers. Each section contains a set of recommendations that test developers and users should follow in their respective activities. It was hoped that distribution of the code and adherence to the principles and procedures enunciated in it would improve the validity and fairness of tests and the manner in which they are administered, scored, and interpreted. Complementing this code is a booklet, *Responsible Test Use* (Eyde et al., in press), an interdisciplinary casebook consisting of actual cases from various contexts in which specific tests were misused by being administered, scored, or interpreted improperly.

Informed Consent and Confidentiality

Improper disclosure of test data, especially data identified by name of examinee, is a continuing cause of concern to professionals in psychological assessment. The expanding use of computers and associated data banks has increased the need for vigilance in ensuring that test scores maintained in electronic files in particular be adequately protected against improper disclosure. Unless otherwise required by law, *informed consent* of the test taker or his or her legal representative is needed to release test results by name of examinee to any other person or institution. Informed consent implies that the individual who has agreed to have personal information released is aware of what the information consists of and with whom it is to be shared. Figure 1-3 (on p. 19) is an informed consent form that should be read and signed by the examinee or responsible party before a psychological examination of that person is conducted. As spelled out in this form, before any tests or other psychometric procedures are administered, examinees are told the nature and purpose of the examination, why they are being tested, who will have access to the information, and how it will be used. In addition to the rights of informed consent and confidentiality, the "least stigmatizing label" should be applied in reporting the presence of certain psychological symptoms, disorders, or other conditions. For example, "mentally impaired" is clearly less personally and socially stigmatizing than "feebleminded," "idiotic," or "moronic," and "adolescent adjustment reaction" is less stigmatizing than "psychopathic personality."

From a legal standpoint, psychological test data are considered a *privileged communication* to be shared with others only on a need-to-know basis. Examinees should be told at testing time why they are being tested, who will have access to the information, and how the information will be used. After being tested, examinees also have a right to know their scores and what interpretations are placed on them. Except under unusual circumstances, as when an examinee is a danger to himself or others, test information is confidential and should not be released without the necessary informed consent. Even with informed consent, the information may be *privileged* in the sense that, other than the client and, in the case of a minor or legally incompetent person, the parent(s) or guardian, only the client's attorney, physician, or psychologist may view it.

A Developing/Selecting Appropriate Tests*

Test developers should provide the information that test users need to select appropriate tests.	Test users should select tests that meet the purpose for which they are to be used and that are appropriate for the intended test-taking populations.

Test Developers Should:

1. Define what each test measures and what the test should be used for. Describe the population(s) for which the test is appropriate.

2. Accurately represent the characteristics, usefulness, and limitations of tests for their intended purposes.

3. Explain relevant measurement concepts as necessary for clarity at the level of detail that is appropriate for the intended audience(s).

4. Describe the process of test development. Explain how the content and skills to be tested were selected.

5. Provide evidence that the test meets its intended purpose(s).

6. Provide either representative samples or complete copies of test questions, directions, answer sheets, manuals, and score reports to qualified users.

7. Indicate the nature of the evidence obtained concerning the appropriateness of each test for groups of different racial, ethnic, or linguistic backgrounds who are likely to be tested.

8. Identify and publish any specialized skills needed to administer each test and to interpret scores correctly.

Test Users Should:

1. First define the purpose for testing and the population to be tested. Then, select a test for that purpose and that population based on a thorough review of the available information.

2. Investigate potentially useful sources of information, in addition to test scores, to corroborate the information provided by tests.

3. Read the materials provided by test developers and avoid using tests for which unclear or incomplete information is provided.

4. Become familiar with how and when the test was developed and tried out.

5. Read independent evaluations of a test and of possible alternative measures. Look for evidence required to support the claims of test developers.

6. Examine specimen sets, disclosed tests or samples of questions, directions, answer sheets, manuals, and score reports before selecting a test.

7. Ascertain whether the test content and norms group(s) or comparison group(s) are appropriate for the intended test takers.

8. Select and use only those tests for which the skills needed to administer the test and interpret scores correctly are available.

FIGURE 1–2 Code of Fair Testing Practices in Education. *(From Fremer, Diamond, & Camara, 1989.)*

B Interpreting Scores

| Test developers should help users interpret scores correctly. | Test users should interpret scores correctly. |

Test Developers Should:

9. Provide timely and easily understood score reports that describe test performance clearly and accurately. Also explain the meaning and limitations of reported scores.

10. Describe the population(s) represented by any norms or comparison group(s), the dates the data were gathered, and the process used to select the samples of test takers.

11. Warn users to avoid specific, reasonably anticipated misuses of test scores.

12. Provide information that will help users follow reasonable procedures for setting passing scores when it is appropriate to use such scores with the test.

13. Provide information that will help users gather evidence to show that the test is meeting its intended purpose(s).

Test Users Should:

9. Obtain information about the scale used for reporting scores, the characteristics of any norms or comparison group(s), and the limitations of the scores.

10. Interpret scores taking into account any major differences between the norms or comparison groups and the actual test takers. Also take into account any differences in test administration practices or familiarity with the specific questions in the test.

11. Avoid using tests for purposes not specifically recommended by the test developer unless evidence is obtained to support the intended use.

12. Explain how any passing scores were set and gather evidence to support the appropriateness of the scores.

13. Obtain evidence to help show that the test is meeting its intended purpose(s).

C Striving for Fairness

| Test developers should strive to make tests that are as fair as possible for test takers of different races, gender, ethnic backgrounds, or handicapping conditions. | Test users should select tests that have been developed in ways that attempt to make them as fair as possible for test takers of different races, gender, ethnic backgrounds, or handicapping conditions. |

Test Developers Should:

14. Review and revise test questions and related materials to avoid potentially insensitive content or language.

15. Investigate the performance of test takers of different races, gender, and ethnic backgrounds when samples of sufficient size are available. Enact procedures that help to ensure that differences in performance are related primarily to the skills under assessment rather than to irrelevant factors.

16. When feasible, make appropriately modified forms of tests or administration procedures available for test takers with handicapping conditions. Warn test users of potential problems in using standard norms with modified tests or administration procedures that result in non-comparable scores.

Test Users Should:

14. Evaluate the procedures used by test developers to avoid potentially insensitive content or language.

15. Review the performance of test takers of different races, gender, and ethnic backgrounds when samples of sufficient size are available. Evaluate the extent to which performance differences may have been caused by inappropriate characteristics of the test.

16. When necessary and feasible, use appropriately modified forms of tests or administration procedures for test takers with handicapping conditions. Interpret standard norms with care in the light of the modifications that were made.

FIGURE 1–2 *(continued)*

D Informing Test Takers

Under some circumstances, test developers have direct communication with test takers. Under other circumstances, test users communicate directly with test takers. Whichever group communicates directly with test takers should provide the information described below.

Test Developers or Test Users Should:

17. When a test is optional, provide test takers or their parents/guardians with information to help them judge whether the test should be taken, or if an available alternative to the test should be used.

18. Provide test takers the information they need to be familiar with the coverage of the test, the types of question formats, the directions, and appropriate test-taking strategies. Strive to make such information equally available to all test takers.

Under some circumstances, test developers have direct control of tests and test scores. Under other circumstances, test users have such control. Whichever group has direct control of tests and test scores should take the steps described below.

Test Developers or Test Users Should:

19. Provide test takers or their parents/guardians with information about rights test takers may have to obtain copies of tests and completed answer sheets, retake tests, have tests rescored, or cancel scores.

20. Tell test takers or their parents/guardians how long scores will be kept on file and indicate to whom and under what circumstances test scores will or will not be released.

21. Describe the procedures that test takers or their parents/guardians may use to register complaints and have problems resolved.

*Many of the statements in the Code refer to the selection of existing tests. However, in customized testing programs test developers are engaged to construct new tests. In those situations, the test development process should be designed to help ensure that the completed tests will be in compliance with the Code.

FIGURE 1–2 *(continued)*

INFORMED CONSENT FOR A PSYCHOLOGICAL EXAMINATION

I, _____ , voluntarily give my

consent to serve as a participant in a psychological examination conducted by _____.
I have received a clear and complete explanation of the general nature and purpose(s) of the examination and the specific reason(s) why I am being examined. I have also been informed of the kinds of tests and other procedures to be administered and how the results will be used.

I realize that it may not be possible for the examiner to explain all aspects of the examination to me until it has been completed. It is also my understanding that I may terminate my participation in the examination at any time without penalty. I further understand that I will be informed of the results and that the results will be reported to no one else without my permission. At this time, I request that a copy of the results of this examination be sent to:

_____

_____

_____   _____
Signature of Examinee   Examiner Prints Name Here

_____   _____
Date   Signature of Examiner

FIGURE 1–3 Form for Obtaining Informed Consent for Administering a Psychological Examination

Not only do legally responsible examinees have the right of access to the findings in their own test reports, but they can also arrange for transmittal of their test scores to educational, clinical, or counseling agencies for any appropriate use. At the same time, every effort must be made to maintain confidentiality of test scores and other personal information. The Family Educational Rights and Privacy Act of 1974 specifies, for example, that test results and other student records maintained by educational institutions receiving federal funds can be made available in a personally identifiable way to other people only with the written consent of the student or his or her parents. However, this act does permit parents and school personnel with a "legitimate educational interest" to review student records, as does Public Law 94-142 in the case of handicapped children.

SUMMARY

The roots of psychological testing and assessment can be traced to ancient Greece and China, although a concerted, scientific approach to the measurement of human differences in abilities and personality was not made until the late nineteenth century in Europe and the United States. The field of psychological and educational testing has grown rapidly during the twentieth century, and tests of various kinds are used extensively in educational, clinical, business, government, and military situations. Of the many sources of information about tests, *The Mental Measurements Yearbooks* are the most comprehensive. Tests are classified in various ways: standardized or nonstandardized, individual or group, speed or power, objective or nonobjective, verbal or nonverbal, paper-and-pencil or performance, and cognitive, affective or psychomotor.

During the past half-century, psychological and educational testing has become a big business, but the growth of the field has been accompanied by questions of adequate training and ethical issues. Information obtained from psychological testing should be kept confidential and, with some exceptions, shared with other people only after the written consent of the examinee or his or her legal guardians or counsel has been obtained.

To counter the misuse of tests, the American Psychological Association, the American Educational Research Association, and the American Personnel and Guidance Association have published ethical codes, a list of standards, and a code of fair testing practices. Adherence to these codes and standards will help ensure that psychological tests and other psychometric instruments are administered, scored, and interpreted by qualified persons in a sensible and sensitive manner.

EXERCISES

1. Identify the contribution(s) to psychological and educational measurement made by each of the following men: Alfred Binet, James M. Cattell, Francis Galton, Hermann Rorschach, Charles Spearman, Lewis Terman, Edward Thorndike, and Robert Woodworth. You should consult books on the history of psychological and educational testing, such as Linden and Linden (1968), DuBois (1970), and Edwards (1974), in order to obtain more complete information.

2. Discuss various ways of classifying psychological tests and other assessment instruments, and evaluate each of them.

3. Examine copies of the *Eleventh Mental Measurements Yearbook* (Kramer & Conoley, 1992), *The Tenth Mental Measurements Yearbook* (Conoley & Kramer, 1989), *The Ninth Mental Measurements Yearbook* (Mitchell, 1985), and *Test Critiques* (Keyser & Sweetland, 1984–1988). These books are available in most college and university libraries. Also obtain a copy of the *Standard for Educational and Psychological Testing* (American Educational Research Association et al., 1985) from your instructor or the library. Describe the various kinds of information contained in these reference sources.

4. Some writers, particularly in the physical sciences, have questioned whether test scores and other forms of psychological and educational measurement actually deserve to be called "measurement." After reading a discussion of the logic of mental measurement (for example, Aiken, 1973, Section III), defend the thesis that mental measurement constitutes true measurement.

5. Assuming that psychologists are both professionals who have the welfare of the public uppermost in mind and scientists whose search for truth does not include the exploitation of other people, why is it necessary to have an explicit code of ethics governing the practice of psychology?

SUGGESTED READINGS

Bowman, M. L. (1989). Testing individual differences in Ancient China. *American Psychologist, 44*, 576–578.

Buros, O. K. (1977). Fifty years in testing: Some reminiscences, criticism, and suggestions. *Educational Researcher, 6*(7), 9–15.

Doyle, K. O., Jr. (1974). Theory and practice of ability testing in Ancient Greece. *Journal of the History of the Behavioral Sciences, 10*, 202–212.

DuBois, P. H. (1970). *History of psychological testing.* Boston: Allyn & Bacon.

Edwards, A. J. (1974). *Individual mental testing. Part I: History and theories.* Scranton, PA: Intext Educational Publishers.

Green, B. F. (1981). A primer of testing. *American Psychologist, 36*, 1001–1011.

Gregory, R. J. (1992). *Psychological testing: History, principles, and applications*, Ch. 1. Boston: Allyn & Bacon.

Linden, K. W., & Linden, J. D. (1968). *Modern mental measurement: A historical perspective.* Boston: Houghton Mifflin.

McReynolds, P. (1986). History of assessment in clinical and educational settings. In R. O. Nelson & S. C. Hayes (eds.), *Conceptual foundations of behavioral assessment*, pp. 42–80. New York: Guilford Press.

Sokal, M. M. (1987). *Psychological testing and American society 1890–1930.* New Brunswick, NJ: Rutgers University Press.

Thorndike, R. M. & Lohman, D. F. (1990). *A century of ability testing.* Chicago: Riverside Publishing Company.

Chapter Two

Test Design and Construction

The amount of effort involved in constructing a psychological or educational test varies with the type of test and the purposes for which it is intended. Most classroom teachers probably spend relatively little time preparing essay or short-answer tests for evaluating pupil progress in a unit of instruction. On the other hand, the tests of ability and personality designed by specialists in psychological measurement usually require the efforts of many people working for extended periods of time.

The procedures employed in constructing a test also vary with the type of test and the aims of the users. Preparing a paper-and-pencil inventory of interests or personality entails different problems than constructing a test of achievement or aptitude. Similarly, the complex procedures followed by professional test designers are unfamiliar to the majority of teachers. Whatever the kind of test or the goals of the users may be, some content planning is necessary before the items comprising the test are written.

PLANNING A TEST

Constructing a test demands careful consideration of its specific purposes. Tests serve many different functions, and the process of test construction varies to some extent with the particular purposes of the test. For example, different procedures are followed in constructing an achievement test, an intelligence test, a test of special aptitude, or a personality inventory. Ideally, however, the construction of any test or psychometric instrument begins by defining the variables or constructs to be measured and outlining the proposed content.

Screening Tests

Constructing an aptitude test to screen applicants for a particular job begins with a detailed analysis of the activities comprising the job. A task analysis, or *job analysis,* consists of specifying the components of the job so that test situations or items can be devised to predict employee performance. These specifications may include *critical incidents,* behaviors that are critical to successful or unsuccessful performance, as well as other information describing job activities. Since the description of a particular job is typically long and involved, the finished test will not measure all aspects of employee performance. It will deal with only a sample of behaviors important to the job, a sample that should, at best, represent all the tasks comprising the job.

Intelligence Tests

Procedures for designing intelligence tests are described in detail in Chapter 6. As in constructing any other test, a pool of items that presumably measure some aspect of the construct "intelligence" is assembled. These items may be constructed according to a specific theory of intelligent behavior or simply with reference to the kinds of tasks that more intelligent people presumably perform more effectively than less intelligent people. The selection of items for the final test may be made on the basis of the relationships of item responses to criteria such as chronological age, as well as the relationships among the test items themselves.

Personality Inventories and Scales

A variety of approaches, some based on common (or educated) sense, others on personality theories, and still others on statistical procedures, has been employed in constructing personality inventories and rating scales. As described in Chapters 10 and 11, many recently published personality inventories have been constructed by combining theoretical, rational, and empirical approaches. One or more of these approaches may be employed at different stages of test development.

Achievement Tests

More attention has been devoted to procedures for constructing scholastic achievement tests than other kinds of tests. This is understandable when we realize that achievement tests are more widely administered than any other type of psychological assessment instrument. Despite the widespread use of achievement tests, classroom teachers, who presumably are well acquainted with their subject matter, typically devote insufficient time to evaluating student progress. Too often teachers view testing as a somewhat disagreeable adjunct to teaching, rather than as an integral, formative part of the educational process. Used effectively, however, the results of testing not only evaluate and motivate students, but also provide information to teachers, school administrators, and parents concerning the extent to which the specific educational objectives have been attained. By providing data on the effectiveness of the school curriculum and teaching procedures, test scores can contribute to the planning of instruction for individual students or entire classes.

Questions for Test Planners

Planners of classroom achievement tests should begin by answering the following questions:

1. What are the topics and materials on which students are to be tested?
2. What kinds of questions should be constructed?
3. What item and test formats or layouts should be used?
4. When, where, and how should the test be given?
5. How should the completed test papers be scored and evaluated?

Questions 1 to 3 will be discussed in this chapter, and questions 4 and 5 in Chapter 3.

Taxonomies of Educational Objectives

Just as the construction of a screening test for use in personnel selection requires a preliminary job analysis, the preparation of a test to measure specific instructional objectives is most effective when the behaviors to be assessed are clearly defined at the outset. Since the mid-1950s, much attention has been given to formal, standard systems of classifying the cognitive, affective, and psychomotor objectives of instruction. The major categories of four such taxonomies of cognitive objectives are listed in Table 2–1. The six principal categories of the first taxonomy, the *Taxonomy of Educational Objectives:*

TABLE 2–1 Illustrative Outlines of Cognitive Objectives

Bloom and Krathwohl (1956)	*Gerlach and Sullivan (1967)*
Knowledge	Identifying
Comprehension	Naming
Application	Describing
Analysis	Constructing
Synthesis	Ordering
Evaluation	Demonstrating

Educational Testing Service (1965)
Remembering
Understanding
Thinking

Ebel (1979)
Understanding of terminology (or vocabulary)
Understanding of fact and principle (or generalization)
Ability to explain or illustrate (understanding of relationships)
Ability to calculate (numerical problems)
Ability to predict (what is likely to happen under specified conditions)
Ability to recommend appropriate action (or some specific practical problem situations)
Ability to make an evaluative judgment

TABLE 2–2   Categories of the *Taxonomy of Educational Objectives: The Cognitive Domain*

   I. *Knowledge* involves the recall of specific facts. Sample verbs in knowledge items are *define, identify, list,* and *name.* A knowledge item is "List the six major categories of *The Taxonomy of Educational Objectives: The Cognitive Domain.*"

   II. Comprehension means understanding the meaning or purpose of something. Sample verbs in comprehension items are *convert, explain,* and *summarize.* A comprehension item is "Explain what the test reviewer means when he says that the test is unreliable."

   III. *Application* involves the use of information and ideas in new situations. Sample verbs in application items are *compute, determine,* and *solve.* A sample application item is "Compute the mean and standard deviation of the following group of scores."

   IV. *Analysis* is breaking down something to reveal its structure and the interrelationships among its parts. Sample verbs are *analyze, differentiate,* and *relate.* A sample analysis item is "Analyze this instructional unit into its several behavioral and content categories."

   V. *Synthesis* is combining various elements or parts into a structural whole. Sample verbs are *design, devise, formulate,* and *plan.* A sample synthesis item is "Design a table of specifications for a test on elementary statistics."

   VI. *Evaluation* is making a judgment based on reasoning. Sample verbs are *compare, critique, evaluate,* and *judge.* A sample evaluation item is "Evaluate the procedure used in standardizing this test."

Source: From *Taxonomy of Educational Objectives: The Classification of Educational Goals: Handbook I: The Cognitive Domain* by Benjamin S. Bloom et al. Copyright © 1956, 1984 by Longman. Longman Publishing Group.

The Cognitive Domain (Bloom & Krathwohl, 1956) are listed in order from least complex to most complex. These categories are not exclusive, but rather progressively inclusive. For example, both "Knowledge" (category I) and "Comprehension" (category II) are basic to "Application" (category III) and are therefore included in the third category. Descriptions of the categories in this taxonomy are given in Table 2–2.

Another taxonomy outlined in Table 2–1, one proposed by Gerlach and Sullivan (1967), emphasizes the examinee's behavior in identifying, naming, describing, constructing, ordering, or demonstrating something. In *identifying* the examinee must indicate which member of a set belongs in a particular category. In *naming,* the correct verbal label for a referent or set of referents must be supplied by the examinee. In *describing,* relevant categories of objects, events, properties, or relationships are reported. In *constructing,* a product is created according to certain specifications. In *ordering,* two or more referents are arranged in a specific order, and in *demonstrating* the examinee performs certain actions to accomplish a specified task.

Following any of the taxonomies outlined in Table 2–1 should encourage the test designer to go beyond simple recognitive or rote memory items and construct a number of items to measure higher-order educational objectives that require thinking. The following items, which may be presented in either essay or objective test format, are illustrative:

What is the formula for computing the standard error of measurement? (*Knowledge*)

Examine the graph and determine how many items must be added to a 50-item test to increase its reliability from .60 to .80. (*Comprehension*)

Compute the standard error of estimate for a test having a correlation of .70 with a criterion having a standard deviation of 10. (*Application*)

Differentiate between a classroom achievement test and a standardized achievement test in terms of what each measures and how each is used. (*Analysis*)

Formulate a theory relating interests to personality; cite appropriate supporting research evidence. (*Synthesis*)

Evaluate the criticisms of Ralph Nader and Allen Nairn concerning the Scholastic Aptitude Test (SAT). (*Evaluation*)

Affective and Psychomotor Objectives

An important function of education is instilling certain attitudes, values, and other affective states in the learner. A completely satisfactory method of classifying the affective objectives of instruction does not exist, but a number of classification systems have been proposed. One such classification system is the *Taxonomy of Educational Objectives: Affective Domain* (Krathwohl, Bloom, & Masia, 1964). The major categories of this taxonomy are I. Receiving or Attending; II. Responding or Participating; III. Valuing or Believing in the Worth of Something; IV. Organizing Values into a System; V. Characterization by a Value of Value Complex.

Taxonomies of educational objectives in the psychomotor domain have also been proposed (for example, Simpson, 1966; Harrow, 1972). The six categories in Harrow's Taxonomy of the Psychomotor Domain, for example, are Reflex Movements, Basic–Fundamental Movements, Perceptual Abilities, Physical Abilities, Skilled Movements, and Nondiscursive Communication.

Table of Specifications

Most test designers do not adhere rigidly to a formal taxonomy in specifying the objectives to be measured. Nevertheless, it is helpful in test planning to construct a two-way table of specifications. In preparing such a table, the behavioral objectives to be assessed are listed as row headings and the content (topical) objectives as column headings. Then the descriptions of specific items falling under the appropriate row and column headings are written in the body (cells) of the table.

A table of specifications should be fairly detailed in terms of the knowledge and skills that examinees are expected to demonstrate, but it is important not to place undue emphasis on one particular objective. It may be easier to construct items that assess knowledge of terms and facts than items measuring the ability to analyze and evaluate, but items in the last two categories should also be included on the test.

Table 2–3 is a table of specifications for a unit on the preparation, administration,

TABLE 2-3   Table of Specifications for a Test on the Preparation and Administration of Tests

	Content (topic)				
Behavioral objective	Test preparation (16%)	Test construction (26%)	Administration (14%)	Scoring (22%)	Item analysis (22%)
Knowledge of terminology	Job analysis; critical incidents; representative sample (3 items)	Matching item; spiral omnibus; response set (5 items)	Rapport; halo effect (2 items)	Strip key; composite score; machine scoring (3 items)	Criterion; internal consistency; test homogeneity (3 items)
Knowledge of specific facts	Categories in "Taxonomy of Educational Objectives" (2 items)	Advantages and disadvantages of essay items and objective items (4 items)	Factors affecting test performance (3 items)	Rules for scoring essay and objective tests (3 items)	Methods of determining item validity; purposes of item analysis (3 items)
Comprehension	Explanation of the purposes of making a test plan (2 items)	(0 items)	(0 items)	Effects of weighting on total score (1 item)	Explanation of relationship between p and D (1 item)
Application	Specifications for a unit on testing (1 item)	Examples of multiple-choice items to measure comprehension, application, analysis, synthesis, and evaluation (4 items)	Directions for a test (2 items)	Correction for guessing; confidence weighting; use of nomograph for scoring rearrangement items (4 items)	Computation of difficulty and discrimination indexes; distribution of responses to distracters (4 items)
Total	(8 items)	(13 items)	(7 items)	(11 items)	(11 items)

and item analysis of tests. Notice that the percentage of the total number of test items to be devoted to each topic is given in parentheses below the particular topic. Once a set of objectives for a course of study has been determined and a topical outline prepared, test items can be constructed to measure the extent to which students have attained the objectives listed for each topic.

Certain types of test items are more appropriate than others for measuring the attainment of specific objectives. Short-answer and completion items lend themselves well to the measurement of knowledge of terminology, but they are inadequate for assessing higher-order cognitive abilities. For this reason, the table of specifications for a test should be referred to in deciding what varieties of items and how many of each are appropriate for a particular test. Practical considerations such as cost, time available for test administration, item arrangement, and testing conditions must also be considered in planning a test.

PREPARING TEST ITEMS

The primary goal of test planning is the preparation of a detailed outline, such as a table of specifications, to serve as a guide in constructing items to assess or predict certain objectives. Once a table of specifications or detailed content outline of the test has been prepared, the next step is to construct the actual items. It is generally recommended that, on objective tests, about 20 percent more items than are actually needed be written initially so that an adequate number of good items will be available for the final version of the test. Commercial testing organizations such as Educational Testing Service employ as item writers persons who possess both knowledge of the subject matter of the test and skill in writing items. Anyone desiring to learn how to construct good test items can profit from inspecting a sample of items in published standardized tests because they are among the best available.

All test items represent procedures for obtaining information about individuals, but the amount and kinds of information vary with the nature of the tasks posed by different types of items. Telling examinees to compare the Battle of the Bulge with the Battle of Hastings demands a different kind of response from that obtained when they are simply told to indicate which of a series of listed events occurred in each battle. Complex integrating and organizing abilities are required by the first item, whereas only recognitive memory is needed to answer the second.

Various methods of classifying items according to format, or the form of response required, have been suggested. *Supply* versus *selection, recall* versus *recognition,* and *constructed response* versus *identification* are ways of differentiating between items on which examinees are required to write or construct an answer and those on which they are asked to indicate which of several alternatives is correct. Another popular method of classifying items is *essay* versus *objective,* examples of which are given in Table 2–4. All essay items are of the supply type in that an examinee's answer is a constructed response.

Objective items, however, may be of either the supply or selection type, depending on whether examinees must construct a response or merely select the best answer from a list of alternatives. The crucial feature of objective items is not the form of the response, but how objectively they can be scored. Two or more scorers of an essay item often

TABLE 2–4 Examples of Various Types of Test Items

I. *Essay Items*
Directions: Write a half-page answer to each item.
1. Contrast the advantages and disadvantages of essay and objective test items.
2. Explain the reasons for performing an item analysis of a classroom test.

II. *Objective Items*
  A. *Short answer*
    Directions: Write the appropriate words(s) in each blank.
    1. The only thing that is objective about an objective test is the _____
    _____ .
    2. What is the first formal step in constructing a test to predict degree of success on a particular job? _____

  B. *True–false*
    Directions: Circle T if the statement is true; circle F if it is false.
    T F 1. The most comprehensive test classification system is that of *The Mental Measurements Yearbooks.*
    T F 2. The social-desirability response set is the tendency to rate an examinee high on one trait simply because he or she is rated high on another trait.

  C. *Matching*
    Directions: Write the letter corresponding to the correct name in the appropriate marginal dash.

_____ 1. group intelligence test	A.	Binet
_____ 2. individual intelligence test	B.	Darwin
_____ 3. interest inventory	C.	Galton
_____ 4. personality inventory	D.	Otis
_____ 5. product–moment correlation	E.	Pearson
_____ 6. sensorimotor tests	F.	Rorschach
	G.	Spearman
	H.	Strong
	I.	Woodworth

  D. *Multiple choice*
  Directions: Write the letter of the correct option in the marginal dash opposite the item.
    _____ 1. Qualifying words such as *never, sometimes,* and *always,* which reveal the answer to an examinee who has no information on the subject of the item, are called
      A. glittering generalities
      B. interlocking adverbs
      C. response sets
      D. specific determiners
    _____ 2. Jimmy, who is 8 years, 4 months old, obtains a mental age score of 9 years, 5 months. What is his ratio IQ on the text?
      A. 88
      B. 90
      C. 113
      D. 120

disagree to some extent on the correctness of a given answer and how many points it should receive. But, barring clerical errors, different scorers of an objective test will assign the same score to a given test paper.

Characteristics of Essay Items

The most important advantage of essay items is that they can measure the ability to organize, relate, and communicate, behaviors that are not so easily assessed by objective items. An essay test also takes less time to prepare, and it is unlikely that examinees will get essay items right by guessing. A shortcoming of essay tests is that the number of questions that can be answered in a typical class period (approximately six half-page answers in 50 minutes) may not provide an adequate sampling of the examinees' subject-matter knowledge. Other shortcomings of essay tests are that scoring them is subjective and time consuming, and they are susceptible to bluffing by verbally adept but uninformed examinees.

A history teacher of my acquaintance once reportedly administered an essay test that included the question, "What were the causes and consequences of the Battle of Hastings?" One phlegmatic student who had not found the time to go back farther than the fourteenth century in studying English history began his answer to the question with the statement, "Far be it from me to comment on the Battle of Hastings, but let us turn our attention to the Hundred Years War." This is a fairly blatant example of the tendency of uninformed examinees to answer a slightly different essay question from the one being asked in order to emphasize what they do know, rather than what they don't.[1]

As a rule, essay items should not be used when it is possible to make the same evaluation with objective items. If essay questions are asked, the item writer should try to make the questions as objective as possible. This can be done by (1) defining the task and wording the items clearly, for example, asking the examinee to "contrast" and "explain" rather than "discuss"; (2) using a small number of items, all of which should be attempted by all examinees; (3) structuring the items in such a way that subject-matter experts will agree that one answer is demonstrably better than another; and (4) having examinees answer each item on a separate sheet of paper.

Short-answer, True–False, and Matching Items

Objective items are not limited to the traditional four (short answer or completion, true–false, matching, and multiple choice), but these are the most popular. Among the advantages claimed for objective tests are that they can be scored easily and objectively, and, because less time is needed to answer each item, they permit a broader sampling of material than essay tests. In preparing objective tests, care should be taken to make the items clear, precise, and grammatically correct. They should be written in language suitable to the reading level of the group for whom the test is intended. All information and qualifications needed to select a reasonable answer should be included in the item, omitting nonfunctional or stereotyped words and phrases.

Although it is tempting to construct objective items by lifting statements verbatim

---

[1]One way of coping with this problem, although laborious to both test takers and scorers, is the famous Chinese examination procedure of having examinees write down everything they know!

from textbooks or other sources, this places a premium on rote memory. Item writers should also be careful to omit irrelevant clues to the correct answers and to avoid interrelated or interlocking items. Items are *interrelated* when the wording of one item provides a clue to the answer to the other item. Items are *interlocked* when it is necessary to know the correct answer to one item in order to answer the other item correctly.

Short-answer Items   A short-answer item is a supply-type task on which examinees are required to complete or fill in one or more blanks of an incomplete statement with the correct words or phrases or to give a brief answer to a question. In terms of the length of the constructed response, short-answer items fall somewhere between essay and recognition items. They are among the easiest items to construct, requiring that examinees supply the correct answer rather than simply recognizing it. Although short-answer items are especially useful for assessing knowledge of terminology, they have serious limitations. They are not appropriate for measuring complex instructional objectives, and because there may be more than one correct answer, scoring is not always entirely objective.

The following guidelines should be followed in constructing short-answer items:

1.   Questions are preferable to incomplete statements.
2.   If an incomplete statement is used, word it so that the blank comes at the end.
3.   Avoid multiple blanks in the same item, especially if they make the meaning of the task unclear.

True–False Items   One of the simplest types of test items to construct, but probably the most maligned by professional testers, is the true–false item. True–false items can be written and read quickly, and so they permit a broad sampling of content. A notorious shortcoming of these items is that they are often concerned with trivial information or are constructed by lifting statements verbatim from textbooks. Consequently, they are said to encourage rote memorization on the part of examinees. Other criticisms of true–false items are that they are often ambiguous, they cannot be used to measure more complex instructional objectives, and, by relying on rote memory, they misdirect efforts to learn. Furthermore, because the total score on a true–false test can be affected by the tendency of an examinee to guess when in doubt or to agree (or disagree), the meaning of the total score may be questionable.[2]

On the average, examinees will get 50 percent of the items on a true–false test right simply by guessing. Scores may be inflated even more when items contain *specific determiners*—words such as *all, always, never,* and *only,* which indicate that the statement is probably false, or *often, sometimes,* and *usually,* which indicate that the statement is probably true.

Despite these shortcomings, true–false items do not have to be trivial or ambiguous and do not necessarily misdirect efforts to learn. In defense of true–false items, Ebel (1970) maintained that "the extent of students' command of a particular area of knowledge is indicated by their success in judging the truth or falsity of propositions related to it"

---

[2]The tendency to agree when in doubt (acquiescence) is an example of a response set. *Response sets* are tendencies on the part of examinees to answer test items on the basis of their form, that is, on the way the items are phrased, rather than on the basis of their content.

(page 112). Ebel argued that such propositions are expressions of verbal knowledge, which he viewed as the essence of educational achievement.

Ebel's defense of true–false items can be questioned, but there is no questioning the fact that well-designed true–false items can measure more than rote memory. For example, by including two concepts, conditions, or events in a true–false item, the examiner can ask if it is true that they are moderately to strongly related (Diekhoff, 1984). Other possibilities are to ask if (1) one concept, condition, or event implies (is a consequence of) the other; (2) one concept, condition, or event is a subset, example, or category of the other; or (3) both concepts, conditions, events are true. Such items can measure understanding as well as significant knowledge of concepts and events.

Whatever the objectives of a true–false test may be, it is advisable to attend to the following suggestions in constructing items of this type:

1. Make certain that the statements deal with important (nontrivial) matters.
2. Make the statements relatively short and unqualifiedly true or false.
3. Avoid negatively stated items, especially those containing double negatives.
4. Avoid ambiguous and tricky items.
5. As a rule, avoid specific determiners. If specific determiners are used to trip up unknowledgeable but testwise examinees, they should be included in true items as often as in false items.
6. On opinion statements, cite the source or authority.
7. Make true and false statements about the same length, and make the number of true statements approximately equal to the number of false statements. It can be argued that, because false items tend to be more discriminating than true items, the number of false statements should be greater than the number of true statements. However, if the teacher follows this practice on successive tests, students may become aware of it and begin to answer "false" when in doubt about the answer.
8. Make wrong answers more attractive by wording items in such a way that superficial logic, popular misconceptions, or specific determiners suggest that the wrong answers are correct. False statements having the ring of truth may also trip up unknowledgeable examinees.

Matching Items   Both true–false and multiple-choice items are, in a sense, varieties of matching items. On all three types of items, a set of response options is matched to a set of stimulus options (premises). The distinction is that true–false and multiple-choice items have only one stimulus option (the *stem* of the item) and two or more response options, whereas matching items have multiple stimulus options and multiple response options. The task on a matching item is to indicate which response options are paired with which stimulus options. Matching is usually one to one (one response per stimulus), but it may well be one to many, many to one, or many to many. Examinees should, of course, be informed as to which of these procedures is applicable on a particular item.

Matching items are easy to construct and cover the material more efficiently than other types of items, but they usually measure only the rote memory of facts. In addition, the necessity of making the options homogeneous (all options of the same kind, such as dates, places, or names) limits the type of material that can be fitted into a matching framework. Some guidelines for constructing matching items are the following:

1. Place the stimulus (premise) and response options in a clear, logical column format, with the stimulus options in the left column and the response options in the right column.
2. Number the stimulus options successively, and place letters (a, b, c, and so on) before the response options.
3. Use between six and fifteen stimulus options, with two to three more response options than stimulus options.
4. Clearly specify the basis for matching.
5. Place the entire item on a single page.

A special type of matching item is the *rearrangement item,* on which examinees are required to sort a group of options into a fixed number of predetermined categories. A particular type of rearrangement item is the *ranking item,* on which a set of options is to be arranged in rank order from first to last (see Table 2–4).

Multiple-choice Items

No one knows who constructed the first multiple-choice test item, but from the viewpoint of psychological assessment it was a momentous event.[3] Multiple-choice items are the most versatile of all objective test items in that they can be used to measure both simple and complex learning objectives at all grade levels and in all subject-matter areas. Although constructing an answer to an essay item may demand greater organizational skill than answering a multiple-choice item, responding correctly to a well-prepared multiple-choice item requires good discriminating ability and not merely skill in recognizing or recalling the correct answer. Scores on multiple-choice items are also less affected by guessing and other response sets than are scores on other types of objective items. Furthermore, useful diagnostic information may be obtained from an analysis of the incorrect options (*distracters*) selected by examinees.

Among the shortcomings of multiple-choice items are that (1) good ones are difficult to construct, especially items on which all options are equally attractive to examinees who do not know the correct answer; (2) they emphasize recognition rather than the recall and organization of information; and (3) they require more time to answer and may sample the subject-matter domain less adequately than true–false items. It has also been alleged, although not proven, that multiple-choice tests favor shrewd, nimblewitted, rapid readers and penalize more thoughtful, profound examinees (Hoffman, 1962).

Guidelines for Writing Multiple-choice Items   The following guidelines should facilitate the construction of high-quality multiple-choice items:

1. Either a question or an incomplete statement may be used as the stem, but the question format is preferred. Place the blank in an incomplete statement stem at the end of the item.

---

[3]Arthur Otis should probably be credited with originating the multiple-choice item format, which appears to have been first used in his group intelligence test in 1916–1917.

THE CHRONICLE OF HIGHER EDUCATION

"Look, Harvey, the only reason you're depressed is that you're letting yourself be bound by conventional standards. I think that writing 5,383 multiple-choice questions is a contribution to literature."

FIGURE 2–1   Test Item Writing as a Passage to Fame.
(Courtesy of Vivian Scott Hixson.)

2. State the specific problem of the question or incomplete statement clearly in the stem and at a reading level appropriate for the examinees, but avoid taking questions or statements verbatim from textbooks.

3. Place as much of the item as possible in the stem. It is inefficient to repeat the same words in every option, and examinees have less difficulty scanning shorter options.

4. Employ opinion questions sparingly; when they are used, cite the authority or source of the opinion.

5. Four or five options are typical, but good items having only two or three options can also be written. With students in the lower grades, three options are preferable to four or five.

6. If the options have a natural order, such as dates or ages, it is advisable to arrange them accordingly. Otherwise, arrange the options in random or alphabetical order (if alphabetizing does not give clues to the correct answer).

7. Make all options approximately equal in length, grammatically correct, and appropriate in relation to the stem. However, do not let the stem "give away" the correct option by verbal associations or other clues.

8. Make all options plausible to examinees who do not know the right answer, but make only one option correct or "best." Popular misconceptions or statements that are only partially correct make good distracters.

9. In constructing each distracter, formulate a reason why an examinee who does not know the correct answer might select that distracter.

10. Avoid, or at least minimize, the use of negative expressions such as "not" in either the stem or options.
11. Although a certain amount of novelty and even humor is appropriate and may serve to interest and motivate examinees, ambiguous or tricky stems and options should not be used.
12. Use "none of the above," "all of the above," or "more than one of the above" sparingly. Also, avoid specific determiners such as "always" or "never."
13. Place the options in stacked (paragraph) rather than in tandem (back to back) format; use numbers to designate items and letters for options.
14. Prepare the right number of items for the grade or age level to be tested, making each item independent of other items (not interlocking or interrelated).
15. Make the difficulty levels of items such that the percentage of examinees who answer the item correctly is approximately halfway between the chance (random guessing) percentage and 100 percent: % correct $= 50 (k + 1)/k$, where k is the number of distracters per item.

Simply following these guidelines, which are primarily the products of logic and experience rather than research, will not ensure the construction of a good multiple-choice test. Rather than blindly obeying a set of rules, the ability to write good items depends as much or more on knowledge of the subject matter of the test, understanding what students should know and are unlikely to know about the subject matter, and the art or skill of asking questions. Even when the guidelines are not followed precisely, multiple-choice items tend to be fairly robust in their ability to measure knowledge and understanding.

Constructing Distracters A critical process in determining the effectiveness of multiple-choice items is the selection or construction of distracters (incorrect options). Either a rational or an empirical approach to item selection may be employed. The *rational* approach requires the test constructor to make personal judgments as to which distracters are appropriate. In contrast, the *empirical* approach consists of selecting distracters according to the number of responses given to the stems of items when they are administered as open-ended statements. There is no consensus as to which approach results in better distracters, but examiner judgment appears to be at least as effective as the empirical approach (Owens, Hanna, & Coppedge, 1970; Hanna & Johnson, 1978).

Constructing Complex Items Test designers usually have more difficulty constructing items to measure understanding and thinking than items that measure straightforward knowledge of the subject matter of the test. Various ways of composing objective items to assess more complex instructional objectives have been proposed. Options such as "all of the above," "none of the above," "two of the above," and "all but one of the above" can make an examinee's choice more difficult. In addition, making all options correct (or incorrect) and requiring examinees to select the best or nearly correct option for each item complicates the task. Other ways of making an examinee's decision more demanding are to (1) include multiple-answer items in which a variable number of options is correct and the examinee must indicate which (if any) options are correct or incorrect; (2) have examinees select an answer and improve on it; and (3) ask examinees to identify

TABLE 2–5   Some Complex Forms of Multiple-choice Items

1. *Classification.* The examinee classifies a person, object, or condition into one of several categories designated in the stem:
   Jean Piaget is best characterized as a _____ psychologist.
   a. clinical
   b. developmental
   c. psychometric
   d. social

2. *If–Then Conditions.* The examinee must decide the correct consequence of one or more conditions being present:
   If the true variance of a test increases but the error variance remains constant, which of the following will occur?
   a. reliability will increase
   b. reliability will decrease
   c. observed variance will decrease
   d. neither reliability nor observed variance will change

3. *Multiple Conditions.* The examinee uses the two or more conditions or statements listed in the stem to draw a conclusion:
   Given that Mary's raw score on a test is 60, the test mean is 59, and the standard deviation 2, what is Mary's z score?
   a. −2.00
   b. −0.50
   c. 0.50
   d. 2.00

4. *Multiple True–False.* The examinee decides whether one, all, or none of the two or more conditions or statements listed in the stem is (are) correct:
   Is it true that (1) Alfred Binet was the father of intelligence testing, and (2) his first intelligence test was published in 1916?
   a. both 1 and 2
   b. 1 but not 2
   c. not 1 but 2
   d. neither 1 nor 2

5. *Oddity.* The examinee indicates which option does not belong with the others:
   Which of the following names does *not* belong with the others?
   a. Alfred Adler
   b. Sigmund Freud
   c. Carl Jung
   d. Carl Rogers

6. *Relations and Correlates.* The examinee determines the relationship between concepts 1 and 2 and indicates which of the concepts (a, b, c, d, etc.) listed in the options is related to concept 3 in the same way that concepts 1 and 2 are related:
   Mean is to standard deviation as median is to:
   a. average deviation
   b. inclusive range
   c. semi-interquartile range
   d. variance

the correct setup (such as an equation or method of solution) on problem-solving tasks. Additional procedures for increasing the complexity of multiple-choice items are illustrated in Table 2–5. All these techniques were designed to make the choice of the correct option a thoughtful, analytical process in which various mental abilities are employed, rather than merely recognitive memory.

ASSEMBLING A TEST

After the items for a test have been prepared, it is always advisable to have them reviewed and edited by another knowledgeable person. Even the most painstaking efforts do not necessarily produce a good test, and a friend or associate can frequently spot errors and make valuable suggestions for improving items.

Assuming that the test designer has constructed a sufficient number of satisfactory items, final decisions concerning several matters must be made before a test is assembled:

1. Is the length of the test appropriate for the time limits?
2. How should the items be grouped or arranged on the pages of the test booklet?
3. Are answers to be marked in the test booklet, or is a special answer sheet to be used?
4. How will the test booklet and answer sheet be reproduced?
5. What information should be included in the test directions?

Test Length

The decision on how many items to include on a test depends on the time limits, the grade and reading level of the examinees, and the length and difficulty of the items. Shorter items and/or those requiring only rote memory for facts can be answered in less time than longer items requiring laborious computations and/or abstract reasoning. On tests of moderate difficulty administered at the secondary school level and beyond, a good rule of thumb is to allow 1 minute for each multiple-choice or short-answer item and 1 minute for every two true–false items. Thus, a 50-item multiple-choice or short-answer test and a 100-item true–false test are usually appropriate for a typical 50-minute class period at the junior or senior high school level. Five or six half-page essay questions can be answered in this same period of time. With these time limits, at least 80 percent or more of the students in a typical secondary school class can be expected to finish the test. These guidelines concerning test length and administration time will need to be revised downward when testing elementary school pupils.

There are, of course, differences among students in the time that it takes them to finish a test. It might be expected that students who are most knowledgeable or skilled in the subject matter of the test would finish first, but this is not always the case. Less informed students may simply guess or "give up" and leave early if permitted to do so. Furthermore, the test-taking habits of high-scoring examinees may lead them to review the test items several times to make certain that they do not miss or misunderstand something. Certain students, both high and low scoring, will also have heard that their first answer is more likely to be correct, and therefore it is not a good idea to reconsider initial answers. All these factors make it difficult to predict how long it will take a student to complete a test. It depends on a complex interaction between the preparedness, personality, and temporary emotional and physical state of the examinee, the nature and difficulty of the test material, and the testing environment (noise and other distractions, behavior of the examiner or proctor, and so on). It is likely that the examiner can make actual time-on-task more uniform across examinees by requiring them to remain in their seats after finishing the test, but even with this restriction individual differences in test completion time will occur.

Arrangement of Items

It is sometimes maintained that examinees show position preferences in answering multiple-choice items, in that certain options (say *b* and *c*) are more likely to be selected than other options (*a* and *d*) as being correct. Although research has failed to demonstrate a significant effect of such position preferences (Wilbur, 1970; Jessell & Sullins, 1975), it is advisable to arrange multiple-choice and true–false items so that the answers follow no set pattern. Putting the options for multiple-choice items in alphabetical order may accomplish this, but a better strategy is to randomize the order of options within items. Adhering to this procedure will ensure that at least the test constructor was unbiased in positioning the correct options. Of course, when "all of the above" and/or "none of the above" are used as options, they should be placed last.

Recommendations for arranging other types of items may also prove helpful. For example, placing short-answer items in groups of five or so reduces errors in taking and scoring a test. On matching or rearrangement items, it is more convenient for examinees and it facilitates scoring if all options appear on the same page. Finally, sufficient space should be provided for answering short-answer and essay items, whether the answers are written in the test booklet or on a separate answer sheet.

Concerning the layout of the test as a whole, it might be expected that the examinee's task would be easier if all items of the same type (multiple choice, true–false, and so on) and items dealing with the same topic were grouped together. Although it is true that arranging items in groups according to type or topic may make test preparation, administration, and scoring simpler, there is no evidence that this practice improves test scores.

It is also reasonable to suppose that test scores will be higher if subsets of items are arranged in order from easiest to most difficult. Success in answering easier items would presumably create positive anticipations of further success and hence encourage examinees to try harder on later, more difficult items. Again, however, research findings have not always confirmed this supposition (Allison, 1984; Gerow, 1980; Klimko, 1984). An occasional easy item may improve performance on subsequent items, but, in general, arranging items in order of difficulty seems to have little or no effect on multiple-choice test scores. There are exceptions to this conclusion, for example, tests that are speeded (Plake et al., 1982) or very difficult (Green, 1984; Savitz, 1985). On either a speeded test or a very difficult test, placing the hardest items at the end of the test seems to improve overall scores somewhat.

A logical conclusion from research findings on the effects of ordering items according to difficulty level is that, in constructing tests of easy to moderate difficulty, test designers would do well to be less concerned with item arrangement and more concerned with making certain that items are well written and measure what they are intended to measure. But when a test is very difficult or speeded, arranging the items in order from easiest to most difficult may ensure more efficient use of examinee time, as well as improve motivation and thereby result in higher test scores.

Answer Sheets

For most classroom tests, especially in the lower grades, it is advisable to have students mark their answers in the test booklets. This results in fewer errors in marking answers.

On objective items, requiring examinees to write the appropriate letters or answers in marginal spaces to the left of the questions also facilitates scoring.

Separate answer sheets, which are easier to score, can be used at the upper elementary school level and beyond. Commercially distributed answer sheets will have to be used if the test is to be machine scored (Figure 2–2). On these answer sheets, examinees indicate their responses by filling in the corresponding numbered or lettered circle or space next to the item number. If the test is to be scored by hand, the classroom teacher can easily make up an answer sheet and have it reproduced in quantity. To illustrate, an answer sheet for a 50-item multiple-choice test might have the following format:

1. a b c d e	26. a b c d e
2. a b c d e	27. a b c d e
. . .	. . .
25. a b c d e	50. a b c d e

Examinees are instructed to mark a slash (/) or a cross (×) through the letter corresponding to the correct answer to each item. SCANTRON answer sheets that can be scored either by machine or by hand are also widely available.

Reproducing a Test

Every educational institution has facilities for reproducing written or printed materials for classroom use. Most grade schools and colleges in the United States have replaced the mimeograph and ditto machines of yesteryear with photocopy machines. These machines can be used to duplicate test booklets in one- or two-sided printing format. If the same type of answer sheet is to be used for different tests, a large quantity can be printed in a single run of the machine and stored for other test administrations.

Upon receiving their test papers, examinees often "plunge ahead" and begin answering items without first reading the general directions. This is particularly true on classroom tests, since many students assume that they already know how to take the test and that reading the directions is a waste of time. Therefore, it is usually advisable for the examiner to read the general directions to the class before distributing the test booklets and answer sheets. After the general directions have been read and any questions answered, the answer sheets can be distributed and the directions for marking answers on the answer sheets read aloud. Then the test booklets should be distributed face down and not turned over by the students until the signal to begin the test has been given. In this way, all examinees will start the test at the same time, and no examinee can claim that he or she scored poorly because the examiner failed to explain how answers should be marked, how much time was available, or other matters concerned with taking the test.

The directions for a test should tell examinees what they are supposed to do and how long they have to do it. More specifically, the directions should indicate in relatively simple language the purpose of the test, the time limits, how answers are to be recorded, and how the test will be scored. The directions should also indicate whether it is advisable

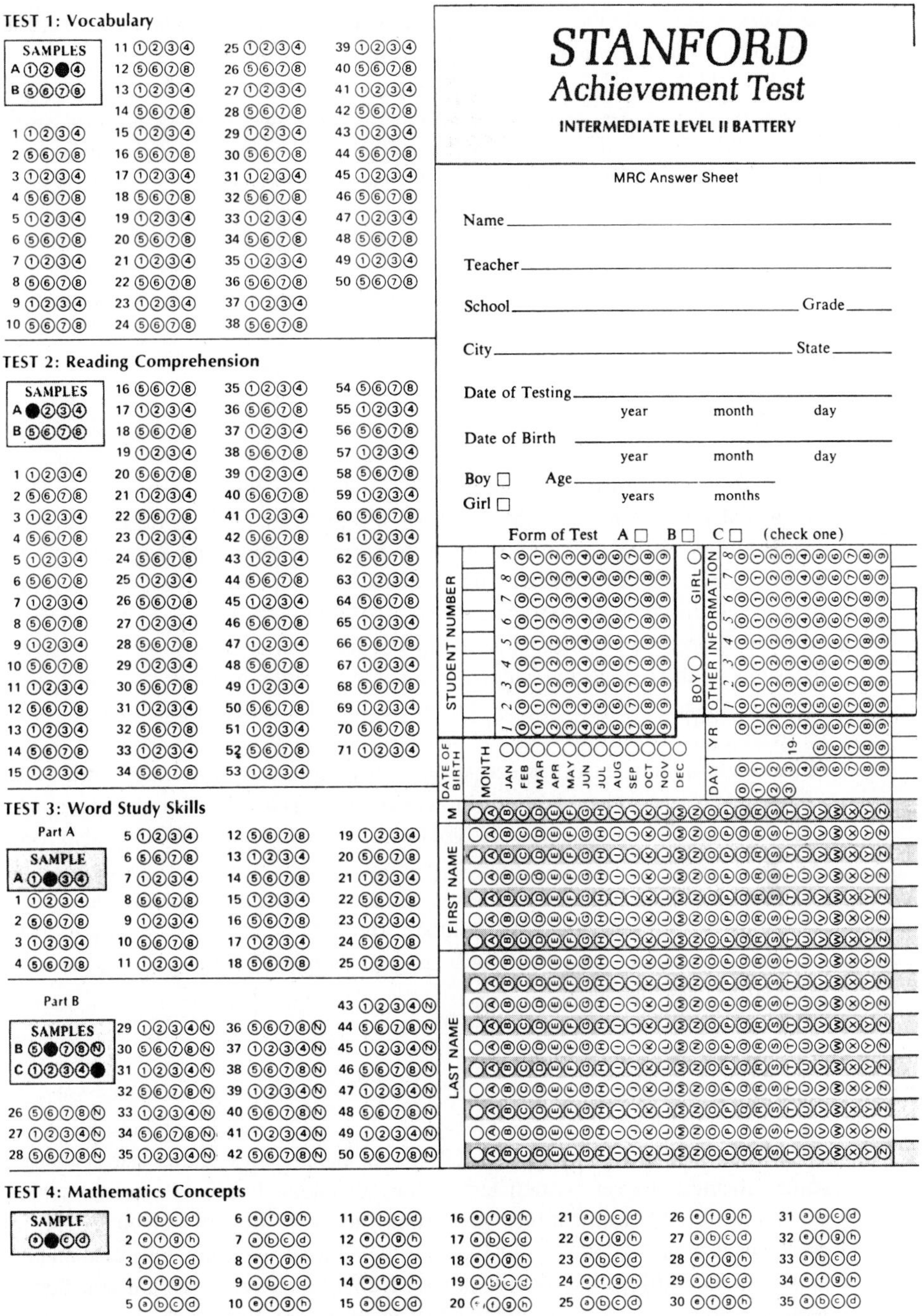

TEST 1: Vocabulary

STANFORD
Achievement Test

INTERMEDIATE LEVEL II BATTERY

MRC Answer Sheet

Name _____

Teacher _____

School _____ Grade _____

City _____ State _____

Date of Testing _____
year   month   day

Date of Birth _____
year   month   day

Boy ☐   Age _____
Girl ☐   years   months

Form of Test   A ☐   B ☐   C ☐   (check one)

TEST 2: Reading Comprehension

TEST 3: Word Study Skills

Part A

Part B

TEST 4: Mathematics Concepts

FIGURE 2–1 Machine-Scorable Answer Sheet.
(Reproduced from MRC Answer Sheet for Stanford Achievement Test: 7th Edition. Copyright © 1982 by Harcourt Brace Jovanovich, Inc. Reproduced by special permission of the publisher.)

to guess when in doubt about an answer. A fairly detailed set of directions for a test on test preparation, administration, and scoring is as follows:

Write your name in the upper right-hand corner of the answer sheet; do not write anything on the test booklet. The purpose of this test is to determine your knowledge and understanding of test preparation, administration, and scoring. There are 50 items, and you will be given 50 minutes in which to complete the test. Indicate your answer to each item by filling in the space on the answer sheet below the letter corresponding to the answer. Your score on the test will be the total number of items that you answer correctly. Therefore, you should make an informed guess when in doubt about the answer. Do not omit any items. If you finish before time is up, please sit quietly until everyone has completed the test.

ORAL TESTING

Oral testing is defined as an evaluation situation in which responses to questions are given orally by examinees; the questions are presented orally, in writing, or both. Oral achievement testing is more common in European educational institutions than in the United States, where oral testing has declined over time and is less common in the higher than in the lower grades (Graham, 1963; Hitchman, 1966).

It has been stated that students do not like oral tests and feel that they are unfair measures of knowledge and understanding. On the other hand, teachers of speech, dramatics, English, and foreign languages often deplore the current inattention to the assessment of spoken language skills and feel that the consequence of this neglect is a multitude of citizens who cannot speak correctly, comprehensibly, or comfortably. While many teachers of languages and other subjects in which the development of oral language skills is important admit the desirability of oral exercises and evaluations, they also recognize that oral tests are inefficient and subjective (Platt, 1961; Crowl & McGinitie, 1974).

Since the early part of this century, oral achievement tests have tended to be perceived as inefficient and lacking in psychometric rigor. They have also been criticized as being too time consuming, as providing a limited sample of responses, and as being poorly planned in most instances.

Advantages of Oral Tests

Despite the shortcomings of oral tests, even their critics admit that such tests possess some advantages over written tests. One advantage is the interactive social situation provided by oral examinations, permitting the evaluation of personal qualities such as appearance, style, and manner of speaking. The face-to-face situation also makes cheating, and perhaps bluffing, less likely. Other advantages of oral tests are that they frequently require responses at a higher intellectual level than written tests and provide practice in oral communication and social interaction (Peterson, 1974). They also encourage more careful review of the test material and can be completed in less time than comparable written examinations. Oral examiners may be better able to follow the thought processes of examinees and to locate the boundaries of their knowledge and understanding of the subject more readily. These boundaries can be determined by asking examinees to explain, defend, or elaborate on their answers. Finally, the time needed to prepare and evaluate oral answers may be less than that for written tests (Glovrozov, 1974; Platt, 1961).

Oral tests are especially appropriate with primary school children and others who have reading or writing deficiencies. Even at higher grade levels, the administration of an occasional oral examination is justifiable when time and/or facilities for duplicating test materials are in short supply (Green, 1975). And in subjects such as speech, foreign languages, and dramatics, oral examinations are crucial.

Oral versus Written Examinations

The fact that scores on oral achievement tests have only moderate correlations with scores on comparable written tests suggests that the two types of evaluation measure different aspects of achievement. In general, knowledge of specific facts can be assessed more quickly with objective written tests, so oral examinations should not contain large numbers of these kinds of questions. On the other hand, as with essay tests, oral tests are more appropriate when the questions call for extended responses (Green, 1975).

Because the achievements or behaviors assessed by oral tests are perhaps just as important as those measured by written tests, it can be argued that more attention should be paid to the major source of error in oral testing: the examiners or evaluators themselves. A thorough knowledge of the subject and a keen awareness of the appropriate responses are needed by examiners of oral tests. Furthermore, the categories used by the examiners in describing or rating examinees' responses should cite specific, observable behaviors, rather than nebulous concepts such as *creative potential, character, general ability,* or *interpersonal effectiveness.* These undefined, and perhaps undefinable, concepts are no more easily assessed by oral tests than by written ones.

SUMMARY

This chapter has been concerned primarily with procedures for constructing and scoring achievement tests, but many of the principles discussed can also be applied to other kinds of psychological and educational assessment instruments.

The first step in constructing an achievement test is to prepare a list of the behavioral objectives to be assessed. A table of specifications giving the number of items needed in each content (topical) category for each behavioral objective should then be constructed. Various taxonomies, or methods of classifying behavioral objectives in the cognitive, affective, and psychomotor domains, have been proposed. The most popular taxonomy of educational objectives has been Bloom and Krathwohl's *Taxonomy of Educational Objectives: Cognitive Domain.*

Both essay and objective tests possess advantages and disadvantages. Essay items are easier to construct, but objective items can be scored more quickly and accurately. Objective tests also provide a more representative sample of subject-matter content. Short-answer, true–false, multiple-choice, and matching questions are varieties of objective test items. Of these, multiple-choice items are the most versatile and popular.

In assembling a test, attention should be given to such factors as test length and format, the method of recording responses, facilities for reproducing the test, and directions for administration. Directions for administering a test include information on the purpose(s), time limits, scoring procedure, and advisability of guessing when in doubt. Oral tests are not employed as much as written tests, but when carefully planned, administered, and evaluated, they can provide information that is not usually obtained by other assessment methods.

EXERCISES

1. Choose a topic for a test in an area of interest to you, state your behavioral and content objectives, construct a table of specifications, and design a 1-hour objective test on the topic using a variety of item types.

2. Design your own classroom system for educational objectives in the cognitive domain. How does your system differ from those described in the text? What particular advantages and disadvantages does it possess?

3. Describe the relative strengths and weaknesses of essay and objective tests. For what purposes and under what conditions is each type of test most appropriate?

4. Why are multiple-choice items generally considered superior to other types of objective test items? Can you think of any situation in which true–false, completion, or matching items would be preferable to multiple-choice items?

5. Write five short-answer (completion) items, five true–false items, and five multiple-choice items on the following selection:

> One reason for the shortage of psychometric data on the elderly is that older people, whose behavior is less susceptible to control by psychologists and educators, are frequently reluctant to be tested. There are many reasons for the uncooperativeness of elderly examinees, including lack of time, perception of the test tasks as trivial or meaningless, and the fear of doing badly and appearing foolish (Welford, 1958). Older adults, to an even greater extent than more test-conscious younger adults, do not relish performing tasks that make them appear foolish or are perceived as having no significance in their lives.
>
> Because elderly people have low motivation to be tested in the first place, sensitivity and tact on the part of psychological examiners are required to obtain valid responses in testing them. Unfortunately, it is often questionable whether technically proficient but young examiners can establish sufficient rapport with elderly examinees to communicate the test directions adequately and stimulate the examinees to do their best (Fletcher, 1972). Relatively few mental testers appear to have sufficient training and experience in the psychological examination of the elderly to do a credible job. Most examiners find, however, that once elderly persons have agreed to be tested, they are as highly motivated as younger examinees to do their best (Welford, 1958).
>
> Even when elderly people are cooperative and motivated to do well, the time limits on many tests, the presence of sensory defects, and the distractibility and easy fatigability of many of these examinees make it difficult for them to perform satisfactorily. For example, one of the most characteristic things about being older is that one's reflexes and physical movements tend to slow down. For this reason, explanations of the declining test scores of the elderly in such areas as learning and memory must take into account the fact that older people do not usually react as quickly as younger people. Although older people are usually at a disadvantage on timed tests, their performance improves significantly when they are given sufficient time to respond. Consequently, on untimed tests the elderly show little or no inferiority in comparison with younger people.
>
> Sensory defects, especially in the visual and auditory modalities, can also interfere with

performance in old age. Special test materials, such as large-face type and trained examiners who are alert to the presence of sensory defects, can be of help. Occasionally, however, an alleged sensory defect may actually be a mask for a problem in reading and auditory comprehension. For example, the writer had the experience of preparing to test an elderly man who, embarrassed by his poor reading ability, conveniently forgot his glasses and hence was unable to read the test materials. (Aiken, 1980, pages 120–121)

6. What are the advantages and disadvantages of oral tests compared with written tests? Under what circumstances are oral tests appropriate? How should they be designed, administered, and scored?

7. Use program 4 ("Preparing an Objective Test") in category 2 ("Programs on Test Construction, Administration, and Scoring") of *Computer Programs for Psychological Assessment* to prepare a short (10-item) multiple-choice test on a subject of interest to you. Then use program 6 in the same category to administer your test to several classmates and score it. The password for program 4 is *makit,* and the password for program 6 is *takit.*

SUGGESTED READINGS

Aiken, L. R. (1982). Writing multiple-choice items to measure higher-order educational objectives. *Educational and Psychological Measurement, 42,* 803–806.

———. (1987). Testing with multiple-test items. *Journal of Research and Development in Education, 20*(4), 44–58.

Albrecht, J. E., & Carnes, D. (1982, November). Guidelines for developing and administering the essay test. *NASSP Bulletin, 66,* 47–53.

Cirn, J. T. (1986, Winter). True/false versus short answer questions. *College Teaching, 34,* 34–37.

Diekhoff, G. M. (1984, April). True–false tests that measure and promote structured understanding. *Teaching of Psychology, 11,* 99–101.

Gerow, J. R. (1980). Performance on achievement tests as a function of the order of item difficulty. *Teaching of Psychology, 7,* 93–94.

Golden, C. J., Sawicki, R. F., & Franzen, M. D. (1990). Test construction. In G. Goldstein & M. Hersen (eds.), *Handbook of psychological assessment,* 2nd ed., pp. 21–40. New York: Pergamon Press.

Nitko, A. J. (1989). Designing tests that are integrated with instruction. In R. L. Linn (ed.), *Educational measurement,* 3rd ed., pp. 447–474. New York: Macmillan.

Thissen, D., Steinberg, L., & Fitzpatrick, A. R. (1989). Multiple-choice models: The distractors are also part of the item. *Journal of Educational Measurement, 26*(2), 161–176.

Weiten, W. (1984). Violation of selected item construction principles in educational measurement. *Journal of Experimental Education, 52,* 174–178.

Chapter Three

Test Administration, Scoring, and Item Analysis

No matter how carefully a test is constructed, the results will be worthless unless it is administered and scored properly. The necessity of having established procedures or guidelines for administering and scoring psychological and educational tests is recognized by all professional organizations concerned with testing. A formal set of guidelines for administering and scoring tests and reporting the results is provided by the *Standards for Educational and Psychological Testing* (American Educational Research Association et al., 1985). The core of this booklet is a list of 180 standards for evaluating, administering, scoring, and interpreting psychological assessment instruments. Five of the standards pertaining specifically to test administration and scoring are listed in Table 3–1.

TEST ADMINISTRATION

The procedure to be followed in administering a test depends on the kind of test (individual or group, timed or nontimed, cognitive or affective), as well as the characteristics of the people to be examined (chronological age, education, cultural background, physical and mental status). Whatever the type of test and the nature of the examinees may be, factors such as the extent to which the examinees are prepared for the test and their level of motivation, anxiety, fatigue, and health can also affect performance.

Just as the preparedness, test wiseness, and motivation of the examinees can affect their scores on a psychological or educational test, factors that vary with the examiner and the situation can also have an influence. The skill, personality, and behavior of the examiner, particularly on individual tests, may be a factor in how well examinees perform. Administration of most individual tests requires that the examiner be formally licensed or certified by an appropriate state agency or supervised by a previously licensed examiner. Such requirements help ensure that psychological examiners possess the requisite knowledge and skills to administer, score, and interpret psychological and educational tests.

Situational variables, including the time and place of testing and environmental

TABLE 3–1   Standards for Test Administration and Scoring

Standard 15.1	In typical applications, test administrators should follow carefully the standardized procedures for administration and scoring specified by the test publisher. Specifications regarding instructions to test takers, time limits, the form of item presentation or response, and test materials or equipment should be strictly observed. Exceptions should be made only on the basis of carefully considered professional judgment, primarily in clinical applications.
Standard 15.2	The testing environment should be one of reasonable comfort and with minimal distractions. Testing materials should be readable and understandable. In computerized testing, items displayed on a screen should be legible and free from glare, and the terminal should be properly positioned.
Standard 15.3	Reasonable efforts should be made to assure the validity of test scores by eliminating opportunities for test takers to attain scores by fraudulent means.
Standard 15.7	Test users should protect the security of test materials. *Comment:* Those who have test materials under their control should take all steps necessary to assure that only individuals with a legitimate need for access to test materials are able to obtain such access.
Standard 15.10	Those responsible for testing programs should provide appropriate interpretations when test score information is released to students, parents, legal representatives, teachers, or the media. The interpretations should describe in simple language what the test covers, what scores mean, common misinterpretations of test scores, and how scores will be used. *Comment:* Test users should consult the interpretive material prepared by the test developer or publisher and should revise or supplement the material as necessary to present the local and individual results accurately and clearly.

Source: From Standards for Educational and Psychological Testing. © 1985 by the American Psychological Testing Association. Reprinted by permission. Further reproduction without the express written permission of the APA is prohibited.

conditions such as illumination, temperature, noise level, and ventilation, may also contribute to the motivation, concentration, and performance of examinees. For this reason, examiners must make careful preparations before administering a test.

Examiner's Duties before Test Administration

Scheduling the Test   In scheduling a test, the examiner should take into account activities that students or other examinees usually engage in at that time. Obviously, it is unwise to test children during lunchtime, playtime, or when other pleasurable activities typically occur or are being anticipated, or even when enjoyable or exciting events have just taken place (such as immediately after a holiday). The testing period should seldom be longer than 1 hour for elementary school children or $1\frac{1}{2}$ hours for secondary school students. Because 30 minutes is about as long as preschool and primary school children can remain attentive to test tasks, more than one session may be required for administering longer tests to young children.

With respect to classroom tests, students should be informed well in advance when and where the test is to be administered, what sort of material it contains, and what kind of test (objective, essay, oral) it is. Students deserve an opportunity to prepare intellectually, emotionally, and physically for a test. For this reason, "pop quizzes" and other unannounced tests are usually not advisable.

Informed Consent   In many states, the administration of an intelligence test or another psychodiagnostic instrument to a child requires the informed consent of a parent, guardian, or someone who is legally responsible for the child. The concept of *informed consent,* which was introduced in Chapter 1, is an agreement made by an agency or professional with a particular person or his or her legal representative to permit the administration of psychological tests and/or obtain other information for evaluative or diagnostic purposes. The requirement of informed consent is usually satisfied by obtaining the signature of the legally responsible person on a standard form supplied by the school district or other relevant agency. The form specifies the purpose(s) of the examination, the uses to be made of the results, the parent's or other guardian's rights, and the procedure for obtaining a copy of the final report and an interpretation of the findings. An illustration of such a form is given in Figure 3–1 (see also Figure 1–3).

Becoming Familiar with the Test   When the examiner is also the author of the test, he or she is obviously familiar with the test material and the procedure for administering it. But because a standardized test is rarely administered by the person who constructed it, the manual accompanying a test must be studied carefully before attempting to administer the test. The examiner should be thoroughly familiar with the directions for administration and the test content. To acquire this familiarity, an examiner should take the test before attempting to administer it to someone else. Finally, it is advisable to review the directions and other procedural matters just before administering a test. Test booklets, answer sheets, and other materials should also be checked and counted beforehand. In particular, *secure tests* bearing serial numbers, such as the Scholastic Aptitude Test and the Graduate Record Examinations, must be inspected closely and arranged in numerical order.

Ensuring Satisfactory Testing Conditions   The test administrator should make certain that seating, lighting, ventilation, temperature, noise level, and other physical conditions are appropriate. A room familiar to the examinees and relatively free from distractions is preferred. A "Testing—Do Not Disturb" sign on the closed door of the examination room may help to eliminate interruptions and other distractions. It is best to administer an individual test in a private room, with only the examiner and examinee (and, if necessary, the parent, guardian, or other responsible person) present. In administering either an individual or a group test, special provisions may also have to be made for physically handicapped or physically different (for example, left-handed) examinees.

Date Signed
Assessment
Plan is Received
Date IEP to be held
_____

LOS ANGELES UNIFIED SCHOOL DISTRICT
Division of Special Education

ASSESSMENT PLAN AND PARENTAL CONSENT FOR ASSESSMENT

Procedural Safeguards
Due Process Procedures
( )Given ( )Mailed
To Parent on:

By: _____

TO THE PARENT/GUARDIAN OF: _____ Date: _____

Birthdate: _____ _____ Primary Language:_____
          Mo.   Day   Yr.   School

English Proficiency_____ Measured by Instrument (Specify)_____ Date:_____

WE REQUEST YOUR CONSENT FOR ASSESSMENT OF YOUR SON/DAUGHTER WHO ( ) MAY BENEFIT FROM SPECIAL EDUCATION OR ( ) IS ALREADY RECEIVING SPECIAL EDUCATION AND ADDITIONAL ASSESSMENT IS NEEDED.

QUALIFIED PROFESSIONALS WHO MAY CONTRIBUTE TO THE MULTIDISCIPLINARY ASSESSMENT ARE INDICATED BELOW BY THEIR INITIALS AND TITLES SUCH AS PSYCHOLOGIST, RESOURCE SPECIALIST, PHYSICIAN, SPEECH SPECIALIST, ADAPTIVE P.E. TEACHER, EDUCATIONAL AUDIOLOGIST, SCHOOL NURSE/PHYSICIAN, SPECIAL EDUCATION TEACHER AND OTHERS. REPRESENTATIVE TYPES OF TESTS ARE LISTED ON THE BACK OF THIS PLAN.

PLEASE REVIEW THE PLAN AND INDICATE IN THE PARENT CONSENT SECTION BELOW WHETHER OR NOT YOU CONSENT TO THIS ASSESSMENT. IF YOU HAVE ANY QUESTIONS ABOUT THE PLAN OR THE PROCEDURAL SAFEGUARDS/DUE PROCESS PROCEDURES YOU RECEIVED WITH THE PLAN, PLEASE CONTACT:

_____   _____   ( )_____
              NAME   TITLE   PHONE

PROPOSED SPECIAL EDUCATION ASSESSMENT PLAN

TYPE AND PURPOSE OF ASSESSMENT	ASSESSMENT RESPONSIBILITIES (Indicate Initials and Title)
ACADEMIC/PREACADEMIC ACHEIVEMENT - To assess basic reading skills and reading conprehension; mathematics calculation and reasoning; spelling; written expression and, if appropriate, pre-reading skills	
COGNITIVE LEVEL - To assess specific skills, learning rate and problem solving ability. NO STANDARDIZED INTELLIGENCE (I.Q.) TESTS WILL BE GIVEN.	
COMMUNICATION/LANGUAGE FUNCTIONING - To measure the ability to understand, relate to and use language/speech clearly and appropriately	
SOCIAL/EMOTIONAL STATUS - To assess level of social maturity, ability to function independently and inter-personal skills.	
MOTOR ABILITIES - To assess the coordination of body movements in large and small muscle activities.	
MEDICAL - To assess general physical condition by a history and physical examination.	
AUDIOLOGICAL ASSESSMENT - To measure the nature and degree of possible hearing loss.	
OTHER Purpose: _____	

PARENT CONSENT FOR ASSESSMENT
PLEASE INDICATE BY A CHECK MARK AND YOUR SIGNATURE

1. ( ) I CONSENT TO THE ASSESSMENT PLAN

2. ( ) I DO NOT CONSENT TO THE ASSESSMENT PLAN

SIGNATURE _____ ( )_____ ( )_____
              Parent/Guardian   Date   Home Phone   Work Phone

In addition, I wish to submit a written report(s) from the following person(s) who has evaluated my son/daughter:

_____   _____
              Name   Title

27.805B (Rev. 6/88)

RETURN THE WHITE COPY AS INDICATED IN THE COVER LETTER. KEEP THE YELLOW COPY FOR YOUR RECORDS

STUDENT FILE COPY

FIGURE 3–1 Los Angeles Unified School District: Assessment Plan and Parental Consent Form for Assessment.
(Reprinted by permission of the Los Angeles Unified School District.)

Minimizing Cheating   Comfortable seating that minimizes cheating should be arranged. Although preferred, it is not always possible to place examinees one seat apart in such a way that cheating is impossible. Preparing multiple forms (different items or different item arrangements) of the test and distributing different forms to adjacent examinees can reduce cheating on group-administered tests. Another possibility is to use multiple answer sheets, that is, answer sheets having different layouts. None of the procedures eliminates the need for proctors, and several roving proctors should be employed whenever a large group of people is tested. Proctors may assist in distributing and collecting test materials, as well as answering procedural questions. The presence of proctors also discourages cheating and unruliness during a test. Proctoring and other procedures designed to guard against cheating are taken quite seriously in the administration of secure standardized tests such as those published by Educational Testing Service.

Examiner's Duties during the Test

Following Test Directions   Carefully prepared test directions, which are read slowly and clearly if given orally, inform examinees of the purpose of the test and how to indicate their answers. Examiners of all standardized tests are required to follow the directions for administration carefully, even when further explanation to the examinees might clarify their task. Departures from the standard directions may result in a different task than the test designers had in mind. If the directions given to a group of examinees are not identical to those given to the group on whom the test was standardized, the scores of the former will not have the same meaning as those of the latter. The result will be the loss of a useful frame of reference for interpreting scores on the test.[1]

Staying Alert   When administering group tests, whether standardized or nonstandardized, the examiner should be alert to cheating, as well as talking and other unnecessary noise. Making certain that a messenger is available in case of medical emergencies or other problems is also a wise precaution. On teacher-made tests or even on standardized tests if the directions permit it, students may be informed periodically of how much time they have left by writing it on a chalkboard or other surface visible to them.

Establishing Rapport   Although it is recommended that the printed directions be followed closely in administering a standardized test, the examiner's behavior can have a significant effect on the motivation of examinees. Sometimes even a smile can provide enough encouragement to anxious or inadequately prepared examinees to stay calm, try

---

[1]Despite the fact that deviations from standard directions eliminate a valuable frame of reference for interpreting test scores (the test *norms*), in clinical or educational contexts, mental testers sometimes go beyond the test directions. This involves attempting to "test the limits" of an examinee's abilities or personal characteristics by employing "dynamic testing" procedures to obtain additional cues for purposes of interpretation or diagnosis. Illustrative of such dynamic assessment are Feuerstein's *learning potential assessment* (Feuerstein et al., 1987) and Embretson's (1987) computer-based approach for finding an examinee's performance level. Both of these approaches involve a test–teach–test format in which the examinee is tested (pretested), then given practice on the test materials, and finally tested again (posttested). The change in performance level from pretest to posttest is calculated as a measure of the examinee's learning potential.

hard, and perform as well as they can. Because the examiner has a better opportunity to observe examinees in individual than in group testing, low motivation, distractibility, and stress are more likely to be detected when administering an individual test. An attempt may then be made to cope with these problems or at least take them into account in interpreting the scores. In a group testing situation, where personal interaction with every examinee is not possible, the examiner is more limited in sensing how well each person is feeling and doing. On both individual and group tests, a good rule to follow is to be friendly but objective. Such behavior on the part of the examiner tends to create a condition of *rapport,* a cordial, accepting relationship that encourages examinees to respond honestly and accurately.

Being Prepared for Special Problems   In some circumstances, examiners need to be especially active and encouraging. A testing situation creates a certain amount of tension in almost anyone, and occasionally an examinee becomes quite anxious. Testing the very young or very old, the mentally disturbed or mentally retarded, or the physically handicapped or culturally disadvantaged presents special problems. In certain situations, questions and answers may have to be given orally, rather than in print, or in a language other than English. Not only must the examiner be familiar with the test material, but also alert, flexible, warm, and objective. Although these qualities are not easily taught, experience in a variety of testing situations plays an important role in acquiring them.

Flexibility   Some flexibility is usually permitted in administering nonstandardized tests and even certain standardized instruments. In testing with these measures, sensitivity and patience on the part of the examiner can provide a better opportunity for handicapped individuals and those with other special problems to demonstrate their capabilities. Other recommended procedures, which have been adapted from well-known instructional techniques, are as follows:

1. Provide ample time for examinees to respond to the test material.
2. Allow sufficient practice on sample items.
3. Use relatively short testing periods.
4. Watch for fatigue and anxiety and take them into account.
5. Be aware of and make provisions for visual, auditory, and other sensory and perceptual–motor defects.
6. Employ a generous amount of encouragement and positive reinforcement.
7. Do not try to force examinees to respond when they repeatedly decline to do so.

Oral Testing   Students frequently regard oral examinations with mixed feelings and often considerable apprehension. Consequently, efforts to calm fears and provide alternative testing methods for those who experience great difficulty coping with oral testing situations can assist in improving the effectiveness of these kinds of tests. Examiners who make special efforts to establish rapport with examinees discover that the latter may even come to enjoy oral tests.

Taking a Test

In general, "pop quizzes" are not considered fair. Students deserve a chance to prepare for a test, so letting them know in advance not only when and where the test will be given, but also what it will cover and what kind of test it will be, is recommended procedure. With respect to the expected format of a test, both classroom and laboratory studies have found that higher scores on recall (essay, short answer) tests result from telling students in advance that a recall test will be administered. It has been found that expecting a recognition (multiple choice, true–false) test leads to greater study of details, whereas expecting a recall test results in greater efforts to remember higher-order units, trends, and themes in the material (Schmidt, 1983).

Classroom studies of recognition tests have found that announcing in advance that this type of test will be given is associated with higher scores on multiple-choice, true–false, or other recognition tests. However, the results of laboratory studies are more complex (Lundeberg & Fox, 1991). Furthermore, other factors, such as mental ability, test wiseness, guessing, and careful reading and consideration of items, appear to have as much effect on test scores as knowing what type of test will be administered.

Test Wiseness When answering objective test items, examinees often employ quite different methods from those intended by the item writer. Not all examinees read the items carefully, and they often fail to use all the information given (Williams & Jones, 1974). This may not be essential in every case, because students often recognize the correct answers to multiple-choice items without having read the material on which the questions are based (Preston, 1964). Sometimes they are able to eliminate wrong options by noting that certain answers are worded incorrectly or are too broad or too narrow. Alliterative associations, grossly unrelated options, inclusionary language, more precise correct alternatives, grammatical cues, and giveaways that are answered in other items are additional cues that can reveal the correct answers to multiple-choice items (Gibb, 1964).

Observations of students taking multiple-choice tests, combined with posttest interviews, indicate that, although they sometimes answer an item simply by eliminating obviously incorrect choices, a more common practice is to make comparative judgments among options. Knowledge of the teacher's idiosyncrasies is also an aspect of test wiseness. *Test wiseness* appears to be a nongeneral, cue-specific ability (Evans, 1984) that develops as students mature and share information on test-taking skills (Slakter, Koehler, & Hampton, 1970). For example, the length, technicality, and exoticness of options act as cues to the correct answers (Chase, 1964; Strang, 1980; Tidwell, 1980). Boys appear to be more testwise than girls (Preston, 1964), and verbal items are more susceptible than numerical items to test wiseness (Rowley, 1974). Some aspects of test wiseness or test sophistication can also be taught (Millman & Pauk, 1969; American College, 1978). At the very least, students should review the suggestions in Table 3–2.

Changing Responses Often examinees must decide whether to change their initial responses to test items. It is sometimes said that, because initial answers tend to be right, going over a test and changing answers that have already been thought about is a waste of time and even counterproductive (Benjamin, Cavell, & Shallenberger, 1984). The results

TABLE 3–2   Suggestions for Improving Your Test Scores through Test Wisdom

1. Don't wait until the day before a test to begin studying for a test that has been announced well in advance.
2. Ask the teacher for old copies of tests that you can legitimately examine.
3. Ask other students what kinds of tests the teacher usually gives.
4. Don't make studying for the test a social occasion; it is usually better to isolate yourself when preparing for a test.
5. Don't get too comfortable when studying. Your body is dumb; it thinks you want to sleep and not study when you lie down or get too comfortable.
6. Study for the type of test (multiple choice, true–false, essay) that is announced.
7. If the type of test that will be administered is not announced, it is probably best to study for a recall (essay) test.
8. Apply the Survey Q3R (survey, questions, reading, recitation, review) technique when studying for a test.
9. Try to form the material you are trying to study into test items, for example, of the multiple-choice type if a multiple-choice test will be given or into essay items if an essay test is scheduled.
10. Read the test directions carefully before beginning the test. If certain information such as time limits, correction for guessing, item weighting, or the like, has been omitted, don't hesitate to ask the test administrator for it.
11. On essay questions, think about the question and formulate an answer in your mind and/or on scratch paper before you begin writing.
12. Pace yourself in taking a test. For example, on a multiple-choice test you should be $1/n$th of the way through the test when $1/n$th of the time has elapsed.
13. Whether or not a correction for guessing is used in scoring the test, don't leave an item unanswered if you can eliminate even one option.
14. Skip more difficult items and come back to them later. Don't panic if you can't answer an item; circle it and come back to it after you have answered other items. Then if you still aren't certain of the answer, make an educated guess.
15. When time permits, review your answers; don't be overly eager to hand in your test paper before time has expired.

---

of a number of investigations indicate, however, that examinees tend to score higher when they reconsider their answers and change those about which they have second thoughts (Smith, White, & Coop, 1979; Vidler & Hansen, 1980). Changing answers tends to raise scores more on difficult tests and with better students, and males tend to do better than females when changing answers (Pascale, 1974). Answers are more likely to be changed from wrong to right than vice versa (Vidler & Hansen, 1980), although the actual number of changed answers tends to be relatively small (Skinner, 1983). In any event, it is recommended that examinees review their initial answers when they have time.

Guessing   Directions for objective tests often include advice concerning whether to omit an item or to guess when in doubt about the correct answer. Guessing, which is more likely to occur when items are difficult or wordy (Choppin, 1975), results in greater score inflation on true–false than on multiple-choice tests. In general, it is advisable for test takers to guess only when they can eliminate one or more options or they have some idea about which option is correct. Because it is almost always possible to eliminate at least one option per item, leaving items blank rather than guessing usually results in lower test scores, whether or not the scores are "corrected" for guessing.

Understandably, examinees guess less when they are informed that a penalty for guessing will be subtracted from their scores than when no directions concerning guessing are given or they are told to guess when in doubt. However, examinees do not always follow or even read the test directions carefully. Even those who read every word of the directions do not always interpret them in the same way. Regardless of what the test directions advise or do not advise, some examinees are reluctant to guess when they are uncertain of the correct answer. This characteristic has been referred to as "intolerance of ambiguity" or "low risk taking."

Examiner's Duties after the Test

After administering an individual test, the examiner should collect and secure all test materials. The examinee should be reassured concerning his or her performance, perhaps given a small reward if he or she is a child, and returned to an appropriate place. In clinical testing, it is usually important to interview a parent or other person who has accompanied the examinee, perhaps both before and after the test. Also after the test, some information on what will be done with the test results and how they are to be used can be provided to the examinee and/or the accompanying party. The examiner will promise to report the results and interpretations to the proper person(s) or agency and to recommend what further action is advisable.

Following the administration of a group test, the examiner should collect the necessary materials (test booklets, answer sheets, scratch paper, pencils, and so on). In the case of a standardized test, the test booklets and answer sheets must be counted and collated and all other collected materials checked to make certain that nothing is missing. Only then are the examinees dismissed or prepared for the next activity and the answer sheets arranged for scoring.

TEST SCORING

Professional test designers do not wait until a test is constructed and administered before deciding what scoring procedure to use. Similarly, if a teacher-made test consists of a series of parts dealing with different content or different types of items, the teacher may wish to obtain separate scores on the various parts, as well as a composite score on the test as a whole. Different numerical scoring weights may be assigned to different responses. Decisions must also be made on such matters as whether to subtract a correction for guessing and whether to report the results in raw-score form or to convert them in some way. For standardized tests, the classroom teacher does not have to make all these decisions; answer sheets can be scored by machine. Even when answer sheets must be scored by hand, scoring stencils provided by the test publisher can be used according to the directions given in the manual.

Scoring Essay Tests

Essay questions can be made more effective by structuring the task clearly so that the interpretation of a question does not vary widely from examinee to examinee. Scoring can then be based on the quality of the answer. Similarly, an attempt should be made to structure and make the scoring of essay items more objective so that a person's score depends less on noncontent, impressionistic factors and more on the level of understanding and ability demonstrated. Scoring on the basis of penmanship rather than the quality of the answers, being overly general (*leniency error*), and awarding a high score on an item simply because an examinee makes high scores on other items (*halo effect*) are among the errors affecting scores on essay tests.

A number of recommendations can be made for scoring essay questions so that the scores will be objective and reliable. To begin, the tester must decide whether to score the question as a whole or to assign separate weights to different components. Whole (*global* or *holistic*) scoring is common, but it is perhaps more meaningful to use an analytic scoring procedure in which points are given for each item of information or skill included in the answer. In the first essay item of Table 2–4, for example, one point might be given for each correct advantage or disadvantage listed and a maximum of five points for the manner in which the answer was organized. The maximum number of points allocated to an item is determined not only by the examiner's judgment of the importance of the item, but also by the assigned length of the answer. When the directions specify a half-page answer, the item should be weighted less than when a whole-page answer is required.

Whatever the scoring weights assigned to specific questions and answers, it is advisable for the examiner to write out an ideal answer to the question beforehand. It is also recommended that the names of examinees be blocked out before test papers are inspected so that the papers can be scored anonymously. Other recommendations are as follows: (1) score all the answers to one question before going on to the next question; (2) score all answers to an item during the same time period; (3) if both style (mechanics quality of writing) and content are to be scored, evaluate each separately; (4) have a second person rescore the paper, and make the final scores the average of the number of points assigned by the two scorers; and (5) write comments next to answers, and mark error corrections on the papers.

Corrections and comments written on classroom test papers are a valuable addition to the number of points or the grade assigned. A student is more likely to learn something if the responses to a test are corrected and commented on, rather than simply being given a number or letter grade.

Scoring Objective Tests

A unique advantage of objective tests is the efficiency and accuracy with which they can be scored. Whereas the scorer of an essay test has to spend hours reading the answers and weighing their correctness, a clerk can score an objective test quickly and accurately with a scoring stencil or machine. Therefore, the test papers can be returned to the examinees soon after the test is administered and while the material is still fresh in their minds.

A strip key or stencil for hand scoring of test booklets or answer sheets can be easily prepared. A strip of cardboard containing the correct answers at positions corresponding to the spaces in the test booklet where answers are to be written makes a satisfactory strip key. A scoring stencil for use with a special answer sheet can be prepared from a blank sheet of paper or cardboard by punching out the spaces where the correct answers should be.

Machine Scoring   Although the tests distributed by National Computer Systems and certain other commercial organizations can be scored only by machine, the majority of answer sheets for commercially distributed tests are scorable by hand or machine. After a test is administered, the answer sheets may be mailed to a special scoring service or returned to the distributor for machine scoring.

Objective tests have been scored by machine for over a half-century, and the increased availability of computers has made test scoring much more rapid, flexible, and economical. Optical scanners connected to computers, which are used by numerous scoring services, can score hundreds of answer sheets in an hour.

Human Scoring Errors   Computer scoring of tests is not completely error free, and it is recommended that test scoring services monitor their error frequencies and issue corrected score reports when errors are found in test scores (American Educational Research Association et al., 1985). Compared with hand scoring, however, the error rates in computer scoring are small indeed.

Considering the fact that the scoring directions for many individual tests of intelligence and personality are not entirely clear-cut, it is not surprising that various scores may be assigned to the same response. Although the variability of scores is probably greater with less experienced scorers, even experienced scorers make mistakes. It has been found, for example, that errors in both administration and scoring occur when either graduate students in psychology or professional psychologists administer individual intelligence tests (Franklin & Stillman, 1982; Ryan, Prefitera, & Powers, 1983). In a number of cases, the errors are of sufficient magnitude to result in misclassifying examinees on the level of intelligence. Other studies have found that scoring is affected by the examiner–scorer's liking for the examinee or perception of the latter as a warm person (Donahue & Sattler, 1971) or as bright or dull (Sattler, Hillix, & Neher, 1970; Sattler & Winget, 1970). Errors in converting raw scores to standard or scaled scores may also occur when the examinee's chronological age is unknown or computed incorrectly.

Scoring Weights for Multiple-choice and True–False Items   It appears reasonable to suppose that on objective tests, as on essay items, the number of points assigned to an answer should vary with the kind of item and the quality of the response. Many studies of the effects of a priori weighting of responses to conventional objective test items, that is, allocating different numbers of points to different item types and different anticipated responses, have been conducted. Some research studies have found a priori weighting to be more discriminating and reliable than conventional scoring (Serlin & Kaiser, 1978; Willson, 1982; Hsu, Moss, & Khampalikit, 1984). The advantages of a priori weighting, however, do not seem to be justified by the increased scoring time and cost (Kansup & Hakstian, 1975). On tests of 20 or more items, simply assigning a score of 1 to each correct response and 0 to each incorrect response is as satisfactory as using differing weights. Thus, the scores on a conventionally scored 50-item multiple-choice or true–false test may range from 0 to 50.

It is possible that assigning different weights to different responses might be more effective if the type of required response were changed. For example, one interesting variation on the true–false format is to have examinees specify the degree of confidence they have in their answers (Ebel, 1965). Table 3-3 illustrates how this confidence weighting procedure works. Although the procedure may represent an improvement over conventional 0–1 scoring of true–false items, the latter is probably satisfactory for most classroom tests.

Scoring Ranking Items   As with true–false and multiple-choice items, short-answer and matching items may be scored by assigning 1 point to each correct response and 0 points to each incorrect response or omission. Because of the large number of different orders in which a group of items can be arranged, the scoring of ranking items presents a special problem. For example, the error of assigning to second place an item that actually belongs in first place is not as serious as placing the same item in fourth place.

Figure 3–2 is a simple computing chart that takes into account the fact that the seriousness of placing an item out of order depends on where it is placed relative to its correct position. To illustrate the use of this chart, assume that five cities are to be arranged in rank order according to population by assigning a rank of 1 to the largest city, 2 to the next largest city, and so on. The names of the five cities are given in the first column of Table 3–4, the correct ranks in the second column, and the ranks assigned by a hypothetical examinee (E) in the third column. The fourth column contains the absolute values of the differences between the correct rank for each city and the rank assigned by the examinee; the sum of the absolute values of the differences is 10.

To determine the score of examinee E on this item, the scorer refers to Figure 3–2, marks a point at the appropriate value (10) on the vertical *Diff* axis and a point on the

TABLE 3–3   Ebel's Confidence Weighting Procedure for True–False Tests

Examinee's response: The statement is	Actual condition of statement	
	True (points)	*False (points)*
Probably true	2	−2
Possibly true	1	0
I have no idea	.5	.5
Possibly false	0	1
Probably false	−2	2

Source: Robert L. Ebel, *Measuring Educational Achievement,* © 1965, p. 131. Adapted by permission of Prentice Hall, Englewood Cliffs, N.J.

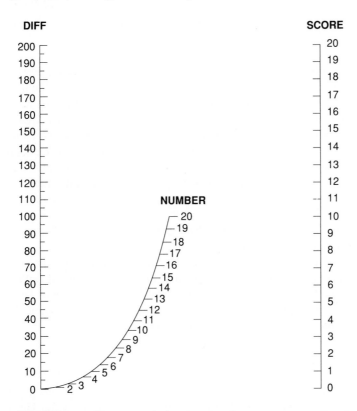

FIGURE 3–2 Nomograph for Scoring Rearrangement Test Items. *(After Aiken, 1970, p. 90)*

TABLE 3–4   Rank Ordering of Sample Rearrangement Item

City	Correct rank	Ranking by examinee E	Absolute value of difference
Philadelphia	4	1	3
Chicago	3	2	1
Los Angeles	2	3	1
San Francisco	5	4	1
New York	1	5	4
			Diff. = 10

curved *Number* scale at the point corresponding to the number of things ranked (5). Then a straight line is drawn from the point marked on the *Diff* axis through the point marked on the *Number* axis and extended to the *Score* axis. This line intersects the *Score* axis at a value of approximately 1, which is examinee A's score on this ranking item. The chart in Figure 3–2 may be used to score ranking items in which the number of things to be ranked is between two and twenty. The minimum score is 0, and the maximum score is equal to the number of things to be ranked.

Correction for Guessing   After the total raw score on an objective test has been determined, the question arises as to whether the score represents an examinee's true standing or whether it has been inflated by successful guessing. Examinees do guess on objective tests, and their chances of improving their scores in this way, especially on items having few options, can be quite high. If an examinee does not know the correct answer and all options are equally attractive, then the chances that the correct option will be selected by guessing are $100/k$ out of 100, where k is the number of options per item. Thus, the chances of blindly guessing the correct answer to a true–false item are 50 out of 100 (since $k = 2$ for true–false items). On a four-option multiple-choice item, however, the chances are only 25 out of 100 of guessing the correct answer. Obviously, guessing the answer to a large number of items will have a more serious effect on the scores on true–false tests than on multiple-choice test scores.

As an attempt to correct for the effects of guessing, on certain standardized tests a portion of the number of wrong answers is subtracted from the number of right answers. The reasoning behind correction-for-guessing formulas need not concern us here, except for the questionable assumption that examinees guess blindly when in doubt. The most popular scoring formula when correcting for guessing is

$$S = R - \frac{W}{k - 1} \tag{3.1}$$

where S is the corrected score, R the number of items that the examinee gets right, W the number of items he or she gets wrong, and k the number of options per item. This formula has been criticized for yielding scores that are too low when examinees are less familiar with the test material, but too high when they are more familiar with the material (Little, 1962, 1966). An alternative formula proposed by Little (1962) is

$$S = R - \frac{W}{2(k - 1)} \tag{3.2}$$

Professional testers generally agree that correction-for-guessing formulas do not really correct for guessing and that they typically have little effect on the rank order of scores. Exceptions occur when the number of unanswered items varies greatly from examinee to examinee and when certain items are more likely to be guessed at than others. The use of these formulas, which is similar to assigning different weights to different items, is not generally recommended in scoring classroom tests. The formulas are probably most helpful in scoring true–false and speeded tests, where guessing is more of a factor, than on other types of tests. Negative scores, which occasionally occur when formula 3.1 is used with true–false tests ($S = R - W$), are usually changed to zeros. In any event, examinees have a right to know if their scores will be corrected for guessing. Information on how a test is scored, including whether a correction for guessing is employed, should be included in the test directions.

Converted Scores   It is usually not worthwhile to alter raw scores on objective tests by differential weighting or correction formulas, but the scores are often changed in other ways to make them more meaningful. As described in the section on norms in Chapter 4, the process of interpreting test scores is facilitated by transforming them to percentile ranks, standard scores, or converted scores.

Scoring Oral Tests   Although errors are more likely in scoring responses to oral than to objective questions, special forms for rating performance can improve the objectivity of scoring oral tests (see Table 3–5). Careful attention to the design of questions, construction of model answers to questions before administering the test, the use of multiple raters or scorers, and training examiners to avoid favoritism and other rater biases can also decrease errors in scoring oral tests. If the time allotted to scoring is not critical, the accuracy with which oral tests are scored can be improved by electronically recording examinees' responses for later playback and (re)evaluation (see Aiken, 1983a).

Score Evaluation and Grading

After a test has been administered and scored, it remains for the scores to be evaluated. In the case of teacher-made tests, score evaluation usually implies the assignment of letter grades or marks. Grade assignment is a rather subjective process, depending not only on

TABLE 3–5   Evaluation of Student Oral Report

Directions: For each of the questions listed below, rate the oral report on a scale of 1 to 10, 1 being very low and 10 being very high. Write the appropriate number (1 to 10) in the marginal dash.

_____   1. What was the level of the student's knowledge of the subject matter of the report?

_____   2. How well organized was the report?

_____   3. How effective was the introduction to the report in capturing your attention?

_____   4. How clearly and distinctly did the student speak?

_____   5. How interesting was the topic?

_____   6. How effectively were audiovisual materials (films, posters, chalkboard, etc.) used?

_____   7. To what extent did the student look at the class during the report rather than looking at her or his notes?

_____   8. How effectively did the student use gestures, body postures, and other nonverbal messages to communicate?

_____   9. To what extent did the student refer to research or other primary sources in presenting the report?

_____   10. How would you rate the closing (summary of major points, presentation of thought questions, etc.) of the report?

Comments:

the test score itself, but also on the expectations of the evaluator and the scores obtained by other students. Some teachers grade strictly on the curve, while others grade in terms of a fixed performance standard or criterion. The majority, however, probably employ a combination of curve and fixed-standard grading. In one curve-grading procedure, the *Cajori method,* A's are assigned to 7 percent of the examinees, B's to 24 percent, C's to 38 percent, D's to 24 percent, and F's to 7 percent. A drawback of this method is its failure to consider the facts that tests vary in difficulty and that the overall ability level of students in different classes is not the same. An alternative curve-grading procedure establishes letter-grade boundaries on classroom tests when the ability level of the class, the class's test performance relative to that of other classes, and the test scores themselves are all taken into account (Aiken, 1983b).

The traditional grading system, in which A is considered excellent or superior, B is above average or good, C is average, D is below average or poor, and F is failing, is a form of score interpretation or performance evaluation. Every public or private organization has standards that its students, employees, or members are expected to meet. The standards may be flexible, but at some time individuals who belong to the organization are usually evaluated on their level of proficiency or participation. The penalty for receiving a negative evaluation may take the form of remedial work, demotion, suspension, or even expulsion. The rewards for receiving a good evaluation include prizes, privileges, and promotions.

Letter grading implies the evaluation of scholastic performance by administering various kinds of achievement tests to students. Scores on other tests of ability and personality also require interpretation if they are to be used for certain purposes: for placement in special classes or jobs, for psychodiagnosis, or for psychological treatment or other interventions. Procedures for interpreting scores on such tests can be very complex, depending on the type of test and the purpose(s) for which it is administered. These procedures are described throughout this book, beginning with the discussion of norms in Chapter 4.

ITEM ANALYSIS

Even after a test has been administered and scored, the examiner cannot always be certain that the test has done its job well. When a test is tried out initially, it is likely that a number of problems will be encountered. This is one reason why commercially distributed tests are tried out first (pilot tested) on a sample of 50 or so people who are representative of the group for whom the test is ultimately intended.

Whatever the type of test—standardized or teacher made, ability or personality—a post-mortem or post hoc analysis of results is just as necessary as it is in medicine or any other human enterprise. Among the questions that need to be answered are the following: Were the time limits adequate? Did the examinees understand the directions? Were the environmental conditions appropriate? Were emergencies handled properly? Rarely is every problem or contingency that arises during a test anticipated. A post hoc analysis can provide information and motivation for meeting similar situations on future administrations of the test. The questionnaire in Table 3-6, administered immediately after students have finished the test, can provide qualitative information on student perceptions

TABLE 3–6 Test Evaluation Form

Course: _____

Directions: Complete this form after you finish the test. Circle your response to each item, and fill in the blanks if appropriate.

Yes No   1. Was the testing environment (seating, temperature, ventilation, etc.) satisfactory? If not, explain. _____

Yes No   2. Did you read the directions carefully before beginning the test?

Yes No   3. Were the directions for the test clear?

Yes No   4. Was the layout of the test (kinds of items, arrangement, answer sheet, etc.) satisfactory? If not, explain. _____

Yes No   5. Did the test cover the assigned material adequately? If not, explain. _____

Yes No   6. Were the test questions of appropriate difficulty? If not, explain. _____

Yes No   7. Did you study enough for the test? Why not? _____

Yes No   8. Did you study the right material? Why not? _____

Yes No   9. Do you think you answered any questions wrong? Which ones? _____

Yes No   10. Did you "guess" at any answers? How many? _____

Yes No   11. Did you omit any items? How many? _____

Yes No   12. Did you have enough time to finish? Why not? _____

Yes No   13. After you finished the test, did you go back and check your answers?

Yes No   14. Were you very anxious (emotionally upset) during the test?

Yes No   15. Was the test fair? Why not? _____

Yes No   16. In general, was this a good test? Why not? _____

_____   17. What grade do you expect to get on this test?

of the fairness of the test, whether they felt prepared for it, whether it met their expectations, and how they responded to the test items.

An analysis of the responses given by a group of examinees to the individual items on a test serves several functions. The major aim of such an *item analysis* is to help improve the test by revising or discarding ineffective items. Another important function served by an item analysis, especially of a classroom achievement test, is to provide diagnostic information on what examinees do and do not know.

Criterion-referenced Tests and Mastery

The procedure employed in evaluating the effectiveness of test items depends to some extent on the purposes of the test. For example, the tester may merely be interested in determining how much an examinee knows of the test material, not in comparing the latter's performance with that of other examinees. In this case a student's performance is compared with a criterion or standard established by the classroom teacher or by institutional policy. The purpose of such *criterion-referenced tests* is not to discover where people score in relation to the scores of other people, but rather to determine where each person stands with respect to certain educational objectives. A particular type of criterion-referenced test designed to measure the attainment of a limited range of cognitive skills is known as a *mastery test.* A person's score on a mastery test, or on any other criterion-referenced test, is expressed as a percentage of the total number of items answered correctly; a perfect score indicates 100 percent mastery of the test material.

Individual Differences and Item Validity

Since it is frequently difficult to obtain agreement on how much an individual should know about a particular subject or what constitutes mastery of the subject, a score on a psychological or educational test is more often interpreted by comparing it with the scores of other people. The history of testing is interwoven with the study of individual differences, and psychological tests have been devised primarily to assess the differences among individuals in cognitive and affective characteristics. People differ in their abilities and personalities, and psychologists attempt to measure these differences with tests. The more carefully this is accomplished, the more precisely can behavior be predicted from test scores. Consequently, professional test constructors try to devise items that differentiate among individuals in terms of whatever is being measured. By so doing, the variability of total test scores is increased, and a given score is a more accurate indicator of an examinee's standing in relation to other people.

To assess the usefulness of an item as a measure of individual differences in ability or personality characteristics, testers need some external criterion measure of the characteristic. If the test is being constructed to predict performance on a job or in school, then a suitable external criterion is a measure of job performance (for example, supervisors' ratings) or school achievement (for example, teacher-assigned marks). The *validity* of an item for predicting the particular external criterion measure may be determined by computing the correlation between scores on the item (0's and 1's) and scores on the criterion measure. Different types of correlation coefficients have been used for this purpose, the most common being the *point-biserial coefficient.* A formula for computing the point-biserial coefficient is

$$r_{pb} = \frac{(\overline{Y}_p - \overline{Y})}{s} \sqrt{\frac{nn_p}{(n - n_p)(n - 1)}} \tag{3.3}$$

where n = the total number of examinees, n_p = the number of examinees who pass the item, $\overline{Y}_p$ = the mean criterion scores of examinees who pass the item, $\overline{Y}$ = the mean of all criterion scores, and s = the standard deviation of all criterion scores. The criterion may be an external one or even total scores on the test itself.

To illustrate the computation of the point-biserial coefficient, assume that the total test scores of a group of 30 people have a mean of 75 and a standard deviation of 10.

Also assume that the mean test score of the 17 examinees who answer a certain item correctly is 80. Substituting these numbers in formula 3.3 yields

$$r_{pb} = \left(\frac{80 - 75}{10}\right)\sqrt{\frac{30(17)}{13(29)}} = .58$$

The higher the validity index for an item (item–criterion correlation), the more useful the item is for predicting the criterion. Whether an item will be retained or discarded depends on the size of the validity index. Although items with validity indexes as low as .20 may contribute to the prediction of the criterion, higher validity indexes are preferred. Certainly, an item with a validity index close to .00 or with a negative validity index should be revised or discarded. The usefulness of an item for predicting a specified criterion, however, depends not only on the validity index, but also on the correlation of the item with other items on the test. Items that have high validity indexes but low correlations with other items are best because they make an independent contribution to the prediction of the criterion scores.

Item Difficulty and Discrimination Indexes

On classroom achievement tests, there is usually no external criterion against which to validate items, so a different, *internal consistency* procedure is employed. Although an item analysis of a classroom test, like that of any other test, entails determining the percentage of examinees who pass the item and the correlation of the item with a criterion measure, in this case the criterion consists of total scores on the test itself.

A shortcut procedure is to divide the examinees into three groups according to their scores on the test as a whole: an upper group consisting of the 27 percent of examinees making the highest test scores, a lower group of the 27 percent making the lowest test scores, and the remaining 46 percent in the middle group. When the number of examinees is small, upper and lower 50 percent groups on total test scores may be used. In any event, the following statistical indexes are computed from the scores of the upper and lower groups:

$$p = \frac{U_p + L_p}{U + L} \tag{3.4}$$

and

$$D = \frac{U_p - L_p}{U} \tag{3.5}$$

U_p and L_p designate the numbers of examinees in the upper and lower groups, respectively, who pass the item; U and L are the total number of examinees in the upper and lower groups. The value of p is referred to as an *item difficulty index* and the value of D as an *item discrimination index*. To illustrate the computation of these indexes, assume that 50 people take a test. Then the upper and lower groups can be formed from the top 14 and the bottom 14 examinees on total test scores. If 12 of the examinees in the upper group and 7 of those in the lower group pass item A, then $p = (12 + 7)/28 = .68$ and $D = (12 - 7)/14 = .36$.

The item difficulty index has a range of .00 to 1.00. An item whose $p = .00$ is one that no examinee answered correctly, and an item with $p = 1.00$ is one that all examinees answered correctly. The optimum p value for an item depends on a number of factors, including the purposes of the test and the number of response options. If the purpose of a test is to identify or select only a small percentage of the best applicants, then the test should be fairly difficult and have a low mean value of p. If the test is designed to screen out only a few very poor applicants, then a high mean value of p is best.

The optimum mean values of p corresponding to selected values of k, the number of response options, are given in Table 3–7. Acceptable item difficulty indexes fall within a fairly narrow range, say plus or minus .20 around these values. Although several very easy and several very difficult items are often included on a test, they actually add very little to the overall effectiveness of the test in differentiating among examinees who possess different amounts of knowledge, skill, or understanding of the material.

The item discrimination index (D) is a measure of the effectiveness of an item in discriminating between high and low scorers on the test. The higher the value of D, the more effective is the item in discriminating between high and low scorers on the test as a whole. When D is 1.00, all examinees in the upper group on total test scores and none of those in the lower group answered the item right. Rarely, however, is D equal to 1.00, and an item is usually considered acceptable if its D index is .30 or higher. D and p are not, however, independent indexes, and the minimum acceptable value of D varies with the value of p. A value of D somewhat smaller than .30 is acceptable as p becomes increasingly higher or lower than the optimum value, particularly when the sizes of the upper and lower comparison groups are large (Aiken, 1979b). Furthermore, an item having a low D index is not automatically discarded; it may be possible to save the item by modifying it. Constructing good test items is a time-consuming process, so defective items should be revised if possible.

Group Differences on Speeded Tests

The results of an item analysis often vary substantially with the specific group that is tested, especially when the number of examinees is small. Certain items may be answered

TABLE 3–7 Optimum Mean Item Difficulty Indexes for Test Items Having Various Numbers of Options

Number of options (k)	Optimum means difficulty index (p)
2	.85
3	.77
4	.74
5	.69
Open-ended (essay, short answer)	.50

Source: Constructed from data provided by F. M. Lord, *Psychometrika, 17* (1952), 181–194.

differently by males than by females, by one ethnic group than by another, or by one socioeconomic group than another. In constructing a standardized test, it has become common practice to examine each item and its associated statistics for indications of group discrimination or bias. Simply because the way in which an item is answered is not the same for two groups does not necessarily mean that the item is biased against one of the groups. Technically, an item is biased only when it measures something different—a different characteristic or trait—in one group than in another. If item scores reflect true differences in the ability or other characteristic that the item was designed to measure, the item is technically unbiased.

Problems also occur in the item analysis of speeded tests, on which the time limits are short and not all examinees have time to finish. On a speeded test, items placed near the end of the test are attempted by relatively few examinees. If those who reach and therefore attempt an item are the most able examinees, then the discrimination index (D) will probably be greater than it would be if the time limits were ample. On the other hand, if the most careless responders are more likely to reach and attempt items toward the end of the test, the D values of those items will tend to be smaller than the D values of items located near the beginning of the test. Various procedures have been suggested to take care of the problems encountered in analyzing items toward the end of speeded tests, but none is completely satisfactory (see Anastasi, 1988, pages 224–226).

Conditions of testing other than time limits can also affect the item difficulty and discrimination indexes. Nevertheless, these two indexes provide useful information on the functioning of individual items. In general, it has been found that item analyses can result in significant improvements in test effectiveness (Bodner, 1980). The item discrimination index in particular is a fairly good measure of item quality (Pyrczak, 1973). Along with the difficulty index p, D can serve as a warning that something is wrong with an item. Consequently, these two indexes, together with the nature and size of the group tested, should be recorded on the back of an index card containing the item. Repeating this process for all items yields a library of analyzed test items for constructing future tests.

Internal Consistency versus Validity

The concept of item validity usually refers to the relationship of an item to an external criterion. But D is a measure of the relationship of an item to total test score, rather than to an external criterion. Selecting items having high D values will result in an internally consistent test on which the correlations among items are highly positive. Simply because a test is internally consistent, however, does not mean that it will be highly correlated with an external criterion. To construct a test that yields scores that are highly correlated with an external criterion, we should select items having low correlations with each other but high correlations with the criterion. Thus, selecting items on the basis of the D statistic will result in a different kind of test than one composed of items selected for their high correlations with an external criterion. Which of these procedures is superior depends on the purposes of the test. If an internally consistent measure of a characteristic is desired, the item discrimination index (D) should be used in selecting items. If the most valid predictor of a particular external criterion is needed, the item–criterion correlations should be used. Sometimes a combination of the two approaches is appropriate: A composite test is constructed from subtests having low correlations with each other and substantial correlations with an external criterion, but the items within each subtest are highly intercorrelated.

Criterion-referenced Test Items

Difficulty and discrimination indexes may also be computed on criterion-referenced test items. In this case, the examinees are divided into two groups: an upper group consisting of the U examinees whose total test scores meet the criterion of mastery, and a lower group consisting of the L examinees whose total test scores fail to meet the criterion. For a particular item, U_p is the number in the upper group (above criterion level) who get the item right, and L_p is the number in the lower group (below criterion level) who get the item right. Then the item difficulty index is defined by formula 3.4. Because U and L are not necessarily equal, the item discrimination index is defined as

$$D = \frac{U_p}{U} - \frac{L_p}{L} \qquad\qquad (3.6)$$

An external criterion may also be used in forming the upper and lower groups. In the case of a criterion-referenced achievement test, for example, examinees may be sorted into two groups: those who have received instruction in the subject matter associated with the test (U) and those who have not received such instruction (L). The U and L groups may also consist of the same individuals, both before (L) and after (U) instruction. In either case, formula 3.6 can be used to compute the item discrimination index (Popham, 1981, pages 300–303).

Analysis of Item Distracters

The analysis of multiple-choice items typically begins with the computation of difficulty and discrimination indexes for each item. A second analysis is concerned with the functioning of the $k - 1$ distracters for each item. The algebraic sign and magnitude of the item discrimination index (D) provide some information on the functioning of the distracters as a whole. A positive D value means that examinees in the upper group tended to select the correct answer, while examinees in the lower group tended to select the distracters; the magnitude of D indicates the extent of this tendency. On the other hand, a negative value of D indicates that the distracters as a whole were chosen more frequently by the upper group (on total test scores) than the lower group and that the item needs revising. The sign and magnitude of D, however, do not indicate whether all distracters functioned properly.

The simplest method of determining whether all distracters are working properly is to count the number of times that each distracter is selected as the right answer by examinees in the upper group and by those in the lower group. If, on an otherwise satisfactory item, too many examinees in the upper group or too few of those in the lower group selected a given distracter, that distracter should be edited or replaced. Ideally, all $k - 1$ distracters should be equally plausible to examinees who do not know the correct answer to an item; consequently, every distracter should be selected by approximately the same number of examinees.

Item Characteristic Curves

Even acceptable p and D values do not ensure that an item is functioning effectively across all levels of overall test performance. To be most effective, the proportion of examinees who answer a test item correctly should increase steadily with increases in total scores on the test or subtest. Whether or not a test item is functioning in this manner can be determined by inspecting the characteristic curve of the item. In constructing an *item characteristic curve,* the proportion of examinees who responded to the item with the keyed answer is plotted against scores on an internal criterion (for example, total test scores) or performance on an external criterion (for example, academic or occupational adjustment measures). Once the characteristic curve for a particular item has been drawn, the difficulty level and discrimination index for the item can be determined. The *difficulty level (b)* is the criterion score for which 50 percent of the examinees gave the keyed answer; the *discrimination index (a)* is the slope of the item-response curve at that 50-percent point. In the two item characteristic curves shown in Figure 3–3, item 1 has a lower difficulty level but a steeper slope, and hence a greater discrimination index, than item 1. The similarity of these two indexes to the p and D indexes of traditional item analysis is obvious. However, an item characteristic curve goes further in that it provides a detailed picture of the functional relationship between the proportion of examinees who get the item right and their scores on a criterion measure.

Item-response Theory

An extension of the item characteristic curve approach is *item-response theory (IRT).* An item-response curve is constructed by plotting the proportion of people who answered an item according to the keyed response against estimates of the true standing of these individuals on a unidimensional latent trait or characteristic (see Figure 3–4). These estimates are derived by a mathematical function known a a logistic equation (see Baker, 1985). The precise mathematical equations involved in IRT vary with the assumptions and estimation procedures prescribed by the approach.

An item-response curve can be constructed either from the responses of a large group of examinees to an item or, if certain parameters are estimated, from a theoretical model. In the one-parameter IRT model, known as the *Rasch model,* an item-response curve is drawn by estimating only the item difficulty parameter (b). In the two-parameter model, which is probably the most popular IRT model, construction of an item-response curve involves both difficulty (b) and discrimination (a) parameters. Finally, in the three-parameter model, difficulty (b), discrimination (a), and guessing (c) parameters are estimated. Figure 3–4 illustrates item-response curves constructed according to a two-parameter model. For item $P,$ the difficulty parameter (b) is 1.00, and the discrimination parameter

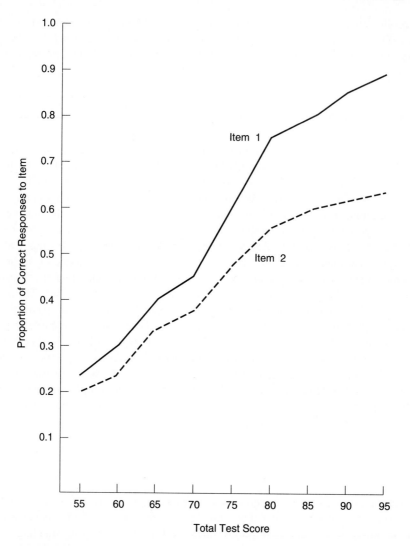

FIGURE 3–3 Two Item Characteristic Curves. See Text for Explanation.

(*a*) is .5; for item *Q*, *b* = .25 and *a* = .75. Therefore, item *Q* is easier but more discriminating than item *P*.

Item-response theory has been applied not only to item analysis, but also to designing tests that have certain characteristics. Procedures for developing, administering, and evaluating tests of ability, and to some extent personality assessment instruments, have benefited greatly from IRT. Because a thorough understanding of the functioning of item-response models requires a fairly sophisticated background in mathematics, the technical details are not included in this text (for a simple, computer-based exposition, see Baker, 1985).

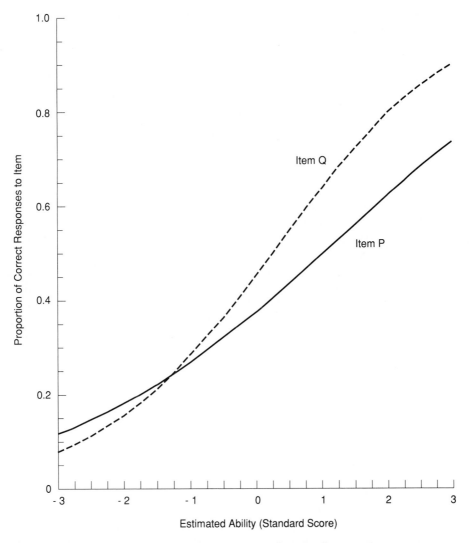

FIGURE 3–4 Two Item Response Curves. See Text for Explanation.

SUMMARY

Procedures for administering and scoring tests vary to some extent with the type of test and the nature of the examinees. It is particularly important for examinees to be prepared for the test, motivated to do well, and relatively free from stress and other disruptive conditions. The examiner should be trained, familiar with the test, and confident that everything is in order before attempting to administer the test. In general, the testing situation should be physically and psychologically comfortable so that examinees will be inclined to do their best.

As a rule, examinees should be informed of the purpose(s) of a test, where and when the test will be administered, the format of the test, and the material with which it will deal. Examiners should follow the test directions carefully, taking precautions to minimize cheating, and be prepared to handle emergencies and other special problems. Some flexibility is usually permitted in administering both teacher-made and standardized tests, but sharp deviations from the directions for administration will invalidate the use of norms on the latter type of test. Examiners should also attempt to establish rapport with examinees, especially on individually administered tests.

Test wiseness, successful guessing, changing answers, and cheating are some of the factors that can inflate scores on objective tests; bluffing, a sophisticated writing style, and good penmanship can do the same on essay tests. The effects of test wiseness are minimized by constructing items carefully, avoiding cues such as item length, specific determiners, grammatical errors, stylistic giveaways, and heterogeneous (nonparallel) options. Correction-for-guessing formulas are sometimes applied to reduce the effects of guessing. With the possible exception of true–false items, however, conventional correction-for-guessing formulas are usually not worth the time or effort to apply in scoring classroom tests.

Essay tests may be scored holistically or analytically, but in either case examinees should be informed as to how the test will be scored. Scoring the responses of all examinees to a specific essay question before going on to the next item is recommended, as is scoring responses separately for content and style. In addition to a numerical score, written comments, corrections, and explanations are often helpful in providing feedback on essay test performance.

Many objective tests are scored by computers or other special machines. Machine scoring is generally superior to hand scoring in terms of speed and accuracy, but less flexible. The scoring of many individual tests of intelligence and personality is not completely objective and may result in serious errors on the part of professional testers and trainees alike.

The effects of assigning different scoring weights for different kinds of objective items or different responses to an item is a topic that has been investigated extensively. In general, a priori scoring weights are not recommended on tests consisting of 20 items or more.

Raw test scores are often converted to percentile ranks or standard scores for purposes of computing averages, making comparisons, and interpreting scores. Scores on classroom tests are also converted to grades, either by using a fixed set of percentages such as those specified by the Cajori method or in a more subjective manner.

The major purpose of an item analysis is to improve a test by revising or discarding ineffective items. Item analysis also provides specific information on what examinees know and do not know.

Test items may be analyzed by comparing item responses with scores on an external criterion, such as teacher-assigned marks or ratings by supervisors, or with an internal criterion measure such as total test scores. If the goal of the test constructor is to produce a test that is most predictive of scores on an external criterion, then the items should be validated against that criterion.

Various statistics are computed to validate test items against external or internal criteria. These statistics, which are indexes of the relationship between dichotomously scored (right–wrong) items and scores on the criterion measure, provide a basis for accepting or rejecting specific items.

Two simple coefficients that may be computed in the item analysis of a teacher-made test are the item difficulty index (p) and the item discrimination index (D). These indexes are applicable to both norm- and criterion-referenced items. The optimum value of p depends on the purposes of the test and the number of options per item. In most situations, a D value of .30 or higher is required for an item to be acceptable.

In addition to computing difficulty and discrimination indexes, test items should be examined for bias, ambiguity, and the effects of speededness. Marked variations from a uniform frequency distribution of responses to the distracters is a sign of a poorly functioning item.

In constructing an item characteristic curve, the proportion of examinees who answer an item in accordance with the keyed response is plotted against scores on an internal (total test scores) or external criterion. An extension of the item characteristic approach known as item-response theory involves inserting difficulty, discrimination, and guessing parameters into a logistic equation or deriving values of these parameters from such an equation. The logistic equation relates the proportion of examinees who answered the item correctly to estimates of their scores on a hypothesized continuum of ability or some other unidimensional trait.

EXERCISES

1. What are the relative advantages and disadvantages of essay and objective tests? Of oral and written examinations?

2. Define *test wiseness,* and describe test-taking behaviors indicative of test wiseness. What can a test designer do to minimize the effects of test wiseness on test scores?

3. Question a group of your fellow students about the techniques they use in selecting answers to items on a multiple-choice test when they are poorly acquainted with the test material. What techniques are most popular, and how effective are they?

4. You have undoubtedly observed that the speed of completing a classroom test can vary markedly from student to student. Some students finish a 2-hour examination in less than 1 hour, while others continue working even after the allotted time has elapsed. From your observations and conversations, what do you believe are the major factors that determine how quickly students finish a test?

5. John takes a 50-item, four-option multiple-choice test. He gets 30 items right, 16 items wrong, and leaves 4 items blank. What is his total score on the test, both corrected and uncorrected for guessing? If all items were of the true–false variety and he gave the same number of correct and incorrect answers as listed above, what would his total score be, both corrected and uncorrected for guessing?

6. A test on British history contains a rearrangement item consisting of a list of seven battles. Students are asked to arrange the seven battles, from first to last, according to their dates of occurrence. The correct order is: Battle of Hastings, Battle of Bunker Hill, Battle of Yorktown, Battle of Trafalgar, Battle of Waterloo, Battle of the Marne, Battle of Britain. John lists these battles in the following order: Waterloo, Hastings, Yorktown, Trafalgar, Marne, Britain, Bunker Hill. What is his score on the item? Jenny lists the

seven battles in the order: Hastings, Waterloo, Yorktown, Bunker Hill, Trafalgar, Marne, Britain. What is her score?

7. Applying the percentages designated by the Cajori method, assign letter grades to the scores in the X distribution in Exercise 2 of Appendix A. Then assign grades to the Y distribution in the same exercise. If the set of *Computer Programs for Psychological Assessment* is available, you can use program 3 ("Grade Assignment by the Modified Cajori Method") in category 2 to solve this problem. Let both the maximum score and the median ability level of the class equal 50.

8. What are the difficulty (p) and discrimination (D) indexes of a test item that was administered to 75 people if 18 people in the upper group (upper 27 percent on total test score) and 12 people in the lower group (lower 27 percent on total test score) get the item right? Note that rounding yields 20 people in the upper group and 20 people in the lower group. Use formulas 3.3 and 3.4.

9. Compute the difficulty (p) and discrimination (D) indexes of an item on a criterion-referenced test taken by 50 people, 30 of whom scored at or above and 20 of whom scored below the criterion level. Of those who scored at or above the criterion level, 20 got the item right; of those who scored below the criterion level, 10 got the item right.

10. The following two-way table indicates whether each of 20 people got each of the 10 items on a four-option multiple-choice test right (r) or wrong (w). Classifying examinees A through J in the upper group and examinees K through T in the lower group on total test scores (see last line of table), compute the difficulty and discrimination indexes for each item. Write these values in the last two columns of the table. By inspecting the p and D indexes, decide which items are acceptable and which items need revising or discarding.

	Examinee																					
Item	A	B	C	D	E	F	G	H	I	J	K	L	M	N	O	P	Q	R	S	T	p	D
1	r	r	r	w	w	w	r	r	r	r	w	r	r	w	w	w	r	w	w	w		
2	r	r	w	r	w	r	w	r	w	r	r	w	w	r	w	w	w	w	r	w		
3	r	w	r	r	r	w	r	w	r	w	w	w	r	r	w	w	r	w	w	w		
4	r	r	r	r	r	r	w	r	w	r	r	w	w	r	r	w	w	w	w	w		
5	r	r	w	r	r	r	r	r	w	w	w	r	w	w	w	w	w	w	w	w		
6	r	r	r	r	r	r	w	r	r	r	r	w	r	r	w	r	w	r	w	r		
7	r	w	w	w	r	r	r	r	w	r	w	w	r	w	r	w	w	r	r	w		
8	r	r	r	r	r	w	w	w	r	w	r	r	w	w	w	r	r	w	w	w		
9	r	r	r	r	w	r	r	w	r	r	r	r	w	r	r	w	w	w	w	w		
10	r	r	r	w	r	r	r	w	r	w	w	w	w	w	w	w	r	w	w	w		
Score	10	8	7	7	7	7	6	6	6	6	5	5	4	4	3	3	3	2	2	1		

11. If the set of *Computer Programs for Psychological Assessment* is available, use program 3 ("Item Characteristic Curves and Item Response Curves") in category 3 ("Programs on Item Analysis and Norms") to plot item characteristic curves for the 10 items in Exercise 10. What conclusions concerning the functioning of these items can you draw from an inspection of the ICC curves?

SUGGESTED READINGS

Aiken, L. R. (1980). Problems in testing the elderly. *Educational Gerontology, 5,* 119–124.

———— (1991). Detecting, understanding, and controlling for cheating on tests. *Research in Higher Education, 32,* 725–736.

Airasian, P. W., & Terrasi, S. (1985). Test administration. In T. Husén & T. N. Postlethwaite (eds.), *International encyclopedia of education,* Vol. 9, pp. 5195–5198. New York: Wiley.

Green, K. (1984). Effects of item characteristics on multiple-choice item difficulty. *Educational and Psychological Measurement, 44,* 551–561.

Hughes, D. C., and Keeling, B. (1984). The use of model essays to reduce context effects in essay scoring. *Journal of Educational Measurement, 21,* 277–281.

Naylor, F. D. (1985). Test-taking anxiety. In T. Husen & T. N. Postlethwaite (eds.), *International encyclopedia of education,* Vol. 9, pp. 5209–5211. New York: Wiley.

Popham, W. J., & Lindheim, E. (1980). The practical side of criterion-referenced test development. *NCME Measurement in Education, 10*(4), 1–8.

Chapter Four

Standardization, Reliability, and Validity

Item analysis is an important step in designing and evaluating a psychological test or other assessment instrument, but it is not the last step. Before a test can be used with some assurance that it is an accurate measure of the psychological construct it is supposed to measure, information concerning the reliability and validity of the test must be obtained. Furthermore, it is useful for purposes of score interpretation to have data available on the performance of a large group of people like those with whom the instrument is to be used. To accomplish this task, the test, inventory, rating scale, or other psychometric instrument must be standardized.

TEST STANDARDIZATION AND NORMS

Any standardized test has standard directions for administration and scoring that should be followed closely, leaving little room for personal interpretation or bias. However, having standard directions for administration and scoring is necessary but not sufficient for a test to be standardized. In addition, the *standardization* of any psychological or educational assessment instrument requires administering the instrument to a large sample of individuals (the *standardization sample*) selected as representative of the *target population* of persons for whom the instrument is intended.

The major purpose of the standardization procedure is to determine the distribution of raw scores in the standardization group (*norm group*). The obtained raw scores are then converted to some form of derived scores, or *norms*. These norms include age equivalents, grade equivalents, percentile ranks, and standard scores. Most test manuals contain tables of norms listing the raw scores and the corresponding converted scores. An examinee's standing on a test is evaluated by referring to the appropriate table of norms and finding the converted score equivalents to the raw score(s). In this way, norms serve not as standards of desirable performance, but simply as a frame a reference for interpreting raw scores. Norms indicate an examinee's standing on the test relative to the distribution of scores obtained by people of the same chronological age, grade, or sex, or other demographic characteristics.

In terms of sample size and representativeness, group tests, and achievement tests in particular, are often standardized more adequately than individual tests. Norms for group tests may be based on as many as 100,000 people, whereas the size of the norm group for a carefully standardized individual test is more likely to be 2000 to 4000. Of course, having a large standardization sample does not guarantee that the sample is representative of the population of interest. To be representative of this *target population,* the sample needs to be carefully selected.

Selecting a Standardization Sample

Norms that serve effectively in the interpretation of test scores must be appropriate for the group or individual being evaluated. For example, a particular fourth-grader's score may surpass that of 80 percent of fourth-grade children and 60 percent of sixth-graders. Although it may be of some interest to compare the student's score with the third- and sixth-grade norms, of primary concern is the student's standing in his or her own (fourth grade) group. Whenever a test score is converted by referring to a table of norms, it is important to note the nature (age, sex, ethnicity, educational and socioeconomic status, geographical region) of the particular norm group and to include this information in all communications regarding that person's test performance. Another important factor to consider is when the norms were obtained. During times of rapid social and educational change, the norms on certain tests can quickly become outdated. For example, changes in school curricula may necessitate restandardizing and perhaps modifying or reconstructing an achievement test every 5 years or so.

The manner in which a standardization sample is selected from the target population varies from simple random sampling to more complex sampling strategies, such as stratified random sampling and cluster sampling. In *simple random sampling,* every person in the target population has an equal chance of being selected. However, randomness does not ensure representativeness. Consequently, a more appropriate way of standardizing a test is to begin by categorizing, or "stratifying," the target population on a series of demographic variables (sex, age, socioeconomic status, geographical region, and the like) presumed to be related to scores on the test. Then the number of individuals selected at random from each category or stratum is made proportional to the total number of persons in the target population who fall in that stratum. Using this *stratified random sampling* procedure, the likelihood of selecting an atypical, or biased, sample is minimized. Then the obtained norms will provide a sounder basis for interpreting scores on the test than norms obtained by simple random sampling.

More economical than stratified random sampling and more likely than simple random sampling to produce a representative sample of the target population is cluster sampling. *Cluster sampling* consists of dividing a designated population of geographical areas or other relevant units into blocks or clusters. Then a specified percentage of the clusters is selected at random, and within each cluster a certain number of subunits (schools, residences, and so on) are randomly chosen. The final step is to administer the test to everyone in each subunit, or at least a random sample of people having certain characteristics.

Administering all items on a test to a stratified random sample or a cluster sample of individuals is tedious and time consuming, so less costly strategies for determining test norms have been proposed. One such strategy is to sample test items as well as individuals. In *item sampling,* different samples of items are administered to different, randomly selected samples of examinees. One group of people answer one set of items, and other groups answer other sets. The process is efficient, in that more items can be administered to a large group of people in a fixed period of time. Item analyses can then be conducted and norms based on the scores of representative samples of examinees can be determined for a wide range of test content. Research employing item-sampling procedures has demonstrated that the resulting norms are very similar to those obtained by the traditional but more laborious procedure of administering the entire test to a large representative sample of individuals (see Owens & Stufflebeam, 1969).

Type of Norms

Figure 4–1, a report of the scores of a student who took the Gates–MacGinitie Reading Tests, illustrates several types of norms: national and local percentile ranks, national and local stanines, grade equivalents (grade norms), and standard scores. Among the norms not shown in this report are age equivalents (age norms) and certain types of standard score norms.

National, Regional and Local Norms   The norms published in test manuals are useful in comparing an examinee's score with those of a sample of people from various localities, sometimes a cross section of the entire nation. But a test administrator is typically more interested in determining how well an examinee has performed in comparison with other students in the school, school system, state, or region, rather than with a national sample. When interest is restricted to the test scores of a particular school, the test administrator will want to convert raw test scores to *local norms* by the procedures discussed in the following sections. Local norms are often used for selection and placement purposes in schools and colleges.

Age and Grade Norms   Among the most popular types of norms, primarily because they are easily understood by test users, are age norms and grade norms. An *age norm* (age equivalent, educational age) is the median score on a test obtained by examinees of a given chronological age; a *grade norm* (age equivalent) is the median score obtained by examinees at a given grade level. Age norms are expressed in years and 12 one-month intervals. For the tenth year, for example, age norms range from 10-0 to 10-11, or 10 years, 0 months to 10 years, 11 months. Grade norms are expressed in 10 one-month intervals; it is assumed that growth in the characteristic of interest during the summer months is inconsequential. For example, the range of grade norms for the fifth grade is 5-0 to 5-9, in one-month intervals from the first to the last month of the school year.

Despite their popularity, age and grade norms have serious shortcomings. The main shortcoming is that growth in cognitive, psychomotor, or affective characteristics is not uniform over the entire range of ages or grades. Thus, a difference of 2 months growth in achievement at grade 4 (say from 4-2 to 4-4) is not educationally equivalent to 2

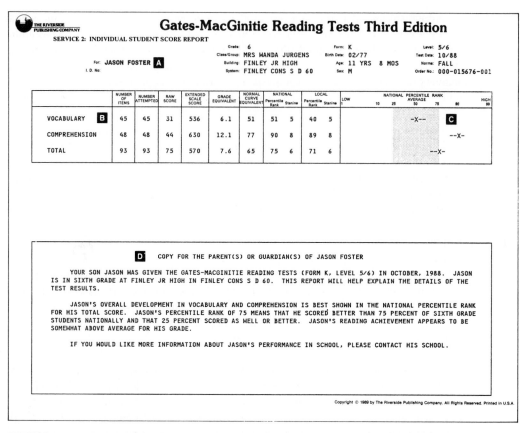

FIGURE 4–1   Individual Student Score Report, Gates–MacGinitie Reading Tests, Third Edition.
(Reproduced from Gates–MacGinitie Reading Tests, Third Edition, Copyright © 1989. Reproduced with permission of The Riverside Publishing Company.)

months' growth in achievement at a later grade level (say from 8-2 to 8-4). Actually, the age and grade units become progressively smaller with increasing age or grade level. Since age and grade norms incorrectly imply that the rate of increase in tested abilities is constant from year to year, their use is frequently discouraged by educational measurement specialists. Norms in which the unit of measurement is less variable are preferred.

Because of their convenience, age and grade norms continue to be used at the elementary school level, where the growth units are more nearly constant across time. Even at this level, however, age and grade norms should be supplemented with the percentile norms or standard score norms for a particular age or grade.

Modal Age Norms   Typically, the students in a given grade on whom grade norms are determined have a rather wide range of ages; the scores of certain students who are actually much older (or younger) than the average student in that grade are included in the norms. To provide a more accurate index of the average score of students at a given grade level, the scores of students who are much older or much younger than the modal age are sometimes omitted, and the median score is computed only on students who are of the appropriate age for that grade. These "restricted" grade norms are referred to as *modal age norms*. Modal age norms, which are found infrequently in current achievement test manuals, are mentioned here primarily for their historical interest.

Mental Age Norms The term *mental age* will be recalled from the brief discussion in Chapter 1 of the history of mental measurement. This concept, which was introduced by Alfred Binet, is a type of age norm employed on various intelligence tests. The mental age score of a particular examinee corresponds to the chronological age of the subgroup of children (all of the same chronological age) in the standardization group whose median score on the test was the same as that of the examinee. It has been the practice in many special schools to group mentally retarded children according to their mental ages, rather than their chronological ages, for purposes of instruction.

Quotients An older practice in testing, which has virtually disappeared, is to convert an examinee's age norm to a quotient by dividing the age score by the person's chronological age and multiplying the result by 100. Thus, the *intelligence quotient (ratio IQ)* on the older Stanford–Binet Intelligence Scale was defined as

$$IQ = 100 \frac{MA}{CA} \qquad (4.1)$$

where MA is the examinee's mental age and CA his or her chronological age in months. Similarly, an *educational quotient* on certain achievement tests was computed as the ratio of educational age (age norm on an educational achievement test) to chronological age in months. By combining the results of an intelligence test with those of an educational achievement test, an *accomplishment quotient* could be computed as the ratio of educational age to mental age. Some of these quotients are still computed in evaluating test scores, but the practice is discouraged by psychological measurement specialists.

Percentile Norms Percentile norms consist of a table of percentages corresponding to particular raw scores. The raw scores are referred to as *percentiles,* and the percentage of the norm group falling below a particular score is the *percentile rank* of that score. For example, referring to columns 2 and 5 of the distribution in Table 4–1, the percentile rank of a score of 775 is approximately 99, and the percentile rank of a score of 475 is approximately 23. Or we may say that the 99th percentile for this group of scores is 775, and the 23rd percentile is 475.

Because percentile norms are often needed for selection and placement purposes in a given school or grade group, the procedure for computing them will be described in some detail. Columns 1 and 3 of Table 4–1 are a frequency distribution of 250 scores obtained on a scholastic aptitude test, and column 2 gives the midpoints of the score intervals. To compute the entry in column 4 (cumulative frequency below midpoint) for a particular interval, the frequencies on all intervals up to that interval are summed. To this sum is added one-half of the frequency on that interval. For example, the entry 227.0 for the interval 650–699 is computed as $1 + 13 + 25 + 38 + 65 + 49 + 27 + \frac{1}{2}(18) = 227.0$. Since the entry for

TABLE 4–1 Percentile Ranks and Standard Scores Corresponding to Midpoints of a Frequency Distribution of Test Scores

(1)	(2)	(3)	(4)	(5)	(6)	(7)	(8)	(9)
Score interval	Midpoint	Frequency	Cumulative frequency below midpoint	Percentile rank	z	Z	z_n	T
750–799	774.5	3	248.5	99.4(99)	2.59	76	2.51	75
700–749	724.5	11	241.5	96.6(97)	2.03	70	1.83	68
650–699	674.5	18	227.0	90.8(91)	1.48	65	1.33	63
600–649	624.5	27	204.5	81.8(82)	0.92	59	0.91	59
550–599	574.5	49	166.5	66.6(67)	0.37	54	0.43	54
500–549	524.5	65	109.5	43.8(44)	−0.19	48	−0.16	48
450–499	474.5	38	58.0	23.2(23)	−0.74	43	−0.73	43
400–449	424.5	25	26.5	10.6(11)	−1.30	37	−1.25	37
350–399	374.5	13	7.5	3.0(3)	−1.86	31	−1.88	31
300–349	324.5	1	0.5	0.2(0)	−2.41	26	−2.88	21

a particular interval in column 4 is the cumulative frequency below the midpoint of that interval, the percentile rank of a given interval midpoint may be computed by dividing the respective number in column 4 by the total number of scores (n) and multiplying the resulting quotient by 100. For the data in Table 4-1, $n = 250$, so each of the percentile ranks in column 5 is equal to 100 times the corresponding cumulative frequency in column 4 divided by 250. For example, the percentile rank of the midpoint 674.5 is 100(227/250) $= 90.8 \approx 91$.

Because percentile norms are easy to compute and to understand, they are common in published tests. Tables of percentile norms within grades, ages, sex, occupations, and other groups are reported for many psychometric instruments. Unfortunately, the problem of unequal score units, which was referred to previously in the discussion of age and grade norms, is not solved by percentile norms. As may be observed graphically on the scale labeled Percentile Equivalents in Figure 4–2, percentile rank units are not equal on all parts of the scale. Percentile ranks are ordinal-level rather than interval-level measures. Notice, for example, that the distance between the percentile ranks 5 and 10 (or 90 and 95) on the Percentile Equivalents scale of Figure 4–2 is larger than the distance between 40 and 45 (or 60 and 65). Although the numerical differences between the ranks are the same, the size of the percentile rank unit becomes progressively smaller toward the center of the scale.

The tendency of percentile rank units to bunch up in the middle and spread out at the extremes of the scale causes difficulty in the interpretation of changes and differences in percentile norms. Thus, the difference in achievement between a person whose percentile rank on an achievement test is 5 and one whose percentile rank is 10 is not equal to the difference in achievement between a person whose percentile rank is 40 and one whose percentile rank is 45. On the percentile rank scale, 10 minus 5 is greater than 45 minus 40, because the unit of measurement for the first difference is larger. With practice, however, it is not difficult to interpret percentile norms. We must simply remember to give greater weight to percentile rank differences at the extremes than to those toward the center of the scale.

Standard Score Norms   Unlike percentile ranks, standard scores represent measurements on an interval scale. *Standard score norms* are converted scores having any desired mean and standard deviation. There are many different types of standard scores: z scores, Z scores, CEEB scores, deviation IQ scores, stanine scores, and T scores.

z Scores   The z score equivalents of a particular distribution of raw scores may be determined by the following formula:

$$z = \frac{X - \overline{X}}{s} \qquad (4.2)$$

where X is a given raw score, $\overline{X}$ is the arithmetic mean, and s is the standard deviation of the distribution of scores. Transforming the distribution of raw scores to z scores results in a new distribution having the same shape, but a different mean and standard deviation from those of the raw score distribution. The mean of z scores is 0, and the standard deviation is 1. The z scores corresponding to the interval midpoints listed in column 2

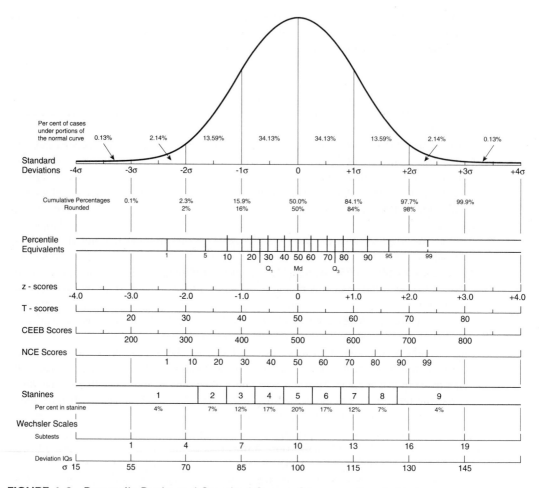

FIGURE 4–2 Percentile Ranks and Standard Scores Corresponding to Various
Points on the Baseline of a Normal Distribution of Scores.
(H. G. Seashore, Methods of expressing test scores,
The Psychological Corporation Test Service Bulletin, *No. 48, 1955.)*

are given in column 6 of Table 4–1. It may be determined by procedures described in
Appendix A that the mean and standard deviation of the distribution of scores in Table
4–1 are 541.50 and 90.30, respectively. Therefore, the z score corresponding to the midpoint
774.5 is $(774.5 - 541.5)/90.3 = 2.58$. The z scores of the other midpoints may be found
in the same way. The z scores corresponding to various points along the base line of the
normal curve are listed in Figure 4–2.

Z scores   The fact that z scores can be negative or positive decimal numbers creates
some difficulty in manipulating these scores. This problem can be solved by multiplying
the z scores by a constant and adding another constant to the products. If the z scores are
multiplied by 10, and 50 is added to the products, a new set of scores, *Z scores,* having

a mean of 50 and a standard deviation of 10, is produced. The new distribution of Z scores also has the same shape as the original raw-score distribution; only the mean and standard deviation have been changed (see column 7 of Table 4–1).

CEEB Scores   Instead of having a mean of 50 and a standard deviation of 10, the scores on the two sections (Verbal and Mathematical) of the College Entrance Examination Board's Scholastic Aptitude Test (SAT) were originally transformed by multiplying the corresponding z scores by 100 and adding 500 to the result. This was done to the results of the tests administered in 1941, yielding a new score distribution having a mean of 500 and a standard deviation of 100. The scores that examinees obtain on the SAT now administered, however, are not transformed each year to give a mean of 500 and a standard deviation of 100. Rather, to have a constant score unit for comparing test results from year to year, since 1941 the SAT scale has been based on the results of the 1941 testing.

AGCT and Wechsler Scores   The score scale on the Army General Classification Test (AGCT), which was formerly employed in selecting and placing American soldiers, had a mean of 100 and a standard deviation 20. In contrast, raw scores on the subtests of the Wechsler intelligence scales were transformed to have a mean of 10 and a standard deviation of 3, while the total scores of the Wechsler norm groups were converted to have a mean of 100 and a standard deviation of 15 (see last two lines of Figure 4–2).

Normalized Standard Scores   All the standard score norms referred to above are simple linear transformations of raw scores; the distribution of converted scores has a different mean and standard deviation from the raw-score distribution, but the shapes of the two distributions are identical. If the raw-score distribution is symmetrical, the converted score distribution will also be symmetrical.

To make the scores from different tests more directly comparable, there is a transformation procedure that not only affects the mean and standard deviation, but also changes the shape of the distribution of raw scores to that of a normal distribution. The conversion of a group of raw scores to *normalized standard scores* begins with the computation of the percentile ranks of the raw scores. Then, from a table of areas under the normal curve (Appendix B), the z score corresponding to each percentile rank is found. For example, assume that the midpoints (column 2) of the distribution in Table 4–1 are to be converted to normalized standard scores. Since the percentile ranks of these midpoints have already been computed (column 5), all that needs to be done is to convert the percentile ranks to proportions (for example, 99.4 becomes .994). Then, from the table in Appendix B, the z scores below which the given proportions of the area lie may be determined. Thus, the z score (z_n) below which .994 of the area lies is 2.51. The other normalized z scores in column 8 of Table 4–1 were determined similarly. To eliminate decimal points and negative numbers, these z_n scores were transformed to T scores by the formula $T = 10z_n + 50$ (column 9). The new normal distribution of T scores has a mean of 50 and a standard deviation of 10.

The z_n scores may be transformed to normalized scores having a desired mean and standard deviation. One popular scale, which has been used by the U.S. Air Force and for grading purposes in certain academic institutions, is the stanine (standard nine) scale. The *stanine scale,* a normalized standard score scale with a mean of 5 and a standard deviation of approximately 2, is represented by the third scale from the bottom in Figure 4–2. There are nine different ranges, or stanines, on the scale. These ranges are represented by the numbers 1 through 9, and, as shown in the figure, a certain percentage of the examinees fall in the interval represented by a given stanine. The stanine scale, however, is not a true standard score scale because the first and ninth stanines are open ended. Notice in Figure 4–2 that the widths of stanines 2 through 8 are equal, indicating equal standard score units, but that stanines 1 and 9 are much wider than the others. One advantage of stanine scores is that they represent ranges rather than specific points. This helps combat the tendency to view test scores as precise, unvarying measures of individual differences. Another procedure having the same effect is to report not only the percentile rank or standard score corresponding to a given raw score, but also a percentile rank or standard score interval within which the examinee's true standing on the test might reasonably be expected to fall. This practice is a recognition of the fact that scores on psychological and educational tests are not exact measurements, but are subject to errors of measurement, a topic discussed in more detail later in the chapter.

Parallel and Equated Tests

In many situations involving applications and research with psychological tests, more than one form of a test is needed. *Parallel forms* of a test are equivalent in the sense that they contain the same kinds of items of equal difficulty and are highly correlated. Therefore, the scores made on one form of the test are very similar to the scores of the same examinees on a second form at the same age or grade level as the first form. The construction of two parallel tests is, unfortunately, a rather expensive and time consuming process. It begins with the preparation of two tests having the same number and kinds of items and yielding the same means and standard deviations when standardized on the same group of people. The resulting parallel forms are then "equated" by converting scores on one form to the same units as those on the other form. This may be done, for example, by the *equipercentile method* of changing the scores on each form to percentile ranks. Then a table of equivalent scores on the two forms is prepared by equating the pth percentile on the first form to the score at the pth percentile on the second form.

Tests may also be equated, or rather made comparable, by anchoring the tests to a common test or pool of items, as is done every year with the Scholastic Aptitude Test (SAT). By using a set of common anchor items on each new form that are the same as a subset of items on at least one earlier form of the test, scores on the new form of the SAT administered each year are equated to at least one earlier form, going all the way back to the form administered to the initial standardization sample in 1941.

Item-response theory (IRT) was discussed briefly in the last chapter in connection with item analysis. The IRT approach, which prescribes methods of calibrating a set of test items on an operationally defined latent trait (usually standard scores on the horizontal axis of an item characteristic curve), has also been applied to the task of equating tests. The procedure is economical in that item sampling, in which randomly selected subsets of items are administered to different randomly selected groups of people, is employed. But whatever the method of attempting to equate two tests may be (equipercentile, item response, linear or nonlinear score transformations), tests that either measure different psychological characteristics or have different reliabilities cannot, strictly speaking, be equated. In almost every case, about the best that can be done is to make the two tests or other psychometric instruments "comparable" (American Educational Research et al., 1985).

RELIABILITY

No assessment device can be of value unless it measures something consistently, or *reliably.* Consequently, one of the first things that should be determined about a newly constructed assessment instrument is whether or not it is sufficiently reliable to measure what it was designed to measure. If, in the absence of any permanent change in a person (due to growth, learning, disease, or injury), test scores vary widely from time to time or situation to situation, the test is probably unreliable and cannot be used to explain or make predictions about a person's behavior. Note that *reliability* does not have the same meaning as *stability;* in determining the reliability of a measuring instrument, it is assumed that the instrument is measuring a relatively stable characteristic. Unlike instability, unreliability is a result of measurement errors produced by temporary internal states, such as low motivation or indisposition, or external conditions, such as a distracting or uncomfortable testing environment.

Classical Reliability Theory

In classical test theory, it is assumed that a person's observed score on a test is composed of a "true" score plus some unsystematic error of measurement. *True score* is defined as the average of the scores that would be obtained if a person took the test an infinite number of times. It should be emphasized that the true score can never be measured exactly, but must be estimated from the person's observed score on the test. It is also assumed in classical test theory that the variance of observed scores (s_{obs}^2) for a group of examinees is equal to the variance of their true scores (s_{tru}^2) plus the variance of unsystematic errors of measurement (s_{err}^2):

$$s_{obs}^2 = s_{tru}^2 + s_{err}^2 \qquad (4.3)$$

Then test reliability (r_{11}) is defined as the ratio of true variance to observed variance, or the proportion of observed variance accounted for by true variance:

$$r_{11} = \frac{s_{tru}^2}{s_{obs}^2} \qquad (4.4)$$

The proportion of observed variance accounted for by error variance, or unaccounted for by true variance, can be determined from formulas 4.3 and 4.4 to be

$$\frac{s_{err}^2}{s_{obs}^2} = 1 - r_{11} \qquad (4.5)$$

The reliability of a test is expressed as a positive decimal number ranging from .00 to 1.00; $r_{11} = 1.00$ indicates perfect reliability, and $r_{11} = .00$ indicates total unreliability.

Because the variance of the true scores cannot be computed directly, reliability is usually estimated by analyzing the effects of variations in administration conditions and test content on test scores. As noted previously, reliability is not influenced by systematic changes in scores that affect all examinees similarly, but only by unsystematic changes that have different effects on different examinees. Such unsystematic factors influence the error variance of the test and hence its reliability. Each of the several methods of estimating reliability (test–retest, parallel forms, internal consistency) takes into account somewhat different conditions that may produce these unsystematic changes in test scores and consequently affect the magnitude of the error variance and hence the test's reliability.

Test–Retest Coefficient

To determine whether an instrument measures consistently from one time to another, a *test–retest* coefficient is determined. This coefficient, also known as a *coefficient of stability,* is found by correlating the scores obtained by a group of people on one administration of the test with their scores on a second administration. The test–retest procedure takes into account errors of measurement resulting from differences in conditions associated with the two occasions on which the test is administered. Because the same test is administered on both occasions, errors due to different samples of test items are not reflected in a test–retest coefficient. Furthermore, differences between conditions of administration are likely to be greater after a long time interval than a short one. As a result, the magnitude of a test–retest reliability coefficient tends to be larger when the interval between initial test and retest is short (a few days or weeks), rather than long (months or years).

Parallel-forms Coefficient

When the time interval between initial test and retest is short, examinees usually remember many of the responses that they made on the initial test. This obviously affects their responses on the second administration. This fact by itself would not change the test's reliability if all examinees remembered equal numbers of responses. But some examinees usually recall more responses than other examinees, reducing the correlation between test and retest. What seems to be needed to overcome this source of error is a parallel form of the test, one consisting of similar items, but not the same items. Then a *parallel-forms coefficient,* also known as a *coefficient of equivalence,* could be computed as an index of reliability.

The parallel forms idea is reasonable in principle: by administering a parallel form after a suitable interval following administration of the first form, a reliability coefficient reflecting errors of measurement due to different items and different times of administration can be computed. To control for the confounding effect of form with time of administration, form A should be administered first to half the group and form B to the other half; then, on the second administration, the first group takes form B and the second group takes form A. The resulting correlation between scores on the two forms, known as a *coefficient of stability and equivalence,* takes into account errors due to different times of administration and different test items.

Internal Consistency Coefficients

Although parallel forms are available for a number of tests, particularly tests of ability (achievement, intelligence, special aptitudes), a parallel form of a test is expensive and often very difficult to construct. Therefore, a less direct method of taking into account the effects on reliability of different samples of test items was devised. This is the *method of internal consistency,* examples of which are the split-half method, the Kuder–Richardson method, and Cronbach's alpha. Errors of measurement caused by different conditions or times of administration, however, are not reflected in an internal consistency coefficient. Consequently, internal consistency coefficients cannot be viewed as truly equivalent to either test–retest or parallel-forms coefficients.

Split-half Method It is often convenient to conceptualize a single test as consisting of two parts (parallel forms), each of which measures the same thing. Thus, a test can be administered and separate scores assigned to every examinee on two arbitrarily selected halves of the test. For example, an examinee may be given one score on the odd-numbered items and a second score on the even-numbered items. Then the correlation (r_{oe}) between the sets of scores is a parallel forms reliability coefficient for a test half as long as the original test. Assuming that the two halves are equivalent, with equal means and equal variances, the reliability of the test as a whole can be estimated by the *Spearman–Brown prophecy formula:*

$$r_{11} = \frac{2r_{oe}}{1 + r_{oe}} \qquad (4.6)$$

To illustrate the use of formula 4.6, assume that the correlation between total scores on the odd-numbered items and total scores on the even-numbered items of a test is .80. Then the estimated reliability of the entire test is $r_{11} = 2(.80)/(1 + .80) = .89$.

Kuder–Richardson Method Obviously, there are many different ways of dividing a test into two halves. Since each way may yield a somewhat different value of r_{11}, it is not clear which halving strategy results in the best reliability estimate. One solution to the problem is to take the average of the reliability coefficients obtained from all half-splits as the overall reliability estimate. Yet, even with a test of, say, 20 items, the assistance of a computer is needed to determine and average the resulting 92,378 split-half coefficients!

Under certain circumstances, the mean of all split-half coefficients can be estimated by one of the following formulas:

$$r_{11} = \left(\frac{k}{k-1}\right)\left[1 - \frac{\sum_{i=1}^{k} p_i(1 - p_i)}{s^2}\right] \qquad (4.7)$$

$$r_{11} = \left(\frac{k}{k-1}\right)\left[1 - \frac{\overline{X}(k - \overline{X})}{ks^2}\right] \qquad (4.8)$$

In these formulas, k is the number of items on the test, $\overline{X}$ is the mean of total test scores, s^2 is the variance of total test scores (computed with n instead of $n - 1$ in the denominator), and p the proportion of examinees giving the keyed response to item i. Formulas 4.7 and 4.8 are known as Kuder–Richardson (K–R) formulas 20 and 21, respectively. Unlike formula 4.7, formula 4.8 is based on the assumption that all items are of equal difficulty; it also yields a more conservative estimate of reliability and is easier to compute than formula 4.7.

To illustrate the application of formula 4.8, assume that a test containing 75 items has a mean of 50 and a variance of 100. Then, by formula 4.8,

$$r_{11} = \left(\frac{75}{74}\right)\left[1 - \frac{50(75 - 50)}{75(100)}\right] = .84$$

Coefficient Alpha   Formulas 4.7 and 4.8 are special cases of the more general coefficient alpha (Cronbach, 1951). *Coefficient alpha* may be defined as

$$\alpha = \left(\frac{k}{k - 1}\right)\left(1 - \frac{\sum_{i=1}^{k} s_i^2}{s_t^2}\right) \tag{4.9}$$

where k is the number of items, s_i^2 the variance of scores on item i, and s_t^2 the variance of total test scores. Although the Kuder–Richardson formulas are applicable only when test items are scored 0 or 1, a coefficient alpha is a general formula for estimating the reliability of a test consisting of items on which two or more scoring weights are assigned to answers.

All internal consistency procedures (split-half, Kuder–Richardson, coefficient alpha) overestimate the reliability of speeded tests, which most examinees do not finish in time. Consequently, internal consistency procedures must be modified to provide reasonable estimates of reliability when a test is speeded. One recommendation is to administer two split halves of the test at different times, but with equal time limits. Then the scores on the two separately timed halves are correlated and the resulting correlation coefficient is corrected by the Spearman–Brown prophecy formula. Test–retest and parallel-forms procedures may also be used to estimate the reliabilities of speeded tests.

The reliability coefficients of affective instruments such as personality and interest inventories are typically lower than those of cognitive tests (achievement, intelligence, and special aptitudes) (see Table 4–2). Occasionally, however, the reliabilities of affective measures are fairly high and the reliabilities of cognitive instruments very modest. How high must the reliability coefficient be for a test to be useful? The answer depends on what we plan to do with the test scores. If a test is used to determine whether the mean scores of two groups of people are significantly different, then a fairly modest reliability coefficient (.60 to .70) may be satisfactory. But if the test is used to compare one person's score with the score of another person, a reliability coefficient of at least .85 should be obtained.

Interscorer Reliability

Barring clerical errors, the scores computed by two different scorers of an objective test paper will be identical. Scoring essay and oral tests and certain other evaluative judgments

TABLE 4–2   Reliability Coefficients Obtained with Various Psychological Assessment Instruments

Type of instrument	Reliabilities		
	Low	Medium	High
Achievement test batteries	0.66	0.92	0.98
Scholastic ability tests	0.56	0.90	0.97
Aptitude test batteries	0.26	0.88	0.96
Objective personality tests	0.46	0.85	0.97
Interest inventories	0.42	0.84	0.93
Attitude scales	0.47	0.79	0.98

Source: G. C. Helmstadter, *Principles of Psychological Measurement,* © 1964, p. 85. Adapted by permission of Prentice Hall, Englewood Cliffs, N. J.

(personality ratings and projective-test scoring, for example) is, however, a fairly subjective process. In evaluating scores involving subjective scorer judgment, it is important to know the extent to which different scorers agree on the numerical values assigned to the responses of different examinees and items. The most common approach to determining this *interscorer or interrater reliability* is to have two persons score the responses of a sizable number of examinees and then to compute the correlation between the two sets of scores. Another approach is to have many persons score the test responses of one examinee or, better still, have many persons score the responses of a number of examinees. The last approach yields an *intraclass coefficient* or *coefficient of concordance,* which is a generalized interscorer or interrater reliability coefficient. Procedures for comparing these indexes are found in many statistics or psychometrics textbooks (Nunnally, 1978). The author (Aiken, 1985) has also provided special procedures for computing test–retest and internal consistency reliability indexes from rating-scale data and for conducting statistical tests of significance of the indexes.

Reliability of Oral Tests

Oral tests are not known for their high reliabilities, but special forms for rating oral performances can improve their objectivity and, hence, their reliability (see Table 3–5). Although oral examinations typically have lower reliabilities than comparable written tests, careful attention to the design of oral questions, the construction of model answers to questions before the test is administered, and the use of multiple raters or scorers can enhance the reliability of these tests. Such procedures have resulted in interscorer reliability coefficients in the .60s and .70s for oral tests administered in certain undergraduate, graduate, and professional school courses (Carter, 1962; Levine & McGuire, 1970; Hitchman, 1966). Other suggestions for improving the reliabilities of oral examinations include requiring examinees to delay answering until they have thought about the question for a while (Meredith, 1978) and electronically recording responses for later playback and reevaluation by scorers.

Variability and Reliability

As with other measures of relationship, reliability tends to be higher when the variance of the variables of interest (test scores, item scores, ratings) is large than when it is small. Because test score variance is related to test length, one method of increasing reliability is to make the test longer by adding items to it. The general Spearman–Brown formula is an expression of the effect on reliability of lengthening a test by adding items of the same type. This formula, a generalization of formula 4.6, is

$$r_{mm} = \frac{mr_{11}}{1 + (m - 1)r_{11}} \tag{4.10}$$

where m is the factor by which the test is lengthened, r_{11} is the reliability of the original, unlengthened test, and r_{mm} is the estimated reliability of the lengthened test. For example, if a 20-item test having a reliability coefficient of .70 is made three times as long by adding 40 more items, the estimated reliability of the lengthened test will be 3(.70)/[1 + 2(.70)] = .875. To determine how many times longer a test of reliability r_{11} must be made to attain a desired reliability (r_{mm}), we can solve formula 4.10 for m:

$$m = \frac{r_{mm}(1 - r_{11})}{r_{11}(1 - r_{mm})} \tag{4.11}$$

In addition to being dependent on the number of items comprising the test, the variance and reliability of a test are affected by the heterogeneity of the group of people who take the test. The greater the range of individual differences on a certain characteristic, the larger will be the variance of the scores on a measure of that characteristic. Consequently, the reliability coefficient of a test or other assessment device will be higher in a more heterogeneous group, which has a larger test score variance, than in a more homogeneous group having a smaller test score variance. The fact that the reliability of a test varies with the nature of the group tested is reflected in the practice of reporting separate reliability coefficients for different age, grade, sex, and socioeconomic groups.

The association between the variance and reliability of a test is also reflected in the fact that tests comprised mostly of items of intermediate difficulty (p values of around .50) tend to be more reliable than tests on which the items are mostly of high or low difficulty. The reason is that items of intermediate difficulty have higher variance, and hence scores on a test consisting of many such items have a higher variance than scores on tests comprised mostly of items of low or high difficulty.

Standard Error of Measurement

The reliability of a test cannot be computed directly from formula 4.4 because the variance of true scores is never known. Given an estimate of a test's reliability, however, the true score variance can be computed from formula 4.4, or, of greater interest, the error variance of the test can be computed from formula 4.5. Solving formula 4.5 for s_{err} gives

$$s_{err} = s \sqrt{1 - r_{11}} \tag{4.12}$$

where s is the standard deviation of test scores and r_{11} is the test–retest reliability coefficient. This statistic, which is known as the *standard error of measurement* (s_{err}), is an estimate of the standard deviation of the normal distribution of test scores that would presumably be obtained if a person took the test an infinite number of times. The mean of this hypothetical obtained score distribution is the person's true score on the test.

To illustrate the computation and meaning of the standard error of measurement, assume that the standard deviation of a test is 6.63 and the test–retest reliability coefficient is .85; then $s_{err} = 6.63\sqrt{1 - .85} = 2.57$. If Joe's raw score on the test is 40, it can be concluded with 68 percent confidence that Joe is one of a group of people with an observed score of 40 whose true scores on the test fall between $40 - 2.57 = 37.43$ and $40 + 2.57 = 42.57$. Or it can be concluded with 95 percent confidence that Joe is one of a group of examinees with observed score 40 whose true scores on the test fall between $40 - 1.96(2.57) = 34.96$ and $40 + 1.96(2.57) = 45.04$.

As can be seen from inspecting formula 4.12, the standard error of measurement increases as reliability decreases. When $r_{11} = 1.00$, there is no error at all in estimating a person's true score from his or her observed score; when $r_{11} = .00$, the error of measurement is a maximum and equal to the standard deviation of observed scores. Of course, a test having a reliability coefficient close to .00 is useless because the correctness of any decisions made on the basis of the scores will be no better than chance.

Percentile Bands

An examinee's score on certain tests is expressed not as a single number, but rather as a score band, or *percentile band,* having a width of one standard error of measurement (or the percentile rank equivalents of s_{err}) on both sides of the examinee's observed test score. This practice is merely an acknowledgment of the fact that a test score is not a fixed, unvarying measure of a characteristic, but only an approximation. The standard error of measurement is an estimate of the average error in that approximation (see Figure 7–10).

When a person's scores on several tests are plotted in the form of a profile, it is useful to draw a band having a width of one or two standard errors of measurement around the score points. Then small differences between the scores of the same person on two different tests or the scores of two persons on the same test are less likely to be viewed as significant. As a rule of thumb, the difference between the scores of two persons on the same test should not be viewed as significant unless it is at least twice the standard error of measurement of the test. On the other hand, the difference between the scores of the same individual on two tests should be greater than twice the larger standard error of measurement before that difference can be interpreted as significant. This is so because the standard error of the difference between scores on two tests is larger than the standard error of measurement of either test alone.

Reliability of Criterion-referenced Tests

The traditional concept of reliability pertains to norm-referenced tests, which are designed primarily to differentiate among individuals who possess various amounts of a specified cognitive or affective characteristic. The greater the range of individual differences in test scores, the higher the reliability of the test. On the other hand, the goal in constructing most criterion-referenced tests is to place examinees into one of two groups. One group consists of examinees whose scores equal or exceed the criterion (mastery) level on the ability being assessed; the other group consists of examinees who did not attain the criterion level. In this situation, traditional correlational procedures for determining test–retest, parallel-forms, and internal consistency coefficients are inappropriate. Instead, the following reliability formula, adapted from a procedure described by Lindeman and Merenda (1979), is appropriate:

$$c = \frac{nb - sf}{nb - sf + vN} \tag{4.13}$$

In this formula, n is the number of examinees who reached the criterion level on *neither* administration of the test, b is the number of examinees who reached the criterion level on *both* administrations of the test, f is the number of examinees who reached the criterion level on only the *first* administration of the test, s is the number of examinees who reached the criterion level on only the *second* administration of the test, v is the smaller value of f or s, and $N = b + f + n + s$.

To demonstrate the application of this c coefficient, assume that, on a criterion-referenced test administered to 100 students, $n = 5$, $b = 75$, $s = 5$, and $f = 15$. Then $v = 5$ and $N = 100$; so the c coefficient becomes

$$c = \frac{5(75) - 5(15)}{5(75) - 5(15) + 5(100)} = .375.$$

The statistical significance of this rather low reliability coefficient can be evaluated by a computer program devised by Aiken (1988).

Generalizability Theory

Since the 1950s, there has been increasing dissatisfaction with the classical test theory that was developed during the first half of this century, and a number of alternative approaches have been proposed. These approaches are based on modern statistical theory and are also influenced by advances in high-speed computing. An example is *generalizability theory,* which considers a test score to be a single sample from a universe of possible scores. The reliability of that score is the precision with which it estimates a more generalized universe value of the score (the "true score"). The computations of generalizability theory involve the application of analysis of variance statistical techniques to determine the generalizability, or dependability, of test scores as a function of changes in the person(s) taking the test, different samples of items comprising the test, the situations or conditions under which the test is administered, and the methods or people involved in scoring the test. A *generalizability coefficient,* which is similar to a traditional reliability coefficient, may then be computed as the ratio of the expected variance of scores in the universe to the variance of scores in the sample. Finally, a "universe value" of the score, similar to the "true score" of classical reliability theory, can be estimated (Cronbach et al., 1972). Despite its greater statistical sophistication, however, generalizability theory has not replaced the classical theory of test reliability and validity.

VALIDITY

Traditionally, the *validity* of a test has been defined as the extent to which the test measures what it was designed to measure. A shortcoming of this definition is the implication that a test has only one validity, which is presumably established by a single study to determine whether the test measures what it is supposed to measure. In actuality, a test may have many different validities, depending on the specific purposes for which the test was designed, the target population, and the method of determining validity. Among the methods by which validity may be assessed are analyzing the content of the test, relating scores on the test to scores on a criterion of interest, and investigating the particular psychological characteristics or constructs measured by the test. All these procedures are useful to the extent that they improve our understanding of what a test measures. If we understand what a test measures, then the scores will provide better information for making decisions concerning the examinees. Furthermore, we need to ask how much the particular test adds to the prediction and understanding of criteria that are already being predicted. This is the notion of incremental validity, to which we shall return later.

Unlike reliability, which is influenced only by unsystematic errors of measurement, the validity of a test is affected by both unsystematic and systematic (constant) errors. For this reason, a test may be reliable without being valid, but it cannot be valid without being reliable. In short, reliability is a necessary, not a sufficient, condition for validity. Technically, the (criterion-related) validity of a test, as indicated by the correlation between the test and an external criterion measure, can never be greater than the square root of the parallel-forms reliability coefficient.

Content Validity

The physical appearance of a test with regard to its particular purposes (*face validity*) is certainly an important consideration in marketing it. The concept of *content validity*, however, refers to more than just face validity. The question of a test's content validity is concerned with whether the content of the test elicits a range of responses representing the entire domain or universe of skills, understandings, and other behaviors that the test is supposed to measure. That universe of behaviors must be specified carefully. Then, if the test is well designed, examinees' responses to the test items will be representative of what their responses would be to the universe of situations sampled by the test.

An analysis of content validity occurs most often in connection with achievement tests, in which case there is usually no external criterion. Content validity is also of concern, although perhaps less so than criterion-related or construct validity, on measures of aptitude, interest, and personality. The content validity of an achievement test is determined by evaluating the extent to which the test represents the objectives of instruction. One way of doing this is to compare the content of the test with an outline or table of specifications concerning the subject matter presumably covered by the test (see Chapter 2). If subject-matter experts agree that the test looks and acts like a measure of the skill or knowledge it is supposed to assess, then the test is said to possess content validity. Such judgments may involve not only the content of the test items, but also an analysis of the processes that examinees are likely to go through in arriving at answers. Obviously, the process of evaluating a test's content validity need not wait until the test has been constructed. Expert judgments as to what items to include are made from the beginning of the test-construction process. By defining the universe of content of the test and the sample of that universe to be included, test constructors are engaging in content validation.

Criterion-related Validity

Basically, all tests are validated by relating scores on the tests to performance on criterion measures, standards or variables with which test performance can be compared. In the case of content validity, the criterion is the judgement of subject-matter experts. Traditionally, however, the term *criterion-related validity* has been restricted to validation procedures in which the test scores of a group of examinees are compared with ratings, classifications, or other behavioral or mental measurements. Examples of criteria against which tests are validated are school marks, supervisors' ratings, and number or dollar amount of sales. Whenever a criterion measure is available at the time of testing, the *concurrent validity* of the test is being determined. When scores on the criterion do not become available ("mature") until some time after the test is administered, the *predictive validity* of the test is the focus of interest.

Concurrent Validity   Concurrent validation procedures are employed whenever a test is administered to people in various categories, such as diagnostic groups or socioeconomic levels, for the purpose of determining whether the average scores of different types of people are significantly different. If the average score varies substantially from category to category, then the test might be used as another, perhaps more efficient, means of grouping people into the various categories. For example, scores on the Minnesota Multiphasic Personality Inventory (MMPI) are useful in identifying specific mental disorders, because it has been found that people who have been diagnosed as having a particular disorder tend to make characteristic scores on certain groups of items (*scales*) on the MMPI.

Predictive Validity   Predictive validity is concerned with how accurately test scores predict criterion scores, as indicated by the correlation between the test (predictor) and a criterion of future performance. Predictive validity is of concern primarily with respect to aptitude or intelligence tests, since pretest scores on these kinds of tests are often correlated with ratings, marks, achievement test scores, and other criteria of later success.

The correlation between a predictor variable and a criterion variable, computed by procedures such as that described in Appendix A for the Pearson r, varies with the specific criterion, but it is seldom greater than .60. Because the proportion of variance in the criterion that can be accounted for by the predictor equals the square of the correlation between predictor and criterion, typically not more than 36 percent of the variation in criterion scores can be predicted from scores on a test or other prediction instrument. This leaves 64 percent of the criterion variance unaccounted for or unpredicted. Considering that the predictive validity of most tests is less than .60, it is understandable why claims concerning the ability of psychological tests to predict behavior must be made cautiously.

Standard Error of Estimate   The section in Appendix A on regression and prediction describes the procedure for finding a regression equation (prediction equation) for predicting the criterion scores of examinees from their scores on a test or other predictor variable. However, a predicted score obtained by substituting a person's test score in a regression equation is only an estimate of the criterion score that the person will actually obtain. If an individual's predicted criterion score is viewed as the mean of a normal distribution of the criterion scores of people having the same score on the predictor test as that individual, then the standard deviation of this distribution is an index of the average error in the predictions. This standard deviation, known as the *standard error of estimate* (s_{est}), is approximately equal to

$$s_{est} = s\sqrt{1 - r^2} \qquad \textbf{(4.14)}$$

where s is the standard deviation of the criterion scores and r the product–moment correlation between the predictor (test) and the criterion.

To illustrate the computation and meaning of s_{est}, suppose that the standard deviation of a criterion measure is 15 and the correlation between test and criterion is .50. Then $s_{est} = 15\sqrt{1 - .50^2} = 13$. If an examinee's predicted criterion score is 50, the chances are 68 out of 100 of obtaining a criterion score between 37 and 63 ($Y_{pred} \pm 1s_{est}$) and approximately 95 out of 100 of obtaining a criterion score between 24 and 76 ($Y_{pred} \pm 2s_{est}$). More precisely, the chances are 68 out of 100 that the examinee is one of a group of persons having a test score of 50 whose criterion scores fall between 37 and 63. Similarly, the chances are approximately 95 out of 100 that the examinee is one of a group of people with a test score of 50 whose obtained criterion scores fall between 24 and 76. This example shows that, when the correlation between test and criterion scores is low, a person's obtained criterion score may be very different from his or her predicted score. For this reason, caution must be exercised in interpreting predicted scores when the correlation between test and criterion is modest. The smaller the correlation coefficient is, the larger the standard error of estimate and the less accurate the prediction from test to criterion.

Factors Affecting Criterion-related Validity   The criterion-related validity of a test can be affected by a number of factors, including group differences, test length, criterion contamination, and base rate. The incremental validity of a test should also be considered in deciding whether to use the test for purposes of selection and placement.

Group Differences   The characteristics of the group of people on whom a test is validated include such variables as sex, age, and personality traits. Referred to in this context as *moderator variables,* these factors can affect the correlation between a test and a criterion measure. The magnitude of a validity coefficient, like that of a reliability coefficient, is also influenced by the degree of heterogeneity of the validation group on whatever the test measures. Validity coefficients tend to be smaller in more homogeneous groups, that is, groups having a narrower range of test scores. Because the size of a correlation coefficient is a function of two variables, narrowing the range of scores on either the predictor or criterion variable will tend to lower the predictive validity coefficient.

Because the magnitude of a validity coefficient varies with the nature of the tested group, a newly constructed test that is found to be a valid predictor of a particular criterion variable in one group of examinees should be cross-validated. *Cross-validation* involves administering the test to a second sample of people to determine whether the test retains its validity across different samples. Due to the operation of chance factors, the magnitude of a validity coefficient usually shrinks somewhat on cross-validation. Consequently, the correlation with the criterion obtained by cross-validating a test is considered in most instances to be a better index of predictive validity than the original test-criterion correlation. Cross-validation, which is one way of determining the validity generalization of a test, may also involve a different (parallel) sample of test items. In any case—different samples of examinees, different samples of test items, or both—there is typically some shrinkage of the validity coefficient on cross-validation. Formulas for "correcting" for such shrinkage have been proposed, but they entail certain assumptions that cannot always be met.

Test Length   Like reliability, validity varies directly with the length of the test and the heterogeneity of the group of people who are tested. Up to a point, scores on a longer test and scores on a test administered to a group of individuals who vary greatly in the characteristics being measured have greater variances. On the other hand, scores obtained on shorter tests or tests administered to more homogeneous groups of people have lower variances. Formulas that correct for the effects of range restriction and curtailed test length on validity have been proposed, but they are appropriate only under certain special circumstances.

Criterion Contamination   The validity of a test is limited not only by the reliabilities of the test and criterion, but also by the validity of the criterion itself as a measure of the particular variable of interest. Sometimes the criterion is made less valid, or becomes *contaminated,* by the particular method of determining the criterion scores. For example, a clinical psychologist who knows that a group of patients have already been diagnosed as "psychotic" may misperceive psychotic signs in the projective test responses of those patients. Then the method of contrasting groups, in which the test scores of the psychotics are compared with those of normals, will yield false evidence for the validity of the test. Such contamination of the criterion (psychotic versus normal) can be controlled by *blind analysis,* that is, by making available to the diagnostician no information about the examinees other than their test scores. Many clinical psychologists maintain, however, that blind analysis is unnatural in that it is not the way in which tests are used in practice. Clinicians typically amass a great deal of data about a client or patient and then attempt to identify consistencies or congruences among the various kinds of data when making a diagnosis or treatment recommendation.

Base Rate   Another factor that can affect the magnitude of a criterion-related validity coefficient is the base rate of the characteristic or behavior of interest in the target population. *Base rate* refers to the proportion of people in the population who manifest the characteristic or behavior of interest. A test designed to predict a particular type of behavior is most effective when the base rate is 50 percent and least effective when the base rate is very high or very low. Thus, psychoticism, brain damage, suicide, and other characteristics or behaviors having low base rates in the population are much more difficult to diagnose or forecast than neuroticism, sexual deviation, spouse or child abuse, and other behaviors having higher base rates.

Incremental Validity   When trying to decide whether administering a particular assessment instrument for predictive or diagnostic purposes is justified by the cost, the concept of *incremental validity* should be taken into account. Incremental validity is concerned with the question of how much more accurate predictions and diagnoses are when the instrument is included than when it is not included in the battery of assessment techniques. It is possible that other methods of assessment (observation, interview, biographical inventory) are less expensive and can adequately fulfill the purposes of assessment by themselves, without administering another assessment instrument.

Construct Validity

Predictive validity is of greatest concern in occupational or educational selection and placement. Ability tests of various kinds, and sometimes personality and interest tests, are used for selection and placement purposes. Of even greater concern with respect to personality tests is construct validity (Cronbach & Meehl, 1955; Jackson, 1971). The *construct validity* of a psychological assessment instrument refers to the extent to which the instrument is a measure of a particular *construct,* or psychological concept, such as anxiety, achievement motivation, extraversion–introversion, or neuroticism. Construct validity, which is the most general type of validity, is not determined in a single way or by one investigation. Rather, it involves a network of investigations and other procedures designed to determine whether an assessment instrument that purportedly measures a certain personality variable is actually doing its job.

Evidence for Construct Validity   Among the sources of evidence for the construct validity of a test are the following:

1.   Experts' judgments that the content of the test pertains to the construct of interest.
2.   An analysis of the internal consistency of the test.
3.   Studies of the relationships, in both experimentally contrived and naturally occurring groups, of test scores to other variables on which the groups differ.
4.   Correlations of the test with other tests and variables with which the test is expected to have a certain relationship and factor analyses of these intercorrelations.
5.   Questioning examinees or raters in detail about their responses to a test or rating

scale in order to reveal the specific mental processes that occurred in deciding to make those responses.

As noted in the above list, various kinds of information may contribute to the establishment of the construct validity of a psychometric instrument. The information may be obtained from rational or statistical analyses of the variables assessed by the instrument and studies of the ability of the instrument to predict behavior in situations in which the construct is known to be operative. Experimental demonstrations such as those used in the construct validation of the Taylor Manifest Anxiety Scale (TMAS) (Taylor, 1953) are particularly important in establishing the construct validity of a test. According to Hullian learning theory, anxiety is a drive, and hence more anxious people should be easier to condition than less anxious people. Assuming that the theory is correct, people with a high anxiety level should acquire a conditioned eyeblink in a light-airpuff–eyeblink classical conditioning situation more quickly than people with a lower level of anxiety. Therefore, if the TMAS is a valid measure of the construct *anxiety*, high TMAS scorers should condition more readily in this situation than low TMAS scorers. The verification of this prediction contributed significantly to establishing the construct validity of the TMAS.

Convergent and Discriminant Validation   A construct validated assessment instrument should have high correlations with other measures of (or methods of measuring) the same construct (*convergent validity*) and low correlations with measures of different constructs (*discriminant validity*). Evidence pertaining to the convergent and discriminant validity of an instrument can be obtained most convincingly by comparing correlations between measures of (1) the same construct using the same method, (2) different constructs using the same method, (3) the same construct using different methods, and (4) different constructs using different methods. This *multitrait–multimethod approach* (Campbell & Fiske, 1959) provides evidence for the construct validity of the instrument when correlations between the same construct measured by the same and different methods are significantly higher than correlations between different constructs measured by the same or different methods. Unfortunately, the results of such comparisons are not always as desired: sometimes correlations between different constructs measured by the same method are higher than correlations between the same construct measured by different methods. This means that the method (paper-and-pencil inventory, projective technique, rating scale, interview, and so on) is more significant in determining whatever is measured than the construct or trait that is presumably being assessed.

SUMMARY

To standardize a test, it should be administered to a representative sample of people under standard (uniform) conditions. Norms computed from the obtained test scores provide a frame of reference for interpreting scores made by people who subsequently take the test. Test norms have traditionally been determined by testing a sample (random, stratified random, cluster) of the population of people for whom the test is intended. Less expensive and more efficient than traditional test-standardization procedures are item-sampling techniques in which not only people but also test items are sampled, with different groups of examinees answering different sets of items.

Depending on the needs and resources of the test users, norms may be computed on local, regional, or national samples. Age and grade norms, which are determined most often for tests of achievement, permit comparing an individual's test score with the average score of children at a certain age or grade level. The main shortcoming of age and grade norms is that growth in achievement or ability is not uniform over age or grade levels. Percentile norms, in which raw test scores are converted to the percentages of examinees in the standardization group who made those scores or lower, also suffer from the problem of unequal score units. Age, grade, and percentile norms are fairly easy to understand and convenient to use, so they will undoubtedly continue to be popular.

Standard score norms are converted scores having a designated mean and standard deviation. Unlike the original measurement represented by age, grade, and percentile norms, standard scores (*z, T, CEEB,* and others) are interval-level measures. Not all standard scores are normally distributed, but they can be converted to normalized scores.

Scores on parallel tests may be scaled to achieve comparability, if not strictly equated, in various ways. Tests have traditionally been equated by the equipercentile method, but more recent approaches entail applications of item-response models.

The reliability of a test is its relative freedom from errors of measurement. In classical test score theory, reliability is defined as the ratio of a test's true score variance to its observed score variance. Because true score variance cannot be computed directly, reliability must be estimated by one of several procedures that take into account various sources of measurement error. Three traditional methods for estimating the reliability of a test or other assessment device are test–retest, parallel forms, and internal consistency. The method of parallel forms, which considers errors due to different times of administration as well as errors due to different samples of test items, is the most satisfactory. However, parallel forms are expensive and time consuming to construct. Internal consistency approaches, which are less appropriate for speeded tests, include split half, Kuder–Richardson, and coefficient alpha.

The standard error of measurement, which varies inversely with the magnitude of the reliability coefficient, is used to compute confidence intervals for true scores on a test. The larger a test's standard error of measurement is, the wider the range of scores that can be said, within a specified degree of confidence, to contain an examinee's true score on the test.

The reliability of a test varies directly with the number of items and the heterogeneity of the group taking the test. Reliability also varies with the difficulty level of the items comprising the test, being maximal with items of intermediate difficulty.

Procedures for determining the consistency among different scorers or raters (interscorer or interrater reliability) and the reliability of criterion-referenced tests were discussed briefly in this chapter. Brief attention was also given to generalizability theory, which conceptualizes a test score as a sample from a population and therefore an estimate of a true score or universe value.

Reliability is a necessary but not a sufficient condition for validity—the extent to which a test measures what it was designed to measure. Information on the validity of a test may be obtained in various ways: by analyzing the test's content (*content validity*), by correlating test scores with scores on a criterion measure obtained at the same time as the test scores (*concurrent validity*), by correlating test scores with scores on a criterion measured at a later time (*predictive validity*), and by a systematic study of the adequacy of the test as a measure of a specified psychological construct (*construct validity*). Achievement tests are usually content validated, whereas predictive validity is of greater interest on aptitude tests. Concurrent and construct validity are important on personality tests.

The amount of error made in predicting a person's criterion score from his or her test score is estimated by the standard error of estimate, which varies inversely with the size of the criterion-related validity coefficient. Both the criterion-related validity coefficient and the standard error of estimate are affected by a number of factors, including group differences, test length, and criterion contamination. The magnitudes of validity coefficients can also be affected by chance factors, and therefore tests used for predictive purposes should be cross-validated. It is also important to consider how much test scores contribute to the process of making good decisions about people (incremental validity).

Information on the construct validity of a test as a measure of a particular psychological construct (characteristic or trait) can be obtained in a variety of ways. Especially helpful is an analysis of correlations between the test and other measures of the same construct obtained by the same or different methods, as well as measures of different constructs obtained by the same or different methods (multitrait–multimethod matrix).

EXERCISES

1. Suppose that George makes a raw score of 65 on an arithmetic test having a mean of 50 and a standard deviation of 10, but makes a raw score of 80 on a reading test having a mean of 75 and a standard deviation of 15. What are George's z scores and Z scores on the tests? Is he better in arithmetic or reading?

2. By referring to a table of areas under the normal curve (Appendix B), find the scores corresponding to the 10th, 20th, 30th, 40th, 50th, 60th, 70th, 80th, and 90th percentile ranks. Then convert the resulting z scores to T scores, *CEEB* scores, stanines, and deviation IQs with a standard deviation of 15.

3. Using Table 4–1 as a model, construct a frequency distribution of the 30 scores listed below (let $i = 3$). Then compute the percentile rank, z, Z, z_n, and T scores corresponding to the interval midpoints:

82	85	70	91	75	88	78	82	95	79	86	90
87	77	87	73	80	96	86	81	85	93	83	89
92	89	84	83	79	74						

4. Why are standard score norms considered superior to age norms, grade norms, and percentile norms?

5. Calculate both split-half (odd–even) and Kuder–Richardson reliability coefficients on the following responses of 10 examinees on a 10-item test, where 1 indicates the right answer and 0 a wrong answer.

					Examinee					
Item	A	B	C	D	E	F	G	H	I	J
1	1	1	0	1	1	0	1	0	1	0
2	1	0	0	0	0	1	0	0	0	1
3	1	1	1	1	1	0	1	0	0	0
4	1	1	1	0	0	1	0	1	0	0
5	1	0	1	1	0	0	0	0	0	0
6	1	1	1	0	1	1	1	0	0	0
7	1	0	1	1	0	0	1	1	0	1
8	1	1	1	0	1	1	0	0	1	0
9	1	1	0	1	1	1	0	1	0	0
10	1	1	1	1	1	0	0	0	1	0
Totals	10	7	7	6	6	5	4	3	3	2

The mean $(\overline{X})$ of the total scores is 5.30, and the variance (s^2) is 5.21.

6. Compute the standard error of measurement (s_{err}) of a test having a standard deviation of 10 and a parallel-forms reliability coefficient of .84. Then use the obtained value of s_{err} to find the 95 percent confidence interval for the true scores corresponding to obtained scores of 40, 50, and 60.

7. A test consisting of 40 items has a reliability coefficient of .80. Approximately how many more items of the same general type must be added to the test to increase its reliability to .90?

8. Plot a set of curves on a single graph illustrating how test reliability (r_{mm}) varies as a function of test length (m) and initial reliability (r_{11}). Use formula 4.10 and values of m equal to 2, 3, 4, 5, and 6 and values of r_{11} equal to .50, .60, .70, .80, and .90. The horizontal axis of your graph should be r_{11} and the vertical axis r_{mm}. Plot one curve for each value of m and draw appropriate conclusions concerning the effects of lengthening a test on the test's reliability.

9. A criterion-referenced test is administered twice to the same group of 100 examinees. The criterion level is reached by 70 examinees on both administration, 10 examinees on the first administration only, 15 examinees on the second administration only, and 5 examinees on neither administration. What is the reliability coefficient of the test?

10. What is the standard error made in estimating grade-point averages from scores on an aptitude test if the standard deviation of the criterion is .50 and the correlation between test and criterion is .60? Interpret the results.

SUGGESTED READINGS

Cronbach, L. J., & Meehl, P. E. (1955). Construct validity in psychological tests. *Psychological Bulletin, 52,* 281–302.

Dudek, F. J. (1979). The continuing misinterpretation of the standard error of measurement. *Psychological Bulletin, 86,* 335–337.

Felner, R. D. (1987). Reliability of diagnoses. In R. J. Corsini (ed.), *Concise encyclopedia of psychology,* pp. 970–971. New York: Wiley.

Green, B. F. (1981). A primer of testing. *American Psychologist, 36,* 1001–1011.

Hambleton, R. K. (1989). Principles and selected applications of item response theory. In R. L. Linn (ed.), *Educational measurement,* 3rd ed. New York: American Council on Education/ Macmillan.

Lyman, H. B. (1991). *Test scores and what they mean,* 5th ed. Englewood Cliffs, NJ: Prentice Hall.

Shavelson, R. J., Webb, N. M., & Rowley, G. L. (1989). Generalizability theory. *American Psychologist, 44,* 922–932.

Sumner, R. (1985). Test norms. In T. Husén & T. N. Postlethwaite (eds.), *International encyclopedia of education,* Vol. 9, p. 5205–5209. New York: Wiley.

von Mayrhauser, R. T. (1992). The mental testing community and validity: A prehistory. *American Psychologist, 47,* 244–253.

PART TWO

ASSESSMENT OF ABILITIES

Chapter Five

Standardized Achievement Tests

Chapters 1 through 4 have been concerned with the background, methodology, and professional status of psychological and educational testing. In the next two sections, specific kinds of cognitive and affective instruments and what they measure are surveyed. Achievement testing, which is referred to as *attainment testing* in the United Kingdom, is discussed in this chapter. Other cognitive instruments, tests of general intelligence and special abilities, are dealt with in Chapters 6 and 7. Affective assessment, including measures of interests, attitudes, values, and personality, are considered in Chapters 9 and 10.

ACHIEVEMENT TESTING IN PERSPECTIVE

Tests of *achievement,* defined as the level of knowledge, skill, or accomplishment in an area of endeavor, are the most popular of all kinds of tests. If we consider all classroom tests constructed by teachers and the standardized tests sold to schools and other organizations, the number of achievement tests administered easily surpasses other types of psychological and educational measures. The majority of standardized achievement tests are in the areas of reading and language arts, although millions of dollars are also spent each year on tests in mathematics, science, social studies, and other subject-matter areas.

Any test of ability—general intelligence, special abilities, or achievement—actually measures what individuals have achieved. The items on tests of intelligence and special abilities, like those on achievement tests, require examinees to demonstrate some accomplishment. Scores on achievement tests may also be used for many of the same purposes as scores on other tests of general or specific abilities. These purposes include not only global and diagnostic assessment of individual abilities, but also evaluation of the effectiveness of instruction or a specific educational program. Finally, achievement tests are often better predictors of school marks than tests of intelligence or special abilities. This does not mean, however, that tests of achievement in a specific subject can entirely replace tests of intelligence and special abilities. The accomplishments or achievements measured by general intelligence tests are usually broader and produced by less formal and presumably less recent learning experiences than those measured by standardized tests of achievement. Achievement tests usually assess knowledge of something that has been explicitly taught. Consequently, scores on these tests tend to be influenced more by coaching than scores on tests of intelligence.

A distinction between achievement tests and tests of intelligence and special abilities can also be made in terms of their emphases. Achievement tests focus more on the present, that is, what a person knows or can do now, whereas tests of intelligence and special abilities focus on the future. They measure *aptitude* for learning, what a person should be able to achieve with further education or training.

Historical Overview

Although the first educational use of written tests was reportedly made at Cambridge, England, in 1702, not until 1845 were such tests administered on a large scale in the United States (Greene, Jorgensen, & Gerberich, 1954). Despite the fact that the number of students had grown too large for the periodic administration of oral examinations in U.S. cities, until the latter half of the nineteenth century, oral testing was the principal method employed in evaluating pupil achievement in this country. In the middle of the nineteenth century, the Boston educator Horace Mann argued persuasively that written examinations, administered and scored under uniform conditions, were more valid measures of achievement than oral examinations. Through Mann's influence, the Boston city schools began giving written examinations to pupils in that city every year. It was hoped that this practice would help to determine "the condition, improvement or deterioration of our schools" (Fish, 1941, page 23). Despite the efforts of Horace Mann and other educators, oral examinations continued for many years to be the principal method of assessing school achievement and were only gradually replaced by written tests.

The first objective test of achievement, one that could be reliably scored, was a handwriting scale constructed by George Fisher, an Englishman, in 1864. Another important step was taken over a quarter-century later by J. M. Rice (1897), who is credited with inventing the comparative test and being the father of educational research in America (Ross & Stanley, 1954, page 38). Rice's first tests were objective spelling tests designed for his classic survey of the spelling abilities of schoolchildren. Research with these tests revealed little relationship between the length of time spent daily in spelling drill and proficiency in that subject. The results of administering a 50-word spelling test to 33,000 children led Rice to conclude that as much was learned in 15 as in 40 minutes of daily instruction in spelling. In later studies, Rice assessed the language skills of 8000 children and the arithmetic achievement of 6000 children. The beginnings made by Rice, whose work is generally viewed as the forerunner of standardized achievement testing, were subsequently built on by E. L. Thorndike and other educational psychologists.

Under the direction of Thorndike, who is considered the father of the educational testing movement (Ross & Stanley, 1954, page 39), a number of standardized achievement tests were published during the early years of the twentieth century. These included C. L. Stone's Arithmetic Test for the Fundamental Operations and Arithmetic Reasoning Test in 1908, S. A. Curtis's Arithmetic Tests Series in 1909, and Thorndike's Scale of Handwriting for Children in that same year. Demonstrations of the unreliability of grades assigned by teachers, even in more exact subjects such as mathematics (Starch & Elliot, 1913), led to an increased interest in objective, standardized testing. By the end of the

1920s, numerous standardized achievement tests were available, including batteries of measures such as the Stanford Achievement Test (1923) for elementary school pupils and the Iowa High School Content Examination (1924). The new multiple-choice format, together with the invention of automated scoring machines, led to a rapid increase in the use of standardized tests for evaluating pupil achievement.

Rather than being motivated solely by educational and scientific concerns, the growth of achievement testing in the United States is attributable in part to the fact that both sides in a political debate over public schools found the advocacy and results of testing to be useful in their arguments (Levine, 1976). As seen in the debate over the proposed nationwide standardized achievement examinations proposed by former president George Bush, even today standardized testing in the schools continues to have significant political ramifications.

Despite the passage of time and hundreds of research studies, the question of the relative merits of essay and objective tests has never been completely settled. In fact, we often hear the allegation that teachers have gone overboard in their use of objective tests to the detriment of students' composition skills. Nevertheless, it is clear that carefully designed objective tests can measure not only memory for facts, but also many of the more complex objectives of education that were formerly presumed to be assessed only by essay examinations. A noteworthy trend in recent years has been toward tests that measure higher-order instructional objectives, such as application, analysis, and evaluation. Another trend has been away from standardized achievement tests that attempt to assess broad educational objectives and toward tests designed specifically for particular textbooks and teaching programs. Finally, in response to the criticism that objective tests foster poor habits of writing and self-expression, greater emphasis is now being placed on standardized essay tests of written expression.

Uses of Achievement Tests

The basic function of achievement tests is to determine how much people know about certain topics or how well they can perform certain skills. Achievement test results inform students, as well as teachers and parents, about students' scholastic accomplishments and deficiencies. Such tests can also motivate students to learn, provide teachers and school administrators with information for planning or modifying the curriculum for a student or group of students, and serve as a means of evaluating the instructional program and staff. Scores on educational tests are obviously not the only means of evaluating the effectiveness of instruction, but they do provide a measure of the quality of education and can thereby contribute to its improvement.

Admittedly, achievement tests do not assess all the objectives or goals proposed by educational philosophers. For example, they do not directly measure such affective variables as delight and confidence in thinking, interest in educational subject matter, pleasure in using skills, enjoyment of reading, learning to learn and to cope with change, or the development of interpersonal and social skills. What these tests can measure, however, and much more accurately than teachers' ratings or other subjective judgments, is the extent to which examinees have attained certain cognitive objectives of instruction (Levine, 1976).

Teacher-made and Standardized Tests   The functions of achievement tests described in the preceding paragraphs apply to both the classroom tests prepared by teachers and the standardized tests constructed by professionals in educational measurement. But teacher-made tests differ from standardized tests in certain important respects. A teacher-made test is more specific to a particular teacher, classroom, and unit of study and is easier to keep up to date than a standardized test. Consequently, a teacher-made test is more likely to reflect the current educational objectives of a given school or teacher. Standardized tests, on the other hand, are built around a core of educational objectives common to many different schools. These objectives represent the combined judgments of subject-matter experts, who cooperate with test-construction specialists in developing tests. Standardized achievement tests also focus more on understanding and thinking processes than on knowledge of specifics. Clearly, teacher-made tests and standardized tests complement rather than replace each other. They measure somewhat different but equally important things, and, depending on the objectives of the particular classroom or school, both kinds of tests should be employed. When a given standardized test does not assess the educational goals of a particular school system, other standardized tests or even a teacher-made test should be considered.

In addition to being more carefully constructed and having broader content coverage than teacher-made tests, standardized achievement tests have norms and are usually more reliable. For these reasons, standardized achievement tests are particularly helpful in comparing individual pupils for the purpose of class placement and in evaluating different curricula by assessing the relative achievements of different groups or schools. The diagnostic function of a test, whereby a person's abilities and disabilities in a certain subject or area are determined, may be served by both teacher-made and standardized tests, although standardized tests are somewhat more effective for this purpose. Decisions pertaining to the individualization of instruction, placement at particular instructional levels, and remedial instruction are also usually made on the basis of scores on standardized rather than teacher-made tests.

Accountability and Performance Contracting   Test scores have been used not only to assess student performance, but also to evaluate teachers and schools. *Accountability,* or holding teachers accountable for their degree of success in teaching students, has been a controversial topic in education for many years. Should teachers, who typically are not permitted to select their students but must attempt to educate whoever is assigned to them, be rewarded when these students are able to attain the objectives of instruction but not rewarded or penalized when they are not? As a result of increasing public concern over the failure of schools to do an adequate job of educating certain students, particular attention has been given in recent years to accountability or responsibility for teaching effectiveness. Efforts have been made in many school systems to specify the competencies that must be attained by students to complete a given grade or course of study or to graduate from high school. Evaluation of instructional effectiveness is then based on the achievement of these competencies.

Accountability and competency-based instruction are associated with *performance contracting,* that is, making the pay checks of teachers commensurate with their degree of success in educating students. If tests are to be employed as a means of determining the extent to which a teacher has fulfilled a contract to teach the course material to students, the same tests may be administered at the beginning and end of the course. Consequently, the greater the gains in student achievement from pretest to posttest, the higher is the teacher's pay.

When combined with other measures of performance, achievement test scores can and should contribute to decisions concerning accountability. However, they have definite limitations when used for this purpose. One serious statistical limitation is that the reliability of the differences between pretest and posttest scores is lower than the reliabilities of the pretest or posttest scores themselves.[1]

Summative and Formative Evaluation   Traditional practice calls for administering an achievement test at the end of a unit or course of study to determine whether students have attained the objectives of instruction. Technically, this procedure is known as *summative evaluation:* a test score is viewed as an end product, or summing up, of large units of educational experience. In contrast to summative evaluation, a need for *formative evaluation* is a consequence of the belief that the processes of instruction and evaluation should be integrated. The purpose of formative evaluation is "to help both the learner and the teacher focus upon the particular learning necessary for movement toward mastery" (Bloom, Hastings, & Madaus, 1971, page 61). When evaluation is formative, testing and other methods of assessing educational progress occur continuously during the process of instruction. A direct result of the concept of formative evaluation is the development of instructional units that include testing as an ongoing, integral part of instruction, rather than a termination of the process. In the way, a learner's performance is continuously monitored during the learning process and can serve to direct his or her review and further learning.

Norm-referenced and Criterion-referenced Measurement   Not only has educational measurement traditionally been summative; it has also been norm referenced rather than criterion referenced. As described in Chapter 4, a person's score on a norm-referenced test is interpreted by comparing it with the distribution of scores obtained from some norm (standardization) group. But a person's score on a criterion-referenced test is interpreted by comparing it with an established standard or criterion of effective performance. This standard may be derived by a consensus of people from all walks of life who are concerned with education—school teachers and administrators, parents, measurement experts, and politicians. In terms of their content, norm-referenced tests are typically broader and contain more complex tasks than criterion-referenced tests. Consequently, the range of individual differences in scores on a norm-referenced test tends to be greater than that on a criterion-referenced test.

Despite differences in the purpose and design of norm- and criterion-referenced tests, a particular achievement test can function as both a norm- and criterion-referenced

---

[1]A formula for the reliability of the differences (r_{dd}) between two sets of scores obtained by the same group of examinees is $r_{dd} = (r_{11} + r_{22} - 2r_{12})/[2(1 - r_{12})]$, where r_{11} is the reliability of the first set of scores, r_{22} the reliability of the second set of scores, and r_{12} the correlation between the two sets of scores. For example, if the reliability of pretest scores is $r_{11} = .90$, the reliability of posttest scores is $r_{22} = .80$, and the correlation between pretest and posttest scores is $r_{12} = .70$, then the reliability of the difference between pretest and posttest scores is $[.90 + .80 - 2(.70)]/2[(1 - .70)] = .50$.

instrument. How much material a student has learned (criterion-referenced function) and how his or her performance compares with that of other students (norm-referenced function) can frequently be determined from the same test (Carver, 1974).

Among the many single-subject criterion-referenced tests that are commercially available are the California Diagnostic Reading Test and the California Diagnostic Mathematics Test (both from CTB/Macmillan/McGraw-Hill). Batteries of criterion-referenced tests, such as the National Proficiency Survey Series and the Cultural Literacy Test (from Riverside Publishing Company) can also be purchased. Another product offered by certain testing companies are single-subject tests combined with matching instructional strategies in those subjects. Examples are the CRC-Mathematics and the CRC-Reading tests (from The Psychological Corporation). Several testing companies also prepare customized criterion-referenced tests or make available banks of criterion-referenced items in a number of subjects. These custom-built tests possess the advantage of being tailored to the objectives of a particular school system, but they also have a number of disadvantages. In addition to the problem of deciding on an acceptable passing score or mastery level on each test, the need for a large number of subtests to measure many different educational objectives necessitates making each subtest relatively short, and hence its reliability is fairly low. Furthermore, the problem of how the reliabilities and validities of the various subtests and the test as a whole should be determined has not been completely resolved.

The National Assessment of Educational Progress A criterion-referenced approach has guided the National Assessment of Educational Progress (NAEP), a continuing nationwide survey of the knowledge, skills, understandings, and attitudes of young Americans. Currently financed by the National Institute of Education and based at Educational Testing Service in Princeton, New Jersey, NAEP involves the periodic assessment of large samples of people in four age groups (9, 13, 17, and 25 to 35 years) in 10 subject areas (art, career and occupational development, citizenship, literature, mathematics, music, reading, science, social studies, and writing). Two or three subjects are assessed in a given year and reassessed on a 3–6 year cycle (see Table 5–1).

A stratified random sampling procedure is employed by NAEP in selecting examinees: a certain number of persons of each sex, socioeducational status, and race are chosen at random from four geographical regions and four types of communities. Although a large number of questions concerning each topic are asked, the procedure of sampling both examinees and items makes only one relatively short testing period (50 minutes) necessary for each person. Adults are assessed individually, and younger persons are assessed on both an individual and a group basis. Because the results are expressed in terms of the percentages of people at each level who possess certain skills and knowledge, the names of those persons do not appear on the test papers.

National Assessment was planned as a continuing program to provide the U.S. public, especially legislators and educators, with information on the status and growth of educational accomplishments in the United States ("The Nation's Report Card") and the extent to which the country's educational goals are being met. These surveys were not designed, as some have feared, to evaluate the achievements of specific schools or school districts or as a means of federal control over public school curricula. The findings, however, have been analyzed by geographical area, size and type of community, sex, parental education,

TABLE 5-1 Subject Areas Assessed by NAEP

Assessment year	Subject area
1969–1979	Science
1970–1971	Reading, Literature
1971–1972	Music, Social Studies
1972–1973	Science, Mathematics
1973–1974	Career and Occupational Development, Writing
1974–1975	Reading, Art, Index of Basic Skills
1975–1976	Citizenship/Social Studies, Mathematics
1976–1977	Science, Basic Life Skills, Reading, Health
1977–1978	Mathematics, Consumer Skills
1978–1979	Writing, Art, Music
1979–1980	Reading/Literature, Art
1981–1982	Science, Mathematics, Citizenship/Social Studies
1984	Reading, Writing
1986	Reading, Mathematics, Science, Computer Competence, Literature, and U.S. History
1988	Reading, Writing, Civics, U.S. History, Geography
1990	Reading, Mathematics, Science, Writing
1992	Reading, Mathematics, Writing

Source: The National Assessment of Educational Progress.

and race. Of particular interest are analyses of the effects of federal support and specific types of programs on educational attainment.

Types of Standardized Achievement Tests

There are four general types of standardized achievement tests: survey test batteries, survey tests in specific subjects, diagnostic tests, and prognostic tests. Some of these tests are designed to be administered individually to one person at a time, but the great majority are group tests. The market for highly specialized tests in a particular subject area is rather limited, so standardized achievement tests typically cover broad content areas and deal with matters of general knowledge. Because the curriculum becomes more specialized in the upper grade levels, administration of standardized achievement tests is less common after junior high school.

Survey Test Batteries   The most comprehensive way of assessing achievement is to administer a *survey test battery,* a group of subject-matter tests designed for particular grade levels. The major purpose of administering a battery of tests is to determine an individual's general standing in a group, rather than his or her specific strengths and weaknesses. Consequently, each test in a survey battery contains a fairly limited sample of the content and skills in a given subject. Because the various tests in a battery are standardized on the same group of examinees and the scores are expressed on the same numerical scale, a person's performance in different subjects can be compared directly.

Although they provide a more comprehensive assessment of pupil achievement than single tests, test batteries have a number of drawbacks. Despite the longer total administration time, the tests comprising a battery are shorter than single-survey tests and consequently tend to have lower reliabilities. Of course, not all the tests in a battery need to be administered to a given group of students; the examiner may select whatever tests yield relevant information pertaining to the goals of assessment.

Single Survey Tests   In addition to the individual subject tests in a survey battery, the examiner has a choice of a number of single-subject tests. These survey tests are usually longer and more detailed than comparable tests in a battery and thereby permit a more thorough evaluation of achievement in a specific area. Single-survey tests, however, typically yield only an overall score and perhaps a couple of subscores and make no real attempt to determine the specific causes of high or low performance in the subject. Because of greater uniformity among different schools in reading and mathematics instruction than in other subjects, standardized tests in these two areas tend to be more valid than, for example, science and social studies tests.

Diagnostic Tests   Certain tests have the diagnostic function of identifying specific difficulties in learning a subject. To construct a *diagnostic test* in a basic skill such as reading, arithmetic, or spelling, performance in the subject as a whole must be analyzed into subskills and then groups of items devised to measure performance in these subskills. Unlike survey tests, which focus on total scores, diagnostic tests yield scores on each of several subskills. Because differences among scores on the various parts of the test are interpreted in making diagnoses, the number of items for measuring a particular subskill must be sufficient (10 or more) to ensure that the differences between part scores are reliable. Unfortunately, the number of items comprising part scores are often small and scores on the parts are correlated, resulting in different scores of low reliability.

Most diagnostic tests are in the area of reading, but diagnostic tests in mathematics and spelling have been constructed. A diagnostic test contains a greater variety of items and usually takes longer to administer than a survey test in the same subject. It may also involve special apparatus, such as a tachistoscope to expose reading material for only a brief period of time and an eye-movement camera to track the direction in which the eyes move in reading.[2]

Administration of a survey test battery is a logical first step in a testing program,

[2]In addition to diagnostic tests in specific subjects such as reading and mathematics, certain individually administered survey or "global" tests are used for educational diagnosis in reading, mathematics, and spelling. Examples are the Kaufman Test of Educational Achievement and the Peabody Individual Achievement Test–Revised, both published by American Guidance Service. Even more global in its diagnostic aims is the Woodcock–Johnson Psychoeducational Battery (by R. W. Woodcock and M. B. Johnson, Teaching Resources Corporation, 50 Pond Rd., Hingham, MA 02043), an individually administered multiple-skills battery designed to assess cognitive ability, scholastic aptitude, academic achievement, and interests in persons from 3 to 80 years of age.

because it gives an overall picture of an examinee's standing in various subjects. If a second assessment of a person's achievement in a particular area is needed, a single test in that specific subject can then be administered. Finally, if it is desirable to make a detailed analysis of an individual's disability in reading or mathematics and to determine the causes of the disability, a diagnostic test should be given.

Prognostic Tests   Prognostic tests, which are designed to predict achievement in specific school subjects, contain a wider variety of items than survey achievement tests in the same subject. They are similar to aptitude tests in their function as predictors of later achievement. For example, the purpose of a *reading readiness test* administered to a kindergartner or first grader is to predict whether the child is prepared to benefit from instruction in reading. At a higher grade level, prognostic tests in mathematics (algebra, geometry) and foreign languages are designed to predict facility in learning those subjects.

Selecting a Standardized Achievement Test

As in constructing a classroom achievement test, selecting a standardized achievement test is basically a matter of finding a test of appropriate difficulty with a content that matches the instructional objectives of the particular organization, class, school, or school system. This means that the level of knowledge or ability of the examinees and the content and objectives of the curriculum must be determined before deciding what test(s) to administer. Furthermore, the reasons for testing and the way in which the scores are to be used should be considered; there is little purpose in administering a test merely because it "looks good" and then filing the unused results in a dusty drawer.

Purposes and Practical Considerations   The manual accompanying a test frequently details its possible uses (pupil evaluation, placement, diagnosis of learning disabilities, readiness to learn, curriculum evaluation) and refers to supporting evidence. Consequently, before a test is selected, the specific ways in which the scores are to be used should be clarified and test manuals consulted to determine what tests are appropriate for these purposes. In addition to reading the manual, prospective purchasers should examine a copy of the test and even take it themselves to determine whether it is suitable for its intended uses. Most testing companies publish specimen sets of tests, consisting of a test booklet, an answer sheet, a manual, a scoring key, and other associated materials; test catalogs are also available on request. These materials are valuable in making decisions about which tests to administer.

Another consideration in selecting a test is the degree of cooperation that can be expected from the school staff in administering the test and interpreting the findings. Also of importance are practical matters such as cost and time for administration, scoring, and analyzing the results. The machine-scoring services provided by commercial testing firms greatly facilitate the scoring and analysis processes and are usually fairly reasonable in cost.

Reliability, Validity, and Norms   Frequently overlooked in selecting an achievement test, but often crucial, are its statistical characteristics. The reliabilities of most achievement tests are in the .80s and .90s, but the meaning of these high coefficients depends on the procedures by which they were obtained. A parallel-forms coefficient is preferable to a test–retest coefficient or an internal consistency coefficient because the last two are more likely to be spuriously high. When an achievement test is administered for the purpose of predicting later achievement, as in the case of a readiness or prognostic test, evidence for its predictive validity is important. But content validity is almost always of greatest concern in the case of an achievement test. Therefore, in deciding whether or not such a test is valid, it is essential to compare the test's content with the objectives of the instructional program of interest. An adequately prepared test manual describes the system for classifying content and behavioral objectives used in constructing the test, and prospective purchasers must decide whether these objectives correspond to their own.

Another statistical characteristic to be examined in selecting any test is the adequacy and appropriateness of the norms. Most well-constructed achievement tests are standardized on representative, national samples, sometimes stratified according to age, sex, geographical region, socioeconomic status, and other relevant variables. Test purchasers who plan to report scores in terms of these norms should make certain that the characteristics of the norm group are similar to those of the students to be examined. For purposes of placement and other comparisons within a given school or school system, local norms may be even more meaningful than national norms.

Test users need to understand that, in plotting a student's academic growth by means of normed scores on a standardized achievement test administered at successive grade levels, it is assumed that the different grade-level groups on which the test was standardized are equivalent. If there is any reason to believe that there were significant differences among the norm groups in variables other than those that are growth related, then a student's grade-norm scores, percentile-rank scores, or standard scores on a test cannot be accurately compared across grade levels.

Another caveat of test purchasing is to exercise caution in selecting a test according to its name. Experienced test users are well aware of the "jingle fallacy" of assuming that instruments having the same name measure the same thing and the "jangle fallacy" of assuming that instruments having different names measure different things. Before deciding what achievement tests to purchase, novices and experienced testers alike can profit from consulting volumes of the *The Mental Measurements Yearbook* and test reviews in professional journals.

ACHIEVEMENT TEST BATTERIES

Achievement test batteries, sometimes referred to as *general educational development* (GED) tests, represent efforts to measure broad cognitive abilities and skills produced by basic educational experiences in core areas. These multilevel batteries of tests assess basic skills in reading, mathematics, language arts, and, at the appropriate grade levels, in study skills, social studies, and science. A battery of tests entitled the Tests of General Educational Development (GED), published by the American Council on Education, was designed to measure the educational achievements of people who have graduated from high school. Many colleges and business organizations, as well as the U.S. armed forces, accept persons who make sufficiently high scores on these "general equivalency diploma" tests on the same basis as they accept high school graduates.

The testing programs of many schools are based on achievement test batteries administered during the fall or spring to grade-school pupils for the purpose of measuring general educational attainments and growth. Such tests have many different uses: grouping (placement), identification of individuals for more detailed study, curriculum evaluation, and curriculum planning. The test results are of interest to teachers, parents, and curriculum advisers and, of course, to the pupils themselves. A limitation of the battery approach is that some of the tests may not correspond to the particular objectives of the school or school system. Furthermore, not all tests in a given battery have equal reliabilities or equal content validities.

Battery Norms

The various subtests comprising a particular level of an achievement test battery are standardized simultaneously on the same group of examinees. Consequently, the resulting unified set of norms permits direct evaluation of an examinee's relative achievement in several subject areas. Since different grade levels of a test battery are standardized on comparable groups of examinees, the scholastic growth of students may be charted by comparing their scores on the tests over a period of several years; however, this should not be done if there is any question about the equivalence or comparability of the different grade-level samples of students on whom the test battery was standardized. Furthermore, the norms against which students' scores are compared should have been obtained from administering the test(s) to the standardization group during the same time of year (fall or spring) as the students whose scores are being evaluated were tested.

Content of Achievement Test Batteries

Elementary School Level   Because of the greater uniformity of instructional content in elementary school, achievement test batteries are administered more frequently at this level. A typical elementary school battery consists of subtests for measuring reading vocabulary, reading comprehension, language usage, spelling, arithmetic fundamentals, and arithmetic comprehension. Subtests to measure study skills, social studies, and science may also be included, but the emphasis at the elementary level is on the measurement of achievement in basic verbal and quantitative skills. Figure 5–1, which gives a breakdown of the scores of one fourth-grader on the Stanford Achievement Test, illustrates the variety of linguistic and quantitative skills measured by an achievement test battery at the elementary school level. Other popular achievement test batteries at this level are the California Achievement Tests, the Comprehensive Tests of Basic Skills, the Iowa Tests of Basic Skills, and the Metropolitan Achievement Tests. These batteries also contain kindergarten and secondary school levels of tests.

STANFORD

ACHIEVEMENT TEST SERIES, EIGHTH EDITION

TEACHER:	JOHN WILLIAMS		STANFORD	OLSAT
		NORMS:	GRADE 4	GRADE 4
SCHOOL:	LAKESIDE ELEMENTARY	GRADE: 4 SPRING	NATIONAL	NATIONAL
		TEST DATE: LEVEL:	INTER 1	E
DISTRICT:	NEWTOWN	4/89 FORM:	J	1

STUDENT SKILLS ANALYSIS
FOR
BRIAN ELLIOTT

TESTS	NO. OF ITEMS	RAW SCORE	SCALED SCORE	NATL PR-S	LOCAL PR-S	GRADE EQUIV	AAC RANGE	NATIONAL GRADE PERCENTILE BANDS
Total Reading	94	70	143	50-5	45-5	4.8	LOW	
Vocabulary	40	27	148	52-5	46-5	5.1	LOW	
Reading Comp.	54	43	143	5	44-5	4.8	LOW	
Total Math	118	58	143	5	45-5	4.6	LOW	
Concepts of No.	34	14	137	32-4	26-4	3.8	LOW	
Computation	44	22	145	50-5	56-5	4.8	MIDDLE	
Applications	40	22	145	50-5	53-5	4.8	MIDDLE	
Total Language	60	47	149	61-6	56-5	5.4	MIDDLE	
Lang Mechanics	30	21	148	60-6	54-5	5.4	MIDDLE	
Lang Expression	30	26	150	62-6	58-5	5.4	MIDDLE	
Spelling	40	22	143	40-5	34-4	4.0	LOW	
Study Skills	30	21	142	50-5	44-5	4.8	LOW	
Science	50	31	139	44-5	38-4	4.6	LOW	
Social Science	50	42	161	82-7	76-6	6.2	MIDDLE	
Listening	45	25	130	49-5	45-5	4.7	LOW	
Using Information	70	35	152	59-5	55-5	5.2	MIDDLE	
Thinking Skills	101	45	146	52-5	53-5	4.9	LOW	
Basic Battery	387	243	143	50-5	45-5	4.8	LOW	
Complete Battery	487	316	145	52-5	47-5	4.9	LOW	

OTIS-LENNON SCHOOL ABILITY TEST	RAW SCORE	SAI	AGE PR-S	AGE NCE	SCALED SCORE	GRADE PR-S	GRADE NCE
Total	72	53	116	84-7	70.9	290	82-7	69.3
Verbal	36	27	117	85-7	71.8	295	83-7	70.1
Nonverbal	36	26	115	82-7	69.3	285	80-7	67.7

AGE 10 YRS 2 MOS

READING GROUP	MATHEMATICS GROUP	COMMUNICATIONS GROUP	LANGUAGE GROUP
GROUP 3	GROUP 2	GROUP 1	GROUP 2

CONTENT CLUSTERS	RAW SCORE/ NUMBER OF ITEMS	BELOW AVERAGE	AVERAGE	ABOVE AVERAGE
Reading Vocabulary	27/ 40		✓	
Synonyms	17/ 24		✓	
Context	5/ 8		•	
Multiple Meanings	5/ 8		✓	
Reading Comprehension	43/ 54		✓	
Recreational	12/ 18		✓	
Toxtual	15/ 18		•	
Functional	16/ 18			✓
Literal	18/ 21			✓
Inferential	22/ 26		✓	
Critical	3/ 7		✓	
Concepts of Number	14/ 34		✓	
Whole Numbers	6/ 16	✓		
Fractions	3/ 4		✓	
Decimals	2/ 3		✓	
Operations and Properties	3/ 11	✓		
Mathematics Computation	22/ 44		✓	
Add and Subtract/Whole Nos	7/ 12		✓	
Multiplication/Whole Numbers	6/ 12		✓	
Division/Whole Numbers	5/ 10		✓	
Add and Subtract/Decimals	2/ 6	✓		
Add and Subtract/Fractions	2/ 4		✓	
Mathematics Applications	22/ 40		✓	✓
Problem Solving	12/ 22		✓	✓
Graphs and Charts	4/ 6		✓	✓
Geometry/Measurement	6/ 12		✓	

CONTENT CLUSTERS	RAW SCORE/ NUMBER OF ITEMS	BELOW AVERAGE	AVERAGE	ABOVE AVERAGE
Language Mechanics	21/ 30		✓	✓
Capitalization	5/ 7		✓	
Punctuation	8/ 11		✓	✓
Applied Grammar	8/ 12		✓	
Language Expression	26/ 30		✓	✓
Sentence Correctness	16/ 20		✓	
Sentence Effectiveness	10/ 10		✓	✓
Spelling	22/ 40		✓	
Study Skills	21/ 30		✓	
Library/Reference Skills	10/ 17		✓	
Information Skills	11/ 13		✓	✓
Science	31/ 50		✓	
Physical Science	9/ 16		✓	
Biological Science	15/ 20		✓	
Earth/Space Science	7/ 14	✓		
Social Science	42/ 50		✓	✓
Geography	12/ 13			✓
History	8/ 8			✓
Political Science	6/ 10		✓	
Economics	9/ 10			✓
Psych/Sociol/Anthro	7/ 9			✓
Listening	25/ 45		✓	
Vocabulary	9/ 15	✓		
Listening Comprehension	16/ 30		✓	
Using Information	35/ 70		✓	
Thinking Skills	45/101		✓	

THE PSYCHOLOGICAL CORPORATION
HARCOURT BRACE JOVANOVICH, INC.

FIGURE 5–1 Sample Skills Analysis Report for Stanford Achievement Test Series.
(Stanford Achievement Test Series, Eighth Edition, Copyright © 1989 by Harcourt Brace Jovanovich, Inc. Reproduced by permission. All rights reserved.)

Secondary School Level Because of greater variability in the academic programs of different high school students, achievement test batteries are less useful at this level. Secondary school test batteries continue to emphasize basic skills in reading, language, and arithmetic, but tests in social studies, science, and study skills are also common. At both the elementary and secondary school levels, achievement tests emphasize general educational development and are not tied to specific courses in particular schools. Illustrative items appearing at successive levels in five of the tests on one achievement battery, the Comprehensive Tests of Basic Skills, are shown in Figure 5–2. Also of interest at the high school level are batteries of tests such as the American College Tests (ACT), which are administered annually for college admissions purposes. The ACT is actually an achievement test battery, but it is somewhat like an aptitude test in that its broad range of content is less related to specific school experiences than that of most achievement tests.

Selected Achievement Test Batteries

Descriptions of all commercially available achievement test batteries can be found in the various editions of the *Mental Measurements Yearbook, Tests in Print, Test Critiques* (Keyser & Sweetland, 1984–1988), and/or in the catalogs available from test publishers (see Appendix D). Among the most prominent achievement test batteries are the California Achievement Tests and the Comprehensive Tests of Basic Skills (both published by CTB/Macmillan/McGraw-Hill), the Iowa Tests of Basic Skills (published by Riverside Publishing Co.), and the Metropolitan Achievement Tests and Stanford Achievement Tests (both published by The Psychological Corporation).

Several achievement test batteries have been designed specifcially to measure the proficiency in basic skills of adults having less than a high school education. Examples are the Tests of Adult Basic Education (CTB/Macmillan/McGraw-Hill) and the Adult Basic Learning Examination (The Psychological Corporation). Both of these multilevel tests, which were standardized on adults, emphasize skills in reading, mathematics, and language.[3]

ACHIEVEMENT TESTS IN SPECIFIC AREAS

Administration of an achievement test battery has priority in a typical school testing program. When more information on pupil achievement in a particular subject is desired, the usual procedure is to follow the battery with the administration of a specific test on that subject. These specific achievement tests have certain advantages over comparable tests in a battery. For example, the fact that a specific subject-matter test contains more

---

[3]Despite the availability of such basic skills tests for adults, a recent survey of 595 U.S. and Canadian companies found that only about one-third of them actually tested their employees for literacy. As a consequence, at least one out of every four employees is functionally illiterate and must "bluff it out" in performing a job requiring reading skills. Another survey of 1328 employers found that 63 percent of them knew that they had workers who could not read, write, perform computations, or comprehend English. Not only are illiterate employees more likely to have accidents, but they are also handicapped in their ability to advance in an organization ("Fewer Firms Testing Employee Literacy," 1992).

Test 1.   READING Vocabulary (Selecting the word that means the same or about the same as the underlined word)

Level 1 (Grades 2.5–4)
<u>mend</u> the tire
○   patch
○   clean
○   change
○   fill

Level 2 (Grades 4–6)
approved his <u>behavior</u>
F   conscience
G   rights
H   decision
J   actions

Level 3 (Grades 6–8)
<u>adequate</u> supplies
F   adjusted
G   actual
H   sufficient
J   extra

Level 4 (Grades 8–12)
complete <u>solitude</u>
F   pacification
G   seclusion
H   confusion
J   classification

Test 3.   LANGUAGE Mechanics (Identifying mistakes in capitalization)

Level 1 (Grades 2.5–4)

In America we   celebrate a holiday   on July 4.   None
○   ○   ○   ○

Level 2 (Grades 4–6)
F   This selection comes   G   from "the silent world,"
H   a book about exciting   J   deep-sea diving adventures.   K   None

Level 3 (Grades 6–8)
A   The villain was   B   finally apprehended   C   Dulles international
                                at   airport
D   near Washington.   E   None

Level 4 (Grades 8–12)
F   When football   G   featured him on its   H   his fame became
    magazine   cover,
J   truly nationwide.   K   None

FIGURE 5–2   Sample Items from Comprehensive Tests of Basic Skills by CTB/ McGraw-Hill
(Copyright © 1968, 1981 by McGraw-Hill. Reprinted by permission of CTB, 2500 Garden Road, Monterey, CA 93940.)

items and has a broader subject content than a single test on an achievement battery makes it likely that the former will more adequately represent the instructional objectives of a wide range of classrooms and schools.

The old song "Reading and writing and' rithmetic, taught to the tune of a hickory

Test 5. LANGUAGE Spelling (Identifying misspelled words)

Level 1 (Grades 2.5–4)
○ full
○ cake
○ football
○ rabit
○ None

Level 2 (Grades 4–6)
A jerney
B event
C contain
D spoon
E none

Level 3 (Grades 6–8)
F recommend
G allowance
H literature
J profit
K None

Level 4 (Grades 8–12)
F constantly
G interpret
H benefit
J explenation
K None

Test 7. ARITHMETIC Concepts

Level 1 (Grades 2.5–4)
What goes in the box?
$5+4= 10-\square$
  0   1   9   10
  ○   ○   ○   ○

Level 2 (Grades 4–6)
What should be next in this series:
57, 64, 71, 78, ____?
  F 79
  G 81
  H 85
  J 88

Level 3 (Grades 6–8)
In 5963.427 the digit in the
hundredths place is
  A 2
  B 5
  C 6
  D 7

Level 4 (Grades 8–12)
If $R<S$ and $S<T$, then

  F $R=T$
  G $R>T$
  H $R<T$
  J $R+S=T$

Test 9. STUDY SKILLS (Using reference materials)

Level 1 (Grades 2.5–4)
Which one of these words would be *first* in abc order?
  pair   paint   polish   point
  ○   ○   ○   ○

Level 2 (Grades 4–6)
Which reference book would you use to find information on: A history of ship-building?
  A almanac
  B dictionary
  C encyclopedia
  D atlas

FIGURE 5–2 *(continued)*

Level 3 (Grades 6–8)

The library catalog subject card for Amusements would be found in the tray labeled
- F A—ALK
- G ALL—ANH
- H ANI—ANS
- J ARO—BAH

Level 4 (Grades 8–12)

In preparing a report about Carl Sandburg, which would be a primary source of information?
- F a collection of his writings
- G a review of a collection of his poems
- H a talk with an old friend of his
- J a biography by a well-known writer

FIGURE 5–2 *(continued)*

stick" is a testimonial to the time-honored prominence of these subjects in the elementary school curriculum—but with less stress on corporal punishment these days. Hundreds of specific subject-matter tests in reading, mathematics, language, science, social studies, the professions, business, and the skilled trades are available. Other areas in which standardized achievement tests have been constructed are health, home economics, industrial arts, library usage, literature, the Bible, music, speech, spelling, and driver education. In addition to traditional norm-referenced survey, diagnostic, and prognostic instruments, there are many criterion-referenced tests in specific subjects. Furthermore, the current emphasis on basic skills competency testing for high school graduation has led to the publication of a number of proficiency tests for assessing the knowledge and skills of junior and senior high students in reading, writing, and mathematics. These "survival skills," as they have been labeled, are considered essential in coping with the demands of everyday living.

Reading Tests

Many learning difficulties experienced by children are related to problems in reading, and this is a frequently stated reason for referring a child for psychoeducational evaluation. Because problems with reading are cumulative and affect performance in almost all schoolwork, it is important to assess reading level and diagnose deficiencies in this subject early and regularly. Because of their many uses, more reading tests are administered than any other type of achievement test. In fact, there are so many different reading tests that a separate volume of the Buros series, *Reading Tests and Reviews II* (Buros, 1975a), has been devoted to them. Various types of reading tests are available; three major categories are survey tests, diagnostic tests, and reading readiness tests. Other ways of classifying reading tests are norm-referenced versus criterion-referenced (or both) and silent versus oral reading.

Survey Reading Tests   The main purpose of administering a survey reading test is to determine a person's overall reading ability. Tests of this type contain sections of vocabulary items and sections of paragraphs or passages about which questions are asked. A measure of word knowledge is obtained from the vocabulary items, whereas speed and level of reading comprehension are measured from the paragraphs. Noteworthy examples of survey reading tests are the Gates–MacGinitie Reading Tests, the Nelson–Denny Reading Test, the Gray Oral Reading Tests–Revised, and the Metropolitan Achievement Tests, Sixth Edition–Reading Survey. The first two tests are published by The Riverside Publishing Company and the last two by The Psychological Corporation.

Diagnostic Reading Tests   Diagnostic reading tests, which are by far the most common type of diagnostic test, attempt to assess many different factors that affect reading: eye–hand coordination, visual and auditory perception, understanding of concepts, and even motivation. They contain subtests on word recognition, reading passages, phonetics and pronunciation, silent and oral reading, spelling, and sound discrimination, all for the purpose of discovering the causes of a student's disability in reading. Because the correlations among these subtests are often substantial, the various skills measured by diagnostic reading tests are not necessarily independent. In addition, the reliabilities of the subtests and the test as a whole are frequently not as high as might be desired. Representative of tests in this category are the California Diagnostic Reading Tests (published by CTB/Macmillan/McGraw-Hill), the Durrell Analysis of Reading Difficulty and the Stanford Diagnostic Reading Tests (both published by The Psychological Corporation), and the Woodcock Reading Mastery Tests (published by American Guidance Service).

Reading Readiness Tests   As a measure of the extent to which a child possesses the skills and knowledge necessary for learning to read, a reading readiness test often predicts achievement in first grade better than a general intelligence test. For this reason, reading readiness tests, which usually take less time to administer than intelligence tests, may be given to kindergartners and first-graders when intelligence test scores are unavailable. Certain reading tests contain both diagnostic and prognostic components. For example, the Woodcock Reading Mastery Tests is not only a diagnostic reading test, but also contains a reading readiness test. Furthermore, reading readiness tests contain many of the same types of items as diagnostic reading tests—measures of visual discrimination, auditory blending and discrimination, vocabulary, letter recognition, and visual–motor coordination. Illustrative of tests in this area are the CTBS Readiness Test (CTB/Macmillan/McGraw-Hill), the Linguistic Awareness in Reading Readiness (American Guidance Service), and the Metropolitan Readiness Tests (The Psychological Corporation). The latter is unique in that it combines a reading readiness test with a mathematics readiness test.

Mathematics Tests

In a manner similar to achievement tests in reading, mathematics achievement tests may be classified as survey, diagnostic, and prognostic.

Survey Mathematics Tests   Since the field of mathematics education has changed a great deal during the past 30 years, a variety of approaches to instruction are represented by current mathematics tests. Certain tests are designed to encompass both modern and traditional emphases in the mathematics curriculum, and instruments reflecting more specialized instructional approaches from primary school through college are available. In general, survey mathematics tests contain items requiring examinees to demonstrate an understanding of quantitative concepts and operations and the ability to apply this understanding in solving problems. Examples of norm-referenced mathematics tests of the survey type are the Mathematics Survey Tests of the Metropolitan Achievement Tests and the Stanford Mathematics Tests (both published by The Psychological Corporation) and the Test of Mathematical Abilities and the Test of Early Mathematics Ability (both published by Publishers Test Service).

Diagnostic Tests in Mathematics   Although less widely used than diagnostic reading tests, diagnostic tests in mathematics also represent attempts to break down a complex subject involving a variety of skills into its constituent elements. The items on diagnostic tests of arithmetic and mathematics are based on an analysis of skills and errors in the subject. Skills and the knowledge required for applications involving numeration, fractions, algebra, and geometry are tapped by these tests. Two examples of diagnostic mathematics tests are the Stanford Diagnostic Mathematics Test and KeyMath. The Stanford Diagnostic Mathematics Test, which is published by The Psychological Corporation, is a group test developed to diagnose the specific strengths and weaknesses in basic mathematics concepts and operations of children grades 1 through 12. KeyMath Revised: A Diagnostic Inventory of Essential Mathematics is an individually administered test published by The American Guidance Service and designed to measure the understanding and application of basic mathematics concepts and skills in kindergarten through grade 9.

Prognostic Tests in Mathematics   A number of tests have been designed to forecast performance in specific mathematics courses, but, compared with prognostic tests in reading (reading readiness tests), they are not widely used. An example of a prognostic test in mathematics is the Orleans–Hanna Algebra Prognosis Test–Revised (The Psychological Corporation). Designed to identify, before instruction begins, which students will be successful and which will encounter difficulties in learning algebra, the Orleans–Hanna assesses aptitude and achievement as well as the interest and motivation in algebra of junior and senior high school students. The questionnaire and work sample items on the test take 40 minutes to complete. The percentile rank and stanine score norms are based on three groups of students: those completing seventh-grade mathematics, those completing eighth-grade mathematics, and those from the first two groups who completed a one-year course in algebra in the following year.

Language Tests

Language, as generally construed, refers to any means of communication. Although language tests are primarily of the verbal type, measures of nonverbal communication for

FIGURE 5–3   Testing with KeyMath Revised.
(Reproduced by permission of American Guidance Service, Inc.)

use with hearing-impaired and, more recently, normal-hearing people have also been developed.

Both oral and written language is taught at all levels, and tests appropriate for the entire range of grades are available. Failure to understand certain concepts can act as a communication barrier between a first-grade pupil and teacher and consequently have a serious effect on the child's school learning. In recognition of this fact, the Boehm Test of Basic Concepts–Revised (for grades K–2) and the Boehm Test of Basic Concepts: Preschool Version (for ages 3–5 years) were designed to measure young children's mastery of basic concepts of space, quantity, and time (see Figure 5–4). A kit of materials to help children master the concepts measured by the tests, the *Boehm Resource Guide for Basic Concept Teaching,* is also available from The Psychological Corporation.

Despite the existence of tests such as the Boehm, most of the achievement tests listed in the language category have been designed for secondary and college students. These instruments, which include both English and foreign language tests, are frequently administered in high schools and colleges for the purpose of placing students in English or foreign language courses appropriate to their level of competence.

English Language Tests   Some of the most severe criticisms of objective tests have come from teachers of English, but it is generally recognized that such tests do a fairly respectable job of measuring knowledge of grammar and vocabulary and, to some extent, skill in oral and written expression. English language skills are assessed as a part of achievement test batteries, but there are also many separate tests of proficiency in English. Examples are the Purdue High School English Test, the Business English Test, and the College English Placement Test (all from the Riverside Publishing Co.). These tests assess

Mark the window that is *above* the door.

Mark the squirrel that is *beginning* to climb.

Mark the dress that is *farthest* from the socks.

Mark the picture that shows *part* of the cat.

FIGURE 5–4   Sample Items from the Boehm Test of Basic Concepts—Revised. The Examinee Marks an × on the Selected Option.
(Copyright © 1986 by The Psychological Corporation. All rights reserved.)

knowledge of vocabulary, grammar, syntax, and spelling. Separate tests of spelling, such as the Test of Written Spelling–2 (pro.ed), are also available.

Listening, speaking, and writing skills are obviously part of English usage, and a number of tests have been developed to measure these skills. A good example of a listening test is the Goldman–Friscoe–Woodcock Auditory Skills Test Battery (from American Guidance Service). Among the measures of students' abilities to articulate speech sounds are the Test of Articulation Performance (pro.ed) and the Goldman–Friscoe Test of Articulation (American Guidance Service). A child's understanding and meaningful use of spoken words, differing aspects of grammar, and ability to speak words correctly and to distinguish between similar-sounding words can be assessed by The Test of Language Development Primary and Intermediate (from American Guidance Service and pro.ed.). Examples of writing tests are the Test of Written Language (pro.ed.) and the Writing Test of the Metropolitan Achievement Test, Sixth Edition (The Psychological Corporation). These two writing tests, for students in grades 2–12, are free-response, work-sample measures in which examinees write stories about a set of pictures shown to them (see Figure 5–5). The stories may be scored on several variables, including theme, vocabulary, syntax, spelling, and style. Many other commercially available achievement tests, such as the Advanced Placement Tests of the College Entrance Examination Board, also contain a writing (essay) component.

Foreign student applicants for admission to U.S. colleges and universities whose native language is not English typically take the Test of English as a Foreign Language (TOEFL). TOEFL is a 3-hour multiple-choice examination (from Educational Testing Service) consisting of three parts: Listening Comprehension, which measures the ability to understanding spoken English; Structure and Written Expression, which measures the ability to recognize language that is not appropriate for standard written English; and

FIGURE 5–5 Sample Pictures from the Test of Written Language–2. The Student Makes up a Story About Each of a Series of Pictures Like These Two. *(Reprinted by permission of pro.ed, Inc., Austin, TX.)*

Vocabulary and Reading Comprehension, which measures the ability to understand non-technical reading material.

Foreign Language Tests   Survey tests of proficiency in a foreign language typically consist of different forms for students who have completed different amounts of training in the language. Certain tests reflect the more traditional grammatical approach to language instruction, whereas others emphasize comprehension of spoken and written language. In addition to survey (placement) tests in foreign languages, there are several prognostic tests. The content of these tests, which are designed to predict success in learning a foreign language, varies with the particular instrument. A typical test includes measures of rote memory, interest in studying a foreign language, sensitivity to grammatical structure, and the ability to associate sounds and symbols. An example of foreign language tests of the survey type is the MLA–Cooperative Foreign Language Tests. These tests, published by the Modern Language Association of America and Educational Testing Service and distributed by CTB/Macmillan/McGraw-Hill, are available in French, German, Spanish, Russian, and Italian. Examples of prognostic tests in foreign languages are the Pimsleur Language Aptitude Battery and the Modern Language Aptitude Test, both published by The Psychological Corporation. These two tests, which consist of exercises in learning the vocabulary and grammar of an artificial language, were designed to predict how easily and rapidly English-speaking students can progress in a typical foreign language program.

Social Studies Tests

Topics in social studies, history, economics, and political science are generally thought of in connection with secondary school and college curricula. Social studies, perhaps in a less formal sense, is also taught in the elementary grades. Representative of tests of achievement in social studies at the secondary school level are the CAT End-of-Course Tests in World History, American History, and Consumer Economics (CTB/Macmillan/McGraw-Hill) and the Emporia American Government Test (Bureau of Educational Measurements).

Science Tests

Instruction in science, like instruction in mathematics, has changed so much since the early 1960s that many of the older tests are inappropriate for today's science curriculum. The Biological Sciences Curriculum Study (BSCS) and the Physical Sciences Study Committee (PSSC) led to the design of specific tests in biology and physics. Comprehensive testing programs in other sciences, such as the American Chemical Society's Cooperative Chemistry Tests, also reflect modern approaches to science education. Many of the older tests have been revised in an attempt to assess performance in either a modern or traditional science program. Examples of tests of instructional effectiveness in specific sciences are the End-of-Course Tests in Biology, Chemistry and Physics (CTB/Macmillan/McGraw-Hill) for senior high students.

Tests for Higher Education and the Professions

Many institutions of higher learning permit students to earn credit for college courses by making acceptable scores on standardized achievement tests such as those administered by the College Board's Advanced Placement Program (APP), College-Level Examination Program (CLEP), and the ACT Proficiency Examination Program. In addition, universities and professional schools use scores on standardized achievement tests as criteria for selecting students. These tests are usually "restricted" or "secure," in the sense that they are sold or rented only to certain organizations for administration in connection with specific educational programs.

A set of 15 standardized achievement tests used in selecting students for graduate programs are the Subject Tests of the Graduate Record Examinations (GRE). The GRE Subject Tests, consisting of tests in major fields of college work, may be taken, along with the GRE General Test, by college students in their senior year who intend to apply for admission to graduate school. Other examples of standardized tests for graduate or professional school admission are the National Teacher Examination (NTE), the Medical College Admission Test (MCAT), the Law School Admission Test (LSAT), the NLN Achievement Tests in Nursing, and the Graduate Management Aptitude Test (GMAT). Certification or licensing as a certified public accountant, physician, lawyer, registered nurse, or professional in certain other fields is also contingent on passing a series of achievement tests (board examinations, bar examinations) in the particular field.

Tests for Business and the Skilled Trades

Business is a school subject in itself, and business education tests are designed to assess a student's knowledge of the subject. In addition to evaluating the degree of accomplishment in a school subject, achievement tests are used in business and industry for purposes of selection, placement, and promotion. Tests of proficiency in typing, filing, word processing, computing, and other office skills are perhaps the most popular of these measures. Examples of tests in this category are the Office Skills (see Figure 5–6) and the Word Processor Assessment Battery (both available from London House).

Tests of knowledge and skill in some particular trade (*trade tests*) are widely used for purposes of employee selection and placement and licensing. A trade test may consist of a series of questions to be answered orally or in writing, or it may be a work-sample task requiring the examinee to demonstrate a particular skill. Examples of trade, or occupational competency, tests are those devised under Educational Testing Service's National Occupational Competency Program. This program has been responsible for the development of dozens of occupational tests. Included among these are proficiency examinations for auto mechanics, bartenders, beauticians, contact lens dispensers, firefighters, foreign service officials, police officers, professional golfers, and many other specialties. A number of these tests involve very different performance from those required by traditional paper-and-pencil examinations. In the test for foreign service officials, for example, there is an "assessment day" on which the candidate's ability to take appropriate action on each of a set of memos and other communications of the sort usually found in an executive's in-basket, as well as his or her ability to handle a leaderless group negotiation

Sample Item   Typing

*Missing person, Ramona Woodstock,
526 Vine, had been told to be home
from visiting Mary Lyne no later
than 2390 hours. Contact of family
was made at 0200 hours and
missing person had not yet returned home.*

Sample Item   Forms Completion

At 8:30 a.m. on Oct. 15, 1977, Today's Sound Center reported a burglary at their location at 3907 Palm Ave., Wista, California. Tel: 689-7734. Four tape decks, two amplifiers, and two cases of blank tape cassettes were reported missing. Rear door was damaged to obtain entry. It is possible arson in adjoining store was intended to divert suspicion of burglary. Offense 789A3 reported.

```
                        CITY OF WISTA
                     POLICE DEPARTMENT

    OFFENSE REPORTED   789A3              CR# _____

    DATE REPORTED  OCT. 15, 1977  TIME REPORTED  8:30 A.M.

    NAME OF VICTIM (FIRM IF BUSINESS)  TODAY'S SOUND CENTER

    ADDRESS OF INCIDENT  3907 PALM AVE., WISTA  PHONE 689-7734

    EXTENT OF LOSS  4 TAPE DECKS    2 AMPLIFIERS
        2 CASES  BLANK  TAPE  CASSETTES
```

Sample Item   Filing

You are to look at the item in the "To Be Filed" column and find the number of the item in the "Existing File" that this new item should *follow*. Mark an "X" on *that* number in the row of circled numbers on the right. If there is no number given for your choice, put an "X" in the *blank* circle.

	Existing File	To Be Filed					
1.	Philip Jenkins						
2.	J. C. Kile	A. B. Reynolds	①	②	③	⊗	○
3.	Thomas Morris Company						
4.	Paulson Company, Inc.	John Jones	②	③	④	⑤	⊗
5.	Sally White						

Sample Item   Coding

In this test you will be given code lists similar to these.

34 male
21 female
M adult
U teenager
Z child

Below the code lists you will find a list of items. Each item is followed by circles containing five possible codes. Your task is to find the correct code combination for the item and mark an "X" in the appropriate circle. Look at the following examples. An "X" has been placed on the answer for example 1. What would you mark for example 2?

Examples:

1. female adult   ⟨34U⟩ ⟨34M⟩ ⟨86Z⟩ ⟨2⊗⟩ ⟨21U⟩
2. male child   ⟨21Z⟩ ⟨34Z⟩ ⟨34U⟩ ⟨21U⟩ ⟨34M⟩

FIGURE 5–6 Sample Items from the Office Skills Tests.
(Reprinted by permission of London House.)

interview, is evaluated. Some of these tasks obviously go beyond the domain of ability testing and into the realm of attitude and personality assessment.

SUMMARY

More tests of achievement—the level of knowledge, skill, or accomplishment in an area of endeavor—are administered than all other types of tests combined. During the twentieth century, written examinations, especially those of the objective variety, have become increasingly more popular. Objective tests can measure not only knowledge of facts, but comprehension and higher-order thinking as well. They have been criticized, however, for fostering poor skills in written composition.

Standardized achievement tests reflect general educational objectives, whereas teacher-made tests are more likely to reflect the goals of a particular teacher or school system. The results of standardized achievement testing are used not only for pupil evaluation, but also for pupil placement, diagnosis of learning difficulties, determination of readiness to learn, and the evaluation of curricula and teaching effectiveness (accountability).

The emphases on formative evaluation, in which testing is an integral part of the instructional process, and criterion-referenced testing are indicative of the changing roles of educational achievement testing. Also of significance is the use of tests in large-scale educational assessment and planning, an example of which is the National Assessment of Educational Progress.

Four types of achievement tests are single-survey tests, survey test batteries, diagnostic tests, and prognostic tests. Survey tests provide an overall appraisal of achievement in a subject, whereas diagnostic tests analyze the specific strengths and weaknesses in a person's knowledge of a particular subject. Readiness, aptitude, and other prognostic tests attempt to forecast achievement by determining a person's ability to learn certain material.

Sources of information concerning achievement tests include publishers' catalogs, test reviews in professional journals, *The Mental Measurements Yearbooks,* and the specimen sets of tests. The reliabilities of achievement tests range from the low .80's to the high .90's. Content validity is of greater concern than other types of validity in evaluating achievement tests.

A wide selection of multilevel achievement test batteries can be purchased. Examples are the Stanford Achievement Tests, the Comprehensive Tests of Basic Skills, and the Iowa Tests of Basic Skills. These batteries are commonly administered in elementary and junior high school. Single-survey tests in reading, mathematics, science, social studies, English, foreign languages, and other areas are also widely administered. Survey reading tests typically measure vocabulary, level of comprehension, and speed of comprehension. The Gates–MacGinitie Reading Tests are illustrative of instruments of this kind.

Diagnostic tests, which are designed to assess an individual's specific strengths and weaknesses in a particular subject, are found in reading, arithmetic, and spelling. Examples are the Woodcock Reading Mastery Test–Revised and the Stanford Diagnostic Mathematics Test. Various reading readiness tests, as well as prognostic tests in mathematics and modern language aptitude tests, are available. Illustrative of tests in these categories are the Metropolitan Readiness Tests in reading, the Orleans–Hanna Algebra Prognosis Test, and the Modern Language Aptitude Test.

Tests in social studies (history, economics, political science) and in the natural sciences (general science, biology, chemistry, physics) are available for a wide range of grades and different types of curricula. Tests for admission to professional schools (NTE, GMAT, MCAT, LSAT) and for business and the skilled trades or occupations are also used extensively.

EXERCISES

1. Compare standardized achievement tests with teacher-made tests, listing the merits and shortcomings of each.
2. What is accountability in education? How is accountability related to performance contracting? List points supporting and opposing performance contracting in the public schools.
3. Distinguish between norm-referenced and criterion-referenced measurement. What are the advantages and disadvantages of each?
4. How does formative evaluation differ from summative evaluation? How do the two approaches to evaluation complement each other? In what way is formative evaluation related to criterion-referenced measurement?
5. Compare the purposes and design of survey tests, diagnostic tests, and prognostic tests.
6. Why is it better to administer an achievement test battery rather than a series of single-subject-matter tests? Why not?
7. Name at least one standardized achievement test in each of the following school subjects: English, science, reading, mathematics, foreign languages.
8. Most departments of psychology and education keep on file specimen sets of standardized achievement tests, including test booklet, answer sheet, scoring key(s), manual, and perhaps other interpretative materials. Once a test is selected, a review outline such as the following should be used. Whenever possible, the student should fill in this outline from information obtained by reading the test manual and examining the test itself. The student should not consult a review of the test in the *Mental Measurements Yearbooks* or journal sources until completing his or her own review, because this might lead to bias or plagiarism.

    Content. List the title, author(s), publisher, date and place of publication, forms available, type of test, and cost. Give a brief description of the sections of the test, the kinds of items of which the test is composed, and the mental operations or characteristics the test is supposed to measure. Indicate how the test items were selected and whether the construction procedure and/or theory on which the test is based are clearly described in the manual.

    Administration and Scoring. Describe any special instructions, whether the test is timed, and, if so, the time limits. Give details concerning scoring: as a whole, by sections or parts, and so on. Indicate whether the directions for administration and scoring are clear.

    Norms. Describe the group(s) (composition, size, and so on) on which the test was standardized and how the samples were selected (systematic, stratified random, and so on). What kinds of norms are reported in the test manual or technical supplements? Does the standardization appear to be adequate for the recommended use of the test?

Reliability. Describe the kinds of reliability information reported in the manual (internal consistency, parallel forms, test–retest, and so on). Are the nature and sizes of the samples on which reliability information is reported adequate with respect to the stated uses of the test?

Validity. Summarize the available information on the validity (content, predictive, concurrent, construct) of the test given in the manual. Is the validity information satisfactory in terms of the stated purposes of the test?

Summary Comments. Give a summary statement of the design and content of the test, and comment briefly on the adequacy of the test as a measure of what it was designed to measure. Does the test manual give satisfactory descriptions of the test design, content, norms, reliability, and validity? What further information and/or data are needed to improve the test and its uses?

SUGGESTED READINGS

Airasian, P. W. (1979). A perspective on the uses and misuses of standardized achievement tests. *NCME Measurement in Education, 10*(3), 1–12.

Green, B. F., Jr. (1978). In defense of measurement. *American Psychologist, 33,* 664–670.

Katz, L. J., & Slomka, G. T. (1990). Achievement testing. In G. Goldstein & M. Hersen (eds.), *Handbook of psychological assessment,* 2nd ed., pp. 123–147. New York: Pergamon.

Kennedy, H. (1980). The first written examinations at Harvard College. *American Mathematical Monthly, 87,* 483–486.

Levine, M. (1976). The academic achievement test: Its historical context and social functions. *American Psychologist, 31,* 228–238.

Millman, J., & Greene, J. (1989). The specification and development of tests of achievement and instruction. In R. L. Linn (ed.), *Educational measurement,* 3rd ed., pp. 447–474. New York: Macmillan.

Nickerson, R. S. (guest ed.). Special issue on educational assessment. *Educational Researcher, 18*(9).

Paris, S. G., et al. (1991). A developmental perspective on standardized achievement testing. *Educational Researcher, 20*(5), 12–20.

Schrader, W. B. (ed.). (1980). Measuring achievement: Progress over a decade. Proceedings of the 1979 ETS Invitational Conference. *New Directions for Testing and Measurement, 5.*

Wood, R. (1985). Achievement tests. In T. Husén & T. N. Postlethwaite (eds.), *International encyclopedia of education,* Vol. 1, pp. 31–35. New York: Wiley.

Chapter Six

Intelligence Testing

From the time of their introduction during the first decade of this century, intelligence tests have been used extensively in the United States and other countries, not only to assist in making academic, vocational, and clinical decisions about people, but also to study group differences in mental abilities. These uses of intelligence tests have stimulated much controversy concerning the nature and meaning of intelligence and the personal and social consequences of relying on these tests. Research on individual and group differences in intelligence has been adequately reviewed in books on differential psychology (Minton & Schneider, 1980; Willerman, 1979), so this topic is not dealt with extensively in this chapter. Rather, the student is introduced to a variety of intelligence tests and how they are used. Intelligence testing is no longer the exclusive occupation of many practicing psychologists, as it was earlier in the century, but the assessment of mental abilities still forms a part of the activities of psychologists in a variety of settings.

HISTORY AND TERMINOLOGY

Intelligence, which is a common word today, was almost unknown in everyday speech a century ago. During the latter part of the nineteenth century, the philosopher Herbert Spencer and the gentleman-scientist Francis Galton, who were stimulated by Charles Darwin's writings on the origin of species differences, reintroduced the ancient Latin term *intelligence* to refer to individual differences in mental ability. These men and their followers believed that there exists in human beings an inborn degree of general intelligence, which is distinct from special abilities.

Unlike Spencer, Galton was not content to philosophize about the nature of intelligence. He attempted to demonstrate its hereditary basis by studies of family trees, and he devised several tests of sensory discrimination and reaction time that it was hoped would measure the components of intelligence. These and other sensorimotor tests (measures of movement speed, muscular strength, pain sensitivity, weight discrimination, and the like) were studied extensively by the American psychologist J. McKeen Cattell, but they proved to be relatively useless as predictors of accomplishment in schoolwork and other tasks that presumably require intelligence.

Radically different from the analytic procedure of trying to measure the components of intelligence was the approach taken by the French psychologist Alfred Binet. Defining intelligence as "the capacity to judge well, to reason well, and to comprehend well," Binet and Simon (1916, page 192) maintained that a person's intelligence is manifested in performance on a variety of tasks and can be measured by responses to a sample of those tasks. Because his work in designing the first successful intelligence tests was motivated by the problem of identifying mentally retarded children in the Paris school system, it is natural that the sample of tests selected by Binet was heavily loaded with school-type tasks.

Binet and his associate, Simon, published their first set of intelligence tests (30 short tests arranged in order from easiest to most difficult) in 1905. Further work led to the publication in 1908 of a revised Binet–Simon scale consisting of 58 tasks arranged at age levels from 3 to 13 years. The tasks were grouped by age level corresponding to what Binet's research had indicated normal children of a given age could do. A child's mental age (MA) on the tests was determined by the number of tests he or she passed at each level; a mental age strikingly lower than the child's chronological age was indicative of mental retardation. A final revision of the scale was published in 1911 (Table 6–1), but after Binet's untimely death during that same year the scene of later development of the Binet test shifted to the United States.

Definitions of Intelligence

Many new tests of intelligence have been developed since Binet's early work, and much research and theorizing on the nature of intelligence have taken place. Intelligence has been viewed by educators as the ability to learn, by biologists as the ability to adapt to the environment, by psychologists as the ability to deduce relationships among objects and events, and by information theorists as the ability to process information (Wechsler, 1975). Certain writers have objected to the term *intelligence,* with its connotation that general mental ability is innate, and have proposed that it be replaced with a term such as *general scholastic ability* or *general educational ability.*

Not all tests discussed in this chapter are specifically labeled *intelligence tests;* rather, they have been proposed as measures of *general mental ability.* In this sense, they are to be distinguished from the measures of *special abilities* considered in Chapter 7. The distinction between tests of general mental ability (intelligence) and tests of special abilities is, however, not sharp, and certain scholastic ability tests described in the present chapter might fit equally well in Chapter 7.

Items on intelligence tests represent attempts to assess individual differences in the effects of experiences common to nearly everyone, particularly in Western culture. It is assumed that, when exposed to the same experiences, people of higher intelligence will benefit more from those experiences than people of lower intelligence. Consequently, to the extent that test makers are successful, differences among individuals' scores on intelligence tests should be more a matter of variations in basic mental ability than variations in experience.

TABLE 6–1 The Fifty-Four Tests on Alfred Binet's 1911 Mental Age Scale

Age 3
Points to nose, eyes, and mouth.
Repeats two digits.
Enumerates objects in a picture.
Gives family name.
Repeats a sentence of six syllables.

Age 4
Gives own sex.
Names key, knife, and penny.
Repeats three digits.
Compares two lines.

Age 5
Compares two weights.
Copies a square.
Repeats a sentence of ten syllables.
Counts four pennies.
Unites the halves of a divided rectangle.

Age 6
Distinguishes between morning and
 afternoon.
Defines familiar words in terms of use.
Copies a diamond.
Counts 13 pennies.
Distinguishes pictures of ugly and pretty
 faces.

Age 7
Shows right hand and left ear.
Describes a picture.
Executes three commands given
 simultaneously.
Counts the value of six sous, three of
 which are double.
Names four cardinal colors.

Age 8
Compares two objects from memory.
Counts from 20 to zero.
Notes omissions from pictures.
Gives day and date.
Repeats five digits.

Age 9
Gives change from 20 sous.
Defines familiar words in terms superior
 to use.
Recognizes all the (nine) pieces of
 money.
Names the months of the year in order.
Answers or comprehends "easy
 questions."

Age 10
Arranges five blocks in order of weight.
Copies two drawings from memory.
Criticizes absurd statements.
Answers or comprehends "difficult
 questions."
Uses three given words in not more than
 two sentences.

Age 12
Resists suggestion as to length of lines.
Composes one sentence containing
 three given words.
Names 60 words in 3 minutes.
Defines three abstract words.
Discovers the sense of a disarranged
 sentence.

Age 15
Repeats seven digits.
Finds three rhymes for a given word in
 1 minute.
Repeats a sentence of 26 syllables.
Interprets pictures.
Interprets given facts.

Adult
Solves the paper-cutting test.
Rearranges a triangle in imagination.
Gives differences between pairs of
 abstract terms.
Gives three differences between a
 president and a king.
Gives the main thought of a selection that
 he has read.

Individual versus Group Tests

Despite their common aim of measuring a unitary capacity, not all tests of general intelligence are alike. On some tests, the order of the items is mixed or alternated and there is a single time limit; on the tests, the items are grouped as sets of separately timed subtests.

The most common way of classifying intelligence tests is by the dichotomy *individual* versus *group*. Individual intelligence tests, which are administered to one examinee at a time, are somewhat different in focus from group intelligence tests, which can be administered simultaneously to many examinees. The focus of individual tests is more global or holistic, their major purpose being to assess a general trait (Tyler & Walsh, 1979). The focus of group tests, on the other hand, tends to be narrower: to predict academic or occupational performance. Furthermore, administering an individual intelligence test is usually more time consuming than administering a group test. However, the examiner of an individual test can pay more attention to the examinee, and, consequently, encourage and observe him or her more closely. In addition, scores on individual tests are not as dependent on reading ability as are scores on group tests.

The greater economy of administering a group test in certain situations is seen in the fact that many more group than individual tests are given. Also, in spite of what advocates of individual tests have sometimes declared, group tests are not necessarily less reliable and valid than individual tests. When the criterion is achievement in schoolwork (grades or achievement test scores), occasionally group tests of intelligence have even higher validity coefficients than individual intelligence tests, ranging between .50 and .70.

Group intelligence tests are more often used for initial screening in school and businesses, to be followed by individual testing in cases where the examinee scores low and/or more information on his or her strengths and weaknesses is required. Individual intelligence tests are preferred by psychologists in clinics, hospitals, and other settings where clinical diagnoses are made and where they serve not only as measures of general mental ability, but also as a means of obtaining insight into personality functioning and disabilities.

INDIVIDUALLY ADMINISTERED TESTS

The instruments stemming from the work of Alfred Binet, Lewis Terman, and David Wechsler have been the most popular individually administered tests of intelligence. Over the years, the tests developed by Terman and Wechsler have been used to evaluate the intellectual abilities of children and adults in a wide variety of circumstances. Other individual tests, some representing variations or extensions of the Stanford–Binet and Wechsler series, have been designed specifically to assess the mental abilities of young children and persons with linguistic and/or physical handicaps.

Older Editions of the Stanford–Binet Intelligence Scale

There were three English translations and adaptations of the Binet–Simon scale in the United States. One was prepared by H. H. Goddard of the Vineland Training School, one by Frederic Kuhlmann of the University of Minnesota, and a third by Lewis Terman of Stanford University. The most popular of these revisions, the Stanford–Binet Intelligence Scale, was published by Terman in 1916.

The 1916 Scale   Like the earlier Binet–Simon scales, the 1916 Stanford–Binet was an age scale on which the tests were grouped into chronological age levels. Terman selected items from the Binet–Simon scales as well as completely new items representing a broad sample of tasks that presumably require intelligence. Efforts were also made to include tasks that were not so dependent on specific school learning experiences.

One criterion for including an item on the Stanford–Binet was that an increasing percentage of children at successive age levels should be able to answer the item correctly. For certain statistical reasons having to do with maintaining a fairly constant intelligence quotient (IQ) scale across age levels, the percentage-passing requirement was lower for items included in subtests at higher-year levels than for items at lower-year levels. In any event, the percentage-passing criterion served as an objective means of assuring that every item on the test was placed at an appropriate age level(s).

An examinee's mental age (MA) and intelligence quotient on the Stanford–Binet depended on the number of subtests passed at successive age levels. The IQ was determined by dividing the examinee's mental age (MA), the total number of months of credit earned on the test, by his or her chronological age (CA) in months, and then multiplying the resulting quotient by 100. In symbols, this *ratio IQ* was computed as

$$IQ = 100 \left(\frac{MA}{CA}\right) \tag{6.1}$$

For many years, the Stanford–Binet Intelligence Scale was a standard against which other intelligence tests were evaluated. Nevertheless, the test had a number of shortcomings. For example, the 1916 version of the scale was standardized on only 1000 children and 400 adults. The sample was, by present-day standards, not selected carefully and was certainly not representative of the U.S. population of the time. Two other shortcomings of the 1916 scale were its inadequacies in testing adults and very young children and the lack of a second form to permit retesting. Therefore, in 1937, Terman and his associate, Maud Merrill, published a revised, updated version of the Stanford–Binet.

The 1937 Scale   The 1937 version of the Stanford–Binet Intelligence Scale had more *floor* and *ceiling* than the 1916 scale, two parallel forms (L and M), and more adequate standardization. The 1937 scale was standardized in stratified fashion on 100 children at each half-year age interval from ages 1½ through 5½ years, 200 children at each year age interval from 6 through 14 years, 100 children at each year age interval from 6 through 14 years, and 100 persons at each year age interval from 15 through 18. Equal numbers of boys and girls were tested in 17 communities of 11 states, but the sampling was limited to native-born whites who, as a group, were somewhat above average in socioeconomic status. Consequently, the sample was not truly representative of the entire U.S. population.

Three criteria were used for including an item on the scale: (1) the item was judged to be a measure of intelligent behavior, (2) the percentage of children passing the item accelerated with chronological age, and (3) children who passed the item had a significantly higher mean mental age than those who failed the item. Items were grouped at half-year intervals (levels) from Year II through Year V and at yearly intervals from Year VI through Year XIV; there was also an Average Adult level and three Superior Adult levels (Superior

Adult I, II, and III). The six subtests at each level from Year II through Year V were allotted 1 month credit each; from Year VI through Year XIV, the subtests were allotted 2 months' credit each, and the six subtests at Superior Adult levels I, II, and III were each assigned 4, 5, and 6 months' credit, respectively.

In testing a child with the Stanford–Binet, the examiner first established the child's *basal age* on the test. The basal age was the highest year level at which the child passed all subtests. Testing then continued until the *ceiling age*, the lowest year level at which the child failed all subtests, was reached. Mental age was computed by adding to the basal age the number of months' credit received for passing each subtest up to the ceiling age. Then the IQ was computed by formula 6.1.

The 1960 Scale   The third edition of the Stanford–Binet Intelligence Scale, published in 1960, consisted of an updating of the best items from the 1937 L and M forms. Like its predecessors, the third edition was used to measure the intelligence of individuals from age 2 years to adulthood. The procedure for administering the test was similar to that for the 1937 scale, although certain changes were introduced. There was an alternative subtest at each age level for use when a particular subtest was not administered or was administered incorrectly. Administration time could also be shortened in certain instances by giving only four selected subtests instead of six at each year level. Another change was the provision for deviation IQs. The ratio IQ, like any other age norm, did not satisfy the requirements of equality of age units. Furthermore, it was meaningless when applied to adults because there was no satisfactory answer to the question of what chronological age should be used as the denominator of the MA/CA ratio when examining adults. Fourteen years, 16 years, and 18 years were all suggested as the age at which mental growth ceases and thereby would be appropriate to use as a denominator in computing the IQ. Because of such problems in determining the ratio IQ, it was decided to change from a ratio IQ to a deviation IQ scale having a mean of 100 and a standard deviation of 16. The older ratio IQ was still reported on occasion, and tables for computing it were supplied in the 1960 Stanford–Binet manual.

The standardization group for the 1960 Form L–M of the Stanford–Binet consisted of 4500 children aged 2½ through 18 years who had taken either Form L or M of the 1937 scale between 1950 and 1954. Realizing the need for updated norms, the publisher arranged for the test to be administered in 1972 to a stratified national sample of 2100 children (100 children at each half-year interval from 2 through 5½ years and at each year interval from 6 through 18 years). The sample was more representative than earlier normative samples of the general U.S. population. Based on the 1972 standardization, a revised manual for the third edition was published in 1973 (Terman & Merrill, 1973). Reported in this manual were test–retest reliability coefficients of over .90 and, as with the first two editions, moderate correlations with school grades and achievement test scores (.40 to .75) were given.

Fourth Edition of the Stanford–Binet

The fourth edition of the Stanford–Binet Intelligence Scale (SB–IV) was authored by R. L. Thorndike, E. Hagen, and J. Sattler and published by Riverside Publishing Company in 1986. This instrument was constructed with the needs of clinical, school, and other psychologists who use intelligence test information in mind. This most recent version of the Stanford–Binet maintains historical continuity with the older versions, but in terms of its theoretical and psychometric bases, content, and testing procedure, it represents a distinct departure from its predecessors. Like many modern tests, SB–IV was constructed by using sophisticated psychometric procedures, such as item-response theory (Rasch scaling) and ethnic-bias analysis. In addition, it was designed not only to assist in identifying mentally retarded and mentally gifted individuals, but also to provide diagnostic information concerning specific learning disabilities. With respect to sex and ethnic bias, items judged to be unfair or that showed atypical statistical differences between the sexes or ethnic groups were omitted.

Theoretical Model and Tests   A three-level hierarchical model forms the theoretical basis of SB–IV. The model consists of a general intelligence factor (g) at the first level, three broad factors (crystallized abilities, fluid-analytic abilities, and abstract-verbal reasoning) at the second level. The verbal and quantitative reasoning factors at the third level comprise the crystallized abilities factor at the second level, and the abstract-visual factor at the third level comprises the fluid-analytic abilities factor at the second level.

Like its predecessors, the fourth edition of the Stanford–Binet purports to measure intelligence from age 2 to adulthood. There are 15 tests: three to four tests in each of the three broader categories of Level 3 (Verbal Reasoning, Abstract/Visual Reasoning, Quantitative Reasoning), plus three Short-Term Memory tests. Each test is arranged in a series of levels consisting of two items each; almost all tests include sample items for familiarizing examinees with the nature of the specific test task.

Administration   Total testing time for the entire scale is approximately 75 minutes, varying with the age of the examinee and, hence, the number of tests taken. The adaptive or multistage nature of the scale calls for giving the Routing (Vocabulary) Test first to determine the entry level on the other tests. The entry level on the Routing Test is determined by the examinee's chronological age (CA) and the *basal level* is the highest level at which the examinee passes both items at two consecutive levels. Administration of the Routing Test continues until the examinee fails three or four items at two consecutive levels, the higher of which is the *critical level*. The entry level for the remaining 14 tests is determined from a table by a combination of the critical level on the Routing Test and the examinee's CA. Administration of each test begins at the entry level, continuing downward until the examinee passes both items at two consecutive levels and upward until he or she fails three or four items at two consecutive levels. The higher of these levels is the examinee's *ceiling age* for that test.

Scoring   The raw scores on each of the 15 tests consist of the number of items passed. Raw scores on each test are converted, within each age group, to standard age scores having a mean of 50 and a standard deviation of 8. Raw scores on the four areas (Verbal Reasoning, Abstract/Visual Reasoning, Quantitative Reasoning, Short-Term Memory), which are the sum of the raw scores on the three of four tests comprising that area, are converted to standard age scores having a mean of 100 and a standard deviation of 16.

9-74539

RECORD BOOKLET
Stanford-Binet Intelligence Scale: Fourth Edition

Name *John C.*

Sex *M*

Ethnicity NA H B (W/NH) O/AA PI Other _____

	YEAR	MONTH	DAY
Date of Testing	86	6	29
Birth Date **B**	72	1	18
Age	14	5	11

School *Hillview High School*

Grade *9th* **A**

Examiner *Robinson*

Father's Occupation: *Civil engineer*

Mother's Occupation: *Social worker*

FACTORS AFFECTING TEST PERFORMANCE
Overall Rating of Conditions **C**

Optimal	Good	(Average)	Detrimental	Seriously detrimental

D

	RAW SCORE	STANDARD AGE SCORE ✳
Verbal Reasoning		
1 Vocabulary	27	47
6 Comprehension	39	61
7 Absurdities *(Est. ceiling)*	31	57 (Est.)
14 Verbal Relations		
Sum of Subtest SAS's ③		165
Verbal Reasoning SAS		(111)
Abstract/Visual Reasoning		
5 Pattern Analysis	40	56
9 Copying		
11 Matrices	14	48
13 Paper Folding & Cutting		
Sum of Subtest SAS's ②		104
Abstract/Visual Reasoning SAS		(105)
Quantitative Reasoning		
3 Quantitative	19	39
12 Number Series	6	37
15 Equation Building		
Sum of Subtest SAS's ②		76
Quantitative Reasoning SAS		(73)
Short-Term Memory		
2 Bead Memory	28	51
4 Memory For Sentences	32	60
8 Memory For Digits *(Est. basal)*	12	47 (Est.)
10 Memory For Objects	9	55
Sum of Subtest SAS's ④		213
Short-Term Memory SAS		(108)
Sum of Area SAS's		397

COMPOSITE SCORE ✳

Test Composite . . . . (99)
  Partial Composite 109
  Partial Composite based on *VR, A/VR, STM*

	1	2	3	4	5	
Attention						
a) Absorbed by task				✓		Easily distracted
Reactions During Test Performance						
a) Normal activity level				✓		Abnormal activity level
b) Initiates activity			✓			Waits to be told
c) Quick to respond		✓				Urging needed
Emotional Independence						
a) Socially confident			✓			Insecure
b) Realistically self-confident				✓		Distrusts own ability
c) Comfortable in adult company			✓			Ill-at-ease
d) Assured				✓		Anxious
Problem-Solving Behavior						
a) Persistent				✓		Gives up easily
b) Reacts to failure realistically			✓			Reacts to failure unrealistically
c) Eager to continue				✓		Seeks to terminate
d) Challenged by hard tasks			✓			Prefers only easy tasks
Independence of Examiner Support						
a) Needs minimum of commendation				✓		Needs constant praise and encouragement
Expressive Language						
a) Excellent articulation			✓			Very poor articulation
Receptive Language						
a) Excellent sound discrimination			✓			Very poor sound discrimination

Was it difficult to establish rapport with this person?
  Easy ✓ . . . . Difficult

✳ Be sure that all Standard Age Scores (SAS's) are based on the tables in the *Guide* with the number 9-74502 on the cover.

The Riverside Publishing Company

Robert L. Thorndike
Elizabeth P. Hagen
Jerome M. Sattler

1986 The Riverside Publishing Company. All rights reserved

FIGURE 6–1 Front Cover of Record Booklet of the Stanford–Binet Intelligence Scale: Fourth Edition.
(Reproduced with permission of the Riverside Publishing Company from p. 7 of Stanford–Binet Intelligence Scale Examiner's Handbook: An Expanded Guide for Fourth Edition Users by E. A. Delaney and T. F. Hopkins. Copyright 1987. © The Riverside Publishing Company.)

Finally, an overall composite score consisting of the sum of the four area scores is converted to a standard age score scale having a mean of 100 and a standard deviation of 16. The range of the overall composite standard age scores is 36 to 164, which is equivalent to a z-score range of -4 to $+4$ (see Figure 6–1).

Standardization   The fourth edition of the Stanford–Binet was standardized on 5013 individuals between the ages of 2 years and 23 years, 11 months in 47 states and the District of Columbia. The standardization sample was 48 percent male and 52 percent female, 75 percent white, 14 percent black, 6 percent Hispanic, 3 percent Asian/Pacific Islander, and 2 percent other ethnic groups. Student examinees were also stratified according to their relative standing in their school class. Despite efforts to select a standardization sample that was truly representative of the U.S. population, the sample contained disproportionate numbers of individuals at the upper socioeconomic and educational levels. An attempt was made to correct for this problem in scoring the test, but it was not completely successful. Other problems are that the factors measured by the scale are not uniform across age levels, and the reliability information provided by the manual is insufficient. However, split-half and test–retest coefficients, computed on measures obtained over a time interval of 2 to 8 months, indicate that the reliabilities of the 15 tests, the four areas, and the composite are satisfactory.

Wechsler Tests

Although subtests at the adult level have been included on the Stanford–Binet since the 1937 revision, the test was not a very satisfactory measure of adult intelligence. Consequently, in 1939, David Wechsler, a psychologist at Bellevue Hospital in New York, designed an individual intelligence test specifically for adults. To this early version of the test (the Wechsler–Bellevue Scale Form I), Wechsler added a second form in 1947 (Wechsler–Bellevue Scale Form II). A complete revision and restandardization of Form I of the Wechsler–Bellevue was published in 1955 by The Psychological Corporation as the Wechsler Adult Intelligence Scale (WAIS). The WAIS itself was revised, restandardized, and republished in 1981 as the Wechsler Adult Intelligence Scale–Revised for assessing the intelligence of adults from 16 through 74 years.

Wechsler Adult Intelligence Scale–Revised (WAIS–R)   As described in Table 6-2, the six verbal (V) and five performance (P) subtests of the WAIS–R are Information (V), Picture Completion (P), Digit Span (V), Picture Arrangement (P), Vocabulary (V), Block Design (P), Arithmetic (V), Object Assembly (P), Comprehension (V), Digit Symbol (P), and Similarities (V). When administering the WAIS–R, verbal and performance subtests are alternated in the order listed above. Within each subtest, the items are arranged in order of increasing difficulty, and testing on a particular subtest is discontinued when the examinee fails a specified number of items in succession. It takes approximately 75 minutes to administer all 11 subtests.

An examinee's raw score on each WAIS–R subtest is converted to a standard score scale having a mean of 10 and a standard deviation of 3. Separate sums of the six scaled scores on the verbal subtests, the five scaled scores on the performance subtests, and the

TABLE 6–2   Descriptions of Subtests on the Wechsler Adult Intelligence Scale–Revised (WAIS–R)

Information. Thirty-three general information questions to be answered in a few words or numbers. Questions are arranged in easy-to-difficult order. Testing begins with item 5; items 1 to 4 are administered if examinee fails either item 5 or 6. Testing is discontinued when examinee fails seven items in a row. Responses are scored 0 or 1. Responses are affected by familial and cultural background.

Picture Completion. Twenty-seven pictures on cards, each having a part missing. Examinee is given 20 seconds per picture to indicate what is missing. Testing begins with item 1 and is discontinued when examinee fails seven consecutive items. Responses are scored 0 or 1. The test was designed to measure visual alertness, memory, and attention to details.

Digit Span. Seven series of digits to be recited forward and seven series to be recited backward. Test on "digits forward" starts with three digits read aloud (one digit per second) by examiner. Examinee is directed to repeat each series right after examiner has finished. Two trials are given on each series length (two different sets of digits). Testing on "digits forward" continues until the examinee fails both trials of a series or succeeds on nine digits forward. On "digits backward" the examinee is directed to say the digits backward after the examiner has finished saying them forward. Testing begins at two digits backward and continues until the examinee has failed both trials of a series or succeeded on eight digits backward. Score on each set of "digits forward" or "digits backward" is 0, 1, or 2; total score is the sum of part scores on "digits forward" and "digits backward." The test was designed to measure immediate rote memory, but scores are affected by attention span and comprehension.

Picture Arrangement. Ten sets of cards, each card containing a small picture. Examinee is directed to arrange the pictures in each set of cards into a sensible story. Time limits are 60 seconds on sets 1 to 4, 90 seconds on sets 5 to 8, and 120 seconds on sets 9 and 10. Testing is discontinued when the examinee fails five consecutive sets. Responses are scored 0, 1, or 2, depending on accuracy. The test measures ordering or sequencing ability, as well as social planning, humor, and ability to anticipate.

Vocabulary. Thirty-seven words to be defined, in order of ascending difficulty. Testing starts with item 1 for examinees having poor verbal ability, otherwise with item 4. Testing is discontinued when the examinee fails six words in a row. Responses to each word are scored 0, 1, or 2, depending on the degree of understanding of the word expressed. The test was designed to measure knowledge of words, a skill that is highly related to general mental ability.

Block Design. Ten red and white geometric designs are presented on cards; the examinee is instructed to duplicate each design with four or nine blocks. Two attempts are permitted on the first two designs, and one attempt on each succeeding design. Testing is discontinued when four designs in a row are failed. Base scoring is 0, 1, or 2 points on designs 1 and 2 and 0 or 2 points on designs 3 to 10, with bonus points being added for rapid, perfect performance. The test was designed to measure the ability to perceive and analyze a visual pattern into its component parts. In terms of its correlations with total scores on the Performance Scale and scores on the test as a whole, "Block Design" is considered to be one of the best performance tests.

TABLE 6–2   (continued)

Arithmetic. Fifteen arithmetic problems in order of increasing difficulty. Testing begins with item 3 and is discontinued after five consecutive failures; items 1 and 2 are given if items 3 and 4 are failed. Fifteen seconds are allowed on problems 1 to 4, 30 seconds on problems 5 to 10, 60 seconds on problems 11 to 14, and 120 seconds on problem 15. Responses are scored 0 or 1, in addition to bonus points for quick, perfect performance on certain problems. The test measures elementary knowledge of arithmetic, together with the ability to concentrate and reason quantitatively.

Object Assembly. Four cardboard picture puzzles presented to the examinee in a prearranged format, with directions to put the pieces together to make something. All four puzzles are presented, time limits being 120 seconds on puzzles 1 and 2 and 180 seconds on puzzles 3 and 4. The score for each puzzle is determined by the number of "cuts" correctly joined; bonus points are given for quick, perfect performance. The test was designed to measure thinking, work habits, attention, persistence, and the ability to visualize a final form from its parts.

Comprehension. Eighteen questions in order of ascending difficulty, requiring detailed answers. Questions are presented until examinee fails six consecutive items. Responses are scored 0, 1, or 2, depending on quality and degree of understanding expressed. The test measures practical knowledge, social judgment, and the ability to organize information.

Digit Symbol. Examinee is directed to fill in each of 93 boxes with the appropriate coded symbol for the number appearing above the box. Testing begins with a practice series, after which the examinee is given 90 seconds to fill in the 93 blank boxes with the correct symbols copied from a key listed above. The score range is 0 to 93 points. The test was designed to measure attentiveness and persistence in a simple perceptual–motor task.

Similarities. Fourteen items of the type "In what way are A and B alike?" Items are presented in order of ascending difficulty until examinee fails five in a row. Responses are scored 0, 1, or 2, depending on quality and degree of understanding expressed. This test is designed to measure logical or abstract thinking—the ability to categorize and generalize.

scaled scores on all 11 subtests are computed. The sums are then converted to three intelligence quotients (Verbal IQ, Performance IQ, Full Scale IQ) by referring to a special table in the manual. These are deviation IQs, expressed as numbers on a standard score scale having a mean of 100 and a standard deviation of 15 (see Figure 6–2).

Standardization   The WAIS–R was standardized on a carefully selected national sample of 1880 adults in nine age groups (16–17, 18–19, 20–24, 25–34, 35–44, 45–54, 55–64, 65–69, 70–74) within the range of 16 through 74 years. The sample in each age category was stratified by sex, geographical region, ethnicity (white versus nonwhite), education, and occupation. Other characteristics, such as urban versus rural residence, were controlled but did not serve as stratification variables; only "normal" adults were included in the sample. Standardization of the WAIS–R differed from that of the WAIS primarily in stratification of the sample by ethnic group and provision for more representative sampling of older adults.

WAIS-R RECORD FORM

WECHSLER ADULT INTELLIGENCE SCALE— REVISED

NAME _James L. Clarke_

ADDRESS _Agoura Hills, CA_

SEX _M_ AGE _24_ RACE _White_ MARITAL STATUS _Single_

OCCUPATION _Shoe store clerk_ EDUCATION _High school graduate_

PLACE OF TESTING _Pepperdine University-Malibu_ TESTED BY _Lewis R. Aiken_

TABLE OF SCALED SCORE EQUIVALENTS*

		RAW SCORE												
		VERBAL TESTS						PERFORMANCE TESTS						
Scaled Score	Information	Digit Span	Vocabulary	Arithmetic	Comprehension	Similarities	Picture Completion	Picture Arrangement	Block Design	Object Assembly	Digit Symbol	Scaled Score
19	—	28	70	—	32	—	—	—	51	—	93	19
18	29	27	69	—	31	28	—	—	—	41	91-92	18
17	—	26	68	19	—	—	20	20	50	—	89-90	17
16	28	25	66-67	—	30	27	—	—	49	40	84-88	16
15	27	24	65	18	29	26	—	19	47-48	39	79-83	15
14	26	22-23	63-64	17	27-28	25	19	—	44-46	38	75-78	14
13	25	20-21	60-62	16	26	24	—	18	42-43	37	70-74	13
12	23-24	18-19	55-59	15	25	23	18	17	38-41	35-36	66-69	12
11	22	17	52-54	13,14	23-24	22	17	15-16	35-37	34	62-65	11
10	19-21	15-16	47-51	12	21-22	20-21	16	14	31-34	32-33	57-61	10
9	17-18	14	43-46	11	19-20	18-19	15	13	27-30	30-31	53-56	9
8	15-16	12-13	37-42	10	17-18	16-17	14	11-12	23-26	28-29	48-52	8
7	13-14	11	29-36	8-9	14-16	14-15	13	8-10	20-22	24-27	44-47	7
6	9-12	9-10	20-28	6-7	11-13	11-13	11-12	5-7	14-19	21-23	37-43	6
5	6-8	8	14-19	5	8-10	7-10	8-10	3-4	8-13	16-20	30-36	5
4	5	7	11-13	4	6-7	5-6	5-7	2	3-7	13-15	23-29	4
3	4	6	9-10	3	4-5	2-4	3-4	—	2	9-12	16-22	3
2	3	3-5	6-8	1-2	2-3	1	2	1	1	6-8	8-15	2
1	0-2	0-2	0-5	0	0-1	0	0-1	0	0	0-5	0-7	1

*Clinicians who wish to draw a profile may do so by locating the subject's raw scores on the table above and drawing a line to connect them. See Chapter 4 in the Manual for a discussion of the significance of differences between scores on the tests.

	Year	Month	Day
Date Tested	1992	4	10
Date of Birth	1968	1	15
Age	24	2	25

SUMMARY

	Raw Score	Scaled Score	Age Scaled Score
VERBAL TESTS			
Information	20	10	(11)
Digit Span	12	8	(8)
Vocabulary	44	9	(10)
Arithmetic	13	11	(11)
Comprehension	15	7	(7)
Similarities	18	9	(9)
Verbal Score		54	
PERFORMANCE TESTS			
Picture Completion	13	7	(7)
Picture Arrangement	6	6	(6)
Block Design	27	9	(8)
Object Assembly	28	8	(7)
Digit Symbol	45	(7)	(7)
Performance Score		37	

	Sum of Scaled Scores	IQ
VERBAL	54	94
PERFORMANCE	37	80
FULL SCALE	91	86

(Ⓤ) THE PSYCHOLOGICAL CORPORATION
HARCOURT BRACE JOVANOVICH, PUBLISHERS

Copyright © 1981, 1955, 1947 by The Psychological Corporation. Standardization Edition Copyright © 1976 by The Psychological Corporation. No part of this form may be copied by any process without permission. All rights reserved.
Printed in U.S.A.

9-991829

FIGURE 6–2 WAIS–R Record Form.
(Reproduced by permission from the Wechsler Adult Intelligence Scale–Revised. Copyright © 1955, 1980 by The Psychological Corporation. All rights reserved.)

Diagnostic Significance of WAIS and WAIS-R Scores   In designing the WAIS, Wechsler planned to obtain more than just an estimate of the examinee's "aggregate or global capacity . . . to act purposefully, to think rationally, and to deal effectively with his environment." A significant difference between a person's verbal and performance IQs and the pattern of scores (scatter) on the 11 subtests was thought to be characteristic of certain types of mental disorders and therefore potentially useful in clinical diagnosis. Unfortunately, the results of research failed to confirm any of Wechsler's hypotheses concerning the diagnostic significance of subtest scatter.

One problem in attempting to analyze subtest scatter on the WAIS–R is the fact that scores on the subtests are not highly reliable and in some instances have substantial correlations with each other. Consequently, the difference between a person's scores on two given subtests must be very large before it can be viewed as significant or meaningful. Large differences between subtest scaled scores and between verbal and performance IQs are, however, of some use in the diagnosis of organic brain damage and psychopathology and in differentiating between intelligence and opportunity. A significantly lower verbal than performance IQ, for example, may be the result of limited linguistic experience or "cultural deprivation."

Wechsler Intelligence Scale for Children-Third Edition (WISC–III)   The Wechsler Intelligence Scale for Children (WISC), a downward extension of the Wechsler–Bellevue Scale Form I, was published in 1949. A revision of the WISC, the WISC–R, was published by The Psychological Corporation in 1974, and a second revision, the Wechsler Intelligence Scale for Children–Third Edition (WISC–III), was published in 1991. The WISC–III, designed for children from 6 through 16 years and 11 months, consists of the six Verbal subtests and the seven Performance subtests listed in Table 6–3. The 10 core subtests can be administered in 50 to 70 minutes, and the supplementary subtests in 10 to 15 minutes. As in the case of the WAIS–R, the Verbal and Performance subtests of the WISC–III are administered alternately. Verbal, Performance, and Full Scale IQs, based on the same standard score scale as that of the WAIS–R, are determined by summing the scaled score equivalents of raw scores on the five verbal and five performance tests that are administered. Additionally, WISC–III may be scored for four factors: Verbal Comprehension, Perceptual Organization, Freedom from Distractibility, and Processing Speed.

TABLE 6–3   Subtests on the WISC-III

Verbal subtests	*Performance subtests*
Information	Picture Completion
Similarities	Coding
Arithmetic	Picture Arrangement
Vocabulary	Block Design
Comprehension	Object Assembly
Digit Span (supplementary)	Symbol Search (supplementary)
	Mazes (supplementary)

The WISC–III was standardized on representative samples of 100 U.S. boys and 100 U.S. girls in each of 11 age groups between 6 and 16 years. The samples were also stratified by geographical region, parental educational level, and race. Other samples of children were tested with both the WISC–III and either the WAIS–R or the WPPSI–R, depending on their ages. Test–retest reliabilities of the WISC–III, obtained by readministering the scale after 4 to 8 weeks, are satisfactory. In addition, a number of validation studies have been conducted with various clinical groups of children.

Wechsler Preschool and Primary Scale of Intelligence–Revised (WPPSI–R)

The third member of the Weschler family of tests, the Wechsler Preschool and Primary Scale of Intelligence, was first published in 1967 and a revision, the WPPSI–R, in 1989. The six verbal and six performance subtests on the WPPSI–R, in order of administration, are Object Assembly (P), Information (V), Geometric Design (P), Comprehension (V), Block Design (P), Arithmetic (V), Mazes (P), Vocabulary (V), Picture Completion (P), Similarities (V), Animal Pegs (P), and Sentences (V). The last two are supplementary subtests. Designed for children aged 3 to 7 years, the WPPSI–R was standardized during 1987–1989 on a national sample of U.S. children from 3 to 7 years old. Other stratification variables employed to make the sample more representative of the U.S. population of 3- to 7-year-olds were sex, ethnicity, and parents' educational and occupational levels. Like

FIGURE 6–3 Photograph of the Wechsler Intelligence Scale for Children, Third Edition. *(Used by permission of Publisher, The Psychological Corporation.)*

the WAIS–R and the WISC–III, the WPPSI–R yields separate Verbal, Performance and Full-Scale IQs based on a standard score scale having a mean of 100 and a standard deviation of 15.

SOMPA   The WISC–R or WPPSI is administered as part of the System of Multicultural Pluralistic Assessment (SOMPA) (from The Psychological Corporation). SOMPA is a two-component approach for assessing the cognitive abilities, sensorimotor abilities, and adaptive behavior of children aged 5 to 11 years. The first component of SOMPA, the Parent Interview, consists of three measures (Adaptive Behavior Inventory for Children, Sociocultural Scales, Health History Inventory) and can be conducted in either English or Spanish. The second component of SOMPA, the Student Assessment Materials, includes Physical Dexterity Tasks, measures of Weight by Height, Visual Acuity, and Auditory Acuity, as well as the Bender Visual Motor Gestalt Test and either the WISC–R or WPPSI. Collectively, the two components of SOMPA represent three models of psychological assessment: a medical model, a social system model, and a pluralistic model. On the basis of information obtained from the various assessments, a child's estimated learning potential (ELP), which takes family background, socioeconomic status, and other cultural factors into account, is determined. Separate norms are available for Anglo, Black, and Hispanic children aged 5 to 11 years.[1] The SOMPA approach, however, is not used as much as it once was, and it may soon be mainly of historical interest.

Other Wide-range Individual Intelligence Tests

Although they are the most popular individual tests of intelligence in the United States, the Stanford–Binet and Wechsler series of tests are by no means the only wide-range batteries for assessing general mental ability. Nor are they the most popular tests of mental ability in other countries. Especially noteworthy in the United Kingdom are the British Ability Scales (BAS), which have been revised and restandardized in the United States as the Differential Ability Scales (DAS) (from The Psychological Corporation). The basic purpose of the DAS, like that of the BAS, is to provide ability profiles for analyzing and diagnosing children's learning difficulties, to assess changes in abilities over time, and to identify, select, and classify children (ages 2½ to 17 years) having learning disabilities. The DAS consists of 19 tests: Similarities, Matrices, Sequential and Quantitative Reasoning, Picture Similarities, Pattern Construction, Block Building, Copying, Matching Letterlike Forms, Recall of Digits, Recall of Designs, Recognition of Pictures, Recall of Objects, Naming Vocabulary, Word Definitions, Verbal Comprehension, Word Reading, Spelling, Basic Number Skills, and Speed of Information Processing. These tests are grouped into four ability areas: verbal, nonverbal, spatial, and diagnostic. Eight to twelve subtests, with a total time of 45 to 65 minutes, are administered at a particular age level. In addition, three achievement subtests (Word Reading, Spelling, and Basic Number Skills), requiring

---

[1]The ELP is an example of "race-norming," which has recently come under fire (see Chapter 12).

a total of 15 to 20 minutes testing time, are included in the battery. Raw scores on each test are converted to ability scores independent of the examinee's age. The ability scores can then be converted to T scores and percentile ranks based on the scores obtained by a sample of 3475 U.S. children matched against 1988 census data. Scores on the various tests are also used to compute Verbal Ability, Nonverbal Reasoning Ability, and General Conceptual Ability scores based on a mean of 100 and a standard deviation of 15.

Another intelligence test battery that has recently been revised is the Detroit Test of Learning Aptitude. The primary edition of this battery (DTLA–P–2), designed for children aged 3 to 9 years, takes 15 to 20 minutes to administer. The subtests include Articulation, Conceptual Matching, Design Reproduction, Digit Sequences, Draw-a-Person, Letter Sequences, Motor Directions, Object Sequences, Oral Directions, Picture Fragments, Picture Identification, Sentence Imitation, and Symbolic Relations. The third edition of the Detroit Tests of Learning Aptitude (DTLA–3), designed for children aged 6 to 17, takes 50 to 90 minutes to administer. The DTLA–3 subtests include Word Opposites, Design Sequences, Sentence Imitation, Revised Letters, Story Construction, Design Reproduction, Basic Information, Symbolic Relations, Word Sequences, Story Sequences, and Picture Fragments. Standard scores, percentile ranks, age equivalents, and various composite scores may be computed on both the DTLA–P–2 and the DTLA–3. Although these two test batteries represent improvements over the first edition of the DTLA, problems with the reliabilities of some of the subtests and the representativeness of the standardization sample remain.

Individual Pictorial Tests

Less ambitious in concept than the Stanford–Binet and Wechsler, but useful when testing time is limited and/or the examinee's reading skills are poor, are intelligence tests that employ only pictures as test materials. Examples are the Peabody Picture Vocabulary Test and the Columbia Mental Maturity Scale.

Peabody Picture Vocabulary Test–Revised (PPVT–R) The test materials on the PPVT–R (from American Guidance Service) are 175 pictorial plates, arranged in ascending order of difficulty by age level and containing four pictures each. The examiner presents a plate, says a word, and instructs the examinee to point to the picture on the plate that best illustrates the meaning of the word. The test, which takes 10 to 20 minutes to administer and score, can be used with a wide age range of examinees (2½ years to adulthood). Since no verbal response is required, the PPVT–R can be given to persons with speech impairments, cerebral palsy, or reading problems and to mentally retarded, withdrawn, or distractible children. Although the original standardization of the test was quite limited, Forms L and M of the revised edition were standardized in 1979 on a national sample of 4200 people from 2½ to 18 years old and 800 adults ranging in age from 19 through 40 years. A study designed to equate PPVT–R scores with those of the original PPVT was conducted on 1849 children aged 3 through 18 years. The test norms are expressed as standard scores, percentile ranks, stanines, and age equivalents.

Columbia Mental Maturity Scale, 3rd Edition (CMMS)   On this test, which is distributed by The Psychological Corporation, the child selects the drawing that does not belong in each series of pictorial and figure drawings. The 92 items on the CMMS are arranged in eight overlapping levels, but only 51 to 65 items are administered to a specific examinee. The CMMS takes 10 to 20 minutes to administer and is appropriate for children aged $3\frac{1}{2}$ to 10 years old. It is particularly suitable for children who are entering nursery school or kindergarten and/or have impaired physical or mental functioning. The CMMS was standardized in the early 1970s on 2600 children, a national quota sample stratified by sex, race, parents' occupation, and geographical residence. Scores are expressed as age deviations, corresponding percentile ranks and stanines, and maturity indexes.

Nonverbal Tests for the Handicapped

Psychometric instruments such as the PPVT–R and the CMMS, which require pointing, manipulating objects, or some other nonverbal response, rather than speaking or writing, are referred to as *nonverbal tests.* Performance on certain tasks on these tests may be facilitated by verbal language, but its use is minimized.

The fact that the Wechsler scales contain separate verbal and performance measures makes these tests more suitable than older versions of the Stanford–Binet for examining persons with physical language and cultural disabilities. The Wechsler performance subtests tend to be more accurate measures of mental ability in hearing-handicapped and culturally different children, whereas the verbal subtests are more valid measures for the blind and partially sighted. A special version of the WISC–R, The Adaptation of WISC–R Performance Scale for Deaf Children (from Office of Demographic Studies, Gallaudet College, Washington, DC 20002), has been designed for deaf children. In testing blind persons, a series of specially designed performance tests known as the Haptic Intelligence Scale for Adult Blind (from Psychological Research, Box 14, Technology Center, Chicago, IL 60616) is sometimes used in conjunction with the WAIS–Verbal Scale.

Adaptations of the Stanford–Binet and other intelligence tests have been used to assess the intelligence of visually impaired persons. A good example is the Perkins–Binet Tests of Intelligence for the Blind (from Perkins School for the Blind, Watertown, MA 02172), which was adapted from the Stanford–Binet Intelligence Scale. The Perkins–Binet, a well-standardized instrument consisting of both verbal and performance items, is available in two forms for children aged 3 to 18 years. Other intelligence tests for the blind include the Blind Learning Aptitude Test and the Haptic Intelligence Scale.

Single-task Tests   One of the oldest nonverbal tests, the Seguin Form Board, was introduced in 1866. It was not until the early part of the twentieth century, however, that Knox, Porteus, and other psychologists made serious efforts to standardize such tests. In addition to many types of form boards, other nonverbal tasks were investigated and standardized. These included puzzles of various kinds, sequential tapping of cubes, matching problems, block designs, and mazes.

Mazes have been employed extensively in the psychological laboratory and the clinic and have been included on a number of standardized tests. The Porteus Mazes, viewed by its designer as a measure of foresight and planning ability, was introduced in 1914. This test, which is distributed by The Psychological Corporation, consists of a series of mazes arranged in order of increasing difficulty. On each maze the examinee is directed to draw the shortest path between the start and finish points without lifting the pencil or entering blind alleys. The Porteus is particularly suitable as a brief test (25 minutes) for the verbally handicapped and has been employed in a number of anthropological studies. It is also reported to be sensitive to brain damage, but, as is true of scores on intelligence tests in general, Porteus scores are affected by education and experience.

Another nonverbal performance task for testing the handicapped consists of block designs such as those on the Wechsler scales and the Differential Ability Scales. One of the earliest of these tests was the Kohs Block Design. The materials on the Kohs are 16 colored cubes and 17 cards with colored designs to be duplicated by the examinee. The Kohs Block Design was especially appropriate for language- and hearing-handicapped children, but it is seldom administered anymore.

Performance Test Batteries   The first battery of standardized performance tests to be distributed commercially was the Pintner–Paterson Scale of Performance Tests (1917). Equally well known is the Arthur Point Scale of Performance Tests, published initially by Grace Arthur in 1925. Two performance test batteries used rather extensively with the speech and hearing handicapped are the Leiter International Performance Scale and the Hiskey–Nebraska Tests of Learning Aptitude (from Marshall S. Hiskey, 5640 Baldwin, Lincoln, NE 68507).

A performance scale that can be administered entirely without using verbal language is the Leiter International Performance Scale (from Stoelting Company). This wide-range test (age 2 to adulthood) consists of 54 blocks arranged in an age scale format. The examinee must select the blocks bearing the proper symbols or pictures and insert them into the appropriate recesses of a frame. The Leiter was developed on various ethnic Hawaiian groups and also employed in studies of native Africans. It is viewed as a measure of intelligence in people of foreign or non-Western cultural background, as well as in illiterates and those having language handicaps with a physical basis. A shorter version of the test, the Arthur Adaptation of the Leiter, was designed for children from 2 to 12 years of age.

Developmental Scales for Infants and Young Children

Testing infants (0 to $1\frac{1}{2}$ years) and preschoolers ($1\frac{1}{2}$ to 5 years) can be difficult because of their short attention span and greater susceptibility to fatigue. Young children may also lack motivation to pursue the test tasks, which frequently assess characteristics that are unstable at any early age. For these reasons, the reliabilities and validities of tests administered at the preschool level tend to be lower than those of tests designed for school-age children. Infant tests in particular are not very valid predictors of later intellectual development. They have very low correlations with scores on intelligence tests administered to the same children in later years (Lewis & McGurk, 1972).

One reason for the low correlations between scores on infant intelligence tests and scores on tests such as the Stanford–Binet administered at a later age is the difference in the types of tasks on the two kinds of tests. Infant tests are primarily measures of sensorimotor development, whereas Binet-type tests are heavily loaded with verbal material. Nevertheless, infant tests are frequently useful in identifying mental retardation and organic brain damage.

Stimulated to some degree by research on child development and education, in the past three decades there has been an upsurge of activity directed toward constructing tests to measure the cognitive abilities of preschoolers. Furthermore, television programs such as "Sesame Street" and "The Electric Company" have made efforts to familiarize young children with tests and to develop their test-taking skills. The success of these programs is revealed by the finding that time spent viewing them is directly related to improvements in test-taking skills.

Older Developmental Scales   Research begun by Arnold Gesell at the Yale Clinic of Child Development in the 1920s led to an extensive series of investigations of infancy and early childhood that continued for 40 years. A guiding assumption of these studies was that human development follows an orderly, sequential pattern of maturation. Normative data on the motor development, language development, adaptive behavior, and personal–social development of children from birth to age 6 were collected. Detailed information on each child was obtained by various methods: home record, medical history, daily record, anthropometric measurements, material observations, reports of the child's behavior at the clinic, normative examination, and developmental ratings. The following excerpt is characteristic of the normative behavioral descriptions provided by Gesell and his co-workers (Gesell & Amatruda, 1941, page 41):

The baby can reach with his eyes before he can reach with his hand; at 28 weeks a baby sees a cube; he grasps it, senses surface and edge as he clutches it, brings it to his mouth, where he feels its qualities anew, withdraws it, looks at it on withdrawal, rotates it while he looks, looks while he rotates it, restores it to his mouth, withdraws it again for inspection, restores it again for mouthing, transfers it to the other hand, bangs it, contacts it with the free hand, transfers, mouths it again, drops it, resecures it, mouths it yet again, repeating the cycle with variations—all in the time it takes to read this sentence.

Scores on the Gesell Developmental Schedules, determined from the presence or absence of specific behaviors characteristic of children at certain ages, were summarized in terms of a developmental age (DA). As with the ratio IQ, a child's DA could be further converted to a developmental quotient (DQ) by the formula $DQ = 100(DA/CA)$. However, Gesell did not in any way consider the DQ as equivalent to an IQ.

The Gesell Developmental Schedules were probably used more by pediatricians than by psychologists from the 1920s through the 1940s. Psychologists, particularly those with a strong psychometric or statistical orientation, criticized the Gesell Schedules as being too subjective and poorly standardized. However, a later version of the scales provided more objective observational procedures. The age range on the revised scales is from 4 weeks to 5 years, and five behavioral categories are covered: adaptive (alertness, intelligence, constructive exploration), gross motor (balance, sitting, locomotion, postural reactions), fine motor (manual dexterity), language (facial expression, gestures, vocalizations), and personal–social (feeding, playing, toilet training). Knobloch and Pasamanick (1974) provided detailed instructions for making and interpreting observations on the revised Gesell Developmental Schedules. Norms for preschoolers (2½ to 6 years) by half-year intervals, but not for infants, have also been published (Ames et al., 1979).

Other noteworthy older tests of infant and preschool development are the Merrill–Palmer Scale (from Stoelting Company) and the Cattell Infant Intelligence Scale (from The Psychological Corporation). The Merrill–Palmer Scale was designed for children from 1½ through 6 years of age, whereas the Cattell, which is a downward extension of the Stanford–Binet, has an age range from 3 months to 2½ years.

Neonatal Behavioral Assessment Scale (NBAS)   Reaching lower in age than either the Merrill–Palmer or the Cattell Scale is the Neonatal Behavioral Assessment Scale (Brazelton, 1973), which has an age range from 3 days to 4 weeks. This popular infant intelligence scale is scored on 26 behavioral items and 20 elicited responses, including measures of neurological, behavioral, and social functioning. Illustrative items are hand–mouth coordination, habituation to sensory stimuli, startle responses, reflexes, stress responses, motor maturity, and cuddliness. Few normative or validity data on the scale have been provided, and the published reliability coefficients are fairly low (Sameroff, 1978).

Bayley Scales of Infant Development   The Bayley Scales (from The Psychological Corporation) are based on the results of an extensive research program (the Berkeley Growth Study) directed by Nancy Bayley. A refinement and extension of early infant tests such as the California First-Year Mental Scale, the Bayley Scales were designed for infants and toddlers (2 to 30 months) and take about 45 minutes to administer. The stratified sample (by age, sex, race, urban versus rural residence, and education of household head) of 1262 children on which the scales were standardized is more representative than those of other infant intelligence tests. Performance on the Bayley Scales is expressed in standard score form as a mental development index and a psychomotor development index having a mean of 100 and a standard deviation of 16.

McCarthy Scales of Children's Abilities   The McCarthy Scales (from The Psychological Corporation), which pick up where the Bayley Scales leave off, were designed for children aged 2½ through 8½ years. These scales yield six measures of intellectual and motor development: verbal, perceptual–performance, quantitative, general cognitive, memory, and motor. The McCarthy Scales were standardized on stratified (by race, region, socioeconomic status, and urban–rural residence) samples of approximately 100 children in each of 10 age groups within the designated age range. Data on the validity of these scales, which were published only after Dorothea McCarthy's death, remain rather meager.

FIGURE 6–4   Photograph of the Bayley Scales of Infant Development Testing Kit. *(Reproduced by permission from Bayley Scales of Infant Development. Copyright © 1969 by The Psychological Corporation. All rights reserved.)*

Kaufman Assessment Battery for Children (K–ABC)   This test battery (from American Guidance Service) was designed by A. S. and N. L. Kaufman primarily to assess the abilities of children aged 2½ through 12½ years to solve problems requiring simultaneous and sequential mental processing. The K–ABC also includes an Achievement Scale to measure acquired skills in reading and arithmetic. Based on extensive research in neuropsychology and cognitive psychology, the K–ABC is said to be especially appropriate for preschool, minority, and exceptional children. As shown in the Individual Test Record in Figure 6–5, scores are obtained in four global areas: Sequential Processing, Simultaneous Processing, Mental Processing Composite (Sequential plus Simultaneous), and Achievement. Thirteen out of a total 16 gamelike subtests comprising the battery are administered to a given child. Testing time is 30 to 50 minutes for preschoolers and 50 to 80 minutes for older children.

The standardization sample for the K–ABC, stratified for race (white, black, Hispanic, Asian, Native-American) and including a representative group of exceptional children, was based on statistics reported in the 1980 U.S. Census. Separate percentile norms were determined by race and by socioeconomic level for white and black children. Split-half reliability coefficients for the four global scales are in the high .80's and .90's, and information on the construct, concurrent, and predictive validities of the K–ABC is presented in the manual.

K·ABC Kaufman Assessment Battery for Children

by Alan S. Kaufman and Nadeen L. Kaufman

INDIVIDUAL TEST RECORD

Name Mary B. Sex F

Parents' names Rita and James

Home address 807 S. Lincoln

Home phone 782-4602

Grade 4 School Central Elementary

Examiner Norma Ehrhardt

SOCIOCULTURAL INFORMATION (if pertinent)

Race black

Socioeconomic background Mother finished 3rd grade, housewife; father finished 6th grade, construction worker

	YEAR	MONTH	DAY
Test date	~~83~~ 82	~~5~~ 17	15
Birth date	72	8	11
Chronological age	10	9	4

Mental Processing Subtests X = 10; SD = 3	Scaled Score Sequential	Scaled Score Simultaneous	Scaled Score Nonverbal	Nat'l %ile rank Table 4	S or W Table 11	age eq. Other data
1. Magic Window						
2. Face Recognition						
3. Hand Movements	10			50		11-9
4. Gestalt Closure		14		91	S	above 12-6
5. Number Recall	11			63		above 12-6
6. Triangles		8		25		8-0
7. Word Order	6			9	W	6-6
8. Matrix Analogies		9		37		9-9
9. Spatial Memory		7		16		8-3
10. Photo Series		9		37		9-9
Sum of subtest scores	27	47				

Transfer sums to Global Scales. *Sum of subtest scores column*

Achievement Subtests X = 100; SD = 15	Standard score ± band of error 90 % confidence	Nat'l %ile rank Table 4	Socio-cultural %ile rank Table 5	S or W Table 11	age eq. Other data	grade eq.
11. Expressive Vocabulary	±					
12. Faces & Places	87 ± 8	19	35		8-9	
13. Arithmetic	92 ± 8	30	70		9-6	
14. Riddles	99 ± 9	47	90	S	10-6	
15. Reading/Decoding	73 ± 8	4	10	W	7-6	2.4
16. Reading/Understanding	67 ± 8	1	5	W	7-3	1.9
Sum of subtest scores	418					

Transfer sum to Global Scales. *Sum of subtest scores column*

Global Scales X = 100; SD = 15	Sum of subtest scores	Standard score ± band of error 90 % confidence Table 2	Nat'l %ile rank Table 4	Socio-cultural %ile rank Table 5	age eq. Other data
Sequential Processing	27	93 ± 8	32	50	11-9
Simultaneous Processing	47	95 ± 6	37	80	9-9
Mental Processing Composite	74	93 ± 6	32	70	9-9
Achievement	418	81 ± 4	10	30	8-9
Nonverbal					

Global Scale Comparisons

	Indicate >, < or ≈		Circle the significance level		
Sequential	≈	Simultaneous (Table 10)	(NS)	.05	.01
Sequential	≈	Achievement (Table 10)	(NS)	.05	.01
Simultaneous	>	Achievement (Table 10)	NS	.05	(.01)
MPC	>	Achievement (Table 10)	NS	.05	(.01)

AGS®

FIGURE 6–5 Individual Test Record of Kaufman Assessment Battery for Children. *(Reproduced by permission of American Guidance Service.)*

GROUP-ADMINISTERED TESTS

During the early part of this century, Lewis Terman regularly taught a course on the Stanford–Binet Intelligence Scale at Stanford University. It was in a section of the course that a student of his, Arthur Otis, reportedly conceived the idea of adapting selected

Stanford–Binet tasks to paper-and-pencil format. Shortly thereafter, many of Otis's adapted tasks and others were combined as the first group intelligence test, the Army Alpha. The Army Alpha and the companion nonlanguage test for non-English speakers and illiterates, the Army Beta, were administered to nearly 2 million U.S. Army recruits during and after World War I for purposes of military selection and classification. The Army Alpha, which consisted of items involving analogies, arithmetic problems, number series completions, synonyms and antonyms, cube analysis, digit symbols, information, and practical judgment, laid the groundwork for later group tests of intelligence and academic aptitude. After World War I, Otis and other psychologists published their own group tests of intelligence, and by the 1930s many such instruments had appeared.

A typical group intelligence test consists of a series of multiple-choice questions arranged in a spiral-omnibus format, or as a series of separately timed subtests. In the *spiral-omnibus format,* several types of items comprising the test are mixed together and arranged in order of increasing difficulty; items with the same degree of difficulty are grouped together. Examples of tests arranged in this fashion are the Otis–Lennon Mental Ability Tests and the Henmon–Nelson Tests of Mental Ability. In contrast to tests having a spiral-omnibus format are those composed of a series of separately timed subtests, such as the Test of Cognitive Skills and the Cognitive Abilities Test.

Multilevel Group Intelligence Tests

The rationale underlying the construction of a multilevel intelligence test is to provide a series of tasks for comparing the intellectual growth of children over several years. The Stanford–Binet and Wechsler instruments are individually administered, multilevel intelligence tests. More extensively used than these are group tests such as the Otis–Lennon Mental Ability Tests, the Test of Cognitive Skills, and the Cognitive Abilities Tests.

Otis Tests The Otis–Lennon Mental Ability Tests (from The Psychological Corporation) are revisions of the earlier tests in the Otis series: the Otis Self-Administering Tests of Mental Ability and the Otis Quick-Scoring Mental Ability Tests. Like their predecessors, the Otis–Lennon tests are composed of a variety of items to measure general mental ability from the last half of kindergarten (Primary I) through grades 10 to 12 (Advanced). Testing time varies from 30 to 45 minutes, depending on which of the six levels is administered. The norms, which are based on a national sample of 200,000 pupils in all 50 states, are expressed as mental ages, deviation IQs, and percentile ranks and stanines by age and grade.

The most recent entry in the Otis series is the Otis–Lennon School Ability Test (OLSAT), also published by The Psychological Corporation. The sixth edition of OLSAT has seven grade levels, ranging from kindergarten through grade 12. Testing time varies by level to a maximum of 75 minutes. Separate verbal and nonverbal scores, in addition to a total score, are obtained.

Test of Cognitive Skills A successor to the California Short Form Test of Mental Maturity and the Short Form Test of Academic Aptitude, the Test of Cognitive Skills (from CTB/Macmillan/McGraw-Hill) is composed of four subtests (Sequences, Analogies,

OLSAT

Otis-Lennon School Ability Test, Sixth Edition

						INDIVIDUAL REPORT FOR BRIAN ELLIOTT AGE 10 YRS 2 MOS

TEACHER: JOHN WILLIAMS

SCHOOL: LAKESIDE ELEMENTARY   GRADE: 4   NORMS: NATIONAL   GRADE 4 SPRING

DISTRICT: NEWTOWN   TEST DATE: 4/89   LEVEL: E   FORM: 1

AGE BASED SCORES	NUMBER OF ITEMS	RAW SCORE	SAI	PR-S (A)	NCE
Total	72	53	116	84-7	70.9
Verbal	36	27	117	85-7	71.8
Nonverbal	36	26	115	82-7	69.3

NATIONAL AGE PERCENTILE BANDS

1 10 20 30 40 50 60 70 80 90 99

(C)

GRADE BASED SCORES	SCALED SCORE	NAT'L PR-S (B)	NAT'L NCE	LOCAL PR-S	LOCAL NCE
Total	290	82-7	69.3	78-7	66.3
Verbal	295	83-7	70.1	81-7	68.5
Nonverbal	285	80-7	67.7	76-7	64.9

NATIONAL GRADE PERCENTILE BANDS

1 10 20 30 40 50 60 70 80 90 99

CLUSTERS	RAW SCORE/ NUMBER OF ITEMS	BELOW AVERAGE	AVERAGE	ABOVE AVERAGE
VERBAL	27/36			✓
Verbal Comprehension	10/16		✓	
Verbal Reasoning	17/20			✓
NONVERBAL	26/36 (D)			✓
Figural Reasoning	12/18		✓	
Quantitative Reasoning	14/18			✓
TOTAL	53/72			✓

Recently this student took the Otis-Lennon School Ability Test (OLSAT). OLSAT measures those reasoning skills that are related to school learning ability. The following is an interpretation of the student's performance on OLSAT.

The student's Total OLSAT score is above average, both in comparison with students of the same age and in comparison with students in the same grade. The verbal and nonverbal part scores are in the above average range.

(E)

The cluster analysis presents performance indicators for this student on each of the clusters in OLSAT. These indicators, which are expressed as above average, average, or below average, describe the student's performance relative to that of other students in the same grade.

Verbal Comprehension refers to the understanding of the structure of language, of relationships among words, and of subtle differences among similar words. Verbal Reasoning refers to the ability to use language for such reasoning tasks as inference, application, and classification. Figural Reasoning involves geometric shapes rather than words. This skill is independent of language. Quantitative Reasoning, which is also independent of language, refers to the ability to reason with numbers and mathematical concepts.

It should be kept in mind that OLSAT scores give only one piece of information about a student. Other factors such as achievement and interests should be taken into account.

Ⓤ THE PSYCHOLOGICAL CORPORATION®
HARCOURT BRACE JOVANOVICH, INC.

FIGURE 6–6 Sample Items from the Otis–Lennon School Ability Test, 5th ed.
(Copyright © 1982 by Harcourt Brace Jovanovich, Inc. All rights reserved.)

Memory, and Verbal Reasoning) at five grade levels (2–3, 3–5, 5–7, 7–9, and 9–12). In addition to age or grade percentile, stanine, and standard scores norms for each subtest, the combined scores on all four subtests may be converted to a Cognitive Skills Index (CSI). Scores on the test may also be used in combination with scores on the Comprehensive Tests of Basic Skills (CTBS–U and V) or the California Achievement Tests (CAT C and D) to determine anticipated achievement at successive elementary and high school grade levels.

Cognitive Abilities Test (CogAT), Form 4   This edition of the Cognitive Abilities Test (from Riverside Publishing Company), a successor to the Lorge–Thorndike Intelligence Tests, consists of a Primary Battery for kindergarten to grade 3 and a Multilevel Edition (A to H) for grades 3 to 12. There are two levels of the Primary Battery: Primary I (K to 2) and Primary II (grades 2 to 3). The Primary Battery and the Multilevel Edition are composed of three parts (Verbal, Quantitative, and Nonverbal) (see Figure 6–7). Each of the three parts contains two subtests on the Primary Battery levels and three subtests on the Multilevel Edition. Working time for each subtest is 12 to 18 minutes on the Primary Battery and 8 to 12 minutes on the Multilevel Edition. Raw scores on the Verbal, Quantitative, and Nonverbal parts may be converted to various types of norms (standard age scores, national grade and age percentile ranks, grade and age stanines). The norms were obtained in the 1985 national standardization of the CogATt, the Iowa Tests of Basic Skills, and the Tests of Achievement and Proficiency.

Administration, Scoring, and Reporting of Group Tests

Group intelligence tests can be administered to small groups of children as young as 5 to 6 years or to adults of any age. When testing young children, the examiner must be particularly careful that the examinees understand the test directions, turn to the right page, start and stop on time, and so forth. In scoring group intelligence tests, raw scores, whether part or global, can be converted to percentile ranks, standard scores, or other numerical units. Because they are fairly short, tests such as the Otis–Lennon are reliable enough to yield only one score; longer tests are needed to provide reliable scores on several parts,

Scores on group tests, even more than on individual tests, should be interpreted cautiously and against a background of other information (school grades and interview–observational data) about the examinee. Report 6–1 illustrates how the findings from a group intelligence rest may be reported and interpreted, along with other relevant information about the examinee. Interpretive profiles of scores can also be prepared by a test-scoring service. Examinees with very low scores should be followed up with additional testing, preferably individual, before diagnostic or placement decisions are made.

Academic Ability and Admissions Tests

Many group intelligence tests have been designed specifically to measure children's aptitudes for scholastic work and are therefore referred to as *academic ability tests.* Some

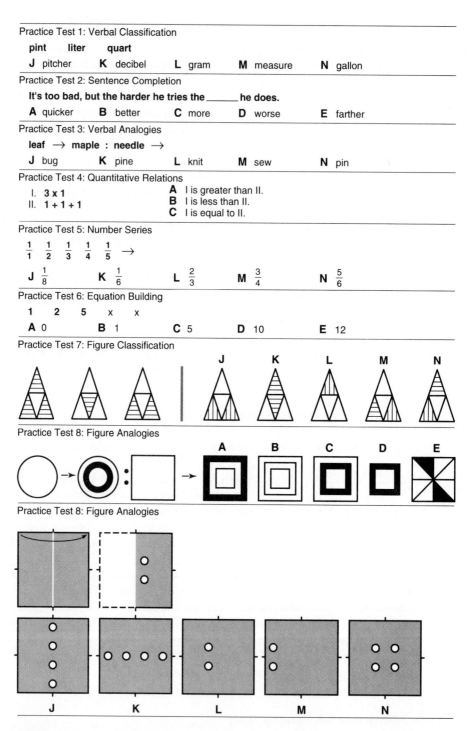

Practice Test 1: Verbal Classification

pint   liter   quart

J pitcher   **K** decibel   **L** gram   **M** measure   **N** gallon

Practice Test 2: Sentence Completion

It's too bad, but the harder he tries the _____ he does.

A quicker   **B** better   **C** more   **D** worse   **E** farther

Practice Test 3: Verbal Analogies

leaf → maple : needle →

J bug   **K** pine   **L** knit   **M** sew   **N** pin

Practice Test 4: Quantitative Relations

I. **3 x 1**
II. **1 + 1 + 1**

A I is greater than II.
B I is less than II.
C I is equal to II.

Practice Test 5: Number Series

$\frac{1}{1}$ $\frac{1}{2}$ $\frac{1}{3}$ $\frac{1}{4}$ $\frac{1}{5}$ →

J $\frac{1}{8}$ **K** $\frac{1}{6}$ **L** $\frac{2}{3}$ **M** $\frac{3}{4}$ **N** $\frac{5}{6}$

Practice Test 6: Equation Building

1   2   5   x   x

A 0   **B** 1   **C** 5   **D** 10   **E** 12

Practice Test 7: Figure Classification

Practice Test 8: Figure Analogies

Practice Test 8: Figure Analogies

FIGURE 6–7   Sample Items from the Practice Test for Levels A–H of the Cognitive Abilities Test.
(Reproduced by permission of Riverside Publishing Company.)

REPORT 6–1   Report of Group Intelligence Test Results

Name of Examinee: Joan R. Blake   Sex: Female
Birth Date: March 11, 1970   Age: 21 years, 11 months
Address: 507 Larkin Street, Orange, CA   Education: College senior
                                         Date of Test: Feb. 14, 1991
Tests Administered: Otis–Lennon School Ability Test, Advanced Form R

Observations and Interview Findings

Joan Blake, a young woman of approximately average height and weight (5'5", 120 pounds), volunteered to take the intelligence test because of a personal interest in her mental abilities and as a favor to the examiner. The test was administered as an assignment in Psychology 429 (Psychological Assessment) at Sentry College during the spring semester of 1991.

At the time of the examination, Joan was in her final semester as an accounting major at Sentry College, having an overall reported grade-point average of 3.2. Joan indicated that she would like to attend graduate school in business eventually to work toward an M.B.A. degree, but that immediately after graduation she planned to be employed full time at an accounting firm in the Los Angeles area.

Joan's father is a college graduate, and her mother had two years of college. Both the father and mother work in the family business, a tax-assistance firm. Joan has reportedly made good grades (B's and A's) throughout her school career but indicated that "I'm no scholar!" She seems to be very practically minded in her interests, as indicated not only by her major but also by her plans and other statements made to the examiner.

Joan showed moderate interest in the test questions and appeared relaxed but involved during the entire testing period. She worked attentively and uninterruptedly during the enture 40 minutes. The testing conditions were good; no disturbances occurred.

Test Results and Interpretations

Joan completed all the test questions during the allotted time (40 minutes), with the following results on the Otis–Lennon:

Raw score = 64
School ability index = 116
Percentile rank (18+ years group) = 84
Stanine (18+ years group) = 7

These scores are approximately average for college seniors, indicating an overall intellectual ability in the "High Average" range for the general population. A brief analysis of the 16 items that she answered incorrectly indicated that Joan has somewhat greater difficulty with nonverbal reasoning than with verbal reasoning. However, there is no significant pattern in the errors made; they appear fairly random.

Conclusions and Recommendations

In a posttest interview, Joan indicated that she had done her best on the test and did not have to hurry to finish on time. In actuality, she completed the test in 35 minutes and spent the last 5 minutes rechecking her answers. Joan indicated that the School Ability Index, which was reported to her by the examiner, was within five pounts of an IQ score that she remembers

REPORT 6–1   *(continued)*

having made on an intelligence test taken in high school. She could not recall the name of the test.

Taking into account the conditions of testing, the examinee's observed behavior, and her statements after the test, the results are considered valid at this time. Joan's career plans and aspirations appear appropriate for her intellectual ability, although she will probably have to work very hard to obtain an M.B.A. from an accredited institution.

Louise J. Brown

Louise J. Brown
Senior Psychology Major
Sentry College

group intelligence tests have a broader focus than this, but even they are similar in content to academic aptitude measures; they are often heavily loaded with verbal, numerical, and other school-type items.

A number of different tests have been used over the years for college admissions purposes, including the American Council on Education Psychological Examination (ACE), the School and College Ability Tests (SCAT), the College Entrance Examination Board's Scholastic Aptitude Test (SAT), and the American College Testing Program Assessment (ACT). The most widely administered of these has been the SAT, which consists of two sections yielding two scores: Verbal (SAT–V) and Mathematical (SAT–M). Verbal analogies, antonyms, information, reading comprehension, and sentence completion items make up the Verbal section; arithmetic, algebra, geometry, charts and graphs, and logical reasoning items make up the Mathematical section. Both sections are scored on a standard score scale having a mean of 500 and a standard deviation of 100, the scores ranging from 200 to 800.[2]

More achievement oriented than the SAT is the second most popular college admissions tests, the American College Test (ACT). The four achievement tests on the ACT are English, Mathematics, Natural Science, and Social Studies. Each test is scored on a standard score scale having a mean of 20 and a standard deviation of 5, the scores ranging from 1 to 36.

The most popular test for admission to graduate school is the Graduate Record Examinations, consisting of a General Test to measure aptitude for graduate work and a Subject Test to measure achievement in a particular subject-matter area. The General Test consists of seven tests of 30-minute duration each. Two of the seven tests are verbal, two are quantitative, two are analytical, and one is reserved for research purposes. The verbal tests consist of analogies, antonyms, sentence completions, and reading comprehension. The quantitative tests consist of quantitative comparisons, discrete quantitative, and data interpretation problems. The analytical tests consist of analytical reasoning and logical

---

[2]To maintain score continuity of meaning and permit year-to-year comparisons of SAT scores, this standard score scale is based on the performance of the 1941 standardization group. The mean scores of today's high school students who take the SAT are somewhat less than 500 on both the Verbal and Mathematical portions of the test.

reasoning exercises. The General Test yields separate Verbal (GRE–V), Quantitative (GRE–Q), and Analysis (GRE–A) scores having the same standard score scale as the SAT. The GRE Subject Tests are 3-hour examinations in any one of 15 different subject-matter fields.

Several other standardized tests are used in selecting students for admission to professional schools, the most widely administered being the Graduate Management Aptitude Test (GMAT), the Law School Admissions Test (LSAT), and the Medical College Admissions Test (MCAT). Although these examinations are primarily achievement oriented, certain sections are similar to those found on tests of academic aptitude.

Nonverbal and Culture-fair Group Intelligence Tests

Performance tests designed as individually administered measures of the intellectual abilities of persons with language or cultural handicaps were discussed earlier in the chapter. Complementary instruments that can be administered on a group basis have been constructed for the physically and culturally disadvantaged. The grandfather of these nonverbal tests was the Army Beta of World War I, which included tasks such as cube analyses, digit symbols, geometrical constructions, mazes, and picture completions. The Army Beta, which also proved useful in testing unskilled civilian workers, was updated, restandardized, and republished in 1978 as the Revised Beta Examination, Second Edition (from The Psychological Corporation). Another example of a nonverbal test suitable for group (or individual) administration is the Goodenough–Harris Drawing Test. Unlike the Revised Beta Examination, which is a multiple-task test, the Goodenough–Harris requires only that the examinee accomplish the task of drawing a human figure.

Goodenough–Harris Drawing Test   This test (from The Psychological Corporation) is a revision of the Goodenough Draw-a-Man Test, together with a similar Draw-a-Woman and an experimental Self-Drawing scale. The man and woman figures that the examinee is instructed to draw are scored for body and clothing details, proportionality among the various body parts (for example, head to trunk), and other characteristics, rather than according to artistic merit. The test is untimed, but it usually takes from 10 to 15 minutes to complete. Norms for children from age 3 to 15 years are reported as standard scores and percentile ranks, separately by sex.

For many years, designers of intelligence tests have been besieged by the criticism that such instruments are loaded with the cultural biases of middle-class Western society. It was the hope of Goodenough and Harris that their test would measure basic intelligence relatively free of cultural influences, but it has become clear that the task of drawing a human figure is significantly affected by specific sociocultural experiences. There have been several other noteworthy, but largely unsuccessful, attempts to develop a culture-free intelligence test, and subsequently the aim was modified to that of constructing a culture-fair test. On a *culture-fair test* of intelligence, efforts are made to include only items related to experiences common to a wide range of cultures. Consequently, items involving specific linguistic constructions and other culture-loaded tasks, such as speed of responding, are not included. In this sense, the Goodenough–Harris test is culturally fair. Two other widely used tests that probably come as close as any others to being culturally fair are the Raven Progressive Matrices and the Culture Fair Intelligence Test.

Raven Progressive Matrices   This test (from The Psychological Corporation) may be administered on either an individual or a group basis. Examinees are required to solve problems involving abstract figures and designs by indicating which of several figures belongs in a given matrix. Developed in Great Britain as a measure of Spearman's general intelligence factor, the Raven is available in two forms. The 1938 form, suitable for grade 8 through adulthood, can be obtained in five black-and-white sets of 12 problems each. The 1947 form, the Raven Children's Coloured Matrices, is available in three sets for children aged 5½ to 11 years and for retarded adults. The Raven tests are untimed, but the 1938 form takes about 45 minutes and the 1947 form 25 to 30 minutes. The percentile norms on both forms of the test were obtained on samples of English schoolchildren and adults, but the samples were small and the norms are now dated. An Advanced Progressive Matrices for adolescents and adults is also available.

Similar to but more recently developed than the Raven Progressive Matrices is the Matrix Analogies Test (from The Psychological Corporation). It consists of nonverbal reasoning items organized in four groups: Pattern Completion, Reasoning by Analogy, Serial Reasoning, and Spatial Visualization. The examinee (ages 5 to 17 years) is tested in 20 to 25 minutes on 64 abstract designs of the standard progressive matrix type, one design per page. The norms are based on a large, representative sample of individuals aged 5 to 17 years living in the United States. Raw scores are converted to standard scores, percentile ranks, and stanines by half-year intervals and to age equivalents ranging from 5 years to 17 years 11 months. A short form of the test, the Matrix Analogies Tests— Short Form, consisting of 34 items, is also available.

Culture Fair Intelligence Test.   Perhaps more familiar to test users in the United States is the Culture Fair Intelligence Test (from the Institute for Personality and Ability Testing). This series of tests is composed of three scales: Scale 1 for children aged 4 to 8 years and adult retardates; Scale 2 for children 8 to 14 years and adults of average intelligence; and Scale 3 for college students, executives, and others of above-average intelligence. As illustrated by the sample problems in Figure 6-8, each scale is composed of four subtests (series, classifications, matrices, and conditions) for measuring the ability to perceive relationships among other things. In addition to these four culture-fair subtests, Scale 1 contains four other subtests to measure cultural information and verbal comprehension. Testing time is 40 to 60 minutes for Scale 1 and 25 to 30 minutes for each of the two forms of Scales 2 and 3.

The Raven Progressive Matrices and the Culture Fair Intelligence Test represent commendable efforts to develop tests on which groups from different cultures score equally well. It is now recognized, however, that it is probably impossible to construct test items whose content is independent of experiences that vary from culture to culture. A not uncommon finding is that middle-class Caucasian groups score higher on the culture-fair tests as well as on more verbal, "culturally loaded" intelligence tests. Furthermore, culture-fair tests are typically poor predictors of academic achievement, job performance, and other indicators of success in Western culture. Consequently, they usually have lower

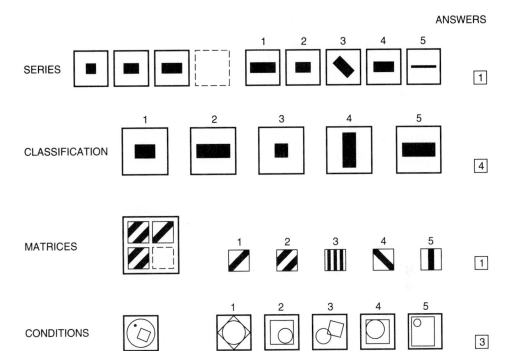

FIGURE 6–8 Sample Items from the Culture Fair Intelligence Test.
(Copyright © 1949, 1960, by the Institute for Personality and Ability Testing, Inc. All rights reserved. Reproduced by permission.)

validities for purposes of selection and placement than general ability tests containing more culturally relevant material.

DISTRIBUTION AND CLASSIFICATION OF INTELLIGENCE TEST SCORES

Scores on intelligence tests, particularly IQ scores, depend, among other things, on which test is administered. A Wechsler (WISC–III or WAIS–R) IQ of 130, for example, is not precisely equivalent to an Otis–Lennon IQ of 130. The specific IQ obtained by an examinee is likely to vary somewhat from one test to another. Consequently, whenever the IQ of a person is reported, it is important to specify the test on which it was obtained.

Despite variations from test to test in the meaning of the intelligence quotient, the shape of the IQ distribution for well-standardized individual intelligence tests is approximately normal (bell shaped). One reason why the distribution is not exactly normal is the hump at the extreme lower end of the curve caused by the low scores of the many children who have suffered accidents or diseases resulting in brain damage. In addition, because of assortative mating (mating among persons possessing similar characteristics), the distribution of intelligence test scores is often flatter than the normal curve. It has been argued that this flatness in the IQ distribution, resulting from a larger number of very low and very high scores than in a normal distribution, is what would be expected if intelligence is substantially influenced by heredity.

Mental Retardation

Alfred Binet's primary reason for constructing an intelligence test was to identify children having little chance of making reasonable progress in regular school classrooms. Therefore, it is not surprising that one of the most popular uses of general intelligence tests has been in diagnosing mental retardation.

According to the American Association on Mental Deficiency (AAMD), "Mental retardation refers to significantly subaverage general intelligence functioning resulting in or associated with concurrent impairments in adaptive behavior and manifested during the developmental period"(Kidd, 1983, pages 243–244). Although this definition does not mandate the use of IQ tests in diagnosing retardation, intelligence test scores, along with measures of academic and vocational achievement, psychomotor skills, socioemotional maturity, and other *adaptive behaviors,* are considered in making the diagnosis. The adaptive behaviors may be assessed by an informal analysis of the person's history and present behavior or by administering a standardized instrument such as the Vineland Adaptive Behavior Scale (from American Guidance Service) or the AAMD Adaptive Behavior Scale (from The Psychological Corporation). The psychological examiner fills out a Vineland or AAMD Adaptive Behavior scale from information supplied by a parent, teacher, or other observer who is well acquainted with the child's behavior.

Socially derogatory labels such as *moron, imbecile,* and *idiot,* which were once used to categorize different degrees of mental retardation, have been discontinued in the United States. In fact, there have been efforts to replace the term mental retardation with a perhaps less pejorative term, such as *mental impairment* or *developmental disability.* In any event, there are various systems of classifying mental retardation, one of the most widely used being that proposed by the American Association of Mental Deficiency (Kidd, 1983):

Mild mental retardation: IQ = 50–55 to approximately 70

Moderate mental retardation: IQ = 35–40 to 50–55

Severe mental retardation: IQ = 20–25 to 35–40

Profound mental retardation: IQ = below 20 or 25

When the child's behavior is sufficiently impaired and judged to be due to deficits in reasoning and judgment, the limit of 70 on the mild mental retardation category may be extended upward to 75 or more if the test is sufficiently reliable. However, the term *marginal intelligence* is sometimes applied to IQs in the 70 to 85 range (Maloney & Ward, 1976).

The AAMD classification system, which is approved by some psychologists but considered confusing by others, is not followed uniformly from state to state. Although an IQ of 75 is generally accepted as the cutoff score, the definition and procedures for identifying mental retardation vary from state to state (Frankenberger, 1984). As advocated by Public Law 94-142 and by the AAMD, adaptive behavior as well as IQ is usually taken into account in making the diagnosis.

Other systems of classifying the degree of mental retardation have been recommended by the National Association for Retarded Children (NARC) and the American Psychiatric Association (APA). The more functional NARC system consists of the following categories: marginally independent (IQ = 50 to 75), semidependent (IQ = 25 to 50), and dependent (IQ = 0 to 25). The APA system, which has been endorsed by the World Health Organization, employs the following categories: mild (IQ = 50 to 70), moderate (IQ = 35 to 49), severe (IQ = 20 to 34), and profound (IQ below 20). Descriptions of the characteristic behaviors of children in these four categories at three periods of development are given in Table 6–4. Another classification system that is sometimes used in schools to emphasize adaptive behavior rather than mental deficiency is *educable mentally impaired* for children who are mildly retarded, *trainable mentally impaired* for those who are moderately retarded, and *severely mentally impaired* for children who are severely mentally retarded.

Mental Giftedness

At the other end of the intelligence continuum from mental retardation is mental giftedness. The most comprehensive study of persons with high IQs was a longitudinal investigation conducted by Terman and Oden (1959). This research, which began in 1921, followed for over 40 years 1500 individuals who as children had made IQs of 140 or higher on the Stanford–Binet Intelligence Scale (Oden, 1968). The purpose of the study was to obtain information on the occupational success, physical and mental health, social adjustment, and other variables associated with high intelligence. The results failed to confirm a number of popular myths concerning the gifted: that bright children are sickly, that they burn out easily ("early ripe, early rot"), and that genius is akin to insanity. As a group, the gifted children in Terman's study were physically superior to children of average intelligence: they were heavier at birth and remained heavier than the average child; they walked and talked earlier and matured at an earlier age than average; and their general health was better than average. Furthermore, they maintained their mental and physical superiority as adults. Follow-up data revealed that they earned more degrees, attained higher occupational success and salaries, had better personal and social adjustment, and were physically healthier than the average adult.

Terman's findings of better adjustment and a lower mental illness rate among the gifted did not go unchallenged. Hughes and Converse (1962) suggested that the fact that the children were selected initially on the basis of teachers' ratings as well as IQ may have biased the sample in favor of better-adjusted persons. Furthermore, Hollingworth (1942) did not find generally superior personal and social adjustment in children having IQs of 180 or above. Finally, as Terman's study demonstrated, intelligence test scores alone are not very good long-term predictors of success. Thus, not one of these gifted children achieved the eminence of an Einstein or a Freud. Clearly, other special abilities, talents, motives, and temperament traits, in addition to environmental contingencies, must be taken into account in forecasting how individual lives turn out.

Another noteworthy investigation of gifted and talented children was the study of

TABLE 6-4 Age-related Behavioral Changes in the Mentally Retarded

Degree of retardation	Preschool age (0–5)	School age (6–21)	Adult (21 and over)
Profound (IQ below 20)	Extreme retardation in all areas; minimal sensorimotor abilities; requires nursing care.	Obviously delayed in all areas of development; responds with basic emotions and may benefit from training in use of limbs and mouth; must be closely supervised.	May be able to walk and talk in a primitive way; benefits from regular physical activity; cannot take care of self, but requires nursing care.
Severe (IQ = 20–34)	Pronounced delay in motor development; little or no speech; benefits from self-help (e.g., self-feeding) training.	Usually walks unless locomotor disability present; can understand and respond to speech; can profit from training in health and other acceptable habits.	Follows daily routines and contributes to self-maintenance; needs direction and close supervision in controlled environment.
Moderate (IQ = 35–49)	Motor development noticeably delayed, particularly in speech; can be trained in variety of self-help activities.	Learns to communicate and take care of elementary health and safety needs; learns simple manual skills but makes little or no progress in reading and arithmetic.	Performs simple unskilled or semiskilled tasks under supervised conditions; participates in simple games and travels alone in familiar places; incapable of self-maintenance.
Mild (IQ = 50–70)	Slower than average to walk, feed self, and talk, but casual observer may not notice retardation.	Learns perceptual–motor and cognitive skills (reading and arithmetic) on third- to sixth-grade level by late teens; can learn to conform socially.	Usually achieves social and vocational skills needed for maintaining self; requires guidance and help when under unusual economic or social stress.

mathematically precocious youth conducted by Julian Stanley and his colleagues (Stanley, Keating & Fox, 1974; Keating, 1976). Among other findings, this study validated the Scholastic Aptitude Test–Mathematical as being superior to teacher's recommendations and other methods of identifying mathematical talent in adolescents. The findings also demonstrated that junior- and senior-high students who are gifted in mathematics can benefit greatly from college-level instruction in the subject. Not only are mathematically precocious youth highly motivated to do superior work in college mathematics, but they also tend to be personally well adjusted and to adapt well to the college environment.

Research and Theory

As noted by Tryon (1991, page 1), "The history of science is largely coextensive with the history of measurement." Nowhere is the implication of the notion that measurement drives research more evident than in the study of individual differences in mental abilities. The intelligence tests devised by Binet and other psychologists during the first half of this century led not only to many practical applications in schools, clinics, the military, and business and industry, but they also stimulated a host of research investigations concerned with the causes and correlates of individual differences in mental abilities. These investigations included studies of the relationships of intelligence test scores to variables such as chronological age, sex, heredity, impoverished or enrichment environments, hormones and drugs, nutrition, climate, socioeconomic status, nationality, and race. Controversy still surrounds the findings of many of these studies, and entire books have been written about the issues and debates stemming from them (see Chapter 12). In addition to research investigations, intelligence testing has led to many different theories of the origin and structure of mental abilities. Some of these theories have guided the development of new assessment instruments. For the most part, however, intelligence testing has remained empirically based, rooted in pragmatism rather than theory.

SUMMARY

Intelligence, an ancient Latin term that was reintroduced during the last century, refers to general mental ability. Various sensorimotor tests were used in early attempts to assess this ability, but the first practical measure of intelligence was devised by Alfred Binet and Theodore Simon during the first decade of the twentieth century. The Binet–Simon scale, a series of school-related tasks arranged in order of ascending difficulty, yielded a mental age score for each examinee. Of the many translations and revisions of the Binet–Simon scale, the Stanford–Binet Intelligence Scale became the most popular. The Stanford–Binet, authored by Lewis Terman, was published originally in 1916 and revised in 1937 and 1960. The test yielded a ratio IQ, defined as IQ $= 100(MA/CA)$, although a deviation IQ could also be computed on the 1960 revision.

The fourth edition of the Stanford–Binet Intelligence Scale represents a major departure from previous editions of the scale. Construction of the fourth edition of the scale involved more sophisticated psychometric theory and procedures and provided for separate scores on 15 tests and four areas, as well as a composite score. The emphasis in designing the fourth edition was not only on the identification of mentally gifted individuals, but also on providing information for diagnosing specific causes of learning difficulties.

For many years the earlier editions of the Stanford–Binet were a standard against which other intelligence tests could be compared. During the past three decades, however, the Wechsler intelligence scales have become increasingly popular. Unlike subtests on the Stanford–Binet, which are grouped according to age levels, subtests on the Wechsler scales are grouped into 10 or so categories according to content. Also, the Wechsler scales provide three kinds of deviation IQs: Verbal, Performance, and Full Scale. In addition to yielding three IQs, the pattern of subtest scaled scores on the WAIS–R may provide clinical information useful in the diagnosis of organic brain damage and certain mental disorders.

Among the many special-purpose, individually administered intelligence tests are pictorial tests such as the Peabody Picture Vocabulary Test and the Columbia Test of Mental Maturity, as well as other single-task tests such as the Porteus Mazes and the Kohs Block Designs. Other nonverbal tests for individuals with language or physical handicaps include performance test batteries such as the Leiter International Performance Scale.

A great deal of research has gone into the construction of various developmental scales for infants and young children. Illustrative of tests in this category are the Bayley Scales of Infant Development and the McCarthy Scales of Children's Abilities. Having a wider age range than either the Bayley or the McCarthy is the Kaufman Assessment Battery for Children (K–ABC). The K–ABC represents a different approach to the assessment of children's problem-solving abilities, one based on the notion of simultaneous and sequential mental processing.

More widely used than individual tests are group-administered tests of intelligence, which can be given to more than one person at a time. These tests stem from the Army Examinations Alpha and Beta of World War I, which were based on the pioneering work of Arthur Otis and other psychologists. Examples of current group intelligence tests are the Otis–Lennon School Ability Test, the Test of Cognitive Skills, and the Cognitive Abilities Test. Certain group tests of academic ability, the Scholastic Aptitude Test (SAT) in particular, are used extensively for college admissions purposes. Nonverbal group intelligence tests for people with language handicaps are also available; an example is a Goodenough–Harris Drawing Test.

Traditionally, it has been assumed that the items on intelligence tests represent common experiences, at least for people in a given culture. It was maintained that the higher a person's innate ability is, the greater the benefit from these common experiences. Not only is this assumption itself questionable, but it has also been recognized that Binet-type tests, which are heavily loaded with verbal materials, are not necessarily fair to examinees from cultures different from that predominant in the Western middle class. Attempts to develop culture-free or even culture-fair intelligence tests, however, have not proved very successful. Illustrative of such attempts are the Raven Progressive Matrices and the Culture Fair Intelligence Test.

The distribution of intelligence test scores in the general population is roughly normal in shape. Persons with IQs in the 90 through 109 range are classified as "average," those with very high IQs are designated as "superior" or "gifted," and those with very low IQs are labeled as "mentally retarded." Both measured intelligence and adaptive behavior are considered in the diagnosis of mental retardation. Neither the mentally retarded nor the mentally gifted are free from adjustment problems, but the former group appears to have more serious difficulties in this regard. Consequently, research and special programs have focused more on the retarded than on the gifted.

EXERCISES

1. What is the ratio IQ of a child who is 8 years, 9 months old if his or her score on the Stanford–Binet Intelligence Scale is equal to a mental age of 6 years, 5 months?

2. Why are deviation IQ scores considered psychometrically superior to ratio IQ scores?

3. Trace the development of the Stanford–Binet Intelligence Scale from Binet's early tests through the fourth edition of the scale.

4. List and describe the three currently available tests in the Wechsler series of intelligence tests, including the age range for which each is appropriate and the subtests on each test.

5. Compare the Wechsler tests with the older and newer editions of the Stanford–Binet in terms of age range, types of abilities measured, fairness of the test to physically or culturally disadvantaged people, and other pertinent features.

6. What intelligence test(s) would you recommend for use with each of the following individuals? (a) A 5-year-old child suspected of being mentally retarded; (b) a group of high school seniors; (c) a 10-year-old child with cerebral palsy; (d) a group of South Sea island aborigines; (e) a normal, English-speaking adult; (f) a 7-year-old totally blind child; (g) an adult schizophrenic; (h) a group of culturally disadvantaged elementary school children.

7. Repeat Exercise 8 of Chapter 5 with a standardized group intelligence test.

8. Select one of the following categories of intelligence tests discussed in this chapter and two representative instruments from the published tests in the category: individual pictorial tests; developmental scales for infants and young children; multilevel group intelligence tests; nonverbal group intelligence tests. Obtain as much information on the two tests in each category as you can from textbooks on testing, the *Mental Measurements Yearbooks,* and other sources (consult *Psychological Abstracts and Education Index* in particular). Write a comparative review of the two tests, focusing on test design and format, procedures for administering and scoring the tests, norms, reliability, validity, and research concerned with the tests. Draw appropriate conclusions regarding the relative merits of the two tests.

9. Describe the classification systems for mental retardation advocated by the American Association on Mental Deficiency, the National Association for Retarded Children, and the American Psychiatric Association.

10. Because the method of diagnosing mental retardation, including the cutoff IQ, varies from state to state, it is possible for a child to be mentally retarded in one state and "borderline" or "low average" in another state. What consequences might this have?

11. If the set of *Computer Programs for Psychological Assessment* is available, run all the programs in Category 5 ("Programs on Problem-Solving and Thinking"). Compare your results with those of your classmates.

SUGGESTED READINGS

Brody, N. (1992). *Intelligence,* 2nd ed. New York: Academic Press.

Chapman, P.D. (1988). *Schools as sorters: Lewis M. Terman, applied psychology, and the intelligence testing movement, 1890–1930.* New York: New York University Press.

Forrest, D. W. (1974). *Francis Galton: The life and work of a Victorian genius.* London: Elek.

Frederiksen, N. (1986). Toward a broader conception of intelligence. *American Psychologist, 41,* 445–452.

Minton, H. L. (1988). *Lewis M. Terman: Pioneer in psychological testing.* New York: New York University Press.

Shurkin, J. N. (1992). *Terman's kids.* Boston: Little, Brown.

Snyderman, M., & Rothman, S. (1987). Survey of expert opinions on intelligence and aptitude testing. *American Psychologist, 42,*137–144.

Sternberg, R. J. (1986). Inside intelligence. *American Scientist, 4,* 137–143.

Wechsler, D. (1975). Intelligence defined and undefined. *American Psychologist, 30,* 135–139.

Wolf. T. H. (1973). *Alfred Binet.* Chicago: University of Chicago Press.

Chapter Seven

Testing Special Abilities

The term *aptitude* has traditionally been defined as a person's capacity to benefit from education or training, whereas *achievement* refers to the degree of ability already attained. The measurement of aptitude focuses on the future, the measurement of achievement on the past. Thus, aptitude tests have been devised primarily to assess potential achievement or to predict future performance in some field of endeavor.

A person's aptitudes are assessed for purposes of academic and occupational counseling and placement. With aptitude test information in hand, a counselor or placement director should be able to do a better job of advising people or placing them in the appropriate programs of education and training or in suitable occupations.

CONCEPTS AND CHARACTERISTICS

During the 1920s, when they first appeared, tests of special aptitudes were viewed as measures of specific innate or hereditary talents that were not based on experience. In a sense, the term *aptitude* is a misnomer if it is meant to imply that what is being measured is an inborn, unchangeable characteristic. Early mental testers did aspire to measure hereditary characteristics, for they assumed that all examinees had equal opportunities to learn the material on which the tests were based. This assumption, however, was incorrect; learning opportunities are never exactly the same for different people.

Aptitude tests are actually measures of achievement, a complex product of the interaction between hereditary and environmental influences. Conversely, if the term *aptitude test* is used to designate a measuring instrument that predicts future accomplishment, then those achievement tests that predict future accomplishment also qualify as measures of aptitude.

Because of confusion over the difference between aptitude and achievement, it has been suggested that the two terms be replaced with the single term *ability*. Then, depending on the purpose for which it is used (to assess current knowledge and understanding or to predict future performance), a test of ability could be either a measure of achievement or aptitude.

It would be a mistake, however, to assume that the distinction between aptitude and achievement is inconsequential. As an illustration of the functional difference between measures of these two variables, consider the results of a study by Carroll (1973). It was found that performance in a foreign language course by students whose precourse scores on a foreign language achievement test were zero could be predicted from their scores on a test of aptitude for learning foreign languages. At the end of the course, the achievement and aptitude tests were readministered. As would be expected if the training improved achievement but had no effect on aptitude, scores on the achievement test increased significantly, but scores on the aptitude test remained essentially unchanged.

General and Specific Aptitudes

The intelligence tests discussed in the last chapter are *general* aptitude tests, in that scores on these tests represent a composite of mental abilities and can be used to forecast achievement and other behaviors in a wide range of situations. But the fact that general intelligence tests measure a hodgepodge of specific aptitudes or abilities is a two-edged sword. In this fact lie both the strength and the weakness of these kinds of tests.

General intelligence tests measure an assortment of abilities and hence they have what Cronbach (1970) referred to as a broad *bandwidth*. Because of their broadness, these tests have proved moderately effective in predicting various criteria. A longer test of one of the special abilities measured by an intelligence test, that is, an instrument with a narrower bandwidth, would have greater *fidelity*. In other words, it would measure whatever it measured more precisely and do a better job of predicting a narrower range of criteria.

Having noted the significant positive correlations among measures of different special abilities, Vernon (1960) concluded that general intelligence is more important than special abilities in determining occupational success. The correlations among tests of special abilities are, however, not particularly high, since people often perform much better on some kinds of tasks than on others. Whether performance varies because of differences in motivation or differences in the special abilities required by certain occupations, or both, is arguable.

Origins of Vocational Testing

One of the forces behind the development of tests of special abilities during the first half of this century was the growth of *scientific management*. Proponents of scientific management in business and industry felt that both employees and employers would benefit if psychological tests could be devised to help match individuals to jobs. Employees would be selected for and placed on jobs that they could perform more effectively, and hence they would be more productive and thereby earn more. Similarly, the selection of more competent employees and placement of them in jobs for which they were best suited would benefit the employer by improving production efficiency.

During the Great Depression years of the 1930s, when matters related to employment (or, rather, unemployment!) became of great concern to government, research and development programs at the University of Minnesota and elsewhere resulted in the construction of a series of special abilities tests for use in vocational counseling and in employee selection and placement. From these programs and subsequent efforts came not only numerous single-ability measures, but also several batteries of tests.

Validity of Special Abilities Tests

Because aptitude tests are designed with differential prediction in mind, it is reasonable to ask how successful they are in predicting who will succeed and who will fail in particular occupations or job training programs. That is, just how valid are vocational aptitude tests? The answer is that, in general, the validities of these tests are not very high. Ghiselli's (1973) summary of the average validity coefficients of different kinds of aptitude tests used to predict performance in various job categories revealed that the coefficients are typically in the .20s and are almost never above the .30s. These very modest coefficients underscore the limitations of tests of special abilities for predicting performance on the job. Despite their limitations, such tests are still helpful in determining what occupation or training program is most suitable for a given person. The tests are certainly limited when used alone, but their value increases when the scores are combined with other kinds of information about individuals.

Even the relatively modest validity coefficients of most special abilities tests are not fixed; they vary with the nature of the criterion, the situation, and the group that is examined. For example, a validity coefficient is likely to be higher when a test is validated against grades in a training program than against ratings of actual on-the-job performance. A validity coefficient also tends to be higher when the test is administered and the criterion data are collected fairly close together in time than when there is a long delay between test administration and the collection of criterion information.

Situational variability in the validity coefficient is seen when the correlation between scores on an ability test and job performance ratings are lower in one manufacturing or service organization than in another. Validity also varies with the characteristics of the group of people who are tested. It may depend on the sex, ethnicity, and socioeconomic status of the examinees, as well as on affective variables such as vocational interests, emotional stability, level of achievement motivation, and values. Such interindividual differences that influence the correlation between a test and a criterion measure are referred to as *moderator variables.*

The fact that the size of a validity coefficient depends on the criterion, the situation, and the group tested underscores the wisdom of validating a test against the specific criterion, in the specific situation in which it is to be used, and with a representative sample of those people for whom it is intended. Although validity coefficients have some cross-situational generality (Schmidt & Hunter, 1977, 1981), it is good practice, from both an economic and a legal standpoint, to conduct a separate validity study in the specific context in which a vocational aptitude test is to be used. There are economic reasons why occupational selection tests need to be valid predictors of on-the-job performance. The bottom line is whether a specific test saves the organization more money than some other personnel-selection procedure. The legal reason for conducting validity studies centers on the question of bias or fairness. For example, it may be that the test-criterion correlation is significantly higher with one ethnic group than another. If so, it is unfair to use the same prediction equation with both groups. The *fairness,* or relative freedom from bias, of a test must be demonstrated if it is to be used for selection or classification purposes, a topic to which we return in Chapter 12.

Performance versus Paper-and-Pencil Tests

The first measures of special abilities to be devised were performance tests that required examinees to construct something or manipulate physical objects in certain ways. These "apparatus" tests are frequently more engaging than paper-and-pencil tests, especially to examinees with reading deficiencies. But the reliabilities of performance tests are typically lower than those of comparable paper-and-pencil tests, and the tests are time consuming and expensive to administer. Furthermore, the correlations between scores on performance tests and scores on paper-and-pencil measures of the same special ability are usually far from perfect. Despite the shortcomings of performance tests, *work-sample tests* (or job-replica tests), which require examinees to complete a sample of tasks similar to those comprising a certain job, are considered to be among the most useful tests of ability in specific occupational contexts.

In-Basket Technique and the Assessment Center

An interesting example of a work-sample test is the *in-basket technique.* This procedure was originally devised as a job replica test for school administrators, but it has also been used in evaluating other kinds of administrators or executives. Candidates for an administrative position are presented with samples of items of the sort typically found in an administrator's in-basket (letters, memos, notes, directives, reports, FAXs) requiring some type of action. They are asked to indicate what action should be taken on each item, and their responses are evaluated according to experts' judgments of the type of administrative action deemed most appropriate.

The Assessment Center approach, which was introduced by the American Telephone and Telegraph Company in the 1950s, combines the in-basket technique with other simulated tasks, such as management games and group problem-solving exercises (as in the Leaderless Group Discussion Test). Interviews, psychological tests, and other methods of appraisal are also applied in this approach. The Assessment Center approach has been used less as a selection technique than as a means of evaluating managerial-level personnel for promotion and classification. Six to twelve candidates are brought to a specific location, where they are observed and assessed by other executives and by each other for several days. The principal criteria on which the candidates are evaluated are degree of active participation, organizational skills, and decision-making ability.

Because the in-basket technique and other simulation tasks are realistic, it might be expected that they would be highly valid. The candidates are, however, aware of being "on stage," and may role-play or in other ways act differently from how they would in an actual administrative situation. Expense and time constraints also prohibit using such simulation techniques for anything other than the assessment of fairly high level managerial personnel.

SENSORY–PERCEPTUAL AND PSYCHOMOTOR SKILLS TESTS

Although they are not psychological tests in the strict sense, tests of sensory–perceptual and psychomotor abilities are important sources of information on an individual's ability to perform certain work-related tasks. There is little relationship between mental and physical abilities, but task performance may depend as much on the latter as the former. Tests of sensory–perceptual and psychomotor abilities are useful as screening devices in the selection, placement, and classification of employees and military personnel for jobs or training programs, as well as in vocational and educational diagnosis and counseling.

Sensory–Perceptual Tests

Performance in school or on the job is obviously affected by vision and hearing, so most educational and work organizations make arrangements for determining the presence of visual and auditory defects. Sensory screening tests are typically administered once a year in the elementary school grades, followed by a more thorough examination of children who appear to have some sensory deficit. In addition, periodic tests of vision and hearing are required, for reasons of safety as well as proficiency, in many business, industrial, and government jobs. Complementing the simple screening instruments that measure a single visual or auditory function are more complex instruments for assessing several different sensory and perceptual functions.

Illustrative Single-purpose Instruments   A single-purpose instrument measures only one function. There are separate single-purpose screening instruments for determining visual acuity, auditory acuity, color vision, and certain other sensory–perceptual functions.

Visual Acuity   One of the oldest instruments for determining visual acuity at a distance is the *Snellen Wall Chart* (Figure 7–1). The standard testing situation requires the examinee to stand 20 feet in front of the chart and read the smallest row of letters that he or she can see clearly, first with one eye and then with the other. If the row of letters is one that a person with normal eyes can read at 20 feet (row 7 in the illustration), then the person's visual acuity in that eye is expressed as 20/20. If the smallest line that the person can read at 20 feet is one that people with normal eyes can read at 40 feet (row 5), then his or her visual acuity is 20/40. If the smallest line that the person can read at 20 feet is one that people with normal eyes can read only by moving up to 15 feet (row 8), then visual acuity in that eye is 20/15. Therefore, a ratio under 1.00 indicates poorer-than-normal visual acuity. It should be cautioned that the chart in Figure 7–1 is much smaller than a standard Snellen Chart.

Auditory Acuity   Auditory acuity is commonly determined with an *audiometer,* an electronic instrument that presents pure tones of varying intensities and frequencies in the normal range of hearing.[1] The procedure employed in determining the hearing threshold

---

[1]A crude assessment of auditory acuity can be made with a "dollar watch," which, depending on how quiet the room is, a person with normal hearing should be able to hear ticking from a distance of 30 to 40 inches from the ear.

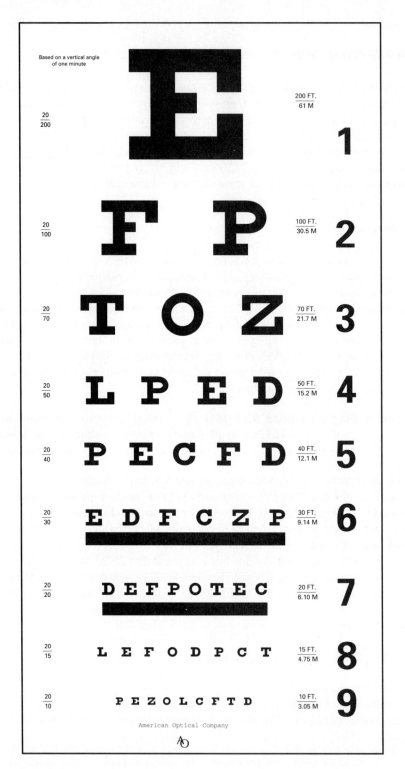

FIGURE 7–1 Snellen Chart.
(Reproduced by permission of American Optical Corporation.)

in each ear is to present a series of tones of a given frequency, first decreasing and then increasing in intensity, until the person no longer reports hearing it on the decreasing series or reports just barely hearing it on the increasing series. The findings may be plotted as an *audiogram,* a graph of the person's auditory threshold at each frequency and for each ear. The normal human ear is most sensitive at a frequency of around 2000 hertz, and the hearing range is from 20 to 20,000 hertz. Individuals with different degrees of deafness typically show relative insensitivity to certain frequencies. A special type of audiometric test, acoustic impedance audiometry, is used to detect middle-ear disorders, which are the major cause of hearing loss in young children.

Color Vision   The ability to distinguish different hues is an important requirement in many occupations, ranging from airplane pilot to yarn inspector. One of the oldest instruments for testing color vision is the Ishihara Test for Color Blindness (from Graham–Field Surgical Company), a set of 14, 24, or 38 cards for identifying color vision deficiency. Each card, referred to as a pseudo-isochromatic plate, consists of an aggregate of dots of different colors. A person with normal color vision perceives the aggregation as a numeral or other form on a background of contrasting dots. But, depending on the nature and severity of the defect, a color-blind person may see only a shapeless collection of dots.

Another color vision test similar to the Ishihara is the Dvorine Color Vision Test (from The Psychological Corporation). This test, which takes approximately 2 minutes to administer, consists of 15 pseudo-isochromatic plates and 8 auxiliary plates for verification purposes. Numbers or geometric figures made of dots must be distinguished from a background of dots of another color. Also noteworthy is the Farnsworth Dichotomous Test for Color Blindness (from The Psychological Corporation). On this test, the examinee is required to arrange, according to color, a series of 15 movable color caps attached to a rack.

Multipurpose Instruments   The acuity and color vision tests discussed above serve essentially only one function, that of determining visual acuity, auditory acuity, or degree and type of color blindness. If more comprehensive testing of sensory capacities is needed, a multipurpose instrument must be employed. Illustrative of multipurpose instruments for visual screening are the B & L Vision Tester (from Bausch & Lomb, Inc.), the Sight Screener (from American Optical Company), the Telebinocular (from Keystone View Company), and the Titmus Vision Tester (from Titmus Optical). The B & L Vision Tester consists of a series of 12 tests in four categories: vertical and lateral phoria (muscular balance of the eyes) at far (20 feet) and near (14 inches) distances; acuity (including six tests) in the right eye, the left eye, and both eyes together; stereopsis (depth perception); and color discrimination. The B & L Vision Tester has been used primarily as a screening instrument in industrial contexts, and profiles for a number of *visual job families* have been determined. A less expensive instrument is the Titmus Vision Tester, which is used primarily for visual screening (acuity and phoria) in public school settings.

Tests of Psychomotor Abilities

Tests of psychomotor skills were among the first measures of special abilities to be constructed. Many of the available tests in this category were introduced during the 1920s and 1930s to predict performance in certain skilled jobs or trades. Subsequently, the Air Force Personnel and Training Research Center made a comprehensive analysis of psychomotor abilities, in particular those skills involved in pilot training. Examples are flight-simulation tasks such as the Link Trainer and the Complex Coordination Test. On the latter task, the examinee uses three controls similar to a stick and rudder to match a pattern of stimulus lights on a vertical panel simulating the movements of an airplane in flight.

An extensive research program conducted by Fleishman (1954, 1972) and his associates found a high degree of specificity in measures of psychomotor skills. The correlations between performance tests and paper-and-pencil tests of psychomotor abilities, as well as the correlations between measures of speed and quality of movement, were generally low. From the pattern of correlations among the various tests, Fleishman identified 11 psychomotor factors: aim, arm–hand steadiness, control precision, finger dexterity, manual dexterity, multilimb coordination, rate control, reaction time, response orientation, speed of arm movement, and wrist–finger speed. He also found that the reliabilities of psychomotor tests were lower on the average (.70's and .80's) than those of other special abilities tests. One reason for the lower reliability coefficients is the fact that performance on psychomotor tests is highly susceptible to practice. Furthermore, the relationships of scores on specific tests to the psychomotor factors changed dramatically from the first trials to the point at which examinees reached proficiency (Fleishman, 1972). Thus, both the scores on psychomotor tests and their meaning are affected by practice.

Generally, tests of psychomotor abilities have not proved very useful in vocational counseling. Due in part to the effects of practice on scores on these tests, the validities tend to be lower than those for tests of mechanical ability or clerical ability. Psychomotor tests have been more helpful in predicting performance in training programs than in forecasting job proficiency. They also have higher validities for predicting success in repetitive jobs such as routine assembly and machine operation than in complex jobs involving higher-order cognitive and perceptual abilities.

To illustrate the available psychomotor skills tests, selected measures of gross movements, fine movements, or a combination of gross and fine movements are described next. The majority of these instruments are appropriate for both adolescents and adults and are scored in terms of the time required to complete the task.

Gross Manual Movements   Two tests designed to measure the speed and accuracy of gross finger, hand, and arm movements are the Stromberg Dexterity Test (from The Psychological Corporation) and the Minnesota Rate of Manipulation Test (from American Guidance Service). On the Stromberg Dexterity Test, the examinee is required to place 54 biscuit-sized, colored discs (red, yellow, blue) in a prescribed sequence as rapidly as possible (Figure 7–2). The Minnesota Rate of Manipulation Test consists of a 60-hole board with blocks that are red on one side and yellow on the other. The test is divided into five subtests, on which the blocks are turned, moved, and placed in certain ways. On the Placing Test portion, for example, the blocks are placed into the holes on the board; on the Turning Test portion the blocks are turned over and replaced in the board.

Fine Manual Movements   Representative of tests requiring the manipulation of small parts are the O'Connor Finger Dexterity Test, the O'Connor Tweezer Dexterity Test, the

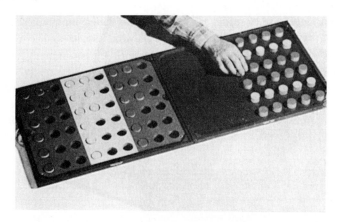

FIGURE 7–2   Photograph of the Stromberg Dexterity Test.
(Copyright 1945, 1951, © 1981 by The Psychological Corporation. Reproduced by permission. All rights reserved.)

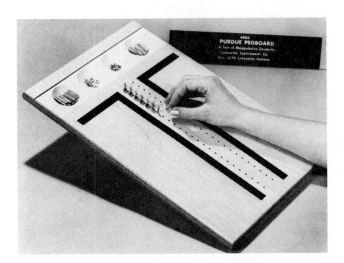

FIGURE 7–3   Purdue Pegboard.
(Courtesy of Lafayette Instrument Company.)

Purdue Pegboard, and the Crawford Small Parts Dexterity Test. On the O'Connor tests (from Stoelting Company), the examinee places small brass pins in the holes of a fiber plate by using the fingers or a pair of tweezers. The Purdue Pegboard (from London House), which is similar to the O'Connor tests, consists of five tasks for measuring manual dexterity and fine finger dexterity. On the first part of this test, the examinee puts pins into holes, first with the right hand, then with the left hand, and finally with both hands. On the second part of the test, the examinee puts a pin into a hole, places a washer and collar over the pin, puts another pin into a hole, and so on (Figure 7–3). The Crawford Small Parts Dexterity Test (from The Psychological Corporation) consists of two parts.

On the first part, examinees use tweezers to insert pins into holes and place collars over them. On the second part, small screws are placed into threaded holes and screwed down with a screwdriver (Figure 7–4).

Gross and Fine Manual Movements   Two psychomotor skills tests involving a combination of finger dexterity and gross movements of the arms and hands are the Pennsylvania Bi-manual Worksample (from American Guidance Service) and the Hand-Tool Dexterity Test (from The Psychological Corporation). Both tests use nuts and

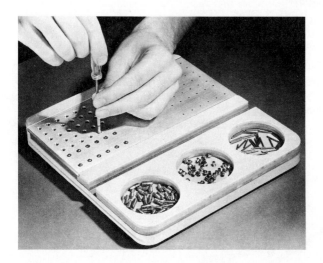

FIGURE 7–4   Photograph of the Crawford Small Parts Dexterity Test, Part II. *(Copyright © 1946, 1956, 1981 by The Psychological Corporation. Reproduced by permission. All rights reserved.)*

FIGURE 7–5   Photograph of the Hand-Tool Dexterity Test. *(Copyright © 1981 by The Psychological Corporation. Reproduced by permission. All rights reserved.)*

bolts. On the Pennsylvania test, the examinee screws 100 nuts onto 100 bolts and places them into the holes of an 8- by 24-inch board. On the Hand-Tool Dexterity Test (Figure 7–5), the examinee is required first to unfasten 12 nuts from 12 bolts of three different sizes mounted on the left side of a frame and then to reassemble the nuts and bolts on the right side of the frame. Scores are expressed as the time needed to complete the task. Norms are given in the manual for various groups of industrial applicants.

MECHANICAL ABILITY

A certain minimum level of psychomotor ability seems to be necessary for almost any industrial occupation, but above that level, spatial perception, mechanical knowledge, and other mental abilities are more important determiners of job success. One of the first and most frequent kinds of special ability to be measured is mechanical ability. There is some evidence for a weak general factor of mechanical ability, but the tests that have been devised to measure it involve a variety of perceptual–motor and cognitive abilities. These are tests of psychomotor skills such as speed and muscular coordination, perception of spatial relations, and comprehension of mechanical relations. The psychomotor components of various mechanical ability tests, like psychomotor tests in general, have low correlations with each other. Nevertheless, total scores on different mechanical ability tests frequently have substantial positive correlations with each other.

One interesting, if not surprising, finding is the presence of sex differences in scores on mechanical ability tests. Males typically score higher on spatial and mechanical comprehension items, whereas females score higher on items requiring fine manual dexterity and certain aspects of perceptual discrimination. These differences become more pronounced in junior and senior high school, and cultural factors undoubtedly play a role in producing them.

Spacial Relations Tests

An intensive analysis of mechanical ability conducted by D. G. Paterson and his co-workers at the University of Minnesota during the late 1920s resulted in the construction of three tests: Minnesota Mechanical Assembly Test, Minnesota Spatial Relations Test, and Minnesota Paper Formboard (Paterson et al., 1930). On the first of these, a work-sample test, the examinee reassembles a set of disassembled mechanical objects. The task requires manual dexterity and space perception, in addition to mechanical comprehension. The second and third instruments in the series are tests of space perception, which has been shown to be an important factor in occupations involving mechanical tasks. As the name implies, tests of space perception measure the ability to visualize objects in three dimensions and manipulate them to produce a particular configuration.

The Minnesota Spatial Relations Test, Revised Edition (from American Guidance Service) consists of four form boards (A, B, C, D). There are two sets of geometrically

There are two or more parts in the upper left-hand corner for each of the problems shown below. Choose from among the five figures labeled A, B, C, D, E, the one that shows how the parts in the upper left-hand corner would look if fitted together. The correct answer is shown for Problem 1.

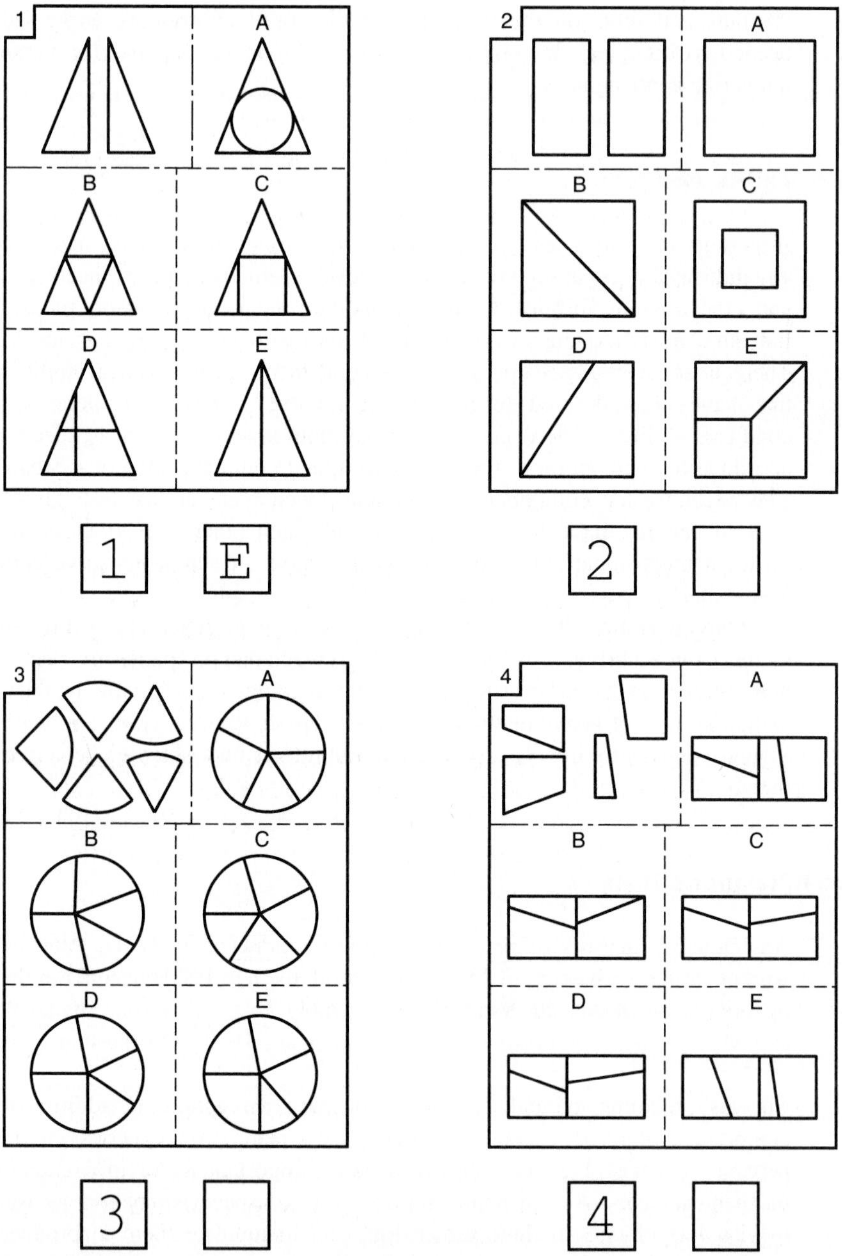

FIGURE 7–6   Sample Items from the Revised Minnesota Paper Formboard.
(Copyright © 1941 by The Psychological Corporation, Cleveland, Ohio, Renewed 1969. All rights reserved.)

shaped blocks; one set fits into the recesses of boards A and B, the other set into the recesses of boards C and D. The test begins with the blocks scattered outside the recesses. The examinee's task is to pick up the blocks and place them in their proper recesses on the board as quickly as possible.

The Revised Minnesota Paper Formboard Test (from The Psychological Corporation) is a paper-and-pencil adaptation of the Minnesota Spacial Relations Test. It consists of 64 multiple-choice items, each containing a frame showing a geometric figure divided into several parts and five answer frames containing an assembled form (Figure 7–6). Examinees select the one answer frame out of five showing how the disassembled geometric figure would look if the parts were fitted together. This test has proved useful in predicting grades in shop and engineering courses as well as supervisors' ratings and production records in inspection, packing, machine operation, and other industrial occupations. Scores on the test are also related to achievement in dentistry and art. Although it was originally devised as a more efficiently administered version of the Minnesota Spatial Relations Test, the Minnesota Paper Formboard is not really the same test; the correlation between the two tests is substantially lower than the parallel-forms reliability coefficient of the latter.

Other Paper-and-Pencil Measures of Mechanical Ability

Spatial relations tests are only one kind of measure of mechanical ability. A second measure is provided by tests of mechanical comprehension, which are concerned with the ability to understand the mechanical principles involved in a range of practical situations. One of the most popular tests in this category is the Bennett Mechanical Comprehension Test (from The Psychological Corporation). This test measures understanding of mechanical relationships and physical laws in practical situations. The items consist of drawings and questions concerning the operation of such relationships or laws (Figure 7–7). Because the average score and reliability of the Bennett are lower for women than for men, separate norms are provided by sex. Evidence of the validity of the Bennett test is found in its modest correlations with performance in a variety of occupations requiring mechanical ability.

CLERICAL AND COMPUTER-RELATED ABILITIES

Like many other categories of ability, clerical ability is not a unitary factor distinct from general intelligence. Although manual dexterity and speed of perceiving similarities and differences are necessary in clerical work, also important are verbal and mathematical abilities, which are aspects of general intelligence. Consequently, many tests of clerical ability contain items similar to those found on general intelligence tests, as well as items to measure perceptual speed and accuracy.

In addition to the more general tests of clerical ability, several tests have been designed to measure stenographic aptitude. Also available are tests of the ability to learn the complex clerical and problem-solving tasks of computer programming and computer operation.

Look at Sample X on this page. It shows two men carrying a weighted object on a plank, and it asks, "Which man carries more weight?" Because the object is closer to man "B" than to man "A," man "B" is shouldering more weight; so blacken the circle under "B" on your answer sheet. Now look at Sample Y and answer it yourself. Fill in the circle under the correct answer on your answer sheet.

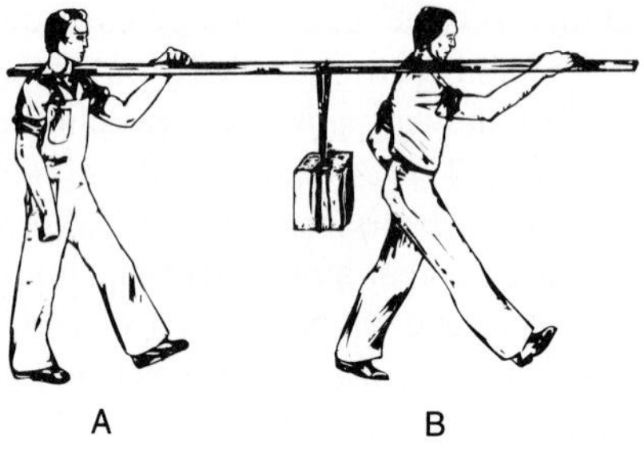

X

Which man carries more weight?
(If equal, mark C.)

EXAMPLES

A B C
X ○ ● ○
A B C
Y ○ ○ ○

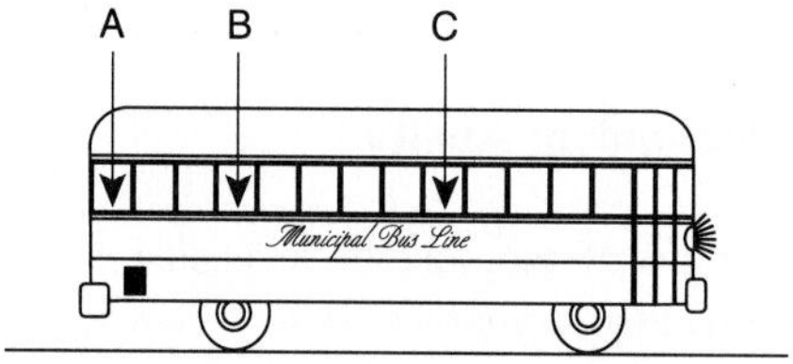

Y

Which letter shows the seat where a passenger will get the smoothest ride?

FIGURE 7–7 Sample Items from the Bennett Mechanical Comprehension Test. *(Copyright © 1942, 1967–1970, 1980 by The Psychological Corporation. All rights reserved.)*

Representative Tests of General Clerical Ability

Commercially distributed tests of clerical ability vary in content from the simple number-and-name checking tasks of the Minnesota Clerical Test to the combined general intelligence and perceptual–motor tasks of the newer Clerical Abilities Measures. The Minnesota Clerical Test (from The Psychological Corporation) was designed for use in selecting clerks, inspectors, and other specialists in occupations involving speed of perceiving and manipulating symbols. The test consists of two parts, Number Comparison and Name Comparison, on which the examinee inspects 200 pairs of numbers and 200 pairs of names for errors and checks identical pairs (Figure 7–8). Both parts of the test are scored by the formula "rights minus wrongs," and the test–retest reliabilities of the scores are in the .70's and .80's. Percentile norms for students, by sex and grade (7 to 12), and for groups of clerical workers and applicants are given in the manual. The scores are moderately correlated with teachers' and supervisors' ratings on clerical work.

In contrast to the Minnesota Clerical Test, which measures only perceptual speed and accuracy, the Clerical Abilities Battery (from The Psychological Corporation) is composed

If the two names or the two numbers of a pair are exactly the same make a check mark (✔) on the line between them; if they are different, make no mark on that line.

Samples done correctly
of pairs of *Numbers*

79542 _____ 79524

5794367 __✔__ 5794367

Samples done correctly
of pairs of *Names*

John C. Linder _____ John C. Lender

Investors Syndicate __✔__ Investors Syndicate

_____

Now try the samples below.

(1) New York World _____ New York World

(2) Cargill Grain Co. _____ Cargil Grain Co.

(3) 66273894 _____ 66273984

(4) 527384578 _____ 527384578

FIGURE 7–8 Sample Items from the Minnesota Clerical Test.
(Copyright © 1933, Revised 1961 by The Psychological Corporation. Reproduced by permission. All rights reserved.)

of seven tests designed to measure a variety of clerical skills: Filing, Copying Information, Comparing Information, Using Tables, Proofreading, Addition and Subtraction, and Reasoning with Numbers. Testing time is 5 to 20 minutes for each subtest, or 60 minutes for all seven. The percentile norms for both forms (A and B) are based on several well-defined clerical populations.

Computer-related Aptitudes

The rapid growth of the computer industry during the past three decades has led to an increased need for computer software, the programs of logical statements that tell the computer what to do to achieve specified objectives. Learning how to program a computer requires a combination of clerical and problem-solving skills that people possess in different degrees. Therefore, it becomes important to identify those who possess a high aptitude for learning computer programming. Responding to this need, measurement specialists have constructed tests of computer-programming aptitude. An example is the Computer Programmer Aptitude Battery (CPAB) (from SRA/London House), which consists of subtests of Verbal Meaning, Reasoning, Letter Series, Number Ability, and Diagramming. The purpose of this 75-minute battery is to evaluate and select applicants for computer-programming courses. Beginners and experienced programmers and systems analysts were used in developing the items, and percentile norms on total and subtest scores are reported for the battery. Validation studies have shown the CPAB to be predictive of job success in a variety of production and service organizations.

Also available are tests that assess the aptitude for operating computers, an example being the Computer Operator Aptitude Battery (COAB) (from SRA/London House). The three subtests of the COAB are Sequence Recognition ("ability to recognize sequences quickly"), Format Checking ("ability to perceive conformity of numbers and letters to a specified format"), and Logical Thinking ("ability to analyze problems and visualize solutions logically"). Testing time for the COAB is 45 minutes. Percentile norms obtained on relatively small samples of experienced computer operators and inexperienced applicants or trainees are listed by subtest and total score in the manual.

One of the most comprehensive of all computer-related aptitude tests is the Computer Aptitude, Literacy, and Interest Profile (CALIP) (from The Psychological Corporation). CALIP consists of 138 attitudinal, reasoning, nonverbal, and visual items grouped into six subtests covering computer aptitude, literacy, and interest. Except for Subtest 1, which is timed at 2 minutes, the subtests are untimed, but take a total of approximately 1 hour. Norms (standard scores for the six subtests, plus a single aptitude quotient obtained from combined scores on four subtests) are based on 1200 individuals between the ages of 12 and 60 selected to be demographically representative of the U.S. population.

ARTISTIC, MUSICAL, AND OTHER CREATIVE ABILITIES

As the phrases *de gustibus non est disputandum* and "beauty is in the eye of the beholder" imply, the ultimate judge of artistic merit is the observer alone. Since taste in art varies greatly from individual to individual, from culture to culture, and from age to age, it is not surprising that criteria of artistic ability are difficult to specify. Notwithstanding the many problems of defining reliable criteria and constructing tests to predict those criteria, a number of tests of visual art ability and musical ability have been published since 1920. However, the majority of these tests are now rarely administered and no longer commercially available.

Art Ability Tests

Some years ago researchers at the University of Minnesota found a positive correlation between scores on spatial perception tests, such as the Minnesota Paper Formboard, and artistic ability (Paterson et al., 1930). Spatial ability, however, is not the only factor included in artistic ability; judgment, manual dexterity, creative imagination, and other factors also play a role. Furthermore, a person who has the ability to recognize good art is not necessarily able to produce it. For this reason, it is important to distinguish between measures of esthetic appreciation (judgment and perception) and work-sample measures of productive skill in art. Illustrative of tests of art judgment and perception are the Meier Art Tests (Art Judgment and Aesthetic Perception) and the Graves Design Judgment Tests. Unlike the Meier Art Judgment Test, which uses famous works of art as stimuli, the Graves Design Judgment Test employs two- and three-dimensional abstract designs to elicit artistic judgments. An example of a performance test in art is the Horn Art Aptitude Inventory.

Musical Ability Tests

As with artistic ability, the correlations between musical ability tests and criteria of accomplishment in music have not been high. There does appear, however, to be a weak general factor of musical ability, and a number of tests have been designed to measure it. Although scores on these tests are positively correlated with intelligence test scores, a high intellectual level is certainly not essential to musical ability. Both young children and the mentally retarded may be quite accomplished musically.

The oldest musical ability test, the Seashore Measures of Musical Talents, was a product of the pioneering research of Carl Seashore and his colleagues at the University of Iowa during the 1920s and 1930s (Seashore, 1939). In contrast to the musical ability tests developed later, the stimulus materials on the Seashore tests consisted of a series of musical tones or notes, rather than meaningful musical selections. However, this analytic, atomistic approach to musical ability was severely criticized, and, as a result, several tests with more complex musical content were developed. Among these are omnibus measures, such as the Wing Standardized Tests of Musical Intelligence, the Drake Musical Aptitude Test, and the Musical Aptitude Profile

Musical Aptitude Profile   These tape-recorded tests (from Riverside Publishing Company) consist of 250 original short selections for violin and cello played by professional musicians. No previous knowledge of music or historical facts is required. The examinee is asked to judge whether a selection and a musical answer are the same or exactly the same or which of the two represents a more musical performance. Three basic musical factors (musical expression, aural perception, and kinesthetic musical feeling) are purportedly measured by the three tests constituting the battery. These three tests are Test T, Tonal Imagery (melody, harmony); Test R, Rhythm Imagery (tempo, meter); and Test S, Musical Sensitivity (phrasing, balance, style). On the first two tests, which have correct answers, the examinee is asked whether two stimuli are alike or different. On the last test, which has multiple scoring, the examinee is asked which of two tape-recorded renditions of a piece of music is more tasteful. This battery of tests is appropriate for grades 4 through 12 and takes 110 minutes to administer.

Gordon's (1967) three-year longitudinal predictive study of the Musical Aptitude Profile (MAP) was one of the most carefully conducted of all investigations of musical ability. Two hundred forty-one fourth- and fifth-grade children in eight classrooms of five cities were tested individually with the MAP and then given weekly instruction in playing musical instruments. The correlation between initial MAP scores and judges' ratings of the children's musical performance was .59 after one year of instruction and .74 after three years of instruction.

Creativity

When intelligence or scholastic aptitude tests are administered to school-age children, the tests usually do a fair job of predicting short-term school achievement and related criteria. These tests, however, were not designed to measure situational variables, lifelong determination, motivation, or nonscholastic talent of the sort that affects creative performance. It is noteworthy that few, if any, of the intellectually gifted children studied by Terman (Terman & Odlen, 1959) attained the eminence of a Winston Churchill, Albert Einstein, or Ernest Hemingway. Nor did any of them become a famous composer, artist, or poet.

It is generally recognized that above-average intelligence is necessary but not sufficient for creative productivity. Beyond a minimum IQ of around 120, creative performance appears to depend more on motivation and special abilities than on general mental ability (MacKinnon, 1962). Therefore, investigations of creativity conducted since 1965 have focused on the identification of other cognitive and affective characteristics that distinguish creative from noncreative people. For example, attempts have been made to develop measures of divergent, as opposed to convergent, thinking ability (Guilford, 1967). On measures of *convergent thinking,* such as problems of the kind found on intelligence tests, there is only one correct answer. In contrast, on tests of *divergent thinking,* examinees are presented with a problem having a number of possible solutions and are scored on the originality of their responses. Thus, rather than having a fixed number of possible answers, items on divergent or creative thinking tests are open ended. Unfortunately, this open-endedness leads to difficulties in scoring and determining the reliability and validity of a creativity test. Among the scoring procedures that have been advocated is evaluating answers for both fluency (number of responses given by the examinee) and novelty (originality or uncommonness of responses given by the examinee).

Single Creativity Tests   The following items are illustrative of those found on single tests of creativity:

1. **Consequences Test.** Imagine all the things that might possibly happen if all national and local laws were suddenly abolished (Guilford, 1954).
2. **Remote Associates Test.** Find a fourth word that is associated with each of these three words: (a) rat–blue–cottage; (b) out–dog–cat; (c) wheel–electric–high; (d) surprise–line–birthday (Mednick, 1962).
3. **Unusual Uses Test.** Name as many uses as you can think of for: (a) a toothpick (b) a brick (c) a paper clip (Guilford, 1954).
4. **Word Association Test.** Write as many meanings as you can for each of the following words: (a) duck (b) sack (c) pitch (d) fair (Getzels & Jackson, 1962.

Creativity Test Batteries   Two widely used batteries of creativity tests are those in the Structure-of-Intellect Abilities and the Torrance Tests of Creative Thinking. The tests in the Structure-of-Intellect Abilities (SOI), several of which are now published by Consulting Psychologists Press as Guilford's Measures of Creativity, are by-products of the factor-analytic research of J. P. Guilford and his co-workers on the nature of human intelligence (Guilford, 1967, 1974). Included in this battery are Consequences and Unusual Uses subtests, four Christensen–Guilford Fluency tests, other verbal subtests such as Simile Interpretation, and nonverbal subtests such as Sketches, Making Objects, and Decorations. The majority of these tests can be administered at the junior high level and beyond, but the scoring is complex. The split-half reliabilities of the tests range from .60 to .90.

The Torrance Test of Creative Thinking (TTCT) (from Scholastic Testing Service) consists of three picture-based exercises (Figural TTCT) and six word-based exercises (Verbal TTCT). An example of the kinds of items on the Verbal TTCT is to "write out all the questions you can think of" about a given picture. On one part of the Figural TTCT, the examinee is asked to make a sketch from a basic line (Figure 7–9). The Verbal TTCT, which takes 45 minutes to administer, is scored on three mental characteristics (fluency, flexibility, and originality). The Figural TTCT, which takes 30 minutes to administer, is scored on five mental characteristics (fluency, originality, elaboration, titles, and closure). The TTCT was restandardized in 1989, and national percentile ranks and standard scores from grade 1 through college and adult level are given in the manual.

Characteristics of Creative People   Thomas Alva Edison held 1093 patents, Albert Einstein published 248 papers, Pablo Picasso averaged over 200 works of art a year, and Wolfgang Amadeus Mozart composed more than 600 pieces of music by the time of his death at age 35. These cases illustrate the high inner drive or intrinsic motivation that creative people reportedly possess (Haney, 1985). Other affective and cognitive traits said to be characteristic of creative people are ideational fluency, flexibility, unconventionalism, social sensitivity, nondefensiveness, a greater willingness to concede faults, and close ties with parents (MacKinnon, 1962).

Based on the results of investigations by MacKinnon (1962) and Wallach and Kogan (1965), it would seem that creativity, especially when accompanied by high intelligence, is not a bad characteristic to possess from a mental health standpoint. However, in a study of prominent British artists (novelists, painters, playwrights, poets, and sculptors), Jamison (1984) found that these artists were much more likely than less creative people to have been treated for mood disorders (mania and depression). Similar findings were obtained by Andreasen (1987) in a study of 30 faculty members in a writers' workshop: 80 percent exhibited depression or some other form of mood disorder, and 43 percent were diagnosed as manic-depressive. The meaning of these findings is not entirely clear, but the least that can be concluded is that creative adults, like gifted children (see Webb & Meckstroth, 1982), are no strangers to unhappiness and poor adjustment.

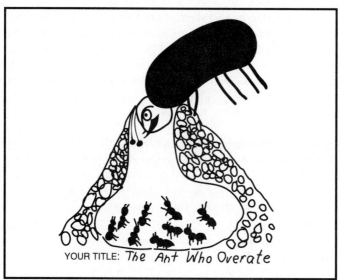

FIGURE 7–9 Sample Items from the Torrance Tests of Creative Thinking. These Drawings from the Figural TTCT Illustrate the Humor That Is Presumably More Characteristic of Creative Persons.
(Copyright © 1984 by Scholastic Testing Service, Inc. Reprinted by permission of Scholastic Testing Service, Inc. from Torrance Tests of Creative Thinking, Streamlined (Revised) Manual, *Figures A and B, by E. Paul Torrance and Orlow E. Ball.)*

Evaluation of Creativity Tests   Although research in the area of creativity and the instruments designed to assess it are intriguing, it is important to heed the criticisms made by McNemar (1964) and other psychologists. It has been noted, for example, that tests of creativity frequently have substantial correlations with IQ tests. Furthermore, the former are apparently no more effective than the latter in predicting "creative performance." All things considered, a reasonable conclusion is that it remains to be demonstrated whether effective measures of creativity can be constructed. Until a test that can predict performance on a generally accepted criterion of creativity is designed, it would be well to heed McNemar's (1964) advice that we not dispose of our general intelligence tests.

MULTIPLE-APTITUDE BATTERIES

Often useful in vocational counseling, as well as in employment classification and place-ment, is the measurement of skills and knowledge in many different areas. An examiner may, of course, decide to administer separate, single tests of several different abilities, but this can be very time consuming. More important, such a collection of single tests will in all likelihood have been standardized on as many different groups of people as there are tests. Because of different norm groups for different tests, it is difficult to compare an examinee's score on one test with his or her score on another test in any meaningful way.

Separate special ability tests certainly have their place, especially in personnel selec-tion and screening. Such tests are, however, less useful in vocational counseling and classification. In an economic system like ours, in which the emphasis in the workaday world has shifted somewhat from selecting only the "cream of the crop" to classifying and placing workers on jobs most suited to their abilities and needs, job classification rather than selection has been increasingly emphasized. Consequently, multiple-aptitude tests, which are designed to match people having particular ability patterns to specific jobs, are seen as potentially more valuable than single tests designed to select only the best and screen out all others. Unlike single tests of special abilities, which may be of either the paper-and-pencil or performance variety, multiple-aptitude batteries do not typically involve any apparatus other than paper and pencil. Therefore, they can be administered simultaneously to a large group of students, job applicants, military inductees, or other people.

Many school systems administer the Differential Aptitude Tests or another multiple-aptitude battery in the eighth or ninth grade. During the junior high years, students are beginning to make career plans and decisions on what courses to take. The information provided by an aptitude test battery can sharpen students' awareness of their strengths and weaknesses and thereby serve as a guide in making occupational and educational decisions. Mental abilities are less specific during the elementary school years, becoming more differentiated with maturity and experience. For this reason, the administration of an expensive, time-consuming, multiple-aptitude battery is usually not recommended prior to the junior high years.

Rather than administering a long series of special abilities tests or a multiple-aptitude battery, a vocational counselor may decide to use a general intelligence test plus one or more tests of special abilities. There is certainly nothing wrong with this strategy. The verbal and quantitative abilities measured by intelligence tests are important in a wide range of activities in Western culture. Consequently, scores on these instruments are among the best overall predictors of academic and occupational success in our society. In addition to evaluating several special abilities, many aptitude batteries contain a built-in general intelligence test. This provides the combined advantages of more efficient administration and comparable norms on all tests.

Score Differences and Profile Interpretation

The statistical procedures of factor analysis (see Appendix A) have been applied in constructing several aptitude test batteries. Examples are the Primary Mental Abilities Test and the Guilford–Zimmerman Aptitude Survey. Even on batteries not constructed by factor-analytic methods, the results of studies employing these methods have usually been taken into account in preparing items and defining test variables.

Items on the Differential Aptitude Tests, a nonfactored battery, were selected so that they would have high correlations with other items on the same subtest, but low correlations with items on other subtests. The final result was a set of internally consistent subtests having low correlations with each other. It was important for the correlations among subtests to be low; otherwise, the overlap among the abilities measured by different subtests would be too great for differential interpretation of subtest scores.

Reliability and Standard Error of Score Differences   The correlations among different subtests in the same battery are often sizable, and the fact that the subtests are fairly short results in relatively low subtest reliabilities. However, not only does the reliability of the differences between scores on two tests vary directly with the reliabilities of the tests, but it also varies inversely with the correlation between the tests (see footnote 1 in Chapter 5). The combined effect of a sizable correlation between two given subtests and low reliabilities of those subtests is low reliability of the differences between scores on the subtests.

When the reliability of the differences between the scores on two subtests is low, the difference between a person's score on the two subtests must be fairly large in order to be viewed as significant. To illustrate this principle, suppose that the reliability of the T scores on the spatial relations test of an aptitude battery is .85 and the reliability of the T scores on the mechanical ability test of the same battery is .90. An approximate formula for the standard error of the differences (s_{ed}) between examinees' scores on the two tests is

$$s_{ed} = s \sqrt{2 - r_{11} - r_{22}} \tag{7.1}$$

where r_{11} and r_{22} are the test–retest reliabilities of the two subtests, and s is the standard deviation of the scores on each test. Recalling that the standard deviation of T scores equals 10, when scores on both tests are expressed as T scores, formula 7.1 becomes $s_{ed} = 10\sqrt{2 - .85 - .90} = 5$. Therefore, to be fairly certain (probability of .95) that the difference between an examinee's scores on these two tests is significant and hence interpretable and not simply due to chance, that difference should be at least 1.96×5 = 9.8 T-score units.

Score Profile The process of interpreting a person's scores on a multiple-aptitude battery consisting of several tests standardized on the same or equivalent norm groups begins by constructing a score profile. A *score profile,* which is a line graph or a bar graph that takes into account the standard errors of measurement of the tests, provides a picture of the person's strengths and weaknesses in various aptitude areas (Figure 7–10). Comparing an individual's profile on a multiple-aptitude battery with the average score profile of people in selected occupations can be of help in vocational counseling and occupational selection and placement. Although workers within the same occupation differ to some degree in the patterns of their abilities, certain job families seem to require a particular set of abilities. Similar profiles on a multiple-aptitude battery indicate similar patterns of abilities.

Not every small difference between two scores on a profile is significant or interpretable, and the elevation of a profile is just as important as its pattern or scatter. As a matter of fact, low scores on aptitude tests tend to be more predictive of performance than high scores; low scores imply failure more often than high scores imply success. The notion that a certain minimum level of ability is required for success in a specific occupation is one that the designers of the General Aptitude Battery stressed. Beyond such a minimum ability, whatever it may be, work habits, interests, and other variables become more important in determining job success.

Differential Aptitude Tests

A number of aptitude test batteries have been designed for and standardized primarily in school situations and used as predictors of scholastic achievement. Most prominent of all test batteries of this type are the Differential Aptitude Tests (DAT) (from The Psychological Corporation). The DAT, which is appropriate for grades 8 through 13, is designed especially for vocational and educational counseling in junior and senior high school. It consists of eight tests: Verbal Reasoning, Numerical Ability, Abstract Reasoning, Clerical Speed and Accuracy, Mechanical Reasoning, Space Relations, Spelling, and Language Usage. Scores are obtained on each of these tests, in addition to an index of scholastic ability, which is the sum of scores on the Verbal Reasoning (VR) and Numerical Ability (NA) tests. The entire battery takes over 3 hours to administer; the time limits range from 6 to 30 minutes per test. A Computerized Adaptive version of the DAT is untimed, but takes an average of 90 minutes to complete. Using item-response theory, the adaptive version presents a subset of test items that are most appropriate for the person being tested. Although the correlations among the eight tests are fairly low, the tests are not measures of "pure factors"; rather, each test assesses a complex of mental abilities.

Standardization and Profile Interpretation Forms V and W of the DAT were standardized on a representative national sample of students in grades 8 through 12, stratified according to size of school district, geographical region, socioeconomic status of community, and type of school (public versus nonpublic). Unlike the Stanford–Binet

INDIVIDUAL REPORT
PROFILE FOR HAND-PLOTTING

DIFFERENTIAL APTITUDE TESTS
G.K. Bennett, H.G. Seashore, A.G. Wesman

FORMS V AND W

Name LEE JOHN   Grade 8   Test date 2/22/83   Form W
Sex M   Norm group { Grade 8 Semester SPRING

N = National
L = Local

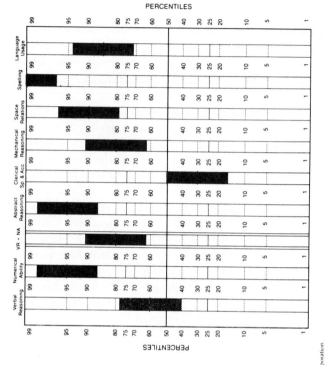

PROFILING YOUR DAT SCORES

The numbers that tell you how you did on each test are in the rows marked "Percentile." The higher the number for any test, the better you did in that area as compared to students in your grade across the country. The first row of percentiles tells where you rank on each test in comparison with students of your own sex. The second row shows how you rank on each test as compared to students of the opposite sex.

If your percentile on one test is 80, you are at the top of 80 percent of the group — only 20 percent made higher scores than yours. If you scored in the 25th percentile, this means about 75 percent of the group did better than you on the test. These percentiles do NOT tell you how many questions (or what percent of them) you answered correctly.

To draw your aptitude profile on the chart, use the percentiles in the first row (own-sex percentiles). There are nine columns to be marked. In each of these make a *heavy short line* across the column at the level of your percentile on that test. (In some cases, the line you draw will match with a dotted or solid line already printed on the chart.) Then blacken each column one-half inch above and one-half inch below the short line you have drawn. You will end up with a solid black bar in each column. (For very high or low percentiles, you will not be able to blacken one-half inch in both directions without running off the chart.) The reason for the bar instead of a single line is that a test is not a perfect measure of your ability. You can be reasonably sure that you stand somewhere within the area covered by the bar.

HOW BIG A DIFFERENCE IS IMPORTANT?

Since tests cannot be perfectly accurate, you should not place too much importance on small differences between the percentiles for any pair of tests. The bars you drew on the chart help show the more important differences.

Look at the bars for any two tests to see whether their ends overlap. If they do not, chances are that you really are better in the kind of ability in which you scored higher. If the bars overlap, but not by more than half their length, the difference may or may not be important. To help you decide, consider whether other things you know about yourself agree with this indication. If they overlap by more than half their length, the difference between the scores can probably be ignored; your ability is really about the same in both areas. You can use this method of looking at the overlap of the bars to compare any two abilities, whether they are listed next to each other or not.

See other side for more information about your profile ▶

Ψ THE PSYCHOLOGICAL CORPORATION

FIGURE 7-10 Sample Profile from the Differential Aptitude Tests, 4th Edition.
(Reproduced by permission, Copyright © 1982, 1972 by The Psychological Corporation. Reproduced by permission. All rights reserved.)

Intelligence Scale, which was designed to eliminate sex differences, there are significant sex differences in DAT scores. For example, girls score higher on Clerical Speed and Accuracy and Language Usage than boys, whereas boys score higher on Mechanical Reasoning and Space Relations than girls. Because of these difference, the percentile and stanine score norms are provided separately by sex as well as by grade level. From the norms, it is possible to construct a profile of an examinee's scores on the various tests for use in academic and vocational counseling (Figure 7–10). The percentile bands represented by the vertical black bars in the same individual DAT profile of Figure 7–10 are equivalent in length to one standard error of measurement on either side of the examinee's observed tests scores. If the vertical bars for two tests do not overlap, then the difference between the examinee's scores on those two tests is considered significant.

Reliability and Validity   The reliability coefficients of tests on the DAT range from .87 to .94, with the exception of Mechanical Reasoning, which has a reliability for girls as low as .70. The manual presents extensive data demonstrating that these tests, and especially the VR + NA composite, are valid predictors of high school and college grades. They also have some value in predicting job level within occupations, but the norms for various occupations are limited. Consequently, the DAT must be used cautiously as a differential predictor of vocational success.

Industrially Oriented Aptitude Batteries

Several multiple-aptitude batteries have been designed especially for selection and placement in business and industry. One of the oldest batteries of this type, which was constructed in the 1930s by the staff of the Minnesota Employment Stabilization Research Institute, consists of tests of general intelligence, as well as numerical, perceptual, mechanical, and psychomotor abilities. Profiles of the average scores on the tests obtained by clerks, mechanical workers, salespersons, and many other occupational groups were established as a set of *occupational ability patterns* (OAPs) with which individual performance could be compared.

General Aptitude Test Battery (GATB)   The OAP approach of the Minnesota psychologists was retained in the development of the General Aptitude Test battery of the U.S. Employment Service. The GATB, designed on the basis of job analyses and a factor analysis of 59 tests, is composed of 8 paper-and-pencil and 4 apparatus tests. These 12 tests in combination yield scores on nine major aptitudes and skills required for occupational success: Intelligence (G), Verbal Aptitude (V), Numerical Aptitude (N), Spatial Aptitude (S), Form Perception (P), Clerical Perception (Q), Motor Coordination (K), Finger Dexterity (F), and Manual Dexterity (M). Raw scores on the nine factors are converted to percentile ranks or standard scores having a mean of 100 and a standard deviation of 20. The standard scores of an examinee can then be compared with those of the 36 or so occupational ability patterns (OAPs) determined from an analysis of the GATB scores of people in over 800 jobs. An OAP consists of a set of minimum GATB scores (cutting scores) considered essential for effective performance in that occupation.

The entire GATB takes 2½ hours to administer and is appropriate for senior high students (usually twelfth-graders) and adults. Test–retest and parallel-forms reliability coefficients of the separate tests range from .80 to .90, with a standard error of measurement of approximately seven points for the standard scores. The validities of the nine aptitude scores and the 36 OAPs for predicting occupational and academic criteria of success range from .00 to .90's. The GATB is one of the most widely used vocational counseling and job placement tools for students in grades 9–12 and adults and probably the most appropriate for that purpose. However, the DAT is better for educational counseling purposes.

Orders and requests for authorization to use the GATB in settings such as vocational rehabilitation centers, state employment services, secondary and postsecondary schools, vocational and technical schools, apprenticeship programs, work-incentive programs, and Job Training Partnership Act programs may be placed with any state employment agency. Test results are processed by National Computer Systems and reported as raw scores for the 12 parts, converted aptitude scores for the different aptitudes, plus 66 OAPs classified by category (High, Middle, Low).

Although the GATB has been the most widely used of all industrially oriented aptitude batteries, a number of other aptitude test batteries deserve mention. These include the OASI Aptitude Survey (from pro.ed), the Employee Aptitude Survey (from EdITS), the Wide Range Employability Sample Test (from Jastak Associates), and the FACT and FIT. Only the last two will be described.

FACT and FIT These two test batteries, the Flanagan Aptitude Classification Tests (FACT) and the Flanagan Industrial Tests (FIT), are available from SRA/London House. The FACT, which was a result of research on the Aviation Cadet Classification Battery during World War II, consists of 16 tests, each corresponding to a job element revealed by an analysis of behaviors critical to job performance. The 16 FACT tests are Arithmetic, Assembly, Coding, Coordination, Components, Expression, Ingenuity, Inspection, Judgment and Comprehension, Mechanics, Memory, Patterns, Precision, Reasoning, Scales, and Tables. An extensive research program designed to validate 38 occupational aptitude scores representing a composite of FACT scores was planned, but only moderate progress was made.

A disadvantage of the FACT is that it takes several hours to administer all 16 tests (5 to 40 minutes per test). However, a subset of the 16 tests may be selected for administration, depending on the examinee's interests and personal history. In general, the FACT program was promising, but valididation data related to the use of the test battery in vocational counseling are meager.

The 18 FIT tests are modifications of the FACT in that they are based on the same job analyses as the FACT battery and measure the same job elements. They take less time (5 to 15 minutes per test) to administer, but are somewhat more difficult than the FACT. Percentile rank and stanine score norms based on relatively small samples of high school and college students are given in the 1965 FIT manual. Reliability estimates for the separate tests range from .50 to .90, but, as with the FACT, validity data are scanty.

A Military-based Test Battery

Beginning with the Army Examinations Alpha and Beta in World War I, over the years the armed services have used various tests to select and classify military personnel. The

Army General Classification Test (AGCT) was administered to millions of military recruits during and after World War II to classify them for skilled and unskilled jobs, to select those who could profit from further training, and to reject those who, because of low mental ability, were considered unfit for military service. Some years after World War II, the Armed Forces Qualification Test (AFQT) replaced the AGCT for screening military applicants.

During the 1970s, the Armed Services Vocational Aptitude Battery (ASVAB) became the uniform selection and classification test for the joint armed services. The 10 ASVAB tests and illustrative items are given in Figure 7–11. The ASVAB tests are grouped into three academic composites (academic ability, verbal, and math) and four occupational composites (mechanical and crafts, business and clerical, electronics and electrical, and health and social), plus an overall measure of general ability.

The ASVAB was designed to identify young men and women who have the requisite abilities to enter the U.S. military and various occupational training programs. It is administered each year to more than 1 million students in grades 11–12 and postsecondary schools. The Kuder–Richardson reliabilities of the ASVAB composite scores are in the .80's and .90's, and evidence for the validity of the battery in predicting success in various military and civilian occupations is substantial. The latest form of the ASVAB was standardized in 1980 on a national sample of 12,000 men and women between the ages of 16 and 23. There is also a microcomputer version of the test, which employs item-response theory and adaptive testing methodology and consequently reduces administration time by about half.

Longitudinal Studies of Aptitude Tests and Careers

One of the great success stories of applied psychology involved the construction of the Aviation Cadet Classification Battery for the Army Air Corps during World War II. The problem facing the Air Corps psychologists was to predict success in learning to fly an airplane. The solution was to construct a battery of instruments, including tests of general information, verbal and mathematical abilities, perceptual–motor skills, mechanical abilities, and an inventory of biographical data. Initially, all candidates took the battery of tests and were accepted for the training regardless of their scores. Subsequently, scores on the tests were correlated with success in completing flying training. Many different tests contributed something to the prediction of success in learning to fly, and, when used in combination as a selection battery, they saved the U.S. government a great deal of money on its pilot-training program. Using these tests for selection purposes also saved airplanes, student pilots, and flight instructors!

Twelve years later, Thorndike and Hagen (1959) located 10,000 men who had taken the Air Corps test battery in 1943. By 1955, this group of men had entered over 100 occupations. The investigators related scores on the Air Corps tests taken 12 years earlier to occupational membership and seven criteria of success in these occupations. Although near-zero correlations were found between scores on the tests and criteria of success within occupations, the average scores obtained by various occupational groups differed significantly. For example, examinees who later became scientists or college professors had scored above average on the tests of general intelligence, numerical ability, and

The ASVAB is used by the armed services to determine qualifications for enlistment as well as most suitable job assignment. Test takers are advised to do their best since ASVAB scores "will determine which job areas you are qualified to enter. The better your scores are, the more opportunities you will have available to you. . . ."

All of the items on the AS-VAB are multiple-choice with four or five possible answers. Score is based on the number right and test takers are encour-aged to guess if they are unsure of the correct response as there is no penalty for guessing. Test takers are further advised to "get a good night's rest before taking the test." Sample items from each of the 10 subtests follow with the answer key printed at the end. To get a feel for the type of questions asked, why not sample these items yourself—even if you perchance didn't get a good night's rest last night.

I. General Science
   Included here are general science questions including questions from the areas of biology and physics.

   1. An eclipse of the sun throws the shadow of the
      A   moon on the sun
      B   moon on the earth
      C   earth on the sun
      D   earth on the moon

II. Arithmetic Reasoning
   The task here is to solve arithmetic problems. Test takers are permitted to use (government supplied) scratch paper.

   2. It cost $0.50 per square yard to waterproof canvas. What will it cost to waterproof a canvas truck that is 15' × 24'?
      A $ 6.67
      B $ 18.00
      C $ 20.00
      D $180.00

III. Word Knowledge
   Which of four possible definitions best defines the underlined word?

   3. Rudiments most nearly means

      A   politics
      B   minute details
      C   promotion opportunities
      D   basic methods and procedures

IV. Paragraph Comprehension
   A test of reading comprehension and reasoning.

   4. Twenty-five percent of all household burglaries can be attributed to unlocked windows or doors. Crime is the result of opportunity plus desire. To prevent crime, it is each individual's responsibility to

FIGURE 7–11   Sample Items from The Armed Services Vocational Aptitude Battery (A SVAB).
(Reprinted by permission of Director of Testing, Headquarters, United States Military Entrance Processing Command, North Chicago, IL, Fort Sheridan, Illinois.)

      A   provide the desire
      B   provide the opportunity
      C   prevent the desire
      D   prevent the opportunity

V. Numerical Operations

This speeded test contains simple arithmetic problems that the test taker must do quickly; it is one of two speeded tests on the ASVAB.

   5. 6 − 5 =
      A   1
      B   4
      C   2
      D   3

VI. Coding Speed

This subtest contains coding items which measure perceptual/motor speed among other factors.

KEY

| green | . . . 2715 | man | . . . 3451 | salt | . . . 4586 |
| hat | . . . 1413 | room | . . . 2864 | tree | . . . 5972 |

	A	B	C	D	E
6. room	1413	2715	2864	3451	4586

VII. Auto and Shop Information

This test assesses knowledge of automobiles, shop practices, and the use of tools.

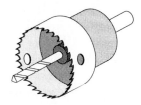

   7. What tool is shown above?
      A   Hole saw
      B   Keyhole saw
      C   Counter saw
      D   Grinding saw

VIII. Mathematics Knowledge

This is a test of ability to solve problems using high school level mathematics. Use of scratch paper is permitted.

   8. If $3X = -5$, then $X =$
      A   −2
      B   −5/3
      C   −3/5
      D   3/5

IX. Mechanical Comprehension

Knowledge and understanding of general mechanical and physical principles are probed by this test.

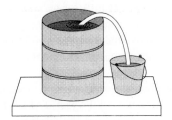

FIGURE 7–11   *(continued)*

9. Liquid is being transferred from the barrel to the bucket by
   A capillary action
   B gravitational forces
   C fluid pressure in the hose
   D water pressure in the barrel

X. Electronics Information
   Here, knowledge of electrical, radio, and electronics information is assessed.

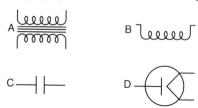

10. Which of the above is the symbol for a transformer?
    A A
    B B
    C C
    D D

Answer Key
 1. B
 2. C
 3. D
 4. D
 5. Why are you looking this one up?
 6. C
 7. A
 8. B
 9. B
10. A

FIGURE 7–11 *(continued)*

perceptual–spacial ability in 1943. On the other hand, examinees who later became machinists or mechanics had scored higher than average on tests of mechanical and psychomotor abilities on the 1943 battery. Nevertheless, the average variability of scores within the same occupation was almost as great as the variability of scores across occupational groups.

   Numerous explanations have been offered for the disappointing results obtained in the Thorndike and Hagen investigations. Perhaps the most important reasons for the failure to predict occupational membership and success more accurately in this case were (1) the wide range of occupations within each occupational group, (2) differences among the variables that were important in the training program and those important on the job, (3) imprecise definitions of occupational success in occupations where pay and promotions had become institutionalized, and (4) contingency or "incidental" factors (Thorndike, 1963).

   The fact that aptitude test scores alone are not accurate predictors of academic and vocational success was also demonstrated by the results of Project TALENT, a nationwide sampling and longitudinal follow-up investigation of the abilities and interests of U.S. high school students. During the spring of 1962, a cross-sectional sample consisting of 440,000 students in high schools throughout the United States took a battery of 22 aptitude and achievement tests and filled out a student activities inventory, an interest inventory, and a student information blank. The students were followed up in 1961, 1965, 1970, and 1980 to determine the relationships of their scores on these measures to their later educational attainments, vocational careers, and social contributions. An analysis of the initial findings into 13 ability factors and 13 motivational factors (Cooley & Lohnes, 1968) indicated that the motivational factors were some of the best predictors of college major and vocational placement. Even when both sets of factors on the TALENT battery were taken into consideration, however, prediction of career choice and other criteria was sill a matter of probability rather than certainty. To improve these probability estimates, the *Career Data Book of Project Talent* was prepared by Flanagan, Tiedeman, and Willis (1973). The *Career Data Book* provides average percentile ranks on the ability and motivation tests of Project TALENT for a variety of occupational groups.

Thus, we see that, although the pattern of scores on a multiple-aptitude test can serve as a rough indicator of an examinee's suitability for a particular job, occupational success cannot be accurately predicted from test scores alone. The range of tasks comprising most jobs is great enough so that people within a fairly wide span of abilities can adapt. Whether a person does adapt and succeed or becomes maladjusted and fails on the job or in other walks of life depends not only on his or her abilities, but also on motivation, interests, and temperament.

SUMMARY

Tests of aptitudes or special abilities focus on the future, that is, on measuring a person's ability to profit from further training or experience in a certain area. Tests of special abilities also have narrower bandwidths than conventional intelligence tests, in that they predict more specific accomplishments. Although certain tests of special abilities are of the work-sample or performance type, paper-and-pencil tests are more widely administered.

A variety of tests exist for measuring visual acuity, auditory acuity, color vision, and other aspects of sensation and perception. In addition, multipurpose instruments for visual screening and for measuring perceptual–motor skills are available.

Psychomotor abilities appear to be highly specific, and scores on tests of these abilities frequently have lower reliabilities than other ability tests; the scores are also very susceptible to practice effects. Illustrative of psychomotor tests are the Minnesota Rate of Manipulation Test for measuring gross manual movements, the Crawford Small Parts Dexterity Test for measuring fine manual movements, and the Bennett Hand-Tool Dexterity Test for measuring both gross and fine manual movements.

Tests of mechanical ability and clerical ability were among the first standardized measures of special abilities to be devised. However, neither mechanical ability nor clerical ability is a unitary psychological dimension. Tests of mechanical ability may involve psychomotor skills in addition to perception and mechanical comprehension. Tests of clerical ability may measure perceptual speed and accuracy, as well as verbal and numerical ability. Examples of tests of mechanical ability are the Bennett Mechanical Comprehension Test and the Test of Mechanical Concepts. Representative tests of clerical ability include the Minnesota Clerical Tests and the Clerical Abilities Battery. A number of tests designed to assess aptitudes for computer programming and computer operation have also been constructed; examples are the Computer Programmer Aptitude Battery and the Computer Operator Aptitude Battery.

A number of tests of artistic and musical ability have been designed since the 1920s. Some of these tests measure art appreciation (judgment and perception), while others assess artistic performance or knowledge of art. Two of the most popular tests of art appreciation are the Meier Art Tests and the Graves Design Judgment Test.

The Seashore Measures of Musical Talents, the oldest published test of musical ability, emphasizes discrimination, judgment, and memory for tones or tonal combinations. Several other musical ability tests (for example, the Wing Standardized Tests of Musical Intelligence and the Musical Aptitude Profile) involve judgment and discrimination of meaningful music. Success in either music or art depends, however, on many factors other than talent. In any case, most of these tests of artistic and musical ability are no longer commercially available.

Creative performance is known to be not only a function of relatively high intelligence, but also of high motivation, special training, and perhaps other psychological abilities. A major problem in developing useful measures of creativity is defining a criterion of creative performance. Tests such as Guilford's Structure-of-Intellect Abilities and the Torrance Tests of Creative Thinking are noteworthy examples of instruments designed to assess creativity, but the problem of specifying an acceptable criterion of creative performance has not been solved. The results of recent research suggest that certain kinds of creative performance are related to mental illness, in particular mood disorders such as manic-depressive psychosis.

Multiple-aptitude batteries are designed to measure individual strengths and weaknesses in a variety of ability areas. Certain multiple-aptitude batteries (for example, the Guilford–Zimmerman Aptitude Survey and the General Aptitude Test Battery) are based on the results of factor analysis, whereas other aptitude batteries (for example, the Differential Aptitude Test) are not. Aptitude test batteries, which are usually not administered prior to the junior high years, are useful tools in academic and vocational counseling, selection, and placement. In general, the most useful battery for academic counseling purposes is the Differential Aptitude Test; the General Aptitude Test Battery is considered best for purposes of vocational counseling. Scores on an aptitude battery alone, however, are inadequate for effective academic or vocational counseling; past performance, interests and motivation, personality characteristics, and situational factors must also be taken into account.

EXERCISES

1. Empirical support for making a distinction between aptitude and achievement was obtained in a cross-sectional investigation by Burket (1973). It was found that, whereas achievement test scores *increased* with increasing grade level when aptitude test scores were held constant, aptitude test scores *decreased* with increasing grade level when achievement test scores were held constant. These findings, combined with those of other investigators (for example, Carroll, 1973), may be interpreted in terms of the following equation: Achievement = Aptitude × Experience.   Explain.

2. Identify at least two tests in each of the following categories: psychomotor abilities, mechanical ability, clerical ability, and creativity.

3. Compare the work of the psychologists in the Employment Stabilization Research Institute at the University of Minnesota during the late 1920s with that of the Army Air Corps psychologists during World War II.

4. What are the advantages and disadvantages of administering an aptitude test battery rather than several single tests of special abilities?

5. How do the purposes of personnel selection and screening differ from those of classification and placement? What kinds of tests are most appropriate for assisting the decision-making process in selection and/or screening? In classification and placement?

6. Write a critical review of any of the separate tests of special abilities described in this chapter, following the outline given in Exercise 8 of Chapter 5.

7. Arrange to visit a local optometrist or ophthalmologist and ask him or her to describe the procedures and instruments employed in testing a person's vision. What aspects of vision are measured routinely by the optometrist, and which are measured only under special circumstances? Write a report of your findings.

8. Arrange to visit the administrative offices of your local school district and interview the school psychologist or director of special education about the psychological tests that they administer. For example, what tests are used in assessing the special abilities or disabilities of students? How often are students tested or screened for visual problems? Write a report of your findings.

9. John makes a T score of 65 on the verbal comprehension test and a T score of 75 on the numerical reasoning test of a multiple-aptitude test battery. If the reliabilities of the two tests are .90 and .85, respectively, can the examiner be 95 percent certain that John is poorer in verbal comprehension than in numerical ability? Support your conclusion with appropriate computations.

10. Run all the programs in Category 6 ("Programs on Special Abilities Tests") of *Computer Programs for Psychological Assessment*. Compare your results with those of your classmates.

SUGGESTED READINGS

Anastasi, A. (1985). Testing the test: Interpreting results from multiscore batteries. *Journal of Counseling and Development, 64,* 84–86.

Burket, G. R. (1973). Empirical criteria for distinguishing and validating aptitude and achievement measures. In D. R. Green (ed.), *The aptitude–achievement distinction.* Monterey, CA: CTB/McGraw-Hill.

Burns, R. B. (1980). Relation of aptitudes to learning at different points in time during instruction. *Journal of Educational Psychology, 72,* 785–795.

Carroll, J. B. (1973). The aptitude achievement distinction: The case of foreign language aptitude and proficiency. In D. R. Green (ed.), *The aptitude–achievement distinction.* Monterey, CA: CTB/McGraw-Hill.

Ghiselli, E. E. (1973). The validity of aptitude tests in personnel selection. *Personnel Psychology, 26,* 461–477.

McGee, M. G. (1979). Human spatial abilities: Psychometric studies and environmental, genetic, hormonal, and neurological influences. *Psychological Bulletin, 86,* 889–918.

Reschley, D. J. (1990). Aptitude tests in educational classification and placement. In G. Goldstein & M. Hersen (eds.), *Handbook of psychological assessment,* 2nd ed., pp. 148–172. New York: Pergamon Press.

Salvia, J., & Ysseldyke, J. E. (1988). *Assessment in special and remedial education,* 4th ed, pp. 220–238, 276–296. Boston: Houghton Mifflin.

Snow, R. E. (1992). Aptitude theory: Yesterday, today, and tomorrow. *Educational Psychologist,* 27(1), 5–32.

Tenopyr, M. L. (1981). The realities of employment testing. *American Psychologist, 36,* 1120–1127.

ASSESSMENT OF PERSONALITY AND PREFERENCES

Chapter Eight

Interests, Attitudes, and Values

Some of the best predictors of academic and vocational success are tests of intelligence and special abilities. These tests are measures of *maximum performance* in that they indicate what a person is capable of achieving under optimum conditions. Questionnaires and inventories of preferences and other affective variables typically do not contribute as much as cognitive tests to the prediction of academic or occupational performance, but they are very helpful in educational and vocational counseling. These measures of *typical performance* often add significantly to information obtained from measures of ability and past performance.

One shortcoming of affective assessment instruments is that they are usually not as objective and therefore not as reliable as cognitive tests. It is even debatable whether the questionnaires, self-report inventories, and other techniques employed as affective measures merit the title of *tests*. Nevertheless, many affective instruments have very respectable reliabilities, appreciable validities for certain purposes, and other characteristics of good tests.

Three affective variables that have received a great deal of research attention are *interests, attitudes,* and *values*. Measures of these variables, which serve both as predictors of outcomes and outcome criteria themselves, are the topic of the present chapter. In Chapters 9 and 10, our survey of affective measures will be completed with an examination of various types of personality assessment procedures and instruments.

INTERESTS AND INTEREST MEASUREMENT

Information on a person's *interests,* or preferences for certain kinds of activities and objects, can be obtained in various ways. The most direct method, simply asking a person what he or she is interested in, has its pitfalls. People often have little insight into what their vocational interests are or what particular occupations entail. Nevertheless, these *expressed interests* are sometimes better predictors than less direct information and should not be overlooked in counseling situations. The results of one extensive investigation showed, for example, that the really large differences between occupational groups were in expressed interests rather than abilities. For example, engineering students scored much higher than average on mechanical–technical and physical science interests, whereas law students scored higher in public service (politics), literary–linguistic activity, business, and sales interests (Flanagan, Tiedeman, & Willis, 1973).

Other methods of determining interests include observing behavior in various situations or participation in various activities, inferring interests from a person's knowledge of special terminology or other information about specific occupations, and administering an interest inventory. The four approaches referred to above (asking for expressions of interests, deducing interests from observed behavior, inferring interests from performance on tests of abilities, and determining interests from paper-and-pencil inventories) are applicable to the assessment of the eight basic interest groups described by Super and Crites (1962). These eight interest groups are scientific, social welfare, literary, material, systematic, contact, esthetic expression, and esthetic interpretation.

Historical Background and Uses

As with tests of special abilities, the development of standardized methods of measuring interests began in an applied context, that of vocational counseling and selection. Some attempts to assess interests were made prior to World War I (for example, Thorndike, 1912; Truman Kelly's doctoral dissertation in 1914), but the work of James Miner marks the beginning of systematic efforts to develop criterion-related and content-validated measures of interests. The interest questionnaire constructed by Miner in 1915 prompted a historic seminar on interest measurement held at Carnegie Institute of Technology in 1919. One result of that seminar was the research of E. K. Strong, Jr. on interest measurement and the development and refinement of the the the first standardized interest inventory, the Strong Vocational Interest Blank for Men. Other noteworthy events in the history of interest measurement were the publication by G. F. Kuder in 1939 of the Kuder Preference Record and the research on objective interest measures conducted by U.S. Army Air Corps psychologists during World War II. Many interest inventories have been published since World War II, but modifications of the inventories developed originally by Strong and Kuder continue to be the most popular.

Today, interest inventories are administered for a number of reasons in a variety of situations. Traditionally, their primary use has been to contribute to occupational and educational counseling in high schools, colleges and universities, and vocational rehabilitation contexts. Interest inventories have also been used extensively in research on individual and group differences, both in basic research for understanding the nature, origins, and effects of interests and in applied research for vocational counseling, selection, and intervention. Other applications of interest inventories include assistance in making avocational choices, midcareer decisions, and preretirement and retirement decisions (Hansen & Campbell, 1985). Although school counselors and psychological researchers are undoubtedly the largest groups of users of interest inventories, the results of these instruments are also helpful to industrial consultants, career-development managers, and human resources practitioners.

Origins and Stability of Interests

The vocational interests of young children typically have an element of fantasy. Children fantasize about being a glamorous, talented, heroic, or adventurous person, but such fantasies may have little to do with abilities or in-depth knowledge of what particular occupations entail. Children normally progress from a fantasy stage through a transition stage of late childhood and early adolescence and finally to a more realistic stage in the development of vocational interests during late adolescence and early adulthood.

Although vocational interests do not become very specific, realistic, or stable until high school or later, the general direction of a person's interests may be apparent rather early in life. Young children tend to engage in activities that they view as appropriate and to avoid activities that they consider inappropriate for themselves (Tyler, 1964). They also make distinctions between people roles and life roles. According to Roe and her coauthors (Roe & Siegelman, 1964; Roe & Klos, 1969), vocational interests, and hence career choices, result from the kinds of relationships children have with their families. A warm, accepting family atmosphere tends to create a people orientation, whereas a cold, aloof family atmosphere is more likely to produce an object orientation in the child. From a social learning perspective, interests are viewed as resulting from differential reinforcement for engaging in certain activities, coupled with imitation and modeling of people who are important to the individual.

Heredity Environment undoubtedly affects interests to a substantial degree, but the findings of a study by Grotevant, Scarr, and Weinberg (1977) suggest that children are born with a hereditary predisposition toward certain interests. From a study of 114 biologically related families, these researchers found many significant correlations between the interest inventory scores of children and those of their parents. In contrast, there were few significant correlations between the interests of parents and children in 109 adoptive families. Biologically related children were more similar in their interest patterns than nonbiologically related children, and the interests of same-sex pairs were more similar than those of opposite-sex pairs of children. The results of a widely cited Minnesota study of identical twins reared apart also indicate that the correlations between the interests of identical twins are greater than those between the interests of other family pairs (Bouchard et al., 1983). Because identical twins have identical heredities, these findings can be interpreted as demonstrating the influence of heredity on interests.

Although it is commonly believed that parental behavior is more influential than heredity in determining the interests of children, Scarr and her colleagues concluded that what parents do after their children are born apparently has little effect on children's interests (Grotevant, Scarr, & Weinberg, 1977). Therefore, rather than trying to lead children into particular interest areas, these researchers recommended that parents provide them with a variety of experiences. Then the children will have a better opportunity to develop whatever interest predispositions or inclinations they have.

Granting that people tend to be interested in things that they do well and that heredity plays an important role in determining abilities and temperament, it can be argued that heredity affects interests by way of abilities, temperament, and physical structure. For example, a person with a genetically based high level of activity but a modest level of intelligence would probably have little interest in becoming a theoretical physicist who spends most of the time indoors thinking about complex scientific problems. But a temperamentally energetic individual with a strong physique might show a greater interest in becoming a professional athlete.

Stability of Interests   Individual patterns of likes and dislikes begin developing long before a person has had experiences with specific occupations. These early interests are relatively unstable, but by the time a child has reached the ninth grade, and almost certainly by the eleventh grade, his or her preferences for specific kinds of activities are fairly constant. Longitudinal studies spanning two decades and more have demonstrated that stability of interests is the rule after the late teens (Strong, 1955). Nevertheless, some people change their interests even in adulthood, and particular caution should be exerted in interpreting the results of interest inventories administered before the ninth grade (Crites, 1969).

Validity of Interest Inventories

Because of the importance of academic and vocational guidance, commercially available interest inventories have been almost as popular as tests of general intelligence and special abilities. Compared with cognitive measures, however, interest inventories are not very good predictors of school grades or occupational success. On the average, scores on interest inventories correlate around .20 to .30 with school marks, whereas general intelligence test scores correlate around .50 with the same criterion (Brokaw, 1956). Scores on interest inventories contribute to the prediction of occupational selection, persistence, and satisfaction, but job success is usually more closely related to abilities than to interests (Kuder, 1963; Campbell & Hansen, 1981). Because people are more likely to avoid occupations they dislike than to enter occupations they like, low scores on interest inventories tend to be more predictive of what a person will not do than high scores are of what he or she will do (Dolliver, Irvin, & Bigley, 1972; Zytowski, 1976).

Faking   As is also true of ability tests, the validity of interest inventories in predicting occupational choice is affected by test-taking factors and examinee characteristics. Intentionally or unintentionally, examinees differ in the extent to which their responses indicate their true interests. On the intentional side, interest inventories can be faked. Bridgman and Hollenbeck (1961) found, for example, that when directed to do so college students filled out an interest inventory (Kuder Form D) in such a way that the responses were very similar to those of people who were employed in specified occupations. Interest inventories are less useful when it is advantageous for examinees to give false reports, which is more likely to occur when the scores are used for selection or employment purposes. But even when the fakability of an interest inventory limits its usefulness as a selection device, faking is much less likely when an inventory is administered for academic and vocational counseling purposes.

Even when examinees might seem to benefit from giving untruthful answers on an interest inventory, they do not necessarily do so. For example, the Strong Vocational Interest Blank was used for many years to select individuals for advanced training in the

U.S. Navy. Under such circumstances, it might be supposed that faking would be a problem. However, the results of a study by Abrahams, Neumann, and Gilthens (1971) indicate that this was not so. The means of scores obtained by a group of young men on the Strong administered as part of a navy scholarship application were found to be quite similar to the means of their scores on the same inventory taken in high school a year before or in college a year after applying for the scholarship. In addition, correlations between the interest score profiles obtained under scholarship application conditions and routine testing conditions were in the .90s. Even though it might have been advantageous for the applicants to produce a more favorable outcome by faking, they apparently did not do so to any appreciable degree.

Response Sets   Although it is not the same as intentional faking, the tendency to respond to the form rather than to the content of items *(response sets)* can also result in inaccurate scores on an interest inventory. Of particular concern are the response sets of *acquiescence* (tendency to agree rather than disagree when in doubt) and *social desirability* (responding in what is perceived to be the more socially desirable direction). One technique designed to minimize these response sets is known as the *forced-choice format.* Items having this format consist of two or more descriptive statements that are equal in social desirability but different in content and validity. On a forced-choice interest item, examinees are directed to indicate which of the activities described in the three or more statements they would most like to do and which they would least like to do. Unfortunately, examinees sometimes find this response format awkward and frustrating.

Socioeconomic Status   One group difference variable that is significantly associated with responses to and, hence, the validity of interest inventories is socioeconomic status. Working-class people do not always have an opportunity to develop their interests or to train for and enter occupations that are most appealing to them. For these individuals, monetary security is seemingly of greater importance than interest satisfaction in determining job selection. This is one reason why, for many years, psychologists showed little inclination to construct vocational interest inventories for people who were planning to enter unskilled, semiskilled, or even skilled occupations. Because working-class people apparently viewed job security and money as more important than satisfying their vocational interests, it seemed unproductive to try to develop interest inventories for nonprofessional occupations. Consequently, early interest inventories were designed almost entirely for use in counseling young people who planned to enter professional occupations. The situation changed somewhat after World War II, but the major focus of interest inventories is still on the professions.

At the high end of the socioeconomic scale are children of the very wealthy, who may have strong vocational interests but for whom familial and societal expectations and traditions frequently prove more influential than individual interests in determining career selection. Children from wealthy families may not be permitted to do what they like, either because the status or monetary rewards of occupations consistent with their interests are not high enough or because parents expect their children to follow in parental footsteps or even surpass the parents' accomplishments. On the other hand, young people from the upwardly mobile middle class are more likely to try to improve their chances of success by entering occupations in which they have strong interests. Hence, vocational interests are usually more important in determining occupational selection, and scores on interest inventories are more predictive of occupational choice, for middle-class than for upper-class and working-class people (McArthur & Stevens, 1955).

STRONG AND KUDER INVENTORIES

The Strong Inventories

As a result of research conducted during the 1920s, E. K. Strong discovered consistent, significant differences in people's reports of what they like and dislike. Strong decided to construct an inventory to assess these individual differences in interests, and he began by constructing a variety of items concerning preferences for specific occupations, school subjects, amusements, activities, and types of people. These items, in addition to a scale for rating one's abilities and characteristics, were then administered to groups of men who were employed in specific occupations. By comparing the responses of these occupational groups to those of men in general, Strong was able to develop several dozen occupational scales consisting of items that significant numbers of men in specific occupations answered differently from men in general. This Strong Vocational Interest Blank for Men was the first standardized and commercially published measure of interests. Several years later, when it became clear that the interests of women were not limited to clerical work, school teaching, nursing, and housewifery, a companion instrument, the Strong Vocational Interest Blank for Women, was published.

For various reasons, including the desire to comply with Title IX of the Civil Rights Act of 1964 and to meet allegations of sexism, in 1974 the men's and women's forms of the Strong Vocational Interest Blank were combined into a single instrument, the Strong–Campbell Interest Inventory (SCII). An attempt was made to remove sex bias in the content of the items and the occupational labels and to create a more unisex inventory. It was recognized, however, that sex bias had been reduced but not entirely eliminated in the SCII.

Format of the Strong Interest Inventory   The latest edition of the instrument originated by Strong is the Strong Interest Inventory (Consulting Psychologists Press & The Psychological Corporation). This inventory, which was published in 1985, consists of 325 items grouped into the following seven parts:

I.   *Occupations.* Each of 131 occupational titles is responded to with like (L), indifferent (I), or dislike (D).

II.   *School Subjects.* Each of 36 school subjects is responded to with like (L), indifferent (I), or dislike (D).

III.   *Activities.* Each of 51 general occupational activities is responded to with like (L), indifferent (I), or dislike (D).

IV.   *Amusements.* Each of 39 amusements or hobbies is responded to with like (L), indifferent (I), or dislike (D).

V.   *Types of People.* Each of 24 types of people is responded to with like (L), indifferent (I), or dislike (D).

VI.   *Preference between Two Activities.* For each of 30 pairs of activities, preference between the activity on the left (L) and the activity on the right (R) or no preference (=) is indicated.

VII. *Your Characteristics.* Each of 14 characteristics is responded to with Yes, ?, or No, depending on whether or not they are self-descriptive.

Although the items, format, and administration procedure of the Strong Interest Inventory were essentially unchanged from the previous edition, the profile was expanded to include 106 occupations represented by 207 occupational scales.

Strong Scales   The Strong Interest Inventory is scored on five groups of measures: Administrative Indexes, General Occupational Themes, Basic Interest Scales, Occupational Scales, and Special Scales. Before attempting to interpret a person's scores on the last four groups of measures, scores on the 10 Administrative Indexes, particularly the Total Responses and Infrequent Responses, should be checked. The numbers of Total Responses and Infrequent Responses are listed at the top left of the upper half of the Strong profile form (see Figure 8–1). If the Total Responses index is less than about 305, the examiner should inspect the answer sheet to ascertain the problem. The Infrequent Responses index, which is based on infrequently selected response choices, is used to determine whether the answer sheet has been marked correctly; a large number of such responses should lead one to question the validity of the Strong profile. The remaining eight administrative indexes are the response percentages given at the bottom right of the lower half of the profile form (see Figure 8–2). If the Like (L), Indifferent (I), or Dislike (D) percentages are outside the 20 to 55 range, then there is an unusual circumstance of some sort that should be investigated before interpreting the profile (Hansen & Campbell, 1985).

As seen in Figures 8–1 and 8–2, the Strong profile is divided into six thematic sections based on Holland's (1985) "vocational personalities" system: Realistic, Investigative, Artistic, Social, Enterprising, and Conventional. The examinee's standard *T* score on each occupational theme is indicated below the label of the theme. The norm group for scoring the general occupational themes consisted of 300 men and 300 women (the general reference sample) whose responses were presumably representative of those of people in general in the United States.

The 23 basic interest scales, one to five of which are listed under each of the six occupational themes, were constructed by grouping items having high intercorrelations. Scores on these basic interest scales represent the strength and consistency of special areas of interest (agriculture, science, music–dramatics, teaching, public speaking, office practices, and so on). Raw scores on the basic interest scales are transformed to a standard score scale and designated as very low, low, moderately low, average, moderately high, high, or very high. Separate scales and scores being provided for men and women.

Listed on the right sides of Figures 8–1 and 8–2 are the names of 207 scales, representing 106 different occupations, and the examinee's standard score on each scale. Each of these occupational scales was constructed by comparing the responses of men or women employed in a particular occupation with the responses of a reference group of men or women in general. All but five of the scales were matched with opposite-sex scales and standardized separately by sex. A person's raw score on a given occupational scale is determined by summing the numerical weights assigned to his or her responses

FIGURE 8–1 Strong Interest Inventory Profile Form, Upper Half.
(Reproduced by special permission of the distributor, Consulting Psychologists Press, Inc., Palo Alto, CA, for the publisher, Stanford University Press, from the Strong Interest Inventory, by E. K. Strong, Jr., Jo-Ida C. Hansen, and David P. Campbell. Copyright 1985 by the Board of Trustees of Leland Stanford Junior University.)

PROFILE REPORT FOR: VANLOO KLAASKE
ID:
AGE: **SEX:** F
DATE TESTED: 04/09/92
DATE SCORED: 4/20/92

OCCUPATIONAL SCALES

STANDARD SCORES — Similarity columns: VERY DISSIMILAR (15), DISSIMILAR (25), MODERATELY DISSIMILAR (30), MID-RANGE, MODERATELY SIMILAR (40), SIMILAR (45), VERY SIMILAR (55)

SOCIAL

GENERAL OCCUPATIONAL THEME - S		
High	65	

BASIC INTEREST SCALES	(STANDARD SCORE)	
TEACHING — Very High	68	
SOCIAL SERVICE — Very High	68	
ATHLETICS — Average	43	
DOMESTIC ARTS — Very High	69	
RELIGIOUS ACTIVITIES — Average	43	

Code F	Code M	Occupation	Score F	Score M	Similarity
SA	[AS]	Foreign language teacher	50	(AS)	Similar
SA	SA	Minister	43	47	Moderately Similar
SA	SA	Social worker	53	56	Similar
S	S	Guidance counselor	46	58	Similar
S	S	Social science teacher	44	51	Moderately Similar
S	S	Elementary teacher	43	45	Moderately Similar
S	S	Special education teacher	49	60	Similar
SRI	SAR	Occupational therapist	55	57	Very Similar
SIA	SAI	Speech pathologist	56	63	Very Similar
SI	[ISR]	Nurse, RN	64	(ISR)	Very Similar
SCI	N/A	Dental hygienist	42	N/A	Moderately Similar
SC	SC	Nurse, LPN	35	51	Mid-range
[RIS]	SR	Athletic trainer	(RIS)	27	
SR	SR	Physical education teacher	16	16	Very Dissimilar
SRE	SE	Recreation leader	39	32	Mid-range
SE	SE	YWCA/YMCA director	46	35	Similar
SEC	SCE	School administrator	48	43	Similar
SCE	N/A	Home economics teacher	39	N/A	Mid-range

ENTERPRISING

GENERAL OCCUPATIONAL THEME - E		
Mod. Low	39	

BASIC INTEREST SCALES	(STANDARD SCORE)	
PUBLIC SPEAKING — Average	43	
LAW/POLITICS — Mod. High	56	
MERCHANDISING — Mod. Low	44	
SALES — Mod. Low	41	
BUSINESS MANAGEMENT — Average	54	

Code F	Code M	Occupation	Score F	Score M	Similarity
E	ES	Personnel director	40	31	Moderately Similar
ES	E	Elected public official	38	26	Dissimilar
ES	ES	Life insurance agent	26	12	Moderately Dissimilar
EC	E	Chamber of Commerce executive	28	21	Moderately Dissimilar
EC	EC	Store manager	24	17	Dissimilar
N/A	ECR	Agribusiness manager	N/A	16	
EC	EC	Purchasing agent	35	21	Moderately Similar
EC	E	Restaurant manager	30	16	Moderately Dissimilar
[AR]	EA	Chef	(AR)	36	
EC	E	Travel agent	25	35	Moderately Dissimilar
ECS	E	Funeral director	40	23	Moderately Similar
[CSE]	ESC	Nursing home administrator	(CSE)	49	
EC	ER	Optician	36	20	Moderately Similar
E	E	Realtor	15	23	Very Dissimilar
E	[AE]	Beautician	24	(AE)	Very Dissimilar
E	E	Florist	20	14	Very Dissimilar
EC	E	Buyer	-2	12	Very Dissimilar
EI	EI	Marketing executive	17	16	Very Dissimilar
EIC	ECI	Investments manager	13	10	Very Dissimilar

CONVENTIONAL

GENERAL OCCUPATIONAL THEME - C		
Average	55	

BASIC INTEREST SCALES	(STANDARD SCORE)	
OFFICE PRACTICES — High	63	

Code F	Code M	Occupation	Score F	Score M	Similarity
C	C	Accountant	22	9	Very Dissimilar
C	C	Banker	27	16	Dissimilar
CE	CE	IRS agent	44	29	Moderately Similar
CES	CES	Credit manager	31	23	Moderately Dissimilar
CES	CES	Business education teacher	28	34	Dissimilar
[CS]	CES	Food service manager	(CS)	43	
[ISR]	CSE	Dietitian	(ISR)	55	
CSE	[ESC]	Nursing home administrator	47	(ESC)	Similar
CSE	CSE	Executive housekeeper	42	41	Moderately Similar
CS	[CES]	Food service manager	38	(CES)	Moderately Dissimilar
CS	N/A	Dental assistant	42	N/A	Moderately Similar
C	N/A	Secretary	34	N/A	Mid-range
C	[R]	Air Force enlisted personnel	31	(R)	Moderately Similar
CRS	[RC]	Marine Corps enlisted personnel	31	(RC)	Moderately Similar
CRS	CR	Army enlisted personnel	32	30	Moderately Similar
CIR	CIR	Mathematics teacher	45	23	Very Similar

ADMINISTRATIVE INDEXES (RESPONSE %)

	L %	I %	D %
OCCUPATIONS	47 L %	21 I %	31 D %
SCHOOL SUBJECTS	67 L %	14 I %	19 D %
ACTIVITIES	55 L %	16 I %	29 D %
LEISURE ACTIVITIES	56 L %	15 I %	28 D %
TYPES OF PEOPLE	38 L %	17 I %	46 D %
PREFERENCES	40 L %	7 = %	53 R %
CHARACTERISTICS	64 Y %	0 ? %	36 N %
ALL PARTS	51 %	16 %	33 %

FIGURE 8–2 Strong Interest Inventory Profile Form, Lower Half.
(Reproduced by special permission of the distributor, Consulting Psychologists Press, Inc., Palo Alto, CA, for the publisher, Stanford University Press, from the Strong Interest Inventory, by E. K. Strong, Jr., Jo-Ida C. Hansen, and David P. Campbell. Copyright 1985 by the Board of Trustees of Leland Stanford Junior University.)

on the scale. The weight assigned to a response depends on the direction in which the item discriminates between men or women employed in that occupation and men or women in general. After all weights assigned to a person's responses to the items on a particular scale have been added, the obtained raw score is converted to a standard *(T)* score. A verbal description (very dissimilar, dissimilar, moderately dissimilar, midrange, moderately similar, similar, very similar) also indicates the degree of similarity between the examinee's score and that of the occupational standardization group.

Two empirically derived scales on the Strong were developed for special purposes (see top left of Figure 8–1). These special scales are Academic Comfort and Intro-version–Extroversion. The Academic Comfort scale was constructed by comparing the responses of high school and college students attaining high marks in school with the responses of those attaining low marks. Scores on the scale are related to the tendency to persist or stay in school. The Introversion–Extroversion scale was constructed by comparing the responses of individuals classified as introverts with those classified as extroverts according to their scores on the MMPI.

Scoring the Strong   The Strong can be scored only by a computer; the item weights and scoring procedure are a trade secret. Completed inventories are sent to Consulting Psychologists Press for computerized scoring, profiling, and interpretation. The results of computer scoring and interpretation are printed as a Strong Interpretive Report. This report, which provides a narrative explanation of the examinee's score pattern, focuses on the three highest General Occupational Themes and related Basic Interest and Occupational Scales; both vocational and avocational pursuits are suggested.

Reliability   Median test–retest reliabilities of the Strong over 2-week, 30-day, and 3-year periods are listed in the manual as .91, .86, and .81 for the General Occupational Themes, .91, .88, and .82 for the Basic Interest Scales, and .92, .89, and .87 for the Occupational Scales. The median internal consistency coefficients are also satisfactory, being in the low .90s. The long-term reliabilities of the Strong Vocational Interest Blank for Men, on which the Strong Interest Inventory is based, are given as .75 over 20 years and .55 over 35 years (Strong, 1955). These figures indicate that interests, as measured by the Strong inventories, are sufficiently stable to be used in the vocational counseling of older adolescents and adults.

Validity   Until his death in 1962, E. K. Strong, Jr., continued his research on the validity of the Strong Vocational Interest Blanks. This work was continued by David P. Campbell and Jo-Ida C. Hansen at the University of Minnesota. In Strong's (1955) follow-up study of the occupations and interests of 663 men who initially took the men's form 18 years earlier when they were in college, their interest scores were good predictors of occupational satisfaction. The results of this study and others demonstrate that interest inventories can be used to predict occupational satisfaction and persistence, but they are poor indicators of how successful a person will be in a particular occupation. Similarly, in academic settings, interest inventories are good predictors of rated satisfaction with one's major or field of study, but poor predictors of course grades (French, 1961).

Kuder Interest Inventories

In contrast to the varied-item format of the Strong Interest Inventory, G. F. Kuder employed a forced-choice item format in all his interest inventories. To construct his first inventory, the Kuder Vocational Preference Record, Kuder administered a list of statements concerned with activities to college students and determined from their responses which items clustered together. As a result, 10 scales of items having low correlations across scales but high correlations within scales were constructed. Then triads of items, each member of a triad belonging to a different interest scale, were formed and administered in forced-choice format. In this way, interests in different areas were pitted against one another.

Each item on the Kuder inventories consists of three statements of activities (see Figure 8–3); the examinee is directed to indicate which of the three activities he or she *most* prefers and which he or she *least* prefers. The responses given to the first item triad in Figure 8–3 indicate that the respondent would most like to visit a museum and least like to visit an art gallery. Of the activities listed in the second item triad, the respondent would most like to collect coins and least like to collect stones.

The forced-choice item format selected by Kuder has both advantages and disadvantages. Although this format tends to minimize certain response sets (acquiescence, social desirability, and so forth), examinees sometimes find that responding to forced-choice items is awkward. Another problem is the ipsative nature of responses to force-choice items. By accepting or rejecting an activity falling on one scale, the respondent does not select or reject an activity falling on another scale. Consequently, respondents' scores on a particular scale are affected by their responses to items on other scales. It is impossible to obtain uniformly high or uniformly low scores across all scales. A typical score pattern consists of high scores on one or more scales, low scores on one or more scales, and average scores on the remaining scales.

Brief descriptions of three Kuder inventories that are currently available (from CTB/Macmillan/MacGraw-Hill) are given in Table 8–1. The two most recently published inventories are the Kuder General Interest Survey (KGIS) and the Kuder Occupational Interest Survey (KOIS).

KGIS Scores and Norms The KGIS, which designed for grades 6–12, yields scores on a person's interests in 10 general areas. Separate percentile norms for four groups

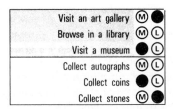

FIGURE 8–3 Examples of Items on Kuder General Interest Survey.
(From the Kuder General Interest Survey, Form E, Answer Sheet, by G. Frederic Kuder. Copyright © 1985, 1976, 1963 by G. Frederic Kuder. Used by permission of the publisher, CTB Macmillan/McGraw-Hill.)

TABLE 8–1   Descriptions of Three Kuder Interest Inventories

Kuder Form C: Vocational Preference Record

Use. For counseling and placement of high school students and adults.

Format. One hundred sixty-eight triads of statements describing activities, one activity in each triad to be marked "Most Liked" and one "Least Liked."

Range and time limit. High school. No time limit; takes 30 to 40 minutes.

Forms and Scoring. CP, hand scored; CM, machine scored.

Scales. Ten interest scales: outdoor, mechanical, scientific, computational, persuasive, artistic, literary, musical, social service, and clerical. One verification (V) score, based on items having extreme response splits.

Standardization data (norms). Percentile ranks for men and women; score profile in 10 interest areas may be plotted on percentile rank scale. Stanines for men and women in 41 occupational families. Manual groups occupations according to major interest area or pair of interest areas.

Reliability. Kuder–Richardson reliabilities of the 10 scales are in the .70s and .80s.

Validity. Several studies of the relationships between Kuder Form C and job satisfaction support its validity.

Kuder Form E: General Interest Survey

Use. Developed as a downward extension and revision of Kuder Form C; useful in vocational counseling of junior and senior high school students to help them make sound choices in school and think about education and careers.

Format. One hundred sixty-eight triads of statements describing various activities, one activity in each triad to be marked "Most Preferred" and one "Least Preferred."

Range and time limit. Grades 6–12. No time limit; takes 30 to 40 minutes.

Forms and scoring. Hand-scored (pin-punch) and machine-scored versions; individual interest scores given on both male and female profiles indicating level of interest in each job family group as compared with either males or females in the grade group.

Scales. Ten interest scales: outdoor, mechanical, scientific, computational, persuasive, artistic, literary, musical, social service, and clerical; one verification (V) score.

Standardization data (norms). In compliance with Title IX regulations, separate percentile norms based on stratified sample of U.S. boys and girls in grades 6–8 and 9–12.

Reliability. Test–retest reliabilities after 6 weeks, by sex and grade level (6–8 and 9–12), in .70s and .80s.

Validity. No long-term evidence of validity available; transparency program designed to help students interpret their Kuder Form E scores.

Kuder Form DD: Occupational Interest Survey

Use. For selection, placement, and counseling in employment centers, personnel agencies, and industrial retraining programs.

Format. One hundred triads of statements describing various activities, one activity in each triad to be marked "Most Preferred" and one "Least Preferred."

Range and time limit. Grade 11 to adult. No time limit; usually takes 30 to 40 minutes.

Scales. Results divided into four sections: Dependability (extent to which results can be relied on); Vocational Interest Estimates [how examinee's attraction to 10 different interest areas (Artistic, Clerical, Computational, Literary, Mechanical, Musical, Outdoor, Persuasive, Scientific, Social Service) compares with those of groups of males

TABLE 8–1   (continued)

and females in general]; Occupational Scales (how examinee's interest pattern compares with those of people in approximately 100 occupations for men and women
combined); and College Major Scales (how examinee's interest pattern compares
with those of students in approximately 40 college majors). Scores on Vocational
Interest Estimates are expressed as percentiles; scores on Occupations and College
Majors are lambda coefficients describing the strength of the relationship between
the responses of the inventory taker and those of people in the specified occupational or college major group.

(males and females in grades 6–8 and males and females in grades 9–12) were obtained
in 1987. The availability of separate sex norms permits examinees to compare their KGIS
scores with those of both boys and girls. Figure 8–4 is a seminarrative report of the
percentile scores obtained by one examinee who took the KGIS. The report format provides
a rank-order listing of percentiles in the 10 interest areas, as well as the three areas in
Holland's six-part classification scheme on which the examinee ranks highest with respect
to other males and with respect to other females. Although the provision of separate sex
norms helps to control for sex bias resulting from combined norms, differences in the
interests of males and females can be seen in the fact that, on the average, boys score
higher on the mechanical, computational, scientific, and persuasive scales, while girls
score higher on the artistic, literary, musical, social service, and clerical scales of the
KGIS.

KOIS Scores and Norms   The KOIS, which was designed for grade 10 through
adulthood, is scored in a different manner from other Kuder inventories. In scoring the
KOIS, the examinee's responses are compared with those of people who are reportedly
satisfied with their occupational choices and with those of college students majoring in
particular fields of study. A person's score on any of the KOIS occupational or college-
major scales is a modified biserial correlation coefficient *(lambda coefficient)* between
his or her responses to the items and the proportion of individuals in the specified
occupational or college major group who endorsed each item. The higher the lambda
coefficient is, the more closely the person's score resembles the interest pattern of the
corresponding occupational group or major. As shown in Figure 8–5, the report of scores
on the KOIS lists the lambda coefficients for occupational and college-major scales by sex
of the norm group. In interpreting a person's lambda coefficients, the highest coefficients are
emphasized; the associated occupations or majors are those in which the examinee has
the greatest interests. However, occupations or majors falling within .06 units of the
highest coefficients should also be considered.

Reliability and Validity of the KGIS and KOIS   The short-term test–retest reliability
coefficients of the KGIS and KOIS scales are in the .80s and .90s, and the scores have
been found to be fairly stable over a decade or more (Zytowski, 1976). In general, the
evidence indicates that the content validities of both interest surveys are adequate. With
respect to the predictive validity of the KOIS, Zytowski (1976) found that over half the

```
S R A ®      KUDER GENERAL INTEREST SURVEY
             Form E Narrative Report
Name    THOMPSON ALEX              Numeric Grid   343434343434343
Sex     M                          Process Number 0001 00011
Level   GRADES 9 - 12              Norm Group     GRADES 9 - 12
```

Recently you took the KUDER GENERAL INTEREST SURVEY, FORM E. You were Ⓐ
asked to indicate which of three activities you most preferred and which
you least preferred. Your V score of 006 indicates that you marked your
answers carefully and sincerely. This means that you can have confidence
in the accuracy of your results.

Your results show how your interest in ten vocational areas compares to
that of other students. The numbers in the charts below indicate the
proportion of students whose interest in these ten areas is less than Ⓑ
yours. Your scores are ranked from highest to lowest and grouped into
HIGH, AVERAGE, and LOW interests. The charts below show which of the
vocational areas fall within each of these groups. The vocational areas
in which your interests are highest extend into the HIGH areas of the
chart; those in which your interests are about the same as other
students extend only into the AVERAGE area; and those that are lowest
extend only into the LOW area.
Ⓓ
Compared to other males: Compared to females:
     Ⓕ
        Low....Avg..High....   Low....Avg..High....
 Ⓖ   Ⓔ
Persuasive 96-------:----:-----   Persuasive 98-------:----:-------
Literary   96-------:----:-----   Scientific 93-------:----:----
Scientific 78-------:----:-   Literary   88-------:----:---
Soc Serv   78-------:----:-   Computat'l 68-------:----:
Musical   66-------:----   Musical   54 -------:---
Computat'l 60-------:----   Mechanical 36-------:-
Artistic   21-------   Soc Serv   33-------:-
Outdoor   18------   Outdoor   24-------
Clerical   14------   Artistic   18------
Mechanical 02-   Clerical   07----
```

Because there are differences in the interests of males and females, Ⓖ
results are provided separately by sex. Generally you will be interested
in the results for your own sex; however, if your interests are
nontraditional, you may learn something from seeing how you compare with
the other sex.

A number of reference books in which you may find occupational          Ⓗ
information are keyed to the following personality type codes: Realistic,
Investigative, Artistic, Social, Enterprising, and Conventional. Your
scores rank you highest on the following:

```
Compared to other males:              Compared to females:

     Enterprising                          Enterprising
     Investigative                         Investigative
     Social                                Social
```

For more information on the vocational areas and scores discussed here,
read your Interpretive Leaflet. If you have any questions regarding
these results, please see your counselor or teacher.

FIGURE 8–4 Sample Interest Profile on Kuder General Interest Survey–
Form E.
(From the Kuder General Interest Survey, Form E, Interest Profile, by G. Frederic Kuder. Copyright © 1985, 1976, 1963 by G. Frederic Kuder. Used by permission of the publisher, CTB Macmillan/McGraw-Hill.)
```

Kuder Occupational Interest Survey Report Form

Name: BYER ALEC J
Sex: MALE   Date: 12/05/86
Numeric Grid No.   SRA No. 00110

1 Dependability: How much confidence can you place in your results? In scoring your responses several checks were made on your answer patterns to be sure that you understood the directions and that your results were complete and dependable. According to these:

YOUR RESULTS APPEAR TO BE DEPENDABLE.

2 Vocational Interest Estimates: Vocational interests can be divided into different types and the level of your attraction to each type can be measured. You may feel that you know what interests you have already — what you may not know is how strong they are compared with other people's interests. This section shows the relative rank of your preferences for ten different kinds of vocational activities. Each is explained on the back of this report form. Your preferences in these activities, as compared with other people's interests, are as follows:

Compared with men		Compared with women	
HIGH		HIGH	
SOCIAL SERVICE	97	SOCIAL SERVICE	87
AVERAGE		MUSICAL	80
MUSICAL	75	AVERAGE	
COMPUTATIONAL	63	COMPUTATIONAL	71
PERSUASIVE	51	MECHANICAL	70
SCIENTIFIC	49	PERSUASIVE	62
MECHANICAL	27	SCIENTIFIC	58
OUTDOOR	25	OUTDOOR	27
LOW		LOW	
ARTISTIC	23	CLERICAL	12
CLERICAL	15	ARTISTIC	11
LITERARY	03	LITERARY	01

3 Occupations: The KOIS has been given to groups of persons who are experienced and satisfied in many different occupations. Their patterns of interests have been compared with yours and placed in order of their similarity with you. The following occupational groups have interest patterns most similar to yours:

Compared with men

ELEM SCH TEACHER	.38
SOCIAL WORKER	.38
AUDIOL/SP PATHOL	.35
MINISTER	.35
COUNSELOR, HS	.35
NURSE	.34
PHARMACEUT SALES	.33
PODIATRIST	.32

THESE ARE NEXT MOST SIMILAR:

NURSE	
NUTRITIONIST	
DIETITIAN	
DENTIST	

Compared with women

AUDIOL/SP PATHOL	.39
RELIGIOUS ED DIR	.37
SOCIAL WORKER	.37
FILM/TV PROD/DIR	.35
INSURANCE AGENT	.35
COUNSELOR, HS	.35
MATHEMATICIAN	.35
DEPT STORE-SALES	.33
COL STU PERS MKR	.32

Compared with men, MOST SIMILAR. (continued)

AUTO SALESPERSON	.30
FILM/TV PROD/DIR	.29
PHYS THERAPIST	.29
PERSONNEL MGR	.28
OPTOMETRIST	.27
LAWYER	.27
PSYCHOLOGIST	.26

THE REST ARE LISTED IN ORDER OF SIMILARITY:

PHYSICIAN	.23
SCIENCE TCHR, HS	.23
CLOTHIER, RETAIL	.23
TRAVEL AGENT	.22
INSURANCE AGENT	.22
PHARMACIST	.22
SCHOOL SUPT	.22
ACCT, CERT PUB	.21
MATH TCHR, HS	.21
REAL ESTATE AGT	.20
DENTIST	.20
FLORIST	.20
BUYER	.19
RADIO STATION MGR	.19
PHOTOGRAPHER	.19
X-RAY TECHNICIAN	.18
TRUCK DRIVER	.18
SUPERVSR, INDUST	.18
PLANT NURSRY MKR	.17
INTERIOR DECOR	.17
POLICE OFFICER	.17
STATISTICIAN	.16
POSTAL CLERK	.16
LIBRARIAN	.16
TV REPAIRER	.16
BANKER	.15
BRICKLAYER	.15
FARMER	.14
EXTENSION AGENT	.14
METEOROLOGIST	.14
VETERINARIAN	.14
BOOKSTORE MGR	.14
CHEMIST	.13
BOOKKEEPER	.13
COMPUTER PRGRMR	.13
WELDER	.13
PLUMBING CONTRAC	.12
PAINTER, HOUSE	.12
MATHEMATICIAN	.12
ARCHITECT	.11
ELECTRICIAN	.11
CARPENTER	.11
MACHINIST	.11
AUTO MECHANIC	.10

Compared with women — THESE ARE NEXT MOST SIMILAR:

PHYSICIAN	.32
DENTAL ASSISTANT	.32
PHYS THERAPIST	.32
BANKER	.31
PSYCHOLOGIST	.31
BEAUTICIAN	.29
ELEM SCH TEACHER	.29
ACCT, CERT PUB	.29
FLORIST	.28
OCCUPA THERAPIST	.28
EXTENSION AGENT	.27
LAWYER	.27
BANK CLERK	.27
SECRETARY	.27
BOOKKEEPER	.23
X-RAY TECHNICIAN	.22

THE REST ARE LISTED IN ORDER OF SIMILARITY:

MATH TEACHER, HS	.20
OFFICE CLERK	.20
VETERINARIAN	.20
ARCHITECT	.19
JOURNALIST	.19
SCIENCE TCHR, HS	.19
ENGINEER	.18
COMPUTER PRGRMR	.18
LIBRARIAN	.17
BOOKSTORE MGR	.17
INTERIOR DECOR	.17

Compared with men, CONT. — REST, CONT.

BLDG CONTRACTOR	.09
PLUMBER	.08
PRINTER	.08
FORESTER	.07
JOURNALIST	.05

4 College Majors: Just as for occupations, the KOIS has been given to many persons in different college majors. The following college majors have interest patterns most similar to yours:

Compared with men

SOCIOLOGY	.36
ELEMENTARY EDUC	.33
PHYSICAL EDUC	.30

THESE ARE NEXT MOST SIMILAR:

PSYCHOLOGY	.25
MUSIC & MUSIC ED	.24
FOREIGN LANGUAGE	.24
POLITICAL SCI	.24
PREMED/PHAR/DENT	.23
HISTORY	.23
ECONOMICS	.23

THE REST ARE LISTED IN ORDER OF SIMILARITY:

BIOLOGICAL SCI	.23
BUSINESS ADMIN	.21
SERV ACAD CADET	.21
MATHEMATICS	.19
AGRICULTURE	.17
ENGLISH	.17
ENGINEERING	.16
PHYSICAL SCIENCE	.15
ANIMAL SCIENCE	.14
ART & ART EDUC	.12
ARCHITECTURE	.12
FORESTRY	.08

Compared with women

ELEMENTARY EDUC	.41
HOME ECON EDUC	.40
SOCIOLOGY	.40
MUSIC & MUSIC ED	.39
PHYSICAL EDUC	.39
DRAMA	.39
FOREIGN LANGUAGE	.37
NURSING	.37
PSYCHOLOGY	.36
HEALTH PROFESS	.36

THESE ARE NEXT MOST SIMILAR:

POLITICAL SCI	.34
HISTORY	.33
BUSINESS EDUC	.33
MATHEMATICS	.33
ENGLISH	.30

THE REST ARE LISTED IN ORDER OF SIMILARITY:

BIOLOGICAL SCI	.23
ART & ART EDUC	.20

Experimental Scales.

U-SCORE 49

M .10	MBI .26	M .29	MBI .26
S .21	F .24	D .42	RO .35

7-3881

FIGURE 8-5 Report of Scores on Kuder Occupational Interest Survey.
(From the Kuder Occupational Interest Survey, Form DD, KOIS Report Form. Copyright © 1985; Science Research Associates, Inc. Reprinted by permission of the publisher.)

individuals who were tested with the KOIS 12 to 19 years earlier had entered occupations on which they had scored within .07 to .12 points of their highest lambda coefficients.

OTHER GENERAL- AND SPECIAL-PURPOSE INTEREST INVENTORIES

Although the Strong and Kuder inventories are the most popular instruments for assessing interests, many other general-interest surveys and special-purpose instruments have been constructed. A number of these instruments focus on vocational interests, but others are concerned with school-related interests, children's interests, the interests of disadvantaged people, and the relationships between interests and personality.

General-Interest Surveys

A useful resource in designing a vocational interest inventory and in vocational counseling is the *Dictionary of Occupational Titles* (DOT) (U.S. Department of Labor, 1991). The DOT is a compendium of the world of work, providing detailed descriptions of almost every available job in the United States and cross-listings for jobs that are related to each other. The DOT has been used in designing, scoring, and interpreting a number of general-interest inventories. A good example is the Jackson Vocational Interest Survey.

Jackson Vocational Interest Survey (JVIS) (Sigma Assessment Systems) The JVIS, based on the results of an extensive research program directed by D. N. Jackson, consists of 289 forced-choice pairs of statements that are descriptive of job-related activities. The statements comprising an item pair refer to two equally popular interests, and examinees are directed to indicate a preference between them. Designed for high school age and beyond, the JVIS takes 45 to 60 minutes to complete. Initial scoring is on 34 basic interest scales representing 26 work-role and eight work-style dimensions. The definitions of these dimensions were refined by referring to job descriptions in the *Dictionary of Occupational Titles*. Another approach to scoring the JVIS is in terms of 10 occupational themes (Expressive, Logical, Inquiring, Practical, Assertive, Socialized, Helping, Conventional, Enterprising, and Communication). These themes are based on Holland's six "vocational personalities" themes and a factor analysis of responses to the JVIS. Scores on the 10 themes are highly reliable (test–retest coefficient between .82 and .92), as are scores on the 34 basic interest scales (median $r = .84$). With respect to the validity of the JVIS, a large study conducted at Pennsylvania State University found that JVIS profiles did a better job of predicting choice of academic major than any previously reported combination of interest and aptitude measures.

Reviews of the JVIS have praised its careful construction and factorially pure scales, but have noted that more evidence for its validity is required (Davidshofer, 1985; Thomas, 1985). The JVIS is also a rather long inventory and takes more time to complete than the Kuder Occupational Interest Survey, which has a similar format.

Special-Purpose Interest Inventories

A number of interest inventories have been designed expressly for a special group of people. Among these groups are children, the disadvantaged, and individuals who are planning to enter nonprofessional occupations.

Inventories for Children   Although the interests of children are often neither highly developed nor realistic, a number of interest measures have been designed especially for this group. The primary purpose of these instruments is to introduce and familiarize children with a wide range of activities and occupations, helping them to focus on future occupations in relation to their current interests, experiences, abilities, and ambitions. Illustrative of such instruments are the Career Awareness Inventory and the Individual Career Exploration, both of which are available from Scholastic Testing Service. Either of the two forms, Elementary for grades 3–6 and Advanced for grades 9–12, of the Career Awareness Inventory can be completed in 60 to 90 minutes. This inventory assesses the child's knowledge of seven areas pertaining to careers, and the results can be used as a basis for class lectures or discussions. There are also two forms of the Individual Career Exploration, a picture form for grades 3–7 and a verbal form for grades 8–12. This instrument, which is based on Roe and Klos's (1969) theory of occupational choice, takes longer to complete than the Career Awareness Inventory (about 2 hours, compared with 60 to 90 minutes).

Inventories for the Disadvantaged   Just as there are special achievement and intelligence tests for the culturally and educationally disadvantaged, certain interest inventories have also been designed especially for these groups. Rather than words, phrases, or statements, these instruments employ as test materials pictures of people engaged in certain activities. Examples are the Geist Picture Interest Inventory, the Reading-Free Vocational Interest Inventory, and the Wide Range Interest-Opinion Test. On each item of the Geist Picture Inventory (Western Psychological Services), examinees circle the one of three pictures that they prefer. The Geist takes about 25 minutes to complete and is scored on 12 areas. On each item of the Reading-Free Vocational Interest Inventory (Publishers Test Service), examinees mark their preferences on each of 55 sets of three drawings depicting job tasks. The drawings represent the kinds of tasks or occupations in which mentally retarded individuals can be productive and proficient (automotive, building trades, clerical, animal care, food service, patient care, horticulture, housekeeping, personal service, laundry, or materials handling).

Broader in scope than the two instruments described above is the Wide Range Interest-Opinion Test (WRIOT) (Jastak Assessment Systems). The WRIOT consists of 150 sets of three drawings of people engaged in a variety of activities with which physically and mentally handicapped individuals are able to identify. The materials are presented in a booklet with three pictures per page or on filmstrip. They can be completed in 40 to 60 minutes by examinees ranging in age from 5 years to adulthood. Likes and dislikes are selected in a forced-choice format, and responses are scored on 18 interest clusters (such as art, sales, management, office work, mechanics, machine operation, and athletics) and eight attitude clusters (examples are sedentariness, risk, ambition, and sex stereotype). Job title lists are available for each of the 18 interest clusters.

Inventories of Interests in Nonprofessional Occupations Although certain scales on the Strong Interest Inventory, the Kuder Occupational Interest Survey, and other general-interest inventories pertain to interests in nonprofessional occupations, none of these inventories was designed specifically for this purpose. Since World War II, a number of inventories focusing on the nonprofessions and somewhat simpler in content and vocabulary than the Strong and Kuder instruments have been constructed. Two examples of carefully designed and standardized instruments in this category are the Career Assessment Inventory–The Vocational Version (National Computer Systems) and the Career Directions Inventory (Sigma Assessment Systems).

The Vocational Version of the Career Assessment Inventory (CAI) was modeled after the Strong inventories and in fact is sometimes referred to as "the workingman's Strong Interest Inventory." Examinees respond on a five-point scale (L = like very much, l = like somewhat, I = indifferent, d = dislike somewhat, and D = dislike very much) to each of the 305 items covering activities, school subjects, and occupational titles. The inventory is written at a sixth-grade level and can be completed in 30 to 45 minutes (Johannson, 1984). Similar to the Strong Interest Inventory, the computer T-score report of the CAI consists of four sections: I. Administrative Indices (Total Responses; Response Consistency; Response Percentages on Activities, School Subjects, and Occupations); II. General Themes (Realistic, Investigative, Artistic, Social, Enterprising, Conventional); III. Basic Interest Area Scales; and IV. Occupational Scales. The 25 Basic Interest Area Scales and the 111 Occupational Scales are grouped under Holland's six themes. Scores on four Special Scales (Fine Arts–Mechanical, Occupational Extroversion–Introversion, Educational Orientation, and Variability of Interests), a computer-generated narrative report, and a counselor's summary are provided. The CAI is well designed from a psychometric viewpoint and has good reliability. On the negative side, McCabe (1985) notes that no predictive validity information is reported in the manual and that the CAI is relatively expensive to score. Overall, however, he rates it as a very important test that fills a significant need and is well developed and engineered to be easily and appropriately used. A revised, updated version of the CAI, designated "The Enhanced Version," was published in 1986 and can be scored on more professional occupations than the Vocational Version.

Interests and Personality

According to a holistic conception of personality, interests and abilities are personality characteristics. But unlike abilities or talents, which are more likely to be perceived as to some degree innate, interests have traditionally been viewed as acquired characteristics produced by fortuitous experiences. A more contemporary conception of interests is that, rather than developing by chance, they are reflections or expressions of deep-seated individual needs and personality traits (Darley & Hagenah, 1955). It follows from this viewpoint that, as psychoanalysts have maintained since Freud's time, vocational selection is influenced by personality traits. It might be surmised, for example, that becoming either a butcher or a surgeon is an expression of strong aggressive or sadistic impulses and that entering show business or the performing arts is reflective of exhibitionistic needs.

With respect to the research evidence linking interests to personality, it has been found that the incidence of psychoneurosis is higher among people with strong literary and esthetic interests, introversion is more common among those with scientific interests, and aggressiveness is related to an interest in selling (Darley & Hagenah, 1955; Osipow, 1983; Super & Bohn, 1970). Two psychologists whose research and theorizing on the relationships of interests to personality has been particularly influential are Anne Roe and J. L. Holland.

Roe's Theory   On the basis of observations and research on careers, Roe (1956) concluded that the primary factor in career choice is whether an individual is person-oriented or nonperson-oriented. Roe's revised theory contains two independent dimensions or continua. Occupational roles are classified on a continuum ranging from orientation to purposeful communication at one end through orientation to resource utilization at the other. On a second continuum, occupational roles range from interpersonal relations at one extreme to orientation to natural phenomena at the other. Although these two basic dimensions are a central feature of the most recent version of Roe's theory of interests, the theory is actually much more elaborate and has influenced the development of several interest inventories. Three of these instruments are the COPS Interest Inventory (EdITS), the Hall Occupational Orientation Inventory (Scholastic Testing Service), and the Vocational Interest Inventory (Western Psychological Services). Each of the last two inventories takes 30 to 40 minutes to complete. The Hall Occupational Orientation Inventory, which focuses on 22 job and personality characteristics, is appropriate for individuals from grade 3 through adulthood. The Vocational Interest Inventory, which is designed for grade 3 through adulthood, consists of 112 forced-choice items focusing on eight occupational areas (Service, Business Contact, Organization, Technical, Outdoor, Science, General Culture, Arts and Entertainment).

Holland's Instruments and Theory   The notion that interest inventories are actually measures of personality is made explicit in J. L. Holland's Self-Directed Search and Vocational Preference Inventory (both from Psychological Assessment Resources). The Self-Directed Search–1985 Revision (SDS) consists of an assessment booklet designed to help the user make a thoughtful evaluation of his or her own interests and abilities and an Occupations Finder for actively exploring the entire range of possible occupations. The six RIASEC scores yielded by the SDS are Realistic, Investigative, Artistic, Social, Enterprising, and Conventional (see Figure 8–6). The norms are incorporated in a three-letter occupational code, and the Occupations Finder contains over 1100 occupational titles keyed to the code.

The Vocational Preference Inventory–1985 Revision is a supplement to the Self-Directed Search and other interest inventories. It is based on Holland's theory that occupations can be described in terms of personality characteristics. Examinees indicate whether they like or dislike each of more than 160 different occupations, and their responses are scored on 11 scales: Realistic, Investigative, Artistic, Scientific, Enterprising, Conventional, Self-Control, Status, Masculinity–Femininity, Infrequency, and Acquiescence. The first six (RIASEC) scores can be used with the SDS Occupations Finder for purposes of career exploration and vocational guidance. Different patterns of high scores on these six types result in assignment of the examinee to different vocational categories. For example,

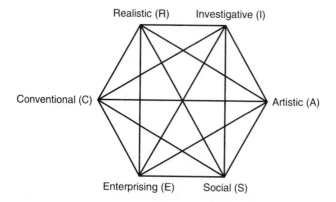

FIGURE 8–6   Holland's Hexagonal Model of Interests.
(From Differential Psychology, by H. L. Minton and F. W. Schneider. Copyright © 1980 by Wadsworth, Inc. Reprinted by permission of the authors.)

a person who scores high on the Conventional, Enterprising, and Social scales falls in the same category as advertising agents and sales representatives.

Sex Differences   Also reflective of personality differences are the sex-stereotyped patterns of scores obtained on the Vocational Preference Inventory, the Vocational Interest Inventory, and other measures of interests. For example, women tend to score higher than men on the Social, Artistic, and Conventional themes of the Vocational Preference Inventory, whereas men tend to score higher than women on the Realistic, Investigative, and Enterprising themes (Gottfredson, Holland, & Gottfredson, 1975; Prediger & Hanson, 1976). Similar sex differences in scores have been found on the Vocational Interest Inventory and the Strong Vocational Interest Blank. It has been argued that such sex differences are due to items that focus on specific activities or materials with which one sex has more experience than the other. Examples are carpentry and automobile-repairing items on Holland's Realistic scale, which are more familiar to males; redesigning the items to include a sewing machine or a blender might make them more familiar to females. It has been alleged, with some justification, that the Strong and other early interest inventories contributed to sex discrimination by directing young women into traditional women's occupations such as teaching, nursing, and clerical work (Diamond, 1979). Responding to the allegation of sex bias, the developers of the Strong Interest Inventory and certain other psychometric instruments constructed a combined form of the men's and women's blanks. Furthermore, combined sex norms, as well as the traditional separate-sex norms, are provided. To eliminate sex differences in responses, certain instruments, such as the revised version of the Vocational Interest Inventory and the Unisex Edition of the ACT Interest Inventory, utilize sex-balanced items. Such items were endorsed by approximately equal percentages of men and women. Perhaps an even more effective way of reducing or eliminating sex differences in scores on interest inventories is to provide equal opportunities, encouragement, and experiences for both sexes in a variety of activities, both traditionally male and traditionally female.

Bem Sex-role Inventory   Concern over sex discrimination, as well as the nature and origin of sex differences in psychological characteristics, has prompted the development of a number of measures of sex role during the past decade or so. The most prominent of these is the Bem Sex-Role Inventory (Consulting Psychologists Press). A short form of the Bem Sex-Role Inventory, which was designed to classify individuals according to their sex-role orientation, consists of 60 words or phrases to be rated on a seven-point scale on which 1 means "never or almost never true" and 7 means "always or almost always true." Twenty of the items refer to characteristics considered significantly more desirable in men than in women (for example, acts as a leader, aggressive, ambitious), 20 items refer to characteristics considered significantly more desirable in women than in men (for example, affectionate, cheerful, childlike), and 20 items are presumably sex neutral (for example, adaptable, conceited, conscientious). Scores on three scales, Masculinity (M), Femininity (F), and Androgyny (A), are determined first. Next the examinee may be placed in one of the following four categories according to his or her scores on the M, F, and A scales: Masculine (above median on M and below median on F), Feminine (above median on F and below median on M), Androgynous (above median on both M and F), or Undifferentiated (below median on both M and F).

Payne (1985) concluded that the short form of the Bem Sex-Role Inventory (Short BSRI) provides promising indexes of stereotypically sex-linked descriptions, which have significant correlations with various indexes of adjustment. The test–retest and internal consistency reliabilities of the Short BSRI are generally satisfactory, but the validity data are meager. In addition, researchers are cautioned not to rely on the forms reported in the manual since they are based solely on samples of Stanford University undergraduates.

Using Interest Inventories in Counseling

Young men and women are frequently unrealistic in making academic and vocational plans. Many more high school students expect to graduate from college than actually do, and the career aspirations of college graduates are often inconsistent with their career possibilities (Flanagan, Tiedeman, & Willis, 1973). Career aims and decisions are affected not only by environmental factors such as the economic situation and the kinds of jobs that are available, but also by psychosocial variables such as sex, socioeconomic status, physical and mental abilities, interests, and knowledge of particular occupations. Consequently, vocational counselors in high schools and colleges should be informed about the world of work—what particular jobs entail—and whether the abilities, interests, and resources possessed by students are appropriate for entering or preparing for certain jobs. Properly trained counselors are prepared to obtain personal data from students and other counselees and to supply them with information on training programs and occupations.

Vocational counseling must be conducted with caution. Both jobs and students are multifaceted and dynamic; they possess many different features, and those features change with time. The job of psychologist, for example, may involve different activities in different situations, and the nature of the job has changed over the years. Even in the same situational context and time period, there is usually enough diversity in most jobs for people with different abilities and interests to adapt and perform adequately.

Despite the need for a flexible, probabilistic approach to vocational counseling, counselors must make some interpretation of scores on psychological tests and inventories. One obvious distinction that counselors should be cognizant of is that between aspirations on the one hand and interests and abilities on the other. Aspirations are often colored by false perceptions of what a particular activity or occupation entails. For example, a child who aspires to become a nurse may picture herself or himself as a Florence Nightingale, ministering to suffering humanity and reaping the praises and love of others. But the same child may be unaware of the fact that since nursing involves a great deal of standing and walking, emptying bed pans, and listening to endless patient complaints, effectiveness as a nurse may depend on the strength of one's foot arches, as well as high olfactory and frustration tolerances.

In interpreting the results of an interest inventory, counselors should be aware of and attempt to clarify the difference between interests and abilities. It is not uncommon for a student to conclude from the results of an interest inventory that he or she has the abilities required to succeed in a certain occupation, when actually all that has been demonstrated is that the student's interests are similar to those of people who are employed in that occupation. Because students sometimes fail to distinguish between interests and abilities, it is unwise to leave the task of interpreting a self-administered inventory to the student. This is especially true of younger students.

The fact that correlations between measures of interests and abilities tend to be rather low indicates that people frequently do not possess the requisite abilities for success in fields in which they are interested, and they may not be interested in fields for which they have the necessary abilities. Consequently, scores on interest inventories should be employed in counseling in the light of other information about the counselee. Other information includes scores on ability tests, accomplishments (grades, awards, extracurricular activities, community service, and the like), experiences, and level of motivation.

Realizing the difficulties of explaining to students, parents, and others the concepts of interests and abilities and how psychological differences among people relate to their academic and vocational goals, experienced vocational counselors should have available many sources of information and explanation about the world of work. In addition to books such as the *Dictionary of Occupational Titles* (4th ed.), the *Occupational Outlook Handbook,* the *Occupational Outlook for College Students,* and *The Guide for Occupational Exploration* (2nd ed.), vocational counselors should have access to the various career exploration and development materials published by commercial testing companies. Examples are the Harrington–O'Shea Career Decision-Making System (American Guidance Service), the WPS Career Planning Program (Western Psychological Services), and the Vocational Exploration and Insight Kit (Psychological Assessment Resources).

ATTITUDE MEASUREMENT

An *attitude* is a learned predisposition to respond positively or negatively to a certain object, situation, institution, or person. As such, it consists of cognitive (knowledge or intellective), affective (emotional and motivational), and performance (behavioral or action) components. Although the concept of attitude is not distinct from that of interest, opinion, belief, or value, there are differences in the manner in which these terms are employed. An *interest* is a feeling or preference concerning one's own activities. Unlike *attitude,* which implies approval or disapproval (a moral judgment), being interested in something simply means that the person spends time thinking about or reacting to it, regardless of whether those thoughts and behaviors are positive or negative. An *opinion* is a specific reaction to certain occurrences or situations, whereas an attitude is more general in its effects on a person's responses toward a broad range of people or events. Furthermore, people are aware of their opinions, but they may not be fully conscious of their attitudes. Opinions are similar to *beliefs,* in that both are judgments or acceptances of certain propositions as facts, but the factual supports for opinions are usually weaker than those for beliefs. Finally, the term *value* refers to the importance, utility, or worth attached to particular activities and objectives, usually as ends but potentially for means as well.

Methods of Measuring Attitudes

Different methods can be used to obtain information on a person's attitude toward something, including direct observation of how the person behaves in relation to certain things. That is, what does the person actually do or say in situations in which the attitude object or event is present? Willingness to do a favor, sign a petition, and make a donation to some cause are examples of behavioral measures of attitudes.

Direct observation of behavior is informative, particularly with certain individuals (for example, young children) or when other methods are considered obtrusive. However, obtaining a representative sample of behavior, across time and situations, is very time consuming and expensive. In addition, behavioral measures of attitudes often yield different results from other methods. Among these methods are projective techniques and attitude questionnaires or scales.

Attitudes may be assessed projectively by showing a set of ambiguous pictures to people and instructing them to make up a story about each picture. Because the pictures can be interpreted in various ways, the stories told by the respondents should reveal something about their attitudes toward the characters, scenes, or situations in the pictures.

The most popular method of measuring attitudes is to administer an attitude scale. An *attitude scale,* consisting of a set of positive and negative statements concerning a subject of interest (a group of people, an institution, a concept), can be constructed by a number of different procedures. One of the first attitude scales was the Bogardus Social Distance Scale (Bogardus, 1925), on which respondents were asked to indicate their degree of acceptance of various racial and religious groups by ranking them. The Bogardus scale proved useful in research on regional differences and other variables associated with racial prejudice, but it permitted attitude measurement on only a ordinal scale and was somewhat crude by present-day standards. Somewhat more precise measures of attitudes were subsequently made possible by the work of Louis Thurstone, Rensis Likert, Louis Guttman, and other psychometricians.

Thurstone Scales

During the late 1920s, Louis Thurstone and his colleagues began attempting to put attitude assessment on the level of interval measurement by using the methods of *pair comparisons* and *equal-appearing intervals*. The first step in constructing an attitude scale by either method is to collect a large number of statements expressing a wide range of positive and negative attitudes toward a given topic. The next step in the method of pair comparisons is for a large number of experts to compare each statement with every other statement and judge which statement in each pair expresses a more positive attitude toward the topic. Because the pair comparisons procedure is rather cumbersome and time consuming, the method of equal-appearing intervals has proved more popular.

The first step in the method of equal-appearing intervals is to have several dozen expert judges sort the 200 or so statements expressing attitudes toward something (person, object, event, situation, or abstraction) into 11 categories, varying from least favorable (category 1) to most favorable (category 11) toward the thing in question. The judges are instructed to think of the 11 categories as lying at equal intervals along a continuum. After all judges have completed the sorting process for all statements, a frequency distribution for each statement is constructed by counting the number of judges who placed the statement in each of the 11 categories. Next the median (scale value) and semi-interquartile range (ambiguity index) for each statement are computed from the frequency distribution for that statement. The final attitude scale consists of 20 or so statements selected in such a way that the 20 scale values are approximately equidistant in numerical value, the range of scale values is as wide as possible, and the ambiguity indexes are low. A portion of one of the many attitude scales constructed by L. L. Thurstone and his colleagues by this method is shown in Figure 8–7. Note that the scale values of the statements shown, which are concerned with attitudes toward capital punishment, range from .1 (highly negative toward) to 11.0 (highly positive toward). An examinee's score on such a scale is the median of the scale values of the statements with which she or he indicates agreement.

Despite the fairly high reliabilities of instruments constructed by the method of equal-appearing intervals, the procedure has been criticized for (1) the great amount of work required in constructing an attitude scale, (2) the lack of uniqueness in a respondent's score, and (3) the effects of the judges' own attitudes on the scale values of statements (Selltiz, Wrightsman, & Cook, 1976). Considering the availability of new time-saving techniques, the first criticism is not so serious. The second criticism refers to the fact that the same score, which is simply the median scale value of the statements checked, may be obtained by checking different statements. The third criticism refers to the fact that not everyone is capable of playing the role of a neutral judge. Bruvold (1975) concluded, however, that careful instruction of the judges reduces the judgmental bias to a level that does not seriously distort the equal-interval properties of these scales. A final criticism, which is not limited to Thurstone-type attitude scales, is that these scales represent measurement at only an ordinal, not an interval, level (Petrie, 1969). Although the actual level of measurement of equal-appearing interval scales probably lies somewhere between the ordinal and interval levels, the matter is debatable.

Likert Scales

As with the method of equal-appearing intervals, Rensis Likert's *method of summated rating* begins with the collection of a large number of statements expressing a variety of positive and negative attitudes toward a specified object or event. Next a group of 100

This is a study of attitude toward capital punishment. Below you will find a number of statements expressing different attitudes toward capital punishment.

√ Put a checkmark if you agree with the statement.
X Put a cross if you disagree with the statement.

Try to indicate either agreement or disagreement for each statement. If you simply cannot decide about a statement you may mark it with a question mark.

This is not an examination. There are no right or wrong answers to these statements. This is simply a study of people's attitudes toward capital punishment. Please indicate your own convictions by a checkmark when you agree and by a cross when you disagree.

Scale Value	Item Number	
(0.1)	12	I do not believe in capital punishment under any circumstances.
(0.9)	16	Execution of criminals is a disgrace to civilized society.
(2.0)	21	The state cannot teach the sacredness of human life by destroying it.
(2.7)	8	Capital punishment has never been effective in preventing crime.
(3.4)	9	I don't believe in capital punishment but I'm not sure it isn't necessary.
(3.9)	11	I think the return of the whipping post would be more effective than capital punishment.
(5.8)	18	I do not believe in capital punishment but it is not practically advisable to abolish it.
(6.2)	6	Capital punishment is wrong but is necessary in our imperfect civilization.
(7.9)	23	Capital punishment is justified only for premeditated murder.
(9.4)	20	Capital punishment gives the criminal what he deserves.
(9.6)	17	Capital punishment is just and necessary.
(11.0)	7	Every criminal should be executed.

FIGURE 8–7 Twelve of the Twenty-four Items on a Scale of Attitudes Toward Capital Punishment.

to 200 people, not necessarily expert judges as required by the method of equal-appearing intervals, indicate on a four- to seven-point scale the extent to which they agree or disagree with each statement. In the typical case of a five-point scale, positively stated items are scored 0 for strongly disagree, 1 for disagree, 2 for undecided, 3 for agree, and 4 for strongly agree; negatively stated items are scored 4 for strongly disagree, 3 for disagree, 2 for undecided, 1 for agree, and 0 for strongly agree. A respondent's total score on the initial attitude item set is computed as the sum of scores for the individual items. After obtaining the total scores of all respondents on the initial item set, a statistical procedure (*t*-test or item discrimination index) is applied to each item. Then equal numbers of positively and negatively stated items (usually 10 of each) that significantly differentiate between respondents whose total scores fall in the upper 27 percent from those whose total scores fall in the lower 27 percent are selected. An attitude scale constructed by this method is shown in Figure 8–8. A person's total score on this scale is the sum of the numerical weights (0, 1, 2, 3, or 4) of the responses that he or she checks.

Not all published attitude scales referred to as Likert-type scales have been constructed by item-analysis procedures (Triandis, 1971). In many cases, a set of declarative statements, each with five agree–disagree response categories, is simply put together as an instrument without any specific theoretical construct in mind or without following the Likert attitude-scaling procedure. Consequently, we cannot be certain that a questionnaire that looks like a Likert scale was actually constructed by the Likert scaling procedure.

Directions: *Please write your name in the upper right-hand corner. Each of the statements on this opinion-naire expresses a feeling or attitude toward mathematics. You are to indicate, on a five-point scale, the extent of agreement between the attitude expressed in each statement and your own personal feeling. The five points are: Strongly Disagree (SD), Disagree (D), Undecided (U), Agree (A), Strongly Agree (SA). Draw a circle around the letter(s) which best indicate(s) how closely you agree or disagree with the attitude expressed in each statement AS IT CONCERNS YOU.*

1.	Mathematics is not a very interesting subject.	SD	D	U	A	SA
2.	I want to develop my mathematical skills and study this subject more.	SD	D	U	A	SA
3.	Mathematics is a very worthwhile and necessary subject.	SD	D	U	A	SA
4.	Mathematics makes me feel nervous and uncomfortable.	SD	D	U	A	SA
5.	I have usually enjoyed studying mathematics in school.	SD	D	U	A	SA
6.	I don't want to take any more mathematics than I absolutely have to.	SD	D	U	A	SA
7.	Other subjects are more important to people than mathematics.	SD	D	U	A	SA
8.	I am very calm and unafraid when studying mathematics.	SD	D	U	A	SA
9.	I have seldom liked studying mathematics.	SD	D	U	A	SA
10.	I am interested in acquiring further knowledge of mathematics.	SD	D	U	A	SA
11.	Mathematics helps to develop the mind and teaches a person to think.	SD	D	U	A	SA
12.	Mathematics makes me feel uneasy and confused.	SD	D	U	A	SA
13.	Mathematics is enjoyable and stimulating to me.	SD	D	U	A	SA
14.	I am not willing to take more than the required amount of mathematics.	SD	D	U	A	SA
15.	Mathematics is not especially important in everyday life.	SD	D	U	A	SA
16.	Trying to understand mathematics doesn't make me anxious.	SD	D	U	A	SA
17.	Mathematics is dull and boring.	SD	D	U	A	SA
18.	I plan to take as much mathematics as I possibly can during my education.	SD	D	U	A	SA
19.	Mathematics has contributed greatly to the progress of civilization.	SD	D	U	A	SA
20.	Mathematics is one of my most dreaded subjects.	SD	D	U	A	SA
21.	I like trying to solve new problems in mathematics.	SD	D	U	A	SA
22.	I am not motivated to work very hard on mathematics problems.	SD	D	U	A	SA
23.	Mathematics is not one of the most important subjects for people to study.	SD	D	U	A	SA
24.	I don't get upset when trying to work mathematics problems.	SD	D	U	A	SA

FIGURE 8–8 Scale for Measuring Attitudes toward Mathematics.
(After Aiken, 1979a. Reprinted by permission of School Science and Mathematics Association, Inc.)

Despite misuses of Likert's method of summated ratings, it has several advantages over Thurstone's method of equal-appearing intervals (Selltiz, Wrightsman, & Cook, 1976). Because it does not require expert, unbiased judges, constructing a Likert scale is easier than constructing a Thurstone scale. Also, unlike Thurstone scales, Likert scales permit the use of items that are not clearly related to the attitude being assessed as long as they are significantly correlated with total scores. Finally, a Likert scale is likely to have a higher reliability coefficient than a Thurstone scale consisting of the same number of items. Like Thurstone scales, however, Likert scales have been criticized for the fact that different patterns of responses can yield the same score and that at best the scores represent ordinal measurement.

Guttman Scales

The Thurstone and Likert attitude-scaling procedures have been widely used, but a third procedure, Louis Guttman's *scalogram analysis,* has been employed less frequently. The purpose of scalogram analysis (Guttman, 1944) is to determine whether the responses to the items chosen to measure a given attitude fall on a single dimension. When the items constitute a true, unidimensional Guttman scale, the respondent who endorses a particular item also endorses every item having a lower scale value. This condition is more likely to be met with cognitive than with attitude statements and other affective items.

As with Bogardus's (1925) approach to attitude-scale construction, the goal of scalogram analysis aims to produce a cumulative, ordinal scale. Guttman realized the difficulty of creating such a true scale with attitudinal items, but he felt that it could be approximated. The extent to which a true scale is obtained is indicated by the *reproducibility coefficient,* computed as the proportion of actual responses that fall into the perfect pattern of a true Guttman scale. That is, what proportion of the respondents who endorse a particular item endorse all items below it on the scale? An acceptable value of the reproducibility coefficient is .90 (see Edwards, 1957).

Other Attitude Measurement Procedures

A number of other procedures have been applied to the process of attitude-scale construction, including the semantic differential technique, Q-technique, and facet analysis. The first two of these are discussed in Chapter 9. The last procedure, *facet analysis,* is a complex, multidimensional approach to item construction and analysis that can be applied to any attitude object or situation (Castro & Jordan, 1977). The procedure has been used to construct attitude-behavior scales pertaining to a number of psychosocial conditions and situations, including mental retardation (Jordan, 1971) and racial–ethnic interaction (Hamersma, Paige, & Jordan, 1973).

It has become increasingly clear during the past three decades or so that attitudes are multidimensional rather than unidimensional variables, requiring more complex assessment procedures than those of Thurstone and Likert. For example, factor analysis (see Appendix A) is now commonly used in constructing attitude instruments (Steiner & Barnhart, 1972; Wiechmann & Wiechmann, 1973). The trend away from unidimensional scales is also seen in the increasing use of complex statistical procedures such as multidimensional scaling (van der Kamp, 1973), latent structure analysis (Lazarsfeld, 1957), latent partition analysis (Hartke, 1979), and the repertory grid technique (Duckworth & Entwhistle, 1974).

Sources and Psychometric Characteristics of Attitude Scales

A volume compiled by Shaw and Wright (1967) describes 176 attitude scales of various types, covering attitudes toward a variety of issues, concepts, groups, and institutions. In addition, a series of books published by the Institute for Social Research at the University of Michigan describes many different scales for assessing social attitudes (Robinson, Shaver, and Wrightsman, 1991), political attitudes (Robinson, Rush, & Head, 1973), and occupational attitudes (Robinson, Athanasiou, & Head, 1974). Several dozen attitude measures in a wide range of areas are also listed in *Tests in Microfiche* and can be ordered from Educational Testing Service.

Several publishers and distributors of psychological assessment instruments (see Appendix D for names and addresses) market attitude questionnaires and scales. For example, the Survey of School Attitudes and the Survey of Study Habits and Attitudes are available from The Psychological Corporation, the Study Attitudes and Methods Survey from EdITS, and the London House Attitude Survey for Business and Industry from London House. As with attitude questionnaires in general, the reliabilities of these survey instruments are generally lower than those of tests of cognitive abilities.

The test–retest and internal consistency coefficients of Thurstone- and Likert-type scales often reach into the .80s and .90s. With respect to validity, scores on attitude scales appear to make a small but significant contribution to the prediction of performance in academic and certain other organizational settings. Attitude measures have not generally correlated very highly with actual behavior, and research reviews have concluded that they are not very accurate predictors of specific behavior (see Gardner, 1975). It has been argued, however, that specific behavior can be predicted from measures of attitude toward the specific behavior, especially when the attitude statements are expressed in behavioral terms (Ajzen & Fishbein, 1977).

SURVEYS OF VALUES

The *values* held by people—the usefulness, importance, or worth attached to particular activities or objects—are related to but not identical to their interests and attitudes. Milton Rokeach (1973), who conducted extensive international and cross-cultural research on the topic, defined a value as "an enduring belief that a specific mode of conduct or end-state of existence is personally or socially preferable to an opposite or converse mode of conduct or end-state of existence" (page 5). This definition implies that values are of two kinds, those concerned with modes of conduct *(instrumental values)* and those concerned with end states *(terminal values)*. Although vocational psychologists have in large measure limited their attention to terminal values, Rokeach defined several subcategories of both instrumental and terminal values and designed an instrument to measure them.

Rokeach Value Survey

Rokeach classified instrumental values as being of two kinds, *moral values* and *competence values*. The former category is concerned with interpersonal modes of conduct, which produce guilt feelings when violated. The latter category, competence values, has to do with intrapersonal, self-actualizing modes of conduct, the violation of which leads to feelings of inadequacy. Terminal values are also further subdivided into *personal values* and *social values*. Personal values, which include such end states as peace of mind and salvation, are self-centered. Social values, which include end states such as equality and world peace, are societally centered.

The Rokeach Value Survey (Consulting Psychologists Press) consists of a series of 18 instrumental and 18 terminal value terms or phrases for assessing the relative importance of these values to people (see Table 8–2). The respondent is directed to place the 18 items in each list in rank order according to their importance to him or her. No other instrument measures as many values, a fact that, coupled with the speed of its administration and scoring and its inexpensiveness, may account for the popularity of the Rokeach Value Survey. Its reliability for comparing different groups, a purpose for which it has been employed in hundred of investigations for more than two decades, is adequate. People of different nationalities and in different walks of life rank the items on the Value Survey differently. For example, Rokeach (1973) reported that Israeli students, perhaps understandably, assigned highest rankings to "a world at peace" and "national security," whereas American students placed higher value on "a comfortable life" and "ambitious."

TABLE 8–2   Items on the Rokeach Value Survey

Instrumental values	Terminal values
Ambitious	A comfortable life
Broadminded	An exciting life
Capable	A sense of accomplishment
Cheerful	A world at peace
Clean	A world of beauty
Courageous	Equality
Forgiving	Family security
Helpful	Freedom
Honest	Happiness
Imaginative	Inner harmony
Independent	Mature love
Intellectual	National security
Logical	Pleasure
Loving	Salvation
Obedient	Self-respect
Polite	Social recognition
Responsible	True friendship
Self-controlled	Wisdom

Reprinted by permission of Consulting Psychologists Press.

Study of Values

Over the past several decades, many different instruments have been constructed by social and vocational psychologists to measure values. Undoubtedly the most popular of these instruments has been the Study of Values (Riverside Publishing Company), a popularity attested to by its administration in numerous research investigations concerned with personality, perception, learning, social psychology, and vocational guidance. Based on Eduard Spranger's classification of people into six value types, the Study of Values (Riverside Publishing Company) assesses the relative strength of an individual's values in six areas: theoretical, economic, esthetic, social, political, and religious. Appropriate for high school students, college students, and adults, the Study of Values is untimed, but takes approximately 20 minutes to complete. On the 30 items of Part I, respondents indicate a relative preference for two activities by dividing up three points among them, or by dividing the three points between affirmative and negative responses. On the 15 items of Part II, respondents rank four choices in order of preference. Scores on the six areas, which are ipsative in nature, are plotted as a profile showing the relative strength of the respondent's values. The manual lists mean scores on each of the six value areas for a sample of over 8000 college students of both sexes and various occupational groups; the most recent norms, based on a nationwide sample of 6000 high school students, were obtained in 1968. Test–retest reliabilities of the separate areas scales over a 2-month interval are in the .80s.

The theoretical foundation, the ipsative nature of the scoring system, and the fair amount of education required to understand the wording of items on the Study of Values have all been criticized (Rabinowitz, 1984). In addition, some of the content seems too old-fashioned for the 1990s, and the norms are obviously dated. Despite these shortcomings, the Study of Values continues to be used for instructional and research purposes.

Vocational Values

Although there is no reason why Rokeach's Value Survey and the Study of Values cannot be used in vocational counseling situations, these inventories were not designed specifically for this purpose. More closely related to work choices and satisfactions are instruments such as the Work Values Inventory, The Values Scale, and the Temperament and Values Inventory. Such vocational values vary from individual to individual and within the same individual from time to time. For example, Super (1973) found that people in upper-level occupations are more motivated by the need for self-actualization, which is an intrinsic goal, whereas extrinsic values are more likely to be subscribed to by people in lower-level occupations.

Work Values Inventory *(Riverside Publishing Company)* This inventory, designed by Donald Super to assess 15 values deemed to be significant in vocational success and satisfaction, consists of 45 Likert-type items. Each of the values (for example, achievement, supervisory relations, independence, esthetics, and creativity) is measured by three items. Each item consists of a statement, and the respondent indicates, on a five-point scale, the degree of importance that he or she attaches to the value represented by the statement. Percentile norms by grade (7–12) for each of the 15 values are based on data collected in the spring of 1968 on a representative national sample of approximately 9000 high school boys and girls. Test–retest reliability coefficients, obtained from retesting 99 tenth graders after 2 weeks, range from .74 to .88 for the 15 scales. Evidence for the content, concurrent, and construct values of the Work Values Inventory is described in the manual.

The Work Values Inventory has been praised for its excellent psychometric foundations and its continuing research uses (Bolton, 1985), but it has not gone uncriticized. The manual needs to be revised and brought up to date by incorporating the findings of research studies conducted since 1970, in particular occupational validity studies based on the current form of the inventory. In addition, reliability data based on college students and adults, not just tenth graders, and new normative data are required.

The Values Scale *(Consulting Psychologists Press)*   Developed by the Work Importance Study, an international consortium of vocational psychologists from America, Asia, and Europe, this instrument possesses characteristics of both the Work Values Inventory and Rokeach's Value Survey. The purpose of the consortium and The Values Scale is to understand values that individuals seek or hope to find in various life roles and to assess the relative importance of the work role as a means of value realization in the context of other life roles. The Values Scale consists of 106 items and takes 30 to 45 minutes to complete. It is scored for 21 values (five items per value): Ability Utilization, Achievement, Advancement, Esthetics, Altruism, Authority, Autonomy, Creativity, Economic Rewards, Life Style, Personal Development, Physical Activity, Prestige, Risk, Social Interaction, Social Relations, Variety, Working Conditions, Cultural Identity, Physical Prowess, and Economic Security. The reliabilities of all scales are adequate for individual assessment at the adult level; the reliabilities of ten scales are high enough for individual assessment at the college level, and the reliabilities of eight scales are adequate at the high school level. The means and standard deviations for three samples (high school, college, and adult), as well as data on the construct validity of the instrument, are given in the manual. The Values Scale appears to have good potential for research on vocational counseling and selection, and particularly for cross-cultural or cross-national comparative studies.

Temperament and Values Inventory *(National Computer Systems)*   Designed by C. B. Johansson and P. L. Webber to complement information obtained from ability tests and vocational interest inventories, this carefully constructed instrument consists of 230 items divided into two sections: 133 true–false items scored on seven Temperament Scales (Personal Characteristics) and 97 Likert-type items scored on seven Values Scales (Reward Values). The seven bipolar Temperament Scales are Routine–Flexible, Quiet–Active, Attentive–Distractible, Serious–Cheerful, Consistent–Changeable, Reserved–Social, and Reticent–Persuasive. The seven Values Scales are Social Recognition, Managerial–Sales Benefits, Leadership, Social Services, Task Specificity, Philosophical Curiosity, and Work Independence. The Temperament and Values Inventory is designed primarily for high school students and adults, takes approximately 30 minutes to complete, and is computer scored and interpreted. The scales were developed on an initial sample of 802 males and females and verified on a separate sample of 456 high school students.

The standard *T*-score scale norms are based on males and females in three age groups (15 to 19, 20 to 25, and 26 to 55 years). Test–retest reliabilities, computed on small samples retested over 1 to 2 weeks, are fairly satisfactory (.79 to .93). Comparisons with other related inventories are made to support the construct validity of the inventory, and data on its ability to differentiate between relatively small samples of individuals in a rather narrow range of occupations is reported to support the claim for concurrent validity.

The Temperament and Values Inventory has received fairly positive evaluations (for example, see Wheeler, 1985; Zuckerman, 1985), especially for its careful construction and well-designed manual. Among its psychometric shortcomings are a lack of long-term reliability data, a need for convergent and discriminant validity studies, and norms based on fairly small and nonrepresentative samples.

SUMMARY

Among the various methods of assessing interests, inventories are the most popular. The serious use of interest inventories in vocational and academic counseling and placement began with the development of the Strong Vocational Interest Blanks in the 1920s and 1930s. Subsequent publication of the Kuder Vocational Preference Record and other interest inventories resulted in increased understanding of interests and improved the accuracy with which they can be measured.

Scores on interest inventories are not very good predictors of vocational success, but they do a better job of forecasting occupational choice and satisfaction. The results of longitudinal studies have shown inventoried interests to be fairly stable, although responses to such inventories can be faked and may be susceptible to response sets.

Interests are generally considered to be learned, but there is some evidence of a hereditary basis in preferences for different types of people, activities, and things. Many investigators view interests as indicative of broader personality characteristics, and several inventories and theories have been developed along these lines.

Early interest inventories were concerned primarily with the interests of adolescents and adults planning to enter professions. Inventories have also been designed to assess and encourage the development of interests in children, the disadvantaged, and people planning to enter skilled or semiskilled occupations. A well-designed instrument for assessing interests in nonprofessional occupations is the Career Assessment Inventory.

The Strong Interest Inventory consists of 325 items grouped into seven categories. It is scored on six general occupational themes, 23 basic interest scales, 207 occupational scales, two special scales, and several administrative indexes. Scoring keys for the occupational scales were developed empirically by comparing the responses of people in general with those of people employed in particular occupations. Scores on the Strong Interest Inventory are fairly reliable and valid predictors of occupational persistence and satisfaction, but not necessarily occupational success.

G. F. Kuder constructed several interest inventories consisting of a series of forced-choice item triads. The Kuder Vocational Preference Record, the Kuder General Interest Survey, and the Kuder Occupational Interest Survey are three instruments of this type. The last of these instruments, like the Strong Interest Inventory, can be scored on a number of empirically derived occupational scales, although the first two are scored only on general-interest scales. All these inventories, also like the Strong Interest Inventory, are appropriate for high school students and adults.

In addition to inventories scored according to broad interest areas, a number of instruments designed to assess the interests of children, the disadvantaged, and people planning to enter nonprofessional occupations are available. The relationships of interests to personality are underscored by the research and instruments of Anne Roe and J. L. Holland. Vocational counseling requires a broad knowledge of the world of work and skilled integration of ability test scores, measures of interest, biographical data, and behavioral observations.

Attitudes are learned predispositions to respond positively or negatively to some object, person, or situation. As such, attitudes are characteristics of personality, although at a more superficial level than temperaments, values, and other individual traits. Attitudes can be assessed in a number of ways, the most popular being attitude scales. Procedures for constructing attitude scales were devised by Thurstone (method of equal-appearing intervals), Likert (method of summated ratings), and Guttman (scalogram analysis). Other attitude-scaling techniques include the semantic differential, Q-sorts, and a variety of multivariate statistical procedures.

Judging by the variety of instruments that has been devised, an individual can have an attitude toward almost anything—any school subject, any vocation, any defined group, any institution, any proposed social action, any practice. The vast majority of the hundreds of attitudes scales and questionnaires listed in various reference sources are unstandardized instruments, designed for a particular research investigation or application. However, a number of standardized instruments for assessing attitudes toward school and school subjects, work and work supervisors, and other kinds of human activities are available from commercial test distributors.

Values, or beliefs concerning the utility or worth of something, may be assessed by inventories such as the Study of Values and the Work Values Inventory. The Rokeach Value Survey and the associated theory have stimulated extensive research on political–ideological values and conceptions of the good life. The Study of Values has been used extensively in research on perception, learning, and motivation. Research on work-related values has resulted in a number of psychometric instruments, such as the Work Values Inventory and The Values Scale.

EXERCISES

1. What are response sets? Why are they of particular concern in designing inventories to measure interests and personality characteristics? What can be done to counter the effects of response sets on scores on these inventories?

2. Arrange with your instructor to take the Strong Interest Inventory or the Kuder Occupational Interest Survey and have it scored by the appropriate agency (Consulting Psychologists Press for the Strong Interest Inventory and CTB/Macmillan/McGraw-Hill for the Kuder OIS).

3. If the set of *Computer Programs for Psychological Assessment* is available, run all the programs in Category 7 ("Programs on Attitudes and Values"). Compare your results with those of your classmates.

4. Defend the thesis that interests are personality characteristics and therefore that interest inventories are measures of personality. Cite specific theories, research findings, and affective instruments in support of your position.

5. Assume that each of 50 judges sorts 200 attitude statements into 11 categories. The number of judges who place statements D, N, and X into each category are listed in the three frequency distributions given next. Compute the scale value (median) and ambiguity index (semi-interquartile range) of each statement by methods described in Appendix A, using the category numbers plus .5 as the upper exact limits of the intervals.

Pile	Statement D	Statement N	Statement X
11	8		
10	10		
9	13	3	
8	9	4	
7	7	6	
6	3	8	
5		13	6
4		10	9
3		6	10
2			17
1			8

6. Make multiple copies of the Mathematics Attitude Scale in Figure 8–8 and administer it to several people. Determine their scores on the four parts of the scale: E (enjoyment of mathematics), M (motivation in mathematics), I (importance of mathematics), and F (fear of mathematics); also determine a Total score. The E score consists of the sum of responses to items 1, 5, 9, 13, 17, and 21; and M score is the sum of responses to items 2, 6, 10, 14, 18, and 22; the I score is the sum of responses to items 3, 7, 11, 15, 19, and 23; and F score is the sum of responses to items 4, 8, 12, 16, 20, and 24. Responses to items 1, 4, 6, 7, 9, 12, 14, 15, 17, 20, 22, and 23 are scored as SD = 4, D = 3, U = 2, A = 1, SA = 0; responses to items 2, 3, 5, 8, 10, 11, 13, 16, 18, 19, 21, and 24 are scored as SD = 0, D = 1, U = 2, A = 3, SA = 4. The T (total) score is the sum of the four part scores (T = E + M + I + F). A high score on the four parts or total score of the Mathematics Attitude Scale indicates a favorable attitude toward mathematics, and a low score indicates an unfavorable attitude toward mathematics. Question your examines on the causes of their attitudes toward mathematics, and summarize your findings.

7. Design your own scale of attitudes toward some concept of interest to you: abortion, euthanasia, religion, communism, the economy, the elderly, and so on. Write or collect 24 statements ranging from highly positive to highly negative toward the concept. Then administer these items in Likert-type format (see Figure 8–8) to a sizable group of people (30 or more) and compute the correlations between item scores and total scores (sum of items scores). Retain the five positive and five negative items that are most highly correlated with total scores for your final scale.

8. Administer the following Educational Values Inventory to several students of various backgrounds and compute their scores. Construct and compare the profiles of scores of the students on the six values scales. Responses to each item on the Educational Values Inventory are scored on a scale of 1 to 5 from left (U or N) to right (E), respectively.

The sum of the scores on items 2, 7, 18, and 21 is the Esthetic Value score; the sum of the scores on items 1, 8, 13, and 24 is the Leadership Value score; the sum of the scores on items 4, 19, 15, and 23 is the Philosophical Value score; the sum of the scores on items 5, 12, 16, and 19 is the Social Value score; the sum of the scores on items 6, 11, 17, and 22 is the Scientific Value score; the sum of the scores on items 3, 10, 14, and 20 is the Vocational Value score.

Educational Values Inventory

Part I   Each of the items in this section refers to a possible goal or emphasis of higher education. Check the appropriate letter after each of the following statements to indicate how important you believe the corresponding goal should be. Use this key: U = unimportant, S = somewhat important, I = important, V = very important, E = extremely important.

1. Ability to lead or direct other people.   U S I V E
2. Appreciation of the beautiful and harmonious things in life.   U S I V E
3. Preparation for a vocation or profession of one's choice.   U S I V E
4. Gaining insight into the meaning and purpose of life.   U S I V E
5. Understanding of social problems and their possible solutions.   U S I V E
6. Understanding of scientific theories and the laws of nature.   U S I V E
7. Acquiring the ability to express oneself artistically.   U S I V E
8. Understanding how to direct others in the accomplishment of
   some goal.   U S I V E
9. Development of a personal philosophy of life.   U S I V E
10. Learning how to succeed in a chosen occupation or field.   U S I V E
11. Learning about scientific problems and their solutions.   U S I V E
12. Understanding people of different social classes and cultures.   U S I V E

Part II   Check the appropriate letter after each of the following items to indicate your estimate of how valuable the particular kinds of college courses are to students in general. Use this key: N = not at all valuable, S = somewhat valuable, V = valuable, Q = quite valuable, E = extremely valuable.

13. Courses concerned with how to direct and organize people.   N S V Q E
14. Courses in one's chosen vocation or professional field.   N S V Q E
15. Courses dealing with philosophical and/or religious ideas.   N S V Q E
16. Courses concerned with understanding and helping people.   N S V Q E
17. Courses in science and mathematics.   N S V Q E
18. Courses in music, art, and literature.   N S V Q E

Part III   Check the appropriate letter after each of the following items to indicate how much attention you feel should be given to each kind of college course in the education of most college students. Use this key: N = no attention at all, L = little attention, M = moderate degree of attention, A = above average attention, E = extensive amount of attention.

19. Courses concerned with how to understand and be of help to
    other people.   N L M A E
20. Courses in the vocational or professional field of your choice.   N L M A E
21. Courses in art, literature, and music.   N L M A E
22. Courses in scientific and mathematical fields.   N L M A E

23. Courses concerned with philosophy and religion.   N L M A E
24. Courses concerned with organizing and directing people.   N L M A E

SUGGESTED READINGS

Aiken, L. R. (1980). Attitude measurement and research. In D. A. Payne (ed.), *Recent develop-ments in affective measurement,* pp. 1–24. San Francisco: Jossey-Bass.

Ashmore, R. D. (1990). Sex, gender, and the individual. In L. A. Pervin (ed.), *Handbook of personality theory and research,* pp. 486–526. New York: Guilford Press.

Davis, D., & Ostrom, T. M. (1985). Attitude measurement. In R. J. Corsini (ed.), *Encyclopedia of psychology,* Vol. 1, pp. 97–99. New York: Wiley.

Deaux, K. (1984). From individual differences to social categories; Analysis of a decade's research on gender. *American Psychologist, 39,* 105–116.

Hansen, J. C. (1990). Interest inventories. In G. Goldstein & M. Hersen (eds.), *Handbook of psychological assessment,* 2nd ed., pp. 173–196. New York: Pergamon Press.

Holland, J. L. (1984). *Making vocational choices,* 2nd ed. Englewood Cliffs, NJ: Prentice Hall.

———. (1986). New directions for interest testing. In B. S. Plake & J. C. Witt (eds.), *The future of testing,* pp. 246–268. Hillsdale, NJ: Lawrence Erlbaum.

Jordan, J. P., & Heyde, M. B. (1979). *Vocational maturity during the high school years.* New York: Teachers College Press.

Osipow, S. H. (1983). *Theories of career development,* 3rd ed. Englewood Cliffs, NJ: Prentice Hall.

Thorndike E. L. (1912). The permanence of interests and their relation to abilities. *Popular Science Monthly, 81,* 449–456.

Chapter Nine

Personality Assessment: Observations, Interviews, and Ratings

The term *personality* has many different meanings. To some, it refers to a mysterious charisma possessed by Hollywood stars and other popular, influential people, but not by everyone. To others, personality is the same as temperament, a natural, genetically based predisposition to think, feel, and act in a particular way. To still others, personality consists of a person's unique mixture of emotional, intellectual, and character traits (honesty, courage, and so forth). And to more behaviorally oriented psychologists, personality is not something internal, but rather an externally observable pattern of organized behavior typical of an individual.

The various definitions of personality have some common ground, but there is also room for disagreement. Perhaps an acceptable compromise would be to define human personality as a *composite of mental abilities, interests, attitudes, temperament, and other individual differences in thoughts, feelings, and behavior.* This definition emphasizes the fact that personality is a unique combination of cognitive and affective characteristics describable in terms of a typical, fairly consistent pattern of individual behavior.

From the last definition, it follows that methods of assessing personality should include a broad range of cognitive and affective variables. Among these variables are the measures of achievement, intelligence, special abilities, interests, attitudes, and values discussed in Chapters 5 through 8. Other emotional, temperamental, and stylistic characteristics, which have traditionally been referred to as *personality variables,* are also important in understanding and predicting human behavior. The observations, interviews, ratings, personality inventories, and projective techniques for assessing this second group of variables are described in this chapter and the next.

FOUNDATIONS OF PERSONALITY ASSESSMENT

As was the case with intelligence testing, personality assessment developed partly from research on individual and group differences. Many antecedents of contemporary personality assessment can be found in the history of abnormal psychology and psychiatry.

Pseudosciences and Other Historical Antecedents

The history of science is replete with examples of beliefs or doctrines that had many strong supporters at one time, but subsequently were proved to be partially or totally incorrect. Among these pseudoscientific doctrines are phrenology, physiognomy, and graphology.

Phrenology, which perhaps no one earnestly believes in today, was taken seriously by Thomas Jefferson and certain other prominent scholars and intellectuals during the late eighteenth and early nineteenth centuries. According to the proponents of phrenology, the development of specific brain areas is associated with certain personality characteristics and mental disorders. Among the personality traits that were supposedly traced to particular protuberances of the skull are agreeableness, combativeness, and acquisitiveness (Figure 9–1). A natural consequence of this belief is that personality can be analyzed by feeling a person's head to determine the location of the "bumps" over brain areas presumably associated with particular characteristics. Phrenology had a great deal of influence on nineteenth-century psychiatry and on *faculty psychology,* a basically incorrect notion that affected the school curriculum. According to faculty psychology, the mind consists of a number of faculties that can be developed by mental exercise (for example, by studying difficult subjects such as Latin, Greek, and geometry), just as the body is developed by physical exercise.

Physiognomy, another pseudoscience, is concerned with determining temperament and character from external features of the body and especially the face. Remnants of physiognomy may be seen in contemporary personnel evaluation and assessment procedures, for example, in the requirement that a photograph be submitted with an employment application and in the Szondi Test. This test consists of six sets of photographs, eight pictures per set, of mental patients having different diagnoses (for example, hysteria, catatonia, paranoia, depression, or mania). Examinees select the two pictures they like most and the two they dislike most in each set. The basic assumption underlying the Szondi Test is that the facial features of the mental patients depicted in the 12 photographs that are selected and the 12 that are rejected have a personal meaning for the examinee. The examinee's needs and personality are presumably similar to those of the patients depicted in the photographs. No consistent evidence for the validity of the Szondi Test in personality analysis or psychiatric diagnosis has been found, and the test has been generally discredited.

Belief in *graphology,* which is concerned with analyzing personality by studying samples of the examinee's handwriting, is perhaps even more widespread than belief in physiognomy. Although it makes sense that handwriting, which is a type of stylistic behavior, is an expression of personality characteristics, even experienced handwriting analysts are not known for the accuracy of their interpretations. Physiognomy and graphol-

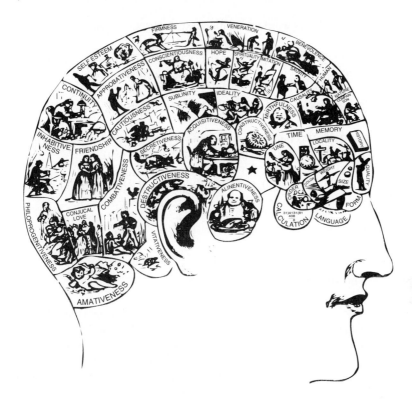

FIGURE 9–1 Phrenologists Chart of Brain Function. Localization of Various
Affective and Cognitive Faculties as Depicted by a Nineteenth-century
Phrenologist. Phrenology Was a PseudoScience, and No One Places Much
Credence in It Today.
(The Bettmann Archive.)

ogy are somewhat more reputable than phrenology, but many of the claims of their
proponents are just as wrong as those of the phrenologists.

Not all nineteenth-century efforts to develop a science of personality assessment
should be labeled as pseudoscience. The efforts of Francis Galton, Emil Kraeplin, and
Alfred Binet, for example, were more reputable, although not always successful in achieving their goals. In 1884, Galton proposed to measure emotions by recording changes in
heartbeat and pulse rate and to assess good temper, optimism, and other personality traits
by observing people in contrived social situations. Kraeplin, who is best known for his
system of classifying mental disorders, developed the word *association technique* in 1892.
Also during the 1890s, Alfred Binet, whose name the reader will recall from the chapter
on intelligence testing, devised methods of studying the personality characteristics of
eminent persons.

Despite a few promising beginnings in the nineteenth century, not until the early
twentieth century, when psychology was applied in clinical, educational, military, and
industrial settings, did personality assessment make genuine progress. Particularly noteworthy during this time were the following events:

1905   Carl Jung uses word-association tests to detect and analyze mental complexes.

1919   Robert Woodworth's Personal Data Sheet, the first standardized personality inventory, is used in U.S. military selection.

1920   Hermann Rorschach's Inkblot Test first published.

1938   Henry Murray publishes *Explorations in Personality,* describing the theoretical foundations of the Thematic Apperception Test.

1942   S. R. Hathaway and J. C. McKinley publish the Minnesota Multiphasic Personality Inventory.

Theories of Personality

Almost everyone has some theory as to why people behave as they do. These theories of human nature and behavior usually consist of overgeneralizations or stereotypes, but they serve as rough guides to expectation and action. Sometimes a person's very survival depends on the ability to understand and predict the behavior of others.

Realizing that everyone is different from everyone else and that human behavior can be very complex, professional personality theorists have learned to be suspicious of commonsense explanations. Certain psychologists, impressed by the individuality and intricacy of human actions, have despaired of discovering general principles or laws to explain personality. They dismiss the *nomothetic approach,* the search for general laws of behavior and personality, as unrealistic and inadequate to the task of understanding the individual. Instead, they advocate an *idiographic approach* of viewing every personality as a lawful, integrated system to be studied in its own right (Allport, 1937).

Many other differences exist among personality theorists, one being the relative emphasis placed on heredity and environment as molders of behavior. Another difference among theorists concerns the extent to which the internal, personal characteristics of the individual, rather than external, situational variables, are the primary determinants of behavior. As these and other points of debate among personality theorists suggest, there is no generally accepted theory of personality. On the contrary, theories and research findings in the field of personality are constantly developing and changing. Heredity versus environment, traits versus situations, and other issues symptomatic of that change are discussed at some length in Chapter 12. But it is important for those who are interested in psychological assessment to be aware of the various theories of personality and to be skeptical of untested ones. Such theories, despite their shortcomings, can serve as guides to the measurement and understanding of personality. Certainly, we must have some frame of reference, some ideas about the dynamics and development of personality and behavior, to interpret individual assessment findings. In this respect, the theories proposed and tested by professional psychologists are probably more useful frames of references than the layperson's commonsense theories.

Type Theories

One of the oldest approaches to understanding personality is the notion of fixed categories or types of people. Galen, a physician in ancient Rome who subscribed to the doctrine of four body humors (blood, yellow bile, black bile, and phlegm) proposed by the Greek physician Hippocrates, hypothesized four types of temperament corresponding to the four humors. The *sanguine type,* with an excess of blood, was purported to be vigorous and athletic, whereas the *choleric type,* with an excess of yellow bile, was easily angered. The *melancholic type,* with an excess of black bile, was generally depressed or sad, and the *phlegmatic type,* with an excess of phlegm, was chronically tired or lazy. Like phrenology and other pseudoscientific theories, the humoral theory is now only of historical interest (but see Figure 9–3 on page 251). Based somewhat more securely on observational data, but still highly tentative and overgeneralized, are the body-type theories of Ernst Kretschmer, Cesare Lombroso, and William Sheldon.

The idea that personality is associated with physique has intrigued many philosophers and poets. Shakespeare indicated as much in several plays; for example:

Let me have men about me that are fat,
Sleek-headed men, and such as sleep a-nights,
Yond Cassius has a lean and hungry look;
He thinks too much; such men are dangerous.

Julius Caesar, Act I, Scene II

Less poetic but more systematic than the writings of famous authors were the descriptions of the scientist Ernst Kretschmer (1925). Kretschmer concluded that both a tall, thin body build (asthenic) and a muscular body build (athletic) are associated with withdrawing tendencies (schizoid personality), whereas a short, stout body build (pyknic) is associated with emotional instability (cycloid personality). A related typology, a three-component somatotype system of classifying human physiques according to the degree of endomorphy (fatness), mesomorphy (muscularity), and ectomorphy (thinness), was proposed by Sheldon, Stevens, and Tucker (1940) (see Figure 9–2).

Although body-type theories are interesting, their scientific status is fairly low because there are so many exceptions to the hypothesized relationships between physique and temperament and also because different interpretations have been given to the relationships. Furthermore, contemporary psychologists object to typologies because they place people in categories and assign labels to them. Not only does labeling overemphasize the internal causation of behavior, but it may also act as a self-fulfilling prophecy through which people become what they are labeled as being. Thus, a person who is labeled an *introvert* may be left alone by would-be friends, causing him or her to become even more socially isolated. Similarly, an *extrovert* may become more outgoing or sociable because other people expect the person to behave in that way.

Trait Theories

Less general than personality types are personality traits. One early personality theorist, Gordon Allport, began his research on traits by listing 17,953 words in the English

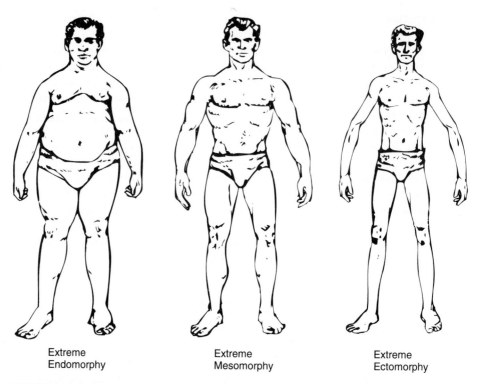

Extreme   Extreme   Extreme
Endomorphy   Mesomorphy   Ectomorphy

FIGURE 9–2 Sheldon's Somatotypes.
*(From Elements of Psychology by David Krech and Richard S. Crutchfield.
Copyright © 1958 by David Krech and Richard S. Crutchfield. Copyright © 1969,
1974 by Alfred A. Knopf, Inc. Reprinted by permission of the publisher.)*

language that refer to characteristics of personality and then reducing them to a smaller
list of trait names (Allport & Odbert, 1936). Allport defined a *trait* as a "neuropsychic
structure having the capacity to render many stimuli functionally equivalent, and to initiate
and guide equivalent (meaningfully consistent) forms of adaptive and expressive behavior"
(Allport, 1961, page 347). To Allport, *personality* consists of the dynamic organization
of those traits that determine a person's unique adjustment to the environment.

Another trait theorist, R. B. Cattell, classified traits in four ways: common versus
unique, surface versus source, constitutional versus environmental mold, and dynamic
versus ability versus temperament. Common traits are characteristic of all people, whereas
unique traits are peculiar to the individual. A person's surface traits are easily observed
in behavior, but source traits can be discovered only by factor analysis (see Appendix
A). Constitutional traits depend on heredity, and environmental-mold traits depend on
environment. Finally, dynamic traits motivate the person toward a goal, ability traits
determine the ability to achieve the goal, and temperament traits pertain to the emotional
aspects of goal-directed activity. Cattell's trait theory, which is much more elaborate than
this brief description suggests, has served as a framework for the construction of several
personality inventories (see Chapter 10).

Many other psychologists, including Henry Murray, J. P. Guilford, and H. Eysenck, have theorized and conducted research on personality traits. The methods of factor analysis have been applied to much of this research, yielding a variety of personality dimensions. The two basic dimensions in Eysenck's system, introversion–extroversion and stability–instability, are depicted in Figure 9–3. The positions of the 32 traits on the axes of this figure indicate the direction and amounts of each of the two basic dimensions comprising each trait.

Psychoanalytic Theory

Sigmund Freud and other psychoanalysts have viewed human personality as a kind of battleground where three combatants, the id, ego, and superego, vie for supremacy. The *id,* a reservoir of instinctive drives of sex and aggression housed in the unconscious part

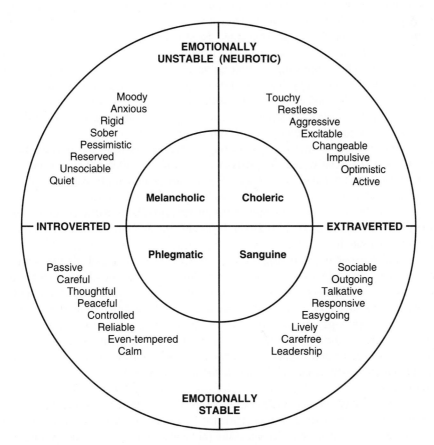

FIGURE 9–3 Eysenck's Dimensions of Personality.
(From Personality and Individual Differences by H. J. Eysenck and M. W. Eysenck, Plenum Publishing, New York, 1958. Reprinted by permission of the publisher.)

of the mind, acts according to the pleasure principle. It runs into conflict with the *superego* (the conscience), which acts according to the moral principle. Although the id is innate, the superego develops as the child internalizes the prohibitions and sanctions that parents place on the behavior of the former. Meanwhile, the *ego,* acting according to the reality principle, attempts to serve as a mediator between the relentless pressures of the id and superego for control. The id says "Now!", the superego says "Never!", and the ego says "Later" to the individual's basic desires. Id impulses and the conflict of id with superego and ego are usually in the unconscious mind, but they are expressed in thoughts and behavior in various disguised forms.

Freud also believed that human personality develops through a series of *psychosexual stages.* During each stage, a different region of the body (erogenous zone) is the center of sexual stimulation and gratification, and at that stage conflicts pertaining to the particular body region predominate. The *oral stage* occurs from birth to $1\frac{1}{2}$ years, during which time pleasure is derived primarily from stimulation of the mouth and lips, as in sucking, biting, and swallowing. During the *anal stage,* from about age $1\frac{1}{2}$ to 3 years, interest and conflict center around the retention and expulsion of feces. Negativism, manifested by defiance of parental orders and frequently associated with the toilet-training situation, is most pronounced during the anal stage. Next in order is the *phallic stage,* from 3 to 6 years, when the body region of greatest interest is the genital area. It is during the phallic stage, when rubbing, touching, exhibiting oneself, and looking are emphasized, that the Oedipus complex develops. The *Oedipus complex,* consisting of a composite of sexual feelings toward the mother and dislike of the father in 3- to 6-year-old boys, was viewed by Freud as a universal phenomenon. The comparable situation in girls, dislike of the mother and love of the father, is the *Electra complex.*

Freud maintained that if a young boy is to progress from the phallic stage to the *latency period* of relative sexual inactivity during middle childhood, the Oedipus complex must either be resolved or repressed. In most instances, it is resolved by the boy's learning to identify with, that is, trying to act like, his father. At the onset of puberty, the child who has successfully navigated through the previous psychosexual stages enters the *genital stage.* Interest in the opposite sex then becomes predominant, ultimately culminating in heterosexual mating.

Freud was one of the first personality theorists to recognize that "the child is father to the man," that deprivation and conflict in childhood frequently have permanent effects on personality. His theory of psychosexual stages maintains that frustration and conflict at a particular stage affect the individual's adult character structure by causing *fixation* (a failure to progress psychosexually beyond a particular stage) or *regression* (a partial or complete return to behavior patterns typical of an earlier stage of development). A person who is fixated at the oral stage, for example, is said to be characterized by overdependency, greed, and passivity. A person fixated at the anal stage is excessively orderly, obstinate, and stingy.

Freud's theory of personality was based almost entirely on uncontrolled clinical observations of approximately 100 patients, and many features of the theory have not been confirmed by research. Certain assumptions, for example, that the Oedipus complex is universal and that there is a latency period in sexual development, are certainly incorrect. Be that as it may, Freud and his followers were certainly correct in pointing out the existence of childhood sexuality and its importance for personality development, the significant role played by unconscious motivation in shaping personality and behavior, and the functions of defense mechanisms in helping the individual to cope with anxiety produced by intrapsychic conflict. The notion that children invariably pass through the sequence of psychosexual stages outlined above and that adult personality is shaped by childhood sexual conflicts is debatable and was modified by later psychoanalysts. Compared with Freud, modern psychoanalysts also place more emphasis on social learning and culture than on biological instincts as determinants of personality.

Phenomenological Theories

Stemming from a philosophical tradition that emphasized the analysis of immediate, personal, subjective experience, phenomenological (humanistic or "self") theorists maintain that trait theorists and others who attempt to analyze personality into a set of components do an injustice to the integrated, dynamic organization of personality. Consequently, phenomenological theorists have been critical of psychoanalytic, trait-factor, and behavioral approaches to understanding personality. In contrast to traditional psychoanalysis, which emphasizes the fundamental importance of sexual and aggressive impulses, the unconscious, and psychosexual stages in development, phenomenologists stress perceptions, meanings, feelings, and the self. Phenomenologists see a person as responding to the world in terms of his or her unique, private perceptions of it. These perceptions are determined by experiences and the meanings attached to those experiences in an effort to fully realize one's potentialities. The part of the environment that is perceived and has meaning for a person is known as the *phenomenal field,* a portion of which (the *self*) is related to the individual in a personal way. Finally, the totality of the good and bad evaluations given by a person to the self are referred to as the *self-concept.*

According to Abraham Maslow, Carl Rogers, and other phenomenological theorists, the individual strives to attain a stage of *self-actualization,* a congruence or harmony between the real self and ideal self. The basic direction of existence is toward self-actualization and pleasant relations with others, but that effort can be inhibited in various ways. Rogers pointed out that most people are not open to or willing to accept the full range of their experiences. In the process of growing up, they learn that they are objects of *conditional positive regard:* parents and other significant persons accept the child's behavior only if it conforms to expected standards (*conditions of worth*). Consequently, the child, who eventually becomes an adult, learns to recognize and accept only a part of his or her experiences. The result is an incompletely functioning individual who cannot become fully functioning unless *unconditional positive regard* is received from other people. This is a condition in which the person is accepted regardless of what he or she is or does.

Clinical practitioners of the phenomenological persuasion have tended to reject objective psychological tests and procedures in favor of case studies and open or unstructured interviews for assessing personality. Carl Rogers was not a great believer in the value of personality assessment devices, and phenomenology or self theory has not been as influential as trait-factor and psychoanalytic theories in the development of personality assessment instruments and procedures. Many instruments for assessing feelings and attitudes toward the self, however, have followed a phenomenological theory of personality. Examples are

Q-sorts (Stephenson, 1953) and inventories such as the Tennessee Self-Concept Scale (Western Psychological Services), the Piers–Harris Children's Self-Concept Scale (Western Psychological Services), and the Coopersmith Self-Esteem Inventories (Consulting Psychologists Press).

Social Learning Theory

Many other theoretical conceptualizations have influenced the development of personality assessment instruments. Among these are George Kelly's (1955) theory of personal constructs and the cognitive–behavioral approaches of social learning theorists such as Julian Rotter, Albert Bandura, and Walter Mischel.

Rotter's Theory   The first *social learning theory* as such was that of Julian Rotter (1954), who attempted to integrate the traditional behavioristic position on the role of reinforcement in learning with the cognitive conceptualizations of Kurt Lewin and other field theorists. Rotter was not the first to note that much human behavior is learned in a social context, but he made a more conscious effort than his predecessors to develop a systematic theory of how this takes place. Rotter distinguished between reinforcements and cognitions: reinforcements result in movement toward or away from a goal, whereas cognitions are internal states such as expectancy and reinforcement value. The term *expectancy* refers to a subjective probability held by a person that a specific behavior performed in a certain situation will lead to reinforcement. Two *generalized expectancies* that have been measured and investigated by Rotter and others are internal–external locus of control (see Chapter 10) and interpersonal trust. *Locus of control* refers to the typical direction from which people perceive themselves as being controlled (internal, or from within oneself, versus external, or by other people). *Interpersonal trust* is concerned with the extent to which the individual believes that others tell the truth.

According to Rotter, reinforcement is important for performance, but not all reinforcements are equally valued by the individual: even when the probabilities of occurrence of different reinforcements are equal, certain objects or actions will have greater *reinforcement value* than others. Both reinforcement value and expectancies are affected by the psychological relevance or meaning of the situation to the individual, which must be understood in order to predict how the person will behave in that situation.

Bandura's Observational Learning Theory   More important for the development of techniques for modifying maladaptive behavior than for influencing the design of personality assessment instruments is Bandura's social learning theory. Conceptualizing psychological functioning as the reciprocal interactions of behavior, person variables (cognitions and other internal states), and environmental variables, Bandura emphasizes the fact that the individual is not a passive "push-button" automaton that only acts when acted upon. People both influence and are influenced by their social environments, in which learning takes place by observation, imitation, and modeling. Unlike more traditional behaviorists, such as Clark Hull and B. F. Skinner, Bandura maintains that much learning takes place without reinforcement, in the absence of rewards and punishments, but that reinforcement is important in determining when the learned behavior will occur. Particularly significant in learning is the process of modeling the behavior of others, the effectiveness of which depends on such factors as the personal characteristics of the model and the learner's motivational level. Aggression, fears, sex-typed behaviors, and many other emotional and stylistic reactions are, according to Bandura, learned by observation and modeling.

Bandura also emphasizes the fact that learning and behavior are mediated by perceptions and cognitions: people use internal, symbolic representations of their environments, and it is these representations that mediate changes in behavior. By visualizing the consequences of certain actions, the individual learns to regulate his or her behavior.

Empirical Approaches to Personality Assessment

Rather than being designed in accordance with a specific theory of personality, many personality assessment instruments have been constructed on a purely empirical basis. For example, the items on the various scales of the Minnesota Multiphasic Personality Inventory (MMPI) were selected on the basis of their ability to distinguish between two contrasting groups of people (normals and selected psychiatric patient groups). No specific theory of personality was implied or involved in this empirical procedure; the MMPI items were simply validated against the specific criterion of psychiatric diagnoses in various samples of mental patients (see Chapter 10).

A number of personality assessment instruments have been developed in the context of investigations of personality and behavior disorders. These efforts, although not completely devoid of theoretical foundations, have not been restricted to one particular theoretical position. Illustrative of such approaches are the researches of the Harvard personologists and psychologists at the Institute for Personality Assessment and Research at Berkeley, California.

Ethical and Measurement Problems

Personality assessment procedures and instruments are used in schools, clinics, hospitals, prisons, and other settings where the results contribute to the process of making decisions about people. Ideally, the results are treated conscientiously and with an awareness of the limitations of the assessments and the needs and rights of examinees. Unfortunately, the ethics of personality assessors are not always as they should be.

Among the methods used in personality assessment are observations, interviews, rating scales, checklists, self-report inventories, and projective techniques. Sometimes these methods have been misapplied by untrained or unethical persons, resulting in a black mark for psychological testing as whole. It is not difficult for individuals who have read a bit of psychology to obtain a few paper-and-pencil instruments and present themselves as personality analysts. Like fortune tellers and other charlatans, these would-be personality analysts deal in generalities, truisms, and other statements that sound specific to a given individual, but actually apply to most people. To demonstrate this "Barnum effect," consider the following "personality profile":

You have a strong need for other people to like you and for them to admire you. You have a tendency to be critical of yourself. You have a great deal of unused capacity which you have not turned to your advantage. While you have some personality weaknesses, you are generally able to compensate for them. Your sexual adjustment has presented some problems for you. Disciplined and controlled on the outside, you tend to be worrisome and insecure inside. At times you have serious doubts as to whether you have made the right decision or done the right thing. You prefer a certain amount of change and variety and become dissatisfied when hemmed in by restrictions and limitations. You pride yourself as being an independent thinker and do not accept others' opinions without satisfactory proof. You have found it unwise to be too frank in revealing yourself to others. At times you are extroverted, affable, social, while at other times you are introverted, wary, reserved. Some of your aspirations tend to be pretty unrealistic (Forer, 1949).

Is this a fairly good description of your own personality? Thirty-seven students in a group of 50 to whom I showed the paragraph rated it as a good or excellent description of their personalities.

It requires training and experience to become a skilled observer and interpreter of human personality. Teachers, personnel managers, and other nonpsychologists can often apply rating scales and checklists in a sensitive, sensible manner, but the administration and interpretation of personality inventories and projective techniques are restricted to psychologists and other professionals with comparable training. Even then, it is questionable whether many of the available personality inventories and projectives should be employed for anything other than research purposes. Personality tests very often focus more on symptoms of maladjustment and mental illness than on adjustment and mental health. Because these topics are very personal and should be handled with great care, we need to be very cautious in administering and interpreting the results of any personality assessment device. Both the examinee's right to privacy and natural concern over his or her own emotional stability and mental health must be respected.

In addition to the question of privacy and other moral issues, the reliability and validity of personality assessment devices pose problems. Responding to test materials in terms of the most socially desirable answers or letting one's answers be determined by whatever role it is felt necessary to assume in the specific testing situation are types of response sets that can invalidate personality assessment procedures. More unobtrusive measures, which are less susceptible to faking or on which the procedure does not unduly interfere with obtaining valid results, may take care of response sets but at the same time introduce problems of quantification and interpretation of the findings.

Interpreting and Reporting Assessment Findings

Even when the most carefully constructed and validated measures of personality are used, it is a cardinal rule that the resulting interpretations should be viewed as hypotheses to be confirmed or disconfirmed by behavioral observations and personal interviews. Certainly, the results of personality assessment are neither exact nor final, and they can be viewed in different ways by different examiners. This becomes embarrassingly obvious when different psychologists or psychiatrists, acting as expert witnesses in a court trial, differ radically in their interpretations of the same assessment findings. Given the subjective nature of most psychological assessments, such embarrassments may be unavoidable when the two parties in a legal dispute have different objectives.

Several additional recommendations concerning the collection and interpretation of personality assessment data, which have been adapted from Sundberg (1977), can be made:

1. Survey the examinee's overall life situation and problems and then obtain more details in areas of particular relevance to the assessment.
2. Be sensitive to the sociocultural and ethnic background of the examinee, as well as his or her age and sex, if relevant.
3. Use more objective, as opposed to subjective, techniques and data whenever possible.
4. Obtain the *right kind* of information, not just *more* information, pertaining to the specific situation and purposes of the assessment.
5. Avoid too much speculation in interpreting results and predicting behavior; be especially careful in making predictions concerning behavior that has a low probability of occurrence.
6. If possible, check your findings and interpretations with other specialists in psychological assessment, and keep a record of your agreements and disagreements, successes and failures.
7. Communicate your findings in a clear, written form in a style that can be understood by the people for whom the report is intended.

Whatever the reasons for a psychological examination may be—the determination of vocational competency, mental abilities, or emotional stability—some kind of written report of the results is usually required. The outline and length of the written report of a clinical case study vary with its purposes and the readers for whom it is intended, but the format presented in Table 9–1 is representative.

When preparing a formal report of a psychological examination, the writer should keep clearly in mind the referral questions or principal complaint(s) (why the person was referred for psychological assessment or sought it out) and how the assessment findings bear on answers to these questions or solutions to these problems. Information on the current mental status and emotional stability, as well as the probable outcomes (prognosis) of the patient's condition, should also be dealt with. The examinee's characteristics and their interrelationships should be described as fully and specifically as possible, avoiding vague generalizations, stereotypes, and banalities. It is also helpful for the writer to have a theory of personality, or at least some psychological framework, to serve as a basis for interpreting the findings. The report should be written in a succinct, clear style that is comprehensible to the reader. A psychological report is of little value if it is not understood or not read by the persons who are in a position to use the information that it contains to help make decisions bearing on the examinee's life and well-being.

OBSERVATIONS

The most widely employed and probably the most generally understood and acceptable method of personality assessment is some form of observation. When using the method

TABLE 9–1   Format of a Psychological Assessment Report

Name of Examinee: _____ Sex: _____

Birth Date: _____ Age: _____ Education: _____

Referred by: _____

Place of Examination: _____ Date of Exam: _____

Examined by: _____ Date of Report: _____

Tests Administered: _____

_____

Reason for Referral. State briefly why the examinee was referred for psychological testing. What was the purpose of the referral, and what person or facility made it?

Observations and Interview Findings. Briefly describe the appearance and behavior of the examinee during the examination. Give the examinee's own story, as well as that of other observers if available. Describe the examinee's physical and psychological history and characteristics, educational and employment situation. In the case of children in particular, information on the home and family (social status, characteristics of parents, siblings, etc.) is important. Serious sensory or psychomotor handicaps, as well as the presence of emotional disorder should also be noted.

Results and Interpretaions. Give a detailed description of the results of the tests or other instruments administered and how they should be interpreted. If the examiner is interpreting the results according to a particular theory of personality, make certain that the reader understands the language and assumptions of the theory. Be as specific and individualized as possible in interpreting the results. Describe the examinee's characteristics, his or her approach to the tasks, level of motivation and emotionality, and any other factors that might have affected the results.

Conclusions and Recommendations. Briefly describe the conclusions (descriptive, dynamic, diagnostic) stemming from the observational, interview, and standardized or unstandardized test data. What recommendations are warranted by the results? Include appropriate interpretive cautions, but don't "hedge" or deal in generalities. Additional psychological assessment (be specific), neurological or other medical examinations, counseling or psychotherapy, special class placement and training, vocational rehabilitation and institutionalization are among the recommendations that might be made. If a handicap or disability exists, is it remediable?

                                                                Name and Signature of Examiner

of observation, which is basic to all science, the observer simply takes note of events, such as human behavior, and perhaps makes a record of what is observed. The most common procedure is the *uncontrolled observation* of behavior "on the wing" with no attempt to restrict it to a particular situation or set of conditions. Observing the activities of children on a playground and the behavior of people in a waiting line are examples of such uncontrolled, or *naturalistic,* observation. An illustration of uncontrolled observation in the world of work is the *critical incidents technique* (Flanagan, 1954). Supervisors and others who are familiar with a particular job are asked to identify specific behaviors that are critical to job performance or that distinguish between good and poor workers. These behaviors, or *incidents,* are critical because they have either highly positive or highly negative consequences. Examples are "secures machinery and tidies up place of work when finished" and "follows up customers' requests promptly." Identification of a large number of such incidents supplies valuable information on the nature of the job and the requirements for effective performance.

Observation as a Research Method

Observations may be uncontrolled and yet systematic and objective. For example, teachers can be trained to make objective observations of the behavior of schoolchildren and accurate records (*anecdotal records*) of whatever behavior seems significant. A well-trained teacher–observer indicates in the anecdotal record precisely what was observed and distinguishes the observation from the interpretation placed on it. The observer realizes that when Johnny pinches Mary it is not invariably an act of aggression.

Improving the Accuracy of Observations   Training observers to be as objective as possible, by not letting their own personal biases and needs affect what they observe and separating observation from interpretation, is one of several recommended guidelines for improving the validity of observational data. Another recommendation is to observe a limited number of specific behaviors, which are defined beforehand. Employing several observers and collecting a large, representative sample of observations can also improve the accuracy of the observational method. Obtaining a representative sample of behavior is, however, time consuming and expensive. To reduce the volume of data collected in continuous observation, the *incident sampling technique* of noting and recording only specific incidents, say of aggressive behavior, is appropriate. Further improvements in the efficiency of observation may be obtained by *time sampling*—making a series of observations lasting only a few minutes each over a period of a day or so (Wright, 1960).

Participant Observation   Also relatively uncontrolled is *participant observation,* in which the observer is a part of the observational situation. Participant observation has been used extensively by cultural anthropologists, so much so that at one time it was quipped that a typical aborigine family consisted of a mother, a father, two children, and a cultural anthropologist! Realizing that they must take into account the likelihood that the observer's own behavior will affect the reactions of other people in the situation, proponents of this research method argue that active involvement in a situation can provide insights unobtainable by other means.

Controlled Observations and Situational Testing

In addition to relatively uncontrolled observations, prearranged, contrived, or controlled observations are made with the purpose of determining how people (and animals) behave in various situations. For example, a developmental psychologist may set up an observational situation beforehand to determine if a child will cheat or behave honestly under a prearranged set of circumstances.

A classic research study that used a controlled observational procedure known as *situational testing* was the Character Education Inquiry of Hartshorne and May (1928). In this series of investigations, children were surreptitiously provided with an opportunity to demonstrate their honesty, altruism, and other character traits. For example, to test a child's honesty, the investigators placed the child in a situation where some coins could be stolen and in another situation where test answers could be copied, presumably without being detected. Among the findings of the study were that older children, less intelligent children, children of lower socioeconomic status, and more emotionally unstable children tended to be less honest in all the situations. Perhaps the most important outcome of the investigations was that honesty and other character traits varied as much with the situation as with the individual. In other words, a child's honesty, altruism, and other character traits were typically highly dependent on the situation in which the child was observed.

Situational testing for use in the military was introduced by the Germans and subsequently adapted by the British and U.S. armed services during World War II. A series of simulated situational tests administered by the U.S. Office of Strategic Services (OSS) was designed to select espionage agents, and, as in the Hartshorne and May (1928) studies, deception of the candidates was involved. For example, in the "wall problem," a group of men was given the task of crossing a canyon. Unknown to the candidate, the men assigned to assist him were "plants," rather than other candidates. One of these plants acted as an obstructor by making unrealistic suggestions and insulting or worrisome remarks; another plant pretended not to understand the task and passively resisted directions from the candidate. The real candidate, not realizing that the others were in league with the examiners, was observed during his efforts to complete the task in the face of these frustrating circumstances. It was difficult to determine the effectiveness of these procedures as selection devices, however, and they were never adequately validated.

Situational testing has been used in other assessment programs, for example, in the selection of clinical psychologists (Kelly & Fiske, 1951). One interesting variation is the Leaderless Group Discussion (LGD) test in which a group of examinees discusses an assigned topic for 30 to 50 minutes while the performances of individual members of the group are being rated by observers. The ratings of these observers, as well as ratings made by the other examinees, may be in terms of the ascendance, task facilitation, and socialiability shown by the examinee. In spite of the real-life quality of situational testing, it is never possible to duplicate the real situations in detail. Even in the OSS assessment program, examinees realized that the tests were rigged. For these and other reasons, the reliabilities and predictive validities of situational tests are frequently too low to justify the cost.

Unobtrusive Observation   In situational testing, the behavior of the examinee may be observed through a one-way mirror. By remaining unseen, the observer does not intrude on or affect the behavior of the individuals who are being observed. Whenever people realize they are being observed, they may behave unnaturally or act as if they are on stage (role play). For this reason, observations for the purposes of personality assessment are usually made as unobtrusively as possible. In *unobtrusive observation,* the performer is unaware of the observer's presence, and therefore the performer's behavior is not influenced by the knowledge that he or she is being watched. Either controlled or uncontrolled observation may be unobtrusive and, under certain circumstances even participant observation can be relatively unobtrusive.

Clinical Observations

A clinical or school psychologist who is examining a child interacts with the latter as a special kind of participant observer. Consequently, the examiner must be careful not to let his or her own presence and actions provoke atypical responses in the child. As implied in the report form in Table 9–1, the examiner's observations, which must be as unobtrusive as possible, are an important part of the psychological report. The following observational description is typical in a brief psychological assessment report:

Michael is an attractive child with long, straight brown hair and freckles. He seemed a bit anxious during the examination, squirming around in his chair, but not excessively. He tended to give up easily on more difficult tasks, and revealed other signs of low frustration tolerance (sighing deeply, reluctance to try). However, he was fairly cooperative during the test and mildly interested in the tasks; he showed signs of fatigue toward the end of the examination. In general, he was attentive and energetic, responding when told to in a brief, occasionally uncertain manner. He did not smile during the entire time.

Much of what is known about personality dynamics and mental disorders has been obtained from observations of people in clinical settings. Clinical observations are obviously not completely objective: both parties, the therapist and the patient, in a clinical situation affect each other's behavior. Consequently, the accuracy of clinical observations and the interpretations given to them should be verified by other people and procedures.

An alert clinical observer notes a variety of details: what the examinee is wearing and whether he or she is well groomed; if and how the examinee shakes hands and looks at the examiner; how the examinee sits, stands, and walks; what facial expressions, body movements, and voice tones are characteristic. These are nonverbal behaviors and, when interpreted properly, can provide better insight into personality than a record limited to what the individual actually says.

Nonverbal Behavior

Most people realize that interpersonal communication is not entirely verbal, but they are usually unaware of the extent to which movements of their hands, eyes, and mouth, as well as body postures and voice tones, are interpreted as messages. As indicated in the following quotation, Freud was very cognizant of these nonverbal cues: "He that has eyes to see and ears to hear may convince himself that no mortal can keep a secret. If his lips are silent, he chatters with his fingertips; betrayal oozes out of him at every pore" (Freud, 1905, page 94).

A great deal of research has been conducted on nonverbal behavior, including *kinesics* (movements of body parts), *proxemics* (distance between communicants), and *paralinguistics* (tone of voice, rate of speaking, and other nonverbal aspects of speech). According to the findings of one investigation (Mehrabian & Weiner, 1967), 65 to 90 percent of the meaning in interpersonal communications comes from nonverbal cues. It has been found that certain types of nonverbal cues are more important than others in message transmission. Kinesics are particularly important, followed by proxemics, paralinguistics, and even culturics (style of dress, culturally based habits or customs, and the like). Most people are probably right more often than wrong in interpreting nonverbal messages, although mistakes do occur. The poker-faced gambler and the glad-handed salesman or politician are renowned for their ability to deceive others with nonverbal behavior. Nonverbal behaviors and characteristics (*nonverbals*) are interpreted more accurately when the observer has some knowledge of the specific situation or context in which the behavior occurs. In addition, some people are better than others at interpreting nonverbals, an ability that appears to be related to personality, but not to intelligence.

The PONS   To assess individual differences in the ability to interpret nonverbal communications, Rosenthal et al. (1979) devised a test, the Profile of Nonverbal Sensitivity (PONS). The PONS consists of a 45-minute film in which viewers are presented with a series of scenes such as facial expressions or spoken phrases heard as tones or sounds, but not as words. After each scene is presented, the viewer selects an appropriate descriptive label out of two. The authors of the PONS report that men and women who score high on the test tend to have fewer friends, but warmer, more honest, and more satisfying sexual relationships than those who score low.

Reasoning that sensitivity to nonverbal messages is an important ability for diplomats to possess, David McClelland used the PONS in an applicant screening program for the U.S. Information Agency. Short taped segments from the test were played to USIA job applicants, who were then asked to indicate what emotion was being expressed. It was discovered that applicants who scored high on the PONS were considered significantly more competent by their colleagues than those who scored low (Rosenthal et al., 1979, pages 304–306).

Unmasking the Face   Another contribution to the assessment of nonverbal behavior is the Facial Action Coding System (FACS) (Consulting Psychologists Press). Designed by Paul Ekman and Wallace Friesen, the FACS material consists of 135 photographs of various facial expressions for training observers in scoring dozens of facial Action Units. Also useful in training observers to judge emotion from facial expressions are Friesen and Ekman's Pictures of Facial Affect (Consulting Psychologists Press). These are 110 black-and-white pictures expressing fear, anger, happiness, sadness, surprise, or disgust (plus a neutral expression).

Self-observation and Content Analysis

Observing oneself, which most people typically spend some time doing, is an appealing data-collection method in both research and clinical contexts. The appeal of the method lies in both its economy and the fact that it is one of only a few ways to get at private thoughts and feelings.[1] A problem with self-observations is that they are likely to be even more biased than observations made by others; people are seldom entirely objective in describing their own thoughts and behavior (Wolff & Merrens, 1974). However, as with observations made by others, people can be trained to make more objective, systematic observations of themselves (Thoreson & Mahoney, 1974). Thus, they can learn to distinguish what they are actually feeling, thinking, or doing from what they should or would like to feel, think, or do.

By keeping a continuous written record of one's thoughts, feelings, and actions, a

---

[1]Some others are hypnosis, narcoanalysis, and free association.

wealth of self-observational data can be accumulated. Unfortunately, it is not always clear what to do with such an abundance of data, that is, how to analyze or interpret it. As seen in the *content analysis* of diaries, autobiographies, letters, drawings, and other personal documents, important insights into personality and behavior can be gained from interpreting self-observational data (Allport, 1965). But the complexity and laboriousness of content analysis have kept this interpretative approach from being applied routinely in clinical or other applied contexts.

Biographical Data and Employment Situations

The information provided by completed application blanks and other self-report forms is useful in clinical and educational contexts; however, the most systematic research application of biographical data has occurred in employment situations. Much of this information is highly factual and objective (applicant's name, birthdate, marital status, and so on), but a substantial amount is obtained from self-observations and the respondent's impressions of the personal and social environment.

Applications and Recommendations   One of the first things that a job applicant is required to do is write a letter of application and/or fill out an application blank. A completed application blank is both a formal request for employment and a brief description of the applicant's fitness for the job. Following a series of identifying questions (name, address, employment desired, and so forth), detailed background information (education, physical handicaps, military record, previous employment and experience) is requested. In most cases, a section of the blank is also provided for references.

Information from an applicant's listed references, whether obtained by letters, telephone calls, interviews, or questionnaires, can be useful despite some obvious limitations. Letters of recommendation have perhaps the greatest limitation in that they often provide an incorrect picture of the applicant. Because former employers or other reference sources are often reluctant to make negative statements about a person in writing, one telephone call is sometimes worth a dozen letters of recommendation. In fact, laudatory letters of recommendation are so much the rule that personnel administrators and other selection officials often become oversensitized to anything less than very positive written statements concerning an applicant. There is also a tendency to interpret short letters as indicative of disapproval of the applicant and longer letters as more complimentary.

Biographical Inventories   A completed applicant blank provides a human resources (personnel) department with an efficient, inexpensive way of determining whether an applicant meets the minimum requirements for a job. If it is not filed away and forgotten, it can also serve as an information guide for any subsequent interviews of the applicant. Furthermore, the background, experience, and other information provided by a completed application form can be numerically weighted and used in a statistical way to predict quality of work, absenteeism, turnover, and other criteria of job performance. More formal *biographical inventories,* or biodata forms, which are comprised of a variety of items pertaining to the life history of the applicant (such as family relationships, friendships, extracurricular activities, and interests), have been designed and used by Exxon, the U.S.

Office of Personnel Management, and other production and service organizations. A great deal of research on these longer forms of weighted application blanks has been conducted during the past 25 years (see Owens, 1976). Catalogs of life history items, from which personnel administrators or recruiters may construct their own biographical inventories, have even been prepared (Glennon, Albright, & Owens, 1966).

Not only do biographical inventories have substantial content validity; they are also effective predictors of performance in a variety of job contexts ranging from unskilled work to high-level executive responsibilities. However, legal problems are associated with requests for certain kinds of information (age, sex, ethnicity, religion, marital status, number of children) on application forms and biographical inventories or in interviews. This is unfortunate because many of these items are the most predictive of on-the-job performance. Although information provided from application forms and biographical inventories has fairly high validity, applicants may object to certain items as being too personal or otherwise offensive (Rosenbaum, 1973). Consequently, we would expect answers to these kinds of items (about personal finances, family background, and other intimate details) to be less accurate than less sensitive information.

INTERVIEWS

Interviewing is one of the oldest and most widely used methods of personality assessment. Not only does it yield much of the same kind of data as observations, but information on what a person says as well as what he or she does is obtained. The interviewee's nonverbal behavior, including body postures and poise, gestures, eye movements, and the quality and pattern of speech, is important and should be noted. The major emphasis in interviewing, however, is on the content of the verbal statements made by the interviewee. For this reason, an interview may be defined as a "face-to-face verbal interchange in which one person, the interviewer, attempts to elicit information or expressions of opinion or belief from another person or persons" (Maccoby & Maccoby, 1954, page 449). The information obtained in an interview consists of details of the interviewee's background or life history, in addition to data concerning feelings, attitudes, perceptions, and expectations.

Interviews are used in various contexts and for a wide range of purposes. In research contexts, they are used for polling, surveys, and to obtain in-depth information on personality and behavior to test some hypothesis or theoretical proposition. In employment situations, interviews are used for selection and screening, evaluation or appraisal, troubleshooting, and termination. In clinical contexts, intake interviews of patients and their relatives are essential in collecting case history information for making medical and/or psychological diagnoses (diagnostic interviews). In addition, therapeutic interviews are a part of the psychological treatment process, and exit interviews are designed to determine whether a institutionalized individual is ready to be released.

Whatever the context and purposes of interviewing may be, it requires skill and sensitivity and may be quite time consuming and laborious. Interviewing is as much an art as a science, and some individuals are more effective than others in establishing rapport and getting interviewees to open up. The interviewer's approach varies with the purpose and context of the interview, but, as in any interpersonal situation, the outcomes depend on the personality and actions of both participants. Thus, an interview is not a one-way, question-and-answer situation in which the interviewer remains unaffected; in almost every case it is a dynamic, two-way interchange in which the participants mutually influence one another.

Interviewing can be an end in itself, but it may also function as a "get acquainted" or warming-up process designed as a lead-in to other assessment procedures. Most clinical and counseling psychologists like the face-to-face closeness of the interview because it enables them to get a "feel" for the patient or client and his or her problems and characteristics. Clinical psychologists, personnel psychologists, employment counselors, and other human service professionals usually justify the time and expense of an interview with the belief that private information obtained in this way is not available by any other means. Applicants, counselees, and patients usually express feelings of being more involved when interviewed than when they are merely asked to fill out paper-and-pencil questionnaires or application blanks and are not given an opportunity to communicate their problems, needs, opinions, and circumstances in a face-to-face situation.

Interviewing Techniques and Structure

A personal interview can take place anywhere, but it is usually better to conduct it in a quiet room free from distractions. Both the interviewer and interviewee should be comfortably seated and facing each other. Because interviewing is a complex interpersonal skill and to some extent a function of the interviewer's interpersonal style, effective interviewing is not easily taught. Attention to the following recommendations, however, can improve one's interviewing skills.

Professional interviewers are usually friendly but neutral, interested but not prying in reacting to the interviewee. They are warm and open, nonjudgmentally accepting the interviewee for what he or she is without showing approval or disapproval. They do not begin with leading questions of the "How often do you beat your wife?" type, or ask questions that imply a certain answer (for example, "You still do that, don't you?"). By properly timing the questions and varying the nature of the questions according to the situation, good interviewers are able to develop a conversation that flows from topic to topic. Pauses or silences cause them no discomfort: they allow the interviewee sufficient time to answer a question completely, and they listen to the answer without interrupting. In addition, they pay attention not only to what the interviewee says, but also to the manner in which it is said. Realizing that the interviewer's behavior (activity level, amount and speed of talking, and the like) tends to be imitated by the interviewee, interviewers are patient and comfortable and do not hurry the interviewee. Skilled interviewers also check their understandings, impressions, and perceptions of the interviewee's statements by asking for clarification or repetition. They may rephrase the interviewee's answers to clarify them and make certain that they do not misunderstand, or they may ask direct questions to fill in the gaps. Effective interviewers are, however, not voyeurs who unrelentingly probe or relish the discussion of certain topics and consciously or unconsciously reinforce the interviewee's statements pertaining to those matters.

Although the characteristics of good interviewers described above are generally applicable, specific techniques vary with the theoretical orientation (behavioral, client centered, psychoanalytic, and so on) of the interviewer, as well as the goals and stage of the interview. Most interviewers outside of clinical contexts, as well as many clinicians, are fairly eclectic in their orientation, following no particular theory of personality but applying relevant concepts from a variety of theories.

Structured versus Unstructured Interviews   The degree to which an interview is *structured* should depend primarily on the goals of the interview, but it is also important to consider the interviewee and interviewer. Some interviewees respond more readily to a relatively unstructured, open-ended approach; other offer more relevant information when the interview follows an *interviewing guide* and is very structured in the questions asked. In addition, certain interviewers feel more comfortable and accomplish more using the highly structured procedure of asking a series of questions similar to those found on an application blank or personal history form. Less experienced interviewers typically find it easier to handle a structured interview, the results of which can be more easily quantified for purposes of analysis. On the other hand, many experienced interviewers prefer greater flexibility in the content and timing of interview questions, in other words, less structure.

It requires more skill and time to conduct an interview in an unstructured or open-ended manner, but the interviewer can follow up interesting leads or concentrate on details of greater significance. To accomplish this, the interviewer encourages the interviewee to feel free to discuss his or her problems, interests, behaviors, or whatever else is relevant to the goals of the interview. Those goals also affect the amount of structure used in an interview. When answers to a large number of specific questions are needed, as in employ- ment selection situations, then a fairly structured interview is appropriate. When the goal is to obtain an in-depth picture of the individual's personality or to define the nature of certain problems and their causes, a more unstructured interview is called for. Whether highly structured or relatively open ended, the sequence of questions in an interview should usually proceed from general to specific and from less personal to more personal topics. Most professional interviewers are able to vary their approach with the personality of the interviewee and the objectives of the interview. They begin by asking a series of nonthreatening, open-ended questions to establish rapport and get the conversation going, and then become more specific in their questioning as the interview progresses.

Interview Topics and Questions   The specific questions asked depend on the pur- poses of the interview, but it is helpful to plan for an interview by outlining the topics to be covered, if not the specific questions to be asked. A topical outline for a life history interview is given in Table 9–2. A complete life history interview, whether conducted in a clinical, social service, employment, or research situation, requires obtaining the kinds of information listed in this table. Not all these topics need be covered in a specific situation; the interviewer can concentrate on those areas that are considered most important. In any event, the specific interview questions, framed in language with which the inter- viewee is familiar and comfortable, can be developed from the outline in Table 9–2.

Clinical Interviews

In clinical interviews conducted for intake purposes at a social agency or mental hospital, diagnostic interviews to determine the causes and correlates of an individual's problems

TABLE 9–2   Information to Obtain in a Life History Interview

What are the interviewee's name, address, and date and place of birth?

What is the purpose(s) of the interview (employment, personal counseling, and the like)?

How can the interviewee's family (parents, siblings, other family members) and socio-cultural group be described?

What is the interviewee's medical history (present health, health history, major health problems)?

What is the interviewee's developmental history (physical, intellectual, speech, emotional, and social development; irregularities or problems in development)?

What education and training has the interviewee had (schools attended, performance level, adjustment to school), and what are his or her plans for further education and training?

What jobs or positions has the interviewee held, and how well did he or she perform? Any particular job problems?

What are the interviewee's primary interests, hobbies, and recreations?

Has the interviewee ever been in trouble with the law (what, when, where, why)?

What is the interviewee's marital history (marriages, marital problems and divorce(s), children)?

What are the interviewee's self-perceptions? Is he or she self-accepting or dissatisfied with self? Why?

What are the interviewee's attitudes toward his or her past, present, and future life?

and therapeutic interviews (counseling, psychotherapy), it is recommended that, among other things, the interviewer:

Assure the interviewee of confidentiality of the interview.

Convey a feeling of interest and warmth (rapport).

Try to put the interviewee at ease.

Try to get in touch with how the interviewee feels (empathy).

Be courteous, patient, and accepting.

Encourage the interviewee to express his or her thoughts and feelings freely.

Adjust the questions to the cultural and educational background of the interviewee.

Avoid psychological or psychiatric jargon.

Avoid leading questions.

Share personal information and experiences with the interviewee (self-disclosure) if appropriate and timed accurately.

Use humor sparingly, and only if appropriate and not insulting.

Listen without overreacting emotionally.

Attend not only to what is said, but also to how it is said.

Take notes or make a recording as inconspicuously as possible.

Of course, many of these recommendations are not restricted to clinical interviews but apply to many other types of verbal interchanges as well.

When conducted properly, a diagnostic or therapeutic interview can provide a great deal of information about the interviewee: the nature, duration, and severity of his or her problems; how the problems are manifested (inwardly or outwardly); what past influences are related to present difficulties; the interviewee's resources and limitations for coping with the problems; the kinds of psychological assistance the interviewee has had in the past; and the kinds of assistance that are expected and might be of help now.

Behavioral Interviewing   Behavioral interviewing is a type of clinical interviewing in which the focus is on obtaining information to plan a program of behavior modification. As discussed later in the chapter, this entails describing, in objective behavioral terms, the problem behaviors of the interviewee, as well as their antecedent conditions and reinforcing consequences. To conduct such an interview successfully, the interviewee must be encouraged (and taught if necessary) to respond in specific behavioral terms, rather than in the more customary language of motives or traits. After obtaining the necessary information to develop a behavior modification program, the program must then be explained to the client, and he or she must be motivated to follow it.

Stress Interviewing   The usual role of cordiality toward the interviewee is suspended in a *stress interview*. The goal of stress interviewing, which is used in clinical, selection, and interrogation contexts, may be to determine the interviewee's ability to cope or solve a specific problem under emotionally stressful conditions. Stress interviewing may also be appropriate when time is short or when the interviewee is very repetitious, emotionally unresponsive, or very defensive. An attempt is made to produce a valid emotional response—to get beneath the superficial social mask (*persona*) of the interviewee—by asking probing, challenging questions in a kind of police interrogation atmosphere. A great deal of professional expertise is obviously required to make a stress interview appear realistic and not get out of control.

Methode Clinique and Morality Research   The clinical method of interviewing, in which the interviewer asks probing questions to test the limits or obtain in-depth information about a person, was employed extensively by Sigmund Freud, Jean Piaget, and many other famous psychologists. The use of clinical interviewing in research, referred to as the *methode clinique*, requires considerable skill.

An example of a research instrument involving the use of the *methode clinique* is Lawrence Kohlberg's Moral Judgment Scale. Kohlberg (1969, 1974) maintained that the development of personal morality progresses through three ascending levels, consisting of two stages each. At the lowest level (*premoral level*), moral judgments are guided either by punishment and obedience or by a kind of naive pleasure–pain philosophy. At an intermediate level (*morality of conventional rule conformity*), morality depends either on the approval of other people ("good boy–good girl" morality) or on adherence to the precepts of authority. In the first stage of the last level (*morality of self-accepted moral principles*), morality is viewed in terms of acceptance of a contract or democratically determined agreement. In the second stage of the last level, the individual has developed an internal set of principles and a conscience that directs his or her judgment and behavior.

The Moral Judgment Scale is administered by presenting to the examinee nine hypothetical moral dilemmas and obtaining judgments and reasons for the judgment pertaining to each dilemma. One such dilemma, that of Heinz and the druggist, is as follows:

In Europe, a woman was near death from a special kind of cancer. There was one drug that the doctors thought might save her. It was a form of radium that a druggist in the same town had recently discovered. The drug was expensive to make, but the druggist was charging ten times what the drug cost him to make. He paid $200 for the radium and charged $2000 for a small dose of the drug. The sick woman's husband, Heinz, went to everyone he knew to borrow the money, but he could only get together about $1000 which is half of what it cost. He told the druggist that his wife was dying, and asked him to sell it cheaper or let him pay later. But the druggist said, "No, I discovered the drug and I'm going to make money from it." So Heinz got desperate and broke into the man's store to steal the drug for his wife. (Kohlberg & Elfenbein, 1975)

Scoring in terms of the levels or stages consists of making rather subjective evaluations of the examinee's responses in terms of the levels or stages.

Personnel Interviews

Almost all production and service organizations use interviews, not only for employee selection, classification, and placement purposes, but also for counseling, troubleshooting, termination (exit interview), and research. Because the interviewing process is expensive and time consuming, it is reasonable to wonder if it is the most efficient procedure for obtaining data on job applicants. Much of the information from a structured interview, which is the preferred approach in most employment settings, can be obtained from an application blank or questionnaire. But job applicants are often more willing to reveal matters of significance in the personal atmosphere of an interview than in writing. In any event, a personnel interview is the final step in the employee selection process for all but the lowest-level jobs in the great majority of organizational settings.

Employment interviewers usually have available a variety of other information about an applicant, including that supplied by the completed application form, letters of recommendation, test scores, and the like. The interviewer's task is to integrate the information obtained from all these sources and the personal interview to make a recommendation or job decision concerning the applicant.

An employment interviewer must be cautious in asking questions concerning private matters, not only because they may place the interviewee under an emotional strain, but also because it may be illegal to ask them. Interpretive guidelines issued by the Equal Employment Opportunity Commission indicate that it is permissible to ask the following questions in the employment interview:

How many years experience do you have?
(To a housewife) Why do you want to return to work?
What are your career goals?
Who have been your prior employers?
Why did you leave your last job?

Are you a veteran? Did the military provide you with job related experience?

If you have no phone, where can we reach you?

What languages do you speak fluently?

Can you do extensive traveling?

Who recommended you to us?

What did you like or dislike about your previous jobs?

What is your educational background? What schools did you attend?

What are your strong points? Weaknesses?

Do you have any objection if we check with your former employer for references?

On the other hand, is considered legally unacceptable to ask the following questions:

What is your age?

What is your date of birth?

Do you have children? If so, how old are they?

What is your race?

What church do you attend?

Are you married, divorced, separated, widowed, or single?

Have you ever been arrested?

What kind of military discharge do you have?

What clubs or organizations do you belong to?

Do you rent or own your own home?

What does your wife (husband) do?

Who lives in your household?

Have your wages even been attached or garnished?

What was your maiden name (female applicants)?

Reliability and Validity of Interviews

The interview is an important psychological tool, but it shares with observational methods the problems of reliability and validity. Reliability demands consistency, but interviewers vary in their appearance, approach, and style, and, consequently, the impressions they make on interviewees. These differing impressions result in differences in behavior: with one interviewer a person may be friendly and outgoing, whereas with another he or she becomes hostile and remote. In addition, the interviewer's perceptions of the interviewee can be distorted by his or her own experiences and personality (Raines & Rohrer, 1960).

The reliability of an interview is usually determined by comparing the ratings given to the interviewee's responses by two or more interviewers. The resulting interrater reliability coefficient varies with the specificity of the questions asked and the behaviors rated and is higher for structured and semistructured than for unstructured interviews (Schwab & Heneman, 1969; Bradley & Caldwell, 1977; Disbrow, Doerr, & Caulfield, 1977). But even in the case of fairly specific, objective questions asked in a structured format, the reliability coefficients are moderate, usually no higher than .80.

Because the interviewer is the assessment instrument in an interview, many of the reliability problems of interviews are associated with the characteristics and behavior of the interviewer. The interviewer is almost always in charge in an interviewing situation. The personality and biases of the interviewer are usually more important than those of the interviewee in determining what kinds of information are obtained. The socioemotional tone of the interview is determined more by the interviewer's actions than by those of the interviewee: the interviewer usually talks more, and the length of the interviewee's answers is directly related to the length of the interviewer's questions. In addition to being overly dominant, the interviewer may fail to obtain complete, accurate information by asking the wrong questions, by not encouraging or not allowing enough time for complete answers, and by incorrectly recording the responses.

Other shortcomings of interviewers are the tendency to give more weight to first impressions and to be affected more by unfavorable than by favorable information about an interviewee. Errors that affect ratings also occur in interviewers' judgments. An example is the *halo effect* of making judgments, both favorable and unfavorable, on the basis of a "general impression" or a single prominent characteristic of the interviewee. This effect occurs when a person who is actually superior (or inferior) on only one or two characteristics is given an overall superior (or inferior) evaluation. In addition, the *contrast error* of judging an average interviewee as inferior if the preceding interviewee was superior or as superior if the preceding interviewee was inferior can occur.

Because an interviewer's impressions are influenced by the neatness, posture, and other nonverbal behaviors of the interviewee, as well as the latter's verbal responses, prospective interviewees would do well to prepare themselves, both mentally and physically for interviews. In the case of employment interviews, interviewees should have some knowledge of the organization and its philosophy. They should be prepared to give a synopsis of their background and aspirations, but refrain from controversial comments and engaging in bad habits such as smoking or nailbiting during the interview.

A consistent finding of research pertaining to the validity of the interview as an employment selection or clinical diagnostic technique is that it is overrated (Arvey, 1979; Reilly & Chao, 1982). Interviews can be made more valid, but they must be carefully planned or structured, and the interviewers need to be extensively trained. Interview findings are also more valid when the interviewer focuses on specific (job or clinical) information and when answers are evaluated question by question, preferably by at least two evaluators, rather than as a whole. To facilitate this process, the entire interview should be recorded on audiotape or videotape for later playback and evaluation. In this way, the task of interpreting an interviewee's responses can be separated more effectively from the actual interviewing process.[2]

RATING SCALES

Information obtained from observations and interviews, whether formal or informal, can be recorded in a variety of ways. Because of the large mass of data produced in lengthy

---

[2]It can be argued that even a videotape recording and especially an audiotape recording of the interview is insufficient in that the pictures and words are not always clear and the emotional tone and contextual variables are frequently missed in an electronic recording. The point is well taken. A keen human observer who takes good notes is usually needed to supplement an electronic recording of an interview.

observational and interviewing sessions, the findings are almost always summarized in some form. Together with a condensed written description, a rating scale or checklist serves as a useful device for summarizing observational and interview findings. Unlike the items on a checklist, which require only a yes–no decision, rating scale items require the respondent to make an evaluative judgment on an ordered series of categories.

Rating Scales

The rating scale, which was introduced by Francis Galton during the latter part of the nineteenth century, is a popular assessment device in schools, employment settings, and many other situations. Ratings may be made either by the ratee (the person being rated) or another rater and are generally considered to be less precise than personality inventories and more superficial than projective techniques. Nevertheless, various types of rating scales are used extensively in assessing a wide range of behavioral and personality characteristics.

Numerical Rating Scale   On this types of rating scale, the person (or the object or event) is assigned one of several numbers corresponding to particular descriptions of the characteristics being rated, such as "supervisory ability" or "interpersonal effectiveness." All that is required is for the ratings to be made on an ordered scale on which different numerical values are assigned to different locations. An example of an instrument containing ten rating scales, four of which are concerned with rating instructors, is the College Course and Instructor Evaluation Questionnaire in Table 9–3.

Semantic Differential   Another kind of numerical rating scale is the *semantic differential,* a technique employed frequently in research in personality and social psychology. Osgood, Suci, and Tannenbaum (1957) introduced this technique in their studies of the cannotative (personal) meanings that concepts such as "father," "mother," "sickness," "sin," "hated," and "love" have for different people. The procedure begins by asking a person to rate a series of concepts on several seven-point, bipolar adjectival scales. For example, the concept of "MOTHER" might be rated by making a checkmark on the appropriate line segment on each of the following three scales:

BAD   _____ : _____ : _____ : _____ : _____ : _____ : _____   GOOD

WEAK   _____ : _____ : _____ : _____ : _____ : _____ : _____   STRONG

SLOW   _____ : _____ : _____ : _____ : _____ : _____ : _____   FAST

After all concepts of interest have been rated on the various scales, the responses to each concept are scored on several "semantic dimensions" and compared with the rater's

TABLE 9–3 College Course and Instructor Evaluation Form

Course: _____ Instructor: _____

Part I. Circle or check the appropriate number to the right of each statement to indicate how descriptive that statement is of this course or instructor. Circle any number from 1 (Not at All Descriptive) to 5 (Very Descriptive). Circle NA if the statement is not applicable to this course.

	Not at All Descriptive			Very Descriptive	Not Applicable
1. The course is well organized.	1	2	3	4	5	NA
2. The course objectives have been defined and met.	1	2	3	4	5	NA
3. The textbook and other reading assignments are appropriate in content.	1	2	3	4	5	NA
4. The papers, reports, and/or other written or oral assignments are reasonable and fair.	1	2	3	4	5	NA
5. The tests and other evaluations are appropriate and fair.	1	2	3	4	5	NA
6. The instructor has a thorough knowledge of the subject matter.	1	2	3	4	5	NA
7. The instructor shows interest in and enthusiasm for the course	1	2	3	4	5	NA
8. The instructor has been available when needed outside of class.	1	2	3	4	5	NA
9. Overall, the instructor is an excellent teacher.	1	2	3	4	5	NA
10. Overall, this is an excellent course.	1	2	3	4	5	NA

273

responses to the remaining concepts. The main connotative meaning (semantic) dimensions that have been determined by factor analyses of ratings of a series of concepts on a large number of these adjectival scales are "evaluation," "potency," and "activity." A *semantic space* may then be constructed by plotting a person's scores on the rated concepts on each of these three dimensions. Concepts falling close to each other in the semantic space presumably have similar connotative meanings for the rater.

Graphic Rating Scale   Another popular type of scale is a *graphic rating scale*, an example of which is:

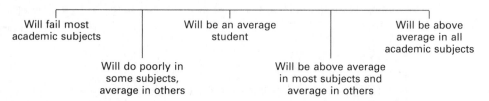

The rater makes an × or check mark on each of a series of lines such as this containing descriptive terms or phrases pertaining to a certain characteristic or trait. Typically, a verbal description of the lowest degree of the characteristic is given at the extreme left of the line. A description pertaining to the highest degree of the characteristic is given at the extreme right, and intermediate points on the line contain descriptions referring to intermediate degrees of the characteristic.

Standard Rating Scale   On a *standard rating scale,* the rater supplies or is supplied with a set of standards against which the persons being rated (the *ratees*) are to be compared. An example of a standard rating scale is the *man-to-man* (or *person-to-person*) *scale,* which is constructed for rating individuals on a specified trait such as "leadership ability." The rater is asked to think of five people falling at different points along a hypothetical continuum of leadership ability. Then the rater compares each ratee with these five individuals and indicates which of them is most like the ratee in leadership ability.

Behaviorally Anchored Scales   Developed by Smith and Kendall (1963) and based on Flanagan's (1954) critical incidents technique, behaviorally anchored scales represent attempts to make the terminology of rating scales more descriptive of actual behavior and hence more objective. Understandably, terms such as *anxiety, self-confidence, aggressiveness,* and other nouns or adjectives used in traditional trait-oriented rating scales may be interpreted differently by different raters. This is particularly true when raters receive little or no training in how to interpret such terms. A tongue-in-cheek illustration of a behaviorally anchored scale for rating five employee performance factors is given in Table 9–4.

A behaviorally anchored rating scale is constructed by convening a group of individuals who possess expert knowledge of a particular job or other situation. Then, through discussion and painstaking deliberation, these individuals attempt to reach a consensus on a series of behaviorally descriptive critical incidents from which an objective, highly

TABLE 9–4 Tongue–in–Cheek Behaviorally Anchored Rating Scale for Employee Appraisal

Performance factors	Far exceeds job requirements	Exceeds job requirements	Meets job requirements	Needs some improvement	Does not meet minimum requirements
Quality	Leaps tall buildings with a single bound	Must take running start to leap over tall buildings	Can leap over only a short building or medium with no spires	Crashes into buildings when attempting to jump over them	Cannot recognize buildings at all, much less jump
Timeliness	Is faster than a speeding bullet	Is as fast as a speeding bullet	Not quite as fast as a speeding bullet	Would you believe a slow bullet?	Wounds self with bullets when attempting to shoot gun
Initiative	Is stronger than a locomotive	Is stronger than a bull elephant	Is stronger than a bull	Shoots the bull	Smells like a bull
Adaptability	Walks on water consistently	Walks on water in emergencies	Washes with water	Drinks water	Passes water in emergencies
Communication	Talks with God	Talks with the angels	Talks to himself	Argues with himself	Loses those arguments

Adapted from *The Industrial–Organizational Psychologist, 17*(4), 1980, p. 22, and used with permission.

reliable rating scale can be constructed. Behavioral descriptions that survive repeated reevaluation by the group, or by other groups, may then be prepared as a series of items to be rated. We might expect that the emphasis on objectively observable behavior and the concentrated group effort, which are features of behaviorally anchored scales, would make these scales psychometrically superior to other rating scales. In addition, the fact that the technique requires group involvement and consensus in constructing the scale, and hence a greater likelihood of group acceptance, would seem to be an advantage. However, a review of relevant research literature concluded that behaviorally anchored scales are not necessarily an improvement over graphic rating scales (Schwab, Heneman, & De Cotiis, 1975).

Forced-choice Rating Scale   The person-to-person scale is reportedly preferred by U.S. Army raters to the more complex but less biased *forced-choice rating scale.* In the latter method, raters are presented with two or more descriptions and are told to indicate the one that best characterizes the person to be rated. If there are three or more descriptions, raters may also be asked to indicate which is least descriptive of the ratee. In the case of four descriptions, for example, an item consists of two equally desirable and two equally undesirable statements. The rater marks both the statement that is most descriptive and the one that is least descriptive of the ratee. Only one desirable statement and one undesirable statement discriminate between high and low ratees on the criterion, but the raters presumably do not know which of the four statements these are. A hypothetical example of a four-statement forced-choice item for rating "leadership" is:

       _____ Assumes responsibility easily.
       _____ Doesn't know how or when to delegate.
       _____ Has many constructive suggestions to offer.
       _____ Doesn't listen to others' suggestions.

Can you tell which statement is keyed as "desirable" and which one is keyed as "undesirable"?

Errors in Rating   Raters sometimes find the forced-choice format cumbersome, but it is considered to be fairer than the person-to-person rating technique. It has the advantage of controlling for certain errors in rating, such as constant errors, halo effect, contrast error, and proximity error. *Constant errors* occur when the assigned ratings are higher (*leniency* or *generosity error*), lower (*severity error*), or more often in the average category (*central tendency error*) than they should be. The *halo effect* refers to the tendency of raters to respond to the general impression made by the ratee or to overgeneralize by assigning favorable ratings on all traits merely because the ratee is outstanding on one or two traits. A halo effect may also be negative, in which case one bad characteristic spoils the ratings on all other characteristics. Related to the halo effect is the *logical error* of assigning a person similar ratings on characteristics that the rater believes to be logically associated.

The term *contrast error* has been used in at least two different senses. In one sense it refers to the tendency to assign a higher rating than justified if the immediately preceding ratee received a very low rating or to assign a lower rating than justified if the preceding ratee received a very high rating. In a second sense, *contrast error* refers to the tendency of a rater to compare or contrast the ratee with the rater in assigning ratings on certain behaviors or traits. Finally, when committing the *proximity error,* the rater tends to assign similar ratings to a person on items that are located close together on the printed page. Likewise, if a person is consistently rated high, low, or average on the majority of a set of items located close together on the printed page, the person may receive similar ratings on other items situated near these items.

Improving Ratings It is not easy to make reliable and valid judgments of people under any circumstances and particularly when the behaviors or characteristics are poorly defined or highly subjective. Not only are personal biases likely to affect ratings, but raters frequently are not sufficiently familiar with the ratee to make accurate judgments. Training in how to make ratings more objective—by being aware of the various kinds of errors that can occur in rating, becoming more familiar with the persons and traits being rated, and omitting items that the rater feels unqualified to judge—can improve the accuracy of ratings. Combining the responses of several raters is also a recommended way of balancing out the response biases of individual raters. Finally, careful attention to the design of rating scales—defining the points clearly with precise behavioral descriptions of the characteristics to be rated—can also improve the validity of ratings.

Standardized Rating Scales Although a large number of rating scales are home-grown devices designed to be used in specific applied or research settings, many standardized scales for assessing the behavior of children and adults are commercially available. Scales for rating the developmental progress of mentally retarded and other handicapped persons are especially popular. Representative of such instruments are the AAMD Adaptive Behavior Scales, which are available from several test distributors. Both the School Edition and the Residential and Community Edition of the AAMD scales are designed to assess the abilities of mentally retarded, emotionally disturbed, and developmentally disabled persons to cope with the natural and social demands of the environment. Helpful in assessing the vocational adjustment of mentally retarded individuals are the Vocational Adaptation Rating Scales (Western Psychological Services). Two other examples of standardized behavior rating scales for handicapped children are the Pupil Rating Scale Revised, used to screen for learning disabilities, and the Connors' Rating Scales, which identify hyperactive children. Both of these scales are distributed by The Psychological Corporation.

CHECKLISTS

A *checklist* is a relatively simple, highly cost effective, and fairly reliable method of describing or evaluating a person. More easily constructed than rating scales or personality inventories and sometimes just as valid, checklists can be administered as self-report or observer-report instruments. In completing a checklist, the respondent is instructed to mark the words or phrases in a list that apply to the individual being evaluated (oneself or another person). When a number of judges or checkers evaluate a person on the same items of a checklist, that person's score on each item can be set equal to the number of judges who checked it.

In certain employment situations, useful checklists for appraising job performance have been constructed from a set of critical incidents pertaining to job behavior. Checklists for special purposes or for use in specific contexts can also be prepared in clinical, research, and other situations. The problem with such home-grown instruments is that they are rarely adequately validated or standardized, reliability data are meager, and consequently it is uncertain whether the checklist is serving its intended purposes. For this reason, it is better to examine the many commercially available checklists before constructing one. Two of the most popular checklists are the Mooney Problem Check Lists and the Adjective Check List.

Mooney Problem Check Lists   Among the oldest of the published checklists are the Mooney Problem Check Lists (The Psychological Corporation). Each of the four forms of the Mooney, J (for junior high school pupils), H (for high school pupils), C (for college students), and A (for adults), consists of a list of 210 to 330 problems in areas such as health and physical development, home and family, boy and girl relations, morals and religion, courtship and marriage, economic security, school or occupation, and social and recreational. Examinees are asked to underline problems that are of some concern to them, circle the number of the problems of most concern, and then write a summary of their problems. The Mooney checklists can be scored for the number of problems in each area, but no national norms have been published. Responses are either interpreted impressionistically or compared with locally obtained norms. The Mooney manual reports test–retest reliability coefficients of .90 or better for ranks (order of importance) of the problem areas for each examinee. The case for the validity of the Mooney instruments, as with problem checklists in general, is usually made on the basis of content.

Adjective Check List   In contrast to the nonnormative approach of the Mooney Problem Check Lists, the Adjective Check List (Consulting Psychologists Press) consists of 300 adjectives arranged alphabetically from *absent-minded* to *zany*. Examinees take 15 to 20 minutes to mark those adjectives they consider to be self-descriptive. Responses may then be scored on the 37 scales described in the 1983 manual: 4 modus operandi scales, 15 need scales, 9 topical scales, 5 transactional analysis scales, and 4 origence–intellectence (creativity and intelligence) scales. Scores on the first four, or modus operandi, scales (total number of adjectives checked, number of favorable adjectives checked, number of unfavorable adjectives checked, communality) pertain to the manner in which the respondent has dealt with the checklist. The need scales (scales 5 to 19) are based on Edwards's (1954) descriptions of 15 needs in Murray's (1938) need-press theory of personality. Each of the topical scales (scales 20 to 28) assesses a different topic or component of interpersonal behavior (for example, counseling readiness, personal adjustment, creative personality, and masculine attributes). The transactional analysis scales (scales 29 to 33) are described as measures of the five ego functions in Berne's (1966) transactional analysis. The origence–intellectence scales (scales 34 to 37) are described as measures of Welsh's origence–intellectence (creativity and intelligence) dimensions of personality.

For purposes of interpretation and counseling, raw scores on the ACL scales are converted to standard *T* scores. As an illustration, the 37 *T* scores and the associated profile of the case described in Report 9–1 are given in Table 9–5. The *T* scores are interpreted with reference to norms, based on 5238 males and 4144 females, listed in the 1983 manual. Profiles and associated interpretations for six sample cases, one of which

TABLE 9–5 Scales and Illustrative *T* Scores on Adjective Check List

Scale name and designation	T *scores for* Report 9-1
Modus operandi	
1 Total number of adjectives checked (No. Ckd)	37
2 Number of favorable adjectives checked (Fav)	62
3 Number of unfavorable adjectives checked (Unfav)	59
4 Communality (Com)	68
Need scales	
5 Achievement (Ach)	57
6 Dominance (Dom)	50
7 Endurance (End)	53
8 Order (Ord)	57
9 Intraception (Int)	57
10 Nurturance (Nur)	44
11 Affiliation (Aff)	53
12 Heterosexuality (Het)	46
13 Exhibition (Exh)	44
14 Autonomy (Aut)	49
15 Aggression (Agg)	58
16 Change (Cha)	58
17 Succorance (Suc)	41
18 Abasement (Aba)	56
19 Deference (Def)	49
Topical scales	
20 Counseling readiness (Crs)	55
21 Self-control (S-Cn)	48
22 Self-confidence (S-Cfd)	59
23 Personal adjustment (P-Adj)	53
24 Ideal self (Iss)	64
25 Creative personality (Cps)	63
26 Military leadership (Mls)	52
27 Masculine attributes (Mas)	54
28 Feminine attributes (Fem)	69
Transactional analysis	
29 Critical parent (CP)	62
30 Nurturing parent (NP)	48
31 Adult (A)	56
32 Free child (FC)	46
33 Adapted child (AC)	41
Origence–intellectence	
34 High origence, Low intellectence (A-1)	47
35 High origence, High intellectence (A-2)	64
36 Low origence, Low intellectence (A-3)	44
37 Low origence, High intellectence (A-4)	63

Source: Adapted from *The Adjective Check List Manual* by Harrison G. Gough, Ph.D., and Alfred B. Heilbrun, Jr., Ph.D. Copyright 1983. Published by Consulting Psychologists Press, Inc.

is summarized in Report 9–1, are also provided. The manual reports test–retest coefficients for the separate scales ranging from .34 for the high-origence, low-intellectence scale to .77 for the aggression scale (median of .65) and also describes many uses of the ACL and research investigations in which it has been used.

Reviews of the ACL have been fairly positive, concluding that the instrument is well developed and has had its greatest usefulness in self-concept studies (Teeter, 1985; Zarske, 1985). The internal consistency reliabilities of most of the 37 scales are reasonably high, but data on their test–retest reliabilities are limited. Furthermore, the scales are significantly intercorrelated and should therefore not be interpreted as independent factors. A factor analysis which I conducted on the 15 need scales (scales 5 to 19) revealed three factors: Self-Confidence or Ego Strength, Goal Orientation, and Social Interactiveness or Friendliness. The ACL has been used principally with normal people, and its validity in psychodiagnosis and treatment planning has not been determined.

REPORT 9–1   Case Description Accompanying Adjective Check List Scores in Table 9–5

This 19-year-old undergraduate student majoring in biology maintained an A– grade average and planned to go to graduate school. She was brought up in a close-knit, large family, and had warm feelings about her parents and her childhood. Before college, she had always lived in small towns or semirural areas. Coming to an urban college required quite an adjustment, but she liked the excitement and stimulation of city life. She retained her religious beliefs and regularly attended church. She viewed herself as a political and economic conservative. Her life-history interviewer described her in the following way:

> She is an intelligent, vivacious, attractive young woman, enthusiastic about her life at the university. Although she views herself as introverted, her behavior is more extroverted; she was talkative, outgoing, candid, and not hesitant to assume a leadership role. Her parents were strict, expected the children to assume responsibilities, and placed a high value on academic achievement. She described her mother as a demanding, extremely shy woman who participated in social activities from a sense of duty. She said her father was somewhat intimidating, but affectionate; she feels closer to him now than she did when she was growing up. Being at school—away from home and the relative isolation of that environment—is very exciting.

Scores on her ACL profile are in agreement with the case-history data and staff evaluations. Moderate elevations occur on the scales for Achievement, Self-Confidence, and Personality Adjustment, and scores of 60 or greater on the scales for Ideal Self, Creative Personality, and A-2 (high origence, high intellectence). The ACL profile also revealed scores of 60 or greater on the scales for Favorable, Communality, Femininity, Critical Parent, and A-4 (low origence, high intellectence). Although the staff rating of 54 on Femininity was above average for the sample of 80 students included in this project, it is not as high as the score of 69 on her self-descriptive ACL. Because she had scores greater than 50 on *both* Masculinity and Femininity, she is in the androgynous cell in the interaction diagram between the two scales. The profile also reveals elevated scores on *both* Favorable and Unfavorable, which suggests she is more complex, internally differentiated, and less repressive than her peers.

A number of checklists are designed to identify behavioral problems in children. Examples are the Behavior Problem Checklist (Quay & Peterson, 1983), the Child Behavior Checklist (Achenbach, 1978; Achenbach & Edelbrock, 1983), the Louisville Fear Survey Schedule (Miller et al., 1976), and the Home Situations Questionnaire (Barkley, 1981). The items on these checklists are answered by parents or other people who know the child well. The psychometric characteristics of all four of these checklists appear adequate, and they are widely used in programs for treating children with problems (Ollendick & Green, 1990).

Q-Sorts and the Rep Test

Q-sorts are similar to rating scales, but they also possess certain features of checklists. The *Q-sort technique,* which was pioneered by Stephenson (1953), requires the examinee or an acquaintance to sort a set of personality statements into a series of piles ranging from "most characteristic" to "least characteristic" of the examinee. The sorter is asked to arrange the statements so that a certain number will fall in each pile and result in a normal distribution of statements across piles.

Q-sort statements may be written especially for a specific investigation, but standard decks of statements are available. A commercially distributed set is the California Q-Sort (Consulting Psychologists Press), consisting of 100 cards containing statements descriptive of personality. An adaptation of the California Q-Sort for use with children is the 10-item California Child Q-Set (see Block, 1978).

Certain investigations of changes in self-concept resulting from psychotherapy or other experiences have required the research subjects to make before-and-after Q-sorts of a series of statements to describe their feelings and attitudes (for example, Rogers & Dymond, 1954). In several investigations, each subject was asked to make separate Q-sorts according to his or her perceived real self and ideal self. The two sorts were then compared to determine the congruence between the two perceived selves (Rogers & Dymond, 1954). If the real- and ideal-self sorts were more similar after than before psychotherapy, the therapy was presumed to be successful.

Rather than asking the examinees to sort statements, they may be asked to sort a set of persons into various categories. An example of this approach is the Role Construct Repertory (Rep) Test. According to Kelly (1955), people are like scientists in that they conceptualize or categorize their experiences in what appears to them to be a logical way. Unfortunately, many people perceive or construe the world incorrectly and thereby develop a faulty system of constructs. The aim of the Rep Test is to identify the system of personal constructs that a person uses to interpret his or her experiences. The examinee sorts into various conceptual, self-selected categories those people who are important to him or her in certain ways. Performance on the test is analyzed by noting how many constructs are used by the examinee, what those constructs are, what characteristics of people are emphasized by those constructs (physical, social, and so on), and which people are most like or most different from the examinee. Interpreting the results of the Rep Test in terms of the examinee's "system of personal constructs," which serves as an internal frame of reference for perceiving and understanding the world, is a laborious, subjective process. This fact, plus the meager amount of data concerning the test's validity, has resulted in infrequent use of the Rep Test for clinical or research programs.

BEHAVIOR ANALYSIS AND ASSESSMENT

Behavior modification is a term that comprises a set of psychotherapeutic procedures, based on learning theory and research, designed to change inappropriate behavior to more personally and/or socially appropriate behavior. The inappropriate behaviors may consist of excesses, deficits, or other inadequacies of action that are correctable through behavioral techniques such as systematic desensitization, counterconditioning, and extinction. Among the maladaptive behaviors that have received special attention by behavior modifiers are specific fears (or phobias), smoking, overeating, alcoholism, drug addiction, underassertiveness, bedwetting, chronic tension and pain, and sexual inadequacies. Although these target behaviors have typically been rather narrowly defined, more cognitively inclined behavior therapists have also tackled less specific problems, such as negative self-concept and identity crisis. Furthermore, the target behaviors consist not only of nonverbal movements, but also of verbal reports of thoughts and feelings.

Behavior Analysis

Behavior therapists have attempted to understand behavior by studying the antecedents, including both the social learning history and current environment, and the results or consequences of that behavior. A fundamental principle of behavior modification, which is based on laboratory studies of operant learning, is that behavior is controlled by its consequences. Therefore, in designing a program to correct problem behavior, we must identify the reinforcing consequences that sustain the behavior in addition to the conditions that precede and trigger it. Following this approach, the process of behavior modification is preceded by a *functional analysis* of the problem behavior(s), consisting of an A–B–C sequence in which A stands for the antecedent conditions, B the problem behavior, and C the consequences of that behavior. B is modified by controlling for A and changing C. The antecedents and consequences of the target behavior may be overt, objectively observable conditions or covert mental events reported by the person whose behavior is to be modified.

Behavioral Assessment

Behavioral assessment has multiple functions, including (1) the identification of target behaviors, alternative behaviors, and causal variables; (2) the design of intervention strategies; and (3) the reevaluation of target and causal behaviors (Haynes, 1990). Various procedures have been employed for these purposes, including observations, interviews, checklists, rating scales, and questionnaires completed by the patient or a person acquainted with the patient. On occasion, behavior modifiers have even used responses to projective tests as samples of behavior (see Maloney & Ward, 1976).

Observational Methods   The observational procedures employed in a behavior analysis involve taking note of the frequency and duration of the target behaviors and the particular contingencies (antecedents and consequences) of their occurrence. Depending on the context and the age of the patient, behavior observations can be made and recorded by teachers, parents, nurses, nursing assistants, or any other person who is acquainted with the patient.

Self-observation and Self-monitoring   Perhaps the easiest and most economical way to determine how frequently and under what conditions a particular target behavior occurs is *self-observation*. Although self-observation is not always reliable, people can be trained to make accurate and valid observations of their own behavior (Kendall & Norton-Ford, 1982). In self-observation for purposes of behavioral analysis and modification, the person is instructed to carry at all times materials such as index cards, a note pad, a wrist counter, and a timer to keep a record of occurrences of the target behavior and the time, place, and circumstances under which it occurs. The self-observational procedure, referred to as *self-monitoring*, can be fairly reliable when the patient is carefully trained. Interestingly, the very process of self-monitoring, that is, observing and tabulating occurrences of specific behaviors in which one engages, can affect the occurrence of those behaviors, sometimes in a therapeutic way (Ciminero, Nelson, & Lipinski, 1977). For example, heavy smokers tend to smoke less when they keep track of how often, how long, and in what circumstances they smoke.

Behavioral Interviewing   Behavioral interviewing is a type of clinical interviewing in which the focus is on obtaining information to plan a program of behavior modification. This entails describing, in objective behavioral terms, the problem behaviors of the interviewee, as well as the antecedent conditions and reinforcing consequences. To conduct such an interview successfully, the interviewee must be encouraged (and taught if necessary) to respond in specific behavioral terms, rather than in the more customary language of motives and traits. After obtaining the necessary information to develop a program of behavior modification, the program must be explained to the client and he or she must be motivated to adhere to it.

Other Psychometric Techniques   Several additional procedures for behavioral assessment have been proposed (for example, see Haynes & Wilson, 1979; Kendall & Korgeski, 1979; Hersen & Bellack, 1982; Ciminero, Calhoun, & Adams, 1986; Ollendick & Green, 1990; Haynes, 1990). The specific assessment procedures and instruments used vary with the therapeutic techniques and goals. A representative approach is that advocated by Cautela and Upper (1976), who begin by determining the frequency and intensity of the target behavior(s), what triggers the behavior (antecedents), and what effects the behavior has (consequences). These antecedents and consequences, both motor and mental, are identified by observing and interviewing the person, as well as significant other people, and administering various questionnaires, rating scales, and inventories. Many questionnaires, checklists, and inventories, some of which are commercially available, may be employed in behavior analysis. An example is the Fear Survey Schedule (EdITS). Unfortunately, there is no standard, generally recommended battery of assessment instruments for this purpose. The great majority of psychometric instruments administered in behavior analysis are somewhat makeshift devices that are inadequately standardized and frequently fail to meet the reliability and validity requirements of good psychological assessment procedures.

SUMMARY

The temperamental, emotional, and stylistic traits or characteristics known as personality variables are neither as stable nor as precisely measurable as cognitive variables. Attempts to assess these characteristics go back to antiquity, but a genuine scientific approach did not get underway until the late nineteenth and early twentieth centuries.

Although certain instruments have been designed on a purely empirical basis, many personality assessment devices have been constructed in the context of some theory of personality. Psychoanalytic, trait-factor, and phenomenological theories have been particularly influential in this regard. More recently, behavior theory has also stimulated the development of a number of devices for assessing characteristic behaviors.

Observations and interviews are the most widely used, but not necessarily the most valid, methods of assessing personality. Observations may be controlled or uncontrolled and interviews structured or unstructured. Observing and interviewing can be made more objective by training observers and interviewers. It is also important to collect observational and interview data as unobtrusively as possible and to pay attention to both the verbal and nonverbal components of interpersonal communications.

Special observational procedures include the anecdotal record, time sampling, incident sampling, and situational testing. A special type of interviewing is stress interviewing, an approach that requires a great deal of training in order to be effective. Interviews are conducted for various purposes, but certain kinds of interview questions are considered illegal in personnel selection.

Various types of rating procedures (numerical scales, graphic scales, standard scales, behaviorally anchored scales, and forced-choice scales) have been employed in psychological assessments. Of the various types, graphic rating scales have probably been the most popular. A numerical rating scale of particular interest is the semantic differential. Semantic differentials are used to determine the connotative meanings that selected concepts have for people.

Errors in rating, such as constant errors (leniency or generosity error, severity error, central tendency error), the halo effect, the logical error, the contrast error, and the proximity error, can be reduced by careful training of raters and the use of certain formats in designing rating scales.

A checklist of personal characteristics or problems is a popular, efficient method of recording observations of oneself and others. A variety of checklists are commercially available, including instruments for noting and evaluating adaptive behavior, mental status, depression, anxiety, personal problems, personal history, health problems, marital evaluation, sexual abuse, preschool behavior, and for a more general analysis of personality. Of all checklists, the most popular have been the Mooney Problem Check Lists and the Adjective Check List.

Numerous behavior assessment instruments have been constructed for use in behavior analyses preceding applications of behavior modification procedures. These instruments are designed to reveal a person's social learning history and the antecedents and consequences of certain maladaptive target behaviors. Administration of several such instruments, in addition to extensive observation (self and other) and interviewing, is a diagnostic first step in planning a program of behavior modification.

EXERCISES

1. Describe the major concepts of trait theory, psychoanalytic theory, phenomenological (self) theory, and social learning theory. Which theories have made the most significant contributions to personality assessment? Which theory is most appealing to you in terms of its explanatory power and congruence with your own personal theory of human personality and behavior?

2. Defend physiognomy and graphology as legitimate areas of investigation and application in personality assessment. Why are they more reputable than phrenology and astrology?

3. Show the personality description on page 256 to several of your friends. How many agreed that it was a fairly accurate description of their personalities? Why do you think that this was so?

4. Select a person in one of your classes as a subject for observation, preferably someone whom you do not know and toward whom you have neutral feelings. Observe the person over a period of three or four class meetings, inconspicuously recording what he or she does and says. Try to be as objective as possible, looking for consistent, typical behaviors, as well as noting responses that occur infrequently. At the end of the observation period, write a two- to three-page characterization of the person. Without having access to any other information about this person (what other students say about the person, how well he or she does in college, and the like), how would you describe his or her personality and characteristic behavior? Finally, check your observations against those of other people who know or have observed this person. After this experience of close observation using a time sampling technique, how do you feel about objective observation as a method of assessing personality? Is it valid and useful?

5. Ask six people, one at a time, to make facial expressions indicative of each of the following emotions: anger, disgust, fear, happiness, sadness, and surprise. Make notes on the facial expressions, differentiating among the various emotions. Did your "actors" find the task difficult? Was there appreciable consistency from person to person in the expressions characterizing a particular emotion? Were certain emotions easier to express and more consistently expressed than others?

6. Referring to the discussion of interviewing procedures in this chapter and other interviewing guidelines available to you, conduct a structured personal interview of someone whom you do not know well. Write up the results as a formal report, giving identifying information, a summary of the interview findings, and recommendations pertaining to the interviewee.

7. Consult a dictionary or thesaurus and select a sample of 50 adjectives referring to traits or characteristics of personality. Try to choose a mixture of positive and not-so-positive terms that are not synonyms or antonyms. Make multiple copies of the alphabetized list of terms, with a short blank line after each adjective, and administer the list to a sample of students. Ask the students to check each adjective that they believe to be generally descriptive of themselves. Summarize the results, comparing them with what you already know about the persons from other reports and observations.

8. If the set of *Computer Programs for Psychological Assessment* is available, run program 3

("Professor Personality Ratings") in category 8 ("Programs on Personality Assessment"). Compare your results with those of your fellow students in the course. Were they similar or different? Why?

SUGGESTED READINGS

Aiken, L. R. (1988). *Assessment of personality,* Chs. 4–5. Boston: Allyn & Bacon.

———. (1993). *Personality: Theories, research, and applications.* Englewood Cliffs, NJ: Prentice Hall.

Argyle, M. (1975). *Bodily communication.* New York: International Universities Press.

Cone, J. D., & Foster, S. L. (1982). Direct observation in clinical psychology. In P. C. Kendall & J. N. Butcher (eds.), *Handbook of research methods in clinical psychology,* Ch. 10. New York: Wiley.

Edelbrock, C., & Costello, A. J. (1990). Structured interviews for children and adolescents. In G. Goldstein & M. Hersen (eds.), *Handbook of psychological assessment,* 2nd ed., pp. 308–323. New York: Pergamon.

Hersen, M., & Bellack, A. A. (eds.) (1982). *Behavioral assessment: A practical handbook,* 2nd ed. New York: Pergamon.

———, & Turner, S. M. (1985). *Diagnostic interviewing.* New York: Plenum.

Ollendick, T. H., & Green, R. (1990). Behavioral assessment of children. In G. Goldstein & M. Hersen (eds.), *Handbook of psychological assessment,* 2nd ed., pp. 403–422. New York: Pergamon.

Rorer, L. G. (1990). Personality assessment: A conceptual survey. In L. A. Pervin (ed.), *Handbook of personality theory and research,* pp. 693–720. New York: Guilford Press.

Sciassi, I. (1984). Psychiatric interviews and mental status examinations. In G. Goldstein & M. Hersen (eds.), *Handbook of psychological assessment,* pp. 259–275. New York: Pergamon.

Wiens, A. N. (1990). Structured clinical interviews for adults. In G. Goldstein & M. Hersen (eds.), *Handbook of psychological assessment,* 2nd ed., pp. 324–344. New York: Pergamon.

Wiggins, J. S., & Pincus, A. L. (1992). Personality: Structure and assessment. In M. R. Rosenzweig & E. W. Porter (eds.), *Annual Review of Psychology, 43.* Palo Alto, CA: Annual Reviews, Inc.

Chapter Ten

Personality Assessment: Inventories and Projective Techniques

Rating scales, checklists, and related psychometric devices have contributed to the assessment and understanding of human personality. They have not, however, received as much professional attention as the two categories of instruments discussed in the current chapter. The origins of the instruments considered in the last chapter are also, in the main, different from those discussed in this chapter. Although a number of rating scales and checklists originated in clinical situations, the majority were designed for educational and employment contexts. Personality inventories have also been used in nonclinical situations, but they, like projective techniques, have focused primarily on personality adjustment and psychopathology. The design and applications of these assessment devices have been extended to include the evaluation and investigation of normal personality, but the emphasis of earlier inventories and projectives on psychopathology has continued in many contemporary instruments.

There are dissimilarities, in both construction and application, between personality inventories and projective techniques. Designers of the first type of instrument have concentrated more on the psychometric qualities of their measures, whereas projectivists have tended to be less concerned with reliability, validity, and norms and more concerned with the richness of impressionistic interpretation and the clinical analysis of responses. Nevertheless, personality inventories and projectives serve similar purposes—sometimes for screening applicants in educational and employment contexts, but more often for diagnosis in mental health clinics, hospitals, and counseling centers.

PERSONALITY INVENTORIES

Inventories of adjustment and temperament, more generally referred to as *personality inventories,* consist of items concerning personal characteristics, thoughts, feelings, and behavior. As on an interest inventory, rating scale, or checklist, respondents mark those items on a personality inventory that they judge to be descriptive of themselves. Such an instrument usually yields scores on several variables, although there are many single-score or single-purpose inventories. Examples of such single-purpose instruments are the Beck Depression Inventory and the Beck Hopelessness Scale (National Computer Systems and The Psychological Corporation). However, a typical personality inventory measures a broad range of variables and is usually more carefully constructed and standardized than a rating scale or checklist.

Truthfulness in Responding

The problem of truthfulness in responding can be a serious problem on a personality inventory. Not only may respondents be unwilling to tell the truth, but they may not even know the truth about themselves and hence fail to give accurate answers to items. Research evidence indicates that people can respond to personality inventories in a distorted fashion when instructed to do so. However, perhaps for fear of being detected or for whatever reason, people do not lie or fake as much in counseling or job-placement situations as we might suspect (Schwab & Packard, 1973). On some inventories, special validation scoring keys have been prepared to detect dissimulation or faking. These keys do not always reveal when an examinee is lying, but they have been shown to be very effective in certain situations (Norman, 1963).

Intentional deception, either to make oneself appear worse (faking bad) or better (faking good), is, of course, not the only factor affecting the accuracy of responses to a personality inventory. Invalid scores may result from faking answers or not knowing the answers to certain questions, but response tendencies or sets such as acquiescence, social desirability, overcautiousness, and extremeness can also affect the validity of scores. Of particular concern are the response sets of *acquiescence* (the tendency to agree rather than disagree when in doubt) and *social desirability* (the tendency to respond in a more socially acceptable manner). As with faking good and faking bad, special scoring keys have been devised on certain inventories to detect or compensate for these response sets. Typically, the scores on the "validity scales" determined by applying these keys to a person's responses are examined before evaluating the content scores or diagnostic scales. However, even personality inventories that are scored on such validity scales can still be susceptible to faking and response sets, often leading to faulty interpretation of scores on the diagnostic scales. Therefore, personality inventories should probably be used in decision making only when examinees have nothing to gain by failing to answer thoughtfully and truthfully.

Norms, Reliability, and Validity

Unlike most rating scales and checklists, personality inventories are usually scored with reference to a set of norms based on the responses of selected groups of people. Because the standardization samples are sometimes very small and unrepresentative of the target population, such norms must be interpreted cautiously. Furthermore, scores and norms for some personality inventories, particularly those consisting of items having a forced-choice format, are *ipsative* in nature. When scores are ipsative, an examinee's score on one scale is affected by his or her scores on the remaining scales. This creates problems in comparing the scores of different people or groups on a particular scale or variable.

The fact that affective variables appear to be more influenced than cognitive variables by situational factors (Mischel, 1968) leads to greater instability in measures of personality than in measures of ability. Coupled with the problems of defining personality characteristics and designing acceptable measures of those characteristics, the instability of personality measurements typically results in lower reliabilities of scores on personality inventories than for scores on tests of intelligence or special abilities.

Personality inventories also have very limited validities for the most part. One factor that limits the validities of many inventories are their low reliabilities. The presence of faking and response sets also contributes to the low validities of many inventories for purposes of clinical diagnosis and classification. Another factor that can affect the validity of a personality inventory is the tendency for users to fall victim to the "jingle fallacy" of believing that subsets of items (scales) having similar names on different inventories necessarily measure the same variable. This can occur, for example, when the "anxiety" and "hostility" scales of one inventory have only moderate correlations with similarly labeled scales on other inventories. Moreover, even when a high correlation is found between scales on two different inventories, the possibility that the correlation is illusory in that it is the result of a common response set must be considered.

Early Inventories

The Personal Data Sheet, which was constructed by R. S. Woodworth to screen U.S. Army recruits for emotional disorders during World War I, was the first personality inventory of any consequence. This single-score instrument consisted of 116 yes–no questions concerning abnormal fears, obsessions, compulsions, tics, nightmares, and other feelings and behaviors. Four illustrative items from the Woodworth Personality Data Sheet are:

Do you feel sad and low-spirited most of the time?

Are you often frightened in the middle of the night?

Do you think you have hurt yourself by going too much with women?

Have you ever lost your memory for a time? (DuBois, 1970, pages 160–163)

Another early personality inventory of the single-score variety was the A–S Reaction Study, a multiple-choice instrument designed by G. W. Allport and F. H. Allport in 1928 to measure a person's disposition to be ascendant or submissive in everyday social relationships.

The first multiscore, or multiphasic, adjustment inventory was the Bernreuter Personality Inventory (1931). The Bernreuter consisted of 125 items to be answered "yes," "no," or "?" by high school or college students or adults in 25 minutes or so. By assigning different numerical weights to various items, six scores were obtained: Neurotic Tendency, Self-sufficiency, Introversion–Extroversion, Dominance–Submission, Sociability, and Confidence.

Many other personality inventories have been published since 1930. Supplementing the logical–rational procedure of selecting items on the basis of their content validity are the statistical procedures of factor analysis and criterion keying. A combination of these methods has also been applied in constructing certain inventories. For convenience, illustrative instruments will be described under three separate headings: content-validated inventories, factor-analyzed inventories, and criterion-keyed inventories.

Content-validated Inventories

The items on content-validated inventories were selected because they appeared to the test designer(s) to measure certain personality traits or characteristics that were considered important. This has sometimes been called the "rational" or "a priori" method of personality test construction. The construction of an inventory by this method is frequently guided, at least to some extent, by a formal or informal theory of personality. Illustrative of inventories that are associated with certain conceptions or theories of personality are the Edwards Personal Preference Schedule, the Myers–Briggs Type Indicator, and the Jenkins Activity Survey.

Edwards Personal Preference Schedule *(The Psychological Corporation)*   The Edwards Personal Preference Schedule (EPPS), which consists of 225 pairs of statements pertaining to individual likes and feelings, is one of the most widely researched of all personality inventories. Each forced-choice statement pair pits two psychogenic needs against each other; examinees are instructed to indicate which statement is more descriptive or characteristic of themselves. In an effort to control for the social desirability response set, the two statements comprising each item were selected to be approximately equal in social desirability. An example of an item on the EPPS is:

A. I like to do things by myself.
B. I like to help others do things.

Based on Henry Murray's need system, the EPPS is scored for the 15 needs listed as scales 5 to 19 in Table 9–5; a consistency score and a profile stability score are also obtained. Percentile and *T* score norms for each scale are based on over 1500 students in 29 colleges and approximately 9000 adults in 48 states; separate norms for high school students are also available. Split-half reliabilities of the scores range from .60 to .87 and test–retest reliabilities from .74 to .88.

As is true of all forced-choice inventories, scores on the EPPS are *ipsative* rather than *normative* and must be interpreted accordingly. By endorsing statements pertaining to certain needs, the respondent also rejects statements concerned with other needs. The result is that a person's score on one need is relative to his or her scores on other needs, and therefore scores on the various need scales are not statistically independent. The ipsative nature of scores on forced-choice inventories such as the EPPS creates problems of score interpretation and data analysis.

Although the forced-choice format of the EPPS controls to some extent for the social desirability response set (Feldman & Corah, 1960; Wiggins, 1966), many examinees find the format awkward and difficult. In addition, the validity of the EPPS scales as measures of psychological needs is questionable. For example, the scores do not correlate very highly with other measures of similar variables.

Myers–Briggs Type Indicator (MBTI) (Consulting Psychologists Press)   This personality inventory is composed of a series of two-choice items concerning preferences or inclinations in feelings and behavior. There are four forms (G, F, K, and J), with 126 to 290 items per form. Based on Carl Jung's theory of personality types, the MBTI is scored on four bipolar scales: Introversion–Extroversion (I–E), Sensing–Intuition (S–N), Thinking–Feeling (T–F), and Judging–Perceptive (J–P). Combinations of scores on these four two-part categories result in 16 possible personality types. Thus, an ENFP type is a person whose predominant modes are Extrovert, Intuition, Feeling and Perceptive. On the other hand, an ISTJ type is a person whose predominant modes are Introvert, Sensing, Thinking, and Judging. Unfortunately, no measures of test-taking attitude are provided, a shortcoming that could lead to mistakes in diagnosis and screening (Willis, 1984).

Percentile norms for the four indicator scores, based on small samples of high school and college students, are given in the MBTI manual (Myers & McCaulley, 1985). Split-half reliabilities of the four scores are reported as being in the .70s and .80s, and a number of small-scale validity studies are also described. Although the conceptualization of personality in terms of types is not viewed favorably by many U.S. psychologists, an impressive array of materials on the Myers–Briggs Type Indicator has been published (Consulting Psychologists Press). Included in these materials are books, computer software, and the Myers–Briggs Type Development Indicator. These materials should be studied extensively by the user as a background for obtaining the necessary skills to administer and interpret the MBTI.

Jenkins Activity Survey (The Psychological Corporation)   The psychological examination of patients who manifest symptoms of coronary heart disease has revealed a pattern of behavior known as Type A. This behavior pattern is characterized as aggressive, ambitious, extremely competitive, preoccupied with achievement, impatient, and restless, with chronic feelings of being challenged and under pressure. Contrasting with the Type A pattern are Type B people, who do not show a proneness to coronary disorder. Type B's are more relaxed, easygoing, and patient; they speak and act more slowly and evenly (Jenkins, Zyzanski, & Rosenman, 1979). Compared with Type B's, Type A individuals manifest a significantly higher incidence of heart attacks, even when differences in age, serum cholesterol level, smoking frequency, and blood pressure are taken into account.

The A and B types can be divided into four subtypes (A1 and A2, B3 and B4), depending on the degree to which Type A or Type B characteristics are manifested. A1 people show most Type A characteristics to an intense degree, behaviors that are entirely absent in B4 people. A2 and B3 people are intermediate between the A1 and B4 extremes in their behavior. These four behavior patterns have been assessed by means of either a clinical interview or a personality inventory, the Jenkins Activity Survey (JAS). The JAS, a 52-item self-administered inventory designed for adults (25 to 65 years), takes about 20 minutes to complete. It is scored on three factorially independent scales: Speed and Impatience (Factor S), Job Involvement (Factor J), and Hard Driving and Competitive (Factor H). Illustrative items from each of the three scales are:[1]

1. When you listen to someone talking, and this person takes too long to come to the point, do you feel like hurrying him along?
2. How often do you bring your work home with you at night or study materials related to your job?
3. Nowadays, do you consider yourself to be:
   a. Definitely hard-driving and competitive?
   b. Probably hard-driving and competitive?
   c. Probably more relaxed and easy-going?
   d. Definitely more relaxed and easy-going?

The JAS was standardized on 2588 middle- to upper-level managers between the ages of 48 and 65 in 10 large California corporations. Results obtained from structured interviews and through retrospective and predictive studies of coronary heart disease are cited as proof of the validity of the JAS. Despite its wide usage and a number of positive features, the JAS was viewed by Blumenthal (1985) as still in the experimental phase. The reliabilities, validities, and norms of this inventory are tentative, the scoring system is complex, and controls for test-taking attitude are lacking. Blumenthal (1985) concluded that use of the JAS should be limited to research and that clinical judgment is a more accurate method of selecting individuals who are prone to coronary heart disease.

Factor-analyzed Inventories

The common goal of researchers who apply factor-analytic techniques to the analysis of personality has been to isolate a relatively small number of personality factors or traits that can account for variations in scores on different inventories and then construct a measure of each factor. The first published application of factor analysis to the study of personality was made by Webb (1915). Webb had large groups of males in schools and colleges rate 40 or more qualities that they considered to have "a general and fundamental bearing on the total personality." Treatment of the data by an early form of factor analysis led Webb to conclude that "consistency of action resulting from deliberate volition, or 'will,' is the most basic characteristic of personality."

J. P. Guilford, whose research and development work began in the late 1930s and early 1940s (Guilford, 1940; Guilford & Martin, 1943), deserves credit for being the first psychologist to construct a personality inventory by using factor-analytic techniques. The construction of his initial inventories, the Guilford–Martin Inventory of Factors, Guilford–Martin Personnel Inventory, and Inventory of Factors STDCR, which were influenced by Jung's introversion–extroversion types, involved correlating scores on a

---

[1]Reproduced by permission from the Jenkins Activity Survey. Copyright (c) 1979, 1969, 1965 by The Psychological Corporation, San Antonio, Texas. All rights reserved.

large number of existing personality tests. Guilford's tests were carefully reviewed by Louis Thurstone and Thelma Thurstone, who then constructed their own personality inventory, the Thurstone Temperament Schedule (1949–1953). This 140-item inventory was scored on seven traits (Active, Vigorous, Impulsive, Dominant, Stable, Sociable, Reflective), but the reliabilities of these trait measures were not very high.

Guilford–Zimmerman Temperament Survey *(Consulting Psychologists Press and National Computer Systems)* Following Thurstone and Thurstone's analysis of Guilford's data, the latter reanalyzed his earlier results and published a 10-factor composite of his three earlier inventories. Known as the Guilford–Zimmerman Temperament Survey (GZTS), this inventory was designed for high school through adult levels and was scored on 10 trait scales: General Activity, Restraint, Ascendance, Sociability, Emotional Stability, Objectivity, Friendliness, Thoughtfulness, Personal Relations, and Masculinity. Three verification keys for detecting false and careless responding are also provided. Percentile and standard score norms for the 10 scales, which have moderate reliabilities, are based mainly on samples of college students. Although still in print, the GZTS has never been as popular as the more clinically oriented Minnesota Multiphasic Personality Inventory.

Cattell's Questionnaires Perhaps the most comprehensive series of inventories for assessing personality in both children and adults was designed by R. B. Cattell. Cattell began his personality research with a list of 17,953 personality-descriptive adjectives, which Allport and Odbert (1936) had gleaned from the dictionary. By combining terms having similar meanings, the list was first reduced to 4504 "real" traits and then to 171 trait names; subsequent factor analyses of scores on these trait dimensions produced 31 surface traits and 12 source traits of personality. Cattell devised a number of measures of these traits and four others isolated in his later work, but his major instrument is the 16 Personality Factor Questionnaire (16 PF) (Institute for Personality and Ability Testing). Two parallel forms of the 16 PF at each of three vocabulary proficiency levels (educationally disadvantaged through newspaper-literate adults), in addition to a tape-recorded form for the educationally disadvantaged, were published.

The personality variables measured by the 16 PF are listed in Report 10–1. In addition to 16 primary traits of personality, the 16 PF can be scored for three validity or test-taking attitude scales [Motivational Distortion (MD) or "faking good," Faking Bad, and Random response], as well as a number of combined scores or patterns. Standard score norms (sten scores) for the 16 PF scales, based on large, representative samples of high school students, college students, and adults, are given in a special supplement supplied with the manual. Separate norms are provided for males, females, and males and females combined in three groups (high school seniors, college students, and adults). These sten scores, which range in value from 1 to 10, have a mean of 5.5 and a standard deviation of 2. Sten scores of 4 and below are defined as low and sten scores of 7 and above as high.

Scores on the 16 PF may be interpreted by the profile-matching technique of comparing the examinee's scores with those of selected groups, for example, delinquents or neurotics. A second interpretive technique, known as criterion estimation, involves the use of statistical equations in which each score is multiplied by a specified numerical weight to predict

N A R R A T I V E   S C O R E   R E P O R T
for The Sixteen Personality Factor Questionnaire--16 PF

This report is intended to be used in conjunction with professional judgment. The statements it contains should be viewed as hypotheses to be validated against other sources of data. All information in this report should be treated confidentially and responsibly.

NAME-John Sample   January 3, 1992
ID NUMBER-   AGE-29; SEX-M

VALIDITY SCALES

```
SCORES      1 2 3 4 5 6 7 8 9 10
Raw Sten
  1    2    [====]                   Faking good is very low.
  5    8    [===========]            Faking bad is high.
```

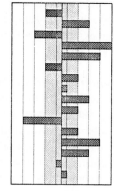

```
  SCORES                        16 PF    PROFILE
Raw Sten      LEFT MEANING  1 2 3 4 5 6 7 8 9 10  RIGHT MEANING      %
     U  C
  8  4  4   A   Cool, Reserved                    Warm, Easygoing   23
 10  8  8   B Concrete Thinking                   Abstract Thinking 89
 10  2  3   C    Easily Upset                     Calm, Stable      11
 22 10 10   E   Not Assertive                     Dominant          99
 21  9  9   F   Sober, Serious                    Enthusiastic      96
 11  4  4   G      Expedient                      Conscientious     23
 19  7  7   H     Shy, Timid                      Venturesome       77
  9  6  6   I   Tough-Minded                      Sensitive         60
 11  8  8   L       Trusting                      Suspicious        89
 16  7  7   M      Practical                      Imaginative       77
  4  2  2   N     Forthright                      Shrewd             4
 15  8  7   O   Self-Assured                      Self-Doubting     77
 15  9  9   Q1  Conservative                      Experimenting     96
 14  8  8   Q2 Group-Oriented                     Self-Sufficient   89
 12  5  5   Q3  Undisciplined                     Self-Disciplined  40
 14  7  6   Q4       Relaxed                       Tense, Driven    60
```

average

Note: "U" indicates uncorrected sten scores. "C"indicates sten scores cor-
       rected for distortion (if appropriate). The interpretation will pro-
       ceed on the basis of corrected scores. This report was processed using
       male adult (GP) norms for Form A.

SECOND-ORDER FACTORS   COMPOSITE SCORES

Extraversion..average (5.9)   Adjustment....above average (6.5)
Anxiety.......above average (7.1)   Leadership....average (5.6)
Tough Poise...average (4.9)   Creativity....very high (9.0)
Independence..extremely high (10.0)
Control.......below average (4.2)   Profile Pattern Code = 2323

REPORT 10-1

Name: John Sample   -2-   January 3, 1992

PERSONAL COUNSELING OBSERVATIONS

Adequacy of adjustment is above average (6.5).
Effectiveness of behavior controls is below average (4.2).

INTERVENTION CONSIDERATIONS

The influence of a controlled environment may help. Suggestions include:
A graded series of success experiences to improve self-confidence.
A structured, active program to reduce anxiety.

PRIMARY PERSONALITY CHARACTERISTICS OF SPECIAL INTEREST

Capacity for abstract skills is high.
Involvement in problems may evoke some emotional upset and instability.
In interpersonal relationships, he leads, dominates, or is stubborn.
His style of expression is often lively, optimistic, and enthusiastic.
He tends to project inner tension by blaming others, and becomes jealous or suspicious easily.
In his dealings with others, he is emotionally natural and unpretentious, though somewhat naive.
He is experimenting, has an inquiring mind, likes new ideas, and tends to disparage traditional solutions to problems.
Being self-sufficient, he prefers tackling things resourcefully, alone.

BROAD INFLUENCE PATTERNS

His attention is directed about equally toward the outer environment and toward inner thoughts and feelings. Extraversion is average (5.9).
At the present time, he sees himself as somewhat more anxious than most people. His anxiety score is above average (7.1).
In comparison with those who tend to approach problems coolly and dispassionately or those who emphasize the emotional relationships involved, he is average (4.9).
His life style is independent and self-directed, leading to active attempts to achieve control of the environment. In this respect, he is extremely high (10.0).
He tends to be very expedient and to pursue his own wishes rather than the expectations of others. Thus, he may lack restraint and may fail at times to meet his responsibilities. This tendency is above average (6.8).

REPORT 10–1   (continued)

certain behaviors or classifications. A somewhat less complex interpretative procedure begins with an inspection of the examinee's scores on the three validity scales to determine whether the scores are sufficiently valid to warrant interpretation. If so, then scores on the second-order factors (Introversion Versus Extroversion, Low Anxiety Versus High Anxiety, Tender-minded Emotionality Versus Tough Poise, Subduedness Versus Independence) are examined, followed by an analysis of the 16 primary factors (Karson & O'Dell, 1976). The following example shows how a clinical psychologist interpreted a specific pattern of sten scores on the 16 PF, using no other information than the person's age (23) and sex (female):[2]

Factor	A	B	C	E	F	G	H	I	L	M	N	O	Q1	Q2	Q3	Q4	MD
	:	:	:	:	:	:	:	:	:	:	:	:	:	:	:	:	:
Score	3	8	6	10	8	4	4	7	5	10	9	8	7	8	1	6	4

This is an extremely dominant and aggressive young lady who shows a severe inability to bind anxiety ($Q_3 = 1$). Her relatively high F of 8 indicates marked immaturity coupled with relatively low group conformity (G = 4) and high superego introjection (O = 8). Her average ego strength (C = 6) suggests that she has some good capacity for improved personal adjustment. This, and her good intelligence (B = 8), both indicate that she may be able to respond to psychotherapy. Her extremely high dominance (E = 10) and relatively high Q_1 of 7 suggest that she would be a difficult person to live with in view of her critical, castrating tendencies. She is seen as a highly sophisticated person who apparently needs to learn to get more gratification from people rather than from things. Her extraordinarily high tendency toward fantasy activity (M = 10) suggests that too much of her potential energy is perhaps wasted on impractical daydreams rather than put to constructive use. It is hoped that her employment does not require careful attention to details and attending to the task at hand, since she is not cut out for this type of work. Her 16 PF profile suggests that she is a sporadic individual with a variable level of ego functioning who is unable consistently to apply her energies to the task at hand. She might well be able to use some psychotherapy.

The low to moderate reliabilities of the 16 PF are a serious shortcoming. The split-half reliabilities of the 16 factors are as low as .54, and the equivalence coefficients (correlations between primary factor scales on different test forms) are also low. Test–retest coefficients over short time intervals (dependability coefficients) are in the .70s and .80s, which are lower than those of many other personality inventories. Evidence for the validity of the 16 PF is found in the results of numerous research investigations, many of which were cross-cultural in nature (see Gynther & Gynther, 1976). A case for the construct validity of the questionnaire is made on the basis of multiple correlations between scores on items loading significantly on a factor and scores on the factor itself (direct construct validity) or multiple correlations between scores on the primary factors and scores on other factors (indirect construct validity).

An attractive feature of the 16 PF is the computer report of scores, including a score profile, personal counseling observations, intervention considerations, primary personality characteristics of significance, broad influence patterns, and vocational observations (see Report 10–1). Unfortunately, the 16 PF norms, in addition to the reliability and validity information, are rather dated. Be that as it may, the 16 PF is widely used in counseling and research, enterprises for which it would presumably be even more valuable if it were restandardized (Wholeben, 1985).

Three inventories designed by Cattell as downward extensions of the 16 PF are the High School Personality Questionnaire (for ages 12 through 18), the Children's Personality Questionnaire (for ages 8 through 12), the Early School Personality Questionnaire (for ages 6 through 8), and the Preschool Personality Questionnaire (for ages 4 through 6). Like the 16 PF, these questionnaires have some problems with reliability, but are generally well-constructed and have proved useful in educational and research contexts. Cattell also designed several single-score instruments (for example, IPAT Anxiety Scale Questionnaire, IPAT Depression Scale, and Neuroticism Scale Questionnaire) as measures of more general factors of personality. By factor analyzing 16 PF items related to psychological disorders, 12 new factors were obtained, and a new inventory, the Clinical Analysis Questionnaire, was then constructed to assess scores on these 12 factors in clinical populations.

Eysenck Personality Questionnaire (EPQ) *(EdITS)*   This revision of the Eysenck Personality Inventory (1963–1969) and the Junior Eysenck Personality Inventory (1963–1970) represents a more parsimonious conception of personality than the inventories of Guilford and Cattell. Hans Eysenck's earlier inventories (the Maudsley Personality Inventory and the Eysenck Personality Inventory) were scored for two basic dimensions of personality, Neuroticism (N) and Extroversion (versus Introversion) (E), that emerged from his factor-analytic research. A measure of a third dimension, Psychoticism (P), and a Lie Scale (L) were added in designing the EPQ. The EPQ has a wide age range (7 through adulthood) and takes only 10 to 15 minutes to complete.

Test–retest reliabilities for the N, E, P, and L scales of the EPQ range from .78 to .89 over a 1-month interval; internal consistency coefficients are in the .70s and .80s. Norms on the two forms (A and B), based on U.S. college students and adults, are appropriate for individuals aged 16 years and above. Norms on the Junior EPQ were obtained from samples of 7- to 15-year-old children.

The EPQ and its predecessors have been used extensively in personality research, but less frequently in clinical and other applied contexts. Eysenck (1965, 1981) has used scores on the introversion–extroversion and neuroticism factors in particular to predict how individuals will react in certain experimental situations. He has also related personality patterns to body type (for example, introverts are taller and leaner than extraverts).

Perspective on Factor Analysis in Personality Assessment   Many other personality inventories, some of which are described in the next section, have been constructed using factor-analytic methodology. However, most personality researchers do not believe that factor analysis, regardless of its mathematical sophistication, yields true dimensions of personality in any substantive sense. Rather, by revealing internal consistencies and differences among test items and scales, it helps clarify the relationships among personality constructs or variables.

With respect to the criterion-related validities of personality inventories constructed by factor analysis, they tend to be low or unknown. Consequently, these instruments are generally less helpful in making behavioral predictions and decisions (diagnostic, intervention, training, and the like) in clinical and other applied psychological contexts than content-validated and criterion-keyed inventories. Nevertheless, applications of factor analysis to inventory construction and even more basic research on the nature of human personality remain appealing to certain psychologists. There is fairly good agreement that a large number of personality inventories measure at least the two factors defined by Eysenck, extroversion–introversion and neuroticism (emotionality). In addition, there is substantial support for a five-factor model of personality. These factors are listed as extroversion or surgency, agreeableness, conscientiousness, emotional stability, and culture by Goldberg (1980) and as neuroticism, extroversion, openness, agreeableness, and conscientiousness by Costa and McRae (1986).

Costa and McRae (1986) define their five factors as follows:

neuroticism—worrying vs. calm, insecure vs. secure, self-pitying vs. self-satisfied;

extroversion—sociable vs. retiring, fun-loving vs. sober, affectionate vs. reserved;

openness—imaginative vs. down to earth, preference for variety vs. preference for routine, independent vs. conforming;

agreeableness—soft-hearted vs. ruthless, trusting vs. suspicious, helpful vs. uncooperative;

conscientiousness—well-organized vs. disorganized, careful vs. careless, self-disciplined vs. weak willed.

The five factors appear to be highly consistent across different groups of people and situations.

NEO–PI and NEO–FFI   An analysis of personality in terms of the five-factor model is provided by the NEO Personality Inventory (NEO–PI) and a shortened version, the NEO Five-Factor Inventory (NEO–FFI). These two inventories were designed by P. T. Costa and R. McCrae and are distributed by Sigma Assessment Systems. The NEO–PI is comprised of 181 items rated on a five-point scale and takes about 30 minutes to complete; the NE–FFI has 60 items and takes 10 to 15 minutes. Both inventories are scored for the three N–E–O domains (factors) of Neuroticism (N), Extroversion (E), and Openness to Experience (O); scores on Agreeableness (A) and Conscientiousness (C) are also obtained. Each of the N–E–O domains can be subdivided and scored in turn on six different facets: Anxiety, Hostility, Depression, Self-consciousness, Impulsiveness, and Vulnerability for domain N; Warmth, Gregariousness, Assertiveness, Activity, Excitement-Seeking, and Positive Emotions facets for domain E; Fantasy, Aesthetics, Feelings, Actions, Ideas, and Values facets for domain O.

The internal consistency reliabilities of the NEO inventories range from .85 to .93 for NEO–NPI and from .74 to .89 for NEO–FFI. Test–retest reliabilities computed over a 6-month period range from .86 to .91 for the domain (factor) scales and from .66 to .92 for the facet scales of NEO–PI. Evidence for the validity of the inventories is somewhat scanty, but correlations with other personality inventories, experts' ratings, and sentence-completion test scores are reported in the NEO–PI manual.

Minnesota Multiphasic Personality Inventory

Analogous to the construction of the Strong Interest Inventory, criterion-keyed personality inventories are composed of items or scales that differentiate between two or more criterion groups. An early instrument of this kind was the A–S Reaction Study; items on this inventory were retained only if they differentiated between groups of individuals who had been rated as ascendant or submissive by their peers. The most famous criterion-keyed personality inventory, however, is the Minnesota Multiphasic Personality Inventory (MMPI), which was first published by by S. R. Hathaway & J. C. McKinley in the early 1940s.

Description of the MMPI   The original MMPI was designed to assess personality characteristics indicative of psychological abnormality; the 550 statements on the inventory are answered "yes," "no," or "cannot say." The statements are concerned with attitudes, emotions, motor disturbances, psychosomatic symptoms, and other reported feelings and behaviors indicative of psychiatric problems. Each of the nine scales on which the MMPI was scored consisted of items that distinguished between the responses of a specified psychiatric patient group and a control group of normal people. These scales were cross-validated by comparing the responses of the psychiatric patients with those of various groups of normal individuals. The nine clinical scales, together with the Si (Social Introversion) scale and the four validity scales (?, L, F, K) are described in Table 10–1. Many special scales (for example, accident proneness, anxiety, ego strength, and originality) were developed from the MMPI item pool during the course of nearly 2000 research investigations over 40 years. The majority of these special scales have rarely been used, two noteworthy exceptions being the Taylor Manifest Anxiety Scale and the Welsh A Scale.

Before attempting to interpret scores on the clinical or special scales of the MMPI, attention is directed to scores on the four validity scales (see Table 10–1). The first of these, the raw question (?) score, is the total number of items that the examinee answers "cannot say" or leaves unanswered. A high question score is interpreted as defensiveness in responding. The raw lie (L or "fake good") score is the number of items that the examinee answers in such a way as to be placed in a more favorable light. The infrequency (F or "fake bad") score is the number of items answered by the examinee in such a way as to place himself or herself in a less favorable light. The K score, a fraction of which is applied as a correction factor to the raw scorers on clinical scales 1, 4, 7, 8, and 9, is a measure of overcriticalness or overgenerousness in evaluating oneself. High scorers on the K scale tend to deny personal inadequacies and deficiencies in self-control; low scorers are willing to say socially undesirable things about themselves.

MMPI–2   The MMPI was first published in 1943, so by the 1980s the norms and some of the item content had become out of date. A revision of the inventory was undertaken to provide new, up-to-date norms; broaden the item pool to include content not represented in the original version; revise and reword the language of some of the existing items that were dated, awkward, or sexist; and provide separate forms of the inventory for adults and adolescents. All 550 of the original MMPI items were retained in the Adult and Adolescent revised versions, although 14 percent of the original items were changed

TABLE 10–1   Descriptions of Validity and Clinical Scales on the Original MMPI

Validity (or Test-taking Attitude) Scales

   ? (Cannot Say) Number of items left unanswered.

   L (Lie) Fifteen items of overly good self-report, such as, "I smile at everyone I meet." (Answered True)

   F (Frequency or Infrequency) Sixty-four items answered in the scored direction by 10 percent or less of normals, such as, "There is an international plot against me." (True)

   K (Correction) Thirty items reflecting defensiveness in admitting to problems, such as, "I feel bad when others criticize me." (False)

Clinical Scales

   1 or Hs (Hypochondriasis) Thirty-three items derived from patients showing abnormal concern with bodily functions, such as, "I have chest pains several times a week."(True)

   2 or D (Depression) Sixty items derived from patients showing extreme pessimism, feelings of hopelessness, and slowing of thought and action, such as, "I usually feel that life is interesting and worthwhile." (False)

   3 or Hy (Conversion Hysteria) Sixty items from neurotic patients using physical or mental symptoms as a way of unconsciously avoiding difficult conflicts and responsibilities, such as, "My heart frequently pounds so hard I can feel it." (True)

   4 or Pd (Psychopathic Deviate) Fifty items from patients who show a repeated and flagrant disregard for social customs, an emotional shallowness and an inability to learn from punishing experiences, such as, "My activities and interests are often criticized by others." (True)

   5 or Mf (Masculinity–Femininity) Sixty items from patients showing homoeroticism and items differentiating between men and women, such as, "I like to arrange flowers." (True, scored for femininity.)

   6 or Pa (Paranoia) Forty items from patients showing abnormal suspiciousness and delusions of grandeur or persecution, such as, "There are evil people trying to influence my mind." (True)

   7 or Pt (Psychasthenia) Forty-eight items based on neurotic patients showing obsessions, compulsions, abnormal fears, and guilt and indecisiveness, such as, "I save nearly everything I buy, even after I have no use for it." (True)

   8 or Sc (Schizophrenia) Seventy-eight items from patients showing bizarre or unusual thoughts or behavior, who are often withdrawn and experiencing delusions and hallucinations, such as, "Things around me do not seem real" (True) and, "It makes me uncomfortable to have people close to me." (True)

   9 or Ma (Hypomania) Forty-six items from patients characterized by emotional excitement, overactivity, and flight of ideas, such as, "At times I feel very 'high' or very 'low' for no apparent reason." (True)

   0 or Si (Social introversion) Seventy items from persons showing shyness, little interest in people, and insecurity, such as, "I have the time of my life at parties." (False)

Source: After Sundberg (1977). The items quoted are simulated MMPI items. The MMPI scale names and abbreviations are from Minnesota Multiphasic Personality Inventory. Copyright © by the Regents of the University of Minnesota, 1942, 1943 (renewed 1970). Reproduced by permission of the University of Minnesota Press. ("Minnesota Multiphasic Personality Inventory" and "MMPI" are registered trademarks of the University of Minnesota, Minneapolis, Minnesota.)

because of dated language or awkwardness in wording. Words or phrases more characteristic of the 1940s (for example, streetcar, sleeping powder, and drop the handkerchief) were omitted, and other modifications were made to update statements (for example, "I like to take a bath" became "I like to take a bath or shower"). As with the items on the original form, the items on the revised MMPI were written at a sixth-grade level. The Adult Version (MMPI–2) contains 154 new experimental items designed to assess certain areas of psychopathology not well represented in the original MMPI (such as eating disorders, Type A personality, and drug abuse). The Adolescent Version contains 104 new items concerned specifically with adolescent problems. In addition, the tendency for normal adolescents in a temporary state of turmoil to score like adult psychopaths on the original MMPI has been corrected.

Designed to be more suitable for nonclinical as well as clinical uses, MMPI–2 consists of 567 true–false questions at an eighth-grade reading level and takes about 90 minutes to complete. The four validity scales and the ten basic clinical scales are scored from the first 370 items, whereas the supplementary content and research scales are scored on items 371 to 567 (see Table 10–2). Many of the content and research scales are holdovers from the original MMPI.

As seen in Figure 10–1, MMPI–2 is scored on the same clinical scales as its predecessor. However, the T scores for eight of the clinical and other (content) scales have been made uniform so that a given T score is now comparable from scale to scale. The uniform T scores were devised because, due to differences in score distributions, the traditional T scores on different scales were not strictly comparable. Not only do uniform T scores remove these differences, but, unlike normalized T scores, they preserve the general shape of the original distributions of T scores.

To provide a more representative sample of the U.S. adult population than the original MMPI, MMPI–2 was standardized on 2600 U.S. residents aged 18 to 90 (1138 males and 1462 females) selected according to statistics obtained from the 1980 census on geographic distribution, ethnic and racial composition, age and educational levels, and marital status. Reliability data reported in the MMPI–2 manual (Hathaway & McKinley, 1989) are based on relatively small samples (82 men and 111 women); test–retest coefficients of the basic scales range from .58 to .92. Some of the low reliability coefficients, coupled with the fairly sizable standard errors of measurement, indicate that differences in scores on the various scales should be interpreted cautiously.

Profile Interpretation   Figure 10–1 is a profile of scores on the MMPI–2 obtained by the 60-year-old businessman described in Report 10–2. Although a generally high profile on the clinical scales suggests serious psychological problems, a high T score on a given clinical scale is not necessarily indicative of the disorder with which the scale is labeled. For this and other reasons, the clinical scales are now referred to by their numerical designations. Rather than being based on a single score, a psychiatric diagnosis or personality analysis is made on the basis of the pattern displayed by the entire group of scores. Therefore, the process of profile interpretation begins with profile coding.

Several systems for coding score profiles on the MMPI have been devised, with those of Hathaway and Welsh being the most popular. The coding process begins by arranging the numerical designations of the nine clinical scales and the Social Introversion scale (scale 0), from left to right, in descending order of their T scores. Performing this ranking

TABLE 10–2   Scales on MMPI–2

Basic Validity and Clinical Scales

– Validity:
  (L) Lie, (F) Infrequency, (K) Defensiveness.
  (?) Cannot Say is reported as a raw score.

– Clinical:
  (1) Hs   Hypochondriasis
  (2) D   Depression
  (3) Hy   Conversion Hysteria
  (4) Pd   Psychopathic Deviate
  (5) Mf   Masculinity–Femininity
  (6) Pa   Paranoia
  (7) Pt   Psychasthenia
  (8) Sc   Schizophrenia
  (9) Ma   Hypomania
  (0) Si   Social Introversion

Supplementary Scales

A   Anxiety
R   Repression
Es   Ego Strength
MAC-R   MacAndrew Alcoholism–Revised
F_B Back F
TRIN   True Response Inconsistency
VRIN   Variable Response Inconsistency
O-H   Overcontrolled Hostility
Do   Dominance
Re   Social Responsibility
Mt   College Maladjustment
GM   Gender Role–Masculine
GF   Gender Role–Feminine
PK   Post-Traumatic Stress
         Disorder–Keane
PS   Post-Traumatic Stress
         Disorder–Schlenger
Si_1 Shyness/Self-consciousness
Si_2 Social Avoidance
Si_3 Alienation–Self and Others

Content Scales, newly developed for the MMPI-2

ANX   Anxiety
FRS   Fears
OBS   Obsessiveness
DEP   Depression
HEA   Health Concerns
BIZ   Bizarre Mentation
ANG   Anger
CYN   Cynicism
ASP   Antisocial Practices

Harris–Lingoes Subscales

D_1 Subjective Depression
D_2 Psychomotor Retardation
D_3 Physical Malfunctioning
D_4 Mental Dullness
D_5 Brooding
Hy_1 Denial of Social Anxiety
Hy_2 Need for Affection
Hy_3 Lassitude–Malaise
Hy_4 Somatic Complaints
Hy_5 Inhibition of Aggression
Pd_1 Familial Discord
Pd_2 Authority Problems
Pd_3 Social Imperturbability
Pd_4 Social Alienation
Pd_5 Self-alienation
Pa_1 Persecutory Ideas
Pa_2 Poignancy
Pa_3 Naivete
Sc_1 Social Alienation
Sc_2 Emotional alienation
Sc_3 Lack of Ego Mastery, Cognitive
Sc_4 Lack of Ego Mastery, Conative
Sc_5 Lack of Ego Mastery, Defective
        Inhibition
Sc_6 Bizarre Sensory Experiences
Ma_1 Amorality
Ma_2 Psychomotor Acceleration
Ma_3 Imperturbability
Ma_4 Ego Inflation

Wiener–Harmon Subtle–Obvious Subscal

D-O   Depression, Obvious
D-S   Depression, Subtle
Hy-O   Hysteria, Obvious
Hy-S   Hysteria, Subtle
Pd-O   Psychopathic Deviate, Obvious
Pd-S   Psychopathic Deviate, Subtle
Pa-O   Paranoia, Obvious
Pa-S   Paranoia, Subtle
Ma-O   Hypomania, Obvious
Ma-S   Hypomania, Subtle

TABLE 10–2   (continued)

TPA	Type A
LSE	Low Self-esteem
SOD	Social Discomfort
FAM	Family Problems
WRK	Work Interference
TRT	Negative Treatment Indicators

process for the profile in Figure 10–1 yields 1267039845. Both Hathaway's and Welsh's profile coding systems require placing a prime (') after the number of the last scale having a *T* score of 70 or greater and a dash (-) after the number of the last scale having a *T* score of 60 or greater. The numerical designations of scales having *T* score values within 1 point of each other are underlined, and scores on the L, F, and K scales are placed after the profile code. The complete Welsh code for the profile in Figure 10–1 is 12-670 39/ 845/*LK*:F.

A number of interpretive computer programs based on prerecorded rules for the configural or pattern analysis of MMPI and MMPI–2 scores have been developed. Despite the seeming expertise and plausibility of many of these computer-based interpretations, we must be careful not to overmechanize the process of profile interpretation. Machines, as well as people, make mistakes, but we are often readier to trust the former than the latter.

In interpreting an MMPI or MMPI–2 profile, special attention is given to scales having high *T* scores (above 65 or 70). Scale 2 is considered to be a measure of depression and scale 7 a measure of anxiety, tension, or alertness to unknown danger. Since depression and anxiety are the most common symptoms of mental disorder, psychiatric patients typically have high scores on scale 2, scale 7, or both. High scores on both scales 2 and 7 point to a combination of anxiety and depression. Other patterns of high scores indicate other symptoms. For example, high scores on scales 4 and 9 suggest impulsiveness, low frustration tolerance, rebelliousness, and hostile aggression. High scores on scales 6 and 8 point to withdrawal, apathy, and paranoid delusions.

Special terms have become associated with certain patterns of high scores on the MMPI clinical scales. Scales 1, 2, and 3 are referred to as the "neurotic triad," because high scores on these scales are so often associated with psychoneurotic problems. When the *T* scores on all three scales are above 70, but scale 2 is lower than scales 1 and 3, the picture is referred to as a "conversion V" and associated with a diagnosis of conversion hysteria. At the other end of the profile, scales 6, 7, 8, and 9 are referred to as the "psychotic tetrad"; high scores on these four scales are associated with psychotic problems. When the *T* scores on these four scales are all above 70, but the *T* scores on scales 7 and 9 are lower than those on scales 6 and 8, the picture is referred to as a "paranoid valley" and is suggestive of a diagnosis of paranoid schizophrenia.

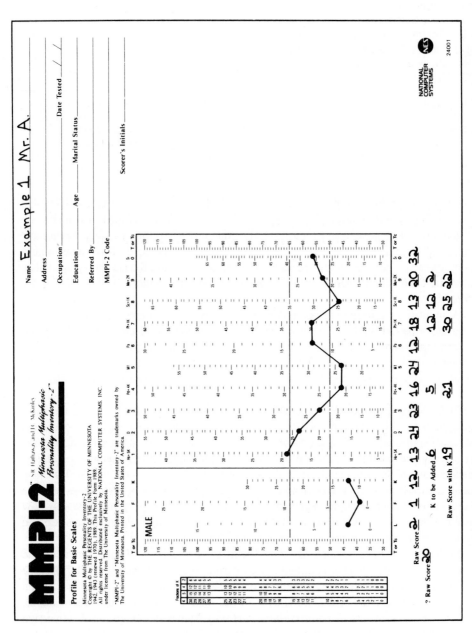

FIGURE 10–1 Sample Profile of Scores on MMPI–2. See Report 10–2.
(From Minnesota Multiphasic Personality Inventory–2, copyright © The Regents of the University of Minnesota, 1942, 1943 (renewed 1979, 1989). All rights reserved.)

REPORT 10–2 Interpretive Report of Scores on MMPI–2 Profile in Figure 10–1

Mr. A was seen in a medical outpatient service complaining of a variety of abdominal pains and distress. He is a sixty-year-old businessman, white, married, with two years of college. Little evidence could be found for an organic basis for his complaints, and he was referred for psychological assessment.

The profile he obtained on the MMPI–2 is shown in Figure 10–1; the code is 12-670 39/ 845/LK:F. All the traditional validity indicators are below the mean and suggest that he was very cooperative with the test. There is no evidence of defensiveness or of intention to distort his self-presentation on the inventory. His L and K scores fell in the ranges that raise the possibility that he was deliberately faking a poor adjustment, but his score on the F scale does not indicate that this is true. The correlates of these validity indicators suggest that this man is open, conventional, likely to display his problems, but is not in the midst of a serious emotional crisis.

On scale 1, his highest clinical score, he earned a T score of 66. A score in the high range on this scale suggests that he is rather self-centered and demanding, pessimistic and defeatist in his view of the future, and is likely to overreact to any real problems. It is likely Mr. A will have numerous physical complaints that will shift to different places on his body.

His second highest score is on scale 2 and it falls in the moderate range. This score also suggests that he is pessimistic and discouraged about the future. He is dissatisfied with himself or the world, is worrying and moody. His temperament is introverted, but he is a responsible and modest individual.

Three other scores fall within the moderate range: scales 6, 7, and 0. These scores also characterize Mr. A as responsible, hard-working, and reserved.

Individuals with 12/21 profiles show an exaggerated reaction to physical disorders, are prone to fatigue, and are often shy, irritable, seclusive, and depressed. Visceral pain, overconcern with bodily functions, and lack of insight are prominent features.

The scale-by-scale analysis of this man's profile highlights some hypochondriacal and depressive trends in an introverted, moody, and hard-working man. The code type characteristics are present but only to a moderate degree, as would be expected for profile elevations of this magnitude.

These characterizations are clearly borne out in the background information about Mr. A. He was married at the age of 25 to his present wife; there have been no marital difficulties. However, Mrs. A has recently quit her job, which resulted in a loss in the family income. They have one child, a son age 25, who is living away from home.

Mr. A has consulted his family physician very frequently in the last year and has made three visits to a Veterans Administration outpatient clinic in the last few months. In addition to his abdominal symptoms, Mr. A has had problems sleeping, complains of chronic fatigue, a loss of interest in sex, and recurring fears of death. He has also lost considerable weight and has had difficulty concentrating in his work. Sedatives have not been helpful. The present diagnostic impression is that Mr. A is suffering from dysthymia (moderate depression) with hypochondriacal features.

Other Criterion-keyed Personality Inventories

Like the Stanford–Binet in intelligence testing, the MMPI has been a parent instrument for a number of other personality inventories. One of these offspring was the Minnesota Counseling Inventory (MCI), which was based on the MMPI and the older Minnesota Personality Scale. In contrast to the MMPI, which has a psychiatric orientation, the MCI was designed as a measure of adjustment in boys and girls in grades 9 through 12. The MCI is now out of print, having been replaced to a large extent by the California Psychological Inventory.

California Psychological Inventory *(Consulting Psychologists Press)*   Of the many empirically validated, MMPI-like inventories that have been devised for "normal" people, the most popular and extensively researched is the California Psychological Inventory (CPI). Designed by Harrison Gough, one-half of the 480 true–false statements on the original version of this inventory of adolescent and adult personality characteristics was taken from the MMPI and the remaining half was new. Unlike the MMPI clinical scales, which emphasize maladjustment and psychiatric disorders, the CPI scales stress more positive, normal aspects of personality.

CPI Scales   The original CPI is scored for the starred (*) scales listed in Table 10–3, three of which, Well-being, Good Impression, and Communality, are validity scales. The first two validity scales were constructed from items that tended to be responded to in a certain way by normal people who were either asked to fake bad (Well-being) or fake good (Good Impression), whereas the Communality score is simply a count of highly popular responses. Eleven of the fifteen remaining scales, like those of the MMPI, were selected by comparing the responses of different groups of people; the other four scales (Social Presence, Self-acceptance, Self-control, and Flexibility) were content validated.

Norms, Reliability, and Validity   The CPI has been more extensively standardized than any other criterion-keyed inventory and, with the exception of the MMPI, is the most thoroughly researched. Its standard score norms are based on the responses of 6000 males and 7000 females of varying ages and socioeconomic status. The test–retest reliability coefficients for all scales except Psychological-mindedness and Communality range from .57 to .77 for high school students over a period of 1 year. Coupled with the fact that the correlations among CPI scales are rather high, the relatively low reliabilities point to problems of differentiating among an examinee's scores on different CPI scales. The situation is somewhat better with respect to differentiating among the mean scale scores of different groups of examinees. Megaree (1972) summarized the results of a variety of studies and discussed the questions of profile interpretation and interactions among the CPI scales. The majority of the validity coefficients for single scales are low, but the usefulness of the CPI as a predictor of grades, delinquency, dropouts, parole violations, and other criteria can be improved by combining scores on several scales by means of multiple-regression equations.

Revised CPI   The revised version of the CPI, published in 1986, consists of 462 items retained or reworded from the original 480-item CPI. Two new scales, Empathy

TABLE 10–3 Basic Scales on the Revised CPI

Interpersonal Style and Manner of Dealing with Others
  *Dominance
  *Capacity for status
  *Sociability
  *Social presence
  *Self-acceptance
  Independence
  Empathy

Internalization and endorsement of Normative Conventions
  *Responsibility
  *Socialization
  *Self-control
  *Good impression
  *Communality
  *Tolerance
  *Well-being

Cognitive and Intellectual Functioning
  *Achievement via conformance
  *Achievement via independence
  *Intellectual efficiency

Thinking and Behavior
  *Psychological-mindedness
  *Flexibility
  *Femininity–Masculinity

Special Scales and Indexes
  Managerial Potential
  Work orientation
  Leadership potential index
  Social maturity index
  Creative potential index

Reprinted by permission of Consulting Psychologists Press.
*Scales on original version of CPI.

and Independence, were added to the original eighteen scales. The Revised CPI can also be scored on the Five Special Scales and Indices listed in Table 10–3.

Another way of classifying the CPI scales is in terms of three conceptual groups. The first group, the folk-concept measures, consists of the 18 original scales plus the Empathy and Independence scales. The second group of measures is comprised of the special-purpose scales, indexes, and regression equations developed by Gough and others (Social Maturity, Type A Living Style, and others). The third group represents a theoretical model containing three major themes: role, character, and competence. Vectors 1, 2, and 3 (v.1, v.2, v.3) assess these three themes (see Figure 10–2). The role or interpersonal orientation (internality versus externality) theme, which is the interpersonal presentation of self inherent in the Capacity for Status, Dominance, Self-acceptance, Sociability, and Social Presence scales, is measured by the new 34-item structural scale v.1. The character

Three Major Vectors

Interpersonal orientation (from externality
to internality)
Normative perspective (from norm-favoring
to norm-questioning)
Realization (from lower to higher levels)

Results in Four Types . . .

Alphas (externally oriented, norm-favoring)
Betas (internally oriented, norm-favoring)
Gammas (externally oriented, norm-questioning)
Deltas (internally oriented, norm-questioning)

And Seven Levels

1 . . . . 2 . . . . 3 . . . . 4 . . . . 5 . . . . 6 7

1 = poor integration and little or no realization of the positive potential of the type	7 = superior integration and realization of the positive potential of the type

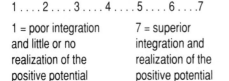

FIGURE 10–2   Structure of the Revised CPI.
(Reprinted by permission of Consulting Psychologists Press.)

(norm favoring versus norm questioning) theme, involving intrapersonal values of the sort assessed by the Responsibility, Socialization, and Self-control scales, is measured by the new 36-item structural scale v.2. The competence or realization theme, involving the Achievement via Conformance, Achievement via Independence, Intellectual Efficiency, Well-being, and Tolerance scales, is measured by the new 58-item structural scale v.3. The three structural scales have zero correlations with each other, but are significantly related to the folk-concept scales.

Scores on v.1 and v.2 were classified separately for 1000 males and 1000 females to create the fourfold typology shown in Figure 10–3. Note the descriptions of the alpha, beta, gamma, and delta personality types in the four quadrants of this figure. In a word, alphas are described as "manipulative," betas as "conventional," gammas as "alienated," and deltas as "conflicted." As depicted in Figure 10–2, the third structural scale (v.3) is divided into seven competence levels; Figure 10–3 is a cross-section at level 4 of v.3. Level 1 is described as "poor integration and little or no realization of the positive potential of the type" and level 7 of v.3 as "superior integration and realization of the positive potential of the type" (the "type" being alpha, beta, gamma, or delta). Levels 2 through 6 are assigned descriptions intermediate between these two extremes. Thus, various scores on v.1, v.2, and v.3 can be combined to produce a total of 4 types × 7 levels = 28 different personality configurations.

Personality Inventory for Children   Because of the low reading comprehension of most children, self-report personality inventories are less reliable and valid when used with

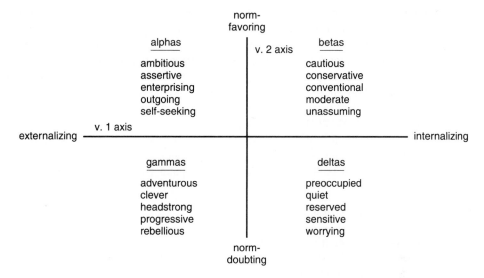

FIGURE 10–3 Theoretical Model for the v.1 and v.2 Structural Scales of the California Psychological Inventory. The Figure Depicts the Role (v.1) and Character (v.2) Type Quadrants at Level 4 (Average) on Competence (v.3). *(Reprinted by permission of Consulting Psychologists Press, Inc., from the Manual of the California Psychological Inventory, Revised Edition, copyright 1987.)*

children. Although there are a number of inventories on which children rate themselves, for example, the Children's Personality Questionnaire (The Psychological Corporation), instruments on which adults rate children are perhaps more valid. An example is the Personality Inventory for Children (PIC). This MMPI-based inventory of 660 true–false items concerning child behavior is completed by a parent, usually the mother, or other caretaker of the child. The PIC was standardized on 2400 normal boys and girls ranging in age from 6 to 16 years and 200 normal boys and girls aged 3 to 5 years. The 16 primary scales on which the PIC is scored consist of 3 validity scales (Lie, F or deviant responding, and Defensiveness), 12 clinical scales, and a screening scale (Adjustment) to identify children needing psychological evaluation. Scores on 17 experimental scales may also be determined. The clinical scales were designed to identify certain emotional and interpersonal problems, in addition to assessing the child's cognitive development and the psychological climate of the family. The scores are profiled separately by sex and age group (3 to 5 and 6 to 16 years) and can be interpreted by computer (see Wirt & Lachar, 1981). A Revised Format PIC, in which the items are rearranged into four parts to provide meaningful results without the parent having to respond to all 600 items, was published in 1982.

Millon Clinical Multiaxial Inventory (MCMI) *(National Computer Systems)* This inventory and a revision of it, both designed by Theodore Millon, consist of 175 brief, self-descriptive true–false statements written at an eighth-grade level. These inventories are appropriate for clinical patients aged 17 years and older. In revising the

MCMI to produce the MCMI–II, 45 of the items were reworded or replaced and the number of clinical scales was increased to 22, with three correction scales (see Table 10–4). The designations of these scales follow the personality theory described in Millon's *Modern Psychopathology* (1969) textbook, a theory that also influenced the development of the third edition of the *Diagnostic and Statistical Manual of Mental Disorders* (DSM–III) (American Psychiatric Association, 1980). MCMI–II was also designed to coordinate with the categories of personality disorders and clinical syndromes incorporated in the revised version of DSM–III (DMS–III–R).

Administration of the MCMI–II follows a procedure similar to that for the MMPI and CPI, but requires less time (25 to 30 minutes) than the last two inventories. The MCMI–II must be scored by National Computer Systems. Raw scores on the various

TABLE 10–4   MCMI–II Scales

Modifier Indices (Correction Scales)
  Scale X   Disclosure
  Scale Y   Desirability
  Scale Z   Debasement

Clinical Personality Pattern Scales
(DSM–II–R Axis II)
  Scale 1   Schizoid
  Scale 2   Avoidant
  Scale 3   Dependent
  Scale 4   Histrionic
  Scale 5   Narcissistic
  Scale 6   Antisocial
  Scale 6B   Aggressive–Sadistic
  Scale 7   Compulsive
  Scale 8A   Passive–Aggressive
  Scale 8B   Self-defeating

Severe Personality Pathology Scales
  Scale S   Schizotypal
  Scale C   Borderline
  Scale P   Paranoid

Clinical Syndrome Scales (DSM–III–R Axis I)
  Scale A   Anxiety Disorder
  Scale H   Somatoform Disorder
  Scale N   Bipolar: Manic Disorder
  Scale D   Dysthymic Disorder
  Scale B   Alcohol Dependence
  Scale T   Drug Dependence

Severe Clinical Syndrome Scales
  Scale SS   Thought Disorder
  Scale CC   Major Depression
  Scale PP   Delusional Disorder

scales are weighted and converted to *base rate scores,* which take into account the incidence of a particular characteristic or disorder in the general population. By determining the incidence of a particular personality disorder or trait in a specific population, raw scores can be transformed in such a way that the ratio of the number of correct classifications (valid positives) to the number of incorrect classifications (false positives) is maximized. In addition to a list of scores and a score profile, a narrative interpretation is provided. The narrative portion of the report gives a statement concerning the validity of the responses, provides interpretations for both Clinical Syndromes and Personality Patterns, and lists statements involving noteworthy responses by the examinee; parallel DSM–III–R multiaxial diagnoses, and therapeutic implications.

The norm group for the MCMI–II consisted of a sample of 1292 men and women patients throughout the United States who were being treated for a variety of problems in clinics, hospitals, and private practices. The average test–retest reliabilities of the scales range from .81 to .87 over 1 week and from .67 to .82 over 5 weeks; internal consistency coefficients average .82 to .90. Some evidence for the validity of the scales is found in their correlations with a number of psychiatric checklists and inventories.

Jackson's Inventories

More recent efforts to construct personality inventories have taken place in an atmosphere of renewed interest in personality research and a greater appreciation of its complexities. Rather than relying on a single approach—content (rational), theoretical, factor analytic, or empirical—the development of new assessment instruments has involved a combination of procedures. Representative of this new level of sophistication in personality test construction are the inventories designed to D. N. Jackson. Jackson's overall approach to inventory construction began with detailed descriptions of the characteristics to be measured. Next a large pool of items was written or collected and administered to a sizable, representative sample of people. Using the trait descriptions prepared at the outset, judges' ratings of the examinees on these traits were also obtained. In analyzing the data, the item responses of separate samples of examinees were subjected to different item analyses. A statistical, computer-based procedure was employed to ensure that correlations among the items constituting a given scale were high, but that correlations among different scales were low.

Personality Research Form (PRF) *(Sigma Assessment Systems)* The PRF is a true–false personality inventory designed for grade 6 through adulthood. The PRF takes 35 to 75 minutes to complete, depending on the form. There are five forms: Form E consists of 352 items, parallel Forms AA and BB of 440 items each, and parallel Forms A and B of 300 items each. Based on Henry Murray's trait theory of personality, each of the 15 scales of Forms A and B and the 22 scales of Forms AA, BB, and E consists of 20 items. Many of these scales bear the same names as those listed in the description of the Edwards Personal Preference Schedule. In addition to the content scales, all forms are scored on an Infrequency scale consisting of rarely marked items; Forms AA, BB, and E are also scored on a Social Desirability scale.

The PRF was standardized on 1000 men and 1000 women in 30 colleges. Internal consistency and test–retest reliability coefficients for the 14 content scales common to all five forms cluster around .80, but the reliabilities of the six additional content scales on Forms AA, BB, and E fall into the .50s. Validity coefficients obtained by correlating the content scales with ratings on behavior and a specially devised trait-rating form are in the .50s. Evidence for convergent and discriminant validity is also reported in the PRF manual.

Jackson Personality Inventory (Sigma Assessment Systems)   Like the PRF, the Jackson Personality Inventory (JPI) was designed for adolescents and adults. It is comprised of 320 true–false items and takes about 1 hour to complete. The JPI has a more social or interpersonal orientation than the PRF, providing a method of predicting behavior in a variety of practical settings (business, industrial, educational, recreational), as well as in clinical and counseling situations. The construction methodology for the JPI was even more sophisticated than that for the PRF. Separate item analyses of a large item pool administered to two samples of people were conducted to maximize content variances in relation to social desirability variance, to maximize item variance, and to minimize the overlap among scales.

The JPI is scored on the following 15 substantive, or content, scales, plus an Infrequency scale:

Anxiety	Innovation	Self-esteem
Breadth of Interest	Interpersonal Affect	Social Adroitness
Complexity	Organization	Social Participation
Conformity	Responsibility	Tolerance
Energy Level	Risk Taking	Value Orthodoxy

Norms on samples of 2000 males and 2000 females from 43 North American colleges and universities, in addition to separate high school norms, are available. Internal consistency reliability coefficients for the separate scales range from .75 to .95, averaging around .90. With respect to the validity of the JPI, the correlations of scores on the 15 scales with ratings of the same traits are moderate (.38 with peer ratings, .56 with self-ratings, and .70 with relevant adjective checklist variables). Correlations with other criteria (occupational preference, attitude toward marijuana use, and so forth) are listed in the manual. Like the Personality Research Form, the Jackson Personality Inventory has good potential. Neither inventory has experienced widespread use, so their potentials have yet to be realized.

PROJECTIVE TECHNIQUES

Projective technique is a term coined by Lawrence Frank (1939) for ambiguous stimuli on which respondents can "project" their inner needs and feelings. Projective techniques are composed of relatively unstructured stimuli and/or tasks that an examinee is asked to describe, tell a story about, complete, or respond to in some other manner. In contrast to the more direct personality inventories and rating scales, projective techniques are usually less obvious in their intent and therefore presumably less subject to faking and response sets. Because projectives are relatively unstructured in content and open ended in terms of the responses obtained, it is assumed that the structure imposed on the stimulus material or task is a reflection or *projection* of the examinee's own individual perception of the world. It is also assumed that, as the task becomes less structured, the responses are more likely to reveal important facets of personality.

According to their advocates, projective techniques can tap deeper layers of personality, of which even the examinee may be unaware. Projectives do not, however, provide an "open Sesame" to the unconscious or an X-ray of the mind. Furthermore, their lack of structure is a two-edged sword in that it can result in a wealth of responses that are difficult to evaluate. As a consequence of scoring problems, most projective techniques fail to meet conventional standards of reliability and validity. The validity coefficients of projectives obtained using assorted criteria are generally low, reflecting situational factors as well as subjectivity in scoring and interpretation.

Because projectives attempt to get at unconscious processes, interpretation of responses to the test materials have been greatly influenced by psychoanalytic theory. It is therefore not surprising that the periods of greatest increase in the use of projective techniques was 1940 to 1960, a time when psychoanalytic thinking exerted a particularly strong influence on personality theory and research. In addition to being influenced by psychoanalysis and other psychodynamic theories, psychologists who interpret projective test protocols usually try to form an overall impression of the examinee's personality by searching for consistencies and outstanding features in the pattern of responses. As a consequence, administering and scoring a typical projective test requires more training and sensitivity than for a self-report inventory. Even so, psychologists who are presumably well trained in these techniques frequently disagree in their interpretations of responses to projectives. For these reasons, the interpretations described in the following sections, and analyses of responses to projectives in general, should be viewed as hypotheses or possibilities, rather than substantiated fact. Consider the following interpretations of figure drawings:

Large size: Emotional expansiveness or acting-out behavior

Small size: Emotional constriction, withdrawal or timidity

Erasures around buttocks of male figure; long eyelashes on male figure: overt or latent homosexuality

Overworking of lines: tension and aggressive behavior, possible delusional thinking

Distorted or omitted facial or other body features: conflict pertaining to that feature or organ

These interpretations may seem plausible and reasonable, but they are based to a large extent on stereotypes or illusory correlations and are more often wrong than right. Clinical psychologists and psychiatrists should not make the mistake of concluding that something is true simply because it appears reasonable. Rather, they should view interpretations (both theirs and others') of projective responses only as suggested explanations that may or may not be confirmed by other sources of information about a person.

Word Associations and Construction Techniques

Various projective techniques have been devised to detect less obvious motives, conflicts, problems, and other covert intrapersonal characteristics. Of these, semistructured techniques such as word associations and sentence completions are perhaps closest to self-report inventories in terms of design and format.

Word Associations   The method of word association was introduced by Francis Galton (1879) and first applied clinically by Carl Jung (1910) to detect neurotic conflicts. A series of words is read aloud to the examinee, who has been instructed to respond to each word with the first word that comes to mind. Clinical applications of the technique involve interspersing among neutral words emotionally loaded words or words of special significance to the examinee. Long response times or bizarre associations may be symptomatic of emotional disturbance. The degree to which certain words are emotionally arousing may also be determined by measuring skin conductance, muscle tension, respiration rate, blood pressure, pulse rate, voice tremors, or other physiological reactions to the stimulus words.

As with all projective techniques, the responses on a word-association test should be interpreted against a backdrop of other information concerning the person. A general principle that has guided psychoanalytic interpretations of language is that nouns are more likely than verbs to be disguised expressions of needs and conflicts. This is so because, according to Freudian theory, it is easier to alter the object of a desire (a noun) than its direction (a verb).

Many clinical psychologists prefer to make up their own word lists, but standardized lists are available. An example is the Kent–Rosanoff Free Association Test, a standard list of 100 words and the corresponding associations of 1000 adults. The Kent–Rosanoff, published originally in 1910, is one of the oldest psychological tests in use.

Sentence Completions   Asking a person to complete specially prepared incomplete sentences is a flexible, easily administered projective technique first described by Payne (1928). A variety of sentence fragments related to possible areas of emotion and conflict can be constructed, illustrative of which are the following:

My greatest fear _____.

I only wish my mother had _____.

The thing that bothers me most _____.

It is assumed that the respondent's wishes, desires, fears, and attitudes are reflected in the content of his or her completion responses.

Despite the fact that they are more obvious than many other projective techniques, sentence completions are considered to be one of the most valid of all projective techniques for diagnostic and research purposes (Goldberg, 1965). The reliability and validity of sentence completions are higher when objective, rather than impressionistic, scoring and interpretations are employed. As with the MMPI and other criterion-keyed instruments, empirical keys can be constructed for both word associations and sentence completions.

Sentence completion tests may be constructed for a particular clinical case or personality research study, but a half-dozen or so instruments of this kind are commercially available. Examples are the Activity Completion Technique (Psychological Assessment Resources), the Bloom Sentence Completion Survey (Stoelting Co.), the Geriatric Sentence Completion Form (Psychological Assessment Resources), and the Rotter Incomplete Sentences Blank (The Psychological Corporation). The 60 sentence stems of the Activity Completion Technique cover the areas of Family, Interpersonal, Affect, and Self-Concept. The Bloom consists of two 40-stem forms (student and adult) covering eight areas (age mates or other people, physical self, family, psychological self, self-directedness, education and work, accomplishment, and irritants). The 30-item Geriatric Sentence Completion Form, designed for older adults, is scored on four content domains: physical, psychological, social, and temporal orientation. Finally, the 40 sentence fragments on each of the three forms (high school, college, and adult) of the Rotter blank are scored in three categories: conflict or unhealthy responses, neutral responses, and positive or healthy responses.

Rosenzweig Picture-frustration Study *(Psychological Assessment Resources)* Another projective device that requires examinees to construct verbal responses to partially verbal stimuli is the Resenzweig Picture-frustration Study (Rosenzweig, 1978). Each of the three forms (child, adolescent, and adult) of this instrument consists of 24 cartoons; each cartoon depicts an individual in a frustrating situation. The directions are to indicate, by writing in the balloon above the frustrated person's head, the first verbal response that comes to mind as being made by this anonymous person (Figure 10–4). Responses are scored according to the direction of aggression and

FIGURE 10–4 Item from Rosenzweig Picture-frustration Study.
(Copyright 1964 by Saul Rosenzweig. Reproduced by permission.)

the type of aggression expressed. Included under direction of aggression are extraggression (outwardly, or toward the environment), intraggression (inwardly, toward oneself), or imaggression (avoidance or nonexpression of aggression). Included under type of aggression are obstacle-dominance or O-D (the frustrating object stands out), etho-defense or E-D (the examinee's ego predominates to defend itself), and need-persistence or N-P (the goal is pursued despite the frustration). Interpretation of scores is in terms of frustration theory and the available norms on the instrument. The Rosenzweig Picture-frustration Study has been used in a large number of research investigations worldwide on the nature of frustration and its correlations with other variables (see Rosenzweig, 1978).

Projective Drawings   Procedures requiring oral or written responses to words and sentences are only one of many construction tasks that qualify as protective techniques. Other nonverbal materials that have been employed are clay paints, building materials, and colored chips. Handwriting analysis, although it has not received wide acceptance among psychologists, also has its proponents (Holt, 1974). Even more popular have been drawings of people and other objects, such as on the Draw-a-Person Test (Machover, 1971) and the House–Tree–Person Technique.

On the Draw-a-Person Test, an examinee's drawings of people of the same and opposite sex are interpreted in terms of the placement of various features of the drawings (sex, quality, position, clothing, and so forth). Specialists in the technique maintain that there is a tendency for examinees to project impulses that are acceptable to them onto the same-sex figure and impulses unacceptable to them onto the opposite-sex figure. Particular aspects of the drawings are considered to be indicative of certain personality characteristics or psychopathological conditions. Large eyelashes on persons in the drawings are said to be indicative of hysteria; many clothing details suggest neurosis; large drawings indicate acting out of impulses; and dark, heavy shading suggests strong aggressive impulses. Small drawings, few facial features, or a dejected facial expression point to depression; few body periphery details indicate suicidal tendencies; and few physical features suggest psychosis or organic brain damage (Kaplan & Sadock, 1989).

Rorschach Psychodiagnostic Technique

The Swiss psychiatrist Hermann Rorschach was not the first person to use inkblots to study personality, but he provided the first widely accepted set of blots and a standard approach to administering them and interpreting the responses.

The stimulus materials for the Rorschach Psychodiagnostic Technique, which were published initially in 1921, are ten $5\frac{1}{2}$ by $9\frac{1}{2}$ inch cards. Each card contains one bilaterally symmetrical, black-and-white (five cards), red-and-gray (two cards), or multicolored (three cards) inkblot similar to the one in Figure 10–5. The cards are presented individually and viewed at no greater than arm's length, but turning the card is permitted. The examinee is told to report what he or she sees in the blot or what it might represent. To illustrate, a young woman in her senior year of college gave the following response to the inkblot in Figure 10–5 10 seconds after it was shown:

FIGURE 10–5   Inkblot Similar to Those on the Rorschach Psychodiagnostic Technique.

My first impression was a big bug, a fly maybe. I see in the background two face-like figures pointing toward each other as if they're talking. It also resembles a skeleton, the pelvis area. I see a cute little bat right in the middle. The upper half looks like a mouse.

After all the cards have been presented, the examiner may start over with Card I and ask the examinee what features (shape, color, shading, and so on) of the card determined his or her responses. Following this *inquiry* period, there may be a further *testing the limits* period to discover whether the examinee can see certain things in the cards.

A number of scoring methods for the Rorschach have been proposed, the most recent one being John Exner's (1978, 1986; Exner & Weiner, 1982) revised scoring compendium. Every response given to a Rorschach card may be scored on several categories:

Location, where it was seen: the whole blot (W), a common detail (D), an uncommon detail (Dd), or, if the white space on the card was used in responding, WS, DS, or DdS.

Determinant, what aspects of the blot determined the response: form (F), color (C), shading–texture (T), shading–dimension (V), shading–diffuse (Y), chromatic color (C), achromatic color (C'), movement (M), or combinations of these.

Content: anatomy (An), blood (Bl), clouds (Cl), fire (Fi), geography (Ge), nature (Na), and so forth.

Popularity: whether the response is a popular or an original one.

The number of responses falling in each category and certain ratios computed from them guide the interpretation of the test protocol as a whole. For example, several good "whole" (W) responses are considered indicative of integrated or organized thinking, whereas color responses suggest emotionally and impulsivity; many detailed responses indicate compulsivity; white-space responses point to oppositional tendencies; and movement responses reveal imagination. The ratio of the number of human movement responses to the number of color responses (*experience balance*) is said to be related to the degree to which a person is thought minded rather than action oriented. The ratio of the number of form responses to the number of color responses is an index of the extent to which the respondent is controlled by cognition rather than emotion. Also important in evaluating a Rorschach protocol is the accuracy of responses, that is, how well the responses fit the respective parts of the blots (good, poor, and indeterminate). Delays in responding may be interpreted as anxiety, a small number of color and movement responses as depression, and several shading responses as self-control. Many original responses having poor form and other indicators of confused thinking suggest a psychotic process.

One of the most reliable scores on the Rorschach, a rough index of mental ability, is a simple count of the total number of responses to the 10 inkblots. Responses may also be interpreted in terms of their content, but the process is very subjective. For example, unreal characters such as ghosts and clowns are interpreted as indicative of an inability to identify with real people and masks as role playing to avoid exposure. Food is interpreted as dependency needs or emotional hunger, death as loneliness and depression, and eyes as sensitivity to criticism.

Thousands of articles have been published on the Rorschach Technique, but is has not fared well in reliability and validity studies. Considering the length of time required to administer and score the test, it is unsatisfactory when judged by conventional psychometric criteria. The Rorschach remains popular among clinical psychologists and psychiatrists, however, and it will probably continue to be so until a demonstrably superior method for the depth analysis of personality has been devised.

Holtzman Inkblot Technique

The Holtzman Inkblot Technique (HIT) (The Psychological Corporation) represents an attempt to construct a more objective and precise inkblot test than the Rorschach. The two parallel forms of the HIT (A and B) consist of 45 blots each; the examinee is limited to one response per blot. Each of the blots was selected on the basis of its high split-half reliability and its ability to differentiate between normal and pathological responses to the blot. The HIT blots are more varied than those on the Rorschach: some are asymmetrical, and some have colors and different visual textures. The HIT can be scored on the 22 response categories developed by computer analysis of hundreds of test protocols. The percentile norms for these 22 scores are based on eight groups of examinees, normal and pathological, ranging in age from 5 years to adulthood.

Because the construction and standardization of the HIT were more like those of a personality inventory than the Rorschach, it is not surprising that the reliability of the HIT is higher than that of the Rorschach. As with the Rorschach, however, a great deal of work on the validity of the HIT remains to be done. The validity of projectives in general for assisting in the task of making decisions about people has not been adequately demonstrated, and in spite of its limitations the Holtzman Inkblot Technique is one of the few instruments in this category that come even close to meeting the psychometric standards of a good test.

Apperception Tests

Less structured than word associations and incomplete sentences, but more structured than inkblots, are pictures or other materials about which the examinee is asked to tell a story. The majority of these *apperception tests* employ pictures of people or animals, but one (the Hand Test) is composed of pictures of hands and another (the Auditory Apperception Test) of auditory stimuli. Nearly all apperception tests call for open-ended responses, but at least one (Iowa Picture Interpretation) has a multiple-choice format. The directions for the various picture-story tests are similar: the examinee is asked to tell a story about each picture, including what is going on at the moment, what led up to it, and what the outcome might be.

Thematic Apperception Test (TAT) *(The Psychological Corporation)*   Next to the Rorschach, the most popular projective technique in terms of research citations and clinical usage is the Thematic Apperception Test. The TAT materials consist of 30 black-and-white picture cards (four overlapping sets of 19 cards each for boys, girls, men, and women) depicting people in ambiguous situations, plus 1 blank card. The usual administration procedure is to ask the examinee to tell a complete story about each of 19 picture cards selected as appropriate for his or her age and sex and the single blank card. Examinees are asked to devote approximately 5 minutes to each story, telling what's going on now, what thoughts and feelings the people in the story have, what events led up to the situation, and how it will turn out. For example, one of the pictures shows a young woman in the foreground and a weird old woman with a shawl over her head grimacing in the background. The following story was told by a young college woman in response to this picture:

This is a woman who has been quite troubled by memories of a mother she was resentful toward. She has feelings of sorrow for the way she treated her mother; her memories of her mother plague her. These feelings seem to be increasing as she grows older and sees her children treating her the same way that she treated her mother. She tries to convey the feeling to her own children, but does not succeed in changing their attitudes. She is living the past in her present, because this feeling of sorrow and guilt is reinforced by the way her children are treating her.

From stories such as this, the skilled examiner gains information about the dominant needs, emotions, sentiments, complexes, and conflicts of the storyteller and the pressures to which he or she is subjected. TAT responses can be especially useful in understanding the relations and difficulties between a person and his or her parents.

As with other projective techniques, when interpreting the TAT it is assumed that respondents project their own needs, desires, and conflicts into the stories and the characters. Interpreting these stories is a fairly subjective, impressionistic process centered on an analysis of the needs and personality of the main character (the *hero* or *heroine*), who presumably represents the examinee, and the environmental forces (*press*) impinging on the main character. The frequency, intensity, and duration of the story are all taken into account in the interpretation.

The following are illustrative of the TAT responses or signs that certain psychologists consider indicative of mental disorders of various kinds. Slowness or delays in responding may indicate depression. Stories by men that involve negative comments about women or affection for other men may point to homosexuality. Overcautiousness and preoccupation with details are suggestive of obsessive–compulsive disorder.

Although the usual methods of scoring and interpreting the TAT are highly impression-istic, the scores determined by one of the more systematic scoring procedures are fairly reliable and can be interpreted in terms of norms based on standardization studies (see Bellak, 1986). Asking a person to tell stories about pictures would also seem to have potentially greater validity in personality studies than asking for responses to inkblots. TAT stories are, however, affected by the particular environmental context in which the test is taken, and they do not always differentiate between normal and mentally disordered persons (Eron, 1950). Furthermore, many psychologists maintain that amorphous stimuli such as inkblots are more effective than picture stories in revealing unconscious conflicts and repressed desires. This claim has never been adequately verified, and the validity of picture stories is less disputed than that of responses to inkblots. Even so, the TAT has not proved to be as popular as the Rorschach for purposes of psychiatric diagnosis.

Modifications of the TAT   The TAT has been used with a wide range of ethnic and chronological age groups, and various modifications have been constructed for blacks, children, and the elderly. On the assumption that blacks identify more closely with pictures of other blacks than with those of whites, 21 of the original TAT pictures were redrawn with black figures and published as the Thompson Modification of the TAT. Two other special versions of the TAT are the Senior Apperception Test and the Children's Appercep-tion Test.

Senior Apperception Technique (The Psychological Corporation and Psy-chological Assessment Resources)   The 16 stimulus pictures on this test, which was designed specifically for older adults, reflect themes of loneliness, uselessness, illness, helplessness, and lowered self-esteem, in addition to positive and happier situations. As in the case of the Gerontological Apperception Test (Wolk & Wolk, 1971), a similar instrument, responses to the pictures on the Senior Apperception Technique reflect serious concerns about health, getting along with other people, and being placed in a nursing or retirement home. Both tests have been criticized for inadequate norms and possible stereotyping of the elderly.

Children's Apperception Test (The Psychological Corporation and Psycho-logical Assessment Resources)   Based on the perhaps questionable premise that young children (3 to 10 years) identify more closely with animals than with humans, the CAT consists of 10 pictures of animals in various situations. An extension of the CAT to older children, the CAT–H, is composed of pictures of humans in situations paralleling those of the CAT animal pictures. The stories on both the CAT and CAT–H are interpreted from the viewpoint of psychodynamic theory, specifically in terms of conflicts, anxiety, and guilt. A checklist, the Haworth Schedule of Adaptive Mechanisms, is available to assist in interpreting CAT and CAT–H stories.

Other Apperception Tests   Unfortunately, the lack of representativeness and variety of the stimulus materials and the lack of psychometric rigor in design, standardization, and validation for which the TAT has been criticized also apply to the modifications described above. Somewhat sounder from a psychometric viewpoint than the Children's Apperception Test are the Michigan Picture Test and the Children's Apperception Story-Telling Test.

The Michigan Picture Test–Revised (The Psychological Corporation) is one of the best picture story tests for older children (8 to 14 years), because a genuine effort was made to meet the requirements of adequate standardization and reliability. Seven of the 15 pictures (one blank) on the test are appropriate for both sexes, with 4 being exclusively for girls and 4 for boys. Responses to the social and emotional situations depicted in the pictures are scored for a "Tension Index" (needs for love, extropunitiveness–intropunitiveness, succorance, superiority, submission, and personal adequacy), "Direction of Force" (whether the central figure acts or is acted on), and "Verb Tense" (tense of verbs used by examinee). Although interscorer reliability coefficients are moderately high and the results of cross-validation studies have been reported, evidence for the validity of the test is inadequate.

More recently published than the Michigan Picture Test is the Children's Apperceptive Story-Telling Test (CAST) (pro.ed and Psychological Assessment Resources). Based on Adlerian theory and designed to evaluate the emotional functioning of children aged 6 through 13, CAST consists of 31 colorful pictures to which children make up stories (see Figure 10–6) (Schneider, 1989; Schneider & Perney, 1990). CAST was constructed to be

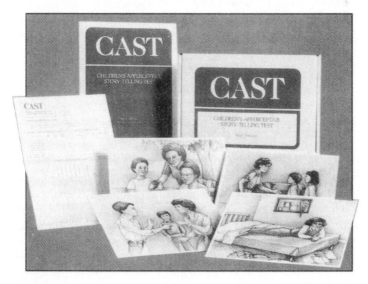

FIGURE 10–6   Sample Materials on the Children's Apperceptive Story-telling Test.
(Reprinted by permission of pro.ed.)

racially sensitive and was standardized on a sample of 876 U.S. children selected as representative. The test is scored on four factors (adaptive, nonadaptive, immature, and uninvested). Internal consistency and test–retest reliability coefficients of the factor scores are reported as being in the .80s and .90s. Some evidence for the content, criterion-related, and construct validity, including score profiles for several clinical groups of children (attention deficit, conduct, anxiety, opposition, and depressive disorders), are reported in the manual.

Problems with Projectives

Although some projectives are better than others, as this brief overview has shown, these techniques leave much to be desired from a strictly psychometric standpoint. Among their shortcomings are inadequacies of administration, scoring, and standardization. The lack of objectivity in scoring and the paucity and deficiency of representative normative data are particularly bothersome to specialists in psychometrics. Nevertheless, repeated criticisms from these specialists have not greatly dampened the enthusiasm of clinical psychologists and psychiatrists for projective techniques. For example, a survey of the members of the Society for Personality Assessment found that the Rorschach and the TAT were ranked second and fourth, respectively, in terms of usage among all psychometric instruments (Piotrowski, Sherry, & Keller, 1985). Other popular projectives were the Sentence Completion, Draw-a-Person, House–Tree–Person, Bender–Gestalt, and Children's Apperception Tests.

It may appear as if clinicians, like many laypersons, view projective techniques as possessed of a kind of magic or mystique, making them capable of revealing human personality in greater depth and detail than more consciously controllable and hence fakable personality inventories, rating scales, and interviews. Whatever the reasons may be, research indicates that most people place more faith in personality descriptions based on projective techniques than they do on interpretations based on scores from personality inventories (Snyder, 1974).[3] Many psychometricians view this faith as somewhat misplaced.

OBJECTIVE MEASURES OF PERSONALITY

A definition of personality that includes both affective and cognitive factors has been advocated by certain psychologists for many years. Although measurement specialists have tended to separate the two domains, interest in combined cognitive and affective instruments has grown. Furthermore, dissatisfaction with traditional, self-report techniques for assessing personality has led to a greater emphasis on less obvious but more structured physiological, perceptual, cognitive, and behavioral measures. These indirect, relatively objective indexes of personality are favored because the responses are not so much under

---

[3]Perhaps soap operas, murder mysteries, and other "human interest" programs on television and in the other media have made people more suspicious of others and more inclined to accept deep, convoluted explanations for behaviors that are usually explicable in terms of fairly ordinary human motives.

conscious control, cannot be easily faked, and are not as greatly influenced by response sets as are scores on traditional assessment procedures.

Physiological Measures

Many types of instruments have been applied to measure physiological responses produced by stressful or arousing situations. Among these are responses obtained by a polygraph ("lie detector"), which measures blood pressure, respiration rate, and the electrical resistance of the skin (galvanic skin response, or GSR).[4] Changes in blood chemistry, brain waves, pupillary diameter, finger and penis volume, muscle tension, and voice tone or tremors have also been analyzed. These reactions, which are regulated by the autonomic, reticular, and other parts of the nervous system, are frequently used as indexes of emotional arousal. They are, however, rather imprecise measures of response intensity and reveal little or nothing about the specific emotion or feeling being experienced. An occasional investigation has found certain physiological or biochemical differences between emotions such as fear and anger (for example, Funkenstein, King, & Drolette, 1957), but research generally has failed to reveal any reliably distinctive physiological response patterns associated with different emotions or personality characteristics. It may be that further research involving biofeedback of physiological state, for example, will yield information of value in personality assessment, but it is unlikely that such methods will replace paper-and-pencil inventories and other traditional assessment procedures.

Perceptual and Cognitive Measures

A significant amount of research has found moderate relationships between personality characteristics and certain aspects of perception and cognition. For example, it has been demonstrated that, compared with extroverts, introverts are more vigilant, more sensitive to pain, more easily bored, more cautious, and more disrupted by overstimulation (Wilson, 1978). Speed of responding on several perceptual and learning tasks (for example, word recognition, identification of incomplete figures, dark adaptation, and conditioning) is also related to personality (Eysenck, 1962; Eysenck & Rachman, 1965). The majority of these tasks are, however, rather crude measures, and they show no immediate signs of replacing traditional personality assessment devices.

[4]Polygraph tests have been used extensively in industry to screen out dishonest workers and by government to detect security risks. Despite their wide usage, it has been estimated that polygraph tests are accurate in only about 65% of the cases and are more likely to declare innocent people guilty than they are to find guilty people innocent (Lykken, 1983). Since the passage in 1988 of federal legislation banning the use of polygraph tests in job interviews in government and the private workplace, a number of questionnaires and other paper-and-pencil tests have been devised to detect cheating and other forms of dishonesty in job situations ("Company Expects to Prosper Finding Cheaters," 1988). It is too early to evaluate the effectiveness of these devices, but their popularity is an indication of the seriousness with which the problem of dishonesty is viewed by officials in industry and government.

Field Independence and Dependence   One of the most systematic series of investigations of the relationships between personality and perception was conducted by Herman Witkin and his colleagues (Witkin et al., 1962; Witkin & Goodenough, 1977). Three tests (Body Adjustment Test, Rod and Frame Test, and Embedded Figures Test) were used in these studies to classify individuals as field independent or field dependent. On the Body Adjustment Test, the examinee is seated in a chair located in a tilted room and directed to adjust the chair to a true vertical position. On the Rod and Frame Test, the examinee is seated before a luminous rod situated in a luminous square frame in a darkened room and instructed to adjust the rod to the true vertical position when the rod and frame are tilted in opposite directions. On the Embedded Figures Test, the speed with which the examinee can locate simple figures in a series of complex forms is determined (Figure 10–7). According to Witkin, these three tests measure much the same thing: the ability to differentiate aspects or parts of a complex, confusing whole. People who are able to find the upright position accurately and the embedded figures quickly are *field independents;* those who have difficulty finding the upright position and locating the embedded figures are *field dependents.*

Of particular interest is the fact that field independents and field dependents tend to have different personalities. Witkin's description of a typical field-independent person is that of a secure, independent, more psychologically mature, self-accepting individual who is active in dealing with the environment, tends to use intellectualization as a defense mechanism, and is more aware of his or her inner experience. On the other hand, a typical field-dependent person is less secure, psychologically immature, passive, less attuned to his or her inner experience, and tends to use repression and denial as defenses. Sex and sociocultural differences in these two perceptual styles have also been found. Boys are typically more field independent that girls, and members of hunting and foraging cultures are more field independent than those in sedentary, agricultural societies (Witkin & Berry, 1975). In terms of child-rearing practices, the parents of field independents are usually less restrictive and less authoritarian than those of field-dependent children.

Witkin's research program represents only one of many areas of investigation concern with the relationships of personality to the ways in which people attend to, process, store, and use information from the environment in solving problems. It has also been found that people differ in the broadness of the categories employed in classifying their experiences, a variable that is related to other personality characteristics (Block et al., 1981). The findings of numerous investigations in which cognitive, affective, and perceptual variables were combined indicate that cognition and affect are actually inseparable, interwoven processes.

Objective Analytic Test Batteries   The fact that measures of cognition and affect overlap a great deal is seen clearly in the Objective Analytic Test Batteries (Institute for Personality and Ability Testing). These tests were designed by R. B. Cattell and J. M. Schuerger to measure 10 source traits: ego strength, anxiety, independence, extroversion, regression, control, cortertia, depression, and two others). Identified in Cattell's research on personality, these traits are assessed by a variety of perceptual, cognitive, and behavioral tasks that on the surface seem more like aptitude tests than personality measures. The tasks include measures of perceptual–motor rigidity, picture perception, endurance of difficulty, criticalness of judgment, humor appreciation, and musical preferences.

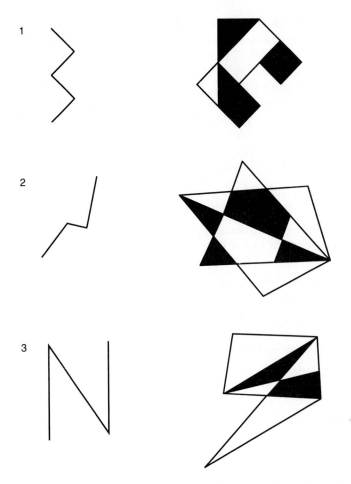

FIGURE 10-7   Sample Embedded Figures Test Item. People Who Have Difficulty Locating the Figures at the Left in the Complex Patterns at the Right May Be Characterized as Field Dependent.
(From Witkin et al. "Field Dependent and Field Independent Cognitive Styles and Their Educational Implications," Review of Educational Research, 47, 1–64. Copyright 1977 by The American Educational Research Association. Adapted by permission of the publisher.)

Cognitive Styles   The term *cognitive style* has been applied to the collection of strategies or approaches to perceiving, remembering, and thinking that an individual comes to prefer in trying to understand and cope with the world. Among the cognitive styles that have received particular research attention are the reflective versus impulsive style and the internal versus external locus of control style. Both the reflective–impulsive and internal–external locus of control dimensions are correlated with numerous personal and sociocultural variables. The *reflective versus impulsive* style, as measured by the Matching

Familiar Figures Test (Kagan et al., 1964) (see Figure 10–8), is concerned with whether, when faced with a problem or task, a person tends to be slow and accurate (reflective) or quick and inaccurate (impulsive) in finding a solution. The *internal versus external locus of control* style, as measured by Rotter's (1966) I–E Scale, refers to whether a person believes that rewards in life are the consequence of his or her own behavior (internal locus of control) or are controlled by forces outside oneself (external locus of control). Some examples of items on the I–E Scale are:

1A. Many of the unhappy things in people's lives are partly due to bad luck.
1B. People's misfortunes result from the mistakes they make.

2A. No matter how hard you try, some people just don't like you.
2B. People who can't get others to like them don't understand how to get along with others.

3A. In the case of the well-prepared student, there is rarely if ever such a thing as an unfair test.
3B. Many times exam questions tend to be so unrelated to course work that studying is really useless.

4A. Becoming a success is a matter of hard work; luck has little or nothing to do with it.
4B. Getting a good job depends mainly being in the right place at the right time.

5A. The average citizen can have an influence in government decisions.
5B. This world is run by the few people in power, and there is not much the little guy can do about it. (Reprinted with permission from Rotter, 1966)

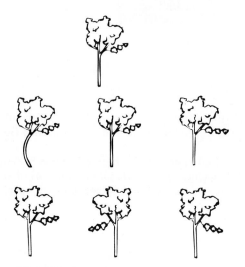

FIGURE 10–8 Sample of Types of Items on the Matching Familiar Figures (MFF) Test. On This Item the Examinee Is Instructed to Select Which of the Six Pictures in the Second or Third Row Is Identical to the Picture at the Top.
(From Jerome Kagan, "Reflection–Impulsivity: The Generality and Dynamics of Conceptual Tempo," Journal of Abnormal Psychology, 71, 17–24. Copyright © 1966 by the American Psychological Association. Reprinted by permission of the author.)

You should be able to tell which statement in each pair indicates an internal locus of control and which indicates an external locus of control orientation.

SUMMARY

Personality inventories and projective techniques have traditionally been used in clinical contexts to identify personal problems and diagnose psychopathology. However, a number of inventories and projectives have been designed for or extended to the analysis of normal personality.

The first personality inventory of note was the Woodworth Personal Data Sheet, but numerous single-score and multiscore inventories have been constructed since that instrument made its debut during World War I. These inventories measure the examinee's standing on certain adjustment, temperament, trait, or psychiatric variables. The items and scales on some personality inventories are based on a rational or theoretical frame of reference. The selection of items for and the scoring of other inventories are determined by the results of factor analysis or empirical studies of the ability of items to differentiate among various criterion groups.

Examples of inventories based on personality theory are the Edwards Personal Preference Schedule, the Myers–Briggs Type Indicator, and the Jenkins Activity Survey. Among the inventories based on the results of factor analysis are the Guilford–Zimmerman Temperament Survey, the 16 Personality Factor Questionnaire, and the Eysenck Personality Questionnaire.

The most famous personality inventory, and the one on which the greatest amount of research has been conducted, is the Minnesota Multiphasic Personality Inventory (MMPI). The MMPI, which is a criterion-keyed inventory, was designed to differentiate among various groups by analyzing differences in the responses on nine clinical scales of normals and patients having specific psychiatric diagnoses. The MMPI may be scored on several other scales as well, including four validating scales (?, L, F, K). The validating scales on the MMPI and other personality inventories are scored to determine whether the examinee has filled out the inventory properly and to adjust content scores for faking and response sets. The MMPI was updated and restandardized in the 1980s, and a revised version, the MMPI–2, was published in 1986.

The criterion-keyed procedure by which the MMPI was constructed was also employed in constructing the California Psychological Inventory, the Personality Inventory for Children, and related instruments. Other more noteworthy personality inventories designed on the basis of criterion keying, as well as theory and sophisticated psychometric procedures, include the Millon Clinical Multiaxial Inventory (MCMI) and the Jackson Personality Inventory.

The most unstructured of all personality assessment devices are projective techniques. Various kinds of projective techniques have been devised, including word associations, sentence completions, drawing human figures, responses to inkblots, and making up stories to pictures. Proponents of projective techniques maintain that inventories and other self-report instruments fail to get at deeper layers of personality because people either do not know or will not reveal their characteristics and problems. Since the scoring of projectives is usually very impressionistic or subjective, difficulties have been encountered in determining the validity of these instruments.

The two most popular projective techniques are the Rorschach Psychodiagnostic Technique and the Thematic Apperception Test. Also noteworthy are the Rosenzweig Picture-frustration Study, the Rotter Incomplete Sentences Blank, the Holtzman Inkblot Test, and picture-story tests for children, seniors, and nonwhite ethnic groups.

Efforts have been made to devise methods of assessing personality that are less fakable than self-report instruments and more valid than projective techniques. The majority of these physiological, perceptual, cognitive, and behavioral tests are, unfortunately, somewhat crude, or at least narrow, measures of personality. For the present, these "objective" tests show no signs of replacing traditional personality assessment methods (observations, interviews, checklists and ratings, personality inventories, and projective techniques).

The results of research on perceptual and cognitive styles, in particular field independence–dependence, reflectivity–impulsivity, and internal–external locus of control, demonstrate that cognition and affect are interactive rather than independent processes and that cognitive and affective assessment instruments overlap in what they assess. These research investigations have been concerned with determining the relationships of personality variables to the perceptual–cognitive processes of attending to, encoding, and using information.

EXERCISES

1. In what sense is it appropriate to refer to measures of interests, attitudes, and personality as "tests"? In what sense is it inappropriate to do so?

2. With respect to the matter of faking on personality inventories, write five true–false items that you think would be answered true more often by fakers than by nonfakers. Then write five items that would be answered false more often by fakers than by nonfakers.

3. Describe the social desirability response set. Then write five true–false items that you feel will provide a good measure of this response set.

4. Arrange to take the California Psychological Inventory, the Jackson Personality Inventory, or another personality inventory and have your scores interpreted by a qualified person. Are your scores consistent with your own assessment of yourself? What criticisms of the inventory do you have to offer?

5. Compare personality inventories with projective techniques, describing both the positive and negative features of each kind of instrument and the conditions under which each is most appropriately administered.

6. It has been said that interpreting responses to a projective test often reveals more above the interpreter than about the examinee. Does this imply that a good way to analyze an individual's personality would be to have him or her interpret fictitious responses to projective stimuli?

7. Following the procedure outline in Exercise 8 of Chapter 5, prepare a critical review of any of the personality inventories described in this chapter or any other personality test of interest to you. Compare your review with a review of the test in the *Mental Measurements Yearbook* or *Test Critiques.*

8. Construct a 10-item self-concept inventory using a true–false format. On half the state-

ments the keyed answer should be "true," and on the other half it should be "false." Administer your Self-Concept Inventory to several students, and compute their total scores (0 to 10) as the number of responses given in the keyed direction. Did you find generally low or generally high scores? How variable were the scores? What evidence can you provide to validate your Self-Concept Inventory?

9. Construct an alphabetical list of 25 nouns pertaining to subjects of interest to people in your age bracket (college, grades, graduation, failure, sex, marriage, religion, mother, father, career, health, and so on). Read your list to 12 acquaintances and ask each person to respond to each word on the list as quickly as possible with the first word that comes to mind. Record the response time (in seconds) and the response to each word. Summarize the results in terms of the number of responses of a given kind made to each stimulus word, average response times, and insights provided into the personalities of the respondents. Review the section on "Word Associations" in this chapter before drawing any conclusions. (Also run program 6 in Category VIII of "Computer Programs for Psychological Assessment.")

10. Construct 10 incomplete sentences pertaining to matters of concern to college students. Type (double space) your 10 sentence fragments on a sheet of paper and make 10 copies. Administer your sentence-completion test to 10 college students, instructing them to complete every sentence fragment with a word or phrase that has a personal meaning or refers to a matter of concern to them. Study the responses given to the sentence fragments, and try to analyze them in terms of the personalities of the respondents. Write a report summarizing your findings. (Also run program 5 in Category VIII of "Computer Programs for Psychological Assessment.")

11. Construct two incomplete stories that you believe will reveal something about the respondent's personality when he or she is asked to complete the stories. Try out your stories on several of your classmates or friends. Does the content of the completed stories suggest anything significant about the respondent's personality? Do you consider this technique of personality assessment to be reliable and valid? Why or why not?

12. Construct an inkblot picture by putting a large drop of black ink in the middle of an $8\frac{1}{2}$ by 11-inch sheet of white paper. Fold the sheet in half so that the ink is inside, crease the sheet in the middle, and press it flat. Then open it up and let the blot dry. Repeat this procedure with other sheets until you obtain five fairly detailed, symmetrical inkblots. Then administer your inkblot test to several people, asking them to tell you what they see in each blot, where on the blot they see it, and what it is about the blot that caused them to make that response. Record the responses of each examinee to each inkblot, and then see if you can tell anything about the examinee's personality from the responses to the five inkblots (refer to the section in this chapter on "Inkblots"). Compare the test results with your personal knowledge of the individual and any other test results that are available. Summarize your findings in a report. (Also run programs 1 and 4 in Category VIII of "Computer Programs for Psychological Assessment.")

SUGGESTED READINGS

Barnett, D. W. (1986). Personality assessment and children: A critical appraisal and emerging trends. *Special Services in the Schools, 2,* 121–140.

Erdberg, P. (1990). Rorschach assessment. In G. Goldstein & M. Hersen (eds.), *Handbook of psychological assessment,* 2nd ed., pp. 387–402. New York: Pergamon.

Groth-Marnat, G. (1990). *Handbook of psychological assessment,* 2nd ed., Chs. 9–11. New York: Wiley.

Gynther, M. D., & Green, S. B. (1982). Methodological problems with self-report inventories. In P. C. Kendall & J. N. Butcher (eds.), *Handbook of research methods in clinical psychology,* pp. 335–386. New York: Wiley.

Hogan, R., & Nicholson, R. A. (1988). The meaning of personality test scores. *American Psychologist, 43,* 621–626.

Keller, L. S., Butcher, J. N. & Slutske, W. S. (1990). Objective personality assessment. In G. Goldstein & M. Hersen (eds.), *Handbook of psychological assessment,* 2nd ed., pp. 345–386. New York: Pergamon.

Newmark, C. S. (ed.) (1985). *Major psychological assessment instruments,* Chs. 1–5. Boston: Allyn & Bacon.

———, (ed.). (1989). *Major psychological assessment instruments,* Vol. II, Chs. 1–6. Boston: Allyn & Bacon.

PART FOUR

APPLICATIONS, ISSUES, AND DEVELOPMENTS

Chapter Eleven

Psychological Assessment in Applied Settings

Tests and other psychological assessment instruments and procedures are used extensively for research purposes not only in psychology and education, but in many other sciences and professions as well. For example, an anthropologist planning to conduct a field study of some primitive culture might pack with other essential equipment a set of Rorschach inkblots, a Draw-a-Person Test, and other assorted test materials to measure the cognitive abilities and personality characteristics of the natives. Likewise, a medical researcher may decide to administer a personality inventory or rating scale as part of a study of factors affecting the incidence and prognosis of a certain disease.

Psychometric psychologists contribute their expertise in test selection and design, in addition to statistical analysis, as members of research teams in many different situations. This is so because, whatever the area of research may be, psychological measures of various kinds can serve as independent, control, concomitant, moderator, or dependent variables. Research is an important area of application in psychological assessment, and it plays a role even when the primary purpose of the activity is not research. First and foremost, psychologists are observers, investigators, and explorers of human behavior, activities that entail research even if not in a formal sense. Of course, psychological assessment is not limited to research uses. Otherwise, many students for whom "research" is anathema would never become practicing psychologists. Even more extensively than in research, tests and other psychometric procedures are used for purposes of selection, classification or diagnosis, and, more generally, evaluation in a multitude of situations in which decisions about people, programs, and procedures must be made.

Previous chapters of this book have been concerned with the methodology and tools of psychological testing and assessment. Although applications of testing are certainly not overlooked in those chapters, they are not dealt with at length. The purpose of the present chapter is to make up for that deficiency by a more detailed treatment of psychological assessment in several applied contexts: educational, occupational, clinical, health, legal, and environmental. The discussion is by no means exhaustive, since entire books have been written on the applications of psychological tests in any one of these contexts.

Instead, the focus is on a few areas within each situation in which tests have been used most extensively. Although applications of psychological tests in all these contexts have been criticized, often vociferously and unremittingly, consideration of these criticisms is postponed until the next chapter.

ASSESSMENT IN EDUCATIONAL CONTEXTS

The primary reason why tests are administered in schools, colleges, and other educational situations is to evaluate the extent to which students have acquired certain knowledge and skills, either in or out of school. The knowledge should involve not only simple recall of memorized facts, but also some degree of understanding and an ability to apply what has been learned to various situations and circumstances. Likewise, the learned skills, which include cognitive, psychomotor, and social skills, should be generalizable or transferrable to other arenas of life. In the process of assessing these abilities not only are individual persons (students, teachers, administrators, and the like) evaluated, but also groups of people (classes, schools, school districts, states, and even nations) and the programs or intervention procedures by which changes in knowledge and ability are brought about.

In this section we shall consider four areas on which educational assessment has focused in recent years: neuropsychological testing, measuring student competency, measuring teacher competency, and evaluating educational and therapeutic programs. An analysis of efforts that have been made and are still being made in these four areas should provide a useful overview of the ways in which psychological assessment tools have been applied in schools, colleges, and adult education programs. Our survey begins with neuropsychological testing, a topic that, it can be argued, properly belongs in the section on clinical testing. However, our emphasis will be on neuropsychological testing in special education, rather than in the diagnosis of personality disorders.

Neuropsychological Disabilities

The grandfather of modern intelligence tests, the Binet–Simon Intelligence Scale, was designed primarily for testing mentally handicapped children. The term *handicapped,* however, has been used in a more general way to refer to persons with physical, mental, cultural, or even emotional disabilities. Because the procedures employed in testing non-handicapped or "normal" individuals are frequently unsuitable or unfair in testing the handicapped, special methods and tests have been devised. A number of these tests, in particular tests for the physically handicapped, are described in Chapters 5 and 6. In this section we shall consider instruments and procedures for assessing one subgroup of the handicapped, the neuropsychologically impaired.

Damage to the central nervous system may not be detectable with CAT scans, EMR scans, PET scans, and other medical tests, but its effects are nevertheless seen in behavioral disturbances or changes. Proficiency in diagnosing and treating deficits in neuropsychological abilities requires a long training program and extensive experience, and even then it is sometimes as much of an art as a science.

Neuropsychological abilities include sensation, motor speed and strength, perception and perceptual–motor integration, language, attention, abstracting ability, flexibility of thinking, orientation, and memory (Grant & Reed, 1982). Brain-injured children experience deficits in one or more of these abilities. Thus, a brain-injured child is

a . . . child who before, during, or after birth has received an injury to or suffered an infection of the brain. As a result of such organic impairment, defects in the neuromotor system may be present or absent; however, such a child may show disturbances in perception, thinking, and emotional behavior, either separately or in combination. These disturbances prevent or impede a normal learning process. (Strauss & Lehtinen, 1947, page 4)

A number of tests and test batteries that can contribute to the assessment of neuropsychological disorders have been described in previous chapters. Several test publishers, including Psychological Assessment Resources, The Psychological Corporation, and Western Psychological Services, have an entire series of older and newer tests for neuropsychological assessment. These single tests and test batteries have been designed specifically for neurological screening and/or the assessment of brain damage.

Because brain-injured children are typically more hyperactive, impulsive, distractible, and emotionally unstable than normal children, special preparations must be made when testing the brain injured. Not only should such a child be informed of the examination a few days in advance, but noise and other sources of distraction in the testing room should be kept to a minimum. Perceptual–motor deficits, coordination defects, short attention span, and uncooperativeness, which are more common in brain-injured children, also contribute to testing difficulties and therefore demand careful preparation, patience, and understanding on the part of the examiner.

Perceptual–Memory Tests   As noted above, distortions of both perception and memory are characteristic of brain-injured individuals. Among the single tests that tap both perceptual and memory functions are the Bender Visual Motor Gestalt Test, the Memory for Designs Test, and the Benton Revised Visual Retention Test. These three tests are usually administered as supplements to individual intelligence tests or other longer psychological examinations.

The Bender Visual Motor Gestalt Test (The Psychological Corporation & American Guidance Service) consists of nine geometric designs on 4- by 6-inch white cards. The examinee is directed to copy the designs, which are presented individually. Notable departures of the copies from the originals, or errors, are interpreted in terms of perceptual deficits. Children 8 years or older and of normal intelligence usually make no more than two errors. Errors in making the drawings that suggest organic brain damage include shape distortions; rotating the design; problems with integrating the design; disproportionate, overlapping, or fragmented drawings; and perseverations. A restandardization of the Bender, including norms for ages 5 through 10 years, was published in 1975; the scores are highly correlated with IQ up to ages 9 to 10 (Koppitz, 1975).

The Memory for Designs Test (MFD) (Psychological Test Specialists) is similar to the Bender except that the examinee attempts to draw copies of 15 geometric designs from memory. Research findings indicate that the MFD, which can be administered in 10 minutes to individuals aged 8½ through 60 years, is useful in identifying organic brain damage (Graham & Kendall, 1960). The Benton Revised Visual Retention Test (The Psychological Corporation) also consists of a set of geometric designs (10 each in three forms) that the examinee is asked to draw from memory after having seen them briefly. The Benton, which takes about 5 minutes, is based on the assumption that impairments in visual perception, visual memory, and visuoconstructive abilities result from neurological deficits.

Other measures that have been used to detect brain damage are tests involving hidden figures, the detection of patterns, and sustained attention or concentration. Screening devices such as the Quick Neurological Screening Test–Revised (The Psychological Corporation) and the Stroop Neuropsychological Screening Test (Psychological Assessment Resources) provide preliminary indexes to determine whether a child should be referred for a complete neurological examination. In addition to these tests, instruments designed to identify or diagnose aphasia, face recognition, form discrimination, and other specific neuropsychological problems are available. However, a comprehensive assessment of neuropsychological functioning requires the administration of a battery of specialized tests.

Neuropsychological Test Batteries   Although conventional intelligence tests such as the WAIS–R and WISC–III are helpful in identifying neuropsychological deficits, a series of tests such as those comprising the Halstead–Reitan Neuropsychological Test Battery, the Reitan–Indiana Neuropsychological Test Battery, the Luria–Nebraska Neuropsychological Battery, or the Contributions to Neurological Assessment is needed to measure adaptive abilities that are not assessed by intelligence tests.

The Halstead–Reitan Neuropsychological Test Battery (Reitan, 1969; Psychological Assessment Resources) contains the first five measures listed in Table 11–1, but several of the remaining six measures may also be included in the total battery. These tests measure a number of sensory abilities, perceptual–motor speed and dexterity, expressive and receptive language functions, memory, concept formation, and abstract reasoning. Any of these abilities may be affected by damage or dysfunction of the central nervous system or the sense receptors and muscles connected to it. A related battery of tests, the Reitan–Indiana Neuropsychological Battery for Children (Reitan, 1964), also includes a variety of sensorimotor and perceptual tests for several sensory modalities and response modes. Among the more complex tests included in the battery are the Category Test and the Trail Making Test. On the Category Test, the examinee deduces general principles from information presented on slides. On the Trail Making Test, the examinee draws lines to connect numbered and lettered circles (from 1 to A, from 2 to B, and so on, alternating numbers and letters). Administration of all tests in the battery is time consuming, requiring between 6 and 8 hours.

The Luria–Nebraska Neuropsychological Battery (Western Psychological Services) was designed to assess cerebral dominance; tactile, visual, and motor functions; perception and reproduction of pitch and rhythm; receptive and expressive speech; reading, writing, and arithmetic; memory; concept formation; and other intellectual processes. Two forms of the battery are available; Form I consists of 269 items, and Form II contains 279 items. Both forms can be scored by computer, but Form I can also be scored by hand. Like the Halstead–Reitan, the Luria–Nebraska is used for more extensive neuropsychological screening for brain damage. Although the Luria–Nebraska takes only about one-third as

TABLE 11–1   Tests and Procedures of the Halstead–Reitan Test Battery

Test	Description
Category Test	Measures abstract reasoning and concept formation; requires examinee to find the rule for categorizing pictures of geometric shapes
Tactual Performance Test	Measures kinesthetic and sensorimotor ability; requires blindfolded examinee to place blocks in appropriate cutout on an upright board with dominant hand, then nondominant hand, then both hands; also tests for incidental memory of blocks
Speech Sounds Perception Test	Measures attention and auditory–visual synthesis; requires examinee to pick from four choices the written version of taped nonsense words
Seashore Rhythm Test	Measures attention and auditory perception; requires examinee to indicate whether paired musical rhythms are the same or different
Finger Tapping Test	Measures motor speed; requires examinee to tap a telegraph keylike lever as quickly as possible for 10 seconds
Grip Strength	Measures grip strength with dynamometer; requires examinee to squeeze as hard as possible; separate trials with each hand
Trail Making (parts A, B)	Measures scanning ability, mental flexibility, and speed; requires examinee to connect numbers (part A) or numbers and letters in alternating order (part B) with a pencil line under pressure of time
Tactile Form Recognition	Measures sensory–perceptual ability; requires examinee to recognize simple shapes (e.g., triangle) placed in the palm of the hand
Sensory Perceptual Exam	Measures sensory–perceptual ability; requires examinee to respond to simple bilateral sensory tasks (e.g., detecting which finger has been touched, which ear has received a brief sound); assesses the visual fields
Aphasia Screening Test	Measures expressive and receptive language abilities; tasks include naming a pictured item (e.g., fork), repeating short phrases; copying tasks (not a measure of aphasia) included here for historical reasons
Supplementary	WAIS-R, WRAT-R, MMPI, memory tests such as Wechsler Memory Scale or Rey Auditory Verbal Learning Test

From Robert J. Gregory, *Psychological Testing: History, Principles, and Applications,* Copyright © 1992 by Allyn and Bacon. Reprinted with permission.

much time to administer as the Halstead–Reitan, it has been criticized for relying too heavily on language skills and for failing to properly detect aphasia and certain other neuropsychological disorders.

Contributions to Neuropsychological Assessment (Oxford University Press), designed by A. L. Benton and others, is a test battery that emphasizes a flexible sequential approach to neuropsychological assessment. The specific tests that are administered are determined by the patient's complaint and the questions arising during the examination. The battery consists of 12 tests divided into two categories: Tests of Orientation and Learning (Temporal Orientation, Right–left Orientation, and Serial Digit Learning) and Perceptual and Motor Tests (Facial Recognition, Judgment and Line Orientation, Visual Form Discrimination, Pantomime Recognition, Tactile Form Perception, Finger Localization, Phoneme Discrimination, Three Dimensional Block Construction, and Motor Impersistence). These tests were developed over a period of two decades and have been fairly extensively standardized and validated on brain-diseased patients.

Diagnosing Learning Disabilities   Not all children who score average or above on general intelligence tests do well in school. In addition to those who have pronounced physical handicaps, emotional disturbances, or low motivation are children of adequate intelligence who apparently have none of these problems, but still experience difficulties in reading, arithmetic, spelling, writing, and/or other basic academic skills. Examples are the reading disability known as *dyslexia* and the impairment in learning mathematics known as *dyscalculia.* The term *learning disability* or *specific learning disability* has been applied to such conditions, and the emphasis has been on identifying and diagnosing learning problems that cannot be explained by mental retardation, cultural deprivation, mental disorder, or sensory loss (see Report 11–1). Research on learning disabilities and the development of psychological instruments for use in diagnosis and remediation programs were stimulated by the passage of Public Law 94-142, the Education for All Handicapped Children Act, in 1975.

   Although eligibility criteria for providing learning disability services vary from state to state, one guideline for identifying learning disabled children in the State of California is that the child's ability (as measured, for example, by a general intelligence test) should be at least 1.5 standard deviations above his or her achievement (as measured by standardized achievement tests). Children diagnosed as learning disabled, whose actual performance levels do not keep pace with their estimated potential, are frequently inattentive and deficient in language functions, most often in reading, a foundation skill for scholastic achievement. Classroom teachers may be able to detect such conditions through careful observation or administration of group intelligence tests and more specialized instruments, such as the McCarthy Screening Test (The Psychological Corporation), the Pupil Rating Scale (Grune & Stratton), and the Slingerland Screening Tests for Identifying Children with Specific Language Disability (Western Psychological Services). However, the administration of a comprehensive battery of tests to determine the nature and extent of a child's learning disability and his or her educational needs requires the skills of a trained psychologist.

   A variety of cognitive, perceptual, motor, and even affective instruments may be included in a battery of tests to diagnose learning disabilities. These include the WISC–III, Peabody Picture Vocabulary Test, Wechsler Memory Scale, Bender Visual Motor Gestalt Test or Benton Visual Retention Test, Goodenough–Harris Drawing Test, Woodcock–Johnson Psychoeducational Battery, Porch Index of Communicative Ability in Children, Diagnostic Arithmetic Test, Frostig Developmental Test of Visual Perception, the Gray Oral Reading Tests, the Wide Range Achievement Test, the Southern California Sensory Integra-

REPORT 11–1 Perceptual-Motor Learning Disability

William was an 11-year-old boy in the sixth grade of a suburban school. His family had moved recently to the school district; he had spent his first five years at a school in the metropolitan system, where he was reportedly a good student with few problems. Teacher reports from his fifth-grade teacher revealed some concern about his abilities in spelling and arithmetic. Since entering the sixth grade in the suburban system, he had been identified as a mild behavior problem, talking to other children while the teacher was speaking, rebelling against the teacher's discipline, and regularly refusing to turn in both classroom and homework assignments. Neither the teacher nor the parents understood this apparent change in William's behavior, and his parents were concerned that William was "paying us back for moving to the suburbs."

Psychological Evaluation

William was of tall and slender build, with a mildly ungainly appearance. He appeared to be an alert and intelligent young man who was quite capable of taking care of himself. He was well aware of the purpose of the evaluation, and although mildly suspicious of the examiner in the first interview, he subsequently revealed an inclination to speak honestly and candidly about his school difficulties. Although he felt that he had sometimes been unfairly treated and misunderstood by his previous teacher, he harbored little resentment toward school and showed good capacity for viewing his difficulties in school in an objective fashion. William was quite skilled verbally, he related well to the examiner, and rapport was soon established.

William was given a number of tests, including the WISC, the Developmental Test of Visual-Motor Integration (Beery-Buktenica), the Wide Range Achievement Test, the Bender-Gestalt, the Rorschach, the Thematic Apperception Test (TAT, 8 cards), and the Sentence Completion Test. On all tests, William was diligent and hardworking; he was motivated toward achievement and was easily ego-involved by the challenge of a testing situation. There were dramatic differences, however, in his capacity to perform verbal tests as opposed to nonverbal tests. On verbal tests, William appeared immensely challenged and involved, and his problem-solving postures were quite appropriate; on nonverbal tests, he was easily confused and became aimless and anxious. This evidence of differential functioning was substantiated by the results of all testings.

On the WISC, William achieved a Verbal Scale IQ of 120, a Performance Scale IQ of 90, and a Full Scale IQ of 107. Verbal skills were in the superior range, whereas nonverbal skills were at the lower end of the average range. The disparity between verbal and nonverbal skills was consistent and quite debilitating. William's visual memory and visual perceptual-motor abilities were much less advanced than auditory/verbal channels were, representing a learning disability of some magnitude.

On the Beery, William achieved a visual-perceptual-motor integration age equivalent of 9 years 4 months, some 2 years behind his chronological age level. The Bender-Gestalt, which requires an even greater degree of perceptual-motor organization than the Beery, likewise revealed serious deficits in perceptual-motor abilities.

William's learning disability manifested itself on the Wide Range Achievement Test as follows: reading—grade norm of 6.3; spelling—grade norm of 4.2; arithmetic—grade norm of 4.2. Spelling and arithmetic are learning areas that depend heavily on intact visual memory and visual organization, and they were therefore the areas most affected by William's disability.

Projective personality tests indicated that William was a well-integrated youngster who did not display any significant degree of emotional disturbance. There was no evidence of any emotional overlay that could be attributed to previously undetected learning disability. It would seem that his previous schooling experiences had been very supportive and that his

REPORT 11–1   (continued)

teachers had instinctively responded quite appropriately to his learning problems. With the transfer to a new school, William's learning problems had become more apparent to him as he found himself considerably behind his peers in certain areas. The mild behavioral and discipline problems reported in his new school very likely represented William's response to the anxiety associated with his increasing awareness of his inability to manage certain areas of learning. It could be expected that the identification of his learning problems and appropriate assistance would forestall the development of further behavior or discipline difficulties.

Recommendations

The examiner felt that William was in need of special remedial help in both spelling and arithmetic. Since William was well-integrated in his current classroom, and since he had excellent verbal/auditory skills, it was considered best both for his educational growth and for his interpersonal growth that he remain in his regular classroom. As such, it was recommended that William be placed in a supplementary itinerant program that could provide special tutorial assistance in spelling and arithmetic.

Source: Suran, B. B. & Rizzo, J. V. 1979, pp. 257–258. Glenview, Ill: Scott, Foresman. Reproduced by permission.

tion Tests, and primary levels of other achievement test batteries (Stanford Achievement Test, CIRCUS, and Metropolitan Readiness Tests).

Testing Students for Academic Competency

"Tests Find Students' Skills Appalling"

"Report Gives Poor Marks to Students' Skills"

"U.S. Pupils Near Bottom in Math, Science"

As suggested by these newspaper headlines, U.S. public schools and their students are in trouble. A summary of the results of 20 years of assessing the knowledge and skills of young Americans reveals persisting deficiencies in reading, writing, science, mathematics, history, civics, and other subject areas (see Table 11–2). Scholastic achievement is low among white, black, and Hispanic students alike, and particularly so in the last two groups. Although black and Hispanic students in the United States improved in reading, mathematics, and science during the 1980s, they remain significantly behind white students, who themselves are below average compared with students in other developed countries.

National concern with the low test scores of U.S. high school graduates has led the great majority of states to institute a requirement that students pass a *functional literacy* (or minimum competency) examination before being granted a high school diploma. The 240-item Florida examination, which was developed in response to the concern that too many children were being "socially promoted," was designed to measure basic skills in the three R's applied to real-life situations (making change, writing checks, calculating interest, and the like). Students take the examination initially in the eleventh grade and have four chances to pass. Those who are unable to pass by the end of the twelfth grade

TABLE 11–2 Highlights of Findings from 20 Years of NAEP

▶ Students can read at a surface level, getting the gist of material, but do not read analytically or perform well on challenging reading assignments.

▶ Small proportions of students write well enough to accomplish the purposes of different writing tasks; most do not communicate effectively.

▶ Only small proportions of students develop specialized knowledge needed to address science-based problems, and the pattern of falling behind begins in elementary school.

▶ Students' grasp of the four arithmetic operations and beginning problem-solving is far from universal in elementary school; by the time students near high-school graduation, half cannot handle moderately challenging mathematics material, including computation with decimals, fractions, and percents.

▶ Students have a basic understanding of events that have shaped American history, but they do not appear to understand the significance and connections of those events.

▶ Similarly, students demonstrate an uneven understanding of the Constitution and American government and politics; their knowledge of the Bill of Rights is limited.

Reprinted with permission of the National Assessment of Educational Progress.

are given a certificate of completion to show that they attended high school, but it does not have the same status as a diploma.

Despite compromises and efforts to make it more palatable, minimum competency or functional literacy testing continues to be the subject of debate. Because substantially larger percentages of black than white students failed the Florida examination for high school students, the test was alleged to be discriminatory against minorities. In a legal case challenging the competency testing (*Debra P.* v. *Turlington,* 1984), the Florida examination was alleged to be racially biased; it was also maintained that adequate preparation time had not been given and that using the test to group students for remediation purposes would reinstate segregation in the public schools. However, use of the test was upheld ("Florida Skills Test Upheld," 1983). On the other side are critics who feel that passing an eighth-grade-level test is an inadequate standard for high school graduation and that minimum competency may well become the maximum. Two other dangers of minimum-competency testing are that teachers will end up teaching to the test, and enforcers of the requirements are periodically besieged by outraged parents whose children have failed the tests.

Detractors notwithstanding, the use of tests to assess competency in basic skills, a minimum score on which is required for high school graduation, is an idea whose time has arrived. In fact, in many states, accountability through evaluation of student performance is an annual event resulting in publication in the local newspaper of achievement test score averages by school and grade level. A move to make such evaluation more useful in educational decision making and resource allocation is indicated by calls to expand the role of the National Assessment of Educational Progress so as to make "The Nation's Report Card" a report of educational achievement by state and locality, and not simply a report on the nation as a whole (Alexander & James, 1987). During recent years there has also been a great deal of discussion among politicians and professionals concerning the possibility and procedures for establishing national educational standards and constructing national tests in English, mathematics, science, history, and geography to be administered on a national level in the fourth, eighth, and twelfth grades. Such a set of standards and the accompanying tests would presumably provide a source of motivation and a guide for improving learning at the public school level and a way to determine the extent of progress in reaching the standards.

Value-added Testing

Another idea related to accountability and competency testing that has gained momentum in recent years is that of value-added education and the associated assessment procedures of value-added testing. In *value-added testing,* students' achievements in academic subjects and life skills such as analyzing a newspaper column, a mathematical table, or a television advertisement are assessed before and after a certain period of formal education and study. The difference between initial and final scores is a measure of the value added by the educational experience. Value-added testing is mandated by law and controlled by state coordinating boards in South Dakota and Tennessee. Individual institutions of higher learning in certain other states, for example, Northeast Missouri State University, have also instituted value-added testing. Entering students at Northeast Missouri take either the ACT Freshman College Entrance Examination or the ACT College Outcome Measures Project. The latter requires students to analyze newspaper advertisements, articles, and speeches to demonstrate their mastery of life skills. Retesting at the end of the sophomore year, when students still have sufficient time to make up deficiencies, reveals how much they have learned in the general education curriculum.

Teachers and Testing

Testing in the schools is conducted by school psychologists, guidance counselors, directors of special education, and, most often, by teachers themselves. Teachers are involved with formal and informal evaluations of students from their very first day in the classroom. Such evaluations entail not only observations, classwork and homework of various kinds, and teacher-made tests, but also many different types of standardized tests. The extensive use of standardized tests in the schools opens up the possibility of errors in both administration and interpretation. Many of the mistakes made in administering tests and interpreting the results can be attributed to lack of training, lack of concern, or both on the part of test users. Consequently, it is a matter of some importance for teachers, counselors, clinicians, and others who make extensive use of tests to be properly trained and informed.

Teacher Training in Testing   The majority of prospective teachers have some exposure to educational testing during their college education, but typically the exposure is rather superficial. For example, in a study conducted some years ago, Goslin (1967) found that less than 40 percent of the teachers surveyed had taken more than one course in educational measurement, and a large number reported having had no formal training at all in the subject. Unfortunately, it is doubtful whether the situation has changed much during the past quarter-century.

A large percentage of teachers do not understand what is being measured by the tests they administer in their classrooms nor do they know the meanings of the standardized scores entered into a student's permanent record. They often draw sweeping conclusions on the basis of a single test score, failing to take into account the child's developmental history, social competency, or home environment. Therefore, it is essential that more attention be given to this aspect of teacher training. For example, teachers need to realize that scores on tests of intelligence and special aptitudes should be interpreted in terms of the probabilities that examinees will succeed in particular vocations or programs of study. Far too often test scores are viewed as fixed measures of children's mental status on the one hand or completely meaningless on the other.

Testing the Teachers   Increasing public concern over the quality of education in the United States has led to another form of involvement of teachers with testing. Almost all the 50 United States have implemented some form of teacher evaluation system. A majority of states require a passing score on a specified test for students to enter a teacher education program, and almost all states use tests for teacher certification. Tests are also administered for purposes of recertification and the allocation of merit pay.

Custom-built tests are administered for teacher certification purposes in certain states, whereas other states use tests designed by commercial testing organizations. In the latter category are the National Teacher Examinations (NTE), the Pre-Professional Skills Test (PPST), and the California Basic Education Skills Test (CBEST). These examinations cover basic skills in reading, writing, and mathematics, knowledge of the subject matter that the applicant wishes to teach, and knowledge of professional education (curriculum theory, psychology of instruction, and the like). In addition to the tests, several states have implemented formal observation systems for beginning teachers. In these states, beginning teachers are given assistance in teaching for a trial period, after which a recommendation is made to the state that determines whether the candidate will receive regular certification (Rudner, 1988).

The results of a national public opinion poll conducted some years ago indicated that a majority of the general public favor the use of competency tests for teacher certification or licensing (Gallup, 1979). In addition, both of the nation's two largest teacher unions, the National Education Association and the American Federation of Teachers, have expressed support for testing all beginning teachers to make certain that they meet a reasonable standard of competency. Supporters of a national test for prospective teachers argue that it would be a better indicator of teacher quality and would professionalize the teaching force. By improving the quality of teachers, such a test would also have the effects of raising teachers' salaries and improving schools (Doyle & Hartle, 1985).

Teacher competency tests have not gone unchallenged, and legal battles concerning the matter have taken place in several states. A continuing problem concerns the passing standard on the tests: if it is set reasonably high, then large numbers of minority candidates are likely to fail; if it is set too low, individuals of low ability will be permitted to enter the teaching profession. In addition, certain professional educators are dissatisfied with the nature of the examinations. Popham (1984) argued that the current tests are not useful in designing instructional programs for teachers, and he advocated the use of criterion-referenced teacher competency tests that will "become beacons for instructional design." Other authorities believe that a blend of tests using computer technology, direct observations of classroom performance, portfolios with documentation of teaching performance and other items, as well as standardized paper-and-pencil tests, may ultimately be used to evaluate prospective and experienced teachers for hiring and promotion.

Program Evaluation

In addition to evaluating student and teacher competencies, tests are often used to evaluate the effectiveness of educational and other intervention programs. Although psychological and educational assessment plays an important role in evaluating educational instruction, psychological treatment effectiveness, and other procedures designed to change behavior, such programs should not be designed unilaterally by specialists in psychometrics and research, but in collaboration with professionals (educators, human service and mental health workers, and the like) in the area of intervention. The contribution of measurement specialists is, however, an important one of recommending and/or designing instruments to evaluate program outcomes.

Difficulties in measuring change and other technical problems in evaluating the effectiveness of behavioral interventions resulted in the creation of a new kind of specialty, *program evaluation.* The goal of program evaluation is to make judgments concerning the utility or value of educational, psychosocial, and other social intervention programs. Various guides or models of program evaluation have been proposed, including the CIPP (context, input, process, product) model, discrepancy evaluation, and adversary evaluation. Numerous books have been written on the topic of program evaluation during the past few years (for example, Borich & Jemelka, 1981; Rossi & Freeman, 1985; Posavec & Carey, 1992), but only a brief description of one approach will be given here.

The comprehensive model proposed by Rossi and Freeman (1985) characterizes the overall process of program evaluation in terms of four successive stages: planning, monitoring, impact assessment, and economic efficiency assessment. During the first or *program planning* stage, the extent of the problem (for example, drug dealing and use in the schools), the goals, and the target population of the program are identified. After the goals and target population have been specified, a decision is made on whether the program can be properly implemented. Once a decision has been made to go ahead, the *program monitoring* stage begins. During this stage, the implementation or operation of the program is continually monitored to determine whether the program is providing the designated resources and services to the target population.

At the third, or *impact assessment,* stage, the actual outcomes are evaluated to see if the program goals have been attained. Various statistical and nonstatistical methods are applied to determine whether the outcomes are significant and in the direction(s) predicted. Other unintended or unexpected outcomes are also evaluated at the impact-assessment stage, but, even when statistically significant, they may not be of sufficient practical significance. Consequently, it is the purpose of the fourth stage, *economic efficiency assessment,* to determine whether the results of a program are worth the costs incurred in implementing it. This is a matter of cost–benefit analysis, in which the costs of the program are weighed against its potential benefits to the individual and society. For example, it may be concluded that, although the program works, the monetary and other resources required to implement it can be used more effectively elsewhere. When the results of the cost–benefit analysis are in favor of the program, it acts as a signal to go ahead and put the program in place. But even after the program has been initiated, its effectiveness should be evaluated and reviewed periodically.

Although the various models of program evaluation differ in their details, they all attempt to determine the goals, resources, procedures, and management of a program in order to arrive at a sound judgment of its merit. Indicative of interest in these efforts and public support for them is the existence of centers for research and development in educational evaluation and other types of program evaluation at major U.S. universities. The findings of studies conducted at these centers and the services offered by them provide a more rational basis for answering questions pertaining to the processes and outcomes of various types of social programs.

ASSESSMENT IN INDUSTRIAL–ORGANIZATIONAL CONTEXTS

Psychological assessment in industry and other organizational contexts contributes to a variety of activities, including the selection of new employees, training new employees and retraining old employees, and the continuing appraisal of all employees. These uses of tests to help make evaluations and decisions concerning employees are among the activities of personnel psychologists. Psychological assessment also contributes to the decision-making processes in another business-oriented area, consumer psychology. Consumer psychologists are concerned with research on the psychological processes underlying the acquisition, consumption, and disposition of goods, services, and ideas, as well as the applications of research findings on these topics (Mowen, 1989). There are other areas of industrial–organizational psychology in which psychological assessment plays a role, but we shall limit our discussion to these two, personnel and consumer psychology.

Personnel Selection and Classification

Since antiquity people have been selected, classified, and placed in positions to perform various organizational duties. Often, however, the procedures followed in personnel selection, classification, and placement have been haphazard and unsystematic. The ancient Chinese were reportedly the first to use systematic procedures to evaluate people for public service jobs (DuBois, 1970). The principal method of assessing the skills and abilities of government employees in ancient China consisted of a series of oral examinations administered every three years. Other nations have used a variety of techniques for personnel selection and appraisal, many of which were based on casual observation and intuition. For example, great importance was sometimes given to head shape, eye movements, and overall body appearance. Cultural and familial origins were also significant in determining who was appointed to a position, hired for a specific job, or accepted for a certain educational program.

Screening   Personnel selection has traditionally been concerned with identifying, from a pool of applicants, those who are most able to perform certain designated tasks. In this approach, psychological tests have been used, together with nontest information (personal history, physical characteristics, recommendations, and so on), to help select applicants who can perform particular jobs satisfactorily now or after appropriate training.

A personnel selection procedure may be fairly simple or very complex, depending on the nature of the organization and the task for which individuals are being selected. The most straightforward approach is the sink-or-swim strategy in which all who apply are selected or admitted, but only those who perform effectively are retained. In some ways this is an ideal selection strategy, but it is also expensive to both the organization and the applicants. Consequently, almost all organizations use some kind of *screening* procedure by which applicants who are clearly unsuitable for the task (job, program, and so on) are rejected immediately. If the screening instrument is a psychological test of some sort, applicants who make a specified minimum score (*cutoff score*) or higher are accepted, whereas those whose scores fall below the cutoff are rejected. There is a certain impersonality in this procedure, and it may occasionally seem unkind from the applicant's perspective. However, both product-making and service-providing organizations must run efficiently to accomplish their goals. Obviously, they run most efficiently when the members of the organization perform their specific duties most effectively.

Classification and Placement   Initial screening is usually followed by the *classification* and assignment of those who have been selected into one of several occupational categories. Classification decisions may involve grouping people on the basis of their scores on more than one psychological test, such as classifying military inductees into occupational specialties on the basis of their scores on the Armed Services Vocational Aptitude Battery (ASVAB). Screening and classification are frequently followed by the *placement* of those who have been selected at a particular level of a specific job or program.

The process of personnel selection usually consists of a sequence of stages entailing a series of yes–no decisions based on information provided by application forms, letters of reference, telephone calls, personal interviews, psychological tests, and other predictors of occupational or educational success. The purpose of collecting this information is identical to that of any other application of psychology: to make accurate predictions of future behavior from data on past and present behavior. The more reliable and valid the information is, the greater the likelihood of making correct predictions of on-the-job or in-the-program behavior and hence the sounder the selection decisions. The reliability and validity of psychological assessment instruments and procedures for making selection decisions cannot, of course, be determined merely by inspecting the assessment materials. Reliability and validity must be evaluated empirically, which is one of the primary tasks of the personnel psychologist.

An Expectancy Table   When tests are used for purposes of selection, it is not essential to determine the test-criterion correlation and the regression equation linking predicted criterion scores to test scores. Correlational methods are applicable to the construction of theoretical expectancy tables, but an empirical expectancy table can be constructed without computing a correlation coefficient or any other statistic except frequencies and percentages. Assume that Table 11–3 was constructed from a joint frequency distribution of the scores of 250 job applicants on an Occupational Selection Test (OST) and the ratings given to the applicants by their work supervisors 6 months after being hired. The OST score intervals are listed on the left side of the table, and the ratings (on a scale of 1 to 8) are listed across the top. The nonitalicized frequencies in the cells of the table are the numbers of employees who obtained OST scores within a specified 5-point range and the rating indicated at the top of the given column. For example, 10 employees whose OST scores were between 81 and 85 were given a rating of 5 by their supervisors, whereas 14 employees whose OST scores fell between 66 and 70 were given a rating of 4.

The italic numbers in parentheses in Table 11–3 are the percentages of people having OST scores in a given interval whose ratings were equal to the value in the given cell or higher. Thus, 85 percent of the employees whose OST scores fell in the interval 81 to 85 received ratings of 5 or higher, and 61 percent of those having OST scores between 66 and 70 had ratings of 4 or higher.

TABLE 11–3 Empirical Expectancy Table

Occupational selection test score	Supervisor's rating							
	1	2	3	4	5	6	7	8
96–100						(100) 1		(67) 2
91–95					(100) 2		(82) 5	(36) 4
86–90				(100) 1	(94) 8	(50) 3	(33) 4	(11) 2
81–85				(100) 4	(85) 10	(48) 7	(22) 5	(4) 1
76–80			(100) 6	(88) 12	(63) 16	(31) 13	(4) 2	
71–75		(100) 4	(94) 7	(83) 25	(45) 21	(12) 6	(5) 3	
66–70		(100) 5	(87) 10	(61) 14	(24) 7	(5) 2		
61–65	(100) 1	(96) 6	(72) 8	(40) 5	(20) 4	(4) 1		
56–60	(100) 2	(85) 5	(46) 4	(15) 2				
51–55	(100) 1							

To illustrate how this kind of information is applied to the process of occupational selection, assume that John, a potential employee from a group similar to those on whom Table 11–3 was constructed, makes a score of 68 on the Occupational Selection Test. Then it can be estimated that his chances of receiving a rating of 4 or higher on job performance by his supervisor 6 months after beginning the job are 61 out of 100, but his chances of obtaining a rating of 6 or higher are only 5 out of 100. If 4 is an acceptable rating, then John will be hired, but he is not expected to become a highly rated employee.

Factors Affecting the Accuracy of Prediction   As discussed in the section on test validity in Chapter 4, the accuracy with which an applicant's criterion score can be predicted depends on the size of the correlation between predictor and criterion scores. The predictive accuracy of a test is also affected by a number of other factors, including false positive and false negative errors, the selection ratio, and the base rate.

If the cutoff score on a test is set very low, there will be many incorrect acceptances, or *false positives.* These are applicants who were selected but do not succeed on the job or in the program. On the other hand, if the cutoff score is set very high, there will be many incorrect rejections or *false negatives.* These are applicants who were not selected but would have succeeded if they had been. Since the purpose of personnel selection is to obtain as many "hits" as possible, to reject potential failures and select potential successes, setting a cutoff score must be done carefully.

To illustrate these concepts, refer again to Table 11–3. Suppose that the cutoff score on the OST is set at 66 and that a 4 is considered a minimum acceptable job performance rating. Then $4 + 5 + 6 + 7 + 10 = 32$ of the employees represented in Table 11–3 will be classified as false positives: they scored at least 66 on the OST, but had performance ratings of less than 4. On the other hand, $5 + 2 + 4 + 1 = 12$ employees are false negatives because they scored below 66 on the OST, but received performance ratings of 4 or higher. Observe that if the cutoff score on the OST is raised the result will be a decrease in the number of false positives, but an increase in the number of false negatives. The opposite effect, an increase in false positives but a decrease in false negatives, will occur if the cutoff score on the OST is lowered.

Establishing a cutoff score on a test or test composite depends not only on the validity of the test(s), but also on the *selection ratio,* the proportion of applicants to be selected. The lower the selection ratio is, the higher the cutoff score, and vice versa. Since the cutoff score affects the number of false positive and false negative errors, we might argue that the selection ratio should be determined by the relative seriousness with which these two types of errors are viewed. Is it a more serious error to accept an applicant who will fail (false positive) or to reject an applicant who would have succeeded (false negative)? Such errors should be taken into account, but at least as important in determining the selection ratio is the total number of applicants. For example, when the labor market is tight, the number of applicants is small. Then the selection ratio will need to be high and, consequently, the cutoff score on the test must be low in order to select the desired number of applicants. On the other hand, in a free, or open, labor market, the selection ratio is low, so the cutoff score on the test needs to be fairly high.

Figure 11–1 illustrates the relationship of the selection ratio and the validity of a selection test to the percentage of applicants selected who will succeed in a particular job or program. The job or program is one in which 50 percent of the applicants who have

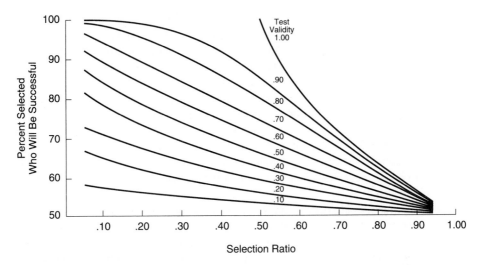

FIGURE 11–1   Relationship of Test Validity and Selection Ratio to Percentage of Selected Applicants Who Will Be Successful.
(After Ernest J. McCormick and Daniel R. Ilgen, Industrial and Organizational Psychology, 8th edition, © 1985, p. 135. Reprinted by permission of Prentice Hall, Englewood Cliffs, New Jersey.)

already been selected are successful. This figure, which as been adapted from a portion of the Taylor–Russell tables (Taylor & Russell, 1939), shows that the percentage of successful applicants increases as the test validity coefficient increases and the selection ratio decreases. Charts such as this one permit a personnel officer to determine what percentage of selected employees can be expected to be successful when a certain proportion of applicants is selected by using a test having a specified validity coefficient.

Another important factor affecting the accuracy with which a test can identify people who will behave in a certain way is the base rate. The *base rate* is the proportion of people in the population of interest who would behave in a specified manner (for example, perform a given job satisfactorily) if given an opportunity to do so. A test designed to predict a particular type of behavior is most effective when the base rate is 50 percent and least effective when the base rate is either very high or very low. For example, a test designed to select people for a highly complex job, which relatively few people can perform satisfactorily, would not be as effective as a test designed to select people for a job that half the applicant population can perform satisfactorily. The concept of base rate is not limited to personnel selection; it is also important in clinical diagnosis. For example, because the incidence of suicide in the general population is very low, a test designed to identify potential suicides would not be very effective. However, a test designed to identify neurotics should do better because the percentage of neurotics is much higher than the percentage of suicides.

Multiple Cutoff and Multiple Regression   Deciding where to set the cutoff score on a selection or placement test is a complicated statistical and judgmental process. In addition to the factors discussed above, the cutoff score and the usefulness of a test in general are affected by other information available on the applicant.

Frequently, a set of test scores and other measures are combined in making selection and classification decisions. One procedure for combining scores, referred to as *successive hurdles* or *multiple cutoff*, is to set separate cutoff scores on each of several measures. Then an applicant must score at the cutoff point or higher on each separate measure in order to be selected. The multiple cutoff approach is most appropriate in prediction situations in which a high score on one measure does not compensate for a low score on another measure. For example, the ability to differentiate between tones of different pitch is essential to effective performance as an orchestra conductor. Regardless of how high his or her intellectual ability may be, a person who is tone deaf will not do well in that profession.

A more mathematical approach to combining the scores of a large sample of people on several measures is to determine a *multiple-regression equation* in which different statistically assigned weights are applied to scores on different tests. Once these weights are computed, a single predicted criterion score for each applicant can be computed by multiplying the applicant's score by the appropriate regression weights. For example, a multiple-regression equation employed for admission purposes at one college was

$$Y_{pred} = .002(SAT\text{-}V) + .001(SAT\text{-}M) + .030(HSR) - 2.00$$

where Y_{pred} designates freshman year grade-point average, SAT-V and SAT-M are the Verbal and Mathematical scores on the Scholastic Aptitude Test, respectively, and HSR is a T score measure of rank in high school graduating class. Assume that an applicant's scores on the two sections of the SAT are 600 and 500 and his or her high school rank (HSR) is 70. Then, according to the equation, the applicant's predicted grade-point average is

$$Y_{pred} = .002(600) + .001(500) + .030(70) - 2.00 = 1.8$$

which is equivalent to a low C.

In the multiple-regression approach, a high score on one predictor variable can compensate for a low score on another predictor variable. Consequently, this approach should not be employed when a minimum score on any of the predictors is essential for effective performance on the criterion. When the multiple-regression approach is used, a *multiple correlation coefficient (R)*, an index of the relationship of a weighted combination of the predictor variables to the criterion measure, should be computed. R ranges from .00 to 1.00 and is interpreted in a manner similar to the product–moment correlation (r) (see Appendix A).

Consumer Behavior

Psychological tests administered for personnel selection purposes are more likely to be measures of cognitive and psychomotor abilities than they are to be personality inventories or other affective instruments. Be that as it may, the biographical data blanks and interview or observation forms employed in personnel screening, classification, placement, and performance appraisals are also helpful in assessing personal characteristics related to job performance. Furthermore, personality inventories, projectives, and situational tests of various kinds are also administered in assessment centers to evaluate executive personnel for selection and promotion purposes.

The inventories and other measures of interests and values discussed in Chapter 8 have important functions in occupational decision making, that of vocational counseling and introducing young people to the wide range of job or career possibilities. Finally, affective instruments such as attitude scales and opinion questionnaires are commonly found in industrial–organizational situations, where they are helpful in assessing employee morale, employee grievances, and other personal and interpersonal factors affecting productivity and job satisfaction.

One of the most extensive uses of measures of interests, attitudes, personality traits, and other affective variables is seen in the study by consumer psychologists of individual differences in behavior, values, and life-style of consumers. Other activities of consumer psychologists include the identification of attitudes, opinions, interests, values, personality traits, and life-styles associated with preferences for and the purchasing of specific products and services. Known as *psychographics,* these research activities are directed toward describing the psychological profiles, or characteristic patterns of behavior and thinking, that differentiate one consumer group from another. If these efforts are successful, markets can be segmented according to types of consumers, and product promotion activities can be directed toward that segment of the market. To illustrate, in a study of how the opinions, interests, and activities of people are related to their eating preferences, Sadalla and Burroughs (1981) classified foods into five categories: vegetarian, gourmet, health, fast, and synthetic (processed bacon or cheese snacks, instant eggs or drinks, and the like). Groups of individuals who preferred foods in each category rated themselves and were rated by other people on a variety of personal preferences and behavior. Both sets of raters agreed in characterizing people who preferred vegetarian foods as "noncompetitive, sexual, and liking crafts and folk dancing." Those who preferred gourmet foods were described as "users of drugs who live alone, are liberal, and like glamour sports and gambling." Those who preferred fast-foods were described as "religious, logical, conservative, and wearers of polyester clothing who have no favorite hobbies, but have a particular liking for fast-food hamburgers." It is not difficult to see how this kind of information might be useful in deciding how to package, advertise, and sell specific products.

Although many different measures of personality and preferences have been administered in psychographic studies, two of the most popular approaches are AIO inventories and VALS. There is no single AIO inventory; the statements on such an inventory are designed to analyze differences in the activities, interests, and opinions of specified target groups. For example, the following AIO statements were endorsed frequently by 18- 24-year-old men who both drink and drive (Lastovicka et al., 1987):

It seems like no matter what my friends and I do on a weekend, we almost always end up at a bar getting smashed.

A party wouldn't be a party without some liquor.

I've been drunk at least five times this month.

352Applications, Issues, and Developments

Being drunk is fun.

The chances of an accident or losing a driver's license from drinking and driving are low.

Drinking helps me to have fun and do better with girls.

A few drinks will have no noticeable effect on my coordination and self-control.

More theoretically based than AIO inventories is the VALS approach developed at the Stanford Research Institute. The VALS (an acronym for values and lifestyles) approach is based on a four-part typology, need driven, outer directed, inner directed, and integrated, with eight more detailed types. Figure 11–2 shows the hierarchical nature of this typology, with the need driven at the bottom, the integrated at the top, and the separate outer-directed and inner-directed loops from the bottom to the top. *Need-driven* people, who spend according to need rather than preference, are subdivided into survivors and sustainers. *Survivors* are characterized as "struggling for survival, distrustful, socially misfitted, and ruled by appetites," whereas *sustainers* are "concerned with safety, insecure, compulsive, dependent, following, and want law and order." *Outer-directed* consumers, who are extensive purchasers and are sensitive to what other people think of them and their purchases, are subdivided into belongers, emulators, and achievers. *Belongers* are characterized as "conforming, conventional, unexperimental, traditional, and formal," *emulators*

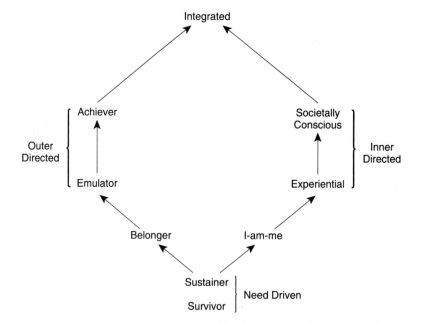

FIGURE 11–2 The VALS Double Hierarchy.
(Reprinted with the permission of Macmillan Publishing Company from The Nine American Lifestyles by Arnold Mitchell. Copyright © 1983 by Arnold Mitchell.)

as "ambitious, show-off, status conscious, upwardly mobile, macho, and competitive," and *achievers* as "achievement-motivated, materialistic, efficient, showing leadership, and desiring comfort." The *inner-directed* group of consumers, who are governed more by their individual needs than externally oriented values, are divided into I-am-me, experimental, and socially conscious subgroups. The *I-Am-Me's* are "fiercely individualistic, dramatic, impulsive, and volatile," the *experimentals* are "driven to direct experience, active, participative, person-centered, and artistic," and the *societally conscious* are characterized by "societal responsibility, simple living, smallness of scale, and inner growth." Finally, the *integrateds,* who represent a kind of optimal integration of outer-directed and inner-directed characteristics, are described as "psychologically mature, with an awareness of what is fitting, tolerant, self-actualizing, and possessing a world perspective." Although widely accepted and used in marketing, VALS is limited by the fact that consumers do not typically fall into a single category and by the proprietary nature of the data base on which VALS is based (Engel, Blackwell, & Miniard, 1989). Alternative psychographic approaches are the Monitor system of Yankelovich, Skelly, & White (see Holman, 1984) and the List of Values (LOV), which is based on Rokeach's theory (see Chapter 8) (Kahle, Beatty, & Homer, 1986).

ASSESSMENT IN CLINICAL CONTEXTS

Although clinical psychologists usually spend more time on treatment, consultation, research, teaching, and other activities than on psychological assessment, a substantial majority of clinicians find objective tests such as the MMPI and projective tests such as the Rorschach useful in psychodiagnosis and treatment planning (Wade & Baker, 1977). Clinical assessment for purposes of identifying and diagnosing behavioral or mental disorders and for planning treatment or other intervention procedures takes place in a variety of settings. These include private practice offices, mental health clinics, mental hospitals, Veterans Administration medical centers, schools, custodial institutions, and forensic settings. Clinical psychologists are called on to conduct psychological evaluations in mental health settings for purposes of diagnosis, treatment, and residential placement; in medical settings as an aid in hospital consultation to clinics in evaluating the psychological aspects of illness; in psychotherapeutic settings as an aid in planning and evaluating the effectiveness of psychotherapy and chemotherapy; in educational settings as an aid in formulating proper remediation measures; in legal settings to assist courts in sanity hearings and planning rehabilitation measures; and in various settings to conduct evaluations required by law, such as cases involving federal compensation.

Once the need for clinical assessment has been recognized, goals can be set and decisions made about what kinds of data are required to attain these goals. The general goals of clinical assessment are to provide an accurate description of the patient's (client's) problem(s), to determine what interpersonal and environmental factors precipitated and are sustaining the problem(s) and to make predictions concerning outcomes with and without intervention. Obtaining the kind of information required in clinical settings often necessitates a thorough case study.

Mental Status Interview and Clinical Case Study

Clinical psychologists are frequently called on to conduct *mental status examinations* to obtain in-depth information about emotional state (affect and mood), intellectual and perceptual functioning (attention, concentration, memory, intelligence, and judgment), style and content of thought process and speech, level of insight into mental status and personality problems, and psychomotor activity, as well as the patient's general appearance, attitude, and insight into his or her condition. Of course, all this information cannot be obtained from psychological tests alone. Detailed interviews of the client (patient) and significant others and careful observations of the client are also required. In conducting a thorough case study, details of the client's background and characteristics are obtained both from the client and significant other persons, and follow-up data are collected over a period of time. Information on the family, the culture, health history, developmental history, educational history, economic history, legal history, and the person's activities and thoughts may all be obtained. After the assessment data have been collected and integrated, a report summarizing the findings concerning the examinee's strengths and weaknesses is prepared, and recommendations for clinical, educational, or vocational interventions may be made.

When a case study is conducted to determine the cause(s) of a specific psychological problem, hypotheses or conclusions pertaining to causation may be formulated and specific recommendations made concerning treatment (psychotherapy, drugs or other medical treatment, special education, and so on). A follow-up assessment to evaluate the effectiveness of the prescribed treatment program should also be conducted after an appropriate time interval.

Despite its yield of potentially useful information for forming an overall picture, as well as an in-depth understanding of the individual, a clinical case study has some notable weaknesses. These include the retrospective nature of the data (memory is seldom completely accurate), the fact that the person conducting the study is frequently biased in selecting and evaluating certain kinds of data or measurements, and the extent to which the findings are generalizable across situations or circumstances encountered by a patient or client. Employing a variety of assessments in a systematic sample of situations and being aware of the likelihood of bias in selection and evaluation can help reduce, but not eliminate, misinterpretations and overgeneralizations.

Psychodiagnosis

Psychodiagnosis is the process of examining a person from a psychological viewpoint to determine the nature and extent of a mental or behavioral disorder. In the traditional *medical model* of mental disorders, the psychodiagnostician observes, interviews, and tests the patient to determine the presence or absence of certain psychological (and physical) symptoms. The diagnostician then compares the patient's symptoms with standard descriptions of abnormal behavior to determine in which category of disorders the patient best fits. The end result of the process is the assignment of a psychiatric classification or label to the patient, as specified in the *Diagnostic and Statistical Manual of Mental*

Disorders–III–R (American Psychiatric Association, 1987). In addition to diagnosing the disorder, a *prognosis,* or a prediction of its likely outcome if treated or untreated, is made.

The ability to make accurate psychodiagnoses requires extensive training and experience, and even then it is fraught with the potential for mistakes. Arkes (1985) describes a number of errors made in psychodiagnosis and other clinical judgments. One source of error is basing clinical judgments on the number of times that a supposed sign or indicator and a disorder have occurred together and overlooking the fact that they have failed to occur together even more often. Another source of error is the *hindsight bias* of believing that, after an event has already occurred, one could have predicted it if asked to do so. A third source of error in clinical judgments is overconfidence in one's judgments, despite evidence to the contrary. Because of selective perception, selective remembering, insufficient experience, inadequate follow-up, and faulty logic, clinicians frequently make diagnostic mistakes.

Case Conference

A written report is only one way in which the results of a psychometric evaluation are communicated to those who have a legitimate right to know. Clinical-case conferences or consultations in mental health contexts and parent–teacher or parent–counselor conferences in school settings may occur both before and after a psychological evaluation. When conducting a posttesting conference with a person who is unsophisticated in psychological testing, such as a typical parent, the psychological examiner should describe, in language appropriate to the listener, the test results and whatever conclusions can reasonably be drawn from them. In general, qualitative rather than quantitative descriptions and interpretations should be employed. The purpose and nature of the tests, why these particular tests were selected, and the limitations of the tests and results should also be discussed. Descriptive statements, rather than labels, and score ranges that take into account the standard error of measurement, rather than specific scores, should be used. Consultation involves a discussion of options and decisions, for treatment, remediation, rehabilitation, or other intervention, and providing information on referral sources. Following the consultation, the examiner should send a copy of the examination report to the referral source and other responsible parties.

Marital and Family Assessment

An estimated 2,362,000 marriages were performed and 1,215,000 divorces were granted in the United States during 1992 (U.S. Department of Health & Human Services, 1993). Although these figures indicate that more people are marrying than are divorcing, due to death or separation many of these marriages last only a short time. Furthermore, thousands of people have children but are never married, and innumerable one-parent families exist. As heard in speeches and discussions in the public forum, it is recognized that a crisis has arisen with regard to the stability of marriages and families in the United States. The consequence of marital and family disruption is that a large portion of the population lives a rootless existence, devoid of traditional values. These individuals find companionship and tutoring in antisocial models who contribute to crime and perpetuate the cycle of instability, violence, and poverty in their own descendants.

Realizing that marital problems are in many cases family problems that involve not only a husband and wife, but children and other members of the family unit as well, the traditional field of marriage counseling has of necessity been superseded in many instances by family counseling. The family is seen as a dynamic social system in which the intercommunications and other activities of all members of the family contribute to marital discord, intrafamilial conflict, and unstable marriages and families, as well as mutual gratification and happiness. Pathology is typically not limited to a single family member, in that "no person is an island unto himself." The family is a dynamic system in which the problems, difficulties, and unhappiness in each member affect the well-being and functioning of the family as a whole. Just as there are pathological individuals, families may themselves become disturbed and require the services of a trained therapist.

A number of psychological assessment instruments have proved useful in identifying, diagnosing, and making prognoses concerning marital and family problems. Instruments are available for (1) premarital advising, (2) identifying the sources and possible solutions for family disagreements and problems, and (3) helping victims of divorce, either parents or children, to pick up the pieces and get on with their lives. Traditional inventories and projectives such as the MMPI, the 16 PF, the Rorschach, and the TAT are frequently administered to analyze marital and family problems. Also available are checklists such as the Marital Evaluation Checklist (Psychological Assessment Resources), inventories such as the Marital Attitude Evaluation (Consulting Psychologist Press), the California Marriage Readiness Evaluation, the Marriage Adjustment Inventory, and the Marital Satisfaction Inventory (all from Western Psychological Services), and special projectives such as the Family Relations Test: Children's Version (Psychological Assessment Resources) and the Family Apperception Test (Western Psychological Services). Another useful psychometric instrument, the Family Environment Scale (Consulting Psychologists Press), was designed to assess the social climate of family systems and how the characteristics of the family interact. This questionnaire can be used to identify family strengths and problems and important issues for family treatment (see Figure 11–3). All these instruments must, of course, be supplemented by sensitive interviewing and observation of couples and family members in face-to-face social interactions.

ASSESSMENT IN HEALTH AND LEGAL PSYCHOLOGY

Two areas in which there has been an increasing demand for psychological services during recent years are those concerned with health-related and legal matters. Both areas have attracted the attention of research psychologists and other professionals who are interested in developing psychometric instruments for research and applications in these areas. A number of universities have instituted graduate programs in health and legal psychology, and measurement and research pertaining to the role of psychology in physical and legal problems are extensive.

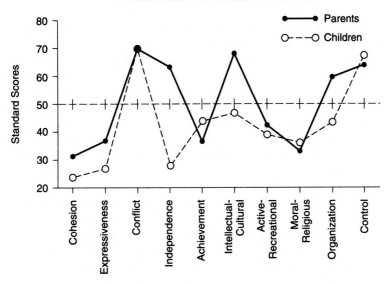

Form R Profiles for Parents and Children

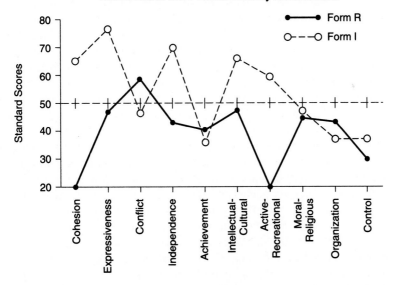

Beth's Actual and Preferred Family Environment

FIGURE 11–3 Profiles for Parents and Children on Form R (Top) and for a Particular Child (Beth) on Forms R and I (Bottom) of the Family Environment Scale.
(Reprinted by permission of Consulting Psychologists Press, Inc., from the Manual of the California Psychological Inventory, Revised Edition, Copyright 1987.)

Health Psychology

Health psychology has been defined as the "educational scientific, and professional contributions of the discipline of psychology to the promotion and maintenance of health, the
prevention and treatment of illness, and the identification of etiologic and diagnostic
correlates of health, illness, and related dysfunction" (Matarazzo, 1980, page 815). Interest
in the role of attitudes, self-efficacy, and other psychological factors or personality variables
in health is not limited to possibly psychosomatic disorders such as duodenal ulcers and
migraine headaches, but includes cardiac disorders, cancer, and other life-threatening
illnesses (see Holroyd, 1979). Psychologists are called on not only to identify psychological
factors related to various medical conditions and to help diagnose specific disorders, but
also to assist in planning intervention or treatment. The field of *behavioral medicine,* a
subspeciality of health psychology, has made significant contributions to the treatment
and management of patients by the use of behavior modification and other procedures.

There are several health-related personality inventories, including the Jenkins Activity
Survey for identifying coronary-prone Type A personalities, the Eating Disorders Inventory
for assessing behavior traits associated with anorexia nervosa and bulimia, and the Millon
Behavioral Health Inventory for assisting in formulating a comprehensive treatment plan
for adult medical patients. The number of commercially available checklists, rating scales,
and other questionnaires concerned with health-related matters has increased markedly
in recent years. Included among these are instruments to inventory health problems in
general and specific health areas, opinions and beliefs pertaining to health, measures of
stress and ways of coping with stress, measures of pain perception and control, and
measures of anxiety, depression, and addictive behavior (alcohol and drugs). Use of these
kinds of instruments is indicative of the growing interest in the field of health psychology,
which includes specializations such as neuropsychology, pediatric psychology, geropsy-
chology, and health enhancement (Weiner, 1983). *Health,* as defined by certain instruments,
connotes more than the absence of disease; health means *positive wellness,* with a focus
on attaining a good *quality of life.*

Among the important topics of research in health psychology are the roles of stress,
learned helplessness, depression, information processing, and coping with illness. For
example, a learned feeling or sense of helplessness has been found to be an important
factor in the coronary-prone personality (Glass & Carver, 1980). According to Dana
(1984), a feeling of personal efficacy or confidence that one's internal and external
environments are predictable and can therefore be controlled is the single most important
mediator of psychological health. An example of an instrument designed to measure the
extent of control or responsibility that one feels toward one's health is the Health Locus
of Control Scale (Wallston, Maides, & Wallston, 1976).

Related to the notion of control is the idea of personal efficacy, which is the opposite
of helplessness and has been found to be an important factor in physical health. A number
of theoretical models have been devised to assist in understanding the development and
consequences of feelings of helplessness and personal efficacy. For example, considerable
research on the topic has been stimulated by attribution theory, which seeks to explain
how people decide, on the basis of samples of an individual's behavior, what the specific
causes of that behavior are (Abramson, Garber, & Seligman, 1980). Two examples of
instruments for assessing attributions in the domain of personal health are the Attributional

Styles Questionnaire (Peterson et al., 1982) and the Health Attribution Test (by J. Achterberg & G. F. Lawlis, Institute for Personality and Ability Testing, 1988).

Another variable that has played a central role in the field of health psychology is that of *stress*. Several years ago, Dana (1984) pointed to the need for more comprehensive measurement of life stress, including identification of the specific stressors, reactions to stress, and an inventory of potential mediators of stress. Dana also noted that what is required is a workable model of psychological health, good functioning, or human wellness. Currently available measures based on various definitions of effective functioning, derived from self-actualization, ego development, and psychosocial development theories, represent a good beginning, but better measures of coping abilities, resistance to stress, and self-efficacy are needed. Among the commercially available instruments with the word *stress* in the title are the Daily Stress Test Inventory (Sigma Assessment Systems) and the Parenting Stress Index (Psychological Assessment Resources). Other stress-related instruments are the Coping Resources Inventory and the Hassles and Uplifts Scales (both from Consulting Psychologists Press). Related to the measurement of stress or stress reactions is *behavioral toxicology*, the assessment of performance under adverse environmental conditions.

Legal Psychology

Legal psychology is that branch of psychology concerned with matters of law enforcement. Psychologists employed in legal contexts are typically clinicians who possess a wide range of skills. They may use tests, questionnaires, and interviewing procedures to help select law-enforcement personnel. They may serve as human relations experts and staff developers who give workshops and in others ways train police officers in techniques of intervening in crises such as domestic arguments and hostage taking. They may counsel or conduct group and individual psychotherapy with officers and their families. They may also contribute to the evaluation of staff development programs in law-enforcement contexts and conduct research on the training and treatment of law-enforcement personnel.

Equally important in terms of its social significance is the branch of legal psychology known as *forensic psychology*, which is concerned primarily with evaluating defendants in court cases to determine whether they are competent to stand trial and whether they are dangerous and/or likely to be recividists. Among the questions asked of forensic psychologists by legal representatives and officials are (Lanyon, 1986):

Is a particular person insane?

What is the likelihood that a person will engage in dangerous or violent behavior?

Who should assume custody of a particular child?

Why did a person commit homicide?

What are the personal characteristics of a particular murderer who has not been apprehended?

How can sex offenders be identified from psychological evaluations and can their future behavior be predicted?

How can one tell whether a particular client will be defensive or honest in testifying?

In addition, psychologists may act as advisors to either the prosecution or defense in the selection of jurors.

In a legal trial or hearing, not only the defendant(s) but other persons connected with a trial or hearing, such as children who have reportedly been abused or whose preferences are important in custody hearings, may also be interviewed and in other ways examined by a psychologist.

Competency and Insanity   The opinions and recommendations of psychologists in matters dealing with the issue of competency (competency to stand trial, civil commitment, understanding of Miranda rights, and related issues) have been increasingly sought in recent years. Competency to stand trial has to do with whether a defendant understands the charges against him or her and can assist in his or her own defense.[1] As stated by the U.S. Supreme Court in *Dusky* v. *United States* (1960), the defendant must possess "sufficient present ability to consult with his lawyers with a reasonable degree of rational . . . [and] factual understanding of the proceedings against him." This means that usually, but not always, persons who are mentally retarded, psychotic, or suffering from debilitating neurological disorders are considered incompetent to stand trial. However, incompetency is not synonymous with *insanity.* Whereas legal insanity pertains to the mental state of the defendant at the time the crime was committed, the condition of incompetency is a continuing one. A person may be found "competent to stand trial" and yet adjudged "not responsible by reason of insanity."

The M'Naughten Rule (see Blau, 1984), the Durham decision (Durham v. United States, 1960), and the Model Penal Code (see Smith & Meyer, 1987) have all influenced legal tests for insanity in the United States. Although the great majority of states permit insanity pleas, several states have completely abolished such pleas. The standard of legal insanity applied most frequently by the judicial system in the United States is the Model Penal Code proposed by the American Law Institute (ALI) and adopted in 1972. As cited by Smith and Meyer (1987), the ALI definition states:

A person is not responsible for criminal conduct, i.e., insane if, at the time of such conduct, as a result of a mental disease or defect, he lacks substantial capacity either to appreciate the criminality (wrongfulness) of his conduct, or to conform his conduct to the requirements of the law. (American Law Institute, 1956)

Among the procedures and tools employed by psychologists in assessing competency are interviewing guides and competency screening instruments such as the Georgetown Screening Interview for Competency to Stand Trial (Bukatman, Foy, & De Grazia, 1971), the Competency Screening Test (Lipsitt, Lelos, & McGarry, 1971), the Competency Assessment Instrument (McGarry et al., 1973), and the Georgia Court Competency Test

---

[1]A kind of partial competence is *testamentary capacity,* which refers specifically to competency to make a will. An individual who possesses testamentary capacity, which is also legally determined, knows the nature and extent of his or her bounty (property), that he or she is making a will, and who his or her natural beneficiaries are.

(Wildman et al., 1980). The Rogers Criminal Responsibility Scales (R–CRAS) (Rogers, 1984, 1986) (Psychological Assessment Resources) may be administered to determine criminal responsibility according to the degree of impairment on psychological variables significant to the determination of insanity under the ALI standard. The five scales on the R–CRAS assess Patient Reliability, Organicity, Psychopathology, Cognitive Control, and Behavioral Control at the time of the crime the patient is alleged to have committed. Neuropsychological tests may also be administered to defendants in insanity pleas.

MMPI and Rorschach   These are the two most commonly administered tests in forensic contexts. In addition to its many other applications in jurisprudence, the MMPI can contribute to the identification of defensiveness (unwillingness to tell the truth) and provide information pertaining to additional matters of personal behavior that are of concern in court trials. The Rorschach is another workhorse in legal settings, but neither the MMPI nor the Rorschach permits unqualified answers and opinions concerning legal affairs. According to some authorities (for example, Lanyon, 1986), what is required are more question-specific instruments, for example, an instrument that can assess the effects of a particular brain injury on criminal behavior. Obviously, psychologists who design and use such instruments should be familiar with the law, as well as being capable test designers and clinicians.

Sex and Violence   With respect to sexual offenses, the Clarke Sex History Questionnaire for Males (Langevin, 1983), which reportedly assesses types and strength of sexually anomalous behavior, may be of help to a forensic psychologist. Perhaps most frequently administered of all psychometric instruments in legal settings, however, is the MMPI. Although no test has been developed that, by itself, can predict violent behavior, the MMPI can contribute to the forecasting of dangerous or violent behavior. A number of behavioral indicators, such as a recent history of violence, substance abuse, breakup of a marriage or love relationship, discipline or termination at work, and access to weapons such as guns can also contribute to the prediction of violent behavior (Hall, 1987). A combination of personal history and test data can be used to derive a probability of violence estimate, which is perhaps better than nothing, but far from exact. Determining the potential for violent behavior is important not only in parole hearings and other matters concerning convicted criminals, but also in the selection and promotion of police officers and other peace-keepers. In the wake of the Rodney King case in California, the question of whether psychological testing can be employed to reduce police brutality has become moot.

Violence may, of course, be expressed against adults or children, but in recent years the legal system and society as a whole have become sensitized to allegations of physical abuse of children. In cases of alleged child abuse, observations, interviews, figure drawing tests, and doll play can contribute to the determination or prediction of violent behavior or of physical or sexual abuse of children and adults.

Child Custody   Psychologists are frequently called on to assess personal injury in worker's compensation cases or other suits and to mediate child custody cases. Child custody evaluations may entail parent interviews focusing on child-rearing practices, as well as the administration of intelligence and personality tests. Measures of the parents' knowledge and attitudes about child-rearing practices may also contribute to decision making in child custody cases. Gordon and Peck's (1989) Custody Quotient, which yields ratings on 10 parenting factors, is helpful in this regard.

Evaluation of children in custody cases may involve administration of standardized psychometric instruments such as the Comprehension subtest of the WPPSI–R or WISC–R, story-telling tests, and the Bricklin Perceptual Scales (Bricklin, 1984). The latter instrument focuses on understanding the child's perceptions of his or her parents in four areas (competence, supportiveness, follow-up consistency, and possession of admirable personality traits). It is customary to talk with the child and perhaps employ other techniques (doll play and figure drawings concerning family living situations and sentence completion tests) to determine whether the child has a preference regarding his or her future living and visitation arrangements. However, it must be acknowledged that the stated preferences and reports of preschoolers with average and below-average intelligence are frequently not very reliable and are influenced too much by recent events to be taken at face value.

ENVIRONMENTAL ASSESSMENT

Because situational factors play an important role in determining behavior, combining environmental assessments with measures of ability and personality should improve the prediction of behavior in specific situations. Data obtained on environmental characteristics may also prove useful in comparing different situations. The effect of the situation on the person, however, does not constitute a one-way street. Different people react to the same situation in different ways, and they select and structure situations in terms of their own personalities. The relationship between the person and the environmental context is reciprocally interactive, or *transactive:* the person both affects and is affected by the environment.

Situations may be weak or strong, in that they may exert a weak or a strong influence on a person's behavior. An example of a strong situation is a religious service or other context in which expected behaviors are fairly clearly prescribed. Another strong situation is when a person is in a different culture or context and doesn't know quite how to behave; usually the problem is resolved by observing and modeling the behavior of other people in that situation. A weak situation is one of which the physical and social environments have weaker effects on a person's behavior. For example, when a person is at home with only his or her spouse or partying with two or three close friends, the situation permits the expression of a greater range of behaviors. In such circumstances, individual characteristics play a more important role than environmental ones.

It can be argued that efforts to construct more effective measures of personality would be more successful if they began with a conceptual model of how personality dispositions and environmental or situational variables interact. Then measures of both sets of variables could be developed to permit a true interactional assessment (McReynolds, 1979). Certainly some situations fit or match particular personalities better than others, and effective person–situation measures must assess the extent of the congruence. In any event, the development of good measures of person–situation interaction requires the combined efforts of specialists in psychometrics and environmental psychology.

Thus far, psychologists are only on the threshold of devising techniques for analyzing and assessing the dynamic, two-way interactions between persons and environments. However, the work of Rudolf Moos and his associates (Moos, 1976, 1979, 1986) on environmental measurement is indicative of how social environments can be conceptualized and evaluated and how the degree of congruence between actual and preferred environments might be assessed.

Recognizing that the ways in which people perceive environments affect their behavior in those environments and that the environments are, in turn, influenced by personal perceptions, Moos directed his efforts toward understanding and assessing human milieus. His assessments of the "personalities" of environments and their effects on individual functioning may be described in terms of three broad dimensions: (1) the nature and intensity of personal relationships, (2) personal growth and self-enhancement influences, and (3) system maintenance and change. In general, it has been found that people are more satisfied and comfortable, are less irritable and depressed, and experience greater self-esteem in environments that they perceive as highly relationship oriented.

Moos maintains that an analysis of environments in terms of the three dimensions listed above can lead to the formulation of criteria for an ideal environment and optimal methods for instituting environmental changes. To provide a means of assessing these dimensions, a number of Social Climate Scales (Consulting Psychologists Press) were constructed by Moos and his collaborators. Each scale consists of 90 to 100 items and yields 7 to 10 scores covering the three dimensions referred to above. Based on the assumption that people can distinguish different dimensions of social environments, the items on each scale are answerable in 15 to 20 minutes by individuals who are functioning in or cognizant of the particular social environment.

Moos and his associates have devised measures of the following social environments: classroom, community-oriented programs, correctional institutions, family, group, military, university residence, ward atmosphere, and work. Different forms of these instruments (Social Climate Scales) measure people's perceptions of the actual social environment (Form R), the ideal social environment (Form I), and the expectations a person has of a particular social environment (Form E); short forms (Form S) taking 5 to 10 minutes to complete are also available. A number of other measures of the characteristics of particular social environments are available, including McKechnie's Environmental Response Inventory (Consulting Psychologists Press), Stern's Classroom Environmental Index, College Characteristics Index, Elementary and Secondary School Index, High School Characteristics Index, and Organizational Climate Index (Evaluation Research Associates), and the Effective School Battery (Psychological Assessment Resources). Unfortunately, none of these instruments, including the ones devised by Moos, is based on an adequate taxonomy of situations relevant to persons (Frederiksen, 1976; Kenrick & Dantchik, 1983).

SUMMARY

This chapter summarizes applications of psychological assessment in seven contexts: educational, personnel, marketing, mental health, physical health, legal, and environmental.

In educational contexts, achievement tests are used to determine the extent to which students have attained the objectives of instruction, to diagnose students' strengths and weaknesses in the subject matter, and to evaluate teachers and educational programs. Diagnostic testing may involve neuropsychological evaluation of handicapped children, including children with sensorimotor and learning disabilities. A variety of psychometric devices, including the Bender Visual–Motor Gestalt Test and other perceptual–memory tests and neuropsychological test batteries such as the Halstead–Reitan Neuropsychological Test Battery and the Luria–Nebraska Neuropsychological Battery are used in diagnosing neuropsychological disorders. Batteries of tests are also administered to diagnose learning disabilities stemming from other conditions.

Requiring that high school students pass an academic competency test before graduation and that teachers pass a professional competency test before being hired are common practices in the United States. Also applied in some colleges and universities is the value-added approach to determine changes in knowledge and skills during the college years. Finally, tests and related assessment instruments are used extensively to evaluate educational programs or curricula and the effectiveness of other intervention procedures and programs.

Psychological assessment in occupational settings is used for purposes of selection, classification, promotion, and periodic appraisals of employees. Some of the statistical procedures applied to achieve these goals, including expectancy tables, selection ratios, multiple-cutoff and multiple-regression techniques, and Taylor–Russell tables, are described.

The section on consumer behavior emphasizes the use of AIO statements and the VALS approach to measure the activities, interests, opinions, values, and life-styles of consumers for purposes of market segmentation and product positioning.

Clinical psychologists administer tests, inventories, rating scales, checklists, and personality inventories for purposes of screening, psychodiagnosis, treatment planning, and research in mental health clinics and other settings. Of particular importance are mental status examinations, which focus on the intellectual, perceptual–motor, and emotional states of patients by means of extensive interviews, questionnaires, and additional psychometric procedures. After completing a psychodiagnostic examination of a person, a clinical case conference is held to explain the results to family members and other persons who have a right to know.

Both health and legal psychologists are trained in clinical–counseling and other psychological skills to perform a variety of tasks in medical or law-enforcement situations. Health psychologists analyze the role of psychological factors in physical illnesses and assist in planning and implementing prescribed treatments for such conditions. Among the many activities of legal or forensic psychologists are the psychological evaluation of offenders and other parties in judicial cases concerned with questions of competency to stand trial, responsibility for criminal acts, and the custody of minors.

Environmental assessment is concerned with analyzing the psychological environments of people and determining how a person's environment affects his or her sense of well-being and functioning effectiveness. Particularly noteworthy among the various environmental assessment instruments are the Social Climate Scales devised by Rudolf Moos and his associates.

EXERCISES

1. List arguments for and against competency testing of (a) high school students, (b) prospective public school teachers, and (c) experienced teachers.

2. Construct an empirical expectancy table from the paired X, Y scores in Table A–2 in Appendix A. Let X be the predictor (row) variable and Y the criterion (column) variable, and use an interval width of 7 for both variables in setting up the score intervals for X and Y.

3. Using the regression equation $Y_{pred} = .44X + 28.64$ for each value of X in Exercise 2, compute the predicted value of Y and construct a theoretical expectancy table with the actual X and predicted Y values. What differences did you find in your empirical and theoretical expectancy tables? How can you explain these differences? Which table would probably be most useful in educational or vocational counseling?

4. Prepare a short paper on "Psychological Testing and the Law," including a discussion of legal statutes pertaining to the usage of tests in education, business and industry, clinics and mental institutions, government, and other organizations. Several references that you should consult and cite in your paper are the following:

   Bersoff, D. N. (1982). The legal regulation of school psychology. In C. R. Reynolds & T. B. Gutkin (Eds.), *The handbook of school psychology.* New York: John Wiley & Sons.

   Bersoff, D. N. (1981). Testing and the law. *American Psychologist, 36,* 1047–1056.

   Lanyon, R. I. (1986). Psychological assessment procedures in court-related settings. *Professional Psychology: Research and Practice, 17,* 260–268.

   Shapiro, D. L. (1991). *Forensic psychological assessment: An integrative approach.* Boston: Allyn & Bacon.

   Smith, S. R., & Meyer, R. G. (1987). *Law, behavior, and mental health.* New York: New York University Press.

5. Consult the yellow pages of several large city telephone directories, such as are found in most college or university libraries, for advertisements concerning psychological services. Look under various headings, including psychologists, psychiatrists, psychotherapists, physicians, counselors, therapists, marriage counselors, education, clinics, or any other headings that occur to you as relevant. What information is given to assist people who require such services? In addition to telephone directories, the County Medical Society, the Mental Health Center, and other local organizations may provide you with a list of psychological service providers.

6. If the set of *Computer Programs for Psychological Assessment* is available, run program 4 ("Multiple Regression Analysis") in category 1 ("Programs on Basic Statistical Methods") using the following data:

   Criterion variable (1): Average grade in computer programming course.

   Predictor variable (2): Analogies Test score

   Predictor variable (3): Average grade in high school

Predictor variable (4): Score on Inventory of Interest in Computers

$r_{12} = .583$ $\overline{X}_1 = 73.8$ $s_1 = 9.1$

$r_{13} = .546$ $\overline{X}_2 = 49.5$ $s_2 = 17.0$

$r_{14} = .365$ $\overline{X}_3 = 61.1$ $s_3 = 19.4$

$r_{23} = .396$ $\overline{X}_4 = 29.7$ $s_4 = 3.7$

$r_{24} = .215$ $N = 100$

$r_{34} = .345$

Using the B coefficients in column 4 of the printout and the value of the intercept, write the regression equation for predicting computer course grades from the other three (predictor) variables. Evaluate the t ratios for testing the significance of the three predictor variables and the F ratio for evaluating the significance of the multiple correlation coefficient (R). Your instructor will help you interpret the results if you have difficulty.

7. Differentiate between the legal concepts of competency and insanity. What psychological assessment instruments or techniques can contribute to decisions concerning competency and insanity?

8. List a dozen different roles that a psychologist may perform in a forensic setting. Which of these are most useful and valid?

9. Many popular articles and television shows have focused on the problem of child abuse and methods of detecting and confirming it. What are some of the techniques employed by psychologists to determine whether or not a child has been abused? How valid are these techniques, and what are their dangers and other shortcomings?

10. Skim several popular magazines to obtain an impression of how women are treated in advertisements. Repeat this exercise with the elderly. What problems did you identify with respect to sexism and ageism in advertising?

SUGGESTED READINGS

Gatewood, R., & Perloff, R. (1990). Testing and industrial application. In G. Goldstein & M. Hersen (eds.), *Handbook of psychological assessment,* 2nd ed., pp. 486–504. New York: Pergamon.

Goldstein, G. (1990). Comprehensive neuropsychological assessment. In G. Goldstein & M. Hersen (eds.), *Handbook of psychological assessment,* 2nd ed., pp. 197–227. New York: Pergamon.

Grant, D., & Reed, R. (1982). Neuropsychological testing. In W. C. Wiederhold (ed.), *Neurology for non-neurologists,* pp. 143–155. New York: Academic Press.

Gregory, W. L., & Burroughs, W. J. (1989). *Introduction to applied psychology,* Chs. 4, 7, 8, 10, 12–15. Glenview, IL: Scott, Foresman.

Grisso, T. (1987). The economic and scientific future of forensic psychological assessment. *American Psychologist, 42,* 831–839.

Linn, R. L. (1986). Educational testing and assessment. *American Psychologist, 41,* 1153–1160.

Matarazzo, J. D. (1990). Psychological assessment versus psychological testing. *American Psychologist, 45,* 999–1017.

Posavac, E. J., & Carey, R. G. (1992). *Program evaluation: Methods and case studies,* 4th ed. Englewood Cliffs, NJ: Prentice Hall.

Shapiro, D. L. (1991). *Forensic psychology and assessment: An integrative approach.* Boston: Allyn & Bacon.

Taylor, H. G., & Fletcher, J. M. (1990). Neuropsychological assessment of children. In G. Goldstein & M. Hersen (eds.), *Handbook of psychological assessment,* 2nd ed., pp. 228–255. New York: Pergamon.

Wise, P. S. (1989). *The use of assessment techniques by applied psychologists.* Belmont, CA: Wadsworth.

Wittenborn, J. R. (1990). Psychological assessment in treatment. In G. Goldstein & M. Hersen (eds.), *Handsbook of psychological assessment,* 2nd ed., pp. 467–485. New York: Pergamon.

Chapter Twelve

Criticisms and Issues in Testing

As witnessed by the number and variety of instruments described in the preceding chapters, the field of psychological and educational assessment has expanded rapidly during this century. The widespread use of group tests of achievement, intelligence, and special abilities in education, business, and government has contributed to the growth of psychological assessment. However, organized labor, maintaining that occupational selection and promotion should be based on experience and seniority rather than measured abilities, has typically been unsupportive of psychological testing. Other spokespersons and sociopolitical organizations have also voiced opposition to certain practices and types of testing.

THE NATURE AND CONSEQUENCES OF CRITICISM

"Testing, Testing, Testing"

"The Shortcomings of Standardized Tests"

"Reliance on Multiple-choice Tests Said to Harm Minorities"

This sample of headings from newspaper and popular magazine articles is indicative of the fairly steady stream of critical stories that have been appearing for years. The bulk of criticism of testing during the past several decades has been concerned with either the content and applications of tests or the social consequences of relying on test scores to make decisions about people. Testing in general has been attacked on the one hand for invasion of the individual's right to privacy and on the other hand for its secretiveness or confidentiality. Ability tests in particular have been faulted for limitations and bias in what they purport to measure. Perhaps because of their less extensive and less crucial applications, personality assessment instruments have not been criticized as much by the general public. The relatively poor measurement characteristics of many personality tests, however, have not escaped critical scrutiny by psychologists and nonpsychologists alike.

Among the nonpsychologists who have denounced personality tests are certain writers and parents who object to particular questions or approaches used in the assessment of personal characteristics, attitudes, and behavior.

With respect to the applications of tests, it has been argued that, rather than fostering equality of opportunity, they have led to a preservation of the status quo and a legitimizing of undemocratic practices by educational institutions, business organizations, and government (Karier, 1972). More specifically, it has been claimed that tests are often useless as predictors of behavior, that they are unfair to minority groups, that the results are frequently misinterpreted and misused, and that they promote a narrow and rigid classification of people according to supposedly static characteristics.

Although criticisms of psychological and educational testing have often resulted in more heat than light, some of the concerns have forced mental testers to reevaluate their practices. Certain criticisms have led to changes of a technical nature, whereas others have prompted a reexamination of the ethics of testing and proposals for an ethical code that would apply to the constructors, distributors, and users of tests.

Legal and ethical issues concerned with the administration of tests and use of the results were discussed briefly in Chapter 1. As noted there, according to the Family Rights and Privacy Act, test results that are maintained by educational institutions may be made available to other people only with the *informed consent* of the student or legally responsible adults. Even when informed consent is granted, test information may be *privileged* in that only certain persons (parents, personal attorney, physician, psychologist, and others) have the right of access to the results.

The concept of privileged communication also applies to both test and nontest information obtained by psychologists. Privileged communication, however, is an all or none matter: if authorized by a client to reveal certain information about a case, a psychologist is also required to reveal, if requested by the court, all available information concerning the client. Furthermore, whenever a psychologist feels that a client represents a clear danger to himself, herself, or others, this information can be released to responsible persons without the client's consent. In fact, as concluded in the case of *Tarasoff* v. *Regents of University of California* (1983), psychologists may be legally obligated to reveal this information; the good of society as a whole supersedes the individual's right to privacy and privileged communication.

The question of whether the administration of various kinds of psychological tests represents a serious invasion of privacy has been debated at length. It can be argued, however, that if the responses to test questions are of sufficient social value then people may have to endure some invasion of their privacy (Marland, 1969). As important as respect for individual rights concerning confidentiality of test scores and invasion of privacy may be, these rights must be balanced against the need for evaluative information of high quality (London & Bray, 1980).

Ideally, psychological assessment findings are treated conscientiously and with an awareness of the limitations of the assessment instruments and the needs and rights of examinees. Unfortunately, the ethics of psychological examiners have not always been as they should be. Therefore, the adoption by the American Psychological Association and other professional organizations of codes of ethics pertaining to testing and sanctions against their violation has represented a step forward in psychological assessment and the practice of psychology in general (American Psychological Association, 1981, 1992; American Educational Research Association et al., 1985).

COLLEGE ENTRANCE EXAMINATIONS

Large-scale testing programs, in which tests are administered to thousands of students each year, have been the special targets of criticism during the past quarter-century. It has been said, for example, that too much school time is spent administering tests that measure only a few of the variables pertaining to academic achievement and other accomplishments. Of all large-scale testing programs, the most influential and most often attacked are college and university entrance examinations. The Scholastic Aptitude Test (SAT), the American College Tests (ACT), and various other instruments fall in this category, but of these it is the SAT that has been the target of greatest criticism.

It has sometimes been alleged that college admissions officers assign too much weight to SAT scores and not enough weight to interview data as indicators of creativity or exceptionality. As revealed by the results of a study of 25,000 students in nine colleges (Willingham & Breland, 1982), there is probably some truth to this allegation. This study, which was conducted by Educational Testing Service, found that three times as much weight was given to high school grades and SAT scores as to personal qualities or extracurricular accomplishments. The most influential personal credential in determining whether or not to admit a student, at least in colleges having strong affirmative action programs, was the minority status of the applicant. Alumni ties, geographical location, and outstanding personal interviews also contributed to a favorable admissions decision in certain cases, but the financial situation of the applicant was a negligible factor.

Other research findings (for example, Ravitch, 1983–1984) indicate that letters of recommendation do not carry as much weight in admissions as might be supposed. Due to lack of confidentiality or a concern about it and a strong interest on the part of the letter writer in having the applicant accepted, almost all such letters tend to be laudatory. For this reason, it has been said that "one telephone call is worth a dozen letters of recommendation." The same leniency error, in addition to variability of grading standards from school to school, affects the usefulness of high school grades as predictors of college success. Personal interviews continue to be of some value in admissions, but they are also limited by the prejudices of the interviewer and the ability of applicants to present themselves.

Despite the fact that few colleges require the submission of SAT scores with an application, the great majority of undergraduate institutions have retained either the SAT or the ACT for admissions and placement purposes. Scores on these tests can also serve as an early warning system and as diagnostic guides for remedial work. The SAT is one of the most carefully designed of all available tests, having high reliability and substantial validity for predicting college grades. These features, however, have not protected the SAT from the rash of criticism to which it has been subjected since the 1950s. Undoubtedly a result, at least in part, of this continuing criticism are changes in the SAT that were implemented in the early 1990s. Among these changes are the addition of a written essay, mathematical questions without hints from multiple-choice answers, more vocabulary testing based on reading passages instead of isolated word exercises, permitting the use of calculators, and fewer questions.

Multiple-choice Tests

During the 1960s, the most vociferous critics of college entrance examinations and other nationally administered educational tests were Hillel Black and Banesh Hoffman. Writing in a less caustic, more constructive vein than Hoffman, Black (1962) offered a number of suggestions for controlling the use of tests in educational institutions. In his book *The Tyranny of Testing* (1962) and in various articles published in popular magazines, Hoffman argued against the use of multiple-choice tests in schools and colleges. His main arguments are as follows:

1. They favor shrewd, nimble-witted, rapid reader.
2. They penalize the subtle, creative, more profound person.
3. They are concerned only with the answer and not the quality of thought behind it or the skill with which it is expressed.
4. They have a generally bad effect on education and the recognition of merit.

Hoffman's method of argument was to display test items that might be interpreted differently by more profound or creative students than by the test constructors. Otherwise, his case was based mainly on hypothetical examples and emotionally loaded arguments, rather than sound evidence.

The criticisms made by Hoffman and other writers did not go unchallenged. After examining the basic assumptions of various critics of educational testing, Dunnette (1963) concluded that most of the assumptions were erroneous and fallacious and due either to a lack of information or a refusal to recognize that tests are the most accurate means available for identifying merit. In another reply to critics of testing, Chauncey and Dobbin (1963) admitted the limitations of tests but maintained that, when used properly, tests can help improve instruction. Furthermore, in the face of mounting criticism, testing organizations did not sit idly by and respond defensively. The College Entrance Examination Board actively sought criticism of its tests and policies by establishing a major commission to investigate itself (College Entrance Examination Board, 1971).

One empirical study designed to look at criticisms of multiple-choice tests examined the relationships between scores on these tests and measures of creativity, nonconformity, the ability to recognize ambiguity, preference for complexity, and test wiseness. The findings were mixed: they neither completely confirmed nor refuted the critics' assertions. As the critics had alleged, test wiseness was positively related to scores on multiple-choice tests of aptitude and achievement. However, contrary to another allegation, the ability to recognize ambiguity was also positively correlated with scores on the tests.

Attacks on objective examinations did not disappear with the 1960s, nor were they limited to nonpsychologists. David McClelland (1973), a prominent psychologist, argued for discontinuing the use of all multiple-choice tests. Rather than continuing to use these measures of what a person already knows as a way of proving his or her capabilities,

McClelland argued that other types of measures, such as those assessing the capacity to learn quickly, should be developed.

A criticism of multiple-choice tests that is difficult to prove or disprove, but that has wide educational and social ramifications, alleges that such tests are not only poor measures of ability and achievement, but that their use also encourages inferior teaching and improper study habits. Consequently, a conclusion of a report of the National Assessment of Educational Progress that standardized tests requiring brief answers are an important factor in the superficiality of students' reading skills demands attention. This report called for teachers to be wary of excessive reliance on objective tests and to reinstate the traditional essay examination, which requires students to explain and support their answers (David, 1981). The effective use of essay items requires that scorers evaluate not only the content of answers, but also the style or skill with which answers are expressed. Writing out an answer to a question does not improve the ability to express oneself in writing unless constructive feedback on the form as well as the content of the answer is given.[1]

Nader–Nairn Criticisms of ETS

The most publicized campaign against objective tests, and college entrance examinations in particular, during the 1980s was directed by consumer advocate Ralph Nader and his "raiders." In his speeches and written reports, Nader criticized the SAT, the GRE, the LSAT, and other standardized tests of ability for not measuring imagination, idealism, determination, and other human attributes that he considered important for the advancement of civilization. Nader maintained that the use of these tests has resulted in the restriction of students' career choices and the misallocation of a great deal of professional talent.

Allan Nairn (1980), an associate of Nader, alleged that scores on the SAT and other ETS tests rank people by social class rather than aptitude, a fact that Nairn felt ETS has attempted to suppress. The result, he argued, is the denial of educational opportunities to lower-class students and hence the preservation of the status quo in higher education. Nairn also concluded that the SAT is a poor predictor of college grades and should be abandoned in favor of various diagnostic measures of skills and competencies. He and his coauthors called for a full disclosure of the questions and answers to the SAT and an admission that the test does not measure any construct so general as "scholastic aptitude."

ETS responded at length to the Nader–Nairn attack (Educational Testing Service, 1980a, 1980b), concluding that tests do not deny opportunities to children of poor and

---

[1]The criticism that multiple-choice tests provide only a glimpse of a student's knowledge at a superficial level and fail to reveal what the student can do with that knowledge has prompted a movement toward performance-based testing, or "authentic assessment," in the public schools. Consisting of open-ended questions and hands-on problem solving in mathematics, science, and certain other subject-matter areas, performance-based tests stress reasoning, analysis, and writing. On such tests, students earn credit not just by obtaining the right answer but by demonstrating how they arrived at the answer. Students may also be required to work in small groups, conducting experiments and sharing interpretations of results, or constructing or producing something through collective efforts. Despite enthusiasm for the new tests, the issues of validity, fairness, cost–benefit ratio, and scoring reliability with respect to performance-based testing remain to be resolved (see Educational Testing Service, 1992).

working-class families and that the SAT in particular is not a poor predictor of achievement in college. ETS officials admitted that no test is a perfect predictor of either academic or life success, nor is it a measure of an individual's value or worth. The SAT and other scholastic ability tests were never intended to measure innate abilities, but rather to assess skills learned in a wide range of school-type activities.

The Nader–Nairn attack on ETS has been continued and extended by the National Center for Fair and Open Testing (FairTest), a testing watchdog group in Cambridge, Massachusetts. FairTest maintains that SAT items are often biased and unfair toward minority groups and women and, consequently, that the tests deprive these groups of equal educational opportunities. Another concern of this group is that it should be unethical to require examinees to take experimental sections on the SAT, the GRE, and other ETS tests consisting of items that are not scored but are used for item tryout purposes. FairTest called on ETS to obtain examinees' consent before having them complete experimental sections of the SAT. FairTest's "Bill of Rights" also emphasizes that test takers have a right to sound test-taking information and tips on test-taking strategies, accurately timed tests administered under quiet conditions, privacy of scores and other personal data, due process for any challenge to the test, and access to data concerning the test's accuracy (Weiss, Beckwith, & Schaeffer, 1989).

Examinees and their parents have a legal right in most states to information regarding examinees' performance on psychological or educational tests, but this does not necessarily mean that actual scores should be reported. Rather, test results should be communicated in such a way that they are not misunderstood or misused and will serve to benefit rather than handicap examinees. This caution applies primarily to tests administered to children for diagnostic purposes in clinical or educational contexts. On the other hand, scores on college entrance examinations are routinely reported to the test taker as well as to those institutions to which he or she indicates that the scores should be sent. In addition, New York State's truth-in-testing law requires that students who take the SAT or other college admissions tests be provided copies of the actual questions and correct answers, as well as copies of their own answer sheets, within a reasonable period of time after taking the test. Two other provisions of the New York State law, which was enacted in 1979, are that (1) test takers be told at the time of application how their scores will be computed, what the tester's contractual obligation to them is, and how scores on the test are affected by coaching and various demographic factors, and (2) the test contractor must file information on and studies of the test's validity with the state commission on education. The law also requires that complete editions of the tests be published so that students can practice taking them.

Critics of testing wish to expand the full-disclosure provisions of the New York law to other states and to other examinations, to encourage the use of novel tests to lessen cultural bias, and to make the testing industry more accountable to its customers. Although over two dozen state legislatures, in addition to the federal government (H.R. 3564 and H.R. 4949), have considered laws similar to the New York legislation, California is the only state other than New York to enact a special statute regulating college entrance examinations. The California law, referred to as the Dunlop Act, requires only that representative samples of tests be provided to the California State Department of Education. Both the New York and California state legislatures have considered additional legislation to tighten regulations pertaining to testing, but only in New York have those efforts met with success.

The New York State law and other pending truth-in-testing legislation affect not only the SAT, the ACT, and other undergraduate admissions tests, but also tests for admission to graduate and professional schools. Although the Law School Admission Council and the Graduate Management Admission Council approved disclosure of the results of their tests (LSAT and GMAT), the American Association of Medical Colleges and the American Dental Association expressed strong opposition to truth-in-testing legislation. The former organization, arguing that the New York law violates the copyright on the MCAT, obtained an injunction in 1979 against implementation of the law. In 1990, a federal court found that the New York State statute, which forces publication of materials from the Medical College Admission Test, violates federal copyright law. Despite this ruling, disclosure of test materials will undoubtedly continue to be standard practice by testing organizations (Blumenstyk, 1990). Current procedures that are designed to ensure fair and open testing have become an accepted part of test construction, administration, and scoring at ETS, ACT, and other organizations that design and market tests.[2]

Concern over truth-in-testing legislation has led to improved monitoring of test questions for cultural or socioeconomic bias. Careful internal review by the ETS professional staff has eliminated bias (ethnic group, sex, and so on) from almost all the 50,000 or so items included on ETS tests each year. Furthermore, the College Entrance Examination Board has adopted a policy of letting students verify their SAT scores and of public disclosure of SAT items one year after the tests have been administered. Test takers can challenge items on the SAT and other ETS tests and how these examinations are administered.

Effects of Coaching on Test Scores

Individual applicants for admission to undergraduate or graduate colleges or professional schools are understandably interested in the possibility of improving their test scores by training or coaching. A result of the increasing importance of large-scale nationwide testing has been the publication of coaching booklets and the establishment of schools that purport to increase a person's score on a particular examination or on standardized tests in general. Whether coaching has a significant effect on SAT and other entrance examinations scores has been a topic of discussion for many years. It is an important issue, for if it were demonstrated that coaching can improve test scores, then young people who could not afford the cost of coaching would be deprived of the same opportunity as their more affluent peers to do well.

[2]With respect to disclosure of psychological test information in court, the 1991 Illinois Confidential Act states that "psychological test material whose disclosure would compromise the objectivity or fairness of the testing process may not be disclosed to anyone including the subject of the test and is not subject to disclosure in any administrative, judicial or legislative proceeding. However, any recipient who has been the subject of the psychological test shall have the right to have all records relating to that test disclosed to any psychologist designated by the recipient" (*APA Monitor,* February, 1991, page 22).

The results of earlier studies indicated that the effects of coaching are quite variable, depending on the similarity of the coached material to the test material, the examinee's level of motivation and education, and other factors. Evidence concerning the effects of coaching on the SAT was reported some years ago by the College Entrance Examination Board (1971). The findings were interpreted as indicating that short-term, intensive drill on items similar to those on the SAT does not lead to significant gains in scores, especially on the verbal section of the test. This conclusion was questioned by a number of people, one of whom, Stanley H. Kaplan, directs the largest test-coaching organization in the United States. In 1979, the Federal Trade Commission (FTC) released a report of a study of the effects of a 10-week coaching program in three of the Kaplan Educational Centers. Admitting that the study had certain methodological flaws, the FTC nevertheless concluded that performance on both the verbal and mathematical portions of the test can be improved by coaching courses. In a review of the findings of the FTC investigation and other studies of coaching, Slack and Porter (1980) maintained that students can raise their SAT scores with training, that the scores are not good predictors of performance in college, and that the test does not measure the capacity to learn.

The FTC study and the Slack and Porter review were subsequently evaluated by ETS. Reanalyzing the data from the FTC investigation, ETS obtained similar findings: inconsistent and negligible effects of coaching for students at two of the Kaplan schools and increases of 20 to 35 points for both verbal and mathematical scores at a third school. Acknowledging that significant increases in test scores may occur when coaching programs involve many hours of course work and assignments, ETS nevertheless maintained that at least part of the gains found at the third school could be attributed to differences in motivation and other personal characteristics (Fields, 1980). Getting only two or three more items correct on the SAT, which could result from many different factors, can increase the verbal or math scores as much as 20 to 35 points.

Subsequent reviews of the effects of coaching (Anastasi, 1981; Linn, 1982; Messick, 1980) concluded that 8 to 12 hours of coaching can improve SAT scores by an average to 10 points, but only after 45 hours of coaching for the SAT-M and 200 hours of coaching for the SAT-V can gains as high as 30 points be expected. John Katzman, president of the test coaching organization Princeton Review, disagreed with these estimates of the effects of coaching and claimed to be able to improve student's SAT scores by up to 200 points. Katzman's approach is to familiarize students with the standard test-writing techniques used by ETS so that they can learn to outsmart the testing service by learning to think the way that ETS does (Biemiller, 1986).[3]

Annual Changes in SAT Scores

Test scores are not fixed, unvarying numbers; they are subject to errors of measurement and to genuine changes in abilities and other personal characteristics. Parents and school officials are usually alert to such changes in test scores from year to year, and decisions

---

[3]Even without formal coaching, a little test sophistication may improve one's score. For example, it has been found that the answer options on certain reading passage items are so poorly designed that a substantial majority of examinees can select the correct answer without reading the passage on which it is based (Jacobson, 1993).

concerning individual instruction, curricular modifications, and the allocation of state funds for instruction are made on the basis of the observed changes. Of particular concern are declines in aptitude and achievement test scores.

During the 1970s, it became increasingly clear that mean scores on the SAT and other standardized tests of mental abilities administered to high school students throughout the United States were declining annually. Although increases in mean SAT scores occurred during the 1950s and 1960s, the mean SAT–Verbal score decreased from 478 in 1963 to 460 in 1970 and 423 in 1980. The decrease in the mean SAT–Mathematics score was not quite as large as that in mean SAT–Verbal score, but still significant—from a mean of 502 in 1963 to 488 in 1970 and 467 in 1980 (see Figure 12–1). Declines occurred for both sexes, for different ethnic groups, and for both higher- and lower-ability students. Although the total number of students taking the SAT fell only 3 percent from 1972 to 1982, there was a 45 percent reduction in the number who scored above 650 on the SAT–Verbal and a 23 percent reduction in the number scoring above 650 on the SAT–Mathematical. Similar downward trends in mean scores occurred on the American College Tests (ACT), the Minnesota Scholastic Aptitude Test, the Iowa Tests of Educational Development, and the Comprehensive Test of Basic Skills.

Various explanations have been given for the decline in test scores during the late 1960s and 1970s. Among the explanations endorsed by sizable percentages of the respondents in a 1976 Gallup poll of the U.S. population were less parental attention, concern and

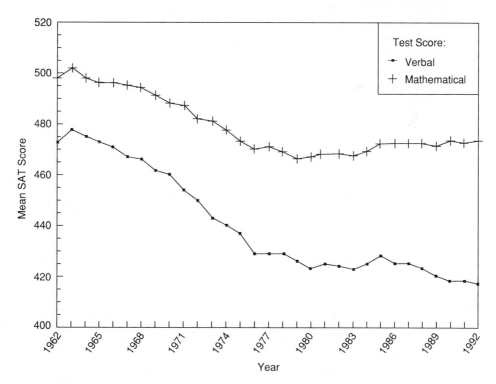

FIGURE 12–1 Changes in Mean SAT Scores from 1962 through 1992. *(Data from College Entrance Examination Board.)*

supervision of children; students not motivated to do well; too much television viewing; society becoming too permissive; and teachers providing less attention to students (Elam, 1978). Other reasons given for the decline in test scores included drugs, sex, lack of economic incentives for obtaining a good education, and spacing of children within families (see Zajonc, 1986).

In a comprehensive review of the data on test-score changes, the report of a special advisory panel failed to find any evidence that the observed decreases were caused by more difficult tests (Austin & Garber, 1982). The panel did conclude that approximately half of the overall decline in scores from 1963 to 1977 was due to changes in the composition of the sample taking the test. Changes in the economic, ethnic, sex, and social class composition of the examinees who took the SAT had, however, already expressed their effects by 1970. Further test-score declines during the 1970s were, according to the advisory panel, caused by more pervasive social forces. Precisely what these forces were and how much influence each had were not clear, but the panel cited such factors as less intellectually demanding high school curricula, diminishing educational standards, lower abilities of teachers, changes in the role and social structure of the U.S. family, television, national disruption during the early 1970s, and lower student motivation. The decline in SAT scores, which appeared to have been arrested by the mid-1980s, was one of the factors stimulating a national debate concerning educational policies.

Demographic Differences

Sex Differences   Over the years, men have consistently outscored women on the SAT–Mathematical, but until 1972 women outscored men on the SAT–Verbal; in 1992 the mean score for men (499) was 43 points higher than that for women (456) on the SAT–Mathematical and 9 points higher on the SAT–Verbal (428 compared with 419). On other tests, such as the NAEP reading tests, girls have continued to score higher than boys, but the gap has narrowed. The causes of the sex differences, which, incidentally, are the reverse of the differences in high-school and college freshman year grade-point averages, are unclear. Authorities are uncertain whether to blame the tests, the schools, biological factors, or some other environmental variable. One possible factor, suggested by Nancy Burton of ETS, is that, on the average, the socioeconomic status of girls who took the SAT in the 1980s was lower than that of boys. Another hypothesis, offered by Margaret Feldman of Ithaca College, is that during the 1980s teenage girls were more worried about dating and possible pregnancies and less committed to schoolwork than they had been in the 1970s (Cordes, 1986).

Whatever the causes of the sex differences in SAT scores may be, the Center for Women Policy Studies maintains that the SAT underestimates the college grades of women and is therefore biased against them. As a result of the gender gap in SATs, it is alleged that young women are less likely than young men to be awarded college scholarships. Nancy Burton of ETS countered, however, that the differences between the average SAT scores of men and women reflect genuine educational differences and that the predictive validity of the test is as high for one sex as for the other. Be that as it may, in response to criticisms by various groups, the New York State Education Department in 1988 stopped awarding college scholarships on the basis of SAT scores alone and began giving equal weight to high school grade-point averages and SATs (Evangelauf, 1989).

Ethnic Group Differences   For the past decade, the relative standings of Asian-Americans, African-Americans, Mexican-Americans, Puerto Ricans, and Anglo-Americans on the SAT have remained fairly constant, although the specific mean scores have changed. In 1992, Anglos scored highest (442), Asian-Americans second highest (413), Mexican-Americans third (372), Puerto Ricans fourth (366), and African-Americans lowest (351) in mean SAT–V score. Asian-Americans scored highest (532), Anglos second highest (491), Mexican-Americans third (423), Puerto Ricans fourth (406), and African-Americans lowest (385) in mean SAT–M score. Although the mean scores for Asians and whites remained fairly constant or even declined slightly, the mean SAT scores of blacks and Hispanics increased somewhat over the 10-year period. Nevertheless, on the average, blacks continued to score approximately 100 points lower than whites on both the SAT–V and SAT–M. Critics maintain that the black–white difference is a result of the fact that the SAT is biased against blacks (Day, 1985), but similar rankings of blacks, Hispanics, and whites have been obtained on the reading, mathematics, and science test scores of the National Assessment of Educational Progress.

Related to, but obviously not specific to, the issue of ethnic differences in college admissions test scores is the requirement that student athletes achieve a minimum total score of 700 on the SAT or 17 on the American College Test (ACT) and a minimum grade-point average of 2.0. This requirement, which was enacted as Proposition 48 by the NCAA in 1983, was modified in 1992 to a minimum GPA of 2.5. The higher required GPA is being phased in over 5-year period, and it will be reduced to as low as 2.0 for students whose SAT or ACT scores are higher than those required by Proposition 48. Although some opponents of the revised rules have described them as discriminating against minorities, representatives of the overwhelming majority of NCAA Division I schools felt that student athletes could meet the requirements (Robbins & Almond, 1992).

Geographical Differences   For some years the U.S. Department of Education has used SAT scores in annual state-by-state comparisons of educational quality, but because of the differing percentages of students in each state who take the test, such comparisons are subject to misinterpretation. For example, in 1989 only 4 percent of high school seniors in Mississippi took the SAT, on which they obtained a mean total score of 1001. However, Mississippi's schools rank close to last among the states on various criteria. On the other hand, the mean total SAT score in New Jersey was 894 in 1989, but 67 percent of that state's high school seniors, representing a much wider range of academic ability, took the test in that year. As ETS has cautioned, because of differences in the percentages of students who take the SAT in various states, not much can be made of such state-by-state comparisons. A fairer state-by-state comparison can be made with the NAEP scores, but there are also serious problems in interpreting the differences in mean scores on the NAEP tests.

OTHER ISSUES IN EDUCATIONAL TESTING

Although matters pertaining to the SAT and other national testing programs have received the most attention in the media, a number of other issues concerning testing in and for the schools are noteworthy. Among these are requiring that students pass a minimum competency test in order to graduate from high school and that prospective teachers pass a test of professional knowledge and skills in order to receive a teaching license or credential. These two topics were considered in some detail in Chapter 11, but a few additional points should be made about teacher testing.

Currently almost all the states require some form of standardized testing of would-be teachers and somewhat over half require students to pass tests or earn a certain score on a standardized entrance examination before they can major in education. Unfortunately, the failure rate on these tests, especially among minority group applicants, is high. In addition, the validity of many of the tests as measures of the knowledge and skills important to teaching has been questioned. The majority of these tests contain not only questions pertaining to professional competence, but also items to assess general academic knowledge and communication skills. Such is the case with the National Teacher Examinations (NTE), the most popular of the teacher tests, which is taken by about 200,000 prospective teachers each year. The NTE in particular has been the object of criticism for some years, but a successor to the NTE was scheduled for introduction by Educational Testing Service in 1992. Unlike the NTE, the new test does not rely exclusively on multiple-choice items; it also includes computer simulations, interactive video, and classroom observation. Plans are also in the works to use different testing methods at various stages of a prospective teacher's educational career, giving the prospect a better chance to show what he or she can do (Fields, 1988). However, it is undoubtedly overly optimistic to expect any test, no matter how modern or unbiased, to eliminate all criticism of competency examinations. People will continue to complain about selection tests that they do not pass or that they, for whatever reasons, believe are unfair or invalid predictors or measures of actual job performance.

Cheating on Tests

As test scores have become more important not only in determining the future educational and professional careers of individuals but also in the political arena for assessing schools and other institutions, the temptation to cheat appears to have increased. The administration of *secure* tests involves standard procedures, such as verifying personal identification, seating examinees in a particular way, careful proctoring, and counting tests and answer sheets to minimize cheating, but none of these procedures can entirely eliminate it. Pressures on students from their parents, teachers, peers, and themselves to score high on standardized tests can lead to stealing copies of the tests, subtly copying answers from other students, and other methods of cheating.

In addition to actually observing students cheat on tests or being told by students that others cheated, circumstantial evidence of cheating may be obtained (1) by noting that the pattern of wrong answers by students seated close to each other is remarkably similar and (2) that an answer sheet contains a very large number of erasures, primarily from changing wrong answers to right ones. The last technique was used in California in the mid-1980s to confirm suspicions arising from dramatic increases in test scores in some schools that not students but teachers were altering students' answers on the California Assessment Program (CAP) tests. The answer sheets from the CAP tests, which measure basic skills in reading, writing, and mathematics and are administered annually in the third, sixth, eighth, and twelfth grades of California public schools, are scored by electronic data scanners. The scanners not only score the answer sheets but also count erasures. By this method and confirmatory clerical work, it was found that in several dozen Los Angeles schools the percentage of erasures on the answer sheets was significantly higher than the expected average of 3 percent. Although the resulting furor and associated media coverage led to strong protests by the teachers' union and a refusal by teachers in some instances to handle CAP tests, a result of these events was investigation of both direct and indirect cheating and tampering with the CAP and CTBS tests.

Tampering by teachers with students' answer sheets could not be convincingly denied, but the question was why did they do it? The general answer seems to be that test scores have come to be used so extensively in our society not only to evaluate individuals, but also schools, school districts, states, and even neighborhoods (for example, real estate agents often cite high test scores in their sales pitches), that the pressure on teachers and schools to show up well is enormous. Not only have the social pressures on everyone connected with the schools resulted in cheating by students and test tampering by teachers, but teachers frequently "teach to the test." An example is the practice in California schools of reviewing with students the booklet "Scoring High on the Comprehensive Tests of Basic Skills," which contains test items that closely resemble those on the CTBS. Teaching to the test and perhaps tampering with the tests are understandable when we consider the extensive publicity given to test scores by schools, the need to justify increased public expenditures on education, and the incentives such as the now defunct "Cash for CAP" program, in which schools were given extra monies by the State of California when students' CAP scores increased.

The time-honored circle in which the state superintendent is badgered by politicians, district superintendents by the state superintendent, school principals by the district superintendent, teachers by their principals, students by teachers and parents, and politicians, principals, and teachers by parents leads to a situation in which someone is "always on your back." Principals and other school administrators, in particular, who do not have tenure and for whom demotion and transfer may be affected by students' test scores, are under a great deal of pressure, which they may direct toward teachers, to have their schools show up well in annual comparisons in city newspapers of the test scores of different schools.

Obviously, students, teachers, and school administrators all require some source of motivation to improve the low estate to which education has sunk in many sections of the United States and some means of evaluating the effectiveness of their efforts. However, the atmosphere of paranoia that reportedly permeated the ranks of teachers and administrators in the Los Angeles School District in light of the test-tampering scandal of 1986–1988 was not good for education in general or educational testing in particular.

Lake Wobegon Effect

In 1987, John Cannell reported that 70 percent of students, 90 percent of the 15,000 school districts in the country, and all 50 states were scoring above the national norms on norm-referenced achievement tests used in elementary schools across the nation (Cannell, 1988). This report led to the term "Lake Wobegon effect," from Garrison Keilor's fictitious Minnesota community "where all children are above average." The results of a study by the U.S. Department of Education that 57 percent of elementary school students scored above the national median in reading and 62 percent above the national median in mathematics supported Cannell's findings. In another survey, conducted by the Friends of Education, it was found that 83 percent of 5143 elementary school districts and 73 percent of 4501 secondary school districts, and all but two states—Louisiana and Arizona—were "above average" in achievement test score (Cannell, 1989).

One explanation of the Lake Wobegon effect is that it is a consequence of tests not being renormed every year. Another possibility is that the effect is the result of teachers coaching students on test questions, allowing them more than the allotted time to take the test, and even altering the completed answer sheets.

Publishers of the achievement tests cited in these surveys (CTB/McGraw-Hill, Riverside Publishing Company, and The Psychological Corporation) responded that it is expensive to renorm tests as frequently as might be desirable and that improved test scores may actually indicate that schools are getting better. Nevertheless, test publishers could undoubtedly do more to emphasize to users of their tests when (the date) and on what samples of students the test norms were obtained. In particular, it should be made clear whether any groups (For example, special education students or those with limited English proficiency) were excluded from the norming sample.

By and large, school officials have failed to respond to Cannell's findings and criticisms, but one school assessment expert asserted that it is unethical and unwarranted to assume that cheating has occurred when test scores increase. This official defended the right of a teacher to examine the content of a test in order to determine in what skill areas students need to improve, but not to "teach to the test" (Landers, 1989).

It is widely recognized that scores tend to creep upward when a particular test battery is used in a school over a period of years. One reason for this increase may be that teachers are teaching to the test, but a more likely explanation is that they are teaching *from* the test (Lenke, 1988). Teachers take note of the tested areas in which the scores are low and attempt to improve students' knowledge and skills in these areas. This is, of course, an appropriate instructional strategy and should not be labeled as cheating. We could also argue that the problem is with norm-referenced tests and that criterion-referenced tests would provide more meaningful information concerning students' academic strengths and weaknesses, information that would be less subject to misinterpretation by psychometrically unsophisticated evaluators. Be that as it may, politicians, parents, and others will undoubtedly continue to demand year-to-year and school-to-school comparative test data to assist in educational decision making.

National Educational Standards and Tests

The nationwide concern that U.S. children are not as well educated in science and mathematics as children in many other countries goes back at least as far as the launching of the Soviet Sputnik in 1957. More recently, the results of internationally administered tests have reawakened that concern by revealing that, compared with children in other countries, 13-year-old U.S. children are near the bottom in mathematics and science. The relative standing of U.S. 9-year-olds is better in science, but near the bottom in mathematics (see Figure 12–2).

In the light of these international comparisons and other test statistics, the federal

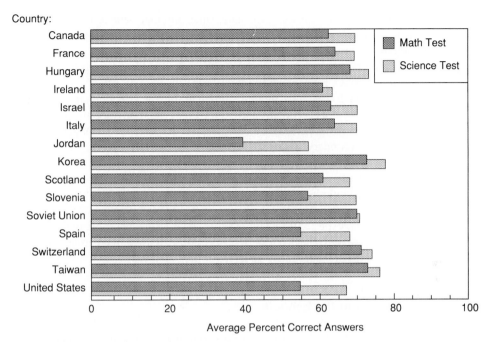

Note 1: Data from Educational Testing Service
Note 2: Soviet Union data are from Russian-speaking schools in 14 republics

FIGURE 12–2   Comparison of Math and Science Scores of 13-Year-Olds in 15 Countries.
(Data from Educational Testing Service.)

government and its advisers began planning for the establishment of a set of national standards in mathematics, science, English, history, and geography. To determine the extent to which such standards were being met, a series of tests in these five subject-matter areas (the "American Achievement Tests") would be constructed and administered to children in the fourth, eighth, and twelfth grades. It has been argued that Americans want to know how well our schools are doing their job and how U.S. children are measuring up to their counterparts in other countries (Merl, 1991). The existence of national educational standards and test, it is hoped, will assist in accomplishing this and restoring public confidence in American education.

Although these aspirations were greeted with some degree of enthusiasm on the part of professional educators and measurement specialists, as well as politicians and the general public, formulating and implementing the plans have proved difficult. Some critics have argued that we need to focus on improving our schools, rather than simply developing more tests. Another related concern is the expense of constructing and administering the tests and acting on the findings to improve instruction. Pointing to the fact that national standards and national tests are already in place in Japan, France, England, Germany, and certain other countries, it seems to many Americans that some sort of national achievement tests will become available, whether or not the individual stages or school districts choose to administer them, by the turn of the century.

In addition to competency testing in the school grades, there is currently a movement underway to develop a national test for determining the extent to which college students are acquiring the skills in critical thinking, problem solving, and communication that they need "to compete in a global economy and exercise the rights and responsibilities of citizenship" (Zook, 1993, p. A3). Spurred by the demand for accountability in higher education, such a National Postsecondary Student Assessment is a controversial topic. However, some sort of evaluative procedure to assess whether the large sums of money that are being spent on higher education are effective in equipping young adults with the analytical skills that are required in the workplace will probably be developed in the near future. Whether the results of these efforts will be a national test or a set of state examinations, the form that such tests will take and how they will be administered and used are debatable issues. Needless to say, the cost of developing such a test or tests will be extensive, but perhaps not as great as the cost of turning out inadequately educated college students.

Intelligence Testing in the Schools

The relationships of education, socioeconomic status, ethnicity, nationality, sex, nutrition, and numerous other psychosocial and biological variables to intelligence test scores have been considered in hundreds of research investigations over the past several decades. A continuing question is concerned with the extent to which whatever is measured by intelligence tests is genetically determined, rather than shaped primarily by environment and experience. The significance of this question and the social and educational implications of the answer have resulted in legal action in certain states. At issue are the utility and biasedness of intelligence tests. Are these tests useful and fair to all groups of children, or are they biased against certain ethnic groups?

Among the legal cases that have been concerned with the use of intelligence tests in the schools are *Hobson* v. *Hansen* (1967), *Diana* v. *State Board of Education* (1970), *Guadalupe* v. *Tempe Elementary District* (1972), *Larry P.* v. *Riles* (1980), *PASE* v. *Hannon* (1980), and *Georgia NAACP* v. *State of Georgia* (1985). In *Hobson* v. *Hansen* the court ruled that group tests of ability discriminated against minority children and hence could not be used to assign students to different ability "tracks." In *Diana* v. *State of California*, the court ruled that traditional testing procedures could not be used for the placement of Mexican-American children in EMR classes and that special provisions (for example, bilingual assessment) must be used to test minority children. The court's decision in *Guadalupe* was to have students tested in their primary language and to eliminate unfair portions of the test. Furthermore, it was decreed that IQ scores must be at least two standard deviations below the mean and that other determiners, such as measures of adaptive behavior, must be included in making decisions as to whether children should be classified as mentally retarded.

In his book *Bias in Mental Testing*, Jensen (1980) asserts that neither verbal nor nonverbal tests of intelligence are biased in any meaningful way against native-born minorities in the United States. He points out that tests of intelligence and other cognitive abilities have predictive validity for all ethnic groups and that the tests are not responsible for differences among these groups. As reflected in the decision in the case of *Larry P. v. Riles* (1979), Judge Robert Peckham of the federal district court of San Francisco disagreed with Jensen. After concluding that IQ tests denied the five black plaintiffs in a class action suit equal protection under the law, Judge Peckham ordered a continuation of his earlier ban on IQ testing for the placement of blacks in educable mentally retarded (EMR) classes in California. Thus, it was ruled that individually administered tests of intelligence are biased against blacks and that the California State Department of Education should not use these tests for educational diagnosis or placement of black children. Contributing to this decision was the fact that a disproportionate number of black children had been assigned to EMR classes, which Judge Peckham labeled "dead-end education." Consequently, it was stipulated that the proportion of black children in EMR classes should match their proportion in the general population of school children. In 1986, Judge Peckham reissued his ruling prohibiting the use of IQ tests in the public schools of California, even when parental consent has been obtained. The court's decision in *Larry P.*, however, did not ban the use of all intelligence tests in California public schools; intelligence test scores can still be used under certain conditions.[4]

Less than a year after the decision in *Larry P.* v. *Riles* was handed down, another federal judge, John F. Grady, rendered a very different decision in a similar case in Illinois. In this case, *PASE (Parents in Action on Special Education) v. Hanson* (1980), it was decreed "that the WISC, WISC–R and Stanford–Binet tests, when used in conjunction with the statutorily mandated '[other criterion] for determining an appropriate educational program for a child' (under Public Law 94-142) . . . do not discriminate against black children" (page 883). As a result, intelligence tests continue to be administered for special class placement in Illinois public schools and in the schools of many other states. Similar to the decision in *PASE* v. *Hannon,* the court ruled in *Georgia NAACP* v. *State of Georgia* (1985) that intelligence tests do not discriminate against black children. Also contrary to the ruling in the *Larry P.* case, it was concluded in the Georgia decision that disproportionate numbers of black children in EMR classes do not constitute proof of discrimination. As a review of these and other court cases concerned with the use of intelligence tests in the schools indicates, the judicial decisions have varied from state to state and with the political climate of the times.

Although the use of intelligence tests may sometimes encourage discrimination and even contribute to a self-fulfilling prophecy, a number of psychologists and educators maintain that there are advantages to using intelligence tests for class placement purposes. Many children who are referred by teachers as being in need of special education are found not to be so when such tests are administered. In fact, if the tests were not used, more minority children would probably be assigned to special education classes. And even those who are placed in such classes on the basis of low test scores often profit from special education to such an extent that their IQs are raised and they become ineligible for those services. Finally, we might ask what happens to children who need special

---

[4]In 1992, Judge Peckham lifted his ban on IQ testing in California public schools on the grounds that it is unfair to those black parents who want the tests to be used in the class placement of their learning disabled children. This ruling effectively nullified the earlier (1986) prohibition against the use of IQ tests in California public schools ("Ban Voided on IQ Tests for Black Pupils," *Los Angeles Times,* September 3, 1992, page A3).

education but are not identified because intelligence tests are not used. How many of those children who fall farther behind every year do so because they are deprived of an appropriate education by being taught in regular classes?

EMPLOYMENT TESTING AND BIAS

Equal in importance to the issues surrounding the use of tests in schools and colleges is the question of the fairness of these instruments for purposes of job selection, placement, and promotion. As a result of the growing concern over civil rights, this matter became increasingly important during the 1960s. Because employment tests had been validated principally on members of the dominant white culture, it was reasonable to ask whether they had any validity for blacks and other minorities. Such was the situation in the *Myart* v. *Motorola* (1964) case, in which the issue was whether a test that was being used for selection purposes was racially discriminatory.

Equal Employment Opportunity Legislation

The Civil Rights Act of 1964 came in the wake of the Motorola case and other criticisms of psychological testing. Title VII of this act specifically prohibits discrimination on the basis of race, color, national origin, sex, or religion. A Supreme Court ruling on Title VII occurred in the case of *Griggs et al.* v. *Duke Power Company* (1971), which was concerned with a suit brought against the Duke Power Company by black employees. The suit challenged Duke Power's earlier requirement of a high school diploma and new hiring and promotion policies requiring a certain minimum score on the Wonderlic Personnel Test and the Bennett Test of Mechanical Comprehension. Chief Justice Burger, who wrote the majority opinion in the case, concluded that "If an employment practice which operates to exclude Negroes cannot be shown to be [significantly] related to job performance, the practice is prohibited" (*Griggs et al.* v. *Duke Power Company*, 1971, page 60). But Justice Burger also found that

nothing in the [Civil Rights] Act precludes the use of testing or measuring procedures; obviously they are useful. What Congress has forbidden is giving these devices and mechanisms controlling force unless they are demonstrably a reasonable measure of job performance. Congress has not commanded that the less qualified be preferred over the better qualified simply because of minority origins. Far from disparaging job qualifications as such, Congress has made such qualifications the controlling factor, so that race, religion, nationality, and sex become irrelevant. (*Griggs* v. *Duke Power Company*, 1971, page 11)

The intent of the Supreme Court decision in *Griggs et al.* v. *Duke Power* and two subsequent cases, *United States* v. *Georgia Power* (1973) and *Albemarle Paper Co.* v. *Moody* (1975), was to require employers to demonstrate that the skills measured by their selection tests and other hiring procedures are job related. In the case of *Washington* v. *Davis* (1976), the court expanded the criterion to which selection test should be related to include performance in job-training programs. An immediate effect of these court decisions was a reexamination, and in some situations a discontinuance, of certain job-selection tests. Nevertheless, Congress subsequently concluded that Title VII of the Civil Rights Act of 1965 had not been adequately enforced and that discrimination against minorities and women was continuing. This conclusion led to a revision of the Civil Rights Act, the Equal Employment Opportunity Act of 1972.

The Equal Employment Opportunity Coordinating Council (EEOCC), which was established by the Equal Employment Opportunity Act, subsequently prepared a set of "Uniform Guidelines on Employee Selection Procedures." These guidelines described procedures for employers, labor organizations, and employment agencies to follow in showing

that any selection procedure which operates to disqualify or otherwise adversely affect members of any racial, ethnic, or sex group at a higher rate than another group, has been validated in accord with these guidelines, and that alternative employment procedures of equal validity which have less of an adverse effect are unavailable. (EEOCC, 1973, page 20)

The guidelines further state that, to be adjudged a valid predictor of performance, the test or combination of tests should normally account for at least half of the reliably measurable skills and knowledge pertaining to the job.

Clearly, the implication of the EEOC guidelines was that employment managers need to conduct validation studies of all their selection procedures, not just psychological tests, to determine if they are significantly related to job success. Substituting more subjective selection procedures in the place of tests is an unsatisfactory alternative. In fact, the court ruled in *Watson* v. *Fort Worth Bank and Trust* (1988) that subjective employment devices such as interviews can be validated and that employees may claim adverse impact resulting from promotion practices based on interviews. Costly though it may be, interviews and other methods that are less objective than tests must be subjected to scrutiny by means of appropriate validity studies. Furthermore, in the case of *Albemarle Paper Co.* v. *Moody* (1975), after finding the company's testing program inadequate, the court maintained that, even if a test is valid but adversely affects the employment of certain groups, the organization should make every effort to find a less biased selection device.

The legal definition of *adverse impact* follows the *four-fifths rule,* according to which a condition of adverse impact is viewed as being present if one group has a selection rate that is less than four-fifths (80%) of that of other groups. For example, if 100 whites and 100 blacks apply for a job and 60 whites are hired, then a condition of adverse impact may be said to exist if fewer than ($\frac{4}{5}$) 60 = 48 blacks are also hired.

The 1978 revision of the EEOC Guidelines on Employee Selection (Equal Employment Opportunity Commission, 1978) is not as strict as the original version of the guidelines in requiring employers to conduct differential validity studies. Like their predecessor, the revised guidelines were designed to require employers to justify the use of tests and other selection procedures that exclude disproportionate numbers of minority group members and women. The guidelines describe in some detail three validation methods on which employers may rely: criterion-related validity, content validity, and construct validity; but they are not clear on how large the validity coefficients must be. In addition, although the revised guidelines state that the use of tests is legitimate when the scores are related to job performance, they do not specify what is meant by "job-related criteria."

Job relatedness is an important concept in this context, because the use of tests that have adverse impact is often justified on the basis of the claim that they are job related. The failure of the EEOC guidelines to make clear what is meant by job-related criteria and other problems of clarity in the guidelines, have prompted many organizations to suspend the use of job-selection tests altogether. The guidelines are considered by many authorities to be technically outdated, and in many cases the required validity studies are too expensive and of questionable value.

Test Fairness

As the EEOC guidelines imply, psychological and educational tests standardized on white samples are unacceptable for use in selecting blacks and other minority group applicants. The use of such tests with groups other than those on which they were standardized raises the issue of test fairness. The guidelines imply that a selection procedure is fair when differences in scores obtained by the procedure are, regardless of the applicant's group membership, reflected in job performance. Also, if the selection rate for any group falls below 80 percent of that for the group having the highest rate, then a condition of "adverse impact" exists. Following the guidelines, employers are required to adopt those selection techniques having the least adverse impact.

The concept of fairness in psychological and educational assessment has a more statistical meaning than implied by the EEOC guidelines. The traditional point of view in psychological measurement is that the *fairness* of a test for different groups depends on whether applicants with the same probability of doing well on the performance criterion have the same likelihood of being selected. According to this definition, even if the mean test score of one group is lower than that of another, the test is not necessarily unfair. Even when blacks or other minorities in the United States attain lower average scores than whites on employment tests, it reveals nothing about the fairness of the tests in the technical sense. Regardless of any difference in mean test scores for two different groups, a job-selection test is said to be fair if it predicts job success equally well for all applicant groups.

After calling attention to a statistical flaw in the traditional (equal regression) definition of test fairness, Thorndike (1971) proposed an alternative definition. Thorndike's *constant ratio* definition specifies that qualifying scores on tests should be established in such a way that different groups of applicants are selected in proportion to the number in each group who are capable of attaining an acceptable level on the performance criterion. For example, if 30 percent of all white applicants and 20 percent of all black applicants are judged capable of performing a given job, then qualifying scores on a selection test should be set in such a way that 30 percent of white applicants and 20 percent of black applicants are hired.

Another appealing definition of test fairness was proposed by Cole (1973). Separate cutoff scores would be established for the two or more different groups of applicants in such a way that the probability of selection is the same for potentially successful applicants in each group. Assume, for example, that two different groups of applicants are composed of 50 and 100 applicants each. If it has been previously determined that 50 percent of all applicants can perform the job satisfactorily, then $50\% \times 50 = 25$ applicants from the first group and $50\% \times 100 = 50$ applicants from the second group should be selected.

A similar quota selection procedure was suggested by Dunnette and Borman (1979). In the Dunnette and Borman proposal, however, the percentage of applicants to be selected is determined beforehand; then separate regression equations are applied to each group.

In a review of the issue written some years ago, Linn (1973) concluded that the various proposals have demonstrated that the fairness of a test is definable in more than one way. The revised (1978) EEOC guidelines also indicate that test fairness is not a fixed concept and that experts disagree on its meaning. Whatever definition of fairness may be preferred, the relative seriousness of errors of incorrectly rejecting and incorrectly accepting applicants must be taken into account in selection. This implies that the fairness of a test is a relative matter, depending on whether it is considered more serious to reject an applicant who would have succeeded (*false negative*) or to accept an applicant who will fail (*false positive*). Social conscience may dictate that the former error is more serious, whereas considerations of safety and profit point to the latter error as being of greater concern.

Even when the test as a whole is viewed as fair, it is possible for individual items comprising the test to be unfair or biased toward a particular group. For example, certain items may present a stereotyped view of minorities and women according to occupation, education, family, and recreation or in any number of other ways (Tittle, 1984). To detect and guard against item bias, test publishers typically conduct judgmental reviews to detect stereotyping and familiarity of test content to particular groups. A variety of statistical procedures has also been employed to detect item bias. The methods described by Cole and Moss (1989) include the use of transformed item-difficulty indexes, biserial correlations to determine item discriminations, item characteristic curves, and variants of chi square, such as the Mantel–Haenszel statistic (Mantel & Haenszel, 1959).

The construction of item characteristic curves (see Chapter 3) is one of the most effective ways of detecting item bias. According to this approach, a test item is unbiased if its characteristic curves are the same for the groups being compared. In other words, examinees of the same ability, regardless of their group membership, have equal probabilities of getting the item right. Experimental studies in which the content of a test is varied to determine if different groups respond differently and factor-analytic studies to ascertain whether the responses of different groups yield the same factors have also been applied to investigate test and item bias (Tittle, 1984; Cole and Moss, 1989).

A kind of compromise approach to item bias was worked out in 1984, when Educational Testing Service agreed to an out-of-court settlement of a suit charging social bias on insurance licensing examinations in Illinois. According to the terms of the settlement, it was agreed that, henceforth, in constructing the insurance examinations, ETS would first use items on which blacks and whites scored most alike. This approach, referred to as the "Golden Rule settlement" after the Golden Rule Insurance Company that was involved in the suit, was subsequently applied in a number of other states. The Golden Rule approach, however, was the subject of considerable debate [see *Educational Measurement, 1987, 6(2)*] and second thoughts by ETS (Anrig, 1987). The rule was also opposed by the Board of Directors of the American Psychological Association (Denton, 1988).

Race Norming

Another practice that was adopted to make the results of selection tests color-blind is *race norming,* in which applicants' test scores are compared only with those of their own ethnic group. Such a practice has been used by the U.S. Department of Labor with scores on the General Aptitude Tests Battery (GATB) as part of the affirmative action policy of that agency. Separate percentile norms are determined for whites, blacks, and Hispanics, and only the in-group percentile ranks of applicants are reported to prospective employers.

Although race norming is no longer practiced as vigorously as it was a few years ago, when more than 30 states race-normed their employment tests, some residual race norming still exists. The charge of reverse discrimination allegedly represented by this practice led to a moratorium on the use of the GATB to allow time to improve the ability of the test to predict job performance or to decide to discontinue using the GATB altogether (Adler, 1991; Hacker, 1991).

Differential Prediction

The traditional definition of test fairness implies that a test unfairly discriminates between two groups if the predicted criterion scores of one group are significantly lower (or higher) than the criterion scores actually attained by that group. This might occur, for example, when the same regression equation is employed for both groups.

Some authorities have argued that in certain job situations a different regression equation should be used with black than with white applicants and/or a different equation with applicants of lower socioeconomic status than with those of highest socioeconomic status. This *moderator variable* approach of employing different regression equations with different groups has been explored in a number of job settings. In a review of five studies conducted during the 1960s, Kirkpatrick et al. (1968) concluded that, for certain jobs, a single regression equation worked equally well with black and white applicants; in other job situations, a single equation was unfair to blacks, unfair to whites, or unfair to both ethnic groups. When separate regression equations for blacks and whites were employed, the validity of the selection procedure improved somewhat in certain instances. Several years later, after reviewing the evidence on the fairness and differential validity of job selection tests, Schmidt and Hunter (1981) concluded that differential validity occurs no more often than would be expected on the basis of chance. Furthermore, when it does occur, the difference is such that the selection system is just as likely to be biased against majority as against minority applicants (Jensen, 1980; Reynolds, 1982). For example, Linn (1973) reported that in 18 of 22 academic contexts in which regression equations have been used, the equations overestimated the actual grade-point averages of black students rather than white students.

Another observation reported by Kirkpatrick et al. (1968) was that different tests seem to work best as predictors of job success in different situations. This implies that, for each job, it is necessary to determine which tests and regression equations work best in predicting job performance. As documented in several publications by Schmidt and his colleagues (for example, Schmidt & Hunter, 1977, 1978, 1981), however, there is a substantial degree of cross-situational generality in the validity of job-selection tests. Some measures possess greater cross-situational validity than others; it has been found, for example, that job replica tests and measures of skills fundamental to the job are more likely to retain their validity when the situational context changes.

Lying, Honesty, and Integrity Testing

Theft is a big problem in U.S. business and industry, with perhaps billions of dollars of materials and products being stolen every year. Consequently, corporation executives are alert to any legal means of detecting dishonesty among employees or applicants.

For years, polygraph (lie-detector) tests, which typically measure heart rate, respiration rate, blood pressure, and the galvanic skin response, were used by business and industrial organizations to identify thieves and liars in their ranks. However, in 1988 the U.S. Congress passed the Employee Polygraph Protection Act, which banned most uses of lie detectors in preemployment interviews in government and the private workplace. Subsequently, a number of paper-and-pencil tests of honesty or integrity were introduced. Although some states have also contemplated banning these tests, a task force of the American Psychological Association concluded that "honesty tests, when used appropriately and in conjunction with additional selection procedures, have demonstrated useful levels of validity as selection procedures" ("APA Task Force," 1991, page 6).

ISSUES IN PERSONALITY ASSESSMENT

During their relatively short history, measures of personality have been attacked repeatedly by psychologists and nonpsychologists alike. Representative of the most extreme negative reactions to these instruments are the writings of Whyte (1956) and Gross (1962, 1965) on the applications of personality assessment in business and industry. In commenting on testimony given before a special subcommittee of the U.S. House of Representatives, Gross (1965) severely criticized personality tests on the grounds of alleged invalidity and immorality.

White and Gross were, of course, not the first persons to criticize personality tests. Indicative of the feelings of some of the lay public toward psychological assessment was the June 1959 burning of certain attitude scales and other questionnaires and tests by order of the Houston School Board. The bonfire was a consequence of the strenuous protest by a group of Houston parents who objected to the fact that schoolchildren had been required, as part of a psychoeducational research study, to respond to items of the following sort:

I enjoy soaking in the bathtub.
A girl who gets into trouble on a date has no one to blame but herself.
If you don't drink in our gang, they make you feel like a sissy.
Sometimes I tell dirty jokes when I would rather not.
Dad always seems too busy to pal around with me. (Nettler, 1959, page 682)

The resulting parental protest led the Houston School Board to order the burning of the answer sheets to six tests and inventories that had been administered to 5000 ninth-graders.

It is certainly understandable how a situation of this kind could develop, particularly when we realize that the public does not always share the scientific attitude and desire to understand human behavior to which psychologists subscribe. Furthermore, it has been alleged that many personality test items, especially those concerned with sex, religion, and morals, are not only personally offensive but also potentially destructive to the character of schoolchildren.

Strong emotional reactions over the meaning and validity of psychological testing and social science research in general also occurred in the debate over Project CAMELOT during the mid-1960s. This project, financed by the U.S. government, was designed to analyze the causes of counterrevolution and counterinsurgency in Latin America. Public awareness of the project resulted in a rather heated reaction by our neighbors to the south, as well as from certain U.S. congressmen. The Project CAMELOT debate, combined with civil suits and attacks on the use of selection tests, led to a congressional investigation of psychological testing in government, industry, and education. One practice examined at length in the congressional inquiry was the administration of personality test items concerning sex and religion to job applicants. Test items of the following types were singled out for special criticism: (1) My sex life is satisfactory; (2) I believe in God; (3) I don't get along very well with my parents. Although the results of hearings concerning personality tests did not lead to an indictment with respect to these tests, the governmental concern manifested by the hearings did prompt psychologists and other assessment specialists to show greater concern for the ethics and values of psychological assessment.

More recently, a similar situation regarding the administration of true–false personality test items occurred in the case of *Soroka* v. *Dayton–Hudson Corp.* (1991). The dispute was concerned with the administration of Psychscreen, a 700-item paper-and-pencil inventory developed from the MMPI and the CPI, to applicants for the position of security guard with Target Stores. Psychscreen had previously been used as a screening test for positions in law enforcement, air-traffic control, and nuclear power plants. Legal council for the plaintiff maintained that questions on Psychscreen of the following type were discriminatory with regard to religious and sexual preferences:

I believe in the second coming of Christ.

I believe there is a devil and a hell in afterlife.

I am very strongly attracted to members of my own sex.

I have never indulged in any unusual sex practices.

(Hager, 1991, page A-20)

Attorneys for Dayton–Hudson Corporation argued that such questions were justified because the position of security guard with Target Stores was not one that emotionally unstable persons, whom Psychscreen was attempting to identify, could perform effectively. However, the appellate court ruled in favor of the plaintiff in concluding that questions on religion and sex violate a job seeker's right to privacy.

On request from the American Psychological Association, which pointed out that the answers to such questions are not interpreted individually as suggesting emotional instability but as a group, the California Supreme Court agreed to review the appellate court's decision (Freiberg & DeAngelis, 1992). It can nevertheless be argued that questions having to do with sexual and religious preferences have no place on employment screening tests, in that the answers may well be misinterpreted by sexually intolerant, religiously bigoted, or psychometrically unsophisticated persons.

Validity Problems

In addition to ethical and moral concerns about personality testing, the technical questions of what is measured by such tests, whether those things are worthwhile measuring, and how best to interpret and apply the results have received a great deal of professional and legal scrutiny during the past three decades. The psychometric qualities of personality tests, and projective techniques in particular, often leave much to be desired. Criterion-keyed inventories tend to have higher validities than other assessment procedures, but the validity coefficients of these instruments often decline substantially when they are administered in situations other than those for which they were intended.

Not only is there a need for more reliable and valid personality tests, but improvements in the theoretical bases of these instruments and in the criteria against which they are validated are necessary. For example, the disease model of mental disorders and the associated diagnostic classification system (DSM–III–R) (American Psychiatric Association, 1987), which is basic to the development and scoring of many personality assessment procedures, is in many respects ambiguous and unreliable. Finally, there is the common problem of misinterpreting the results of personality assessments. Such misinterpretations can happen through failure to consider the base rate, or frequency of occurrence, of the event (criterion) being predicted. Misinterpretations of test results can also result from what is referred to as "clinical insight" or "intuition," but all too often is only a conglomeration of superficial stereotypes, truisms, and other overgeneralizations that may make sense to the personality analyst or diagnostician, but are actually misleading.

Although we cannot help being impressed by the variety of techniques that has been employed in personality assessment, many of these techniques represent relatively crude attempts to measure characteristics of human behavior and should be viewed primarily as research devices, rather than finished psychometric tools. To be sure, personality inventories and projectives have sometimes contributed to selection decisions. For example, the MMPI proved useful in the successful selection program of the Peace Corps during the 1960s. The utility of measures of mental abilities has also been enhanced on occasion by combining them with measures of temperament and motivation. It is generally recognized, however, that none of the available methods of assessing personality is completely satisfactory.

The solution to the validity problem clearly lies in better research and development, but such efforts must be undertaken with a socially responsible attitude and a respect for the rights of individuals. Furthermore, test users should possess a better understanding of statistical and other technical matters pertaining to test design, reliability, validity, and norms. Even when the examiner has adequate knowledge and training and the test is satisfactory for its stated purposes, it is important to keep a record of hits and misses and other indicators of successful and unsuccessful predictions made on the basis of test scores. Over the long run, such information serves as a check on the validity of the test for the stated purposes for which it is used.

Ethnic Bias

Related to both ethical issues and the question of test validity is the matter of whether personality tests are biased against a particular sex, ethnic, or other demographic group. For example, Gynther and Green (1980) maintain that significant differences between the scores of blacks and whites on the MMPI lead to incorrect diagnoses and treatment. However, Pritchard and Rosenblatt (1980) concluded that such differences are exaggerated and that the MMPI is as valid for blacks as for whites. Other than the work of Gynther and his associates, there has been relatively little systematic research on the matter of ethnic-group, social-class, or nationality-group bias in personality test performance. As noted in Chapter 10, however, efforts were made to eliminate gender and ethnic-group bias in constructing the MMPI–2.

Clinical versus Statistical Prediction

One of the most important reasons for obtaining test data is to make behavioral predictions. Unfortunately, personality assessments tend to have rather low predictive validities, a fact that, coupled with their use in personnel screening and clinical diagnosis, has prompted a great deal of research on methods of increasing their validities. The statistical (or actuarial) approach to data collection and behavior prediction consists of applying a statistical formula, a set of rules, or an actuarial table to assessment data. In contrast, the clinical, or impressionistic, approach involves making intuitive judgments or drawing conclusions on the basis of subjective impressions combined with a theory of personality. Furthermore, the data themselves may be either statistically based information, such as test scores, or clinically based information, such as biographical data and personality ratings.

An early review of research comparing the clinical and statistical approaches to prediction concluded that in 19 out of 20 studies the statistical approach was either superior or equal to the clinical approach in effectiveness (Meehl, 1954). Eleven years later, after summarizing data from some 50 studies comparing the two approaches, Meehl (1965) concluded that the statistical approach showed greater predictive efficiency in two-thirds of the studies and was just as efficient as the clinical approach in the remaining studies. A review by Sines (1970) published another 5 years later concurred with Meehl's conclusion: in all but one of the 50 studies reviewed by Sines the actuarial (statistical) approach was found to be superior to the clinical approach in predicting various kinds of behavior.

Although the data summarized by Meehl and Sines provide impressive support for the conclusion that personality diagnoses and behavior predictions are more accurate when a statistical rather than a clinical approach is employed, Lindzey (1965) demonstrated that an expert clinician can sometimes make highly accurate diagnoses. By using only the information obtained from administering the Thematic Apperception Test, a clinical psychologist proved to be 95 percent accurate in detecting homosexuality. In this study the statistical approach of employing only certain objective scores obtained from the TAT protocols was not as accurate as the clinical approach.

Continuing the debate, Holt (1970), argued, on various grounds, against the superiority of the statistical or actuarial approach to personality assessment. Despite Holt's objections, it must be concluded that statistical procedures have generally proved superior to clinical or impressionistic approaches, both in terms of time required and accuracy of prediction. Although the debate on this issue has abated during the past quarter-century, recognition of the efficiency of actuarial methods led to the construction of "cookbooks" and to the current emphasis on computer programs for personality diagnosis and behavior prediction.

Heredity and Environment

The extent to which test scores and personality in general are influenced by heredity and environment has been a topic of dispute for the better part of this century. The issue is far from settled, but contemporary psychologists recognize that both heredity and environment interactively influence performance on both affective and cognitive measures. Correlational statistics computed from the scores on personality inventories (CPI, MMPI, and others) and other measures of personality obtained from individuals with different degrees of kinship have revealed modest but significant contributions of hereditary factors (see Figure 12–3). For example, research on concordance rates for various personality characteristics in identical twins has provided evidence for a significant hereditary influence in intro-version–extroversion, activity level, anxiety, dependence, dominance, emotionality, socia-

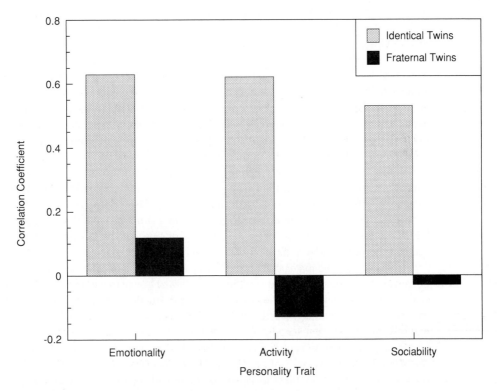

FIGURE 12–3   Average Correlations of Parental Ratings of Identical and Fraternal Twins on Emotionality, Activity Level, and Sociability. *(Data from Buss & Plomin, 1984.)*

bility, and certain other personality traits (Eysenck, 1956; Dworkin et al., 1976; Gottesman, 1966; Scarr, 1969; Buss & Plomin, 1975). There is also considerable evidence for a genetic influence in certain mental disorders (schizophrenia, manic-depressive psychosis) (Kallmann & Jarvik, 1959; Gottesman & Shields, 1973, 1982), but the effects of heredity on personality are far from simple; they vary with age, sex, and other individual differences. Although genetic variables undoubtedly influence personality, they do so by interacting in a complex manner with a person's physical and social environment.

After summarizing evidence for the persistence of various personality characteristics throughout childhood, Thomas and Chess (1977) pointed out that hereditary characteristics both influence and are influenced by personal experience. Parents, other people, and the nonhuman environment as well react differently to children having different physical and temperament traits. These reactions can, in turn, affect the child's genetically based characteristics, thereby demonstrating the interplay between heredity and environment in shaping personality.

Traits versus Situations

Of somewhat more recent origin than the heredity versus environment issue is the dispute over the relative effects of individual traits and social–situational variables on specific behaviors. This argument appears to be resolvable in much the same way as the heredity–environment debate.

The emphasis on situations, as opposed to traits, as determiners of behavior goes back to the Hartshorne and May (1928) studies. Four decades later, Walter Mischel (1968) summarized evidence for the conclusion that, although behavioral correlates of cognitive abilities are fairly consistent across different situations, personal–social behavior is highly dependent on the specific situation. Mischel concluded that inferences regarding personality dynamics or traits are less useful than knowledge of the situation itself in predicting behavior in that situation. He further argued that assessments of generalized traits of personality are not particularly helpful because such traits so often fail to show cross-situational generality. Rather than analyzing personality into a complex of traits or factors, Mischel (1986) proposed a social-learning approach. This approach stresses the fact that people learn to make different responses in different situations and that the accuracy with which an individual's behavior in a specific situation can be predicted must take into account the person's learning history in similar situations.

It is certainly true that social norms, roles, and other group-related conditions can exert powerful effects on people and override temperament or personal style as determiners of individual action and thoughts. As long as the social situation remains fairly constant, people may submerge their idiosyncrasies and adjust their behavior and thinking to the expectations and reward–punishment schedules provided by other people in that situation. It has been amply demonstrated by research in social psychology and by candid television programs that when in Rome all kinds of people "do as the Romans do." Acceptance of this truism does not imply, however, that individual personality plays no role whatsoever in behavior.

Evidence pertaining to the trait–situation controversy is not all in favor of situationism. A number of investigators (for example, Bem & Allen, 1974; Block, 1977; Underwood & Moore, 1981; Chaplin & Goldberg, 1984) have found that the consistency of traits across situations is itself an individual difference variable. In the Bem and Allen investigation, people who believed themselves to be fairly consistent in friendliness and conscientiousness tended to be so; those who identified themselves as less consistent tended to be so.

Research has also demonstrated that some behaviors are more consistent than others. Certain behaviors are narrowly situation specific, whereas behaviors that do not require specific eliciting stimuli occur in a wide range of situations and hence are more reflective of broad personality variables (Funder & Colvin, 1991).

Reviewing Mischel's position and subsequent evidence, a reasonable conclusion is that there is little support for a strict situationist viewpoint regarding personality. Rather, behavior is a joint product of personality characteristics and the particular situation in which the behavior occurs. In certain (strong) situations, the features of the situations themselves are more important in determining how people will behave; in other (weak) situations, personality characteristics are more influential. More generally, it is the interaction between personality and the situation that determines behavior. Future efforts to develop effective measures of personality should be more productive if they begin by providing a conceptual model of how personality dispositions and situational characteristics interact and then proceed to develop measures of both sets of variables to make possible a true "interactional assessment" (McReynolds, 1979).

SUMMARY

The content and applications of standardized tests of ability and personality have come under increasing attack since the 1950s. Standardized tests have been criticized as being invalid measures of what they purport to assess, as representing invasions of the individual's right to privacy, as being unfair to either the favored student or the disadvantaged, and as fostering poor study habits and unethical social and economic practices. Ethical issues in testing are of great concern to psychologists, educators, and other informed persons. Congressional hearings during the 1960s stimulated much discussion and some action on the matters of invasion of privacy and confidentiality in the administration of tests and the treatment of test results.

Multiple-choice items of the type included on college and professional school entrance examinations have been severely criticized. Interest in truth-in-testing legislation is indicative of the demand for the testing industry to become more open and responsible to the public. Also of concern with respect to ability testing have been annual declines in scores on the SAT and other nationally administered tests and the effects of coaching on test scores. Surveys have revealed that testing in the schools is extensive, but that teachers, parents, and students usually lack sufficient information and training to interpret test scores accurately. Competency testing of both high school students and teachers has gained momentum in recent years.

The Civil Rights Act of 1964, the *Griggs* v. *Duke Power* case and related litigation, and the Equal Employment Opportunity Act led to the regulation of test usage in business and industry. The "Uniform Guidelines on Employee Selection Procedures" outlines the characteristics that test and nontest measures should possess in order to be acceptable and valid techniques for employee selection and placement. The question of the fairness of tests for minority and disadvantaged groups has led to new definitions of the concept.

Legal and technical issues stemming from a consideration of the concepts of fairness and differential prediction have alerted professional psychologists, employment managers, and the general public to the need for more responsible use of tests and other psychological assessment procedures.

Personality tests and other affective measures, especially when they are administered in school and employment situations, have been criticized as representing invasions of privacy, as being irrelevant or poor predictors of behavior, and even as suggesting immoral acts to examinees. Psychologists recognize the limitations of these kinds of instruments and, by and large, criticism has had the salutary effect of increasing care in the design of new affective assessment instruments and promoting further research on personality assessment. Such research has led to an emphasis on the interaction between heredity and environment and the interaction between personality traits and situational variables in determining behavior. Other research on affective measurement has pointed to the superiority of the statistical over the clinical approach to data collection and analysis.

EXERCISES

1. Discuss specific objections to standardized tests in general and multiple-choice tests in particular.

2. Describe criticisms of the Scholastic Aptitude Test and the responses of the College Entrance Examination Board and Educational Testing Service to these criticisms.

3. Why might truth-in-testing legislation encourage teachers to "teach to the test"?

4. Review congressional legislation and Supreme Court decisions pertaining to employment testing in business and industry, beginning with Title VII of the Civil Rights Act of 1964.

5. In Appendix E, the fairness of an achievement test is defined as "the extent to which the items on a test are a representative sample of what examinees know," whereas the fairness of an aptitude test is defined as "the extent to which scores on the test are equally predictive of the criterion performance of different groups." However, Thorndike maintains that tests are fair if "the qualifying scores [on the test are] set at levels that . . . qualify applicants in the two groups in proportion to the fraction of the two groups reaching a specific criterion performance." Why do different definitions of test fairness exist, and what are the implications of the various definitions?

6. What is *clinical* prediction, and how does it differ from *statistical* prediction? Which is more effective, and why?

7. Refer to the 30 paired scores in Table A–2 of Appendix A. Assume that X is a score on a job-selection test and Y a job performance rating. Further assume that the 30 paired scores were obtained from a majority group of applicants for the job, whereas the following 30 paired scores were obtained from a minority group of applicants.

X	Y	X	Y	X	Y	X	Y
40	64	34	41	52	46	50	39
62	48	48	44	42	38	32	30
40	32	56	64	18	26	68	42
52	40	48	36	46	34	60	60
36	31	24	54	64	65	44	48

Now assume that 50 percent of the majority group applicants, 25 percent of the minority group applicants, and 40 percent of all applicants are able to perform the job satisfactorily ($Y = 50$ or higher). Is the test fair according to the traditional definition of fairness? According to Thorndike's definition? According to Cole's definition? What are the percentages of false positives and false negatives in each group, and how do these affect the fairness of the test?

8. Investigate the test-coaching schools, test-coaching courses, and published materials on test coaching available in your area. Try to locate a half-dozen or so students who have been coached or prepared for the SAT, the GRE, or some other nationally administered test for a fee. Was the coaching worthwhile? Did it help the students improve their scores on the test? What evidence was cited for the beneficial effects of coaching, if any?

9. Write one or two personality test items (true–false format) that are biased toward men, women, blacks, whites, Americans, Asians, and more highly educated people.

10. If the set of *Computer Programs for Psychological Assessment* is available, run program 2 ("Attitudes Toward Intelligence Testing") in Category 7 (Programs on Attitudes and Values"). Compare your answers with those of other students in the class.

SUGGESTED READINGS

Cannell, J. J. (1988). Nationally normed elementary achievement testing in America's public schools: How all 50 states are above the national average. *Educational Measurement: Issues and Practice, 7*(2), 5–9.

Elliott, R. (1987). *Litigating intelligence: IQ tests, special education, and social science in the courtroom.* Dover, MA: Auburn House.

Eyde, L. D., & Quaintance, M. K. (1988). Ethical issues and cases in the practice of personnel psychology. *Professional Psychology: Research and Practice, 19*(2), 148–154.

Fremer, J., Diamond, E. E., & Camara, W. J. (1989). Developing a code of fair testing practices in education. *American Psychologist, 44,* 1062–1067.

Linn, R. L. (1989). Current perspectives and future directions. In R. L. Linn (ed.), *Educational measurement,* 3rd ed., pp. 1–10. New York: Macmillan.

Pervin, L. A. (1990). Personality theory and research: Prospects for the future. In L. A. Pervin (ed.), *Handbook of personality theory and research,* pp. 723–727. New York: Guilford Press.

Picente, A. E. (1990). Psychological assessment of minority group members. In G. Goldstein & M. Hersen (eds.), *Handbook of psychological assessment,* 2nd ed., pp. 505–520. New York: Pergamon.

Porter, A. C. (1991). Assessing national goals: Some measurement dilemmas. In *The assessment of national educational goals: 1990 ETS Invitational Conference,* pp. 21–42. Princeton, NJ: Educational Testing Service.

Wainer, H. (1988). How accurately can we assess changes in minority performance on the SAT? *American Psychologist, 43,* 774–778.

Chapter Thirteen

Computer-based Assessment and Other Developments

Despite almost continuous criticism, both within and outside the discipline of psychology, psychological testing has continued to prosper and diversify. New tests and test items, coupled with methodological and substantive advances in constructing, administering, scoring and interpreting tests, attest to the dynamic state of the field. Many factors have contributed to this growth, including the expansion of the population, the spread of social services and opportunities to a larger segment of that population, and the consequent need for more efficient methods of selecting, placing, and diagnosing people in employment, education, and clinical contexts. The growth of testing has also been stimulated and facilitated by progress in designing and programming high-speed computing machinery. Computers have been used to analyze psychological test results almost from the onset of their commercial appearance in the mid-1950s, a use that has grown extensively with time.

CHARACTERISTICS OF COMPUTERS

A contemporary digital computer, with its microelectrode, solid-state circuitry packaged in several carry-out boxes, represents a marked improvement over the vacuum-tube monsters of the post-World War II era. Larger mainframe computers, as well as somewhat smaller minicomputers, became available, but the extension of computers to homes and small offices awaited the advent of microcomputers in the mid-1970s.

Hardware and Software

A digital computer consists essentially of three units: an input unit, a central processing unit, and an output unit. A variety of devices are used to enter information or data into the central processing unit (CPU): typewriter or teletype keyboard, optical scanner, magnetic tape or disk reader, light-sensitive or heat-sensitive cathode ray tube (CRT) screen, and (in older computers) punched card or paper tape readers. Information from the CPU can be sent to a CRT screen, to magnetic tape or disk, or to a fast paper printer. The CPU, which is the heart of a computer, also consists of three units: a storage (memory) unit for storing instructions (programs) and data, an arithmetic–logical unit for performing calculations and making logical decisions, and a control unit for following the instructions given in the stored programs. The control unit directs the flow of information from the input unit, uses data from the storage unit, prompts the arithmetic–logical unit to make decisions and perform needed computations, and then sends the results to the output unit(s).

Microcomputers

In a microcomputer, the microprocessor, which consists of an integrated network of thousands of microscopic circuits etched into the surface of a thin layer of silicon, combines the functions of the arithmetic–logical unit. Programmable microcomputers first became available in 1975, followed in 1977 by the APPLE II and in the 1980s by the IBM-PC, the Apple Macintosh, and numerous other brands.

Two types of primary storage are available in a microcomputer: a read-only memory (ROM) to store directions for the microprocessor on how to process input information and a random-access memory (RAM) for temporary storage of information entered by tape or permanent storage device (electromagnetic tape or disk). Typical permanent storage devices for microcomputers are portable $5\frac{1}{4}$ or $3\frac{1}{2}$ inch diameter floppy disks and fixed hard disks located in the computer itself. A standard double-sided floppy disk has a storage capacity of 360 thousand (double density) to 1.44 million (high density) characters and can be randomly accessed at any point on its surface in a matter of milliseconds. Typical hard disks, on the other hand, have a storage capacity of 100 million characters or more.

Computer Programs

The rapid speed, compact size, and relatively modest prices of microcomputers have made it feasible to employ them in many on-site contexts involving testing and other psychological and educational activities. However, a microcomputer, or any other computer for that matter, is not very useful without an appropriate selection of software, the programs that tell the computer what to do. A program, which can be entered into the computer through a keyboard or other input device, consists of a series of instructions on how to enter data or other information, what operations to perform on the data, and where to send the results after the information has been processed. The program is written in a computer language, such as BASICA, Pascal, FORTRAN, or COBOL, and translated by the computer into its own machine language by a special program known as a compiler or by an interpreter.

TABLE 13–1   BASICA Program for Scoring an Objective Test

```
10 REM Program TESTSCOR.  Scores objective tests of 500 items or less.
20 DIM KEE$(500),ANS$(500)
30 CLS
40 REM Scoring key for test is entered.
50 INPUT "Total number of items";N
60 PRINT
70 FOR I=1 TO N
80 PRINT "Enter correct answer to item";I
90 LINE INPUT KEE$(I)
100 NEXT I
110 CLS
120 REM Examinees' responses are entered and scored.
130 PRINT "Press any key to begin scoring answer sheets."
140 IF INKEY$="" THEN 140
150 CLS
160 SCORE=0
170 FOR I=1 TO N
180 PRINT "Answer to item";I;"?"
190 LINE INPUT ANS$(I)
200 IF ANS$(I)=KEE$(I) THEN SCORE=SCORE+1
210 NEXT I
220 PRINT:PRINT "Score =";SCORE:PRINT
230 PRINT:PRINT "Do you want to score another answer sheet--y or n?"
240 ANS$=INKEY$
250 IF LEN(ANS$)=0 THEN 240
260 IF ANS$="y" OR ANS$="yes" THEN 150
270 END
```

Table 13–1 is a very short program written in BASICA and designed to score any objective test (true–false, multiple-choice, short-answer, or a combination of item types) consisting of 500 items or less. Users of this program first type in the number of items on the test and the keyed (correct) response for each item; next the examinee's responses to the items are entered. Then the microprocessor calculates the examinee's score, the score appears on the CRT screen, and the responses of the next examinee may be entered.

One feature of the simple program in Table 13–1 that should be emphasized is the fact that is is interactive, in the sense that there is continuous interaction between the computer and the user. In *interactive mode,* the computer asks questions, and the user answers by typing an appropriate response. Interactive mode contrasts with *batch mode,* in which the responses of all examinees are entered at the same time and then all scores are printed. Interactive mode is usually preferred for purposes of psychological testing because it makes possible the administration, scoring, and interpretation of a test in a single session in which the examinee is actively responding to a series of questions presented on a computer screen.

TEST CONSTRUCTION, ADMINISTRATION AND SCORING

A functional flow chart of the testing process is shown in Figure 13–1 (Baker, 1989). Computers can be of assistance in all stages of this process, including test construction, administration, scoring, analysis, and reporting of results.

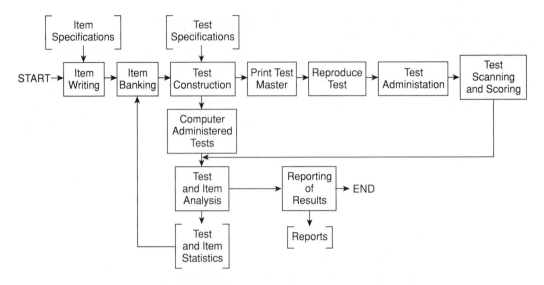

FIGURE 13-1 Functional Flow Chart of the Process of Testing.
*(Reprinted from Educational Measurement, 3rd edition, edited by Robert L. Linn.
Copyright 1989. Used by permission of American Council of Education and The Oryx
Press, 4041 N. Central at Indean School Rd., Phoenix, AZ 85012.)*

Test Construction

The most common application of computers in test construction is using a word-processing
program to assist in typing the items, formatting, checking spelling, and the like. Test
construction is facilitated even more by a combination of word processing and graphics
packages that support true desktop preparation of tests comprised of words and drawings.
Furthermore, commercially available test-generating software packages such as PRISM
(The Psychological Corporation), ExamSystem (National Computer System), and The
Test Bank (Advanced Technology Applications) permit the construction of a variety of
tests having specified content and statistical characteristics. These packages of computer
programs contain banks or pools of test items that can be accessed by entering certain
keywords indicating the content and psychometric characteristics desired in the test.

Banks of items, that can be accessed by computer in designing tests are also available
from textbook publishers for particular subjects and curricula. Examples are the Academic
Instructional Measurement System (The Psychological Corporation), which has banks of
items in mathematics and reading–language arts for grades K–12, and NWEA Electronic
Item Banks and Test Director (Northwest Evaluation Association), which contains item
banks in reading, mathematics, and language usage. In storing or banking an item for
later use, information on the textual and graphical portions of the item, information used
to access the item from different points of view, and psychometric data may all be recorded
on a storage medium such as an interactive videodisc.[1]

---

[1]Less versatile, but substantially less expensive for the classroom teacher or instructor is program BANK-
TEST, a computer program written in BASICA and available free of charge from the author of this textbook.
To obtain a copy of BANKTEST and accompanying instructions, send a self-addressed, stamped mailer to:
Lewis R. Aiken, Ph.D., 12449 Mountain Trail Court, Moorpark, CA 93021.

Administration and Adaptive Testing

It is fairly simple to write a program that follows the traditional test-administration procedure in which the same items are administered to all examinees. Historically, this rigid procedure was not followed precisely on all tests, for example, on various individually administered tests of intelligence and personality. In general, however, little flexibility was permitted in determining which items to administer. The traditional procedure is particularly inefficient on achievement tests, because it requires examinees to answer many items that are either too easy or too difficult for them. Adapting the items that are actually administered to the ability level of the examinee eliminates the presentation of many very easy or very difficult items, thereby saving time and effort.

Item banks or pools for interactive of adaptive (branched, sequential, tailored, or routing) tests can be assembled by computers employing one of the item-response methodologies (latent trait theory, item characteristic curve theory, Rasch model, and so on) (Baker, 1985). In adaptive testing, it is important for the assumptions of item-response theory (IRT) to be met. These assumptions are that (1) all items in a pool measure a single aptitude or achievement dimension, and (2) the items are independent, that is, the answer to one item does not depend on the answer to any other item. Satisfaction of the first assumption, that of unidimensionality, can be verified by factor-analytic procedures and is more likely to be met by item pools or tests derived by factor analysis.

An *adaptive testing* procedure for administering a test of achievement or aptitude works in the following manner. Applying an appropriate statistical model, a pool of test items scaled in terms of their difficulty levels, discriminative indexes, and percentage guessing indexes is assembled for administration by computer. An estimate of the examinee's ability level determines which item(s) will be administered first to that person. Alternatively, items of medium difficulty level are administered first (see Figure 13–2). In any event, the presentation of additional items depends on the examinee's responses to previous items. Testing continues until the estimate of error or level of accuracy in the responses made reaches a specified level. An examinee's test score is determined not merely by counting the number of items answered correctly, but by taking into account the statistical characteristics (difficulty levels and such) of the items.

By making the decision concerning which item to administer contingent on the examinee's response(s) to the previous item(s), adaptive testing makes possible, with no loss of information and equal reliability and validity, the presentation of only a fraction of the number of items required by the traditional testing practice in which every item is administered to every examinee. One disadvantage of adaptive testing is that examinees are not permitted to review and perhaps change their answers after their initial choices have been made.

So far the uses of adaptive testing in assessing general intelligence and special abilities have been limited, but Educational Testing Service, the U.S. Army, and various other organizations have experimented with the interactive, adaptive administration of ability tests, such as the Scholastic Aptitude Test (SAT), the Armed Services Vocational Aptitude Battery (ASVAB), and the Graduate Record Examination (GRE), by computer (Green et al., 1982). It is possible to administer the SAT and other college admission, job qualification,

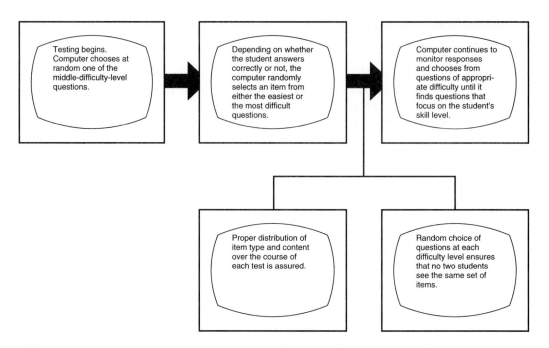

FIGURE 13–2   Question Branch Patterns for The College Board Computerized Placement Tests. The Four Placement Tests in This Series, Reading Comprehension, Sentence Skills, Arithmetic, and Algebra, Are Adaptive Tests Administered on IBM-PC or Compatible Computers.
(Reprinted by permission of The College Entrance Examination Board.)

and military selection tests by computer at sites throughout the world. ETS's Computerized Placement Test, a computer-adaptive placement battery for assessing written communication, learning skills, and mathematics skills, became commercially available in the late 1980s. In the future, the use of graphics, modems, and other input–output devices such as voice encoders and decoders will increase the flexibility and ease with which such tests can be administered.

Although adaptive testing procedures have been used more extensively in achievement and aptitude measurement, applications of adaptive testing methodology to the assessment of personality have also been explored. A particularly useful type of adaptive test is a stratified adaptive test (*stratadaptive test*) (Weiss, 1973, 1985), in which the pool of test items is divided into subsets by difficulty level. Whether a stratadaptive test is designed to assess ability or personality, responding to an item in a certain way (by giving the keyed answer) leads to presentation of another item at a higher stratum. Responding incorrectly (not giving the keyed answer) results in presentation of an item at a lower stratum. Testing may continue until a ceiling stratum, a level at which the examinee answers no items in the keyed direction, is reached. Suppose, for example, that the degree of extroversion characterizing a person is to be assessed. An examinee who endorses an item in the direction keyed for extroversion in one stratum goes on to an item pertaining to extroversion at the next higher stratum (next higher level of the characteristic). Various termination and scoring rules are possible. Thus, the process of presenting items at successively higher strata might continue until the examinee fails to endorse an extroversion item at a given level; his or her score would then be determined by the highest level reached and the item within that level that was endorsed. Similarly, an examinee who fails to endorse an item in the direction keyed for extroversion in one stratum would be presented an extroversion item at the next lower level, and so forth, until he or she endorses an item in the extroversion direction or there are no more strata. In each stratum, items are so arranged that the most discriminating items are presented first (Weiss, 1985; Weiss & Vale, 1987).

In addition to the method (conventional, adaptive, and others) used in selecting the items to be presented, certain cautions concerning the equipment for presenting the test stimuli should be exercised in administering a test by computer. Six recommendations in the *Guidelines for Computer-based Tests and Interpretations* (American Psychological Association, 1986, pages 11–12) that pertain to computerized test administration are as follows:

The environment in which the testing terminal is located should be quite, comfortable, and free from distraction;

Test items presented on the display screen should be legible and free from noticeable glare;

Equipment should be checked routinely and should be maintained in proper working condition;

Test performance should be monitored, and assistance to the test taker should be provided, as is needed and appropriate;

Test taker should be trained on proper use of the computer equipment;

Reasonable accommodations must be made for individuals who may be at an unfair disadvantage in a computer testing situation.

Test Scoring and Reporting

Test-scoring machines have been available for over a half-century. The machines of yesteryear were sensitive only to magnetic marks on paper, so special magnetic pencils were required to mark the answer sheet accompanying the booklet of test questions. The test-scoring machines of today, however, are optical scanners that are sensitive to marks made with ordinary No. 2 pencils.

Although a computer is not required for rapid and efficient scoring or tests, it provides flexibility and further statistical analysis, interpretation, and storage of test scores and other personal data. In addition to processing answer sheets scored locally by an optical scanner (machine on top left of Figure 13–3), answer sheets can either be mailed in or transmitted by telephone line (teleprocessing) to a central scoring service.

The amount of programming needed to use a desktop optical scanner such as the SCANTRON 2100 or the NCS-3000 is fairly simple and permits use of a wide range of features such as item weighting, part scoring, item analysis and flagging, and a printout of various kinds of data, statistics, and graphs. In addition to raw and converted scores, frequency distributions and histograms, test statistics (arithmetic means, standard devia-

FIGURE 13–3 MICROTEST Assessment System. Computer-based System for Administering, Scoring, and Generating Reports for Clinical, Vocational, and Human Resources Assessment Instruments. Shown in the Lower Left Are the MICROTEST Assessment User's Guide and the MICROTEST Assessment Software; in the Upper Left the Sentry 3000 Scanner; in the Center an IBM Personal Computer AT; in the Upper Right a Printer; and in the Lower Right a ScorBox Interface Device.
(Reproduced by permission from National Computer Systems, I. MICROTEST is a trademark of National Computer Systems, Inc.)

tions, internal consistency reliability coefficient), and item statistics (difficulty and discrimination indexes, distributions of responses to options, and the like) are reported.

Test scoring, score analysis, and score reporting may all be accomplished by using an optical scanner connected to a microcomputer with a single software package such as the Microcomputer Scoring System (TESCOR, Inc.). However, a software package that will construct a test according to certain specifications, score it, and analyze and report the results is not yet available. SRA's Micro Test Administration approaches such an ideal, as do the Pitt Educational Testing AIDS (PETA) (Nitko & Hsu, 1987) and MicroCAT (Assessment Systems Corporation, 1988). PETA, the oldest and least expensive of these packages, was designed for use on an APPLE IIe computer as an aid to classroom teachers in constructing tests for up to 10 sections of 50 students in one subject. More sophisticated and substantially more expensive than PETA is MicroCAT, which makes possible the construction, administration, and analysis of tests designed from item-response theory or classical test theory perspectives and administered by adaptive or conventional testing procedures. Even more complex and versatile than MicroCAT, which Baker (1989) refers to as a "first-generation system," are systems that are being designed for the Macintosh and other "second-generation microcomputer systems" having several megabytes of internal memory, advanced graphic and desktop publishing features, and video-display features such as windows. By means of networks of computers situated throughout the country, nationwide test scoring and analysis, as well as on-line testing, can be implemented.

Open-ended and Essay Items

Although the process of programming a computer to administer and score objective tests is fairly straightforward, computerized administration and scoring of responses to open-ended or interlocking questions is more difficult. For example, it is possible to program the administration of certain subtests on the Wechsler Adult Intelligence Scale, but the process is not so easy with scales on which response scoring requires making a subjective judgment of accuracy (Elwood & Griffin, 1972). Even so, efforts to design programs for automated administration of both ability tests such as the Raven Progressive Matrices (Gedye & Miller, 1969) and personality tests such as the One-Word Sentence Completion Test (Veldman, Menaker, & Peck, 1969) or the Holtzman Inkblot Technique (Gorham, Moseley, & Holtzman, 1968) have met with some success. Evaluating responses to essay-type items also poses problems for a computer, although here, too, some progress has been made (see, for example, Page, 1968; Page, Tillett, & Ajay, 1980). Furthermore, progress in devising computer programs to analyze student writing samples and to instruct students in how to write effectively is seen in the development of Bell Writer's Workbench, IBM's Epistle, and UCLA's WANDA programs.

OTHER APPLICATIONS OF COMPUTERS IN PSYCHOLOGICAL ASSESSMENT

The uses of computers in psychological assessment are not limited to test construction administration, scoring, reporting, and statistical analysis. Computers have also been used to interview clients in clinical and employment situations, interpret the results of psychological assessments, and counsel individuals concerning the results of psychological assessments.

Interviewing by Computer

In addition to computer-based test administration and scoring, psychodiagnostic interviewing has been automated by storing in a computer a set of questions and instructions so that the computer asks a question, receives an answer, and decides ("conditionally branches") what question to ask next (Kleinmuntz & McLean, 1968; Kleinmuntz, 1982, pages 199–207). Such branching strategies have been applied effectively in patient data systems at numerous psychiatric hospitals, including those at the University of Wisconsin and the Salt Lake City Veterans Administration Hospital. An example of an interview questionnaire that uses branching to narrow the kind and number of questions asked is the Psychological Systems Questions (Johnson, Giannetti, & Williams, 1978). Furthermore, Spitzer and Endicott (1969, 1974) developed several computer programs known as DI-AGNO that formulate psychiatric diagnoses from structured interview data. Research on these and other programs designed to diagnose psychiatric disorders according to various criteria (Feighner criteria, Research Diagnostic Criteria, DSM–III, and others) has been reviewed by Matarazzo (1983).

Representative of the available computer software packages for psychodiagnostic interviewing and report preparation are the Psychological/Psychiatric Status Interview and the Psychological/Social History Report (both available from Slosson Educational Publications, Inc.), the Diagnostic Interview for Children and Adolescents (available from Multi-Health Systems, Inc.), and the Giannetti On-Line Psychosocial History (GOLPH) (Giannetti, 1987; from National Computer Systems). The first of these packages is designed for an initial psychological or psychiatric interview and the second for a structured psychological intake interview. The third and fourth packages conduct diagnostic interviews structured according to the *Diagnostic and Statistical Manual–III* (American Psychiatric Association, 1980). Software is also available that enables clinicians to develop their own interviews (for example, Q-Fast, from StatSoft) or to modify existing interviews (for example, Psychosocial History Report, from Psychometric Software).

As with other psychometric applications of computers, the advantages of interviewing by computer are efficiency, flexibility, and reliability. Computerized interviews save professional time, permit a broader coverage of topics, are more flexible than rigid questionnaires, and have greater reliability than person-to-person interviews. In general, a high degree of agreement has been found between information obtained by computer interviewing and that elicited from standard psychiatric interviews and questionnaires (Lucas et al., 1977). Being interviewed by a computer is not objectionable to most people. In fact, patients are often more willing to divulge personal information, particularly of a sensitive nature, to an impersonal, nonjudgmental computer than to a human interviewer (Greist & Klein, 1980). On the other hand, it may be necessary to abbreviate or bypass the system in crisis cases, it has limited utility with children and adults of low mentality, and it may not be flexible enough to use with the wide range of problems and symptoms found in psychiatric patients (Haynes, 1984). Other potential disadvantages of computer interviews are that they have difficulty with anything other than structured, verbal information and are unable to tailor the wording of questions (Erdman, Klein, & Greist, 1985). As with adaptive testing, a sequential, unstructured interviewing procedure in which each successive question is influenced by the interviewee's response to a previous question is more difficult to program than the structured interviewing procedure of asking the same questions of every interviewee.

Computer-based Test Interpretation

Even more complex than administering and scoring a test or interview is interpreting the results. The first computer-based test interpretation (CBTI) programs were developed in the early 1960s at the Mayo Clinic, the Hartford Institute of Living, and the University of Alabama (Swenson & Pearson, 1964; Rome et al., 1962; Glueck & Reznikoff, 1965). These programs were designed for scoring, profiling, and interpreting MMPI responses that had been hand recorded on optical scan answer sheets. Subsequently, Fowler (1969) developed a more complex program for automated interpretation of the MMPI. By the mid-1970s, Johnson and Williams (1975) had designed a large-scale computer-based test interpretation system for patients at the Salt Lake City Veterans Administration Hospital, and in 1977 an improved on-line system for interpreting the MMPI was available for use with microcomputers.

An estimated 200 CBTI programs are now in use, among which are programs that score and interpret the results of cognitive abilities tests, neuropsychological tests, and personality tests. A sample report generated by a computer program designed to interpret the 16 PF is given in Report 10–1. Many companies offer computerized test interpretation and reporting services, as well as hardware for computer-based testing. The names and addresses of a sample of these companies are given in Table 13–2. The listing of these services in no way constitutes an endorsement of them; some are satisfactory, and others are not. As noted by Lanyon (1984),

There is a real danger that the few satisfactory services will be squeezed out by the many unsatisfactory ones, since the consumer professionals are generally unable to discriminate among them and are predisposed to believe whatever is printed. Particularly distressing is that the lack of demonstrated program validity has now become the norm, and there appear to be no checks against the further development of this untenable situation. Perhaps the time has now come when federal regulations for this industry are necessary for consumer protection.

The algorithms used to generate computer-based assessment reports range in difficulty from (1) a simple procedure in which a given score or score range is connected to a set of short interpretive paragraphs to (2) complex sets of if–then decision rules in which a particular pattern of subscores leads to a given interpretive statement. However, even the most complex interpretations are usually not as individualized as those produced impressionistically by a clinical or counseling psychologist. The algorithms and decision trees followed in the interpretive programs result in the same data producing the same set of verbal statements, statements that the reader often finds too lengthy and repetitive when printed in report format (Baker, 1989).

Many test interpretation programs are designed to take age, sex, and other demographic information about the examinee into account, but no program considers all the examinee's personal attributes. Consequently, psychological examiners typically supplement CBTI reports with additional interpretive statements gleaned from their observations and experience. As recommended by the *Guidelines for Computer-based Tests and Interpretations* (American Psychological Association, 1986, page 12),

Computer-generated interpretive reports should be used only in conjunction with professional judgment. The user should judge for each test taker the validity of the computerized test report based on the user's professional knowledge of the total context of testing and the test taker's performance and characteristics.

Computer-based test reports are not an adequate substitute for clinical judgment, and a trained clinician should review the report (Butcher, 1978). Computers have been resisted

TABLE 13–2   Representative Companies Providing Computer-based Services and Products for Psychological and Educational Assessment

ADEPT, Inc., Box 1117 L.U. Station, Beaumont, TX 77710

Advanced Technology Applications, 3019 Governor Drive, San Diego, CA 92122 (MICROCAT and THE TEST BANK)

American Guidance Service, 4201 Woodland Road, P.O. Box 99, Circle Pines, MN 55014-1796

Applied Innovations (AI), South Kingston Office Park, Wakefield, RI 02879.

Assessment Systems Corporation, 2233 University Avenue, Suite 440, St. Paul, MN 55114

Behaviordyne, 599 College Avenue, Suite 1, Palo Alto, CA 94306

CFKR Career Materials, Inc., P.O. Box 437, Meadowvista, CA 95722

Caldwell Report, 3122 Santa Monica Boulevard, Santa Monica, CA 90404

Cambridge Software Labs, 45 Highland Road, Boxford, MA 91921

Cattell Research Institute, 1188 Bishop Street 1701, Honolulu, HI 96813

Century Diagnostics, Inc., 2101 East Broadway, Suite 22, Tempe, AZ 85282

Consulting Psychologists Press, Inc., 3803 East Bayshore Road, P.O. Box 10096, Palo Alto, CA 94303

D. C. Heath Software, 125 Spring Street, Lexington, MA 02173

Earthware Computer Services, Box 30039, Eugene, OR 97403

EdSoft, Box 2560, Berkeley, CA 94702

Excelsior Software, Box 2780, Bryan, TX 77805

HMS Software, P.O. Box 49186, Austin, TX 78765

Institute for Practice and Research in Education, School of Education, University of Pittsburgh, SR02 Forbes Quadrangle, Pittsburgh, PA 15260 (PETA)

Institute for Personality and Ability Testing, 1801 Woodfield Drive, Savoy, IL 61874

Integrated Professional Systems, Inc., 5211 Mahoning Avenue, Suite 135, Youngstown, OH 44515

Life Science Associates, 1 Fenimore Road, Bayport, NY 11705

Manumit Psychological Systems, Inc., 2211 East Winston Road, Suite J, Anaheim, CA 92806

Mediax Interactive Technologies, Inc., 21 Charles Street, Westport, CT 06880-5899 (MICROSCALE)

MetriTech, Inc., 111 North Market Street, Champaign, IL 61820

Multi-Health Systems, Inc., 908 Niagara Falls Boulevard N., Tonawanda, NY 14120-2060

National Computer Systems, Professional Assessment Services, P.O. Box 1416, Minneapolis, MN 55440 (computer software and optical scanners)

Northwest Evaluation Association, 5 Centerpointe Drive, Suite 100, Lake Oswego, OR 97035 (Attn: Alan Olson) (item banks)

P.C.A. Diagnostic Laboratory, Inc., 714 South Tillotson, Muncie, IN 47304

Pacific Psychological, 710 George Washington Way, Suite G-3, Richland, WA 99352

Pine Grove Institute, 1188 Montgomery Drive, Santa Rosa, CA 95405

Precision People, Inc., 3452 North Ride Circle S., Jacksonville, FL 32217

pro.ed, 8700 Shoal Creek Boulevard, Austin, TX 78758-6897

Psych Lab, 1714 Tenth Street, Wichita Falls, TX 76301

Psych Solutions Associates, P.O. Box 10262, Baltimore, MD 21234

Psychological Assessment Resources, Inc., P.O. Box 998, Odessa, FL 33556

Psychological Corporation (The), 555 Academic Court, San Antonio, TX 78204-2498 (PRISM)

TABLE 13–2 (continued)

Psychological Software Specialists, 1776 Fowler, Suite 7, Columbia Center North, Richland, WA 99352

Psychologistics, Inc., P.O. Box 3896, Dept. A, Indialantic, FL 32903

Psychometric Software, Inc., P.O. Box 1677, Melbourne, FL 32902-1677

Psychsystems, 600 Reisterstown Road, Baltimore, MD 21208

Reason House, 204 East Joppa Road, Penthouse Suite 10, Towson, MD 21204

Research Psychologists Press, P.O. Box 984, Port Huron, MI 48061

Queue, Inc., 5 Chapel Hill Drive, Fairfield, CT 06432

SCAN-TRON Corporation, 3398E 70th Street, Long Beach, CA 90805 (optical scanners)

Science Research Associates, 155 North Wacker Drive, Chicago, IL 60606 (Microcomputer Test Administration System)

Scientific Psychology, 2477 SW 19th Terrace, Miami, FL 33145

Southern Micro Systems, P.O. Box 2097, Burlington, NC 27216

StatSoft, 2325 East 13th Street, Tulsa, OK 74104

Sunset Software, 11750 Sunset Boulevard, Suite 414, Los Angeles, CA 90049

TESCOR, Inc., 401 Carlisle Drive, Herndon, VA 22020 (Microcomputer Scoring System)

THUNDERWARE, 21 Orinda Way, Orinda, CA 94563 (optical scanners)

Wang Neuropsychological Laboratory, 1720 La Luna Court, San Luis Obispo, CA 93401

Western Psychological Services, 120341 Wilshire Boulevard, Los Angeles, CA 90025

by certain clinicians who consider them to be a threat to the clinician's control over decision making (Young, 1982), but, as Madsen (1986) points out, the importance of clinicians, counselors, and other professionals in personality assessment is not diminished when computers are used to administer, score, and interpret tests.

Comments under the guideline quoted in the last paragraph indicate, however, that "a well-designed statistical treatment of test results and ancillary information will yield more valid assessments than will an individual professional using the same information" (American Psychological Association, 1986, page 13). Consequently, embellishing or altering the computerized interpretation in any way should not be done routinely, but only for good and compelling reasons. Be that as it may, a CBTI narrative is not a comprehensive personality analysis or diagnosis, but rather it serves as an indicator of psychological problems or a verification of problems detected by other means (Eyde & Kowal, 1984).

Concerning the reactions of examinees to computer-based test interpretations, the majority of respondents in one study agreed that computer-based MMPI interpretive reports were at least equal in accuracy to those provided by expert clinicians (Johnson, Gianetti, & Williams, 1978). In another investigation, computer-based MMPI assessments actually outperformed clinicians in differentiating between neurotic and psychotic patients (Goldberg, 1970) and in predicting suicidal or assaultive behavior (Mirabile, Houck, & Glueck, 1970).

Problems and Standards in Computer-based Test Interpretation

Computers, and especially microcomputers, possess many advantages for psychological assessment. In addition to being extremely efficient, they are adaptable to individual differences in mental and physical characteristics and provide prompt scoring and interpretation of assessment results. Despite these advantages, there are some serious problems with the use of computers in testing. Among these are the cost of the system and the inadequacy of software, as well as the fact that computer-based test interpretations may be inappropriate with certain groups of people (young children, the mentally retarded, people in crisis situations, severe psychotics, and others). There is also the problem of maintaining confidentiality when computers collect and store important personal information. Examinees have a legal right to control the release of their test scores and other personal information, a right that may be too easily violated when such information is stored on a computer. Obviously, CBTI reports should be kept confidential, with the examiner and record keeper acting in accordance with the examinee's right to control his or her own personal information (Herr & Best, 1984; Sampson & Pyle, 1983).

With respect to computer-based test scoring and interpretation services, few of the interpretative programs have been adequately validated and many are based on inadequate norms. Reliability is also a problem with some programs. Consequently, buyers must beware of the proliferation of CBTI programs and demand proof that the service providers adhere to the usual standards of reliability, validity, and representative norms. The sale of self-assessment software to the general public is especially disturbing (Niemark, 1984). Many of these programs are inadequately validated, and since no examiner is present to explain the results, the potential for harm exists.

There is also a tendency for computer-generated test reports to be endowed with greater status than they deserve—to be viewed as if they were written in stone—even when the validity of such narratives has not been demonstrated. Accepting test interpretations generated by computers as necessarily valid is an illustration not only of the "power of the machine," but also of the "Barnum effect" of believing that personality descriptions phrased in generalities, truisms, and other statements that sound specific to a given person, but that are actually applicable to almost anyone, are accurate. The tendency to use computer-based test interpretations prematurely is more likely to occur with unqualified users who are given access to the interpretations. As pointed out by Turkington (1984, pages 7, 26),

The most pressing worry of practitioners is the accuracy of computerized test interpretation. . . . Used by those with little training or awareness of test interpretation validity, computerized testing can do more harm than good. . . . Because test scores and interpretations come from a computer, they give a false impression of infallibility. And because the tests are so easy to use . . . many who are untrained will use them incorrectly for decisions involving employment, educational placement, occupational counseling, mental health diagnosis or brain deficiency assessments.

According to Skinner and Pakula (1986), Matarazzo's (1983, page 323) prediction of a "flood of litigation involving unqualified users of the products of this new technology," which in 1986 was said to be "just around the corner," would probably name both the test user and test developer as defendants. For this reason, if for no other, developers of CBTI products and organizations that provide CBTI services should make certain that the users of their products are qualified psychodiagnosticians. CBTI services should also take care that their products are adequately validated and standardized, follow the *Guidelines for Computer-based Tests and Interpretations,* and are made available, with all supporting documentation, to qualified reviewers. Reviews of CBTI products are published in professional journals such as *Computers in Human Behavior, Computers in Human Services, Computers in Psychiatry/Psychology, Computer Use in Social Services,* and the *Journal of Counseling and Development.* After examining these reviews and other documentation on CBTI report products, users would be advised to ask themselves the following questions (Ben-Porath & Butcher, 1986):

> To what extent has the validity of this report been studied?
>
> To what extent does this report rely on empirical findings in generating its interpretation?
>
> To what extent does this report incorporate all of the currently validated descriptive information?
>
> Does the report take demographic variables into account?
>
> Are different versions available for various referral questions?
>
> Is the report internally consistent?
>
> Does the report include practical suggestions?
>
> Is the report periodically revised to reflect newly acquired information?

Finally, it is recommended that students in the human service professions receive adequate computer-based assessment training along the lines outlined by Meier and Geiger (1986). Such training will become increasingly important as new forms of assessment based on administration, scoring, and interpretation by computers are developed. Because the human service professions have traditionally been nontechnically oriented and have usually attracted persons with little computer experience, this requirement is important, but likely to prove difficult to realize.

Computer-based Counseling and Guidance

Related to the use of computers in psychological and educational testing is computer-based counseling. Because many students experience learning problems that require academic counseling, it is not surprising that a number of computer-assisted programs have been developed for this purpose. An example is the Computer-Assisted Study Skills Instruction System (CASSI) (Sampson, 1981). Using this system, students complete assigned lessons and are then assisted in applying the concepts they learn to their academic work.

Career counseling and guidance is another school-related area in which computers have been used extensively. Shatkin (1980) estimated that over 25 computer-assisted guidance systems designed to help students explore their interests, values, attitudes, and abilities and make realistic career decisions were available as of 1980. An example is the System of Interactive Guidance and Information (SIGI and SIGI PLUS), two programs developed by Educational Testing Service to assist students and adults in educational and career planning. By presenting a series of questions and problems, SIGI and SIGI PLUS assist users in defining their values, exploring various strategies for career decision making, and discovering career possibilities. Several sessions with these programs, which users reportedly find enjoyable and profitable, can be followed by discussions with an experienced career counselor. A similar computer-assistance guidance system, DISCOVER and DISCOVER for Adult Learners, is available from The American College Testing Program. In a study of Kapes, Borman, and Frazier (1989), both undergraduate students and counselors in training gave high ratings to the SIGI and DISCOVER systems. These systems have been found to be particularly valuable when used as complements to live career development counseling.

Computers have also been programmed to assist in personality counseling, and a variety of counseling software is available. One of the first such programs was designed by Cassel and Blum (1970) to identify and counsel potentially delinquent youths. Potential delinquents were first identified from their scores on an eight-part Ego-Ideal and Conscience Development Test and then exposed to Computer Assist Counseling to teach them more socially appropriate patterns of behavior. Programs utilizing other approaches to counseling (client centered, psychoanalytic, cognitive, and the like) have been developed since the late 1960s. Perhaps the most comprehensive of these is Wagman's (1980) PLATO DCS, which follows a cognitive framework and logical pattern modeled after the computer. With PLATO DCS clients progress through five sequenced and interrelated processes in attempting to resolve personal dilemmas (Sampson & Pyle, 1983). A significant impediment to continued progress in using computers for treating psychological problems is difficulty in devising computer programs that can interpret natural language (Lawrence, 1986).

Computers as Diagnostic Tools

In speculating on future applications of computers in psychodiagnosis, Sundberg (1977) noted some years ago the significance of research linking the abilities of human observers to the combinatorial processes of computers. Data on literally thousands of human problems occurring in a variety of person–situation contexts could be stored in a computer's memory and referred to on request, suggesting to the assessor several possibilities for exploration in a particular clinical case. Advances in computer simulation of medical cases suggests that computers might also be programmed to simulate various psychological disorders. The results of these simulations could provide a framework for improved understanding and treatment of the disorders. Once enough information on the diagnostic signs has been stored in a computer's memory, it may play a central role in periodic psychological checkups of people. In fact, Sundberg (1977) indicated that computer-based psychological checkups may one day be as common as medical checkups are today.

Research in artificial intelligence on using expert systems to make medical diagnoses (Michaelsen, Michie, & Boulanger, 1985), in which the approaches (heuristics) of experts are distilled into the form of computer programs, suggests that Sundberg's speculations may not be completely fanciful. Furthermore, the pioneering work of Brown and Burton (1978) points to the possibilities of using artificial intelligence techniques to perform educational diagnoses.

Although the routine use of computers for diagnosing educational and psychological problems is obviously a long way off, fifth-generation computers with their parallel architecture, planned for the 1990s, will make the shift from the computer's role of "number cruncher" to knowledge processor and problem solver more feasible. More flexible, fifth-generation computers may also result in the replacement of multiple-choice items by free-response test items. Such machines will be capable of generating open-ended questions and, by being programmed to recognize a set of key words and phrases, of evaluating the typed or spoken answers. In the long run, the expert systems of artificial intelligence with their natural language-processing capabilities will be able to analyze complex verbal responses (Ward, 1985). Computers having this capacity will be able to recognize many right answers, not just one, and score them intelligently. By attaching various input and output devices (audio- and videocassettes, light-, heat-, and touch-sensitive screens, joysticks, dials, psychophysical transducers, and so on) to the computer, test administration and response interpretation of both normal and handicapped individuals on a wide range of cognitive and affective variables should become possible. In classrooms of the future, computers will administer interactive diagnostic tests, keep a record of each student's performance, and track errors to identify patterns and problems. Feedback will be immediate and on-screen, confirming right answers, correcting wrong answers, and suggesting instructional materials that can correct errors (Rounds, Kanter, & Blumin, 1987).

OTHER CURRENT DEVELOPMENTS AND FUTURE PROSPECTS

As witnessed by the large number of tests cited in more recent editions of *The Mental Measurements Yearbook* (Mitchell, 1985; Conoley & Kramer, 1989; Kramer & Conoley, 1992), the quantity of new tests being published continues to rise. Although many of these tests fail to meet the requirements of adequate standardization, reliability, and validity, improvements in the assessment of abilities and personality have been noteworthy. With respect to tests of ability, the concept of multiple aptitudes remains popular, but competency tests, criterion-referenced measurement, and formative evaluation are also being emphasized.

Theory-based Testing

In the past, ability tests have been constructed primarily on an empirical, atheoretical foundation. In the case of tests of intelligence and special aptitude, less concern has been shown with test content and more concern with whether the empirical evidence indicated that the test did what it was designed to do. However, future ability tests promise to be based more on theories of mental abilities, learning, and instruction. The field of intelligence testing is being reshaped by the research of cognitive theorists such as Sternberg (1985) and Pellegrino and Varnhagen (1985), who have attempted to identify the mental stages or cognitive components involved in various kinds of thinking. A test developed by Sternberg focuses on qualities such as creativity and the ability to generate or synthesize ideas and on how individuals acquire knowledge and learn to solve problems (Jacobson, 1986). Certain educational psychologists (for example, Glaser, 1981, 1985) have also attempted to put ability testing on a sounder psychological basis by integrating it with theories of learning and instruction. Furthermore, information-processing analyses of performances that contribute to proficiency in various tasks, conducted by comparing the techniques employed by experts with those used by novices, are leading to an increased understanding of what highly competent performance involves.

Individualized Instruction

Because test scores are measures of differences among individuals in cognitive and affective variables, it seems reasonable to capitalize on these differences by using the scores to allocate people to occupations or educational curricula most appropriate to their abilities and interests. The fact that the effectiveness of a particular type of instructional program depends to some degree on the ability pattern of the learner is widely recognized and the topic of much research. The individualized approach to instruction envisioned by certain educational planners considers each person's unique pattern of abilities and interests in planning his or her educational experiences. Instruction is modular: the student works through only those learning modules from which, according to the results of psychodiagnostic testing, he or she can benefit. Computers can be of assistance at every stage of the individualized instruction process: in diagnosing the needs of the learner, in presenting the instructional material to the learner, in reevaluating the learner's status and needs, and in redesigning the instructional program.

Computer-assisted Instruction

Computer-assisted instruction is not new, but technological advances in computing machinery and programming have made it even more feasible now than in previous years. In computer-assisted instruction (CAI), a computer acts as a private tutor to guide the learner through the lesson in small steps, ask questions, and keep a record of correct and incorrect responses. Learners proceed at their own rate, reading the statements of information and responding to questions based on the information. Stimulus materials may also be presented by colored slides, computer graphics, sound recordings, and other media. Learners usually type their responses into the computer, although touching a light-pen or finger to the CRT screen and voicing the answer are other possible response modes. A joy stick connected to a computer can also facilitate the measurement of perceptual–motor skills. Whatever the response and however it is made, it is evaluated by the computer and confirmed or rejected. If a response is confirmed, the computer usually prints out a verbal reinforcement and proceeds with the regular program. If a response is disconfirmed, the computer tells the learner that it is incorrect, and why, and may then branch to an alternative remedial procedure or program.

Although proponents of CAI are perhaps not as enthusiastic as they once were, computer-assisted instruction has been used to teach a wide range of subject matter and skills, ranging from learning a foreign language to flying a helicopter (Muchinsky, 1983). Among its advantages are that learners can proceed at their own rate and receive immediate feedback regarding the correctness of their answers. The major disadvantages are high cost and, in some instances, poorly designed instructional programs. Furthermore, some students react negatively to a computer-assisted approach to learning.

Educational Diagnosis Revisited

One needed improvement in ability testing is for the tests to be made more diagnostic in nature, a goal that can only be realized with multiscore instruments. Consequently, psychometric seers look forward to less emphasis on single-score tests for predicting educational or vocational performance and greater emphasis on multiscore tests designed with diagnostic purposes in mind. These diagnostic tests of mental abilities may well be of the criterion-referenced (absolute assessment) type, rather than the more traditional norm-referenced (relative assessment) type.

A recent emphasis of Educational Testing Service is on the development of diagnostic tests that, rather than simply measuring what students have learned, will assist them in their efforts to master new fields of knowledge (Trombley, 1986). The diagnostic tests will be individualized and adaptive, including a brief challenge test, probes to identify the component skills of an area in which the student has problems, construction of a profile of the student's strengths and weaknesses, and presentation of remedial instruction. Anrig (1985) sees these diagnostic tests as serving students more than institutions, as aimed primarily at helping individuals learn and succeed rather than simply yielding scores for institutional decision making, and as guiding instruction and self-development on a continuing basis rather than merely comparing performance among test takers.

Personality Assessment

Compared with the technical sophistication of ability testing, personality inventories and other affective measuring instruments are relatively crude. But the potential value of accurate personality assessment in a wide range of situations is unquestioned, and recent progress seen in the psychometrically sophisticated designs of certain personality and interest inventories suggests that general improvements in affective assessment are forthcoming. Some of the current activity involves new methodologies such as structural equation modeling (Bentler & Newcomb, 1986) and taxonometric methods (Meehl & Golden, 1982). Other research is concerned with the administration and interpretation of personality tests, for example, the effects of examiner biases and heuristics on clinical judgment (Dawes, 1986).

According to Ziskin (1986), clinical assessment is currently in an unhealthy state due to the lack of an adequate system for classifying mental disorders, contamination of data by situational effects, evidence that clinical skills do not improve with practice, difficulties in differentiating normal from psychopathic behavior, and problems with computer interpretation of data. Ziskin advocated a broader approach to computer use in clinical diagnosis, including not only the MMPI and similar instruments, but also demographic data and data from structured interviews. He also predicted that in the future greater emphasis will be placed on personal assets (such as good looks) and psychosocial stresses and greater use of structured interviews. Clinicians should also become more aware of the fact that there are limits to what can be discovered about people by means of psychological assessment.

Because of their adaptability to changing conditions and the existence of strong supporters such as James Butcher and John Exner, respectively, it is unlikely that tests such as the MMPI or the Rorschach will be replaced anytime soon. Newer uses for these tests will, in all likelihood, be discovered, and newer tests will force a continuing reevaluation of these and other time-honored clinical instruments. Over a decade ago, Weiner (1983) predicted a bright future for psychodiagnosis, but he cautioned that the realization of such a future demands "continued careful research on psychodiagnostic methods and the expert application of psychological test findings. . . ."

Some years later, Matarazzo (1992) continued to see a bright future for clinical psychodiagnosis with the construction of tests to identify and analyze more specific forms of psychopathology such as panic reactions and depressive disorders. Matarazzo also predicted that newer and better measures of personal competence in adapting to one's environment, including scales of quality of life and adaptive behavior, will be devised. Even more intriguing to Matarazzo than the future of personality assessment are expected developments in physiological measures of intelligence, including indexes derived from intrinsic and evoked brain potentials (EEG and PET) and nerve conduction velocity. Research indicates that these physiological measures are significantly correlated with scores on conventional intelligence tests. However, the physiological indexes will presumably complement rather than replace traditional paper-and-pencil performance tests of intelligence. In addition, new measures of ability based on cognitive theories and research and improvements in tests of neuropsychological functioning are seen on the horizon.

Whatever the future may hold for personality and clinical assessment, there will be a continuing need to evaluate the effectiveness of psychometric instruments and procedures in these areas. Then, as now and in the past, the major questions concerning any personality or clinical assessment will focus on the validity of the assessment methods. To what extent do the methods fulfill their intended purposes—in research, psychodiagnosis, the planning of treatment or other interventions, and evaluation of the effectiveness of such interventions?

Although psychologists, like other forecasters, are not renowned for their ability to peer into the future, a quarter-century after publication of the first edition of this text, the author continues to believe that exciting and productive times lie ahead for psychological testing and assessment. The current situation in this field is very different from what it was at the beginning of the century, when it was reportedly viewed as the only way in which psychologists could make a living outside the classroom and the laboratory. Today testing is no longer the bread and butter of psychology, but certainly it remains and will continue to be an important portion of the meat and potatoes!

SUMMARY

Psychological testing and assessment continue to grow and undoubtedly will remain an important part of applied psychology well into the next century. The increasing automation of psychological assessment and interviewing by means of computers, and especially microcomputers, has made the administration and scoring of tests and other psychometric devices, as well as the interpretation of test results, more objective and efficient. Computer-based testing also tends to be more interesting and motivating to examinees than traditional procedures.

Adaptive testing, in which the sequence of questions presented to an examinee varies with his or her estimated standing on a specified variable and his or her responses to previous questions, substantially reduces testing time. The use of computers for presenting test items and evaluating answers makes adaptive testing a very efficient, although, for the present, a somewhat expensive alternative to the traditional approach of presenting the same items to all examinees.

Computer-based interviewing and test interpretation programs are still relatively new, but substantial progress has been made in this area during the past 30 years. Computer-based test interpretation, which began with the work on interpretive scoring of the MMPI at the Mayo Clinic in the early 1960s, has expanded to include the scoring and interpretation of dozens of cognitive and affective instruments by many commercial organizations.

In addition to their uses in test administration, scoring, and interpretation, psychologists and educators have made extensive use of computers for analyzing research data, for controlling stimulus inputs and response outputs in experiments, and for simulating experiments, environments, and behavior patterns. Two other areas in which computers have been applied with noteworthy success are computer-assisted instruction and computer-based academic and personal counseling. Fifth-generation computers, with their parallel architecture and emphasis on expert systems and artificial intelligence, promise to increase the versatility of psychological assessment procedures far beyond the traditional objective-test format. Theories of cognition and research on the psychophysiological basis of memory, learning, and thinking will also undoubtedly influence the fields of psychological assessment and educational instruction.

Although computers have made and will certainly continue to make significant contributions to psychological and educational assessment, a number of problems have been encountered. Such problems as cost and computerphobia (or "cyberphobia") are perhaps less serious than the problem of confidentiality, which arises when masses of personal data on individuals are stored on computers to which unauthorized persons have access. Recognizing the growing importance of computers in social science research and applications and consequently the potentiality of misuse, a set of *Guidelines for Computer-based Tests and Interpretations* was developed by the American Psychological Association (1986).

Other recent developments in psychological testing and assessment include the revision of older psychometric instruments and the development of many new ones, the growth of qualification and competency testing in educational and employment contexts, continuing interest in linking assessment to instruction, extensions of psychometric methodology and theory (item-response theory, structural equation modeling, adaptive testing), and efforts to create a clearer interface between psychological theories (for example, cognitive theory and psychoanalytic theory) and psychological assessment.

EXERCISES

1. Run the test-scoring program in Table 13–1 on a microcomputer. If you know how to program in BASICA, expand the program in Table 13–1 by having it score each examinee's

test paper and then print out the examinee's name and score as well as the arithmetic mean and standard deviation of the scores.

2. What is *adaptive testing? Stratadaptive testing?* In what ways is adaptive testing superior to traditional objective testing procedures?

3. Using information obtained from reading or personal experience, compare programmed instruction, including computer-assisted instruction, with traditional methods of instruction (lecture, discussion, and the like). What are the advantages and disadvantages of computer-assisted instruction (CAI) compared with other instructional methods?

4. Arrange to take the California Psychological Inventory, the Eysenck Personality Inventory, the 16 Personality Factor Questionnaire, or another computer-scored and computer-interpreted personality inventory and have it sent to an appropriate test-scoring and interpretation service. Does the computer's interpretation correspond to your own analysis of your personality? (*Note:* This exercise should be closely supervised by your course instructor.)

5. Because psychological counseling has traditionally been viewed as involving an interpersonal relationship between a counselor and a counselee, how is it possible to be "counseled" by an inhuman, inanimate computer? In what areas and with what kinds of problems is computer-based counseling most likely to be effective?

6. Describe the ethical issues concerning the use of computers in various phases of psychological assessment: test development, test scoring, test interpretation, and test use. What steps should be taken to make certain that computer technology is used wisely and ethically in psychological assessment?

7. What changes do you forecast as occurring in psychological testing and assessment during the next 50 years? What new kinds of tests and methodologies are likely to be developed? What role will automation (computers in particular) play in these changes?

SUGGESTED READINGS

Butcher, J. N. (1987). Computerized clinical and personality assessment using the MMPI. In J. N. Butcher (ed.), *Computerized psychological assessment,* pp. 161–197. New York: Basic Books.

Golden, C. (1987). Computers in neuropsychology. In J. N. Butcher (ed.), *Computerized psychological assessment,* pp. 344–354. New York: Basic Books.

Green, B. F. (1988). Critical problems in computer-based psychological measurement. *Measurement in Education, 1,* 223–231.

Groth-Marnat, G., & Schumacher, J. (1989). Computer-based psychological testing: Issues and guidelines. *American Journal of Orthopsychiatry, 59,* 257–263.

Honaker, L. M., & Fowler, R. D. (1990). Computer-assisted psychological assessment. In G. Goldstein & M. Hersen (eds.), *Handbook of psychological assessment,* 2nd ed., pp. 521–546. New York: Pergamon.

Jackson, D. N. (1988). Computer-based assessment and interpretation: The dawn of discovery. In T. B. Gutkin & S. L. Wise (eds.), *The computer as adjunct to the decision-making process.* Hillsdale, NJ: Lawrence Erlbaum.

Kramer, J. J. (1988). Computer-based test interpretation in psychoeducational assessment: An initial appraisal. *Journal of School Psychology, 26,* 143–153.

Lanyon, R. I. (1987). The validity of computer-based personality assessment products: Recommendations for the future. *Computers in Human Behavior, 3,* 225–238.

Matarazzo, J. D. (1992). Psychological testing and assessment in the 21st century. *American Psychologist, 47,* 1007–1018.

Tallent, N. (1987). Computer-generated psychological reports: A look at the modern psychometric machine. *Journal of Personality Assessment, 51,* 95–108.

Weiss, D. J., & Vale, C. D. (1987). Computerized adaptive testing for measuring abilities and other psychological variables. In J. N. Butcher (ed.), *Computerized psychological assessment,* pp. 325–343. New York: Basic Books.

Appendix A

Measurement and Statistics

Any kind of physical measures (of size, weight, coloration, and so forth) made on living things will vary across individual members of a given species. Human beings differ physically from each other in many ways—in height, weight, blood pressure, visual acuity, and so on. Similarly, extensive individual differences in the mental characteristics and behavior of humans may be observed. People differ in their abilities, accumulated knowledge, interests, attitudes, and temperament, to name a few psychological variables. Some of these individual differences can be measured more precisely than others, as reflected in the type of measurement scale.

SCALES OF MEASUREMENT

The measurement of physical and psychological variables may be characterized by the degree of refinement or precision in terms of four scales: nominal, ordinal, interval, and ratio. Measurement is on a *nominal scale* whenever numbers are used merely to describe or name, rather than to indicate the order or magnitude of something. Examples of nominal measurement are the numbers on athletic uniforms or numerical designations of demographic variables such as sex (for example, male = 1, female = 2) or ethnicity (for example, white = 0, black = 1, other = 2). Such numbers are a convenient way of identifying individuals or groups, but it makes no sense to compare them in terms of direction or magnitude. Somewhat more refined than nominal measurement is measurement on an *ordinal scale*. The numbers on an ordinal scale refer to the ranks of objects or events in some order of merit. For example, numbers designating the order of finishing in a race or other contest are on an ordinal scale. A third level of measurement is an *interval scale*, on which equal numerical differences can be interpreted as corresponding to equal differences in whatever characteristic is being measured. The Celsius scale of temperature is an example of an interval scale. For example, the difference between 60° C and 40° C is equal to the difference between 30° C and 10° C, both numerically and in terms of temperature (heat). The standard score scale of intelligence (see Chapters 4 and 6) is also considered to be an interval scale.

The highest, or most refined, level of measurement is a *ratio scale,* which has the characteristics of an interval scale in addition to a true zero, a point signifying complete absence of whatever is being measured. When measurement is on a ratio scale, numerical ratios can be interpreted in a meaningful way. For example, the variable of height is measured on a ratio scale. If John is 6 feet tall and Paul is 3 feet tall, it is correct to say that John is twice as tall as Paul. Height, weight, speed, any many other physical variables are measured on ratio scales, but psychological characteristics are not. The scores on psychological tests represent ordinal, or at most interval, rather than ratio measurement. For this reason, even if Frank's IQ score is 150 and Jim's IQ is 50, it is incorrect to conclude that Frank is three times as intelligent as Jim. But if IQs represent interval measurement and Amy has an IQ of 100, then it is correct to state that the difference in intelligence between Frank, and Amy (150 - 100) is equal to the difference in intelligence between Amy and Jim (100 - 50).

FREQUENCY DISTRIBUTIONS

The range and distribution of individual differences in physical and mental characteristics may be depicted by means of a frequency distribution of scores on a test or some other measuring instrument. In its simplest form, a *frequency distribution* is a list of possible scores and the number of examinees who make each score. For example, if a five-item test is administered and an examinee gets one point for each item answered correctly, the possible scores are 0, 1, 2, 3, 4, and 5. If the test is administered to 25 examinees, a frequency distribution of their scores might be depicted as follows:

Score	Number of examinees (frequency)
5	1
4	4
3	9
2	6
1	3
0	2

For example, this frequency distribution shows that two examinees missed all five items, nine examinees answered three items correctly, and one examinee answered all five items correctly.

Score Intervals

When the range of scores on a test is large, say 25 points or more, it may be convenient to group the scores into intervals. To illustrate, intelligence quotient (IQ) scores on the Wechsler Adult Intelligence Scale (WAIS) range from approximately 43 to 152. Computations made on these scores may be simplified by grouping them into intervals of five IQ points, starting with the interval 43–47 and counting up through the interval

148–152 (see column 1 of Table A–1). This gives 22 intervals instead of the 110 (IQs from 43 through 152) that would result if an interval were allotted to every possible score. Using the smaller number of intervals has very little effect on the accuracy of the statistics computed from the frequency distribution of IQ scores, and it is certainly a more efficient way of describing the scores.

Histogram and Frequency Polygon

A useful pictorial way of representing a frequency distribution of scores is to graph the distribution as a histogram or frequency polygon. To begin the construction of a histogram, the exact limits of the score intervals must be determined. The *exact limits* of an interval are computed by subtracting .5 from the lower limit and adding .5 to the upper limit of the interval. For example, the exact limits of the interval 43–47 are 42.5–47.5, and the exact limits of the interval 148–152 are 147.5–152.5. After the exact limits of all intervals have been found, the frequency corresponding to each interval is represented as a vertical bar with a width spanning the exact limits and a height proportional to the number of

TABLE A–1   Frequency Distribution of Full-scale IQs on Wechsler Adult Intelligence Scale

IQ interval	Number of examinees (frequency)
148–152	1
143–147	0
138–142	3
133–137	12
128–132	26
123–127	64
118–122	145
113–117	165
108–112	224
103–107	274
98–102	278
93–97	255
88–92	220
83–87	135
78–82	107
73–77	55
68–72	49
63–67	18
58–62	11
53–57	6
48–52	3
43–47	1

Source: Data from D. Wechsler, *The Measurement and Appraisal of Adult Intelligence,* 4th ed. Baltimore: Williams & Wilkins, 1958, p. 253.

scores falling on that interval. A completed histogram of the frequency distribution in Table A–1 is represented by the adjacent vertical bars in Figure A–1.

For the graphical plot of a frequency distribution to be continuous, the data are often plotted as a series of connected line segments. In Figure A–1, the dashed line segments connecting the midpoints of the score intervals form a frequency polygon of the distribution in Table A–1. Viewed alone, the frequency polygon gives a better picture than the histogram of the overall shape of the frequency distribution.

The Normal Curve

Although the frequency polygon in Figure A–1 looks irregular, it is similar to a symmetrical, bell-shaped curve. More examinees made scores of approximately 100 (actually 98–102) than any other score, and successively fewer examinees made scores greater or smaller than 100. If the frequency polygon were perfectly symmetrical, smooth, and bell shaped, it would look like Figure A–2.

The curve in Figure A–2, which can be described by a mathematical equation, is called a *normal curve*. The scores on the base axis of this normal curve are *standard*

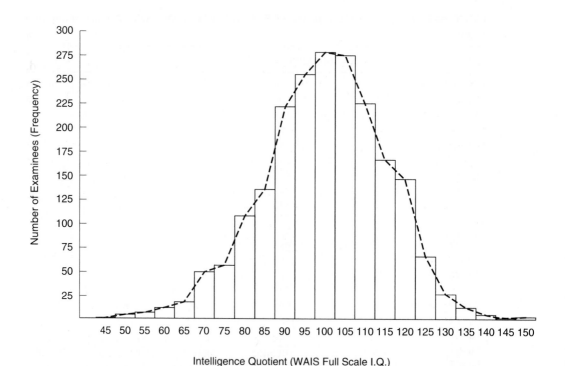

FIGURE A–1 Histogram and Frequency Polygon of Frequency Distribution in Table A–1. *(From D. Wechsler, The Measurement and Appraisal of Adult Intelligence, 4th ed. Baltimore: Williams & Wilkins, 1958, p. 253. © 1958 The Williams & Wilkins Co., Baltimore. Reproduced by permission of Oxford University Press.)*

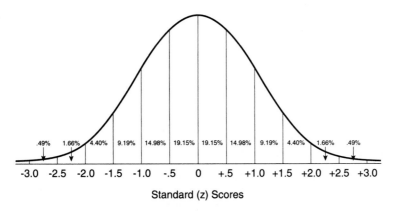

.49%   1.66%   4.40%   9.19%   14.98%   19.15%   19.15%   14.98%   9.19%   4.40%   1.66%   .49%

-3.0   -2.5   -2.0   -1.5   -1.0   -.5   0   +.5   +1.0   +1.5   +2.0   +2.5   +3.0

Standard (z) Scores

FIGURE A–2 Standard Normal Distribution.

scores (*z scores*). These *z* scores, the computation of which is described in Chapter 4, serve as a convenient, standard method of expressing and comparing the scores of the same individual on two or more tests or the scores of two or more examinees on the same test.

A certain percentage of the area under the curve in Figure A–2 lies between any two *z* scores. This percentage may correspond to the percentage of a group of examinees whose raw test scores, when converted to *z* scores, fall within the range of the two *z* scores. For example, 19.15 percent of the area under the curve in Figure A–2 and, consequently, 19.15 percent of a normal distribution of test scores falls between *z* scores of 0 and .5. Only 1.66 percent of the area under the normal curve, however, lies between *z* = +2.0 and *z* = +2.5 (or between *z* =; −2.0 and *z* = −2.5).

Although the theoretical range of *z* scores in a normal distribution is minus infinity (−) to plus infinity (+), over 99 percent of the area under the normal curve (or 99 percent of a normal distribution of test scores) falls between *z* scores of −3.00 and +3.00. Of course, when converting a raw test score to a *z* score, the result is not always one of the 13 *z* scores listed on the base axis of Figure A–2. Therefore, a special table must be provided to determine the percentage of the area falling between any *z* score (see Appendix B).

During the late nineteenth and early twentieth centuries, there was much speculation concerning the normal curve as being an inherent law of nature. The reason for this belief was that the frequency distributions of many biological characteristics are approximately normal in shape. In fact, much of the mathematical theory of statistical inference, which is so important in psychological and educational research, is based on the assumption of a normal distribution of measurements. The reader should be cautioned, however, not to glorify the normal curve. Although many tests are constructed in such a way that the scores are approximately normally distributed, the frequency distributions of other test scores are very asymmetrical, or skewed. A common situation is a *positively skewed* distribution of scores (few high scores and many low scores), representing the results of a test that was perhaps too difficult for the examinees. Less common is a *negatively skewed* score distribution (many high scores and few low scores), which occurs when a test is perhaps too easy for the examinees (Figure A–3).

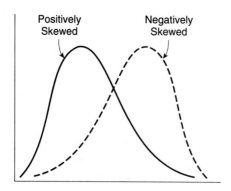

FIGURE A–3   Skewed Frequency Distributions.

MEASURES OF CENTRAL TENDENCY (AVERAGES)

In addition to displaying or plotting the distribution of a set of test scores, it is convenient to have some measure of the typical or *average* score. Three kinds of averages are commonly employed in statistics: the mode, the median, and the arithmetic mean.

Mode

The *mode* of a set of raw test scores is defined as the score obtained by the largest number of examinees. In the five-item test referred to previously, more people (9) made a score of 3 than any other score, so the mode of that group of scores is 3. When test scores are grouped into intervals, the mode is defined as the midpoint of the interval containing the largest number of scores. The score interval 98–102 in Table A–1 contains the largest number of scores (278), so the midpoint of that interval, (98 + 102)/2 = 100, is the mode of that frequency distribution.

As seen in the frequency polygon in Figure A–1, the mode is the maximum point in a frequency distribution. Figure A–1 pictures a *unimodal* distribution, but sometimes there is more than one maximum point. In that case the distribution is said to be *bimodal* if it has two maxima and *multimodal* if it has more than two.

Median

The *median* (Mdn) of a group of scores is the middle score, that is, the score below and above which one-half (50 percent) of the scores fall. Thus, the median of the scores 7, 6, 9, 5, and 3 is 6, because 6 is in the middle when the scores are ranked from highest to lowest. When the number of scores is even, the median is defined as the mean of the two middlemost scores.

Computing the median of a frequency distribution requires several steps, but it can be determined fairly quickly by interpolating within the interval on which the median falls. To illustrate the procedure, the median of the frequency distribution in Table A–1 will be calculated. Since the total number of scores is 2052, the median is the score (IQ) below and above which .50(2052) = 1026 of the scores fall. By successively adding the frequencies in column 2 of Table A–1, it is found that there are 860 scores up through the score interval 93–97. Similarly, there are 1138 scores up through the interval 98–102. To make the distribution of scores continuous, the exact upper limits of the score intervals in the frequency distribution are calculated. In the distribution of Table A–1, 860 scores fall below 97.5 and 1138 scores fall below 102.5. Because the median is the score below which 1026 scores fall, it must lie between 97.5 and 102.5. To find the exact median of these data, we form the ratio

$$(\text{Mdn} - 97.5) / (102.5 - 97.5) = (1026 - 860) / (1138 - 860)$$

This expression reduces to $(\text{Mdn} - 97.5)/5 = 166/278$, which, when solved for the median, gives 100.49.

The procedure for finding the median of a frequency distribution may be expressed more formally (and perhaps more simply!) by the following equation:

$$\text{Mdn} = L + w(.5N - n_b)/n_i \qquad \textbf{(A.1)}$$

In this formula, L is the lower exact limit of the interval containing the median, w is the width of the interval, N is the total number of scores in the distribution, n_b is the number of scores falling below the interval containing the median, and n_i is the number of scores falling on the interval containing the median.

The Summation Operator

Before considering methods for computing the arithmetic mean, the reader should become familiar with the special symbol Σ. This symbol, the Greek letter capital sigma, is used in statistics as a shorthand way of referring to the addition of a series of numerical values assumed by a variable. Thus, $\sum_{i=1}^{n} X_i$ means "the sum of all values of X_i, where i is an index number ranging from 1 to n ($i = 1, 2, 3, \ldots, n$)." In symbols,

$$\sum_{i=1}^{n} X_i = X_1 + X_2 + X_3 + \ldots + X_n$$

To illustrate, let $n = 3$, $X_1 = 2$, $X_2 = 4$, and $X_3 = 1$; then, since in this case $i = 1, 2,$ and 3,

$$\sum_{i=1}^{3} X_i = 2 + 4 + 1 = 7$$

Similarly,

$$\sum_{i=1}^{3} X_i^2 = (X_1)^2 + (X_2)^2 + (X_3)^2 = = (2)^2 + (4)^2 + (1)^2 = 4 + 16 + 1 = 21$$

The sum of the products of two variables, X and Y, is computed as

$$\sum_{i=1}^{n} X_i Y_i = (X_1 Y_1) + (X_2 Y_2) + (X_3 Y_3) + \ldots + (X_n Y_n)$$

If $Y_1 = 3$, $i = 1$, $Y_2 = 5$, and $Y_3 = 2$, this becomes

$$2(3) + 4(5) + 1(2) = 6 + 20 + 2 = 28.$$

Sometimes, when it is clearly understood that the limits of the summation are 1 and n, the index numbers above and below the summation sign and subscripts on the variables are omitted. Thus $\sum_{i=1}^{n} X_i$ may be simplified as ΣX.

Arithmetic Mean

Although the mode is an easily computed measure of central tendency, it is greatly affected by the shape of the score distribution. The median is less affected by the shape of the distribution, and it is the preferred measure of central tendency when the distribution is highly asymmetrical, or skewed. However, the arithmetic mean is the most popular measure of central tendency (average) because the median is cumbersome to work with in statistical theory. To compute the arithmetic mean of a set of scores, the scores (X's) are added, and the resulting sum is divided by the number of scores (n):

$$\bar{X} = \frac{\Sigma X}{n} \tag{A.2}$$

As an exercise, the reader should verify that the mean of the frequency distribution in Table A–1 is 99.96.

PERCENTILES, DECILES, AND QUARTILES

The median is sometimes referred to as the 50th percentile, because 50 percent of the scores fall below the median. The entire frequency distribution of scores may be divided into 100 percentiles, the pth *percentile* being that score below which p percent of the scores fall. For example, the 25th percentile is the score below which 25 percent of the scores fall, and the 75th percentile is the score below which 75 percent of the scores fall. Any percentile can be computed by the same interpolation procedure as that described above for finding the median.

In addition to percentiles, a distribution of scores may be divided into tenths (*deciles*) or fourths (*quartiles*). For example, the fourth decile (or 40th percentile) is the score below which four-tenths of the scores fall, and the third quartile (or 75th percentile) is the score below which three-fourths of the scores fall. Note that the 50th percentile, the fifth decile, and the second quartile are all the same score—the median.

MEASURES OF VARIABILITY

A measure of the average or central tendency is not sufficient by itself to describe a group of test scores. Samples of test scores differ not only in their averages, but also in their degree of spread or variability. Three measures of variability are the range, the semi-interquartile range, and the standard deviation.

Range and Semi-interquartile Range

The simple *range,* defined as the highest score minus the lowest score, is the easiest measure of variability to compute. The range of the data in the five-item problem described earlier is $5 - 0 = 5$, and the range of the IQ scores in Table A–1 is $152 - 43 = 109$. Because it is markedly affected by a single very high or very low score, the range is a poor measure of variability in most instances. A modified type of range known as the *semi-interquartile range* is sometimes used as an index of variability when the distribution of test scores is greatly skewed. The semi-interquartile range, or Q, is computed as one-half the difference between the 75th percentile (third quartile) and the 25th percentile (first quartile).

As an exercise, the reader should verify that, for the frequency distribution in Table A–1, the first quartile is 90.41, the third quartile is 110.33, and, consequently, the semi-interquartile range is $(110.33 - 90.41)/2 = 9.96$. The two quartiles may be found by the same linear interpolation procedure used to compute the median. Because the first quartile is the score below which $.25(2052) = 513$ scores fall, we must interpolate within the score interval 87.5–92.5. To find the third quartile, which is the $.75(2052) = 1539$th score, we interpolate within the interval 107.5–112.5. Thus, the first quartile may be determined by solving for Q_1 in the ratio

$$(Q_1 - 87.5)/(92.5 - 87.5) = (513 - 385)/(600 - 385)$$

and the third quartile may be found by solving for Q_3 in the ratio

$$(Q_1 - 107.5)/(112.5 - 107.5) = (1539 - 1407)/(1631 - 1407)$$

Standard Deviation

The most common measure of variability, the *standard deviation,* is appropriate when the arithmetic mean is the reported average. A formula for computing the standard deviation(s) of a set of scores is

$$\sqrt{\frac{\Sigma X^2 - \frac{(\Sigma X)^2}{n}}{n - 1}} \tag{A.3}$$

As an example, let us compute the standard deviation of the scores 7, 6, 9, 5, and 3. Using these five numbers, $\Sigma X = 30$ and $\Sigma X^2 = 200$, so

$$\Sigma X^2 - (\Sigma X)^2/n = 200 - (30)^2/5 = 20$$

Dividing 20 by $n - 1 = 4$ yields 5, the *variance* of the numbers. The square root of the variance ($\sqrt{5} = 2.24$) is the standard deviation of these scores.

CORRELATION AND REGRESSION

Francis Galton is credited with pioneering work on the method of correlation ("co-relation"). In the field of testing, this method has been employed extensively for analyzing data, and it is also very important in the statistical theory of mental test scores. The method of correlation is concerned with determining the extent to which two sets of measures, such as intelligence test scores and scholastic achievement marks, are related. The magnitude and direction of the relationship between two variables is expressed as a numerical index known as the *correlation coefficient*. Although there are many different types of correlation coefficient, the Pearson *product–moment coefficient,* or r, is the most popular. The value of r ranges from -1.00 (a perfect inverse relationship between the two variables) to $+1.00$ (a perfect direct relationship between the two variables.

Computing the Product–Moment Coefficient

Table A–2 rates the computations required to determine the correlation between the scores of 30 examinees on two measures, X and Y. Measure X may be an ability test of some sort and measure Y a rating of performance on the job. Thus, examinee 1 has a score of 44 on measure X and a score of 69 on measure Y, while examinee 2 has an X score of 38 and a Y score of 46. The column headings indicate the steps in computing r:

1. Compute X^2, Y^2, and the XY products for each examinee (columns 4, 5, and 6).
2. Sum the X, Y, X^2, Y^2, and XY columns (columns 2 through 6) and substitute these values into the following formula:

$$r = \frac{n \Sigma XY - (\Sigma X)(\Sigma Y)}{\sqrt{n \Sigma X^2 - (\Sigma X)^2} \sqrt{n \Sigma Y^2 - (\Sigma Y)^2}} \tag{A.4}$$

Since $\Sigma X = 1498$, $\Sigma Y = 1511$, $\Sigma X^2 = 79{,}844$, $\Sigma Y^2 = 79{,}641$, and $\Sigma XY = 77{,}664$,

$$r = \frac{40(77,664) - (1498)(1511)}{\sqrt{30(79,844) - (1498)^2} \ \sqrt{30(79,641) - (1511)^2}} = .52$$

The Meaning of Correlation

The method of correlation is useful in the field of psychological testing for a number of reasons, among which is the fact that correlation implies predictability. The accuracy with which an individual's score on measure Y can be predicted from his or her score on measure X depends on the magnitude of the correlation between the X and Y scores. The closer the correlation coefficient is to an absolute value of 1.00 (either $+1.00$ or -1.00), the smaller the average error that is made in predicting Y scores from X scores. For

TABLE A–2 Computing Sums for Determining the Correlation between X and Y

Examinee	X	Y	X^2	Y^2	XY
1	44	69	1,936	4,761	3,036
2	38	46	1,444	2,116	1,748
3	56	51	3,136	2,601	2,856
4	54	44	2,916	1,936	2,376
5	66	53	4,356	2,809	3,498
6	52	49	2,704	2,401	2,548
7	46	43	2,116	1,849	1,978
8	36	35	1,296	1,225	1,260
9	44	37	1,936	1,369	1,628
10	60	69	3,600	4,761	4,140
11	22	31	484	961	682
12	72	47	5,184	2,209	3,384
13	56	45	3,136	2,025	2,520
14	52	41	2,704	1,681	2,132
15	50	39	2,500	1,521	1,950
16	64	65	4,096	4,225	4,160
17	40	36	1,600	1,296	1,440
18	28	59	784	3,481	1,652
19	68	70	4,624	4,900	4,760
20	48	53	2,304	2,809	2,544
21	32	51	1,024	2,601	1,632
22	74	63	5,476	3,969	4,662
23	42	54	1,764	2,916	2,268
24	50	52	2,500	2,704	2,600
25	40	49	1,600	2,401	1,960
26	58	48	3,364	2,304	2,784
27	62	60	3,844	3,600	3,720
28	54	64	2,916	4,096	3,456
29	60	55	3,600	3,025	3,300
30	30	33	900	1,089	990
Sums	1498	1511	79,844	79,641	77,664

example, if the correlation between tests X and Y is close to $+1.00$, it can be predicted with confidence that a person who scores high on variable X will also score high on variable Y and that a person who scores low on X will also score low on Y. On the other hand, if the correlation between the X and Y variables is close to -1.00, it can be confidently predicted that a person who scores high on X will score low on Y and that a person who scores low on X will score high on Y. The closer the value of the correlation coefficient is to $+1.00$ or -1.00, the more accurate these predictions will be; the closer the correlation coefficient is to .00, the less accurate will be the prediction of Y from X or X from Y. When the correlation coefficient equals .00, predicting an individual's score on one measure from his or her score on the other measure will be no more accurate than chance.

Although correlation implies prediction, it does not imply causation. The fact that two variables are related does not mean that either variable is necessarily a cause of the other. Both variables may be under the influence of a third variable, and the correlation between the first two variables is a reflection of this common cause. For example, it can be demonstrated that the mental ages of a group of children who vary in chronological age is slightly positively correlated with the shoe sizes of the children. Obviously, neither mental age nor shoe size is a cause of the other. Rather, the positive correlation between these two variables is due to the effects on both of a third variable, body growth or maturation. Thus, the fact that variables X and Y are significantly related makes the prediction of one variable from the other variable more accurate than random guessing. However, it provides no information on whether the two variables are causally related.

Regression and Prediction

The product–moment correlation coefficient, which is a measure of the *linear* relationship between two variables, is actually a by-product of the statistical procedure for finding the equation of a straight line that best depicts the magnitude and direction of relationship between the two variables. To illustrate the meaning of this statement, the X, Y pairs of values listed in Table A–2 have been plotted as a graph in Figure A–4. Clearly, all the X, Y points cannot fall on any one straight line, but a straight line can be fitted to the points in such a way that the sum of the squared vertical distances of the points from that line will as small as possible. The equation for this best-fitting line is

$$Y_{\text{pred}} = r \left(\frac{s_y}{s_x}\right) (X - \overline{X}) + \overline{Y} \qquad \text{(A.5)}$$

where Y_{pred} is the predicted value of Y, r is the correlation coefficient between X and Y, s_x and s_y are the standard deviations of X and Y, and $\overline{X}$ and $\overline{Y}$ are the means of X and Y, respectively. From the data in Table A–2, the values of the five statistics are computed as $r = .52$, $s_x = 13.19$, $s_y = 11.04$, $\overline{X} = 49.93$ and $\overline{Y} = 50.37$. Entering these numbers into formula A.5 and simplifying yields the linear equation $Y_{\text{pred}} = .44X - 28.64$ This is the equation for the straight line (the *regression line*) drawn through the score points in Figure A–4. Using this equation, a person's score on variable Y can be predicted with better than chance accuracy from his or her score on variable X. For example, as illustrated

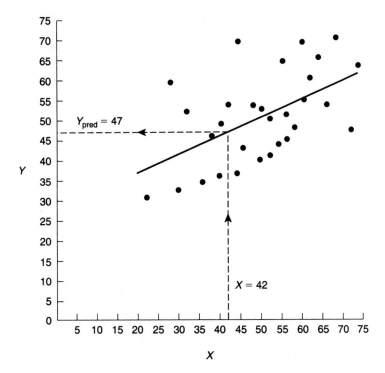

FIGURE A–4   Graphical Plot of Data in Table A–2, Showing Line of Regression of Y on X.

by the horizontal and vertical dashed lines in Figure A–4, if $X = 42$, $Y_{pred} = .44(42) + 28.64 = 47.12$. This means that, if a person scores 42 on the X variable, the best estimate of his or her score on the Y variable is approximately 47.

FACTOR ANALYSIS

As conceived by Karl Pearson and Charles Spearman, the major purpose of *factor analysis* is to reduce the number of variables in a group of measures by taking into account the overlap (correlations) among the various measures. In the field of psychological testing, the problem is to find a few salient factors that can account for the major part of the variance of a group of scores on different tests. All the many different procedures for extracting these factors from test scores are based on a fundamental theorem. The theorem states that the observed (total) variance of a test (s^2_{obs}) is equal to the sum of the variance due to factors that the test has in common with other tests (s^2_{com}), the variance specific to the test itself (s^2_{spe}), and the variance produced by errors of measurement (s^2_{err}). Consequently, formula 4.3 may be rewritten as

$$s^2_{obs} = s^2_{com} + s^2_{spe} + s^2_{err} \tag{A.6}$$

In formula A.6, what was referred to in Chapter 4 as the true variance of a test (s^2_{tru}) has been partitioned into common-factor variance and specific-factor variance. The portion of the observed variance due to common factors is called the test's *communality,* whereas the portion of the observed variance due to specific factors is its *specificity.* From these definitions and formulas 4.4 and A.6, we may write the equation

$$\text{reliability} = \text{communality} + \text{specificity} \tag{A.7}$$

One component of this equation, the communality of a test, is obtained from the results of a factor analysis involving that test. Then, if the reliability of the test is known, its specificity can be computed by subtraction. An illustrative factor analysis should help clarify these matters.

Factor Analysis of the WAIS–R

One way to begin a factor analysis of the scores of *n* people on a group of tests is to compute the correlations among all the tests and cast them into the form of a matrix. This has been done in Table A–3 with the average intercorrelations among the 11 WAIS–R subtests for nine ages ($n = 1880$). Notice that the matrix is symmetric; that is, the correlations in a given row are identical to those in the corresponding column. In addition, there are no entries on the diagonal running from upper left to lower right in the matrix.

The question of what values to place on the diagonal of the matrix—the reliabilities of the tests, estimates of their communalities, or all 1.00's—depends on the particular factor-analysis procedure or theory followed by the researcher. In one type of factoring procedure, Thurstone's *centroid method,* estimates of the communalities of the tests are placed on the diagonal of the correlation matrix. On the other hand, the *principal axis method* requires the diagonal entries to be 1.00's. Without belaboring the question of what values to place on the diagonal of the correlation matrix, it should be emphasized that the choice affects both the number of factors extracted and the obtained weights (*factor loadings*) of each test on each factor.

Factoring the Correlation Matrix

The intermediate result of a typical factor analysis is an original (unrotated) factor matrix such as the one in columns A, B, and C of Table A–4. Observe that in this case the factor-analysis procedure has reduced the number of variables or psychological dimensions from 11, which is the total number of subtests on the WAIS–R, to 3, the number of common factors extracted. The decimal numbers in each column of the factor matrix are the loadings of the 11 WAIS–R subtests on that factor. For example, the Information subtest has a loading of .82 on factor A, but loadings of only $-.31$ and $-.14$ on factors B and C, respectively. Each factor loading is the correlation between a particular subtest and one of the factors. The square of the loading of a given subtest on a factor is the proportion of the total variance of the subtest scores that can be accounted for by that factor. Thus, $(.82)^2 = .67$ means that 67 percent of the variance of Information subtest scores can be accounted for by factor A. But only $(-.31)^2 = .10$, or 10 percent, of the Information

TABLE A–3 Matrix of Average Intercorrelations for WAIS–R Subtests for Nine Ages

Subtest	1	2	3	4	5	6	7	8	9	10	11
1. Information		0.46	0.81	0.61	0.68	0.66	0.52	0.50	0.50	0.39	0.44
2. Digit Span	0.46		0.52	0.56	0.45	0.45	0.37	0.37	0.43	0.33	0.42
3. Vocabulary	0.81	0.52		0.63	0.74	0.72	0.55	0.51	0.52	0.41	0.47
4. Arithmetic	0.61	0.56	0.63		0.57	0.56	0.48	0.46	0.56	0.42	0.45
5. Comprehension	0.68	0.45	0.74	0.57		0.68	0.52	0.48	0.48	0.40	0.44
6. Similarities	0.66	0.45	0.72	0.56	0.68		0.54	0.50	0.51	0.43	0.46
7. Picture completion	0.52	0.37	0.55	0.48	0.52	0.54		0.51	0.54	0.52	0.42
8. Picture arrangement	0.50	0.37	0.51	0.46	0.48	0.50	0.51		0.47	0.40	0.39
9. Block design	0.50	0.43	0.52	0.56	0.48	0.51	0.54	0.47		0.63	0.47
10. Object assembly	0.39	0.33	0.41	0.42	0.40	0.43	0.52	0.40	0.63		0.38
11. Digit symbol	0.44	0.42	0.47	0.45	0.44	0.46	0.42	0.39	0.47	0.38	

From the manual of the Wechsler Adult Intelligence Scale—Revised. Copyright 1981, 1955 by The Psychological Corporation. Reproduced by permission. All rights reserved.

TABLE A–4 Original and Rotated Factor Matrices Produced by Principal Components Factor Analysis and Varimax Rotation of Correlation Matrix in Table A–3

Subtest	Original (unrotated) factor matrix			Rotated factor matrix			Communality
	A	B	C	A'	B'	C'	
Information	0.82	−0.31	−0.14	0.81	0.21	0.29	0.78
Digit span	0.65	−0.11	0.59	0.27	0.11	0.83	0.78
Vocabulary	0.86	−0.31	−0.10	0.82	0.22	0.34	0.84
Arithmetic	0.78	−0.08	0.24	0.49	0.28	0.59	0.67
Comprehension	0.80	−0.28	−0.16	0.79	0.23	0.26	0.74
Similarities	0.81	−0.19	−0.16	0.75	0.30	0.25	0.71
Picture completion	0.73	0.25	−0.26	0.48	0.64	0.11	0.66
Picture arrangement	0.68	0.10	−0.22	0.51	0.49	0.13	0.52
Block design	0.74	0.42	0.06	0.26	0.72	0.38	0.74
Object assembly	0.64	0.60	−0.08	0.14	0.85	0.19	0.77
Digit symbol	0.64	0.13	0.36	0.23	0.37	0.61	0.56

subtest scores can be accounted for by factor B. Similarly, $(-.14)^2 = .02$, or 2 percent, of Information subtest scores can be accounted for by factor C.

The sum of the cross-products of the corresponding factor loadings of any two subtests in Table A–4 is an estimate of the correlation between those two subtests. For example, the correlation between the Information and Digit Span subtests is estimated from the loadings in the original factor matrix to be

$$.82(.65) + (-.31)(-.11) + (-.14)(.59) = .48$$

This is a fairly close approximation to the actual correlation of .46 (see Table A–3). The accuracy with which the correlation matrix is reproduced by estimates determined from the factor loadings depends on the completeness of the obtained factors in accounting for the total variance among the subtests.

Rotating the Factors

To simplify the interpretation of the obtained factors by increasing the number of high and low positive loadings in the columns of the factor matrix, a procedure known as *factor rotation* is applied to the original factor matrix. Methods of rotating factors are very complex and will not be dealt with here. However, depending on the particular rotation method, we can obtain either uncorrelated factors (*orthogonal factors*) or correlated factors (*oblique factors*). Certain factor analysts prefer orthogonal rotation, whereas others have argued for oblique rotation. The rotated factor matrix in Table A–4 (columns A', B', C') was produced by orthogonal rotation of the original factor matrix (columns A, B, C), so factors A', B', and C' are uncorrelated.

Interpreting the Factors

After all statistical computations required by factoring and rotation have been completed, the researcher or test designer faces the task of interpreting the factors. This is accomplished by inspecting the pattern of high and low loadings of each test on the different factors, remembering that the higher the loading is, the more important is the factor on the given test. As shown in Table A–4, the Information, Vocabulary, Comprehension, and Similarities subtests have loadings of over .70 on factor A'. Because these are verbal subtests, factor A' might well be labeled a *verbal* factor. But several of the remaining subtests also have appreciable loadings on factor A', so this factor actually comes close to what is meant by a *general intellective factor* (g). The Picture Completion, Picture Arrangement, Block Design, and Object Assembly subtests have moderate to high loadings on factor B'. Considering the kinds of tasks comprising these four subtests, factor B' may be labeled a *spatial–perceptual* or *spatial imagery* factor. The Digit Span, Arithmetic, and Digit Symbol subtests, all three of which involve numbers, have moderate to high loadings on factor C'. Therefore, a good name for factor C' is *facility with numbers.*

Communality and Specificity

The last column in Table A–4 contains the communalities of the 11 subtests, computed as the sum of squares of the rotated factor loadings on a given subtest. For example, the communality of the Information subtest is $(.81)^2 + (.21)^2 + (.29)^2 = .78$, so 78 percent of the variance of scores on the Information subtest can be accounted for by factors A', B', and C'. If the reliability of the Information subtest is known, formula A.7 can now be used to compute the subtest's specificity. Also, subtracting a test's communality from 1.00 yields the proportion of the total test variance that is attributable to a combination of specific factors and error variance. For the Information subtest, this figure is $1.00 - .78 = .22$; that is, 22 percent of the total variance of the scores on the Information subtest can be explained by specific factors and errors of measurement.

SUMMARY

The statistical analysis of test scores begins with the construction of a frequency distribution of the number of examinees making each score or falling within a certain score range. Frequency distributions may be represented pictorially as histograms and frequency polygons. The normal curve is a theoretical frequency polygon that is basic to much test theory, and it may be used for determining certain types of norms. Nonnormal, asymmetrical frequency distributions may be skewed to the right (positively skewed) or skewed to the left (negatively) skewed.

Three measures of the central tendency or average of a group of scores, the mode (most frequently occurring score), the median (score below which 50 percent of the scores fall), and the arithmetic mean (sum of the scores divided by the number of scores), can be computed from raw scores or from a frequency distribution. Three measures of variability or spread of a group of scores are the range, the semi-interquartile range, and the standard deviation. Of these, the standard deviation is the most popular measure of variability and the most appropriate when the arithmetic mean is the reported average. Raw scores can be converted to standard z scores, percentiles, quartiles, and deciles.

The product–moment correlation coefficient, which is a number between -1.00 (perfect negative correlation) and $+1.00$ (perfect positive correlation), is a measure of the magnitude and direction of relationship between two variables. A significant correlation between two variables facilitates the prediction of a person's score on one variable from his or her score on the other variable. However, correlation should not be construed as implying causation; a significant relationship is not necessarily a causal one.

Correlations among variables may also be used in the statistical procedures of factor analysis to determine the dimensions or factors that different tests have in common. A factor analysis of the scores obtained from a large sample of persons on a group of tests or items involves extracting the factors, rotating the factor axes, and interpreting the rotated factors. Factors are interpreted by inspecting the loadings of the various tests on the factor axes. Computation of the communality (common factor variance) and specificity (specific factor variance) can also aid in the process of factor interpretation.

EXERCISES

1. The following is a frequency distribution of the test scores obtained by a group of 50 students:

Test score interval	Number of students
96–100	6
91–95	8
86–90	15
81–85	10
76–80	7
71–75	4

Draw a histogram and a frequency polygon, and then compute the arithmetic mean, median, standard deviation, 25th percentile, 75th percentile, and semi-interquartile range for these data.

2. Referring to Appendix B, find the percentage of the area under the normal curve falling below each of the following z scores: -2.575, -2.33, -1.96, -1.645, .00, 1.645, 1.96, 2.33, and 2.575. Next, find the z scores below which 10, 20, 30, 40, 50, 60, 70, 80, and 90 percent of the area under the normal curve falls.

3. Consider the following pairs of X, Y scores for 30 individuals:

X	Y	X	Y	X	Y	X	Y	X	Y
32	46	28	23	37	28	36	21	42	27
35	26	32	20	27	13	31	14	39	46
20	8	45	24	37	22	35	18	34	16
41	42	29	13	23	34	43	47	33	30
25	28	46	40	30	31	34	27	29	26
38	25	40	37	36	39	39	32	24	7

Compute the following statistics: arithmetic mean and standard deviation of X, arithmetic mean and standard deviation of Y, product–moment correlation between X and Y, and the regression line for predicting Y from X. Make a graphical plot (a *scattergram*) of the X, Y points, and draw the regression line of Y on X.

4. Whenever the frequency distribution of a group of scores is markedly skewed in either a positive (to the right) or a negative (to the left) direction, the median is considered to be a better, that is, less biased, measure of central tendency (average) than the arithmetic mean. Why?

5. The following is an SPSS/PC+ computer program for conducting a factor analysis of the average for all ages of the subtest scaled scores on the WISC–III. Run this program on a microcomputer that has the SPSS/PC+ software and print out the results.

```
DATA LIST MATRIX FREE
 /INF SIM ARI VOC COM DIS PIC COD PIA BLD OBA SYS MAZ.
SET PRINTER=ON.
VARIABLE LABELS INF 'INFORMATION'/SIM 'SIMILARITIES'
 /ARI 'ARITHMETIC'/VOC 'VOCABULARY'/COM 'COMPREHENSION'
 /DIS 'DIGIT SPAN'/PIC 'PICTURE COMPLETION'/COD 'CODING'
 /PIA 'PICTURE ARRANGEMENT'/BLD 'BLOCK DESIGN'
 /OBA 'OBJECT ASSEMBLY'/SYS 'SYMBOL SEARCH'/MAZ 'MAZES'.
N 200.
BEGIN DATA.
1.
 .66 1.
 .57  .55 1.
 .70  .69  .54 1.
 .56  .59  .47  .64 1.
 .34  .34  .43  .35  .29 1.
 .47  .45  .39  .45  .38  .25 1.
 .21  .20  .27  .26  .25  .23  .18 1.
 .40  .39  .35  .40  .35  .20  .37  .28 1.
 .48  .49  .52  .46  .40  .32  .52  .27  .41 1.
 .41  .42  .39  .41  .34  .26  .49  .24  .37  .61 1.
 .35  .35  .41  .35  .34  .28  .33  .53  .36  .45  .38 1.
 .18  .18  .22  .17  .17  .14  .24  .15  .23  .31  .29  .24 1.
END DATA.
FACTOR READ=COR TRIANGLE
 /VARIABLES=INF TO MAZ.
FINISH.
```

Using the factor loadings of the rotated factor matrix and the reliability coefficients given on page 444, compute the communality and specificity of each subtest and interpret the factors. Refer to the section on factor analysis in this appendix and the descriptions of the subtests given in Chapter 6.

Subtest	Average reliability	Subtest	Average reliability
Information	.84	Vocabulary	.87
Similarities	.81	Comprehension	.77
Arithmetic	.78	Digit Span	.85
Picture Completion	.77	Object Assembly	.69
Coding	.79	Symbol Search	.76
Picture Arrangement	.76	Mazes	.72
Block Design	.87		

6. Obtain a copy of the set of the computer programs accompanying this textbook, *Computer Programs for Psychological Assessment*, from your instructor. Then solve Exercises 1, 2, and 3 using the appropriate programs (3, 1, 5) in category 1 ("Programs on Basic Statistical Methods"). On Exercise 1, use the interval midpoints for the raw scores.

Appendix B

Table of Areas Under the
Normal Curve

To find the cumulative area under the curve to the left of the value of z, find the value of z in the first column and first row of the table. The decimal number at the intersection of the appropriate row and column is the desired proportion of area under the curve. For example, to find the area below $z = 1.57$, locate the row labeled 1.5 and the column labeled 0.07. At the intersection of that row and column is 0.9418, so 94.18 percent of the area under the curve falls below $z = 1.57$. To find the z score below which a certain proportion of the area under the curve falls, find that proportion in the body of the table. Then find the value of z in the corresponding row and column. For example, to find the value of z below which 67 percent of the area falls, locate 0.6700, which is at the intersection of the row labeled 0.4 and the column labeled 0.04. Therefore, the desired value of z is 0.44.

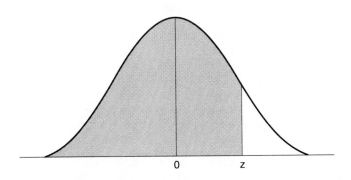

z	.00	.01	.02	.03	.04	.05	.06	.07	.08	.09
−3.0	.0013	.0013	.0013	.0012	.0012	.0011	.0011	.0011	.0010	.0010
−2.9	.0019	.0018	.0018	.0017	.0016	.0016	.0015	.0015	.0014	.0014
−2.8	.0026	.0025	.0024	.0023	.0023	.0022	.0021	.0021	.0020	.0019
−2.7	.0035	.0034	.0033	.0032	.0031	.0030	.0029	.0028	.0027	.0026
−2.6	.0047	.0045	.0044	.0043	.0041	.0040	.0039	.0038	.0037	.0036
−2.5	.0062	.0060	.0059	.0057	.0055	.0054	.0052	.0051	.0049	.0048
−2.4	.0082	.0080	.0078	.0075	.0077	.0071	.0069	.0068	.0066	.0064
−2.3	.0107	.0104	.0102	.0099	.0096	.0094	.0091	.0089	.0087	.0084
−2.2	.0139	.0136	.0132	.0129	.0125	.0122	.0119	.0116	.0113	.0110
−2.1	.0179	.0174	.0170	.0166	.0162	.0158	.0154	.0150	.0146	.0143
−2.0	.0228	.0222	.0217	.0212	.0207	.0202	.0197	.0192	.0188	.0183
−1.9	.0287	.0281	.0274	.0268	.0262	.0256	.0250	.0244	.0239	.0233
−1.8	.0359	.0351	.0344	.0336	.0329	.0322	.0314	.0307	.0301	.0294
−1.7	.0446	.0436	.0427	.0418	.0409	.0401	.0392	.0384	.0375	.0367
−1.6	.0548	.0537	.0526	.0516	.0505	.0495	.0485	.0475	.0465	.0455
−1.5	.0668	.0655	.0643	.0630	.0618	.0606	.0594	.0582	.0571	.0559
−1.4	.0808	.0793	.0778	.0764	.0749	.0735	.0721	.0708	.0694	.0681
−1.3	.0968	.0951	.0934	.0918	.0901	.0885	.0869	.0853	.0838	.0823
−1.2	.1151	.1131	.1112	.1093	.1075	.1056	.1038	.1020	.1003	.0985
−1.1	.1357	.1335	.1314	.1292	.1271	.1251	.1230	.1210	.1190	.1170
−1.0	.1587	.1562	.1539	.1515	.1492	.1469	.1446	.1423	.1401	.1379
−0.9	.1841	.1814	.1788	.1762	.1736	.1711	.1685	.1660	.1635	.1611
−0.8	.2119	.2090	.2061	.2033	.2005	.1977	.1949	.1922	.1894	.1867
−0.7	.2420	.2389	.2358	.2327	.2296	.2266	.2236	.2206	.2177	.2148
−0.6	.2743	.2709	.2676	.2643	.2611	.2578	.2546	.2514	.2483	.2451
−0.5	.3085	.3050	.3015	.2981	.2946	.2912	.2877	.2843	.2810	.2776
−0.4	.3446	.3409	.3372	.3336	.3300	.3264	.3228	.3194	.3156	.3121
−0.3	.3821	.3783	.3745	.3707	.3669	.3632	.3594	.3557	.3520	.3483
−0.2	.4207	.4168	.4129	.4090	.4052	.4013	.3974	.3936	.3897	.3859
−0.1	.4602	.4562	.4522	.4483	.4443	.4404	.4364	.4325	.4286	.4247
−0.0	.5000	.4960	.4920	.4880	.4840	.4801	.4761	.4721	.4681	.4641
0.0	.5000	.5040	.5080	.5120	.5160	.5199	.5239	.5279	.5319	.5359
0.1	.5398	.5438	.5478	.5517	.5557	.5596	.5636	.5675	.5714	.5753
0.2	.5793	.5832	.5871	.5910	.5948	.5987	.6026	.6064	.6103	.6141
0.3	.6179	.6217	.6255	.6293	.6331	.6368	.6406	.6443	.6480	.6517
0.4	.6554	.6591	.6628	.6664	.6700	.6736	.6772	.6808	.6844	.6879
0.5	.6915	.6950	.6985	.7019	.7054	.7088	.7123	.7157	.7190	.7224
0.6	.7257	.7291	.7324	.7357	.7389	.7422	.7454	.7486	.7517	.7549
0.7	.7580	.7611	.7642	.7673	.7704	.7734	.7764	.7794	.7823	.7852
0.8	.7881	.7910	.7939	.7967	.7995	.8023	.8051	.8078	.8106	.8133
0.9	.8159	.8186	.8212	.8238	.8264	.8289	.8315	.8340	.8365	.8389
1.0	.8413	.8438	.8461	.8485	.8508	.8531	.8554	.8577	.8599	.8621
1.1	.8643	.8665	.8686	.8708	.8729	.8749	.8770	.8790	.8810	.8830
1.2	.8849	.8869	.8888	.8907	.8925	.8944	.8962	.8980	.8997	.9015
1.3	.9032	.9049	.9066	.9082	.9099	.9115	.9131	.9147	.9162	.9177

1.4	.9192	.9207	.9222	.9236	.9251	.9265	.9279	.9292	.9306	.9319
1.5	.9332	.9345	.9357	.9370	.9382	.9394	.9406	.9418	.9429	.9441
1.6	.9452	.9463	.9474	.9484	.9495	.9505	.9515	.9525	.9535	.9545
1.7	.9554	.9564	.9573	.9582	.9591	.9599	.9608	.9616	.9625	.9633
1.8	.9641	.9649	.9656	.9664	.9671	.9678	.9686	.9693	.9699	.9706
1.9	.9713	.9719	.9726	.9732	.9738	.9744	.9750	.9756	.9761	.9767
2.0	.9772	.9778	.9783	.9788	.9793	.9798	.9803	.9808	.9812	.9817
2.1	.9821	.9826	.9830	.9834	.9838	.9842	.9846	.9850	.9854	.9857
2.2	.9861	.9864	.9868	.9871	.9875	.9878	.9881	.9884	.9887	.9890
2.3	.9893	.9896	.9898	.9901	.9904	.9906	.9909	.9911	.9913	.9916
2.4	.9918	.9920	.9922	.9925	.9927	.9929	.9931	.9932	.9934	.9936
2.5	.9938	.9940	.9941	.9943	.9945	.9946	.9948	.9949	.9951	.9952
2.6	.9953	.9955	.9956	.9957	.9959	.9960	.9961	.9962	.9963	.9964
2.7	.9965	.9966	.9967	.9968	.9969	.9970	.9971	.9972	.9973	.9974
2.8	.9974	.9975	.9976	.9977	.9977	.9978	.9979	.9979	.9980	.9981
2.9	.9981	.9982	.9982	.9983	.9984	.9984	.9985	.9985	.9986	.9986
3.0	.9987	.9987	.9987	.9988	.9988	.9989	.9989	.9989	.9990	.9990

Appendix C

Answers to Quantitative Exercises

Chapter 3

5. Uncorrected score = number right = 30
   Corrected score = rights − wrongs/3 = 30 − 16/3 = 25
   If items are true–false: uncorrected score = number right = 30, and corrected score = rights − wrongs = 14.

6. Since the sum of the absolute values of the differences between the correct ranks and John's ranks is 12, from Figure 3–2 we find that his score is approximately 4. In Jenny's case, the sum of the absolute values of the differences is 6, and her score is approximately 6.

7. Test X:

Grade	Range	Number
A	44 and above	2
B	38–43	7
C	31–37	12
D	25–30	6
F	24 and below	3

Test Y:

Grade	Range	Number
A	44 and above	3
B	33–43	5
C	22–32	13
D	11–21	7
F	10 and below	2

8. Since $.27 \times 75 = 20.25$, there are 20 people in the upper group and 20 in the lower group. Therefore, $p = (18 + 12)/40 = .75$ and $D = (18 − 12)/20 = .30$. The item is in the acceptable ranges of both p and D.

9. $U = 30$, $L = 20$, $U_p = 20$, and $L_p = 10$, so $p = (20 + 10)/50$ and $D = 20/30 - 10/20 = .17$.

10.

Item	1	2	3	4	5	6	7	8	9	10
p	.50	.45	.45	.55	.40	.75	.50	.50	.60	.40
D	.40	.30	.30	.50	.60	.30	.20	.20	.40	.60

Table 3–7 gives the optimum mean p value of a four-option multiple-choice item as .74. Taking $\pm .20$ around this value, the p value of acceptable items should be in the range from .54 to .94. The D value of acceptable items should be .30 or higher. Only items 4, 6, and 9 meet the specified requirements, so the remaining items should be revised or discarded.

Chapter 4

1. George's score on the arithmetic test is $z_a = (65 - 50)/10 = 1.50$; his z score on the reading test is $z_r = (80 - 75)/15 = .33$. His Z scores on the two tests are $Z_a = 65$ and $Z_r = 53$. George is better in arithmetic than in reading.

2.

% Rank	z	T	CEEB	Stanine	Deviation IQ
10	−1.28	37	372	2	81
20	−0.84	42	416	3	87
30	−0.52	45	448	4	92
40	−0.25	48	475	4	96
50	0.00	50	500	5	100
60	0.25	52	525	6	104
70	0.52	55	552	6	108
80	0.84	58	584	7	113
90	1.28	63	628	8	119

3.

Score interval	Midpoint	Fre-quency	Cumulative frequency below midpoint	Percentile rank	z	Z	Z_n	T
96–98	97	1	29.5	98.33	1.95	70	2.13	71
93–95	94	2	28	93.33	1.50	65	1.50	65
90–92	91	3	25.5	85.00	1.05	61	1.04	60
87–89	88	5	21.5	71.67	0.60	56	0.57	56
84–86	85	6	16	53.33	0.15	52	0.08	51
81–83	82	4	11	36.67	−0.30	47	−0.34	47
78–80	79	4	7	23.33	−0.75	42	−0.73	43
75–77	76	2	4	13.33	−1.20	38	−1.11	39
72–74	73	2	2	6.67	−1.65	33	−1.50	35
69–71	70	1	0.5	1.67	−2.10	29	−2.13	29

5. $r_{oe} = 0.226$, $r_{11} = 0.369$
   $KR_{20} = 0.610$, $KR_{21} = 0.580$

6. $s_{err} = 4.00$
   95% confidence interval for $X = 40$ is 32.16.16–47.84.
   95% confidence interval for $X = 50$ is 42.16–57.84.
   95% confidence interval for $X = 60$ is 52.16–67.84.

7. Solving formula 4.11 for m,

$$m = \frac{r_{mm}(1 - r_{11})}{r_{11}(1 - r_{mm})}$$

Therefore, if $r_{11} = 0.80$ and $r_{mm} = 0.90$, $m = \dfrac{0.90(1 - 0.80)}{0.80(1 - 0.90)} = \dfrac{0.18}{0.08} = 2.25$

Multiplying n by m gives $40 \times 2.25 = 90$. Therefore, 50 more items of the same general type must be added to the test to increase its reliability coefficient to 0.90.

8.

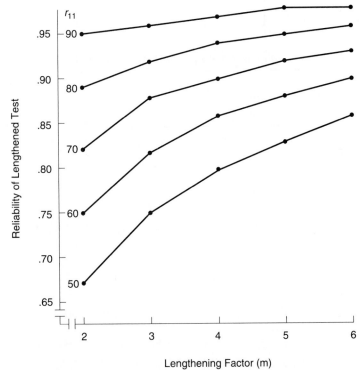

Reliability of a Lengthened Test as a Function of Initial Reliability (r_{11}) and Lengthening Factor (m). *Reliability increases as the test is lengthened, the amount of increase being greater when the initial reliability is lower. The increase in reliability as a function of lengthening gradually levels off as the test is increasingly lengthened.*

9. For this problem, $N = 100$, $b = 70$, $f = 10$, $s = 15$, and $n = 5$. Substituting these values in formula 4.13 yields

$$c = \frac{5(70) - 10(15)}{5(70) - 10(15) + 10(100)} = .167$$

10. $s_{est} = s\sqrt{(1 - r^2)} = .50\sqrt{(1 - (.60)^2)} = .50(8) = .4$

The chances are two out of three that the examinee's obtained criterion score will fall within .4 of his predicted score on the criterion.

Chapter 6

1. $IQ = 100(MA/CA) = 100(77/105) = 73$

Chapter 7

9. Yes, because $s_{est} = 10\sqrt{2 - .90 - .85}$.

Chapter 8

5.

Statement	Scale value (median)	Ambiguity index (Q)
D	8.96	1.14
N	5.19	1.22
X	2.50	1.01

Chapter 11

2. Empirical Expectancy Table

Criterion Variable (Y)

		28-34	35-41	42-48	49-55	56-62	63-70
P r e d i c t o r V a r i a b l e (X)	71-78			(100) 1			(50) 1
	63-70				(100) 1		(67) 2
	56-62			(100) 2	(67) 2	(33) 1	(17) 1
	49-55		(100) 2	(67) 1	(50) 2		(25) 1
	42-48		(100) 1	(80) 1	(60) 2		(20) 1
	35-41		(100) 2	(50) 1	(25) 1		
	28-34	(100) 1			(67) 1	(33) 1	
	21-27	(100) 1					

3.

X	Y_{pred}	X	Y_{pred}
44	48.00	64	56.80
38	45.36	40	46.24
56	53.28	28	40.96
54	52.40	68	58.56
66	57.68	48	49.76
52	51.52	32	42.72
46	48.88	74	61.20
36	44.48	42	47.12
44	48.00	50	50.64
60	55.04	40	46.24
22	38.32	58	54.16
72	60.32	62	55.92
56	53.28	54	52.40
52	51.52	60	55.04
50	50.64	30	41.84

Theoretical Expectancy Table

		Criterion Variable (Y)					
		28-34	35-41	42-48	49-55	56-62	63-70
P r e d i c t o r V a r i a b l e (X)	71-78					(100) 2	
	63-70					(100) 3	
	56-62				(100) 5	(17) 1	
	49-55				(100) 6		
	42-48			(100) 3	(40) 2		
	35-41			(100) 4			
	28-34		(100) 1	(67) 2			
	21-27		(100) 1				

The cell frequencies in the empirical expectancy table are much more scattered throughout the table than those in the theoretical expectancy table. Since the Y scores in the theoretical expectancy table were predicted by means of a linear regression equation, the frequencies in this table are clustered more closely around a straight line, and the Y scores are less variable than those in the empirical expectancy table. Assuming that the empirical expectancy table is based on a representative sample, because it makes no assumptions concerning the Y distribution or the relationship between X and Y it would probably be more useful in educational and vocational counseling.

6. $Y_{pred} = .225X_2 + .152X_3 + .401X_4 + 41.488$
   $t_2 = 5.22, t_3 = 3.87, t_4 = 2.07, df = 96$

All the t values are statistically significant; hence each of the three predictor variables is making a significant contribution to the prediction of the criterion. $R = .693, F = 29.65, df = 2,96$; the overall F ratio and hence the multiple correlation coefficient (R) are statistically significant.

Chapter 12

7. The regression equation for predicting Y from X is $Y_{pred} = .44X + 28.34$ for the majority group and $Y_{pred} = .43X + 24.57$ for the minority group; the corresponding correlation coefficients are .52 and .47. The slope and correlation statistics indicate that the test may be a slightly more accurate predictor for the majority group than for the minority group, but not significantly so. Thus, it may be concluded that the test is not appreciably biased according to the traditional definition of fairness.

   If we assume that 50 percent of the majority group and 25 percent of the minority group can perform the job, then $.50(30) = 15$ examinees in the majority group and $.25(20) = 5$ examinees in the minority group should be selected if the test is fair. If the cutoff score is set at $X = 52$, then 7 minority group members and 15 majority group members will be selected; if it is set at $X = 53$, then 5 minority and 13 majority group members will be selected. Either cutoff score would slightly favor the minority group according to Thorndike's definition.

   If we assume that 40 percent of the entire group of 50 examinees is capable of performing the job, then $.40(30) = 12$ majority group members and $.40(20) = 8$ minority group members should be selected if the test is fair according to Cole's definition. Any cutoff score that will yield a total number selected close to 20 will tend to favor the majority group according to this definition. Thus, using this procedure, the test is slightly biased toward the majority group.

   Combining the scores of the majority and minority groups yields a correlation between X and Y of $r = .517$ and the regression equation

$$Y_{pred} = .460X + 25.639$$

Now, if the cutoff score is set at $X = 50$, the number of false positive and false negative errors in each group will be as follows:

	False positives	False negatives
Majority group	6 (20%)	6 (20%)
Minority group	5 (25%)	2 (10%)

These percentages are based on the total number of applicants in each group. The total percentage of errors is 5 points greater for the majority group than for the minority group, but the percentage of false positives is greater in the minority group and the percentage of false negatives is greater in the majority group. In this case, the question of bias is complex, depending on which type of error is considered more serious.

Chapter 13

1.

```
10 REM Program TESTSCOR.  Scores objective tests of 500 items or less.
20 DIM KEE$(500),ANS$(500),NAM$(500),SCOR(500)
30 CLS
40 REM Scoring key for test is entered.
50 INPUT "Total number of items";N
60 PRINT
70 FOR I=1 TO N
80 PRINT "Enter correct answer to item";I
90 LINE INPUT KEE$(I)
100 NEXT I
110 CLS
120 REM Examinees' names and responses are entered, and responses are scored.
130 PRINT "Press any key to begin scoring answer sheets."
140 IF INKEY$="" THEN 140
150 CLS
160 INPUT "How many answer sheets do you wish to score";M
170 FOR J=1 TO M
180 CLS
190 LINE INPUT "Examinee's name: ";NAM$(J)
200 SCOR(J)=0
210 FOR I=1 TO N
220 PRINT "Answer to item";I;"?"
230 LINE INPUT ANS$(I)
240 IF ANS$(I)=KEE$(I) THEN SCOR(J)=SCOR(J)+1
250 NEXT I
260 SUM=SUM+SCOR(J)
270 SS=SS+SCOR(J)*SCOR(J)
280 NEXT J
290 STD=SQR((SS-SUM*SUM/M)/(M-1))
300 CLS
310 PRINT "     Name                        Score"
320 FOR J=1 TO M
330 PRINT NAM$(J);TAB(34);SCOR(J)
340 NEXT J
350 PRINT:PRINT "Mean =";SUM/M
360 PRINT "Standard Deviation =";STD
370 END
```

Appendix A

1.

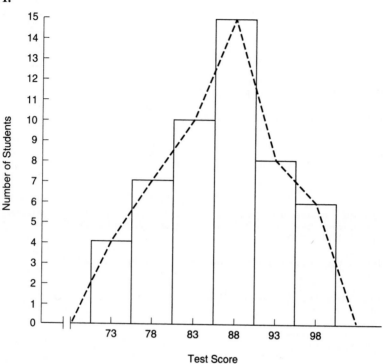

Test Score

$$\overline{X} = 86.40, \text{ Mdn} = 86.83, \text{ mode} = 88, s = 7.17$$

$$P_{25} = Q_1 = 80.50 + 5\left(\frac{12.5 - 11}{10}\right) = 81.25$$

$$P_{75} = Q_3 = 90.50 + 5\left(\frac{37.5 - 36}{8}\right) = 91.44$$

$$Q = \frac{Q_3 - Q_1}{2} = \frac{91.44 - 81.25}{2} = 5.10$$

2. .5%, 1%, 2.5%, 5%, 50%, 95%, 97.5%, 99%, 99.5%
   $-1.28, -.84, -.52, -.25, .25, .52, .84, 1.28$

3. $\overline{X} = 34.00, s_X = 6.58$
   $\overline{Y} = 27.00, s_y = 11.03$
   $r_{y,x} = 0.54, Y_{\text{pred}} = 0.91X - 3.78$

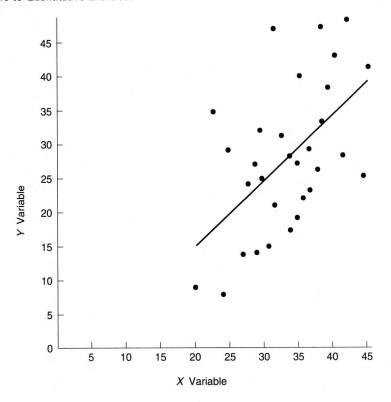

5.

Subtest	Factor 1	Factor 2	Communality	Specificity
Information	.74342	.32519	.65843	.19157
Similarities	.69121	.38976	.62968	.18032
Arithmetic	.73396	.19086	.57513	.19587
Vocabulary	.78308	.32751	.72048	.13952
Comprehension	.64430	.37102	.55279	.21721
Digit Span	.64616	.03258	.41858	.36142
Picture Completion	.26255	.69232	.54824	.22176
Picture Arrangement	.30753	.60523	.46088	.26912
Block Design	.37365	.72545	.66589	.18411
Object Assembly	.18198	.77792	.63827	.06173
Coding	.45880	.17974	.24280	.47720
Mazes	.10234	.66022	.44636	.27364

Appendix D

Major U.S. Distributors of Assessment Materials

American College Testing Program, 2201 N. Dodge Street, P.O. Box 168, Iowa City, IA 52243. Ph. 319/337-1000

American Guidance Service, 4201 Woodland Road, P. O. Box 99, Circle Pines, MN 55014-1796. Ph. 800/328-2560

Assessment Systems Corporation, 2233 University Avenue, Suite 440, St. Paul, MN 55114. Ph. 612/647-9220

CPPC, 4 Conant Square, Brandon, VT 05733. Ph. 800/433-8234

CPS, Inc., P.O. Box 83, Larchmont, NY 10538. Ph. 800/433-8324

CTB/Macmillan/McGraw-Hill, 2500 Garden Road, Monterey, CA 93940-5380. Ph. 800/538-9547

Consulting Psychologists Press, Inc., 577 College Avenue, Palo Alto, CA 94306-1444. Ph. 800/624-1765

DLM Teaching Resources, One DLM Park, P.O. Box 4000, Allen, TX 75002. Ph. 800/527-4747

EdITS/Educational and Industrial Testing Service, P.O. Box 7234, San Diego, CA 92167. Ph. 619/222-1666

ETS Test Collection (30-B), Educational Testing Service, Rosedale Road, Princeton, NJ 08541-0001. Ph. 609 734-5686

GED Testing Service, One Dupont Circle, N.W., Washington, DC 20036. Ph. 202/939-9490

Grune & Stratton, Inc., 465 South Lincoln Drive, Troy, MO 63379.

Hawthorne, 800 Gray Oak Drive, Columbia, MO 65201. Ph. 800/542-1673

Industrial Psychology International Ltd., 111 North Market Street, Champaign, IL 61820. Ph. 217/398-1437

Institute for Personality and Ability Testing, Inc., 1801 Woodfield Drive, Savoy, IL 61874. Ph. 800/225-4728

Jastak Associates, Inc., P.O. Box 3410, Wilmington, DE 19804-0250. Ph. 800/221-WRAT

London House, 1550 N. Northwest Highway, Park Ridge, IL 60068. Ph. 800/237-7685

McCann Associates, Inc., 603 Corporate Drive West, Langhorne, PA 19047. Ph. 215/860-8637

Merrill (Charles E.) Publishing Company, 1300 Alum Creek Drive, Box 508, Columbus, OH 43216. Ph. 800/848-1567

Metritech, Inc., 111 North Market Street, Champaign, IL 61820. Ph. 800/747-4868

NCS Professional Assessment Services, P.O. Box 1416, Minneapolis, MN 55440. Ph. 800/
   NCS-7271

pro.ed., 8700 Shoal Creek Boulevard, Austin, TX 78758-6897. Ph. 512/451-3246

Psychological Assessment Resources, Inc. (PAR), P.O. Box 998, Odessa, FL 33556. Ph. 800/
   331-8378

Psychological Corporation (The), 555 Academic Court, San Antonio, TX 78204-2498. Ph.
   800/228-0752

Psychological Test Specialists, Box 9229. Missoula, MT 59807

Psychometric Affiliates, Box 807, Murfreesboro, TN 37133-0807. Ph. 615/898-2565

Publishers Test Service, 2500 Garden Road, Monterey, CA 93940-5380. Ph. 800/649-9547

Riverside Publishing Company (The), 8420 Bryn Mawr Avenue, Chicago, IL 60631. Ph. 800/
   323-9540

Scholastic Testing Service, Inc., 480 Meyer Road, P.O. Box 1056, Bensenville, IL 60106-
   1617. Ph. 800/642-6STS

Sigma Assessment Systems, Inc., P.O. Box 610984, 1110 Military Street, Port Huron, MI
   48061-0984. Ph. 800/265-1285

Slosson Educational Publications, Inc., P.O. Box 280, East Aurora, NY 14052. Ph. 800/828-
   4800

SOI Systems, P.O. Box D, Vida, OR 97488

SRA/London House, 9701 W. Higgins Road, Rosemont, IL 60018. Ph. 800/221-8378

Stoelting Company, 620 Wheat Lane, Wood Dale, IL 60191 Ph. 708/860-9700

Western Psychological Services, 12031 Wilshire Boulevard, Los Angeles, CA 90025. Ph. 800/
   648-8857

Wonderlic Personnel Test, Inc., 820 Frontage Road, Northfield, IL 60093-8007. Ph. 800/323-
   3742

Appendix E

Glossary

The following definitions of important terms in psychological and educational testing are not meant to be comprehensive. For a more complete understanding of the concepts behind the terms, the reader should refer to the appropriate sections of this book and to other sources of information on testing. The definitions will suffice, however, as a reference or review source on basic concepts in the field of psychological testing and assessment.

Ability test. A test that measures the extent to which a person is capable of performing a certain task or occupation.

Academic aptitude. The ability to learn school-type tasks; also called *scholastic aptitude*. Many intelligence tests are measures of academic aptitude.

Accommodation. In Piaget's theory of cognitive development, the modification of schema as the result of experience.

Accountability. Holding teachers accountable for the educational progress of their students. See *Performance contract*.

Achievement. Degree of success or accomplishment in a given subject or other task.

Achievement test. Measure of the degree of accomplishment or learning in a subject or task.

Acquiescence response set (style). Tendency of a person to answer affirmatively ("yes" or "true") on personality test items and in other alternative response situations.

Actuarial approach. Combining quantified clinical information according to empirically established rules, and then making behavioral predictions or diagnoses on the basis of the results.

Adaptive behavior. The extent to which a person is able to interact effectively and appropriately with his or her physical and social environment.

Adaptive testing. Testing procedure, usually computer based, in which the specific items presented vary with the estimated ability or other characteristics of the examinee and his or her responses to previous items.

Adjustment.   Ability to cope in social situations and achieve satisfaction of one's needs.

Affective assessment.   The measurement of noncognitive (nonintellective) variables or characteristics. Affective variables include temperament, emotion, interests, attitudes, personal style, and other behaviors, traits, or processes typical of an individual. See *Cognitive assessment.*

Age norm.   The median score on an aptitude or achievement test made by children of a given chronological age.

Alternate-forms reliability.   An index of reliability determined by correlating the scores of individuals on one form of a test with their scores on another form. See *Parallel forms.*

Analogies test.   A test that requires the examinee to determine a relationship, similarity, or difference between two or more things; for example, "Roses are red as violets are to (a) blue (b) green (c) orange (d) yellow."

Anchor test.   A common set of items on each of several forms of a test used to equate scores on the several forms.

Anecdotal record.   A written record of behavioral observations of a specified individual. Care must be taken to differentiate between observation and interpretation if the record is to be objective.

Apgar rating.   A rating score, determined at 1 minute and at 5 minutes after birth, for evaluating neonates. A rating of 0 to 2 is assigned to measurements of heart rate, respiration, muscle tone, reflexes, and color; a sum of ratings between 7 and 10 is normal.

Apparatus test.   Tests on which examinees must construct something or in other ways manipulate physical objects, for example, screwing nuts onto bolts or stacking blocks. See *Performance test.*

Aptitude.   Capability of learning to perform a particular task or skill. Traditionally, aptitude was thought to depend more on inborn potential than actual practice.

Aptitude test.   A measure of ability to profit from additional training or experience, that is, become proficient in a skill or other ability.

Arithmetic mean.   A measure of the average or central tendency of a group of scores. The arithmetic mean is computed by dividing the sum of the scores by the number of scores.

Assessment.   Appraising the presence or magnitude of one or more personal characteristics. Assessing human behavior and mental processes includes such procedures as observations, interviews, rating scales, checklists, inventories, projectives, and tests.

Assessment center approach.   Technique, used primarily in the selection of executive personnel, for assessing the personality characteristics and behavior of a small group of individuals by having them perform a variety of tasks during a period of a few days.

Assimilation. In Piaget's theory of cognitive development, the process of fitting new experiences into preexisting mental structures.

Assortative mating. Nonrandom mating between individuals possessing similar characteristics.

Attitude. Tendency to react positively or negatively to some object, person, or circumstance.

Attitude scale. A paper-and-pencil instrument, consisting of a series of statements concerning an institution, situation, person, event, and so on. The examinee responds to each statement by endorsing it or indicating his degree of agreement or disagreement with it.

Audiometer. An instrument for measuring auditory acuity that presents pure tones of varying intensities and frequencies in the normal range of hearing. Hearing is tested in each ear, the results being plotted as an audiogram, a graph of the examinee's auditory acuity at each frequency and for each ear.

Aunt Fanny error. Accepting as accurate a trivial, highly generalized personality description that could pertain to almost anyone, even one's "Aunt Fanny."

Automated assessment. Use of test-scoring machines, computers, and other electronic or electromechanical devices to administer, score, and interpret psychological assessments.

Average. Measure of central tendency of a group of scores; the most representative score.

Bandwith. L. J. Cronbach's term for the range of criteria predictable from a test; the greater the number of criteria that a test can predict, the broader is its bandwidth. See *Fidelity.*

Barnum effect. Belief in a personality description phrased in generalities, truisms, and other statements that sound specific to a given person but are actually applicable to almost anyone. Same as *Aunt Fanny error.*

Basal age. The highest year level of an intelligence test, such as the Stanford–Binet, at and below which an examinee passes all subtests. See *Ceiling age.*

Base rate. Proportion of a specified population of people who possess a characteristic of interest. The base rate should be taken into account when evaluating the effectiveness of a psychometric instrument in identifying and diagnosing people who have that characteristic.

Battery of tests. A group of aptitude or achievement tests measuring different things but standardized on the same population, thus permitting comparisons of a person's performance in different areas.

Behavior analysis. Procedures that focus on objectively describing a particular behavior and identifying the antecedents and consequences of that behavior. Behavior analysis may be conducted for research purposes or to obtain information in planning a behavior modification program.

Bias. Any one of a number of factors that cause scores on psychometric instruments to be consistently higher or lower than they should be if measurement were accurate. Illustrative of factors that result in bias is the *leniency error,* the tendency to rate a person consistently higher than he or she should be rated.

Bimodal distribution. A frequency distribution having two modes (maximum points). See *Frequency distribution; Mode.*

Biographical inventory. Questionnaire composed of items designed to collect information on an individual's background, interests, and other personal data.

Cardinal trait. According to G. W. Allport, a disposition or theme so dominant in a person's life that it is expressed in almost all of his or her behavior (for example, power striving, self-love).

Case study. Detailed study of an individual, designed to provide a comprehensive, in-depth understanding of personality. Information for a case study is obtained from biographical, interview, observational, and test data.

Ceiling age. The minimum age or year level on a test, such as the Stanford–Binet, at which an examinee fails all subtests. See *Basal age.*

Central tendency. Average, or central, score in a group of scores; the most representative score (for example, arithmetic mean, median, mode).

Central tendency error. General tendency to avoid extreme judgments in appraising or assessing a person and to assign ratings in the middle categories of a continuum or scale.

Central trait. G. W. Allport's term for the tendency to behave in a particular way in various situations, but less general or pervasive than a *cardinal trait* Examples of central traits are sociability and affectionateness.

Cerebrotonia. In W. H. Sheldon's temperament typology, the tendency to be introversive and prefer mental to physical or social activities; most closely related to ectomorphic body build.

Checklist. List of words, phrases, or statements descriptive of personal characteristics; respondents endorse (check) those items characteristic of themselves (self-ratings) or other people (other-ratings).

Classification. Assigning individuals to specified groups or categories on the basis of personal data obtained from various sources (observations, interviews, tests, inventories, and the like).

Clinical approach. Approach to behavioral prediction and diagnosis in which psychologists assign their own judgmental weights to the predictor variables and then combine them in a subjective manner to make behavioral forecasts or diagnoses.

Cluster sampling. Sampling procedure in which the target population is divided into sections or clusters, and the number of units selected at random from a given cluster is proportional to the total number of units in the cluster.

Coaching.   Short-term instruction designed to improve the test scores of prospective test takers. The instructional activities include practice on various types of items and test-taking strategies.

Coefficient alpha.   An internal consistency reliability coefficient, appropriate for tests comprised of dichotomous or multipoint items; the expected correlation of one test with a parallel form containing the same number of items. See *Kuder–Richardson formulas.*

Coefficient of determination.   The squared coefficient of correlation; proportion of variation in the dependent variable accounted for by variation in the independent variable.

Coefficient of equivalence.   A reliability coefficient (correlation) obtained by administering two different forms of the same test to a group of examinees. See *Alternate-forms reliability.*

Coefficient of internal consistency.   Reliability coefficient based on estimates of the internal consistency of a test (for example, split-half coefficient and alpha coefficient).

Coefficient of stability.   A reliability coefficient (correlation) obtained by administering a test to the same group of examinees on two different occasions. See *Test–retest reliability.*

Coefficient of stability and equivalence.   A reliability coefficient obtained by administering two forms of a test to a group of examinees on two different occasions.

Cognition.   Having to do with the processes of intellect: remembering, thinking, problem solving, and the like.

Cognitive assessment.   Measurement of intellective processes, such as perception, memory, thinking, judgment, and reasoning. See *Affective assessment.*

Cognitive style.   Strategies or approaches to perceiving, remembering, and thinking that a person comes to prefer in attempting to understand and cope with the world (for example, field independence–dependence, reflectivity–impulsivity, and internal–external locus of control).

Communality.   Proportion of variance in a measured variable accounted for by variance that the variable has in common with other variables.

Component processes.   R. Sternberg's theory that cognitive processes or mental components fall into five classes: metacomponents, performance components, acquisition components, retention components, and transfer components.

Composite score.   The direct or weighted sum of the scores on two or more tests or sections of a test.

Computer-assisted instruction (CAI).   Individualized instructional procedures in which a computer is used to present the material to be learned, to ask questions, and to evaluate answers.

Concrete operations stage.   In Piaget's theory of cognitive development, the stage (7 to 11 years) during which the child develops organized systems of operations by the process of social interaction, with a corresponding reduction in self-centeredness.

Concurrent validity.   The extent to which scores obtained by a group of individuals on a particular psychometric instrument are related to their simultaneously determined scores on another measure (criterion) of the same characteristic that the instrument is supposed to measure.

Construct validity.   The extent to which scores on a psychometric instrument designed to measure a certain characteristic are related to measures of behavior in situations in which the characteristic is supposed to be an important determinant of behavior.

Content analysis.   Method of studying and analyzing written (or oral) communications in a systematic, objective, and quantitative manner to assess certain psychological variables.

Content validity.   A psychometric instrument, such as an achievement test, is said to have content validity if a group of experts on the material with which the instrument is concerned agree that the instrument measures what it was designed to measure.

Contrast error.   In interviewing or rating, the tendency to evaluate a person more positively if an immediately preceding individual was assigned a highly negative evaluation or to evaluate a person more negatively if an immediately preceding individual was given a highly positive evaluation.

Convergent validity.   Situation in which an assessment instrument has high correlations with other measures of (or methods of measuring) the same construct. See *Discriminant validity.*

Correction for attenuation.   Formula used to estimate what the validity coefficient of a test would be if both the test and criterion were perfectly reliable.

Correction for guessing.   A formula, applied to raw test scores, to correct for the effects of random guessing by examinees. A popular correction-for-guessing formula consists of subtracting a portion of the number of items answered incorrectly from the number answered correctly by the examinee.

Correlation.   Degree of relationship or association between two variables, such as a test and a criterion measure.

Correlation coefficient.   A numerical index of the degree of relationship between two variables. Correlation coefficients usually range from -1.00 (perfect negative relationship), through 0.00 (total absence of a relationship), to $+1.00$ (perfect positive relationship). Two common types of correlation coefficient are the product–moment coefficient and the point-biserial coefficient.

Creativity test.   A test that assesses original, novel, or divergent thinking.

Criterion. A standard or variable with which scores on a psychometric instrument are compared or against which they are evaluated. The validity of a test or other psychometric procedure used in selecting or classifying people is determined by its ability to predict a specified criterion of behavior in the situation for which people are being selected or classified.

Criterion contamination. The effect of any factor on a criterion such that the criterion is not a valid measure of an individual's accomplishment. Intelligence test scores are frequently used to predict grades in school, but when teachers use intelligence test scores in deciding what grades to assign, the grades are not a valid criterion for validating the intelligence test; the criterion has become contaminated.

Criterion-referenced test. A test designed with very restricted content specifications to serve a limited range of highly specific purposes. The aim of the test is to determine where the examinee stands with respect to certain (educational) objectives. See *Norm-referenced test.*

Criterion-related validity. The extent to which a test or other assessment instrument measures what it allegedly measures, as indicated by the correlation of test scores with some criterion measure of behavior.

Critical incident. A measure of performance, used primarily in industrial–organizational contexts, in which an individual's overall criterion score is determined by the extent to which behavior thought to be critical for effective performance in a given situation is manifested.

Cross-validation. Readministering an assessment instrument that has been found to be a valid predictor of a criterion for one group of persons to a second group of persons to determine whether the instrument is also valid for that group. There is almost always some shrinkage of the validity coefficient on cross-validation, since chance factors spuriously inflate the validity coefficient obtained with the first group of examinees.

Crystallized intelligence. R. B. Cattell's term for mental ability (knowledge and skills) acquired through experience and education.

Culture-fair test. A test composed of materials to which all sociocultural groups have presumably been exposed. Thus, the test should not penalize any sociocultural group simply because of lack of relevant experience. Efforts to develop culture-fair tests have not been very successful.

Cutoff score (cutting score). All applicants falling below the cutoff score on a criterion are rejected, and all applicants falling at or above the cutoff score are accepted. The cutoff score depends on the validity of the test, the selection ratio, and other factors

Data bank. A repository or collection of data, usually computer based or computer accessible, on a specific subject or research project. The data in a data bank are usually made available to interested, authorized persons.

Derived score. A score obtained by performing some mathematical operation on a raw score, such as multiplying the raw score by a constant and/or adding a constant to the score. See *Standard scores; T scores; z score.*

Developmental quotient (DQ).   An index, roughly equivalent to a mental age, for summarizing an infant's behavior as assessed by the Gesell Developmental Schedules.

Deviation IQ.   Score on an intelligence test obtained by converting an examinee's raw score on the test to a score on a distribution having a mean of 100 and a specified standard deviation.

Diagnostic interview.   An interview designed to obtain information on a person's thoughts, feelings, perceptions, and behavior; used in making a diagnostic decision about the person.

Diagnostic test.   An achievement test composed of a number of areas or skills constituting a certain subject, with the purpose of diagnosing an individual's relative strengths and weaknesses in the areas. Diagnostic tests are available in reading, arithmetic, and spelling.

Discriminant validity.   Situation in which a psychometric instrument has low correlations with other measures of (or methods of measuring) different psychological constructs.

Distracters.   Any of the incorrect options on a multiple-choice item.

Ectomorph.   In W. H. Sheldon's somatotype system, a person with a tall, thin body build; related to the cerebrotonic (thinking, introversive) temperament type.

Educable mentally retarded (EMR).   Children characterized by a mild degree of mental retardation (IQ = 50–70). Such children are capable of obtaining a third- to sixth-grade education and can learn to read, write, and perform elementary arithmetic operations. See *Trainable mentally retarded.*

Electroencephalograph (EEG).   Electronic apparatus designed to detect and record brain waves from the intact scalp.

Electromyograph (EMG).   Electronic apparatus designed to measure muscular activity or tension.

Empirical scoring.   A scoring system in which an examinee's responses are scored according to a key constructed from responses made by people in certain criterion groups, such as schizophrenics or physicians. This scoring procedure is employed with various personality and interest inventories.

Endomorph.   In the W. H. Sheldon somatotype system, a person with a rotund body shape (fat); related to the viscerotonic (relaxed, sociable) temperament.

Equilibration.   In Piaget's theory of cognitive development, the process by which a child comes to "know" and understand the environment by interacting with it. Equilibration involves the processes of assimilation and accommodation.

Equipercentile method.   Traditional method of converting the score units of one test to the score units of a parallel test. The scores on each test are converted to percentile ranks, and a table of equivalent scores is produced by equating the score at the *p*th percentile on the first test to the score at the *p*th percentile on the second test.

Equivalent forms.   See *Parallel forms.*

Essay test.   A test on which the examinee is required to compose rather lengthy answers to questions. The answers are evaluated subjectively by the teacher or another evaluator. See *Objective test.*

Estimated learning potential (ELP).   An estimate of a child's ability to learn, derived from measures obtained in the System of Multicultural Pluralistic Assessment (SOMPA). The ELP takes into account not only the child's IQ on the Wechsler Intelligence Scale for Children–Revised (WISC–R) or Wechsler Preschool and Primary Scale of Intelligence (WPPSI), but also family size, family structure, socioeconomic status, and degree of urban acculturation.

Evaluation.   To judge the merit or value of an examinee's behavior from a composite of test scores, observations, and reports.

Expectancy effect.   Effects of teacher expectations on the IQ scores of pupils. More generally, the effects of a person's expectations on another person's behavior.

Expectancy table.   A table giving the frequency or percentage of examinees in a certain category (score interval) on a predictor variable (test) who would be expected to fall in a certain category (score interval) on the criterion.

Extrovert.   Jung's term for individuals who are oriented, in their thoughts or social orientation, toward the external environment and other people rather than toward their own thoughts and feelings.

Face validity.   The extent to which the appearance or content of the materials (items and the like) on a test or other psychometric instrument is such that the instrument appears to be a good measure of what it is supposed to measure.

Factor.   A dimension, trait, or characteristic of personality revealed by factor analyzing the matrix of correlations computed from the scores of a large number of people on several different tests or items.

Factor analysis.   A mathematical procedure for analyzing a matrix of correlations among measurements to determine what factors (constructs) are sufficient to explain the correlations.

Factor loadings.   In factor analysis, the resulting correlations (weights) between tests (or other variables) and the extracted factors.

Factor rotation.   A mathematical procedure applied to a factor matrix for the purpose of simplifying the matrix for interpretation purposes by increasing the number of high and low factor loadings in the matrix. Factor rotation may be either *orthogonal,* in which the resulting factor axes at right angles to each other, or *oblique,* in which the resulting factor axes from acute or obtuse angles with each other.

Fairness.   On an aptitude test, the extent to which scores on the test are unbiased (equally predictive of the criterion performance of different groups).

False negative.   Selection error or diagnostic decision error in which an assessment procedure incorrectly predicts a maladaptive outcome (for example, low achievement, poor performance, or psychopathology).

False positive.   Selection error or diagnostic decision error in which an assessment procedure incorrectly predicts an adaptive outcome (for example, high achievement, good performance, or absence of psychopathology).

Fantasy stage.   The earliest stage in the development of interests, in which a child's interest orientations are not based on an accurate perception of reality.

Fidelity.   The narrowness of the *bandwidth* of a test or other measuring instrument. A test with high *fidelity* is a good predictor of a fairly narrow range of criteria. See *Bandwidth.*

Field dependence.   A perceptual style in which the perceiver depends primarily on cues from the surrounding visual environment, rather than kinesthetic (gravitational) cues, to determine the upright position in H. A. Witkin's rod-and-frame test.

Field independence.   A perceptual style in which the perceiver depends primarily on kinesthetic (gravitational) cues, rather than visual cues from the surrounding environment, to determine the upright position in H. A. Witkin's rod-and-frame test.

Fluid intelligence.   R. B. Cattell's term for inherent, genetically determined mental ability, as seen in problem solving or novel responses.

Forced-choice item.   Item on a personality or interest inventory, arranged as a dyad (two options), triad (three options), or tetrad (four options) of terms or phrases. The respondent is required to select an option viewed as most descriptive of the personality, interests, or behavior of the person being evaluated and perhaps another option perceived to be least descriptive of the personality, interests, or behavior of the person being evaluated. Forced-choice items are found on certain personality inventories (for example, Edwards Personal Preference Schedule), interest inventories (Kuder General Interest Survey), and rating forms to control for response sets.

Formal operations.   The final period (11 to 15 years) in Piaget's cognitive development sequence, in which the child can now use logic and verbal reasoning and perform higher-level, more abstract mental operations.

Formative evaluation.   Evaluation of performance for the purpose of improving instruction or determining areas of strength and weakness for enrichment or remedial instruction. See *Summative evaluation.*

Frequency distribution.   A table of score intervals and the number of cases (scores) falling within each interval.

Generalizability theory.   A theory of test scores and the associated statistical formulation that conceptualize a test score as a sample from a universe of scores. Analysis of variance procedures are used to determine the generalizability from score to universe value, as a function of examinees, test items, and situational contexts. A generalizability coefficient may be computed as a measure of the degree of generalizability from sample to population.

Grade norm.   The average of the scores on an aptitude or achievement test made by a group of children at a given grade level.

Graphic rating scale.   A rating scale containing a series of items, each consisting of a line on which the rater places a check mark to indicate the degree of a characteristic that the ratee is perceived as possessing. Typically, at the left extremity of the line is a brief verbal description indicating the lowest degree of the characteristic and at the right end, a description of the highest degree of the characteristic. Brief descriptions of intermediate degrees of the characteristic may also be situated at equidistant points along the line.

Graphology.   The analysis of handwriting to ascertain the character or personality of the writer.

Group test.   A test administered simultaneously to a group of examinees by one examiner. See *Individual test.*

Guess-who technique.   Procedure for analyzing group interaction and the social stimulus value of group members, in which children are asked to "guess who" in a classroom or other group situation possesses certain characteristics or does certain things.

Halo effect.   Rating a person high on one characteristic merely because he or she rates high on other characteristics.

Heritability index (h^2).   The ratio of the test score variance attributable to heredity to the variance attributable to both heredity and environment in combination.

Hierarchical model.   P. Vernon's "tree" model of intelligence, consisting of a general factor (g) at the highest level, two major group factors, verbal–educational (v:ed) and practical–mechanical–spatial (k:m), at the second level, and a number of minor group factors at a third level.

Ideal self.   In Carl Rogers' phenomenological theory, the person whom the individual would like to be (the self he or she would like to possess).

Idiographic approach.   Approach to personality assessment and research in which the individual is viewed as a lawful, integrated system in his or her own right. See *Nomothetic approach.*

In-basket technique.   A supervisor or executive evaluation technique in which the candidate is required to indicate what action should be taken on a series of memos and other materials of the sort typically found in a supervisor's or executive's in-basket.

Incident sampling.   As contrasted with *time sampling,* an observational procedure in which certain types of incidents, such as those indicative of aggressive behavior, are selected for observation and recording.

Individual test.   A test administered to one examinee at a time.

Informed consent.   A formal agreement made by an individual, or the individual's guardian or legal representative, with an agency or another person to permit use of the individual's name and/or personal information (test scores and the like) for a specified purpose.

Intelligence. Many definitions of this term have been offered, such as "the ability to judge well, understand well, and reason well" (Binet) and "the capacity for abstract thinking" (L. M. Terman). In general, what is measured by conventional intelligence tests is the ability to succeed in schoolwork and similar verbal–numerical types of tasks.

Intelligence quotient (IQ). A derived score, used originally in scoring the Stanford–Binet Intelligence Scale. A ratio IQ is computed by dividing the examinee's mental age (MA), as determined from a score on an intelligence test, by his or her chronological age (CA), and multiplying the result by 100. A deviation IQ is computed by multiplying the z score corresponding to a raw score on the intelligence test by the standard deviation of the deviation IQs and adding 100 to the product.

Intelligence test. A psychological test designed to measure an individual's aptitude for scholastic work or other kinds of activities involving verbal ability and problem solving.

Interest inventory. A test or checklist, such as the Strong–Campbell Interest Inventory and the Kuder General Interest Survey, designed to assess an individual's preferences for certain activities and topics.

Interlocking items. Test items on which an examinee's response to one item is affected by or contingent upon his or her response to a previous item.

Internal consistency. The extent to which the items comprising a test measure the same thing. The reliability of a test computed by the Spearman–Brown, Kuder–Richardson, or Cronbach alpha formulas is a measure of the test's internal consistency.

Interval scale. A measurement scale on which equality of numerical differences implies equality of differences in the attribute or characteristic being measured. The scale of temperature (Celsius, Fahrenheit) and, presumably, standard scale scales *(z, T),* are examples of interval scales.

Interview. Systematic procedure for obtaining information by asking questions and, in general, verbally interacting with a person (the *interviewee*).

Introvert. Jung's term for orientation toward the self; primary concern with one's own thoughts and feelings rather than with the external environment or other people; preference for solitary activities.

Inventory. A set of questions or statements to which the individual responds (for example, by indicating agreement or disagreement), designed to provide a measure of personality, interest, attitude, or behavior.

Ipsative measurement. Test item format (for example, forced choice) in which the variables being measured are compared with each other so that a person's score on any variable is affected by his or her scores on other variables measured by the instrument.

Item. One of the units, questions, or tasks comprising a test.

Item analysis.   A general term for procedures designed to assess the usefulness of a test item. See *Item discrimination index* and *Item difficulty index.*

Item difficulty index.   An index of the easiness or difficulty of an item for a group of examinees. A convenient measure of the difficulty of an item is the proportion (p) of examinees who select the correct answer.

Item discrimination index.   A measure of how effectively an item discriminates between examinees who score high and those who score low on the test as a whole or some other criterion measure.

Item-response (characteristic) curve.   Graph showing the proportion of examinees who get an item right, plotted against an internal (total test score) or external criterion of performance.

Item sampling.   Procedure for selecting subsets of items from a total item pool; different samples of items are administered to different groups of examinees.

Job analysis.   A general term for procedures used to determine the factors or tasks making up a job. A job analysis is usually considered a prerequisite to the construction of a test for predicting performance on a job.

Kuder–Richardson formulas.   Formulas used to compute a measure of the internal consistency reliability of a test from a single administration of a test having 0 to 1 scoring.

Language test.   A test composed of verbal or numerical items (that is, items involving the use of language). See *Nonlanguage test.*

Latent trait theory.   Any one of several theories (for example, item characteristic curve theory, Rasch model) and their associated statistical procedures that relate an examinee's test performance to his or her estimated standing on some hypothetical latent ability trait or continuum; used in item analysis and test standardization.

Leaderless group discussion (LGD).   Six or so individuals (for example, candidates for an executive position) are observed while discussing an assigned problem to determine their effectiveness in working with a group and reaching a solution.

Learning disability.   Difficulty in learning to read, write, spell, or perform arithmetic or other academic skills by a person whose score on an intelligence test (IQ) is average or above.

Leniency error.   The tendency to rate an individual higher on a positive characteristic and less severely on a negative characteristic than he or she actually should be rated. See *Bias.*

Likert scale.   Attitude scale in which respondents indicate their degree of agreement or disagreement with a particular proposition concerning some object, person, or situation.

Linear regression analysis.   Procedure for determining the algebraic equation of the best-fitting line for predicting scores on a dependent variable from one or more independent variables.

Local norms.   Percentile ranks, standard scores, or other norms corresponding to the raw test scores of a relatively small, local group of examinees. See *National norms* and *Norms*.

Locus of control.   J. B. Rotter's term for a cognitive–perceptual style characterized by the typical direction (internal or self versus external or other) from which individuals perceive themselves as being controlled.

Looking-glass theory.   After C. H. Cooley, the idea that the self is formed as a result of the reflected appraisals of other people, that is, the individual's perception of how others view her or his person and behavior.

Man-to-man (person-to-person) scale.   Procedure in which ratings on a specific trait (for example, leadership) are made by comparing each person to be rated with several other people whose standings on the trait have already been determined.

Mastery test.   See *Criterion-referenced test.*

Matching item.   A test item requiring examinees to indicate which of several options in one list is (are) the correct match(es) or answer(s) for each of several options in a second list.

Measurement.   Procedures for determining (or indexing) the amount or quantity of some construct or entity; the assignment of numbers to objects or events.

Median.   Score point in a distribution of scores below and above which 50 percent of the scores fall.

Mental age (MA).   An examinee's derived score on an intelligence test such as the Stanford–Binet. The examinee's mental age corresponds to the chronological age of a representative sample of children of the same chronological age whose average score on the test is equal to the examinee's score. See *Intelligence quotient.*

Mentally gifted.   A person significantly above average in intellectual functioning, variously defined as an IQ of 130 or 140 and above.

Mental retardation.   Below average intelligence, usually indicated by an IQ of below 70. The DSM–III–R categories of mental retardation include mild, moderate, severe, profound, and unspecified.

Mesomorph.   W. H. Sheldon's term for a person having an athletic physique; correlated with a somatotonic temperament (active, aggressive, energetic).

Mode.   An average; the most frequently occurring score in a set or frequency distribution of scores.

Moderator variable.   Demographic or personality variable (for example, age, sex, cognitive style, compulsivity) affecting the correlation between two other variables (for example, aptitude and achievement).

Multilevel test.   A test designed to be appropriate for several age levels; a separate test is constructed for each level.

Multiple abstract variance analysis (MAVA).   Statistical procedure, devised by R. B. Cattell, for computing the relative effects of heredity and environment in determining a particular personality characteristic.

Multiple-choice item.   A test item consisting of a stem (statement, question, phrase, or the like) and several response options (usually three to five), only one of which is correct.

Multiple correlation coefficient (R).   A measure of the overall degree of relationship, varying between -1.00 and $+1.00$, of several variables with a single criterion variable. For example, the multiple correlation of a group of scholastic aptitude tests with school grades is typically around .60 or .70, a moderate degree of correlation.

Multiple cutoff.   Selection strategy in which applicants are required to make at least specified minimum scores on several selection criteria in order to be accepted (employed, admitted, and so on).

Multiple regression analysis.   Statistical method of analyzing the contributions of two or more independent variables to the prediction of a dependent variable.

Multitrait–multimethod matrix.   Matrix of correlation coefficients resulting from correlating measures of the same trait by the same method, different traits by the same method, the same trait by different methods, and different traits by different methods. The relative magnitudes of the four types of correlations are compared in evaluating the construct validity of a test.

National norms.   Percentile ranks, standard scores, or other norms based on a national sample. See *Local norms* and *Norms*.

Neuropsychological assessment.   Measurement of cognitive, perceptual, and motor performance to determine the location and extent of brain damage.

Nominal scale.   The lowest level of measurement, in which numbers are used merely as descriptors or names of things, rather than designating order or amount.

Nomination technique.   Method of studying social structure and personality in which students, workers, or other groups of individuals are asked to indicate the persons with whom they would like to do a certain thing or the person(s) whom they feel possesses certain characteristics.

Nomothetic approach.   A search for general laws of behavior and personality that apply to all individuals. See *Idiographic approach*.

Nonlanguage test (nonverbal test).   A test consisting of nonverbal or other nonlanguage materials. The examinee is not required to use spoken or written language, but constructs, manipulates, or responds to the test materials in nonverbal ways.

Nonverbal behavior.   Any behavior in which the respondent does not make word sounds or signs. Nonverbal behavior serving a communicative function includes movements of large (macrokinesics) and small (microkinesics) body parts, interpersonal distance or territoriality (proxemics), tone and rate of voice sounds (paralinguistics), and communications imparted by culturally prescribed matters relating to time, dress, memberships, and the like (culturics).

Normal distribution.   A smooth, bell-shaped frequency distribution of scores, symmetrical about the mean and described by an exact mathematical equation. The test scores of a large group of examinees are frequently distributed in an approximately normal manner.

Normalized scores.   Scores obtained by transforming raw scores in such a way that the transformed scores are normally distributed and have a mean of 0 and a standard deviation of 1 (or some linear function of these numbers).

Norm group.   Sample of people on whom a test is standardized.

Norm-referenced test.   A test on which the scores are interpreted with respect to norms obtained from a sample of examinees. See *Criterion-referenced test.*

Norms.   A list of scores and the corresponding percentile ranks, standard scores, or other transformed scores of a group of examinees on whom a test has been standardized.

Objective test.   A test scored by comparing the examinee's responses to a list of correct answers determined beforehand, in contrast to a subjectively scored test. Examples of objective test items are multiple choice and true–false.

Oblique rotation.   In a factor analysis, a rotation in which the factor axes are allowed to form acute or obtuse angles with each other. Consequently, the factors are correlated. See *Orthogonal rotation.*

Observation method.   Observing behavior in a controlled or uncontrolled situation and making a formal or informal record of the observations.

Odd–even reliability.   The correlation of total scores on the odd-numbered items with total scores on even-numbered items of a test, corrected by the Spearman–Brown reliability formula.

Omnibus test.   A test containing a variety of items designed to measure different aspects of mental functioning.

Operation.   In J. P. Guilford's Structure-of-Intellect Model, one of five possible types of mental processes (cognition, memory, divergent thinking, convergent thinking, evaluation). In Piaget's theory of cognitive development, an operation is defined as any mental action that is reversible (can be returned to its starting point) and integrated with other reversible mental actions.

Oral examination.   A test on which examinees answer orally, rather than in writing; the questions may be presented either orally or in writing.

Ordinal scale.   Type of measurement scale on which the numbers refer merely to the ranks of objects or events arranged in order of merit (for example, numbers designating order of finishing in a contest).

Orthogonal rotation.   In a factor analysis, a rotation that maintains the independence of factors; that is, the angles between factors are kept at 90° and hence the factors are uncorrelated. See *Oblique rotation.*

Out-of-level testing.   Administering a test designed primarily for one age or grade level to examinees who are below or above that level.

Parallel forms.   Two tests that are equivalent in the sense that they contain the same kinds of items of equal difficulty and are highly correlated. The scores made by examinees on one form of the test are very close to those made by them on the other form of the test.

Participant observation.   An observational technique in which the observer attempts to minimize the intrusiveness of his or her person and observational activities by becoming part of the group being observed, for example, by dressing and behaving like the other group members.

Percentile.   The *p*th percentile of a group or frequency distribution of scores below which *p* percent of the examinees' test scores fall. See *Median* and *Percentile rank.*

Percentile band.   A range of percentile ranks within which there is a specified probability that an examinee's true score on a test will fall.

Percentile norms.   A list of raw scores and the corresponding percentages of the test standardization group having scores below the given percentile.

Percentile rank.   The percentage of scores, falling below a given score in a frequency distribution or group of scores; the percentage corresponding to this given score.

Performance contract.   A formal agreement according to which teachers' pay is based on the educational gains achieved by their students. See *Accountability.*

Performance test.   A test on which the examinee is required to manipulate various physical objects; performance tests are contrasted with paper-and-pencil tests.

Personality.   The sum total of the qualities, traits, and behaviors that characterize a person's individuality and by which, together with his or her physical attributes, the person is recognized as a unique individual.

Personality inventory.   A self-report inventory or questionnaire consisting of statements concerned with personal characteristics and behaviors. On a true–false inventory, the respondent indicates whether or not each test item or statement is self-descriptive; on a multiple-choice or force-choice inventory. the respondent selects the statements that are self-descriptive.

Personality profile.   Graph of scores on a battery or set of scales of a personality inventory or rating scale. The elevation and scatter of the profile assist in the analysis of personality and the diagnosis of mental disorders.

Personality test.   Any one of several methods of analyzing personality, such as checklists, personality inventories, and projective techniques.

Phenomenology.   Study of objects and events as they appear to the experiencing observer;

type of psychotherapy (Rogers, Maslow, and others) that emphasizes the importance of self-perceptions and impressions of others in determining personality and behavior.

Phi coefficient. A coefficient of correlation, frequently used in item analysis, that indicates the degree of relationship between two dichotomized variables. The phi coefficient is based on the assumption that the variables are truly dichotomous. See *Point-biserial coefficient.*

Phrenology. Discredited theory and practice of Gall and Spurzheim relating affective and cognitive characteristics to the configuration (bumps) of the skull.

Physiognomy. A pseudoscience that maintains that the personal characteristics of an individual are revealed by the form or features of the body, especially the face.

Placement. Assigning examinees to groups or classes according to their scores on a test.

Pluralistic model. In the System of Multicultural Pluralistic Assessment, a combination made up of the Student Assessment Materials and the Parent Interview. A child's scores on the various measures are interpreted by comparing them with the scores of other children having a similar sociocultural background.

Point-biserial coefficient. Correlation coefficient computed between a dichotomous variable and a continuous variable; derived from the product–moment correlation coefficient.

Power test. A test with ample time limits so all examinees have time to attempt all items. However, many of the items are difficult and sometimes arranged in order of difficulty from easiest to hardest. See *Speeded test.*

Predictive validity. Extent to which scores on a test are predictive of performance on some criterion measure assessed at a later time; usually expressed as a correlation between the test (predictor variable) and the criterion variable.

Preoperational stage. In Piaget's theory of cognitive development, the egocentric stage of development (2 to 7 years) when the child acquires language and other symbolic representations.

Profile (psychograph). A graph depicting an individual's scores on several parts of the same test. By inspecting an achievement test profile, an examiner can obtain information about the examinee's areas of strength and weakness; inspection of a profile of scores on an interest or personality inventory provides information on the interests and personality characteristics of the examinee.

Program evaluation. Procedure(s) for arriving at judgments concerning the economic and social value of educational intervention, psychological treatment, or other social programs. The thorough evaluation of a program involves a series of stages, from planning and monitoring the program through assessing its impact and economic efficiency.

Projective technique. A relatively unstructured personality test on which the examinee responds to materials such as inkblots, ambiguous pictures, incomplete sentences, and other materials by telling what he or she perceives, making up stories, or constructing and arranging sentences and objects. Because the material is fairly unstructured, whatever structure the examinee imposes on it is interpreted as a projection of his or her own personality characteristics (needs, conflicts, fears, and the like).

Psychometrics. Theory and research pertaining to the measurement of psychological (cognitive and affective) characteristics.

Q **data.** R. B. Cattell's term of personality data obtained from questionnaires.

Q **technique.** Personality assessment procedure that centers on sorting cards or other materials (*Q* sorts) that contain self-descriptive statements into categories on some continuum and correlating the responses of different individuals or the same individuals at different times.

Quartile. A score in a frequency distribution below which either 25% (first quartile), 50% (second quartile), 75% (third quartile), or 100% (fourth quartile) of the total number of scores fall.

Questionnaire. A list of questions concerning a particular topic administered to a group of individuals to obtain information concerning their preferences, beliefs, interests, and behavior.

r. A symbol for the Pearson product–moment correlation coefficient.

Random sample. A sample of observations (for example, test scores) drawn from a specified population (target population) in such a way that every member of the population has an equal chance of being selected in the sample.

Range. A crude measure of the spread or variability of a group of scores computed by subtracting the lowest score from the highest score.

Rapport. A warm, friendly relationship between examiner and examinee. It is important to establish rapport at the beginning of testing so that the examinee will be motivated to respond truthfully and to his or her best ability.

Rasch model. One-parameter (item difficulty) item-response model for scaling test items for purposes of test design and analysis. The Rasch model is based on the assumption that the indexes of guessing and item discrimination are negligible parameters. As with other item-response models, the Rasch model relates examinees' performance on test items (percentage passing) to their estimated score on a hypothetical ability scale or other specified trait continuum.

Rating scale. A list of words or statements concerning traits or characteristics, sometimes in the form of a continuous line divided into sections corresponding to degrees of the characteristics, on which the rater indicates judgments of either his or her own behavior and traits or the behavior and traits of another person (ratee).

Ratio IQ. An intelligence quotient obtained by dividing an examinee's mental age score on an intelligence test (for example, an older edition of the Stanford–Binet) by his or her chronological age and multiplying the result by 100. See *Deviation IQ.*

Ratio scale. A scale of measurement, having a true zero, on which equal numerical ratios imply equal ratios of the attribute being measured. Psychological variables are typically not measured on ratio scales, but height, weight, energy, and many other physical variables are.

Readiness test. A test that measures the extent to which an individual possesses the skills and knowledge necessary to learn a complex subject such as reading or writing.

Real self. In C. R. Rogers' phenomenological theory, a person's perception of what he or she really is, as contrasted with what he or she would like to be *(ideal self).*

Realistic stage. Final stage in the development of vocational interests, usually occurring during late adolescence or early adulthood. The individual has a realistic notion about what particular occupations entail and the vocation he or she would like to pursue.

Recall item. In contrast to a recognition item, a recall item is one that requires examinees to recall or supply some bit of information rather than simply identifying the correct answer in a list of possible answers. See *Recognition item.*

Recognition item. A test item on which examinees are required to recognize or identify the correct answer in a list of possible answers (for example, multiple-choice or true–false items). See *Recall item.*

Regression equation. A linear equation for forecasting criterion scores from scores on one or more predictor variables, a procedure often used in selection programs or actuarial prediction and diagnosis.

Regression toward the mean. Tendency for a test score or other measure to move closer to the mean on retesting; the more extreme the original score is, the greater the movement toward the mean, in either the higher or lower direction, will be on retesting.

Reliability. The extent to which a psychological assessment instrument measures anything consistently. A reliable instrument is relatively free from errors of measurement, so the scores examinees obtain on the instrument are close in numerical value to their true scores.

Reliability coefficient. A numerical index, between 0.00 and 1.00, of the reliability of an assessment instrument. Methods for determining reliability include test–retest, parallel forms, and internal consistency.

Representative sample. A subset of measurements selected from a population in such a way that the sample is like the population in all significant ways.

Response sets (styles). Tendencies for individuals to respond in relatively fixed or stereotyped ways in situations in which there are two or more response choices, such as on personality inventories. Tendencies to guess, to answer true (acquiescence), and to give socially desirable answers are among the response sets that may affect test scores.

Scatter diagram (scattergram). A graphical plot of the paired *X–Y* values of two variables; a correlation diagram.

Schema. In Piaget's theory of cognitive development, a mental structure (grasping, sucking, shaking, and the like) that is modified (accommodated) as a result of experience.

Scholastic aptitude. The ability to learn the kinds of information and skills taught in school.

Scholastic aptitude test. Any test, such as the SAT or SCAT, that predicts the ability of a person to learn the kinds of information and skills taught in school-type situations.

Scientific management. System of management, pioneered by F. W. Taylor, that emphasizes finding the "one best way" of accomplishing a task, that is, the most efficient and least fatiguing production method.

Scoring formula. A formula used to compute raw scores on a test. Common scoring formulas are Score $=$ Number Right and Score $=$ Number Right $-$ Number Wrong/$(k - 1)$, where k is the number of answer options per item.

Screening. A general term for any selection process, usually not very precise, by which certain applicants are accepted and other applicants are rejected.

Secure test. A test administered under conditions of tight security to make certain that only persons who are supposed to take the test actually take it and that copies of the test materials are not removed from the examination room(s) by unauthorized persons.

Selection. The use of tests and other devices to select those applicants for an occupation or educational program who are most likely to succeed in that situation. Applicants who fall at or above the cutoff score on the test are selected (accepted); those who fall below cutoff are rejected.

Selection ratio. The percentage of applicants who are selected or will be selected or hired for a particular position.

Self-concept. An individual's evaluation of his or her self, as assessed by various psychometric instruments.

Self-fulfilling prophecy. Tendency for a person's expectations and attitudes concerning future events or outcomes to affect their occurrence, for example, the tendency for children to behave in ways in which parents or teachers expect them to behave.

Self-report inventory. A personality or interest inventory comprised of a series of items that the examinee indicates as being characteristics (true) or not characteristic (not true) of himself or herself.

Semantic differential. A rating scale, introduced by C. Osgood, for evaluating the connotative meanings that selected concepts have for a person. Each concept is rated on a 7-point, bipolar, adjectival scale.

Semi-interquartile range (Q). A measure of the variability of a group of ordinal-scale scores, computed as half the difference between the first and third quartiles.

Sensorimotor stage. The first period in Piaget's theory of cognitive development, during which the child learns to exercise simple reflexes and to coordinate various perception.

Sensorimotor tests.   Tests designed to measure sensory, perceptual, and psychomotor abilities or a combination of such skills.

Sentence completion test.   A personality (projective) test consisting of a series of incomplete sentences that the examinee is instructed to complete as quickly as possible.

Sequential mental processing.   Mental process in which a series of items is processed sequentially, in serial order. An example of a sequential task is attempting to recall a series of numbers. See *Simultaneous mental processing.*

Sequential testing.   Testing procedure in which an examinee's answers to previous items determine which items will be presented next; also referred to as *adaptive* or *tailored testing.*

Simultaneous mental processing.   Mental process in which several bits or pieces of information are synthesized or integrated simultaneously. See *Sequential mental processing.*

Situation(al) test.   A performance test in which the examinee is placed in a realistic but contrived situation and directed to accomplish a specified goal. Situation tests are sometimes employed to assess personality characteristics such as honesty and frustration tolerance.

Skewness.   The degree of asymmetry in a frequency distribution. In a positively skewed distribution, there are more scores to the left of the mode (low scores), as when a test is too difficult for the examinees. In a negatively skewed distribution, there are more scores to the right of the mode (high scores), as when a test is too easy for the examinees.

Snellen chart.   A chart containing letters of various sizes, designed to measure visual acuity at a distance.

Social desirability response set.   Response set or style affecting scores on personality inventories. It refers to the tendency on the part of an examinee to respond to the assessment materials in a more socially desirable direction, rather than responding in a manner that is truly characteristic or descriptive of his or her personality.

Sociogram.   Diagram consisting of circles representing persons in a group, with lines drawn indicating which people chose (accepted) each other and which people did not choose (rejected) each other. Terms used in referring to particular elements of a sociogram are *star, clique, isolate,* and *mutual admiration society.*

Sociometric technique.   Method of determining and describing the pattern of acceptances and rejections in a group of people.

Somatotonia.   Athletic, aggressive temperament type in W. H. Sheldon's three-component system of personality; most closely correlated with a mesomorphic (muscular) body build.

Somatotype.   Classification of body build (physique) in W. H. Sheldon's three-component system (endomorphy, mesomorphy, ectomorphy).

Source traits.   R. B. Cattell's terms for organizing structures or dimensions of personality that underlie and determine surface traits. See *Surface traits.*

Spearman–Brown formula. A formula for estimating what the reliability of a test would be if its length were increased by a factor m.

Specific determiners. Words such as *sometimes, never, always,* and *occasionally* that may reveal the answer to a true–false item to examinees who do not know the answer.

Specificity. The proportion of the total variance of a test due to factors specific to the test itself.

Speeded test. A test consisting of a large number of fairly easy items, but having a short time limit so that almost no one completes the test in the allotted time. Many tests of clerical, mechanical, or psychomotor ability are of the speeded variety.

Spiral omnibus test. A test consisting of a variety of items arranged in order of ascending difficulty. Items of a given type or content appear throughout the test, intermingled with other types of items of similar difficulty, in a spiral of increasing difficulty.

Split-half coefficient. An estimate of reliability determined by applying the Spearman–Brown formula for $m = 2$ to the correlation between two halves of the same test, such as the odd-numbered items and the even-numbered items.

Standard deviation. The square root of the variance, used as a measure of dispersion or spread of a group of scores.

Standard error of estimate. The standard deviation of obtained criterion scores around the predicted criterion score; used to estimate a range of actual scores on a criterion variable for an individual whose score on the predictor variable is equal to a specified value.

Standard error of measurement. An estimate of the standard deviation of the normal distribution of test scores that an examinee would theoretically obtain by taking a test an infinite number of times. It can be stated that, if an examinee's obtained test score is X, then the chances are two out of three that he or she is one of a group of people whose true scores on the test fall within one standard error of measurement of X.

Standard scores. A group of scores, such as z scores, T scores, or stanine scores, having a desired mean and standard deviation. Standard scores are computed by transforming raw scores to z scores, multiplying the z scores by the desired standard deviation, and then adding the desired mean to the product.

Standardization. Administering a carefully constructed test to a large, representative sample of people under standard conditions for the purpose of determining norms.

Standardized test. A test that has been carefully constructed by professionals and administered with standard directions and under standard conditions to a representative sample of people for the purpose of obtaining norms.

Stanine. An open-ended standard score scale consisting of the scores 1 through 9, having a mean of 5 and a standard deviation of approximately 2.

State anxiety. A temporary state of anxiety, precipitated by a specific situation.

Statistic. A number used to describe some characteristic of a sample of test scores, such as the arithmetic mean or standard deviation.

Stem (of an item). The part of an objective test item that poses the question or sets the task. A multiple-choice item consists of a stem and two or more response options, one of which is the correct answer.

Stratified random sampling. Sampling procedure in which the population is divided into strata (for example, men and women; blacks and whites; lower class, middle class, upper class), and samples are selected at random from the strata; sample sizes are proportional to the number of people in each stratum.

Stress interview. Interviewing procedure in which the interviewer applies psychologically stressful techniques (critical and hostile questioning, frequent interruptions, prolonged silences, and the like) to break down the interviewee's defenses and determine how he or she reacts under pressure.

Structured interview. Interviewing procedure in which the interviewee is asked a series of preplanned questions.

Subtest. A portion or subgroup of items on a test (for example, a group of items measuring the same function or items at the same age level or difficulty level.

Summated rating, method of. Method of attitude-scale construction devised by R. Likert. Examinees rate a large number of attitude statements on a 5-point scale according to the degree of positivity or negativity of each statement toward the topic in question. Twenty or so statement are selected by certain statistical criteria to comprise the final attitude scale.

Summative evaluation. Evaluation at the end of an instructional unit or course of study as a sum total or final product measure of achievement.

Supply item. An objective test item requiring examinees to supply the correct answer, in contrast to a recognition item in which examinees select an answer from a list of possibilities. See *Recall item.*

Surface traits. Publicly manifested characteristics of personality; observable expressions of source traits. See *Source traits.*

Survey test. An achievement test designed primarily to assess an individual's general skill or understanding in a subject such as reading or arithmetic, rather than his or her specific strengths and weakness in those subjects. See *Diagnostic test.*

***T* scores.** Converted, normalized standard scores having a mean of 50 and a standard deviation of 10. *Z* scores are also standard scores with a mean of 50 and a standard deviation of 10, but in contrast to *T* scores they are not normalized.

Table of specifications. A two-way outline of a test in which behavioral objectives of the test are listed on the rows and content (topical) objectives on the columns. Descriptions of specific items are given in the body of the table.

Target behaviors. Specific, objectively defined behavior observed and measured in behavioral assessment. Of particular interest are the effects on these behaviors of antecedent and consequent events in the environment.

Target population.   The population of interest in standardizing a test or other assessment instrument; the norm group (sample) must be representative of the target population if valid interpretations of (norm-referenced) scores are to be made.

Template-matching technique.   Daryl Bem and David Funder's conceptualization of a situation template as a pattern of behavior characterizing the way that a person (person I) is ideally expected to behave in that situation. The extent to which another person (person J) behaves similarly in the same situation depends on the match between the personality characteristics of persons I and J.

Test.   Any device used to evaluate the behavior or performance of an individual. Psychological tests are of three kinds: cognitive, affective, and psychomotor.

Test anxiety.   A feeling of fear or uneasiness that one will not do well on a test. Although severe test anxiety can interfere with effective test performance, a moderate degree of test anxiety is normal and does not greatly disrupt test performance.

Test–retest reliability.   A method of assessing the reliability of a test by administering it to the same group of examinees on two different occasions and computing the correlations between their scores on the two occasions.

Time sampling.   Observational sampling procedure in which observations lasting only a few minutes are made over a period of a day or so.

Trade test.   A vocational achievement test of an individual's knowledge or ability to perform a specific job.

Trainable mentally retarded (TMR).   Children in the moderately retarded range of IQs (approximately 36 to 50), who usually cannot learn to read and write, but can perform unskilled tasks under supervision. See *Educable mentally retarded.*

Trait.   A cognitive, affective, or psychomotor characteristic possessed in different amounts by different people.

Trait anxiety.   Generalized level of anxiety expressed in a variety of situations.

Transfer hypothesis (ƒ ability differentiation).   Ferguson's hypothesis that the different abilities isolated by factor analysis are the results of overlearning and differential positive transfer in certain areas of learning.

Transitional stage.   An intermediate state in the development of interest; falls between the fantasy stage of early childhood and the realistic stage of late adolescence and early adulthood.

True–false item.   An objective test item (a statement or proposition) that examinees indicate as being or false.

True score.   The hypothetical score that is a measure of the examinee's true knowledge of the test material. In classical test theory, an examinee's true score on a test is the mean of the distribution of scores that would result if the examinee took the test an infinite number of times.

Type A personality.   Personality pattern characterized by a combination of behaviors, including aggressivity, competitiveness, hostility, quick actions and constant striving; associated with a high incidence of coronary heart disease.

Type B personality.   Personality pattern characterized by a relaxed, easygoing, patient, noncompetitive life-style; associated with a low incidence of coronary heart disease.

Unobtrusive observations.   Observations made without the awareness of the person whose behavior is being observed.

Unstructured interview.   Interviewing procedure in which the questions asked are not preplanned, but vary with the progress or flow of the interview.

Validity.   The extent to which an assessment instrument measures what it was designed to measure. Validity can be assessed in several ways: by analyzing the instrument's content *(content validity),* by relating scores on the instrument to a criterion *(predictive* and *concurrent validity),* and by a more thorough analysis of the extent to which the instrument is a measure of a certain psychological construct *(construct validity).*

Validity generalization.   The application of validity evidence to situations other than those in which the evidence was obtained.

Variability.   The degree of spread or deviation of a group of scores around their average value.

Variable.   In contrast to a *constant,* any quantity that can assume more than one state or numerical value.

Variance.   A measure of variability of test scores, computed as the sum of the squares of the deviations of raw scores from the arithmetic mean, divided by one less than the number of scores; the square of the standard deviation.

Verbal test.   A test with verbal directions requiring oral or written word and/or number answers.

Viscerotonia.   Jolly, sociable temperament type in W. H. Sheldon's three-component description of personality; most closely correlated with the endomorphic (rotund) body build.

Word association test.   A list of words read aloud to an examinee, who has been instructed to respond with the first word that comes to mind. First used in a clinical situation by the Swiss psychiatrist Carl Jung, word association tests are often employed in the analysis of personality.

z score.   Any one of a group of derived scores varying from $-\infty$ to $+\infty$, computed from the formula $z =$ (raw score $-$ mean)/standard deviation, for each raw score. In a normal distribution, over 99 percent of the cases lie between $z = -3.00$ and $z = +3.00$.

Appendix F

Computer Programs for Psychological Assessment

MAIN MENU PROGRAM CATEGORY

1. Basic Statistical Methods
2. Test Construction, Administration, and Scoring
3. Item Analysis and Norms
4. Reliability and Validity
5. Problem Solving and Thinking
6. Special Abilities
7. Attitudes and Values
8. Personality Inventories and Projectives

Category 1: Program on Basic Statistical Methods

1. Normal Curve Probabilities
2. Descriptive Statistics
3. Frequency Distribution and Associated Graphs
4. Multiple Regression Analysis
5. Correlation Coefficient and Regression Equation
6. Percentiles and Percentile Ranks
7. Scatter Diagram and Regression Line Plot

Category 2: Programs on Test Construction, Administration, and Scoring

1. An Arithmetic Test
2. Correcting for Guessing on an Objective Test

3. Grade Assignment by the Modified Cajori Method
4. Preparing an Objective Test
5. Scoring Ranking Items
6. Test Administration and Scoring

Category 3: Programs on Item Analysis and Norms

1. Difficulty and Discrimination Indexes for Classroom Test Items
2. Difficulty and Discrimination Indexes for Criterion-referenced Test Items
3. Item Characteristic Curves and Item Response Curves
4. Point-Biserial Correlation
5. Standard Scores and Percentiles

Category 4: Programs on Test Reliability and Validity

1. Coefficient Alpha
2. Coefficient Kappa Reliability for Criterion Referenced Tests
3. Kuder–Richardson Reliability Coefficients
4. Reliability of Standard Error of Difference Scores
5. Split-half (Spearman–Brown) Reliability
6. Standard Errors of Measurement and Estimate

Category 5: Programs on Problem Solving and Thinking

1. Concept Formation Test
2. Insight Problems
3. Luchins Waterjar Problems
4. Number Series
5. Tower of Hanoi Problems

Category 6: Programs on Special Abilities Tests

1. Anagrams
2. Clerical Speed and Accuracy Test
3. Digit Span Test
4. Hearing Test
5. Phi Phenomenon
6. Searching for Numbers
7. Visual Perimeter Test

Category 7: Programs for Attitudes and Values Inventories

1. Altruism Inventory
2. Attitudes Toward Intelligence Testing
3. College Course and Instructor Evaluation Inventory
4. Educational Values Inventory
5. Mathematics Attitude Inventory
6. Sports Success Inventory

Category 8: Programs on Personality Assessment

1. Dot Pattern Test
2. Five Factor Personality Inventory
3. Professor Personality Ratings
4. Projective Line Drawings
5. Sentence Completion Test
6. Word Association Test

References

Abrahams, N. M., Neumann, I., & Gilthens, W. H. (1971). Faking vocational interests: Simulated vs. real life motivation. *Personnel Psychology, 24*(1), 5–12.

Abramson, L. Y., Garber, J., & Seligman, M. E. P. (1980). Learned helplessness in humans. In J. Garber & M. E. P. Seligman (eds.), *Human helplessness,* (pp. 3–34). New York: Academic Press.

Achenbach, T. M. (1978). The Child Behavior Profile—I. Boys aged 6–11. *Journal of Consulting Psychology, 46,* 478–488.

———, & Edelbrock, C. (1983). *Manual of the Child Behavior Checklist and Revised Child Behavior Profile.* Burlington, VT: University of Vermont, Department of Psychiatry.

Adler, T. (1991, May). Tug-of-war develops over use of GATB. *The APA Monitor,* p. 14.

Aiken, L. R. (1970). Scoring for partial knowledge on the generalized rearrangement item. *Educational and Psychological Measurement, 30,* 87–94.

———. (1973). *Readings in psychological and educational testing.* Boston: Allyn & Bacon.

———. (1979a). Attitudes toward mathematics and science in Iranian middle schools. *School Science and Mathematics, 79,* 229–234.

———. (1979b). Relationships between item difficulty and discrimination indexes. *Educational and Psychological Measurement, 39,* 821–824.

———. (1980). Problems in testing the elderly. *Educational Gerontology, 5,* 119–124.

———. (1983a). *The case for oral achievement testing.* ERIC Document Reproduction Service No. ED 222 578 & TM 820 755.

———. (1983b). Determining grade boundaries on classroom tests. *Educational and Psychological Measurement, 3,* 759–762.

———. (1985). Three coefficients for analyzing the reliability and validity of ratings. *Educational and Psychological Measurement, 45,* 131–142.

———. (1988). KAPPO: A program for assessing the reliability of criterion-referenced tests. *Applied Psychological Measurement, 12*(1), 104.

Ajzen, I., & Fishbein, M. (1977). Attitude-behavior relations: A theoretical analysis and review of empirical research. *Psychological Bulletin, 84,* 888–918.

Albemarle Paper Company v. *Moody.* 10 FEP 11 1181 (1975).

Alexander, L., & James, H. T. (1987). *The nation's report card: Improving the assessment of student achievement.* Washington, DC: National Academy of Education.

Allison, D. E. (1984). The effect of item-difficulty sequence, intelligence, and sex on test performance, reliability, and item difficulty and discrimination. *Measurement and Evaluation in Guidance, 16,* 211–217.

Allport, G. W. (1937). *Personality: A psychological interpretation.* New York: Holt, Rinehart & Winston.

———. (1961). *Pattern and growth in personality.* New York: Holt, Rinehart & Winston.

———. (ed.) (1965). *Letters from Jenny.* New York: Harcourt, Brace, Jovanovich.

———, & Odbert, H. S. (1936). Trait-names, a psycholexical study. *Psychological Monographs, 47*(1).

American College (1978). *Test wiseness: Test taking skills for adults.* New York: McGraw-Hill.

American Educational Research Association, American Psychological Association, & National Council on Measurement in Education (1985). *Standards for educational and psychological testing.* Washington, DC: American Psychological Association.

American Law Institute (1956). *Model penal code.* Tentative Draft Number 4.

American Psychiatric Association (1980). *Diagnostic and statistical manual of mental disorders,* 3rd ed. Washington, DC: Author.

———. (1987). *Diagnostic and statistical manual of mental disorders,* 3rd ed., rev. Washington, DC: Author.

American Psychological Association (1981). Ethical principles of psychologists. *American Psychologist, 36,* 633–638.

American Psychological Association, Committee on Professional Standards & Committee on Psychological Tests and Assessment (1986). *Guidelines for computer-based tests and interpretations.* Washington, DC: American Psychological Association.

American Psychological Association (1992). Ethical principles of psychologists and code of conduct. *American Psychologist, 47,* 1597–1611.

Americans still lag in education. (1992, February 5). *News Chronicle* (Thousand Oaks, CA), p. A-4.

Ames, L. B., et al. (1979). *The Gesell Institute's child from one to six: Evaluating the behavior of the preschool child.* New York: Harper & Row.

Anastasi, A. (1981). Coaching, test sophistication, and developed abilities. *American Psychologist, 36,* 1086–1093.

———. (1988). *Psychological testing,* 6th ed. New York: Macmillan.

Andreasen, N. C. (1987). Creativity and mental illness: Prevalence rates in writers and their first-degree relatives. *American Journal of Psychiatry, 144*(10), 1288–1292.

Anrig, G. R. (1985). Introduction. In *The redesign of testing for the 21st century,* pp. v–vi. Princeton, NJ: Educational Testing Service.

———. (1987). "Golden Rule": second thoughts. *The APA Monitor, 18*(8), 3.

APA task force releases final report on integrity testing (1991, May/June). *Psychological Science Agenda 4*(3), pp. 1, 6. Washington, DC: American Psychological Association.

Archer, R. P., et al. (1991). Psychological test usage with adolescent clients: 1990 survey findings. *Professional Psychology: Research and Practice, 22,* 247–252.

Arkes, H. R. (1985). Clinical judgment. In R. J. Corsini (ed.), *Encyclopedia of psychology,* Vol. 1, pp. 404–405. New York: Wiley.

Arvey, R. D. (1979). Unfair discrimination in the employment interview: Legal and psychological aspects. *Psychological Bulletin, 86,* 736–765.

Assessment System Corporation (1988). *User's manual for the MicroCAT Testing System, Version 3.* St. Paul, MN: Author.

Austin, G. R., & Garber, H. (eds.). (1982). *The rise and fall of national test scores.* New York: Academic Press.

Baker, F. B. (1985). *The basics of item response theory.* Portsmouth, NJ: Heinemann.

———. (1989). Computer technology in test construction and processing. In R. L. Linn (ed.), *Educational measurement,* 3rd ed., pp. 409–428. New York: Macmillan.

Barkley, R. A. (1981). *Hyperactive children: A handbook for diagnosis and treatment.* New York: Guilford Press.

Bellak, L. (1986). *The T.A.T., C.A.T. and S.A.T. in clinical use,* 4th ed. New York: Grune & Stratton.

Bem, D. J., & Allen, A. (1974). On predicting some of the people some of the time: The search for cross-situational consistencies in behavior. *Psychological Review, 81,* 506–520.

Benjamin, L. T., Cavell, T. A., & Shallenberger, W. R. (1984). Staying with initial answers on objective tests: Is it a myth? *Teaching of Psychology, 11,* 133–141.

Ben-Porath, Y. B., & Butcher, J. N. (1986). Computers in personality assessment: A brief past, an ebullient present and an expanding future. *Computers in Human Behavior, 2,* 167–182.

Bentler, P. M., & Newcomb, M. D. (1986). Personality, sexual behavior, and drug use revealed through latent variable methods. *Clinical Psychology Review, 6*(5), 363–386.

Berne, E. (1966). *Principles of group treatment.* New York: Oxford University Press.

Biemiller, L. (1986, January 8). Critics plan assault on admissions tests and other standard exams. *Chronicle of Higher Education,* pp. 1, 4.

Binet, A., & Simon, T. (1916). *The development of intelligence in children,* trans. E. S. Kite. Baltimore: Williams & Wilkins.

Black, H. (1962). *They shall not pass.* New York: Morrow.

Blau, T. H. (1984). *The psychologist as expert witness.* New York: Wiley.

Block, J. (1977). Recognizing the coherence of personality. In D. Magnusson & N. S. Endler (eds.), *Interactional psychology: Current issues and future prospects.* New York: LEA/Wiley.

———. (1978). *The Q-sort method in personality assessment and psychiatric research.* Springfield, IL: Charles C Thomas.

———, et al. (1981). The cognitive style of breadth of categorization: Longitudinal consistency of personality correlates. *Journal of Personality and Social Psychology, 40,* 770–779.

Bloom, B. S., Hastings, J. T., & Madaus, G. F. (1971). *Handbook of formative and summative evaluation of student learning.* New York: McGraw-Hill.

———, & Krathwohl, D. R. (1956). *Taxonomy of educational objectives: Handbook I, The cognitive domain.* New York: David McKay.

Blumenstyk, G. (1990, Jan. 31). Federal court ruling that public disclosure of tests violates copyright law seen a blow to "truth in testing" movement. *Chronicle of Higher Education,* pp. A21, A25.

Blumenthal, J. A. (1985). Review of Jenkins Activity Survey. In J. V. Mitchell, Jr. (ed.), *The ninth mental measurements yearbook,* Vol. I, pp. 743–745. Lincoln, NE: Buros Institute of Mental Measurements of the University of Nebraska—Lincoln.

Bodner, G. M. (1980). Statistical analysis of multiple-choice exams. *Journal of Chemical Education, 57,* 188–190.

Bogardus, E. S. (1925). Measuring social distances. *Journal of Applied Sociology, 9,* 299–308.

Bolton, B. (1985). Work Values Inventory. In D. J. Keyser & R. C. Sweetland (eds.), *Test critiques,* Vol. II, pp. 835–843. Kansas City, MO: Test Corporation of American.

Borich, G. D., & Jemelka, R. P. (1981). *Programs and systems: An evaluation perspective.* New York: Academic Press.

Bourchard, T. J., Jr., et al. (1983, June). *Family resemblance for psychological interests.* Paper presented at meeting of International Congress on Twins Research, London.

Bowman, M. L. (1989). Testing individual differences in Ancient China. *American Psychologist, 44,* 576–578.

Bradley, R. H., & Caldwell, B. M. (1977). Home observation for measurement of the environment: A validation study of screening efficiency. *American Journal of Mental Deficiency, 81,* 417–420.

Brazelton, T. B. (1973). *Neonatal behavioral assessment scale.* Philadelphia: Lippincott.

Bricklin, B. (1984). *Bricklin Perceptual Scales.* Furlong, PA: Village.

Bridgman, C. S., & Hollenbeck, G. P. (1961). Effect of simulated applicant status on Kuder Form D occupational interest scores. *Journal of Applied Psychology, 45,* 237–239.

Brokaw, L. D. (1956). Technical school validity of the Airman Activity Inventory. *AFPTRC Development Report,* 56–109.

Brown, J., & Burton, R. R. (1978). Diagnostic models for procedural bugs in mathematical skills. *Cognition Science, 2,* 155–191.

Brown, W. R., & McGuire, J. M. (1976). Current psychological assessment practices. *Professional Psychology, 7,* 475–484.

Bruvold, W. H. (1975). Judgmental bias in the rating of attitude statements. *Educational and Psychological Measurement, 35,* 605–611.

Bukatman, B. A., Foy, J. L., & De Grazia, E. (1971). What is competency to stand trial? *American Journal of Psychiatry, 127,* 1225–1229.

Burket, G. R. (1973). Empirical criteria for distinguishing and validating aptitude and achievement measures. In D. R. Green (ed.), *The aptitude–achievement distinction.* Monterey, CA: CTB/McGraw-Hill.

Buros, O. K. (ed.) (1970). *Personality tests and reviews.* Highland Park, NJ: Gryphon Press.

———. (ed.) (1975a). *Reading tests and reviews II.* Highland Park, NJ: Gryphon Press.

———. (ed.) (1975b). *Vocational tests and reviews.* Highland Park, NJ: Gryphon Press.

———. (ed.) (1978). *The eighth measurements yearbook,* Vols. 1 and 2. Highland Park, NJ: Gryphon Press.

Buss, A. H., & Plomin, R. (1975). *A temperament theory of personality development.* New York: Wiley.

———, & ———. (1984). *Temperament: Early developing personality traits.* Hillsdale, NJ: Erlbaum.

Butcher, J. N. (1978). Automated MMPI interpretative systems. In O. K. Buros (ed.), *The eighth mental measurements yearbook,* pp. 942–945. Highland Park, NJ: Gryphon.

Campbell, D. P., & Fiske, D. W. (1959). Convergent and discriminant validation by the multitrait–multimethod matrix. *Psychological Bulletin, 56,* 81–105.

———, & Hansen, J. C. (1981). *Manual for the Strong–Campbell Interest Inventory,* 3rd ed. Stanford, CA: Stanford University Press.

Cannell, J. J. (1988). Nationally normed elementary school testing in America's public schools: How all 50 states are testing above the national average (with commentaries). *Educational Measurement Issues and Practice, 7*(1), 3–24.

———, (1989). *The Lake Wobegon Report: How public educators cheat on achievement tests.* Albuquerque, NM: Friends for Education.

Carroll, J. B. (1973). The aptitude–achievement distinction: The case of foreign language aptitude and proficiency. In D. R. Green (ed.), *The aptitude–achievement distinction.* Monterey, CA: CTB/McGraw-Hill.

Carter, H. D. (1962). How reliable are good oral examinations? *California Journal of Educational Research, 13,* 147–153.

Carver, R. P. (1974). Two dimensions of tests: Psychometric and edumetric. *American Psychologist, 29,* 512–518.

Cassell, R. N., & Blum, L. P. (1970). *Computer Assist Counseling (COASCON) for the prevention of delinquent behavior among teenagers and youth.* Milwaukee: Department of Educational Psychology, University of Wisconsin—Milwaukee.

Castro, J. G., & Jordan, J. E. (1977). Facet theory attitude research. *Educational Researcher, 6,* 7–11.

Cautela, J. R., & Upper, D. (1976). The Behavioral Inventory Battery: The use of self-report measures in behavioral analysis and therapy. In M. Hersen & A. S. Bellack (eds.), *Behavioral analysis: A practical handbook,* pp. 27–109. New York: Pergamon.

Chaplin, W. F., & Goldberg, L. R. (1984). A failure to replicate the Bem and Allen study of individual differences in cross-situational consistency. *Journal of Personality & Social Psychology, 47,* 1074–1090.

Chase, C. I. (1964). Relative length of option and response in multiple-choice items. *Educational and Psychological Measurement, 24,* 861–866.

Chauncey, H., & Dobbin, J. E. (1963). *Testing: Its place in education today.* New York: Harper & Row.

Choppin, B. (1975). Guessing the answer on objective tests. *British Journal of Educational Psychology, 45,* 206–213.

Chun, K. T., Cobb, S., & French, J. R. P. (1976). *Measures for psychological assessment.* Ann Arbor, MI: Institute for Social Research, University of Michigan.

Ciminero, A. R., Calhoun, K. S., & Adams, H. E. (eds.) (1986). *Handbook of behavioral assessment,* 2nd ed. New York: Wiley.

———, Nelson, R. O., & Lipinski, D. P. (1977). Self-monitoring procedures. In A. R. Ciminero, K. S. Calhoun, & H. E. Adams (eds.), *Handbook of behavioral assessment.* New York: Wiley.

Cole, N. S. (1973). Bias in selection. *Journal of Educational Measurement, 10,* 237–255.

———, & Moss, P. A. (1989). Bias in test tube. In R. L. Linn (ed.), *Educational measurement,* 3rd ed., pp. 201–219. New York: Mcmillan.

College Entrance Examination Board (1971). *Report of the Commission on Tests.* New York: Author.

Company expects to prosper finding cheaters (1988, Dec. 12). *Los Angeles Times,* p. IV-7.

Comrey, A. L., Bacher, T. E., & Glaser, F. M. (1973). *A source book for mental health measures.* Los Angeles: Human Interaction Research Institute.

Conoley, J. C., & Kramer, J. J. (eds.) (1989). *The tenth mental measurements yearbook.* Lincoln: Buros Institute of Mental Measurements, University of Nebraska—Lincoln.

Cooley, W. W., & Lohnes, P. R. (1968). *Predicting development of young adults.* Project TALENT Five-Year Follow-up Studies. Interim Report 5. American Institutes for Research. Washington, DC: U.S. Office of Education.

Cordes, C. (1986, June). Test tilt: Boys outscore girls on both parts of the SAT. *APA Monitor,* pp. 30–31.

Costa, P. T., Jr., & McCrae, R. R. (1986). Personality stability and its implications for clinical psychology. *Clinical Psychology Review, 6,* 407–423.

Crites, J. O. (1969). Interests. In R. L. Ebel (ed.), *Encyclopedia of educational research,* 4th ed., pp. 678–686. New York: Macmillan.

Cronbach, L. J. (1951). Coefficient alpha and the internal structure of tests. *Psychometrika, 16,* 297–334.

———. (1970). *Essentials of psychological testing,* 3rd ed. New York: Harper & Row.

———, & Meehl, P. E. (1955). Construct validity in psychological tests. *Psychological Bulletin, 52,* 281–302.

———, et al. (1972). *The dependability of behavioral measurements.* New York: Wiley.

Crowl, T. K., & McGinitie, W. H. (1974). The influence of student's speech characteristics on teachers' evaluations of oral answers. *Journal of Educational Psychology, 66,* 304–308.

Dana, R. H. (1984). Personality assessment: Practice and teaching for the next decade. *Journal of Personality Assessment, 48,* 46–56.

Darley, J. B., & Hagenah, T. (1955). *Vocational interest measurement.* Minneapolis: University of Minnesota Press.

David, P. (1981, Nov. 27). Multiple-choice tests under fire: United States: *Times Education Supplement,* 3413: 11.

Davidshofer, C. (1985). Review of Jackson Vocational Interest Survey. In J. V. Mitchell, Jr. (ed.), *The ninth mental measurements yearbook,* Vol. I, pp. 739–740. Lincoln, NE: Buros Institute of Mental Measurements of the University of Nebraska—Lincoln.

Dawes, R. M. (1986). Representative thinking in clinical judgment. *Clinical Psychology Review, 6,* 425–442.

Day, K. (1985, Aug. 13). MBA entrance examinations likely to stay. *Los Angeles Times,* p. IV-2.

Debra v. *Turlington,* 644 F.2d 397 (1981); 730F.2d 1406 (1984).

Denton, L. (1988, August). Board votes to oppose Golden Rule technique. *The APA Monitor,* p. 7.

Department of Health and Human Services (1993, May 19). *Monthly vital statistics report.* Births, marriages, divorces and deaths for 1992. Washington, DC: Author.

Diamond, E. E. (1979). Sex equality and measurement practices. *New Directions for Testing and Measurement, 3,* 61–78.

Diana v. *State Board of Education,* C-70 37 RFT (N.D. Cal 1970).

Diekhoff, G. M. (1984). True–false tests that measure and promote structured understanding. *Teaching of Psychology, 11,* 99–101.

Disbrow, M. A., Doerr, H. O., & Caulfield, C. (1977, March). *Measures to predict child abuse.* Final report of Grant MC-R530351, Maternal and Child Health. Washington, DC: National Institute of Mental Health.

Dolliver, R. H., Irivin, J. A., & Bigley, S. E. (1972). Twelve-year follow-up of the Strong Vocational Interest Blank. *Journal of Counseling Psychology, 19,* 212–217.

Donahue, D., & Sattler, J. M. (1971). Personality variables affecting WAIS scores. *Journal of Consulting and Clinical Psychology, 36,* 441.

Doyle, D. P., & Hartle, T. W. (1985, June 4). Toward a national teachers' test. *Los Angeles Times,* p. II-5.

Doyle, K. O., Jr. (1974). Theory and practice of ability testing in Ancient Greece. *Journal of the History of the Behavioral Sciences, 10,* 202–212.

DuBois, P. H. (1970). *The History of psychological testing.* Boston: Allyn & Boston.

Duckworth, D., & Entwhistle, N. J. (1974). Attitudes to school subjects: A repertory grid technique. *British Journal of Educational Psychology, 44,* 76–83.

Dunnette, M. D. (1963). Critics of psychological tests: Basic assumptions; how good? *Psychology in the Schools, 1,* 63–69.

———, & Borman, W. C. (1979). Personnel selection and classification systems. *Annual Review of Psychology, 30,* 477–525.

Durham, v. *United States,* 214 F.2d 862 (D.C. Cir. 1954).

Dusky v. *United States,* 362 U.S. 402. (Apr. 18, 1960).

Dworkin, R. H., et al. (1976). A longitudinal study of the genetics of personality. *Journal of Personality and Social Psychology, 34,* 510–518.

Ebel, R. L. (1965). *Measuring educational achievement.* Englewood Cliffs, NJ: Prentice Hall.

———. (1970). The case for true–false test items. *School Review, 78,* 373–389.

———. (1979). *Essentials of educational measurement,* 3rd ed. Englewood Cliffs, NJ: Prentice-Hall.

Educational Testing Service (1965). *ETS builds a test.* Princeton, NJ: Author.

———. (1980a). *Test use and validity. A response to charges in the Nader/Nairn Report on ETS.* Princeton, NJ: Author.

———. (1980b). *Test scores and family income. A response to charges in the Nader/Nairn report on ETS.* Princeton, NJ: Author.

———. (1992). *What we can learn from performance assessment for the professions.* ETS Conference on Education and Assessment. Princeton, NJ: Author.

Edwards, A. J. (1974). *Individual mental testing, Part I: History and theories* Scranton, PA: Intext Educational Publishers.

Edwards, A. L. (1954). *Manual—Edwards Personal Preference* Schedule. New York: The Psychological Corporation.

———. (1957). *Techniques of attitude scale construction.* New York: Appleton-Century-Crofts.

Elam, S. M. (ed.). (1978). *A decade of Gallup polls of attitudes toward education: 1969–1978.* Bloomington, IN: Phi Delta Kappa.

Elwood, D. L., & Griffin, H. R. (1972). Individual intelligence testing without the examiner: Reliability of an automated method. *Journal of Consulting and Clinical Psychology, 38,* 9–14.

Embretson, S. E. (1987). Toward development of a psychometric approach. In C. S. Lidz (ed.), *Dynamic assessment: An interactive approach to evaluating learning potential,* pp. 135–164. New York: Guilford Press.

Engel, J. F., Blackwell, R. D., & Miniard, P. W. (1989). *Consumer behavior,* 4th ed. Chicago: Dryden.

Equal Employment Opportunity Commission (1973, Aug. 23). *The uniform guidelines on employee selection procedures.* Discussion draft. Washington, DC: Author.

———, Civil Service Commission, Department of Labor and Department of Justice (1978). Adoption by four agencies of Uniform Guidelines on Employee Selection Procedures. *Federal Register, 43*(166), 38290–38315.

Erdman, P. E., Klein, M. J., & Greist, H. (1985). Direct patient computer interviewing. *Journal of Consulting and Clinical Psychology, 53,* 760–773.

Eron, L. (1950). A normative study of the TAT. *Psychological Monographs, 64* (Whole No. 315).

Evangelauf, J. (1989, Feb. 15). Critics and defenders of admission tests eye court's limit on use. *Chronicle of Higher Eduction,* pp. A1, A32.

Evans, W. (1984). Test wiseness: An examination of cue-using strategies. *Journal of Experimental Education, 52,* 141–144.

Exner, J. E. (1978). *The Rorschach: A comprehensive system. Volume II. Current research and advanced interpretation.* New York: Wiley.

———. (1986). *The Rorschach: A comprehensive system,* Vol. 1, 2nd ed. New York: Wiley.

———, & Weiner, I. B. (1982). *The Rorschach: A comprehensive system.* New York: Wiley.

Eyde, L., & Kowal, D. (1984). Ethical and professional concerns regarding computerized test interpretation services and users. In J. D. Matarazzo (chair), *The use of computer-based test interpretations: Progress in clinical psychology,* Vol. 4, pp. 46–64. New York: Grune & Stratton.

———, et al., (in press). *Responsible test use: Case studies for assessing human behavior.* Washington, DC: American Psychological Association.

Eysenck, H. J. (1956). The inheritance of extraversion–introversion. *Acta Psychologica, 12,* 95–110.

———. (1962). Conditioning and personality. *British Journal of Psychology, 53,* 299–305.

———. (1965). The effects of psychotherapy. *International Journal of Psychiatry, 1,* 97–178.

———. (ed.). (1981) *A model for personality.* New York: Springer.

————, & Rachman, S. (1965). *The causes of neurosis.* San Diego: Robert R. Knapp.

Feldman, M. J., & Corah, N. L. (1960). Social desirability and the forced choice method. *Journal of Consulting Psychology, 24,* 480–482.

Feuerstein, R., et al. (1987). Prerequisites for assessment of learning potential: The LPAD model. In C. S. Lidz (ed.), *Dynamic assessment: An interactive approach to evaluating learning potential,* pp. 35–51. New York: Guilford Press.

Fewer firms testing employee literacy (1992, Aug. 12). *Los Angeles Times,* p. D-5.

Fields, C. M. (1980, June 9). SAT score improvements laid to "motivation." *Chronicle of Higher Education, 20*(15), 4.

————. (1988, Nov. 30). Critics question validity of standardized tests for would-be teachers. *Chronicle of Higher Education, 20*(15), 4.

Fish, L. J. (1941). *One hundred years of examinations in Boston.* Dedham, MA: Transcript Press.

Flanagan, J. C. (1954). The critical incident technique. *Psychological Bulletin, 51,* 327–358.

————, Tiedeman, D. V., & Willis, M. G. (1973). *The career data book.* Palo Alto, CA: American Institutes for Research.

Fleishman, E. A. (1954). Dimensional analysis of psychomotor abilities. *Journal of Experimental Psychology, 48,* 437–454.

————. (1972). On the relation between abilities, learning, and human performance. *American Psychologist, 27,* 1017–1032.

Fletcher, C. R. (1972). How not to interview an elderly clinic patient: A case illustration and the interviewer's explanation. *Gerontologist, 12,* 398–402.

Florida skills test upheld. (1983, May 5). *Los Angeles Times,* pp. 1–2.

Forer, B. R. (1949). The fallacy of personal validation: A classroom demonstration of gullibility. *Journal of Abnormal and Social Psychology, 44,* 118–123.

Fowler, R. D. (1969). Automated interpretation of personality test data. In J. N. Butcher (ed.), *MMP, I Research developments and clinical applications,* pp. 105–125. New York: McGraw-Hill.

Frankenberger, W. (1984). A survey of state guidelines for identification of mental retardation. *Mental Retardation, 22,* 17–20.

Franklin, M. R., & Stillman, P. L. (1982). Examiner error in intelligence testing: Are you a source? *Psychology in the Schools, 19,* 563–569.

Frederiksen, N. (1976). Toward a taxonomy of situations. In N. S. Endler & D. Magnusson (eds.) *Interactional psychology and personality.* Washington, DC: Hemisphere Publishing.

Freiberg, P., & DeAngelis, T. (1992, March). High court to review ruling on hiring tests. *APA Monitor,* pp. 1, 8.

Fremer, J., Diamond, E. E., & Camara, W. J. (1989). Developing a code of fair testing practices in education. *American Psychologist, 44,* 1062–1067.

French, J. W. (1961). Aptitude and interest score patterns related to satisfaction with college major field. *Educational and Psychological Measurement, 21,* 287–294.

Freud, S. (1905, reprinted 1959). Fragment of an analysis of a case of hysteria. In *Collected papers,* Vol. 3. New York: Basic books.

Funder, D. C., & Colvin, C.R. (1991). Some behaviors are more predictable than others. *The Score* (Newsletter of Division 5 of the American Psychological Association), *13*(4), 3–4.

Funkenstein, D. H., King, S. H., & Drolette, M. E. (1957). *Mastery of stress.* Cambridge, MA: Harvard University Press.

Gallup, G. (1979). *The Gallup Poll: Public opinion.* Washington, DC: Scholarly Resources.

Galton, F. (1879). Psychometric experiments. *Brain, 2,* 149–162.

Gardner, P. L. (1975). Attitude measurement: A critique of some recent research. *Educational Research, 17,* 101–109.

Gedye, J. L., & Miller, E. (1969). The automation of psychological assessment. *International Journal of Man–Machine Studies, 1,* 237–262.

Georgia State Conferences of Branches of NAACP v. State of Georgia, Eleventh Circuit Court of Appeals, No. 84-8771 (1985).

Gerlach, V. S., & Sullivan, H. J. (1967). *Constructing statements of outcomes.* Inglewood, CA: Southwest Laboratory for Educational Research & Development.

Gerow, J. R. (1980). Performance on achievement tests as a function of the order of item difficulty. *Teaching of Psychology, 7,* 93–94.

Gesell, A., & Amatruda, C. S. (1941). *Developmental diagnosis.* New York: Paul B. Hoeber.

Getzels, J. W., & Jackson, P. W. (1962). *Creativity and intelligence: Explorations with gifted students.* New York: Wiley.

Ghiselli, E. E. (1973). The validity of aptitude tests in personnel selection. *Personnel Psychology, 26,* 461–477.

Giannetti, R. A. (1987). The GOLPH psychosocial history: Response-contingent data acquisition and reporting. In J. N. Butcher (ed.), *Computerized psychological assessment,* pp. 124–144. New York: Basic Books.

Gibb, B. (1964). Test-wiseness as secondary cue response. (Doctoral dissertation, Stanford University). Ann Arbor, MI: *University Microfilms,* No. 64-7643.

Glaser, R. (1981). The future of testing: A research agenda for cognitive psychology and psychometrics. *American Psychologist, 36,* 923–936.

———. (1985). The integration of instruction and testing. In *The redesign of testing for the 21st century,* pp. 69–79. Princeton, NJ: Educational Testing Service.

Glass, D. C., & Carver, C. S. (1980). Helplessness and the coronary-prone personality. In. J. Garber & M. E. P. Seligman (eds.), *Human helplessness.* New York: Academic Press.

Glennon, J. R., Albright, L. E., & Owens, W. A. (1966). *A catalog of life history items.* Washington, DC: American Psychological Association, Richardson Foundation for the Scientific Affairs Committee, Division 14.

Glovrozov, P. A. (1974, July). Testing pupils orally. *Soviet Education, 16,* 95–105.

Glueck, B. C., & Reznikoff, M. (1965). Comparison of computer-derived personality profile and projective psychological test findings. *American Journal of Psychiatry, 121,* 1156–1161.

Goldberg, L. R. (1970). Man vs. model of man: A rationale, plus some evidence, for a method of improving on clinical inferences. *Psychological Bulletin, 73,* 422–432.

———. (1980, April). *Some ruminations about the structure of individual differences: Developing a common lexicon for the major characteristics of human personality.* Paper presented at the annual meeting of the Western Psychological Association, Honolulu, HI.

Goldberg, P. (1965). A review of sentence completion methods in personality assessment. *Journal of Projective Techniques and Personality Assessment, 29,* 12–45.

Goldman, B. A. & Busch, J. C. (eds.) (1978). *Directory of unpublished experimental mental measures,* Vol. 2. New York: Human Sciences Press.

———, & ———. (eds.). (1982). *Directory of unpublished experimental mental measurements,* Vol. 3. New York: Human Sciences Press.

———, & Mitchell, D. F. (eds.) (1990). *Directory of unpublished experimental mental measurements,* Vol. 5. Dubuque, IA: William C. Brown.

———, & Osborne, W. L. (eds.). (1985). *Directory of unpublished mental measurements,* Vol. 4. New York: Human Sciences Press.

———, & Saunders, J. L. (eds.) (1974). *Directory of unpublished experimental mental measures,* Vol. 1. New York: Human Sciences Press.

Gordon, E. (1967). *A three-year longitudinal predictive validity study of the Musical Aptitude Profile. Studies in the psychology of music,* Vol. 5. Iowa City: University of Iowa Press.

Gordon, R., & Peck, L. A. (1989). *The Custody Quotient.* Dallas, TX: Willington Institute.

Gorham, D. R., Moseley, E. C., & Holtzman, W. W. (1968). Norms for the computer-scored Holtman Inkblot Technique. *Perceptual and Motor Skills Monograph Supplement, 26,* 1279–1305.

Goslin, D. A. (1967). *Teachers and testing.* New York: Russell Sage Foundation.

Gottesman, I. I. (1966). Genetic variance in adaptive personality traits. *Journal of Child Psychology and Psychiatry. 7,* 199–208.

———, & Shields, J. (1973). *Schizophrenia and genetics: A twin study vantage point.* New York: Academic Press.

———, & ———. (1982). *Schizophrenia: The epigenetic puzzle.* New York: Cambridge University Press.

Gottfredson, G. D., Holland, J. L., & Gottfredson, L. S. (1975). The relation of vocational aspirations and assessments to employment reality. *Journal of Vocational Behavior, 7,* 135–148.

Graham, F. K., & Kendall, B. S. (1960). Memory-for-Designs Test: Revised general manual (Monograph). *Perceptual and Motor Skills, 11,* 147–188.

Graham, G. (1963). Denmark's oral examination. *Education, 83,* 306–309.

Grant, D., & Reed, R. (1982). Neuropsychological testing. In W. C. Wiederholt (ed.), *Neurology for non-neurologists,* pp. 143–155. New York: Academic Press.

Green, B. F., et al. (1982). *Evaluation plan for the computerized Adaptive Vocational Aptitude Battery.* Report ONR-RR-82-1, Contract N000114-80-K-304, Office of Naval Research. Arlington, VA: Personnel and Training Research Programs Office. ERIC Document Reproduction Service No. ED 220 497.

Green, J. A. (1975). *Teacher-made tests,* 2nd ed., pp. 122–135. New York: Harper & Row.

Green, K. (1984). Effects of item characteristics on multiple-choice item difficulty. *Educational and Psychological Measurement, 44,* 551–561.

Greene, H. A., Jorgensen, A. N., & Gerberich, J. R. (1954). *Measurement and evaluation in secondary school,* 2nd ed. New York: David McKay.

Gregory, R. J. (1992). *Psychological testing: History, principles, and applications.* Boston: Allyn & Bacon.

Greist, J. H., & Klein, M. H. (1980). Computer programs for patients, clinicians, and researchers in psychiatry. In J. B. Sidowski, J. H. Johnson, & T. A. Williams (eds.), *Technology in modern health care delivery systems,* pp. 161–182. Norwood, NJ: Ablex.

Griggs et al. v. *Duke Power Company.* 401 U.S. 424, 3FEP175 (1971).

Gross, M. L. (1962). *The brain watchers.* New York: Random House.

———. (1965). Testimony before House Special Committee on Invasion of Privacy of the Committee on Government Operations. *American Psychologist, 20,* 958–960.

Grotevant, H. D., Scarr, S., & Weinberg, R. A. (1977). Patterns of interest similarity in adoptive and biological families. *Journal of Personality and Social Psychology, 35,* 667–676.

Guadalupe v. *Tempe Elementary School District,* Stipulation and Order (January 24, 1972).

Guilford, J. P. (1940). *An inventory of factors.* Beverly Hills, CA: Sheridan Supply.

———. (1954). A factor analytic study across the domains of reasoning, creativity, and evaluation. I. Hypothesis and description of tests. *Reports from the Psychology Laboratory.* Los Angeles: University of Southern California.

———. (1967). *The nature of human intelligence.* New York: McGraw-Hill.

———. (1974). *Structure-of-Intellect Abilities.* Orange, CA: Sheridan Psychological Services.

———, & Martin, H. G. (1943). *The Guilford–Martin Inventory of Factors (GAMIN): Manual of directions and norms.* Beverly Hills, CA: Sheridan Supply.

Guttman, L. (1944). A basis for scaling quantitative data. *American Sociological Review, 9,* 139–150.

Gynther, M. D., & Green, S. B. (1980). Accuracy may make a difference, but does a difference make for accuracy? *Journal of Consulting and Clinical Psychology, 48,* 268–272.

————, & Gynther, R. A. (1976). Personality inventories. In I. B. Weiner (ed.), *Clinical methods in psychology.* New York: Wiley.

Hacker, H. K. (1991, June 6). Adjusted federal employment tests stir controversy. *Los Angeles Times,* p. A-5.

Hager, P. (1991, Oct. 29). Court bans psychological tests in hiring. *Los Angeles Times,* p. A-20.

Hall, H. V. (1987). *Violence prediction: Guidelines for the forensic practitioner.* Springfield, IL: Charles C Thomas.

Hamersma, R. J., Paige, J., & Jordan, J. E. (1973). Construction of a Guttman facet design cross-cultural attitude-behavior scale toward racial–ethnic interaction. *Educational and Psychological Measurement, 33,* 565–576.

Haney, D. A. (1985, Feb. 3). Creative people: Their inner drive awes researchers. *Los Angeles Times,* I-2, 9.

Hanna, G. S. & Johnson, P. R,. (1978) Reliability and validity of multiple-choice tests developed by four distractor selection procedures. *Journal of Educational Research, 71,* 203–206.

Hansen, Jo-Ida C., & Campbell, D. P. (1985). *Manual for the SVIB-SCII,* 4th ed. Stanford, CA: Stanford University Press.

Harrington, R. G. (ed.) (1986). *Testing adolescents.* Kansas City, MO: Test Corporation of America.

Harrison, P. L. et al. (1988). A survey of tests used for adult assessment. *Journal of Psychoeducational Assessment, 6,* 188–198.

Harrow, A. J. (1972). *A taxonomy of the psychomotor domain: A guide for developing behavioral objectives.* New York: David McKay.

Hartke, A. R. (1979). Development of conceptually independent subscales in the measurement of attitudes. *Educational and Psychological Measurement, 39,* 585–592.

Hartshorne, H., & May, M. A. (1928). *Studies in the nature of character. Vol. 1: Studies in deceit.* New York: Macmillan.

Hathaway, S. R., & McKinley, J. C. (1989). *MMPI–2.* Minneapolis: University of Minnesota Press.

Haynes, S. N. (1984) Computer-assisted assessment. In R. J. Corsini (ed.), *Encyclopedia of psychology,* pp. 263–264. New York: Wiley.

————. (1990). Behavioral assessment of adults. In G. Goldstein & M. Hersen (eds.), *Handbook of psychological assessment,* 2nd ed. pp. 423–463. New York: Pergamon.

————, & Wilson, C. C. (1979). *Behavioral assessment.* San Francisco: Jossey-Bass.

Herr, E., & Best, P. (1984). Computer technology and counseling: The role of the professional. *Journal of Counseling and Development, 63,* 192–195.

Hersen, M., & Bellack, A. S. (eds.) (1982). *Behavioral assessment: A practical handbook,* 2nd ed. New York: Pergamon.

Hitchman, P. J. (1966, Feb.). The validity and reliability of tests of spoken English. *British Journal of Educational Psychology, 36,* 15–23.

Hobson v. *Hansen,* 269 F. Suppl. 401 (D.D.C. 1967).

Hoffman, B. (1962). *The tyranny of testing.* New York: Crowell-Collier.

Holland, J. L. (1985). *Making vocational choices: A theory of careers: A theory of vocational personalities and work environments,* 2nd ed. Englewood Cliffs, NJ: Prentice Hall.

Hollingworth, L. S. (1942). *Children above 180 IQ.* New York: Harcourt, Brace, Jovanovich

Holman, R. (1984). A values and lifestyles perspective on human behavior. In R. E. Pitts & A. G. Woodside (eds.), *Personal values and consumer psychology,* pp. 35–54. Lexington, MA: Lexington Books.

Holroyd, K. A. (1979). Stress, coping, and the treatment of stress-related illness. In J. R. McNamara (ed.), *Behavioral approaches to medicine: Applications and analysis.* New York: Plenum.

Holt, A. (1974). *Handwriting in psychological interpretations.* Springfield, IL: Charles C Thomas.

Holt, R. R. (1970). Yet another look at clinical and statistical prediction: Or, is clinical psychology worthwhile? *American Psychologist, 25,* 337–349.

Hsu, T.-C., Moss, P. A., & Khampalikit, C. (1984). The merits of multiple-answer items as evaluated by using six scoring formulas. *Journal of Experimental Education, 52,* 152–158.

Hughes, H. H., & Converse, H. D. (1962). Characteristics of the gifted: A case for a sequel to Terman's study. *Exceptional Children, 29,* 179–183.

Jackson, D. N. (1971). The dynamics of structured personality tests. *Psychological Review, 78,* 229–148.

Jacobson, R. L. (1986, July 2). Selective colleges' use of SAT is unshaken by controversy. *Chronicle of Higher Education,* p. 8.

———. (1993, June 16). Researcher finds admissions tests vulnerable to attempts by students to answer "passageless" reading questions. *The Chronicle of Higher Education,* pp. A33–34.

Jamison, K. R. (1984). Manic-depressive illness and accomplishment: Creativity, leadership, and social class. In F. K. Goodwin & K. R. Jamison (eds.), *Manic-depressive illness.* New York: Oxford University Press.

Jenkins, C. D., Zyzanski, S. J., & Rosenman, R. H. (1979). *Jenkins Activity Survey: Manual.* New York: The Psychological Corporation.

Jensen, A. R. (1969). How much can we boost IQ and scholastic achievement? *Harvard Educational Review, 39,* 1–123.

———. (1980). *Bias in mental testing.* New York: Free Press.

Jessell, J. C., & Sullins, W. L. (1975). Effect of keyed response sequencing of multiple-choice items on performance and reliability. *Journal of Educational Measurement, 12,* 45–48.

Johannson, C. B. (1984). *Manual for Career Assessment Inventory,* 2nd ed. Minneapolis, MN: National Computer Systems.

Johnson, J. H., & Williams, T. A.(1975). The use of on-line computer technology in a mental health admitting system. *American Psychologist, 3,* 388–390.

———, Giannetti, R. A. & Williams, T. A. (1978). A self-contained microcomputer system for psychological testing. *Behavior Research Methods and Instrumentation, 10,* 579–581.

Johnson, O. G. (1976). *Tests and measurements in child development: Handbook II.* San Francisco: Jossey-Bass.

———, & Bommarito, J. W. (1971). *Tests and measurements in child development.* San Francisco: Jossey-Bass.

Jordan, J. E. (1971). Construction of a Guttman facet designed cross-cultural attitude-behavior scale toward mental retardation. *American Journal of Mental Deficiency, 76,* 201–219.

Jung, C. G. (1910). The association method. *American Journal of Psychology, 21,* 219–269.

Kagan, J. (1966). Reflective-impulsivity: The generality and dynamics of conceptual tempo. *Journal of Abnormal Psychology, 71,* 17–24.

———, et al. (1964). Information processing in the child: Significance of analytic and reflective attitudes. *Psychological Monographs, 78* (Whole No. 578).

Kahle, L. R., Beatty, S. F., & Homer, P. (1986). Alternative measurement approaches to consumer values: The List of Values (LOV) and Values and Life Style (VALS). *Journal of Consumer Research, 13,* 405–409.

Kallman, F. J., & Jarvik, L. (1959). Individual differences in constitution and genetic background. In J. E. Birren (ed.), *Handbook of aging and the individual.* Chicago: University of Chicago Press.

Kansup, W., & Hakstian, A. R. (1975). Comparison of several methods of assessing partial knowledge in multiple-choice tests: Scoring procedures. *Journal of Educational Measurement, 12,* 219–230.

Kapes, J. T., Borman, C. A., & Frazier, N. (1989). An evaluation of the SIGI and Discover microcomputer-based career guidance systems. *Measurement and Evaluation in Counseling and Development, 22,* 126–136.

Kaplan, H. I., & Sadock, B. J. (1989). *Comprehensive textbook of psychiatry,* No. V. Baltimore: Williams & Wilkins.

Karier, C. J. (1972). Testing for order and control in the liberal corporate state. *Educational Theory, 22,* 154–180.

Karson, D., & O'Dell, J. W. (1976). *A guide to the clinical use of the 16PF.* Champaign, IL: Institute for Personality and Ability Testing.

Keating, D. P. (ed.) (1976). *Intellectual talent: Research and development.* Baltimore: Johns Hopkins University Press.

Kelly, E. L., & Fiske, D. W. (1951). *The prediction of performance in clinical psychology.* Ann Arbor: University of Michigan Press.

Kelly, G. A. (1955). *The psychology of personal constructs.* New York: Norton.

Kendall, P. C., & Korgeski, G. P. (1979). Assessment and cognitive–behavioral interventions. *Cognitive Therapy and Research, 1,* 1–21.

———, & Norton-Ford, J. D. (1982). *Clinical psychology: Scientific and professional dimensions.* New York: Wiley.

Kenrick, D. T., & Dantchik, A. (1983). Interactionism, idiographics, and the social psychological invasion of personality. *Journal of Personality, 51,* 286–307.

Keyser, D. J., & Sweetland, R. C. (eds.) (1984–1988). *Test critiques,* (Vols. I–VII). Austin, TX: pro-ed, Inc.

Kidd, J. W. (1983). The 1983 A.A.M.D. definition and classification of mental retardation: The apparent impact of the CEC-MR position. *Education and Training of the Mentally Retarded, 18,* 243–244.

Kirkpatrick, J. J., et al. (1968). *Testing and fair employment: Fairness and validity of personnel tests for different ethnic groups.* New York: New York University Press.

Kleinmuntz, B. (1982). *Personality and psychological assessment.* New York: St. Martin's Press.

———, & McLean, R. S. (1968). Diagnostic interviewing by digital computer. *Behavioral Science, 13,* 75–87.

Klimko, I. P. (1984). Item arrangement, cognitive entry characteristics, sex, and test anxiety as predictors of achievement examination performance. *Journal of Experimental Education, 52,* 214–219.

Knobloch, H., & Pasamanick, B. (eds.) (1974). *Gesell and Amatruda's developmental diagnosis,* 3rd ed. New York: Harper & Row.

Kohlberg, L. (1969). Stage and sequence: The cognitive-developmental approach to socialization. In D. Goslin (ed.), *Handbook of socialization: Theory and research.* Chicago: Rand McNally.

———. (1974). The development of moral stages: Uses and abuses. *Proceedings of the 1973 Invitational Conference on Testing Problems,* pp. 1–8. Princeton, NJ: Educational Testing Service.

———, & Elfenbein, D. (1975). The development of moral judgments concerning capital punishment. *American Journal of Orthopsychiatry, 45,* 614–639.

Koppitz, E. M. (1975). *The Bender Gestalt Test for young children. Research and application, 1963–1973.* New York: Grune & Stratton.

Kramer, J. J., & Conoley, J. (1992). *The eleventh mental measurements yearbook.* Lincoln: Buros Institute of Mental Measurements, University of Nebraska—Lincoln.

Krathwohl, D. R., Bloom, B. S., & Masia, B. B. (1964). *Taxonomy of educational objectives: Handbook II, The affective domain.* New York: David McKay.

Kretschmer, E. (1925). *Physique and character.* New York: Harcourt, Brace Jovamorich.

Krug, S. E. (ed.). (1988–1989). *Psychware sourcebook,* 3rd ed. Austin, TX: pro-ed, Inc.

Kuder, G. F. (1963). A rationale for evaluating interests. *Educational and Psychological Measurement, 23,* 3–12.

Lake, D. G., Miles, M. B., & Earle, R. B. (1973). *Measuring human behavior: Tools for the assessment of social functioning.* New York: Teachers College Press.

Landers, S. (1989, Dec.). Test score controversy continues. *APA, Monitor,* p. 10.

Langevin, R. (1983). *Sexual strands: Understanding and treating sexual anomalies in men.* Hillsdale, NJ: Erlbaum.

Lanyon, R. I. (1984). Personality assessment. *Annual Review of Psychology, 35,* 667–701.

———. (1986). Psychological assessment procedures in court-related settings. *Professional Psychology: Research and Practice, 17,* 260–268.

Larry P. v. *Riles,* 495 F. Supp. 926(N.D. Cal. 1979), appeal docketed, No. 80-4027 (9th Cir., Jan. 17, 1980).

Lastovicka, J. L., et al. (1987). A lifestyle typology to model young male drinking and driving. *Journal of Consumer Research, 14,* 257–263.

Lawrence, G. H. (1986). Using computers for the statement of psychological problems. *Computers in Human Behavior, 2,* 43–62.

Lazarsfeld, P. F. (1957). *Latent structure analysis.* New York: Bureau of Applied Social Research, Columbia University.

Lenke, J. M. (1988, Apr.). Controversy fueled by district and state reports of achievement test results. . . "Lake Wobegon—or Not?" *The Score,* pp. 5, 13 (Newsletter of Division 5 of the American Psychological Association).

Levine, H. G., & McGuire, C. H. (1970). Validity and reliability of oral examinations in assessing cognitive skills in medicine. *Journal of Educational Measurement, 7,* 63–74.

Levine, M. (1976). The academic achievement test: Its historical context and social functions. *American Psychologist, 31,* 228–238.

Levy, P., & Goldstein, H. (1984). *Tests in education: A book of critical reviews.* New York: Academic Press.

Lewis, M., & McGurk, H. (1972). Evaluation of infant intelligence: Infant intelligence scores— true of false? *Science, 1178*(4066), 1174–1177.

Lindeman, R. H., & Merenda, P. F. (1979). *Educational measurement,* 2nd ed. Glenview, IL: Scott, Foresman.

Linden, K. W., & Linden, J. P. (1968). *Modern mental measurement: A historical perspective.* Boston: Houghton Mifflin.

Lindzey, G. (1965). Seer versus sign. *Journal of Experimental Research on Personality, 1,* 17–26.

Linn, R. L. (1973). Fair test use in selection. *Review of Educational Research, 43,* 139–161.

———. (1982). Admissions testing on trial. *American Psychologist, 37,* 279–291.

Lipsitt, P. D., Lelos, D., & McGarry, A. L. (1971). Competency for trial: A screening instrument. *American Journal of Psychiatry, 128,* 105–109.

Little, E. B. (1962). Overcorrection for guessing in multiple-choice test scoring. *Journal of Educational Research, 55,* 245–252.

———. (1966). Overcorrection and undercorrection in multiple-choice test scoring. *Journal of Experimental Education, 35,* 44–47.

London, M., & Bray, D. W. (1980). Ethical issues in testing and evaluation for personnel decisions. *American Psychologist, 35,* 890–901.

Lucas, R. W., et al. (1977). Psychiatrists and a computer as interrogators of patients with alcohol related illnesses: A comparison. *British Journal of Psychiatry, 131,* 160–167.

Lundeberg, M. A., & Fox, P. W. (1991). Do laboratory findings on test expectancy generalize to classroom outcomes? *Review of Educational Research, 61,* 94–106.

Lyerly, S. B. (ed.) (1978). *Handbook of psychiatric rating scales,* 2nd ed. Rockville, MD: National Institute of Mental Health.

Lykken, D. T. (1983, Apr.). Polygraph prejudice. *APA Monitor,* p. 4.

Maccoby, E. E., & Maccoby, N. (1954). The interview: A tool of social science. In G. Lindzey (ed.), *Handbook of social psychology,* pp. 449–487. Reading, MA: Addison-Wesley.

Machover, K. (1971). *Personality projective in the drawing of the human figure.* Springfield, IL: Charles C Thomas.

MacKinnon, D. W. (1962). The nature and nurture of creative talent. *American Psychologist, 17,* 484–495.

Madsen, D. H. (1986). Computer applications for test administration and scoring. *Measurement and Evaluation in Counseling and Development, 19*(1), 6–14.

Maloney, M. P., & Ward, M. P. (1976). *Psychological assessment: A conceptual approach.* New York: Oxford University Press.

Mantel, N., & Haenszel, W. (1959). Statistical aspects of the analysis of data from retrospective studies of disease. *Journal of the National Cancer Institute, 22,* 719–748.

Marland, S. P. (1969). A customer counsels the testers. *Proceedings of the 1968 Invitational Conference on Testing Problems,* pp. 101–112. Princeton, NJ: Educational Testing Service.

Matarazzo, J. D. (1980). Behavioral health and behavioral medicine: Frontiers for a new health psychology. *American Psychologist, 35,* 807–817.

———. (1983). Computerized psychological testing. *Science, 221,* 323.

———. (1992). Psychological testing and assessment in the 21st century. *American Psychologist, 47,* 1007–1018.

McArthur, C., & Stevens, L. B. (1955). The validation of expressed interests as compared with inventoried interests: A fourteen-year follow-up. *Journal of Applied Psychology, 39,* 184–189.

McCabe, S. P. (1985). Career Assessment Inventory. In D. J. Keyser & R. C. Sweetland (eds.), *Test critiques,* Vol. II, pp. 128–137. Kansas City, MO: Test Corporation of America.

McCall, W. A. (1939). *Measurement.* New York: Macmillan.

McClelland, D. (1973). Testing for competence rather than for "intelligence." *American Psychologist, 28,* 1–14.

McGarry, A. L., et al. (1973). *Competency to stand trial and mental illness.* Washington DC: U.S. Government Printing Office.

McNemar, Q. (1964). Lost: Our intelligence? Why? *American Psychologist, 19,* 871–882.

McReynolds, P. (1979). The case for interactional assessment. *Behavioral Assessment, 1,* 237–247.

Mednick, S. A. (1962). The associative basis of the creative process. *Psychological Review, 69,* 1220–1232.

Meehl, P. E. (1954). *Clinical versus statistical prediction.* Minneapolis: University of Minnesota Press.

———. (1965). See over sign: The first good example. *Journal of Experimental Research in Personality, 11,* 27–32.

———, & Golden, R. R. (1982). Taxometric methods. In P. C. Kendall & J. N. Butcher (eds.), *Handbook of research methods in clinical psychology,* pp. 127–182. New York: Wiley.

Megaree, E. I. (1972). *The California Psychological Inventory Handbook.* San Francisco: Jossey-Bass.

Mehrabian, A., & Weiner, M. (1967). Decoding of inconsistent communication. *Journal of Personality and Social Psychology, 6,* 109–114.

Meier, S. T., & Geiger, S. M. (1986), Implications of computer-assisted testing and assessment for professional practice and training. *Measurement and Evaluation in Counseling and Development, 19*(1), 29–34.

Meredith, R. A. (1978). Improved oral test scores through delayed response. *Modern Language Journal, 62,* 321–327.

Merl, J. (1991, May 26). National school testing faces many roadblocks. *Los Angeles Times,* pp. A1, A34–35.

Messick, S. (1980). Test validity and the ethics of assessment. *American Psychologist, 35,* 1012–1037.

Michaelsen, R. H., Michie, D., & Boulanger, A. (1985). The technology of expert systems. *Byte, 10*(4), 303–312.

Miller, L. C., et al. (1976). Comparison of reciprocal inhibition, psychotherapy, and waiting list control for phobic children. *Journal of Abnormal Psychology, 79,* 269–279.

Millman, J., & Pauk, W. (1969). *How to take tests.* New York: McGraw-Hill.

Minton, H. L., & Schneider, F. W. (1980). *Differential psychology.* Monterey, CA: Brooks/Cole.

Mirabile, C. S., Houck, J.,. & Glueck, B. C., Jr. (1970). Computer beats clinician in prognosis contest. *Psychiatric News, 5*(18).

Mischel, W. (1968). *Personality and assessment.* New York: Wiley.

———. (1986). *Introduction to personality,* 4th ed. New York: Holt, Rinehart & Winston.

Mitchell, J. V., Jr. (ed.) (1983). *Tests in print III.* Lincoln: The Buros Institute of Mental Measurements of the University of Nebraska—Lincoln.

———. (ed.) (1985). *The ninth mental measurements yearbook.* Lincoln: The Buros Institute of Mental Measurements of the University of Nebraska—Lincoln.

Moos, R. H. (1976). *The human context: Environmental determinants of behavior.* New York: Wiley.

———. (1979). *Evaluating educational environments.* San Francisco: Jossey-Bass.

———, & Moos, B. S. (1986). *Family Environment Scale: Manual,* 2nd ed. Palo Alto, CA: Consulting Psychologists Press.

Mowen, J. T. (1989). Consumer psychology. In W. L. Gregory & W. J. Burroughs (eds.), *Introduction to applied psychology,* pp. 181–210.

Muchinsky, P. M. (1983). *Psychology applied to work.* Homewood, IL: Dorsey Press.

Murray, H. A. (and collaborator) (1938). *Explorations in personality.* New York: Oxford University Press.

Myart v. Motorola, 110 Cong. Record 5662-64 (1964).

Myers, I. B., & McCaulley, M. H. (1985). *Manual: A guide to the development and use of the Myers–Briggs Type Indicator.* Palo Alto, CA: Consulting Psychologists Press.

Nairn, A., & Associates. (1980). *The reign of ETS: The corporation that makes up minds.* Washington, DC: Learning Research Project.

Nettler, G. (1959). Test burning in Texas. *American Psychologist, 14,* 682–683.

Niemark, J. (1984). Psycho-Out Software. *Datamation, 30,* 32–40.

Nitko, A. J., & Hsu, T. (1987). *Pitt Educational Testing Aids: Users Manual.* Pittsburgh: IPRE University of Pittsburgh.

Norman, W. T. (1963). Personality measurement, faking, and detection: An assessment method for use in personnel selection. *Journal of Applied Psychology, 47,* 225–241.

Nunnally, J. (1978). *Psychometric theory,* New York: McGraw-Hill.

Oden, M. H. (1968). The fulfillment of promise: 40-year follow-up of the Terman gifted group. *Genetic Psychology Monographs, 77*(1), 3–93.

Ollendick, T. H., & Green, R. (1990). Behavioral assessment of children. In G. Goldstein & M. Hersen (eds.), *Handbook of psychological assessment,* 2nd ed., pp. 403–4220. New York: Pergamon.

Osgood, C. E., Suci, G. J., & Tannenbaum, P. H. (1957). *The measurement of meaning.* Urbana: University of Illinois Press.

Osipow, S. H. (1983). *Theories of career development,* 3rd ed. New York: Appleton-Century-Crofts.

Owens, R. E., Hanna, G. S., & Coppedge, F. L. (1970). Comparison of multiple-choice tests using different types of distractor selection techniques. *Journal of Educational Measurement, 7,* 87–90.

Owens, T. A., & Stufflebeam, D. L. (1969, Feb.). *An experimental comparison of item sampling and examinee sampling for estimating norms.* Paper presented at the meeting of the National Council on Measurement in Education, Los Angeles, CA.

Owens, W. A. (1976). Background data. In M. D. Dunnette (ed.), *Handbook of industrial and organizational psychology.* Chicago: Rand McNally.

Page, E. B. (1968). Analyzing student essays by computer. *International Review of Education,* 210–225.

————, Tillett, P. I., & Ajay, H. B. (1989, June). *Computer measurement of subject-matter essay tests: Past research and future promise.* Paper presented at the meeting of the American Psychological Society, Alexandria, VA.

PASE (Parents in Action on Special Education) v. *Joseph P. Hannon,* No. 74C 3586 (N.D. III. 1980).

Pascale, P. J. (1974). Changing initial answers on multiple-choice achievement tests. *Measurement and Evaluation in Guidance, 6,* 236–238.

Paterson, D. G., et al. (1930). *Minnesota Mechanical Ability Tests.* Minneapolis: University of Minnesota Press.

Payne, A. F. (1928). *Sentence completions.* New York: New York Guidance Clinic.

Payne, F. D. (1985). Review of Bem Sex-Role Inventory. In J. V. Mitchell, Jr. (ed.), *The ninth mental measurements yearbook,* Vol. I, pp. 137–138. Lincoln: Buros Institute of Mental Measurements of the University of Nebraska—Lincoln.

Pellegrino, J. W., & Varnhagen, C. F. (1985). Intelligence: Perspectives, theories, and tests. In T. Husén & T. N. Posthlethwaite (eds.), *The international encyclopedia of education,* Vol. 5, pp. 2611–2618. New York: Wiley.

Peterson, C. J. (1974). Development of oral quizzes in a multimedia approach. *Educational Technology, 14*(4), 47–51.

Peterson, C., et al. (1982). The Attributional Style Questionnaire. *Cognitive Therapy and Research, 6,* 287–300.

Peterson, R. C., & Thurstone, L. L. (1933). *Motion pictures and the social attitudes of children.* New York: Macmillan.

Petrie, B. M. (1969). Statistical analysis of attitude scale scores. *Research Quarterly (AAHPER), 40,* 434–437.

Piotrowski, C., & Keller, J. W. (1989). Psychological testing in outpatient mental health facilities: A national study. *Professional Psychology: Research and Practice, 20,* 423–425.

————, Sherry, D., & Keller, J. W. (1985). Psychodiagnostic test usage: A survey of the Society for Personality Assessment. *Journal of Personality Assessment, 49,* 115–119.

Plake, B. S., et al. (1982). Effects of item arrangement, knowledge of arrangement, test anxiety and sex on test performance. *Journal of Educational Measurement, 19,* 49–57.

Platt, J. R. (1961). On maximizing the information obtained from science examinations. *American Journal of Physics, 29,* 111–122.

Popham, W. J. (1981). *Modern educational measurement.* Englewood Cliffs, NJ: Prentice Hall.

————. (1984, Spring). Teacher competency testing: The devil's dilemma. *Teacher Education and Practice,* 5–9.

Posavec, E. J., & Carey, R. G. (1992). *Program evaluation: Methods and case studies,* 4th ed. Englewood Cliffs, NJ: Prentice Hall.

Prediger, D. J., & Hanson, G. R. (1976). Holland's theory of careers applied to men and women: Analysis of implicit assumptions. *Journal of Vocational Behavior, 8,* 167–184.

Preston, R. C. (1964). Ability of students to identify correct responses before reading. *Journal of Educational Research, 58,* 181–183.

Pritchard, D. A., & Rosenblatt, A. (1980). Racial bias in the MMPI: A methodological review. *Journal of Consulting and Clinical Psychology, 48,* 263–267.

Pyrczak, F. (1973). Validity of the discrimination index as a measure of item quality. *Journal of Educational Measurement, 10,* 227–231.

Quay, H. C., & Peterson, D. R. (1983). *Interim manual for the Behavior Problem Checklist.* Unpublished manuscript, University of Miami.

Rabinowitz, W. (1984). Study of Values. In D. J. Keyser & R. C. Sweetland (eds.), *Test critiques,* Vol. I., pp. 641–647. Kansas City, MO: Test Corporation of America.

Raines, G. N., & Rohrer, J. H. (1960). The operational matrix of psychiatric practice. II. Variability in psychiatric impressions and the projection hypothesis. *American Journal of Psychiatry, 117,* 133–139.

Ravitch, D. (1983–1984, Winter). The uses and misuses of tests. *College Board Review,* pp. 23–26.

Reilly, R. R., & Chao, G. T. (1982). Validity and fairness of some alternative employee selection procedures. *Personnel Psychology, 35,* 1–62.

Reitan, R. M. (1964). *Manual for administering and scoring and Reitan–Indiana Neuropsychological Battery for Children (aged 5 through 8).* Indianapolis: Indiana University Medical Center.

———. (1969). *Manual for administration of neuropsychological test batteries for adults and children.* Indianapolis: Author.

Reynolds, C. R. (1982). The problem of bias in psychological assessment. In C. R. Reynolds & T. B. Gutkin (eds.), *The handbook of school psychology.* New York: Wiley.

Rice, J. M. (1897). The futility of the spelling grind. *Forum, 23,* 163–172, 409–419.

Robbins, D., & Almond, E. (1992, Jan. 9). NCAA tightens academic rules for student-athletes. *Los Angeles Times,* pp. A1, A23.

Robinson, J. P., Athanasiou, R., & Head, K. B. (1974). *Measures of occupational attitudes and occupational characteristics.* Ann Arbor: Institute for Social Research, University of Michigan.

———, Rush, J. G., & Head, K. B. (1973). *Measures of political attitudes.* Ann Arbor: Institute for Social Research, University of Michigan.

———, Shaver, P. R., & Wrightsman, L. S. (1991). *Measures of personality and social psychological attitudes.* New York: Academic Press.

Roe, A. (1956). *The psychology of occupations.* New York: Basic Books.

———, & Klos, D. (1969). Occupational classification. *Counseling Psychologist, 1,* 84–92.

———, & Siegelman, M. (1964). *The origin of interest.* Washington, DC: American Personnel and Guidance Association.

Rogers, C. R., & Dymond, R. F. (eds.) (1954). *Psychotherapy and personality change.* Chicago: University of Chicago Press.

Rogers, R. (1984). *Rogers Criminal Responsibility Scales.* Odessa, FL: Psychological Assessment Resources.

———. (1986). *Conducting insanity evaluations.* Odessa, FL: Psychological Assessment Resources.

Rokeach, M. (1973). *The nature of human values.* New York: Free Press.

Rome, H. P., et al. (1962). Symposium on automation techniques in personality assessment. *Proceedings of the Staff Meetings of the Mayo Clinic, 37,* 61–82.

Rosenbaum, B. (1973). Attitude toward invasion of privacy in the personnel selection process and job applicant demographic and personality correlates. *Journal of Applied Psychology, 58,* 333–338.

Rosenthal, R., et al. (1979). *Sensitivity to nonverbal communication: The PONS test.* Baltimore: Johns Hopkins University Press.

Rosenzweig, S. (1978). *Aggressive behavior and the Rosenzweig Picture-Frustration Study.* New York: Praeger.

Ross, C. C., & Stanley, J. C. (1954). *Measurement in today's schools,* 3rd ed. New York: Prentice Hall.

Rossi, P. H., & Freeman, H. E. (1985). *Evaluation: A systematic approach,* 3rd ed. Beverly Hills, CA: Sage Publications.

Rotter, J. B. (1954). *Social learning and clinical psychology.* Englewood Cliffs, NJ: Prentice Hall.

———. (1966). Generalized expectancies for internal versus external control of reinforcement. *Psychological Monographs, 80* (1, Whole No. 609).

Rounds, J. C., Kanter, M. J., & Blumin, M. (1987). Technology and testing: What is around the corner? *New Directions for Community Colleges,* No. 59, 83–93.

Rowley, G. L. (1974). Which examinees are most favoured by the use of multiple-choice tests? *Journal of Educational Measurement, 11,* 15–23.

Rudner, L. M. (1988). Teacher testing—An update. *Educational Measurement: Issues and Practice, 7,* 16–19.

Ryan, J., Prefitera, A., & Powers, L. (1983). Scoring reliability on the WAIS–R. *Journal of Consulting and Clinical Psychology, 51,* 149–150.

Sadalla, E., & Burroughs, J. (1981). Profiles in eating: Sexy vegetarians and other diet-based social stereotypes. *Psychology Today, 15,* 51–57.

Sameroff, A. J. (ed.) (1978). Organization and stability of newborn behavior: A commentary on the Brazelton Neonatal Behavior Assessment Scale. *Monographs of the Society for Research in Child Development, 43* (5–6, Serial No. 177).

Sampson, J. P. (1981), CASSI: A computer-assisted approach to improving study skills. *NASPA Journal, 18,* 42–147.

———, & Pyle, K. R. (1983). Ethical issues involved with the use of computer assisted counseling, testing, and guidance systems. *Personnel and Guidance Journal, 61,* 283–287.

Sattler, J. M., & Winget, B. M. (1970). Intelligence testing procedures as affected by expectancy and IQ. *Journal of Clinical Psychology, 26,* 446–448.

———, Hillix, W. A., & Neher, L. A. (1970). Halo effect in examiner scoring of intelligence test responses. *Journal of Consulting and Clinical Psychology, 34,* 172–176.

Savitz, F. R. (1985). Effects of easy examination questions placed at the beginning of science multi-choice examinations. *Journal of Instructional Psychology, 12,* 6–10.

Scarr, S. (1969) Social introversion–extraversion as a heritable response. *Child Development, 40,* 823–832.

Schmidt, F. L., & Hunter, J. E. (1977). Development of a general solution to the problem of validity generalization. *Journal of Applied Psychology, 62,* 529–540.

———, & ———. (1978). Moderator research and the law of small numbers. *Personnel Psychology, 31,* 215–232.

———, & ———. (1981). Employment testing: Old theories and new research findings. *American Psychologist, 36,* 1128–1137.

Schmidt, S. R. (1983). The effects of recall and recognition test expectancies on the retention of prose. *Memory and Cognition, 11,* 172–180.

Schneider, M. F. (1989). *Children's Apperceptive Story-telling Test.* Austin, TX: pro.ed.

———, & Perney, J. (1990). Development of the Children's Apperceptive Story-telling Test. *Psychological Assessment: A Journal of Consulting and Clinical Psychology, 2,* 179–185.

Schwab, D. P., Heneman, H. A., III, & De Cotiis, T. A. (1975). *In* Behaviorally anchored rating scales: A review of the literature. *Personnel Psychology, 28,* 549–562.

———, & Heneman, H. G. (1969). Relationship between interview structure and interview reliability in employment situations. *Journal of Applies Psychology, 53,* 214–217.

———, & Packard, G. L. (1973). Response distortion on the Gordon Personal Inventory and the Gordon Personal Profile in the selection context: Some implications for predicting employee behavior. *Journal of Applied Psychology, 58,* 372–374.

Seashore, C. E. (1939). *Psychology of music.* New York: McGraw-Hill.

Selltiz, C., Wrightsman, L. S., & Cook, S. W. (1976). *Research methods in social relations,* 3rd ed. New York: Holt, Rinehart & Winston.

Serlin, R. C., & Kaiser, H. F. (1978). Method for increasing the reliability of a short multiple-choice test. *Educational and Psychological Measurement, 38,* 337–340.

Shatkin, L. (1980). *Computer-assisted guidance: Description of systems.* ETS RR-80-23. Princeton, NJ: Educational Testing Service.

Shaw, M. W., & Wright, J. M. (1967). *Scales for the measurement of attitudes.* New York: McGraw-Hill.

Sheldon, W. H., & Stevens, S. S. (1942). *The varieties of temperament.* New York: Harper & Row.

———, Stevens, S. S., & Tucker, W. B. (1940). *The varieties of human physique.* New York: Harper & Row.

Simpson, E. J. (1966). The classification of educational objectives, psychomotor domain. *Illinois Teacher of Home Economics 10,* 110–114.

Sines, J. O. (1970). Actuarial versus clinical prediction in psychopathology. *British Journal of Psychiatry, 116,* 129–144.

Skinner, H. A., & Pakula, A. (1986). Challenge of computers in psychological assessment. *Professional Psychology: Research and Practice, 17,* 44–50.

Skinner, N. F. (1983). Switching answers on multiple-choice questions: Shrewdness or shibboleth? *Teaching of Psychology, 10,* 220–222.

Slack, W. V., & Porter, D. (1980). The Scholastic Aptitude Test: A critical appraisal. *Harvard Educational Review, 50,* 154–175.

Slakter, M. J., Koehler, R. A., & Hampton, S. H. (1970). Grade level, sex, and selected aspects of test-wiseness. *Journal of Educational Measurement, 7,* 119–122.

Smith, M., White, K. P., & Coop, R. H. (1979). The effect of item type on the consequences of changing answers on multiple-choice tests. *Journal of Educational Measurement, 16,* 203–208.

Smith, P.C., & Kendall, L. M. (1963). Retranslation of expectations: An approach to the construction of unambiguous anchors for rating scales. *Journal of Applied Psychology, 47,* 149–155.

Smith, S. R., & Meyer, R. G. (1987). *Law, behavior, and mental health.* New York: New York University Press.

Snyder, C. R. (1974). Acceptance of personality interpretations as a function of assessment procedures. *Journal of Consulting Psychology, 42,* 150.

Society for Industrial and Organizational Psychology, Inc. (1987). *Principles for the validation and use of personal selection procedures,* 3rd ed. College Park, MD: Author.

Soroka v. *Dayton–Hudson Corp.* 91. L.A. Daily Journal D.A.R. 13204 (Cal. Ct. App. 1991).

Spitzer, R. L., & Endicott, J. (1969). DIAGNO II: Further developments in a computer program for psychiatric diagnosis. *American Journal of Psychiatry* (supp.), *125,* 12–21.

———, & ———. (1974). Can the computer assist clinicians in psychiatric diagnosis? *American Journal of Psychiatry, 131,* 523–430.

Stanley, J. C., Keating, D. P., & Fox, L. H. (eds.) (1974). *Mathematical talent: Discovery, description, and development.* Baltimore: Johns Hopkins University Press.

Starch, D., & Elliott, E. C. (1913). Reliability of grading work in mathematics. *School Review, 21,* 254–259.

Steiner, R. L., & Barnhart, R. B. (1972). Development of an instrument to assess environmental attitudes utilizing factor analytic techniques. *Science Education, 56,* 427–432.

Stephenson, W. (1953). *The study of behavior: Q-technique and its methodology.* Chicago: University of Chicago Press.

Sternberg, R. J. (1985). *Beyond IQ: A triarchic theory of human intelligence.* Cambridge: Cambridge University Press.

Stoloff, M. L., & Couch, J. V. (eds.) (1988). *Computer use in psychology: A directory of software.* Washington, DC: American Psychological Association.

Strang, H. R. (1980). Effect of technically worded options on multiple-choice test performance. *Journal of Educational Research, 73,* 262–265.

Strauss, A. A., & Lehtinen, L. E. (1947). *Psychopathology and education of the brain-injured child,* Vol. 1. New York: Grune & Stratton.

Strong, E. K., Jr. (1955). *Vocational interests 18 years after college.* Minneapolis: University of Minnesota Press.

———. (1977). *Assessment of persons.* Englewood Cliffs, NJ: Prentice Hall.

Super, D. E. (1973). The Work Values Inventory. In D. G. Zytowski (ed.), *Contemporary approaches to interest measurement.* Minneapolis: University of Minnesota Press.

———, Bohn, M. J., Jr. (1970). *Occupational psychology.* Belmont, CA: Wadsworth.

———, & Crites, J. O. (1962). *Appraising vocational fitness.* New York: Harper & Row.

Sweetland, R. C., & Keyser, D. J. (eds.) (1983). *Tests.* Austin, TX: pro.ed., Inc.

———, & ———. (eds.) (1986). *Tests,* 2nd ed. Austin, TX: pro.ed., Inc.

Swenson, W. M., & Pearson, J. S. (1964). Automation techniques in personality assessment: A frontier in behavioral science and medicine. *Methods of Information in Medicine, 3,* 34–36.

Swiercinsky, D. P. (ed.) (1985). *Testing adults.* Kansas City, MO: Test Corporation of America.

Tarasoff v. *Regents of University of California,* 17 Cal. 3d 425 (1983).

Taylor, H. C., & Russell, J. T. (1939). The relationship of validity coefficients to the practical effectiveness of tests in selection: Discussion and tables. *Journal of Applied Psychology, 22,* 565–578.

Taylor, J. A. (1953). A personality scale of manifest anxiety. *Journal of Abnormal and Social Psychology, 48,* 285–290.

Teeter, P. A. (1985). Review of Adjective Check List. In J. V. Mitchell, Jr. (ed.), *The ninth mental measurements yearbook,* Vol. I, pp. 50–52. Lincoln: Buros Institute of Mental Measurements of the University of Nebraska—Lincoln.

Terman, L. M., & Merrill, M. A. (1973). *Stanford-Binet Intelligence Scale: 1972 norms edition.* Boston: Houghton Mifflin.

———, & Oden, M. H. (1959). *The gifted group at mid-life. Genetic studies of genius, V.* Stanford, CA: Stanford University Press.

Thomas, A., & Chess, S. (1977). *Temperament and development.* New York: Brunner/Mazel.

Thomas, R. G. (1985). Review of Jackson Vocational Interest Survey. In J. V. Mitchell, Jr. (ed.), *The ninth mental measurements yearbook,* Vol. I, pp. 740–742. Lincoln: Buros Institute of Mental Measurements of the University of Nebraska—Lincoln.

Thoreson, C. E., & Mahoney, M. J. (1974). *Behavioral self-control.* New York: Holt, Rinehart & Winston.

Thorndike, E. L. (1912). The permanence of interests and their relation to abilities. *Popular Science Monthly, 81,* 449–456.

————. (1918). *The seventeenth yearbook of the National Society for the Study of Education.* Pt. II. Bloomington, IL: Public School Publishing Co.

Thorndike, R. L. (1963). The prediction of vocational success. *Vocational Guidance Quarterly, 11,* 179–187.

————. (1971). Concepts of culture-fairness. *Journal of Educational Measurement, 8,* 63–70.

————, & Hagen, E. (1959). *Ten thousand careers.* New York: Wiley.

Tidwell, R. (1980). Biasing potential of multiple-choice test distractors. *Journal of Negro Education, 49,* 289–296.

Tittle, C. K. (1984). Test bias. In T. N. Husén & T. Postlethwaite (eds.), *International encyclopedia of education,* pp. 5199–5204. New York: Wiley.

Triandis, H. C. (1971). *Attitudes and attitude change.* New York: Wiley.

Trombley, W. (1986, Aug. 26). Test makers now search for answers. *Los Angeles Times,* pp. I-1, 22–23.

Tryon, W. W. (1991). *Activity measurement in psychology and medicine.* New York: Plenum.

Turkington, C. (1984). The growing use and abuse of computer testing. *APA Monitor, 7,* 26.

Tyler, L. E. (1964). The antecedents of two varieties of interest pattern. *Genetic Psychology Monographs, 70,* 177–227.

————, & Walsh, W. B. (1979). *Tests and measurements,* 3rd ed. Englewood Cliffs, NJ: Prentice Hall.

Underwood, B., & Moore, B. S. (1981). Sources of behavioral consistency. *Journal of Personality and Social Psychology, 40,* 780–785.

United States v. Georgia Power Company, 5 FEP 587 (1973).

U.S. Department of Health and Human Services (1992, Apr. 15). *Monthly Vital Statistics Report.* Births, marriages, divorces, and deaths for 1991. Washington, DC: Author.

U.S. Department of Labor. Employment and Training Administration (1991). *Dictionary of occupational titles,* 4th ed. Washington, DC: Government Printing Office.

van der Kamp, L. J. T. (1973). Thurstone revisited: Multidimensional similarity scaling of attitude toward the church. *Educational and Psychological Measurement, 33,* 577–585.

Veldman, D. J., Menaker, S. L., & Peck, R. F. (1969) Computer scoring of sentence completion data. *Behavioral Science, 14,* 501–507.

Vernon, P. E. (1960). *The structure of human abilities,* rev. ed. London: Methuen.

Vidler, D., & Hansen, R. (1980). Answer changing on multiple-choice tests. *Journal of Experimental Education, 49,* 18–20.

Wade, T. C., & Baker, T. B. (1977). Opinions and use of psychological tests. *American Psychologist, 32,* 874–882.

Wagman, M. (1980). PLATO DCS: An interactive computer system for personal counseling. *Journal of Experimental Psychology, 72,* 596.

Wallach, M. A., & Kogan, N. (1965). *Modes of thinking in young children.* New York: Holt, Rinehart & Winston.

Wallston, K. A., Maides, S., & Wallston, B. S. (1976). Health-related information seeking as a function of health-related locus of control and health value. *Journal of Research in Personality, 10,* 215–222.

Ward, W. C. (1985). Measurement research that will change test design in the future. In *The redesign of testing for the 21st century,* pp. 25–34. Princeton, NJ: Educational Testing Service.

Washington v. Davis 426 U.S. 229, 12FEP1415 (1976).

Watkins, C. E., Jr., Campbell, V. L., & McGregor, P. (1988). Counseling psychologists' uses of the opinions about psychological tests: A contemporary perspective. *Counseling Psychologist, 16,* 476–486.

Watson v. Fort Worth Bank and Trust, 487 U.S. 977, 108 S. Ct. 277 (1988).

Weaver, S. J. (ed.) (1984). *Testing children.* Kansas City, MO: Test Corporation of America.

Webb, E. (1915). Character and intelligence. *British Journal of Psychology Monograph Supplement,* III.

Webb, J. T., & Meckstroth, B. (1982). *Guiding the gifted child.* Columbus, OH: Psychology Publishing Co.

Wechsler, D. (1975). Intelligence defined and undefined. *American Psychologist, 30,* 135–139.

Weiner, I. B. (1983). The future of psychodiagnosis revisited. *Journal of Personality Assessment, 47,* 451–461.

Weiss, D. J. (1973, Sept.). *The stratified adaptive computerized ability test. Research Report 73–3.* Minneapolis: University of Minnesota, Psychometric Methods Program.

———. (1985). Adaptive testing by computer. *Journal of Consulting and Clinical Psychology, 53,* 774–789.

———, & Vale, C. D. (1987). Computerized adaptive testing for measuring abilities and other psychological variables. In J. N. Butcher (ed.), *Computerized psychological assessment,* pp. 325–343. New York: Basic Books.

Weiss, J., Beckwith, B., & Schaeffer, B. (1989). *Standing up to the SAT.* New York: Simon & Schuster.

Wheeler, K. G. (1985). Review of Temperament and Values Inventory. In J. V. Mitchell, Jr. (ed.), *The ninth mental measurements yearbook,* Vol. II, pp. 1535–1536. Lincoln: Buros Institute of Mental Measurements of the University of Nebraska—Lincoln.

Wholeben, B. E. (1985). Sixteen Personality Factor Questionnaire. In D. J. Keyser & R. C. Sweetland (eds.), *Test critiques,* Vol. IV, pp. 595–605. Kansas City, MO: Test Corporation of America.

Whyte, W. H., Jr. (1956). *The organization man.* Garden City, NY: Doubleday.

Wiechmann, G. H., & Wiechmann, L. A. (1973). Multiple factor analysis: An approach to attitude validation. *Journal of Experimental Education, 41,* 74–84.

Wiggins, J. S. (1966). Substantive dimensions of self-report in the MMPI item pool. *Psychological Monographs, 80* (Whole No. 630).

Wilbur, P. H. (1970). Positional response set among high school students on multiple-choice tests. *Journal of Educational Measurement, 7,* 161–163.

Wildman, R., et al. (1980). *The Georgia Court Competency Test: An attempt to develop a rapid, quantitative measure of fitness for trial.* Unpublished manuscript, Forensic Services Division, Center State Hospital, Milledgeville, GA.

Willerman, L. (1979). *The psychology of individual and group differences.* San Francisco: W. H. Freeman.

Williams, S. I., & Jones, C. O. (1974). Multiple-choice mathematics questions: How students attempt to solve them. *Mathematics Teacher, 67,* 34–40.

Willingham, W. W., & Breland, H. M. (1982). *Personal qualities and college admissions.* New York: College Entrance Examination Board.

Willis, C. G. (1984). Myers–Briggs Type Indicator. In D. J. Keyser & R. C. Sweetland (eds.), *Test critiques,* Vol. I, pp. 482–490. Kansas City, MO: Test Corporation of America.

Willson, V. L. (1982). Maximizing reliability in multiple-choice questions. *Educational and Psychological Measurement, 42,* 69–72.

Wilson, G. (1978). Introversion/extroversion. In H. London & J. E. Exner (eds.), *Dimensions of personality,* pp. 217–261. New York: Wiley.

Wirt, R. D., & Lachar, D. (1981). The Personality Inventory for Children: Development and clinical applications. In P. McReynolds (ed.), *Advances in psychological assessment,* Vol. 5. San Francisco: Jossey-Bass.

Witkin, H. A., & Berry, J. W. (1975). Psychological differentiation in cross-cultural perspective. *Journal of Cross-Cultural Psychology, 6,* 4–87.

————, & Goodenough, D. R. (1977). Field dependence and interpersonal behavior. *Psychological Bulletin, 84,* 661–689.

————, et al. (1962). *Psychological differentiation.* New York: Wiley.

————, et al. (1977). Field-dependent and field-independent cognitive styles and their educational implications. *Review of Educational Research, 47,* 1–69.

Wolff, W. T., & Merrens, M. R. (1974). Behavioral assessment: A review of clinical methods. *Journal of Personality Assessment, 38,* 3–16.

Wolk, R., & Wolk, R. (1971). *The Gerontological Apperception Test.* New York: Behavioral Publications.

Wright, H. F. (1960). Observational child study. In P. E. Mussen (ed.), *Handbook of research methods in child development.* New York: Wiley.

Young, D. W. (1982). A survey of decision aids for clinicians. *British Medical Journal, 285,* 1332–1336.

Zajonc, R. B. (1986). The decline and rise of scholastic aptitude scores. *American Psychologist, 41,* 862–867.

Zarske, J. A. (1985). Review of Adjective Check List. In J. V. Mitchell, Jr. (ed.), *The ninth mental measurements yearbook,* Vol. I, pp. 52–53. Lincoln: Buros Institute of Mental Measurements of the University of Nebraska—Lincoln.

Ziskin, J. (1986). The future of clinical assessment. In B. S. Plake & J. C. Witt. (eds.), *The future of testing,* pp. 185–201. Hillsdale, NJ: Lawrence Erlbaum.

Zook, J. (1993). Two agencies start work on national test of college students' analytical skills. *Chronicle of Higher Education, 39*(29), A23.

Zuckerman, M. (1985). Review of Temperament and Values Inventory. In J. V. Mitchell, Jr. (ed.), *The ninth mental measurements yearbook,* Vol. II, pp. 1536–1537. Lincoln: Buros Institute of Mental Measurements of the University of Nebraska—Lincoln.

Zytowski, D. G. (1976). Predictive validity of the Kuder Occupational Interest Survey: A 12- to 19-year follow-up. *Journal of Counseling Psychology, 23,* 221–233.

Author Index

Q

R

S

Subject Index

Definitions of many of the terms in this index and other terms pertaining to psychological assessment are given in the Glossary on pages 461–486.

Test Index